Lecture Notes in Computer Science 12232

Founding Editors

Gerhard Goos
Karlsruhe Institute of Technology, Karlsruhe, Germany
Juris Hartmanis
Cornell University, Ithaca, NY, USA

Editorial Board Members

Elisa Bertino
Purdue University, West Lafayette, IN, USA
Wen Gao
Peking University, Beijing, China
Bernhard Steffen ⓘ
TU Dortmund University, Dortmund, Germany
Gerhard Woeginger ⓘ
RWTH Aachen, Aachen, Germany
Moti Yung
Columbia University, New York, NY, USA

More information about this series at http://www.springer.com/series/7408

Emil Sekerinski · Nelma Moreira ·
José N. Oliveira et al. (Eds.)

Formal Methods

FM 2019 International Workshops

Porto, Portugal, October 7–11, 2019
Revised Selected Papers, Part I

 Springer

Editors
Emil Sekerinski
McMaster University
Hamilton, ON, Canada

Nelma Moreira
University of Porto
Porto, Portugal

José N. Oliveira
University of Minho
Braga, Portugal

Workshop Editors *see next page*

ISSN 0302-9743   ISSN 1611-3349   (electronic)
Lecture Notes in Computer Science
ISBN 978-3-030-54993-0   ISBN 978-3-030-54994-7   (eBook)
https://doi.org/10.1007/978-3-030-54994-7

LNCS Sublibrary: SL2 – Programming and Software Engineering

This Springer imprint is published by the registered company Springer Nature Switzerland AG
The registered company address is: Gewerbestrasse 11, 6330 Cham, Switzerland

Workshop Editors

AFFORD
Daniel Ratiu
Argo Ai
Munich, Germany
dratiu@argo.ai

DataMOD
Riccardo Guidotti
University of Pisa
Pisa, Italy
riccardo.guidotti@di.unipi.it

FMAS
Marie Farrell
University of Liverpool
Liverpool, UK
marie.farrell@liverpool.ac.uk

Matt Luckcuck
University of Liverpool
Liverpool, UK
m.luckcuck@liverpool.ac.uk

FMBC
Diego Marmsoler
University of Exeter
Exeter, UK
d.marmsoler@exeter.ac.uk

FMIS
José Campos
University of Minho
Braga, Portugal
jose.campos@di.uminho.pt

HFM
Troy Astarte
University of Newcastle
Newcastle upon Tyne, UK
t.astarte@ncl.ac.uk

NSAD
Laure Gonnord
Claude Bernard University
Lyon, France
laure.gonnord@ens-lyon.fr

OpenCert
Antonio Cerone (D)
Nazarbayev University
Nur-Sultan, Kazakhstan
antonio.cerone@nu.edu.kz

Overture
Luis Diogo Couto
Forcepoint
Ireland
ldcouto@gmail.com

Refine
Brijesh Dongol
University of Surrey
Guildford, UK
b.dongol@surrey.ac.uk

RPLA
Martin Kutrib
University of Giessen
Giessen, Germany
kutrib@informatik.uni-giessen.de

SASB
Pedro Monteiro
University of Lisbon
Lisbon, Portugal
pedro.tiago.monteiro@tecnico.ulisboa.pt

TAPAS
David Delmas
Airbus Operations S.A.S.
Toulouse, France
david.delmas@lip6.fr

Preface

The Third World Congress on Formal Methods (FM 2019) took place during October 7–11, 2019, in Porto, Portugal. The congress comprised nine conferences: the 23rd International Symposium on Formal Methods (FM 2019); the 29th International Symposium on Logic-Based Program Synthesis and Transformation (LOPSTR 2019); the 13th International Conference on Mathematics of Program Construction (MPC 2019); the 21st International Symposium on Principles and Practice of Declarative Programming (PPDP 2019); the 19th International Conference on Runtime Verification (RV 2019); the 26th International Static Analysis Symposium (SAS 2019); the 13th International Conference on Tests and Proofs (TAP 2019); the 7th International Symposium on Unifying Theories of Programming (UTP 2019); and the 13th International Conference on Verification and Evaluation of Computer and Communication Systems (VECoS 2019). The conference also included a Doctoral Symposium, an Industry Day, 2 festschrifts, 16 workshops, and 5 tutorials. In total there were 630 registered participants from 43 countries, 381 presentations from 821 authors, 44 invited speakers, and 13 tool exhibitors. The 16 workshops emerged out of 18 workshop proposals. Three workshops, the Second International Workshop on Dynamic Logic, New Trends and Applications (DaLí 2019), the Third International Workshop and Tutorial on Formal Methods Teaching (FMTea 2019), and the 5th Workshop on Formal Integrated Development Environment (F-IDE 2019), had their proceedings published separately. This two-volume book consists of the proceedings of the other 13 workshops.

Volume 1:

AFFORD 2019
The Third Workshop on Practical Formal Verification for Software Dependability
DataMod 2019
The 8th International Symposium From Data to Models and Back
FMAS 2019
The First Formal Methods for Autonomous Systems Workshop
FMBC 2019
The First Workshop on Formal Methods for Blockchains
FMIS 2019
The 8th International Workshop on Formal Methods for Interactive Systems

Volume 2:

HFM 2019
The First History of Formal Methods Workshop
NSAD 2019
The 8th International Workshop on Numerical and Symbolic Abstract Domains

OpenCERT 2019
   The 9th International Workshop on Open Community Approaches to Education, Research and Technology
Overture 2019
   The 17th Overture Workshop
Refine 2019
   The 19th Refinement Workshop
RPLA 2019
   The First International Workshop on Reversibility in Programming, Languages, and Automata
SASB 2019
   The 10th International Workshop on Static Analysis and Systems Biology
TAPAS 2019
   The 10th Workshop on Tools for Automatic Program Analysis

The diversity of the workshop themes reflects the evolution that formal methods of software development have taken since the first World Congress on Formal Methods in 1999 (Toulouse, France) and the second in 2009 (Eindhoven, The Netherlands). Each workshop has its unique history and style that was left up to the workshop organizers to maintain. We are pleased to have four workshops for the first time: FMAS, FMBC, HFM, and RPLA. In total, 123 papers were accepted after a first round of reviewing for the presentation at FM 2019. Of those, 108 were submitted for a second round of reviewing after the congress and 68 selected for inclusion in these proceedings. The workshop organizers ensured that all papers received at least three reviews. Nine invited abstracts, two invited papers, and one workshop summary are included as well.

We are grateful to the workshop authors, the workshop organizers, the Program and Organizing Committee members of the workshops, the local organizers, the sponsors of the congress, and everyone else involved in the 34 events of the congress for the concerted effort in putting together such a rich program.

Finally, we thank Springer for their immediate willingness to publish the collected FM 2019 workshop proceedings in the LNCS series and their support in the editing process.

May 2020

Emil Sekerinski
Nelma Moreira
José N. Oliveira

Organization

General Chair

José N. Oliveira   University of Minho, INESC TEC, Portugal

Program Chairs

Maurice H. ter Beek   ISTI-CNR, Italy
Annabelle McIver   Macquarie University, Australia

Industry Day Chairs

Joe Kiniry   Galois Inc., USA
Thierry Lecomte   ClearSy, France

Doctoral Symposium Chairs

Alexandra Silva   University College London, UK
Antónia Lopes   University of Lisbon, Portugal

Journal First Track Chair

Augusto Sampaio   Federal University of Pernambuco, Brazil

Workshop and Tutorial Chairs

Emil Sekerinski   McMaster University, Canada
Nelma Moreira   University of Porto, Portugal

Organizing Committee

Luís Soares Barbosa   University of Minho, INESC TEC, Portugal
José Creissac Campos   University of Minho, INESC TEC, Portugal
João Pascoal Faria   University of Porto, INESC TEC, Portugal
Sara Fernandes   University of Minho, INESC TEC, Portugal
Luís Neves   Critical Software, Portugal
Ana Paiva   University of Porto, INESC TEC, Portugal

Local Organizers

Catarina Fernandes	University of Minho, INESC TEC, Portugal
Paula Rodrigues	INESC TEC, Portugal
Ana Rita Costa	INESC TEC, Portugal

Web Team

Francisco Neves	University of Minho, INESC TEC, Portugal
Rogério Pontes	University of Minho, INESC TEC, Portugal
Paula Rodrigues	INESC TEC, Portugal

FME Board

Ana Cavalcanti	University of York, UK
Lars-Henrik Eriksson	Uppsala University, Sweden
Stefania Gnesi	ISTI-CNR, Italy
Einar Broch Johnsen	University of Oslo, Norway
Nico Plat	Thanos, The Netherlands

Contents – Part I

FMAS 2019 - 1st Formal Methods for Autonomous Systems Workshop

FMBC 2019 - 1st Workshop on Formal Methods for Blockchains

FMIS 2019 - 8th Formal Methods for Interactive Systems Workshop

Contents – Part II

Overture 2019 - 17th Overture Workshop

Refine 2019 - 19th Refinement Workshop

RPLA 2019 - Workshop on Reversibility in Programming, Languages, and Automata

SASB 2019 - 10th International Workshop on Static Analysis and Systems Biology

TAPAS 2019 - 10th Workshop on Tools for Automatic Program Analysis

AFFORD 2019 - 3rd Workshop on Practical Formal Verification for Software Dependability

AFFORD 2019 Organizers' Message

The Third Workshop on Practical Formal Verification for Software Dependability (AFFORD) was held in conjunction with FM 2019 (the 3rd World Congress of Formal Methods – FM2019). The second edition was organised in conjunction with the 27th IEEE International Symposium on Software Reliability Engineering - ISSRE 2017 in Toulouse, France. The first edition was held in conjunction with ISSRE 2016 under the name Formal Verification for Practicing Engineers (FVPE).

Formal verification techniques have already shown that they can increase the dependability of software. However, they are only sporadically applied in an industrial context (if at all) and mostly in projects where it is explicitly required by regulatory bodies. A broad adoption of formal verification techniques is not in sight.

The inherent complexity of the systems being built, as well as the complexity of their analyses pose scalability challenges in applying these techniques in real industrial projects. Other important reasons for their low adoption are related to pragmatic aspects such as usability or the cost of applying formal verification. For a large majority of software engineers and developers, formal verification techniques are viewed rather as expert tools and not as engineering tools that can be used on a daily basis. The AFFORD workshop aims to build a community interested in the application of formal verification techniques to increase dependability of software intensive systems, by developing and promoting approaches, techniques and tools that can be understood and applied by practicing engineers – without special education in formal methods. Specifically, we aim to bring together researchers and practitioners interested in lowering the adoption barrier to use formal verification for the development of dependable software. We especially focus on the needs of main-stream developers that do not (necessarily) work on highly safety critical systems but on more main-stream systems that still need to be reliable.

AFFORD'19 had 10 submissions which were rigorously reviewed by three reviewers. We were able to accept 6 papers. The workshop program was composed of a keynote and six presentations of regular papers. The keynote, given by Paolo Masci from the National Institute of Aerospace (NIA), presented an approach for establishing a dialogue between formal methods experts and a multi-disciplinary team of engineers, domain experts, and end users of the system for the purpose of validation and debugging.

We would like to thank all members of the program committee for their support. We also thank the authors and presenters for sharing their experiences with us. We thank everyone for attending the workshop and we hope you all enjoyed the program and continue to help us make the pragmatics of applying formal verification a first-class research topic.

November 2019

Daniel Ratiu
Alexander Romanowsky
Alan Wassyng
Fuyuki Ishikawa

Organization

Program Committee Chairs

Fuyuki Ishikawa	National Institute of Informatics, Japan
Daniel Ratiu	Siemens Corporate Technology, Germany
Alexander Romanowsky	Newcastle University, UK
Alan Wassyng	McMaster University, Canada

Program Committee

Toshiaki Aoki	JAIST, Japan
Paolo Arcaini	NII, Japan
Sebastian Fischmeister	University of Waterloo, Canada
Marc Frappier	Université de Sherbrooke, Canada
Alessandro Fantechi	Università di Firenze, Italy
Stefania Gnesi	ISTI, Italy
Rajeev Joshi	Amazon Web Services, USA
Eunsuk Kang	CMU, USA
Florent Kirchner	CEA List, France
Mark Lawford	McMaster, Canada
Thierry Lecomte	ClearSy, France
Dominique Mery	LORIA, France
Ravi Metta	TCS, India
Vincent Nimal	Microsoft, USA
Marco Roveri	FBK, Italy
Neeray Singh	ENSEEITH, France

Experiences with Streamlining Formal Methods Tools

Paolo Masci[(✉)]

National Institute of Aerospace, Hampton, VA, USA
`paolo.masci@nianet.org`

Abstract. This paper discusses the use of formal methods in the context of multi-disciplinary teams. Success stories are presented based on experiences with industry and regulatory agencies. It will be shown that a pragmatic approach based on the use of prototypes driven by executable formal models represents an effective means to present the formal analysis effort to non-experts of formal methods.

Keywords: Rapid prototyping · Executable formal models

1 Introduction

Successful application of formal methods technologies is not just a matter of skillful use of formal methods tools and mathematical analysis techniques. It also requires establishing a constructive dialogue between formal methods experts and a multi-disciplinary team of developers (e.g., see [16]).

Consider the typical workflow followed by formal methods experts. It includes three main activities: (1) Create a formal model that captures information provided in design documents; (2) Translate natural language requirements into formal properties; (3) Perform the analysis with a formal tool.

In this workflow, formal methods experts need to engage with engineers and domain specialists to gain confidence that: *(i)* Formal models correctly capture the characteristics and functionalities of the system under analysis; *(ii)* Formal properties to be verified of the system correctly capture the intended meaning of requirements given in natural language; *(iii)* Counter-examples produced by the formal tool point out genuine design issues that need fixing, and not artifacts due to approximations used in the formal model.

The current generation of formal tools is not designed to facilitate these engagement activities. The tools provide text-based front-ends, rich of mathematical details that non-experts of formal methods find hard to understand. These elements can create strong communication barriers between formal methods experts and the rest of the team, resulting in important delays in the development life-cycle and overall reduced benefits from using formal methods.

This invited paper reports on a series of success stories where communication barriers were eliminated by *instrumenting formal methods tools with rapid*

© Springer Nature Switzerland AG 2020
E. Sekerinski et al. (Eds.): FM 2019 Workshops, LNCS 12232, pp. 5–11, 2020.
https://doi.org/10.1007/978-3-030-54994-7_1

prototyping capabilities. The intuition is that interactive prototypes based on executable formal models represent a convenient means to present relevant aspects of the formal analysis effort to non-experts of formal methods. The prototypes reproduce the visual appearance and behavior of the real system. They can be used to create scenario-based simulations that can be readily comprehended by engineers and domain specialists.

The rest of the paper is organized as follows. Section 2 describes an approach to instrument existing formal methods tools with rapid prototyping capabilities. Section 3 provides an overview of PVSio-web [9], a prototyping toolkit developed using the presented approach. Section 4 presents success stories based on experiences with using PVSio-web with industry and regulatory agencies. Section 5 presents related work and concluding remarks.

2   Instrumenting Formal Tools with Rapid Prototyping

A convenient approach to instrument existing formal methods tools with rapid prototyping capabilities builds on the use of *formal model animation* and a *client-server architecture.*

Formal model animation is a functionality provided by formal tools for evaluating executable fragments of a formal model. The functionality is typically provided in the form of an interactive command prompt with a read-eval-print loop: an expression is entered in the prompt; the tool evaluates the expression; a result is returned to the prompt. When the formal model captures information on the state of the system and on the events that trigger the evolution of the system state, the eval-print-loop can be used to compute execution traces necessary to drive the behavior of a prototype.

The use of a client-server architecture facilitates the integration of a formal tool with the rendering technology adopted for visual animation of the prototype. *The server back-end* encapsulates the formal tool. The APIs of the server provide means to interact with the read-eval-print loop of the formal tool. *The client front-end* runs the rendering technology and handles user actions performed on the prototype (in the case of prototypes with user interfaces). The visual appearance of the prototype reproduces that of the real system in the corresponding state. State information is provided by the server back-end.

The advantages of this approach are: *(i)* The formal tool can be used as-is—this guarantees that the prototyping capabilities do not affect the soundness of the formal tool; *(ii)* Platform-independence between client and server—the most appropriate platform can be chosen for the prototype front-end, e.g., a tablet, without worrying about whether the platform can support the execution of the formal tool.

3   The PVSio-web Toolkit

PVSio-web [9] is a prototyping toolkit based on PVS [11], a state-of-the-art theorem prover routinely used at SRI International and NASA for the analysis

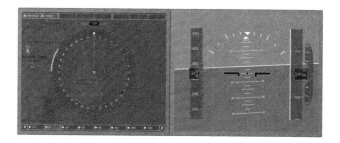

Fig. 1. Screenshots of prototypes generated with the PVSio-web toolkit.

of safety-critical systems, e.g., see [15]. PVS is well known for its expressive specification language based on higher-order logic, as well as for its extensive library of proved properties and decision procedures. Formal model animation is provided by a component called PVSio [10]. Its read-eval-print loop accepts PVS expressions as input, and returns the result of the evaluation as output.

PVSio-web uses Web technologies to instrument the PVSio component with rapid prototyping capabilities. On the client side, HTML, Cascading Style Sheets (CSS) and JavaScript are used for rendering realistic prototypes that closely resemble the *look & feel* of a real system (e.g., see Fig. 1). A picture of the final system can be used as a basis for creating the prototype. CSS transitions are used to perform 2D and 3D transformations necessary for smooth transition between visual states of the prototype. Hotspot areas over the picture identify interactive elements, such as displays and buttons. JavaScript programs monitor and update the hotspot based on state information provided by the server. A library of user interface elements and a web-based IDE are provided to facilitate the creation of the prototypes (see [9] for additional details). On the server side, NodeJS (http://nodejs.org) is used to create process workers that encapsulate PVSio and interact with its read-eval-print loop on-demand, e.g., when the front-end sends an evaluation request following a user action on the prototype.

4   Success Stories with PVSio-web

PVSio-web has been used successfully since 2012 to present the formal analysis effort to a range of different stakeholders, including device developers, human factors specialists, regulatory agencies, procurement staff, and end users. This section presents representative examples.

4.1   Analysis of Commercial Devices

PVSio-web prototypes played a key role in the identification of previously unde-tected software design anomalies in commercial medical devices. An example anomaly is a keypad software error causing the device to erroneously ignore dec-imal point key presses for certain ranges of numbers. This anomaly could result in situations where clinicians accidentally enter a value ten times larger than the intended value.

The anomaly emerged while verifying PVS models of commercial devices in use in hospitals across the US and EU. Most of the models were created by reverse engineering real devices. This involved systematic execution of interaction sequences with the real devices based on information presented in the owner's manuals. When available, the software source code of the device was also used as part of the reverse engineering process. The formal analysis was carried out to verify a human factors principle, *consistency of user actions*. The principle asserts that the same user actions should produce the same results in logically equivalent situations. Failed proof attempts pointed out counter-examples where the property was not satisfied. An example is as follows: entering 100.1 erroneously results in a value of 1,001 (full details of the formal analysis are in [8]). Execution of the same input sequence on the real device confirmed the erroneous behavior observed in the prototype.

In this case, the prototypes facilitated engagement with human factors specialists, medical device trainers, and regulatory officials. The dialogue with human factors specialists was key to develop a correct formalization of the human factors principle. Engagement with medical device trainers and regulatory officials was fundamental to recognize the severity of the design issues identified by the formal analysis.

4.2 Development of a New Product

PVSio-web prototypes were used to introduce formal analysis in the engineering process of a new portable electrocardiography (ECG) monitor produced by a small medical company. The company had limited experience with formal tools.

PVSio-web prototypes were developed to explore different functionalities when the software of the final product was still under development (see Fig. 1, left side). The same prototypes were also used to showcase the device to end users and clinicians when the final product was still unfinished. This allowed developers to gather additional requirements and adjust the software design at reduced cost and effort. Overall, this process resulted in a substantial reduction of the development time.

Formal analysis was used to analyze the modes of operation of the device against given requirements. This resulted in the creation of a reference specification for core software modules. A PVSio-web prototype based on the reference specification was developed to provide developers with a convenient means to explore the reference specification—functionalities could be explored simply by pressing buttons on the user interface of the prototype, and watching the output on the prototype displays.

4.3   Research on Future Systems

PVSio-web prototypes are currently used to support advanced research on flight displays. A new library DAA-Displays of user interface elements has been created for this purpose. The library extends the standard PVSio-web library with visual elements commonly used in flight displays (compass, interactive map, speed and altitude indicators, etc.). New simulation tools were also created to facilitate comparative analysis of different design alternatives.

An example application of the library is based on a Detect-and-Avoid (DAA) system developed at NASA [3]. The DAA system is designed to help the pilot-in-command maintain a safe distance between the ownship and all other aircraft within the ownship's surveillance range. The system uses real-time flight data to project route information and compute potential route conflicts. Maneuvers necessary to avoid conflicts are dynamically presented to the pilot in the form of color-coded *conflict bands* rendered on the flight instruments. Configuration options can be used to fine tune the behavior of the system, e.g., the granularity of maneuvers and the look-ahead time for conflict detection and resolution.

An example prototype of the DAA system is shown on the right side of Fig. 1. These prototypes are useful to discuss the behavior of the DAA system with pilots. This discussion is carried out with the aim to validate the behavior of the DAA system for different configurations, to make sure that generated maneuver recommendations are reasonable and can be followed by pilots.

5   Related Work and Conclusion

This paper discussed a pragmatic approach to facilitate the use of formal methods in the context of multi-disciplinary teamwork. It involves instrumenting formal tools with rapid prototyping capabilities. A series of success stories was presented based on the use of PVSio-web, a prototyping toolkit for PVS.

Others are exploring similar approaches and are experiencing similar success stories with different verification tools. Prototypes based on formal models can be created in the VDM toolset using the Maestro [14] tool. The prototypes have recently been applied to a case study based on ESA's Mars Rover [4]. A tool BMotionWeb [7] introduces prototyping capabilities in the B toolset. Heitmeyer's group created a tool SCR [6] and applied it to perform validation of requirements and specifications. Palanque's group at IRIT routinely uses prototyping tools as part of the formal analysis of flight display systems [12]. Thimbleby uses interactive prototypes to present verification results obtained with Mathematica to non-experts of the analysis tool [13]. The IVY Workbench [2], which builds on the NuSMV model checker, and uses tabular expressions to present formal verification results. This approach proves valuable when discussing requirements and formal analysis results with software engineers. A recent success story involves the use of IVY in the development of a new neonatal dialysis machine [5].

All these success stories clearly indicate the importance of prototyping and formal animation techniques in formal methods. From a tool perspective, future developments should aim to standardize support for rapid prototyping. For example, the Functional Mockup Interface (FMI [1]), which is a de-facto standard technology for integrating different simulation environments, seems to be a promising direction worth exploring in formal tools.

Acknowledgement. Work supported by the System Wide Safety Project, under NASA/NIA Cooperative Agreement NNL09AA00A.

References

1. Blochwitz, T., Otter, M., et al.: Functional mockup interface 2.0: the standard for tool independent exchange of simulation models. In: International MODELICA Conference, no. 76, pp. 173–184. Linköping University Electronic Press (2012). https://doi.org/10.3384/ecp12076173
2. Campos, J.C., Harrison, M.D.: Interaction engineering using the IVY tool. In: SIGCHI Symposium on Engineering Interactive Computing Systems, pp. 35–44. ACM (2009). https://doi.org/10.1145/1570433.1570442
3. Chamberlain, J.P., Consiglio, M.C., Muñoz, C.: DANTi: detect and avoid in the cockpit. In: AIAA Aviation Technology, Integration, and Operations Conference, p. 4491 (2017). https://doi.org/10.2514/6.2017-4491
4. Feo-Arenis, S., Verhoef, M., Larsen, P.G.: The Mars-Rover case study modelled using INTO-CPS. In: 15th Overture Workshop, pp. 130–144. Technical Report CS-TR-1513 (2017). http://pure.au.dk/portal/files/118986058/feo_arenis.pdf
5. Harrison, M.D., et al.: Formal techniques in the safety analysis of software components of a new dialysis machine. Sci. Comput. Program. **175**, 17–34 (2019). https://doi.org/10.1016/j.scico.2019.02.003
6. Heitmeyer, C., Kirby, J., Labaw, B., Bharadwaj, R.: SCR: a toolset for specifying and analyzing software requirements. In: Hu, A.J., Vardi, M.Y. (eds.) CAV 1998. LNCS, vol. 1427, pp. 526–531. Springer, Heidelberg (1998). https://doi.org/10.1007/BFb0028775
7. Ladenberger, L., Leuschel, M.: BMotionWeb: a tool for rapid creation of formal prototypes. In: De Nicola, R., Kühn, E. (eds.) SEFM 2016. LNCS, vol. 9763, pp. 403–417. Springer, Cham (2016). https://doi.org/10.1007/978-3-319-41591-8_27
8. Masci, P., Zhang, Y., Jones, P., Curzon, P., Thimbleby, H.: Formal verification of medical device user interfaces using PVS. In: Gnesi, S., Rensink, A. (eds.) FASE 2014. LNCS, vol. 8411, pp. 200–214. Springer, Heidelberg (2014). https://doi.org/10.1007/978-3-642-54804-8_14
9. Masci, P., Oladimeji, P., Zhang, Y., Jones, P., Curzon, P., Thimbleby, H.: PVSioweb 2.0: joining PVS to HCI. In: Kroening, D., Păsăreanu, C.S. (eds.) CAV 2015. LNCS, vol. 9206, pp. 470–478. Springer, Cham (2015). https://doi.org/10.1007/978-3-319-21690-4_30
10. Muñoz, C.: Rapid prototyping in PVS. Contractor Report NASA/CR-2003-212418, NASA, Langley Research Center, Hampton VA 23681–2199, USA, May 2003. https://ntrs.nasa.gov/search.jsp?R=20040046914
11. Owre, S., Rushby, J.M., Shankar, N.: PVS: a prototype verification system. In: Kapur, D. (ed.) CADE 1992. LNCS, vol. 607, pp. 748–752. Springer, Heidelberg (1992). https://doi.org/10.1007/3-540-55602-8_217
12. Palanque, P., Ladry, J.-F., Navarre, D., Barboni, E.: High-fidelity prototyping of interactive systems can be formal too. In: Jacko, J.A. (ed.) HCI 2009, Part I. LNCS, vol. 5610, pp. 667–676. Springer, Heidelberg (2009). https://doi.org/10.1007/978-3-642-02574-7_75

13. Thimbleby, H., Gow, J.: Applying graph theory to interaction design. In: Gulliksen, J., Harning, M.B., Palanque, P., van der Veer, G.C., Wesson, J. (eds.) DSV-IS/EHCI/HCSE -2007. LNCS, vol. 4940, pp. 501–519. Springer, Heidelberg (2008). https://doi.org/10.1007/978-3-540-92698-6_30
14. Thule, C., Lausdahl, K., Gomes, C., Meisl, G., Larsen, P.G.: Maestro: the INTO-CPS co-simulation framework. Simul. Model. Pract. Theory **92**, 45–61 (2019). https://doi.org/10.1016/j.simpat.2018.12.005
15. Titolo, L., Moscato, M.M., Muñoz, C.A., Dutle, A., Bobot, F.: A formally verified floating-point implementation of the compact position reporting algorithm. In: Havelund, K., Peleska, J., Roscoe, B., de Vink, E. (eds.) FM 2018. LNCS, vol. 10951, pp. 364–381. Springer, Cham (2018). https://doi.org/10.1007/978-3-319-95582-7_22
16. Wassyng, A., Lawford, M.: Lessons learned from a successful implementation of formal methods in an industrial project. In: Araki, K., Gnesi, S., Mandrioli, D. (eds.) FME 2003. LNCS, vol. 2805, pp. 133–153. Springer, Heidelberg (2003). https://doi.org/10.1007/978-3-540-45236-2_9

The Bourgeois Gentleman, Engineering and Formal Methods

Thierry Lecomte[(⊠)]

ClearSy, 320 avenue Archimède, Aix en Provence, France
thierry.lecomte@clearsy.com

Abstract. Industrial applications involving formal methods are still exceptions to the general rule. Lack of understanding, employees without proper education, difficulty to integrate existing development cycles, no explicit requirement from the market, etc. are explanations often heard for not being more formal. This article reports some experience about a game changer that is going to seamlessly integrate formal methods into safety critical systems engineering.

Keywords: B method · Safety platform · Automated proof

1 Introduction

The Moliere's Bourgeois Gentleman claimed that "for more than forty years [he has] been speaking prose while knowing nothing of it". What about imagining engineers claiming the same assertion but about formal methods? Formal methods and industry are not so often associated in the same sentence as the formers are not seen as an enabling technology but rather as difficult to apply and linked with increased costs. Lack of understanding, employees without proper education, difficulty to integrate existing development cycles, no explicit requirement from the market, etc. are explanations often heard for not being more formal. Our experience with formal methods, accumulated over the last 20 years [2–5,7,8], clearly indicates that not every one is able to abstract, refine, and prove mathematically. The Swiss psychologist Piaget claimed that only one third of the population is able to handle abstraction[1]. However we are firmly convinced that formal methods are a fundamental key to ensure safety for our all-connected world. Several years ago, we imagined a new solution smartly combining the B formal method, a diverse compilation tool-chain and a double processor architecture [6]. At that time, our sole objective was to reduce development costs but since then, given the full automation of the process, we are now considering this it as a way to obtain quite easily control-command systems certifiable at the highest levels of safety. This paper briefly presents the technical principles of this platform, the successful experiments/deployments/dissemination before listing the remaining scientific and technological challenges to address in the future.

---

[1] Skill acquired and developed during the so-called Formal Operational Stage.

© Springer Nature Switzerland AG 2020
E. Sekerinski et al. (Eds.): FM 2019 Workshops, LNCS 12232, pp. 12–18, 2020.
https://doi.org/10.1007/978-3-030-54994-7_2

2   CLEARSY Safety Platform

The CLEARSY Safety Platform (abbreviated as CSSP in the rest of the document) is a new technology, both hardware and software, combining a software development environment based on the B language and a secured execution hardware platform, to ease the development of safety critical applications.

It relies on a software factory that automatically transforms function into binary code that runs on redundant hardware. The starting point is a text-based, B formal model that specifies the function to implement. This model may contain static and dynamic properties that define the functional boundaries of the target software. The B project is automatically generated, based on the inputs/outputs configuration (numbers, names). From the developer point of view, only one function (name *user_logic*) has to be specified and implemented properly. The implementable model is then translated using two different chains:

- Translation into C ANSI code, with the C4B Atelier B code generator (instance I_1). This C code is then compiled into HEX[2] binary code with an off-the-shelf compiler (gcc).
- Translation into MIPS Assembly then to HEX binary code, with a specific compiler developed for this purpose (instance I_2). The translation in two steps allows to better debug the translation process as a MIPS assembly instruction corresponds to a HEX line (Fig. 1).

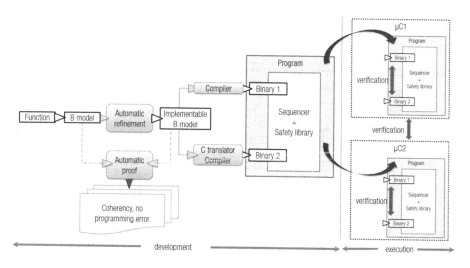

Fig. 1. The safe generation and execution of a function on the double processor.

The software obtained is the uploaded on the execution platform to be executed by two micro-controllers.

---

[2] A file format that conveys binary information in ASCII text form. It is commonly used for programming micro-controllers.

2.1   Safety

These two different instances I_1 and I_2 of the same function are then executed in sequence, one after the other, on two PIC32 micro-controllers. Each micro-controller hosts both I_1 and I_2, so at any time 4 instances of the function are being executed on the micro-controllers. The results obtained by I_1 and I_2 are first compared locally on each micro-controller then they are compared between micro-controllers by using messages. In case of a divergent behaviour (at least one of the four instances exhibits a different behaviour), the faulty micro-controller reboots.

The sequencer and the safety functions are developed once for all in B by the IDE design team and come along as a library. This way, the safety functions are out of reach of the developers and cannot be altered.

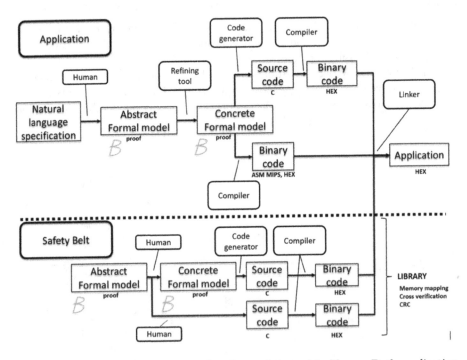

Fig. 2. Process for developing an application and the safety library. Both application and safety belt rely on the B method plus some handwritten code - mainly I/O.

The safety is based on several features such as:

- the detection of a divergent behaviour,
- micro-controller liveness regularly checked by messages,
- the detection of the inability for a processor to execute an instruction properly[3],

---

[3] All instructions are tested regularly against an oracle.

- the ability to command outputs[4],
- memory areas (code, data for the two instances) are also checked (no overlap, no address outside memory range),
- each output needs the two micro-controllers to be alive and providing respectively power and command, to be active (permissive mode). In case of misbehaviour, the detecting micro-controller deactivate its outputs and enter an infinite loop doing nothing.

Some of the tools in Fig. 2 have been "certified by usage" since 1998, but the newest tools of this toolchain have no history to rely on for certification. It is not a problem for railway standards as the whole product is certified (with its environment, the development and verification process, etc.), hence it is not required to have every tool certified. Instead the main feature used for the safety demonstration is the detection of a misbehaviour among the 4 instances of the function and the 2 microcontrollers. This way, similar bugs that could affect at the same time and with the same effects two independent tools are simply neglected. In its current shape, the CLEARSY Safety Platform provides an automatic way of transforming a proven B model into a program that safely executes on a redundant platform while the developer does not have to worry about the safety aspects.

2.2   Target Applications

The execution platform is based on two PIC32 micro-controllers[5]. The processing power available is sufficient to update 50k interlocking Boolean equations per second, compatible with light-rail signalling requirements. The execution platform can be redesigned seamlessly for any kind of mono-core processor if a higher level of performance is required.

The IDE provides a restricted modelling framework for software where:

- No operating system is used.
- Software behaviour is cyclic (no parallelism).
- No interruption modifies the software state variables.
- Supported types are Boolean and integer types (and arrays of).
- Only bounded-complexity algorithms are supported (the price to pay to keep the proof process automatic).

---

[4] Outputs are read to check if commands are effective, a system not able to change the state of its outputs has to shutdown.
[5] PIC32MX795F512L providing 105 DMIPS at 80 MHz.

3 Deployment and Dissemination

3.1 Research and Development

CSSP was initially an in-house development project before being funded[6] by the R&D project LCHIP[7] to obtain a generic version of the platform. This project is aimed at allowing any engineer to develop a function by using its usual Domain Specific Language and to obtain this function running safely on a hardware platform. With the automatic development process, the B formal method will remain "behind the curtain" in order to avoid expert transactions. As the safety demonstration does not require any specific feature for the input B model, it could be handwritten or the by-product of a translation process. Several DSL are planned to be supported at once (relays schematic, grafcet) based on an Open API (Bxml). The translation from relays schematic is being studied for the French Railways.

The whole process, starting from the B model and finishing with the software running on the hardware platform, is expected to be fully automatic, even with "not so simple models" with the integration of the results obtained from some R&D projects[8].

3.2 Education

The IDE is based on Atelier B 4.5.3, providing a simplified process-oriented GUI. A first starter kit, SK_0, containing the IDE and the execution platform, was released by the end of 2017[9], presented and experimented at the occasion of several hands-on sessions organised at university sites in Europe, North and South America. Audience was diverse, ranging from automation to embedded systems, mechatronics, computer science and formal methods. Results obtained are very encouraging:

- teaching formal methods is eased as students are able to see their model running in and interacting with the physical world,
- less theoretic profiles may be introduced/educated to more abstract aspects of computation,
- the platform has demonstrated a certain robustness during all these manipulations and has been enriched with the feedback collected so far.
- CSSP is yet used to teach in M2 in universities and engineering schools.

---

[6] The project is partly funded by BPI France, Région PACA, and Métropole Aix-Marseille, with a strong support from the "Pôles de compétitivité" I-Trans (Lille), SCS (Aix en Provence) and Systematic (Paris).

[7] Low Cost High Integrity Platform.

[8] Project BWARE (http://bware.lri.fr/index.php/BWare_project), to improve automatic proof performances.

[9] https://www.clearsy.com/en/our-tools/clearsy-safety-platform/.

3.3 Deployment

CSSP building blocks are operating platform-screen doors in São Paulo L15 metro (certified in 2018 at level SIL3 by CERTIFER on the inopportune opening failure of the doors), in Stockholm City line (certified in 2019), and in New York city (to be certified in 2019).

A new starter kit, SK_1, released end of 2018 and aimed at prototyping[10], has been experimented by the French Railways for transforming relay-based, wired logic into programmed ones [1] (see Fig. 3).

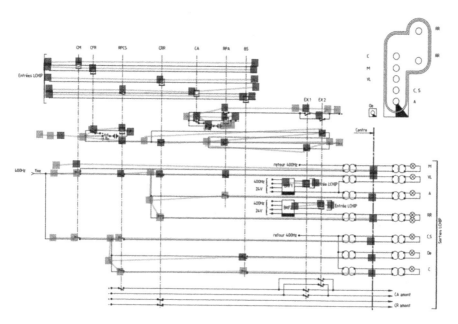

Fig. 3. Example of a relay circuit. Highlighted wires appear in yellow, entered circuit elements appear in green (when energized in default state) and red (otherwise) squares (Color figure online)

This starter kit definitely attracts a lot of attention from industry, from railways but also robotics and autonomous vehicles. With the forthcoming CSSP Core (safety programmable logic controller) by the end of 2019, more deployments in industry are expected.

4 Conclusion and Perspectives

CSSP, combined with improved proof performances and connection with Domain Specific Languages, pave the way to easier development of SIL4 functions (including both hardware and software). The platform safety being out of reach of the

---

[10] It embeds 20 inputs and 8 outputs, all digital.

software developer, the automation of the redundant binary code generation process and the certificates already obtained for products embedding CSSP building blocks, would enable the repetition of similar performances without requiring highly qualified engineers.

Moreover, the hardware platform is generic enough to host a large number of complexity-bounded[11] industry applications, with a special focus on the robotics and autonomous vehicles/systems domains.

However some aspects have to be considered in the near future to ensure a wide dissemination in the target application domains like: improved automatic proof performances to reach 100 % for not-so-complicated software functions, support for continuous values (as opposed to digital ones), support of more powerful, single-core processors, increase of the genericity while keeping the ability to be certified, etc.

References

1. de Almeida Pereira, D.I., Déharbe, D., Perin, M., Bon, P.: B-specification of relay-based railway interlocking systems based on the propositional logic of the system state evolution. In: Collart-Dutilleul, S., Lecomte, T., Romanovsky, A. (eds.) RSS-Rail 2019. LNCS, vol. 11495, pp. 242–258. Springer, Cham (2019). https://doi.org/10.1007/978-3-030-18744-6_16
2. Benveniste, M.V.: On using B in the design of secure micro-controllers: an experience report. Electr. Notes Theor. Comput. Sci. **280**, 3–22 (2011)
3. Burdy, L., Déharbe, D., Prun, É.: Interfacing automatic proof agents in Atelier B: introducing "iapa". In: Dubois, C., Masci, P., Méry, D. (eds.) Proceedings of the Third Workshop on Formal Integrated Development Environment, F-IDE@FM 2016, Limassol, Cyprus, 8 November 2016. EPTCS, vol. 240, pp. 82–90 (2016)
4. Lecomte, T.: Safe and reliable metro platform screen doors control/command systems. In: Cuellar, J., Maibaum, T., Sere, K. (eds.) FM 2008. LNCS, vol. 5014, pp. 430–434. Springer, Heidelberg (2008). https://doi.org/10.1007/978-3-540-68237-0_32
5. Lecomte, T.: Applying a formal method in industry: a 15-year trajectory. In: Alpuente, M., Cook, B., Joubert, C. (eds.) FMICS 2009. LNCS, vol. 5825, pp. 26–34. Springer, Heidelberg (2009). https://doi.org/10.1007/978-3-642-04570-7_3
6. Lecomte, T.: Double cœur et preuve formelle pour automatismes sil4. 8E-Modèles formels/preuves formelles-sûreté du logiciel (2016)
7. Lecomte, T., Burdy, L., Leuschel, M.: Formally checking large data sets in the railways. CoRR abs/1210.6815 (2012)
8. Sabatier, D.: Using formal proof and B method at system level for industrial projects. In: Lecomte, T., Pinger, R., Romanovsky, A. (eds.) RSSRail 2016. LNCS, vol. 9707, pp. 20–31. Springer, Cham (2016). https://doi.org/10.1007/978-3-319-33951-1_2

---

[11] Target complexity is lower than a metro automatic pilot one's.

SEB-CG: Code Generation Tool with Algorithmic Refinement Support for Event-B

Mohammadsadegh Dalvandi[1(✉)], Michael Butler[2], and Asieh Salehi Fathabadi[2]

[1] University of Surrey, Guildford, UK
m.dalvandi@surrey.ac.uk
[2] University of Southampton, Southampton, UK
{mjb,asf08r}@ecs.soton.ac.uk

Abstract. The guarded atomic action model of Event-B allows it to be applied to a range of systems including sequential, concurrent and distributed systems. However, the lack of explicit sequential structures in Event-B makes the task of sequential code generation difficult. Scheduled Event-B (SEB) is an extension of Event-B that augments models with control structures, supporting incremental introduction of control structures in refinement steps. SEB-CG is a tool for automatic code generation from SEB to executable code in a target language. The tool provides facilities for derivation of algorithmic structure of programs through refinement. The flexible and configurable design of the tool allows it to target various programming languages. The tool benefits from xText technology for a user-friendly text editor together with the proving facilities of Rodin platform for formal analysis of the algorithmic structure.

Keywords: Automatic code generation · Event-B · Program verification

1 Introduction

Event-B [1] is a general purpose formal modelling language based on set theory and predicate logic. It has been successfully applied in a wide range of systems including sequential, concurrent and distributed systems. The language is supported by a tool called Rodin [2]. Rodin is an extensible Eclipse-based platform which facilitates modelling and verification of Event-B models. Event-B in its original form does not support code generation. There have been a number of attempts to provide Event-B and Rodin with a code generation tool [6,8,9]. However, the lack of explicit control flow in Event-B made these tools suffer from usability problems. Other issues like the lack of clear and formal relationship between the generated code and the high level formal model decreased the confidence in the code generated by those tools.

This work is a fresh attempt to provide the Event-B toolset with facilities required for formal development and generation of sequential programs. The tool

© Springer Nature Switzerland AG 2020
E. Sekerinski et al. (Eds.): FM 2019 Workshops, LNCS 12232, pp. 19–29, 2020.
https://doi.org/10.1007/978-3-030-54994-7_3

described in this paper is built on our empirical experience with existing Event-B code generation tools in particular [6]. In developing SEB-CG, we have tried to address shortcomings of existing tools and also build on our previous theoretical work on derivation of algorithmic structures and verifiable code generation from Event-B models [3,4]. In designing SEB-CG, we have had the following principles in mind:

- **Extensibility:** The tool should be designed in a way that it is straightforward to extend it to accommodate new target languages.
- **Customisability:** The output of the tool should be highly customisable so that it can be used for generating programs for different domains.
- **Self-Sufficiency:** The tool should be self-sufficient for its core functionalities and its dependency on other Rodin plugins should be minimal.
- **Usability:** The tool should be designed in way that it is intuitive, useful and easy to use.

The above principles have been realised in SEB-CG in various ways. We have provided interfaces for extending the tool and adding support for new programming languages in a clear way. Also it is straightforward to add new translation rules for new target languages. The output of the tool is defined using templates and can be customised by modifying the templates. For instance, the way that a program is structured in terms of procedures and classes can be defined by the user. Unlike some of the previous works that were heavily dependent on other Rodin plugins for some of their core functionalities (e.g. translation rule definitions), SEB-CG has minimal dependency on other Rodin plugins and it has native support for its core functionalities. The scheduling language of SEB-CG is implemented using xText[1]. The xText editor provides a user-friendly environment for writing schedules. We have implemented a number of validation rules using the xText validator which provide the user with live and useful feedbacks including error and warning messages and tips on how to resolve the problem.

The tool and the instructions on how to install and use are provided in http://dalvandi.github.io/SEB-CG. The rest of this paper is devoted to details of the tool and its implementation.

2   Scheduled Event-B

SEB-CG implements the approach introduced in [3,4] which augments Event-B models with explicit control structures. We provided a scheduling language that allows the modeller to specify the control flow of events explicitly. In our approach, starting from the most abstract specification, the modeller provides a schedule associated with each machine. As Event-B refinement continues, the schedule associated with each refinement model should also refine the abstract schedule. We also provided a number of schedule refinement rules that direct the

---

[1] https://www.eclipse.org/Xtext/.

modeller in deriving a concrete program structure from the abstract schedule through refinement. In [4] we provided a number of translation rules for generating code and contracts (logical assertions) from a scheduled Event-B model. Our translation rules transform a concrete scheduled Event-B model to executable code and also generate a number of assertions that allow static verification of code properties.

3   Tool Overview

The SEB-CG tool is implemented as a Rodin plugin. The tool consists of a UI and a code generation core. The UI provides the user with a text editor for writing schedules. It also extends the Rodin explorer to include Schedule elements in a Rodin project folder and also provides a handle to the schedule-specific proof obligation generated by the tool.

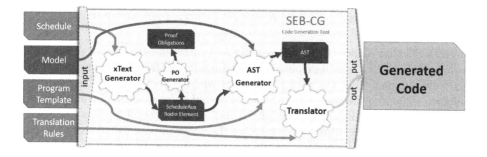

Fig. 1. A high-level overview of SEB-CG

The code generation machinery of the tool is depicted in Fig. 1. As shown, the SEB-CG tool receives four inputs: Schedule, Model, Program Template, and Translation Rules. A brief description of these inputs follows.

Schedule and Model: A *Schedule* is a text file written in the Scheduled Event-B (SEB) language and has *.seb* extension. The SEB language supported by the tool is presented in Appendix A. The schedule file contains a reference to a machine whose events it schedules. This is specified using the `machine` keyword. The name of the schedule is defined using the `schedule` keyword and it should be the same as the schedule file name. The schedule may refine another schedule. This is defined using `refines` keyword. As an example see the schedule presented in Fig. 2. The schedule name is $s3$ and it refines the abstract schedule $s2$. It is scheduling machine $m3$. Once the SEB-CG is invoked on a schedule for a target language, then the tool takes the schedule and the specified machine as inputs.

Program Template: We mentioned earlier that extensibility and customisability are two of the principles of SEB-CG. To realise these principles we have introduced *program templates*. A program template is a convenient feature of

```
schedule s3 refines s2
machine m3
proc binSearch(in:f, in:z, in:v, out:r)
begin
while('f(k) ≠ v')
  {
    if('f(k) < v')
    {
      search_inc
    }
    else
    {
      search_dec
    }
  }
  found
end
```

Fig. 2. An example of a schedule for a binary search algorithm

the SEB-CG that allows the user to specify and customise the output of the tool without the need for making changes to the implementation. It is expected that each new language that the tool is extended with, is provided with a program template. The program templates are not expected to be modified by non-expert users as this may make the output of the tool invalid. Template files are XML files that describe how different elements of the program are ordered and placed in the final generated code. An example of a program template for C is presented in Fig. 3. This template for example places variable declaration (`vardecl`) before procedures (`procedures`).

```
<file name="#MACHINENAME.cpp">
  <vardecl/>
  <procedures>
    <procedure inpar="true" outpar="false" return="true">
    <init/>
    </procedure>
  </procedures>
</file>
```

Fig. 3. An example of a program template for C

We have defined a simple language for templates. The grammar of our Program Template Language (PTL) is given in Appendix B.

Translation Rules: Translation rules define the way in which a scheduled Event-B model is translated to code in a target language. Instead of hard-coding the rules in the implementation of the tool, SEB-CG provides a flexible way for defining translation rules. Each target language has a translation rule file in XML format. Figure 4 depicts a translation rule for a binary operation.

```
<rule type="operator">
  <source> $a - $b </source>
  <target> ($a - $b) </target>
</rule>
```

Fig. 4. An example of a translation rule for C

The grammar of the syntax of the Translation Rule Language (TRL) is given in Appendix C.

4   Tool Components

Figure 1 provides a high level view of the tool core machinery. As can be seen there are four main components in the tool: xText Generator, PO Generator, AST Generator and AST Translator. The work flow of the tool is also depicted in the figure. The rest of this section provides details of various components.

xText Component: We have leveraged the power of xText [7] in the implementation of our tool. Specifically, we have used xText to define the grammar of the scheduling language. xText also provides us with other useful facilities like text editor and a basic validator out of the box. We extended the xText validator with schedule refinement rules so that concrete schedules are checked to be valid refinements of the abstract ones. We have also used the xText generator to translate the textual representation of the schedule to a newly defined Rodin element called ScheduleAux. This translation is performed in order to be able to use the Rodin proof obligation generator easier. ScheduleAux is an internal element and is hidden from the Rodin user.

PO Generator: As explained in [3], there are a number of proof obligations (i.e. guard elimination POs) that a schedule must satisfy. We have extended the Rodin proof obligation generator to generate the required proof obligations based on the schedule (ScheduleAux) and the model (machine and context) that the schedule is referring to.

AST Generator: In order to translate a model to code in a target language, the tool first generates an abstract syntax tree (AST). The AST is generated based on the program template, schedule and the model. The AST represents the overall structure of the program and the hierarchical order of different parts of the program, e.g. classes, procedures, program body, etc. Sequentialisation of event actions [4] are also done by the AST generator as part of the event AST generation.

AST Translator: Once the AST is generated, it is translated to the code in the target language by the AST translator. The AST translator receives translation rules and the generated AST as its inputs and traverses the AST recursively and matches its sub-trees with appropriate rules and outputs the program text.

5   Tool Usage

SEB-CG is designed to be an easy-to-use tool. The GUI is intuitive and consists of a simple text editor. The text editor has syntax colouring and highlighting support and provides live feedback on syntactical warnings/errors. The schedule is also checked in the background to ensure conformance to the refinement rules of [3]. Schedules appear in the Event-B project explorer of Rodin alongside other project elements e.g. machines and contexts. A schedule can only refer to machines in the same project. Since schedules and their respective proof obligations are stored separately from the Event-B model, modifying a schedule does not change its associated model or its proofs.

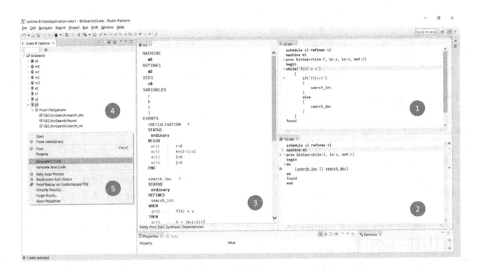

Fig. 5. A screen-shot of the tool

Figure 5 is a screen-shot of the tool. (1) is a schedule editor showing the concrete schedule $s3$ and (2) is another editor showing the abstract $s2$ schedule. Note that $s3$ refines $s2$. We intentionally injected an error into $s2$ by referencing to a wrong machine ($m1$ instead of $m2$) so that the text highlighting is demonstrated. (4) is the Event-B explorer showing schedules $s0, .., s3$ and proof obligations related to $s3$. (5) is the menu that allows the invocation of the code generator for any of the available target languages. Finally (3) is an Event-B machine $m3$, which is scheduled by $s3$, shown using the standard Event-B machine editor.

The recommended practice for using the tool is to start introducing the schedules from the abstract level where the abstract machine is defined and then refine it alongside the machine refinement. The abstract schedule usually contains only abstract scheduling constructs (i.e. choice and iteration). As the refinement continues, the abstract constructs are replaced with concrete ones (i.e. if-branches and while-loops). Although it is possible to define the concrete schedule for the concrete model directly without going through schedule refinement steps, it is a discouraged practice since it is more likely to result in guard elimination POs that cannot be discharged.

Once the refinement has reached a concrete level, both for the model and schedule, the user can invoke the code generator by right-clicking on the concrete schedule element and select the desired target language from the list of available target languages. It is at this time that the tool starts building the AST with respect to the program template, schedule and model. The generated AST together with the translation rules are then fed into the translator and the code is generated. If during the translation phase, the translator does not find a match between a sub-tree and the provided rules, an exception will be thrown and the user will be provided with the pattern of the rule that it was unable to find.

6   Conclusion

In this paper we presented a tool for automatic code generation from scheduled Event-B models. The tool is customisable and extensible and can potentially accommodate a wide range of target languages. Currently the tool has out of the box support for C and Java code generation and it can be extended to include other languages.

As far as we are aware, the only other code generation tool for Event-B that allows introduction of explicit program order is Tasking Event-B [6]. However, comparing to SEB-CG, the Tasking Event-B tool has a restrictive scheduling language (e.g. no support for nested control structures or explicit loop/branch conditions) and has no support for schedule refinement. There exist other code generation tools for Event-B which do not allow introduction of algorithmic structure of the model by the modeller [8,9]. The generated code by these tools may not be optimised and depends entirely on the implementation of the tool and not on a verified algorithmic structure provided by the modeller.

In future, we would like to extend the tool to also generate code contracts (i.e. assertions and pre/post-conditions) as described in [4,5]. The generated contracts will allow the verification of some properties of the generated code (e.g. sequentialisation) using a static program analyser. Extension of the scheduling language to support procedure calls is another feature for the future. We are also interested in further development of our tool to support concurrent program generation.

Acknowledgments. This work was supported by the EPSRC PRiME Project (EP/K034448/1), www.prime-project.org. The first author is currently supported by EPSRC grant EP/R032556/1.

Appendix A   Scheduling Language

⟨*Schedule*⟩   ::= schedule ⟨*ScheduleName*⟩, [refines ⟨*ScheduleName*⟩],
                        machine ⟨*MachineName*⟩,
                        {⟨*Procedure*⟩}

⟨*Procedure*⟩   ::= proc ⟨*ProcName*⟩(⟨*ProcPars*⟩)
                        begin
                        ⟨*ScheduleBody*⟩
                        end

⟨*ScheduleBody*⟩ ::= ⟨*Expression*⟩, {⟨*Expression*⟩}

⟨*Expression*⟩   ::= *Event*
                      | ⟨*ScheduleBody*⟩, {[] ⟨*ScheduleBody*⟩}
                      | do ⟨*ScheduleBody*⟩ od
                      | if(⟨*Cond*⟩){⟨*ScheduleBody*⟩},
                        {elseif(⟨*Cond*⟩){⟨*ScheduleBody*⟩}},
                        [else{⟨*ScheduleBody*⟩}]
                      | while(⟨*Cond*⟩){⟨*ScheduleBody*⟩}

⟨*Cond*⟩   ::= *Predicate*

⟨*ScheduleName*⟩ ::= *String*

⟨*MachineName*⟩ ::= *String*

⟨*ProcName*⟩   ::= *String*

⟨*ProcPars*⟩   ::= ⟨*ProcPar*⟩,{, ⟨*ProcPar*⟩}

⟨*ProcPar*⟩   ::= in : ⟨*Par*⟩
                      | out : ⟨*Par*⟩

⟨*Par*⟩   ::= Event-B variable or constant

Appendix B   Program Template Language

⟨*Template*⟩	::=	`<file name=",` ⟨*Name*⟩, `">,`
		{⟨*TemplateElement*⟩}
		`</file>`

⟨*Class*⟩	::=	`<class name=",` ⟨*Name*⟩ `,">,`
		⟨*ClassElements*⟩,
		`</class>`

⟨*Procedures*⟩	::=	`<procedures>,`
		{⟨*Procedure*⟩},
		`</procedures>`

⟨*Procedure*⟩	::=	`<procedure name=",`⟨*Name*⟩,
		`" inpar=",`⟨*Bool*⟩,`" outpar=",`⟨*Bool*⟩,
		`" return=",`⟨*Bool*⟩,`">,`
		⟨*ProcedureBody*⟩,
		`</procedure>`

⟨*VarDecl*⟩	::=	`<vardecl/>`
⟨*Init*⟩	::=	`<init/>`
⟨*Bool*⟩	::=	true | false
⟨*Name*⟩	::=	⟨*Char*⟩ | ⟨*Ref*⟩, {⟨*Char*⟩ | ⟨*Ref*⟩}
⟨*Char*⟩	::=	a..z | A..Z | 0..9 | _ | - | .
⟨*Ref*⟩	::=	`#SCHEDULENAME` | `#MACHINENAME` | `#PROCNAME`

Appendix C   Translation Rule Language

⟨*Translations*⟩	::=	`<translations language="`, ⟨*LangName*⟩, `">`,
		`{`⟨*Rule*⟩`}`,
		`</translations>`
⟨*Rule*⟩	::=	`<rule type="`, ⟨*RuleType*⟩, `">`,
		`[`⟨*MetaVars*⟩`]`,
		⟨*Source*⟩,
		⟨*Target*⟩,
		`</rule>`
⟨*MetaVars*⟩	::=	`<metavariables>`,
		`{`⟨*Var*⟩`}`,
		`</metavariables>`
⟨*Var*⟩	::=	`<var>`,
		`<id>`,
		`$`, ⟨*VarName*⟩,
		`</id>`,
		`<type>`,
		⟨*VarType*⟩,
		`</type>`,
		`</var>`
⟨*Source*⟩	::=	*Source Expression/Structure*
⟨*Target*⟩	::=	*Translation*
⟨*LangName*⟩	::=	*Name of the target language*
⟨*RuleType*⟩	::=	`class` | `procedure` | `constructor` | `sequence` | `inpar` | `outpar` | `return` | `ifbranch` | `elseifbranch` | `elsebranch` | `loop` | `vardecl` | `identifier` | `type` | `ctype` | `operator`
⟨*VarName*⟩	::=	*Valid Event-B identifier name*
⟨*VarType*⟩	::=	*Valid Event-B type*

References

1. Abrial, J.R.: Modeling in Event-B: System and Software Engineering. Cambridge University Press, Cambridge (2010)
2. Abrial, J.R., Butler, M., Hallerstede, S., Hoang, T., Mehta, F., Voisin, L.: Rodin: an open toolset for modelling and reasoning in Event-B. Int. J. Softw. Tools Technol. Transfer **12**(6), 447–466 (2010)

3. Dalvandi, M., Butler, M., Rezazadeh, A.: Derivation of algorithmic control structures in Event-B refinement. Sci. Comput. Program. **148**(Suppl. C), 49–65 (2017). https://doi.org/10.1016/j.scico.2017.05.010, http://www.sciencedirect.com/science/article/pii/S016764231730120X. Special issue on Automated Verification of Critical Systems (AVoCS 2015)
4. Dalvandi, M., Butler, M., Rezazadeh, A., Salehi Fathabadi, A.: Verifiable code generation from scheduled Event-B models. In: Butler, M., Raschke, A., Hoang, T.S., Reichl, K. (eds.) ABZ 2018. LNCS, vol. 10817, pp. 234–248. Springer, Cham (2018). https://doi.org/10.1007/978-3-319-91271-4_16
5. Dalvandi, M., Butler, M.J., Rezazadeh, A.: Transforming Event-B models to Dafny contracts. ECEASST **72** (2015). http://journal.ub.tu-berlin.de/eceasst/article/view/1021
6. Edmunds, A., Butler, M.: Tasking Event-B: an extension to Event-B for generating concurrent code, February 2011. https://eprints.soton.ac.uk/272006/, Event Dates: 2 April 2011
7. Eysholdt, M., Behrens, H.: Xtext: implement your language faster than the quick and dirty way. In: Proceedings of the ACM International Conference Companion on Object Oriented Programming Systems Languages and Applications Companion, pp. 307–309. ACM (2010)
8. Méry, D., Singh, N.K.: Automatic code generation from Event-B models. In: Proceedings of the Second Symposium on Information and Communication Technology, pp. 179–188. ACM (2011)
9. Wright, S.: Automatic generation of C from Event-B. In: Workshop on Integration of Model-Based Formal Methods and Tools, p. 14. Citeseer (2009)

Compiling C and C++ Programs for Dynamic White-Box Analysis

Zuzana Baranová and Petr Ročkai[✉]

Faculty of Informatics, Masaryk University, Brno, Czech Republic
{xbaranov,xrockai}@fi.muni.cz

Abstract. Building software packages from source is a complex and highly technical process. For this reason, most software comes with build instructions which have both a human-readable and an executable component. The latter in turn requires substantial infrastructure, which helps software authors deal with two major sources of complexity: first, generation and management of various build artefacts and their dependencies, and second, the differences between platforms, compiler toolchains and build environments.

This poses a significant problem for white-box analysis tools, which often require that the source code of the program under test is compiled into an intermediate format, like the LLVM IR. In this paper, we present divcc, a drop-in replacement for C and C++ compilation tools which transparently fits into existing build tools and software deployment solutions. Additionally, divcc generates intermediate and native code in a single pass, ensuring that the final executable is built from the intermediate code that is being analysed.

1 Introduction

Automation is ubiquitous and essential, and this is no different in software engineering. Processes which are automated are cheaper, they reduce the chances of human error and are generally much more repeatable than processes which involve manual steps. Program compilation is one of the earliest software engineering tasks to have been automated. In addition to its intrinsic merits, build automation forms a key component in other process automation efforts within software engineering: automatic testing, continuous integration and continuous deployment, to name a few.

Another area of software engineering which can greatly benefit from automation is correctness and performance analysis of programs. Of course, this is a highly non-trivial problem and is the focus of intense research. However, neither program source code nor the resulting machine code is very convenient for automated analysis: instead, tools prefer to work with intermediate representations,

This work has been partially supported by the Czech Science Foundation grant No. 18-02177S.

E. Sekerinski et al. (Eds.): FM 2019 Workshops, LNCS 12232, pp. 30–45, 2020.
https://doi.org/10.1007/978-3-030-54994-7_4

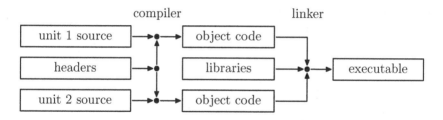

Fig. 1. The process of building an executable from 2 source files.

such as LLVM.[1] Analysis tools fall into two coarse categories: static and dynamic. The latter are usually significantly more difficult to integrate into the workflows of large software projects – a deficiency which we aim to address.

Programming languages come in two basic flavours: interpreted and compiled. In the former case, the program is executed directly in its source form. However, interpretation is often deemed inefficient and many programs are written in languages which are first translated into *machine code*. Individual source files are *compiled* into *object code* (a form of machine code which is suitable for *linking* – the process of combining multiple compilation units to form a single program). The process that encompasses both compilation of the individual translation units, as well as the subsequent linking is then known as *building* (see Fig. 1). A number of programs and/or libraries may result from a single build.

Since the build process is often complex, software implemented in compiled languages – especially C and C++ – usually ships with comprehensive *build instructions* which are automatically processed by a *build system*. Besides simply invoking the compiler and the linker, those build instructions often deal with building the software on different platforms and operating systems, locating build-time *dependencies*[2] and checking that a suitable version is correctly installed and so on.

1.1 Motivation

One of the first tools which is discovered in the configuration phase of a build is the system C compiler: it is common practice to use the compiler to perform subsequent platform checks. It is typically assumed that the compiler used in the configuration phase of the build is the same as the compiler used to build the software package itself.[3]

---

[1] Of course, tools which work with machine code, known as black-box tools, do exist, but their use in software development is limited – they are mainly used in software forensics. In this paper, we focus on white-box methods, which work with source code or an intermediate representation thereof.

[2] A separate (often third-party) software package which needs to be installed in the system before the build can proceed – usually a library, sometimes a tool used in the build process.

[3] Not doing so could lead to configuration mismatches between the two compilers causing build failures, or worse, miscompilation.

Naturally, we would like to take advantage of existing build automation to obtain intermediate code (in our case LLVM IR) which can then be used for correctness and performance analysis. In ideal circumstances, such analysis would also be fully automated and incorporated into the continuous integration process. However, even when employed in mostly manual processes, it is extremely useful to always have an up-to-date intermediate form available. For this reason, we would like to seamlessly and automatically produce this intermediate form alongside standard libraries and executables. We met these goals to a very high degree with the presented tool divcc, reusing existing build systems, and producing the intermediate representation (LLVM IR) along with the executable.

There are a large number of tools which can benefit from improving the process of obtaining LLVM bitcode for entire programs. Tools that perform dynamic analysis can benefit the most.[4] Some of the tools in this category that use LLVM as their input representation are: the symbolic executor KLEE [3], the slicing-based bug hunting tool Symbiotic [4], the software model checker DIVINE [2] or the MCP model checker [13]. Likewise, stateless model checkers for weak memory models like Nidhugg [1] and RCMC [6] would be significantly easier to use on test cases that use external libraries. Similar benefits apply to bounded model checkers like LLBMC [11] or the LLVM-based IC3 tool VVT [5].

An important consideration is that very few of these tools offer comprehensive support for the standard C library, while support for the C++ standard library or for the widely used POSIX interfaces is even less frequent. Unfortunately, using a tool like divcc to build the system C library (libc) into a usable bitcode form is still a daunting task and it is not clear whether such bitcode could be sensibly used with any of the abovementioned tools.

Linking an analysis-friendly C library into the bitcode version of the program (providing bitcode definitions of functions that normally come from the system libc) effectively side-steps the problem. One of the goals of divcc is to make such substitution easy: in Sect. 3.5, we describe a variant of divcc, which supplies the bitcode for standard C and C++ libraries provided by DiOS [10]. DiOS is a small model operating system that can be used as a foundation for programs built with divcc, in the sense that it provides the standard C and C++ libraries (as is expected of operating systems) – mainly libc, but also libm, libc++, libpthread and libc++abi. Importantly, the combined tool dioscc (which integrates divcc with DiOS) provides the libraries directly in the form of LLVM bitcode, making it easy to combine them with other bitcode (the product of the user source files) and include them in compilation. More information about DiOS can be found in [10] Out of the tools mentioned above, DiOS and the libraries it includes have been successfully ported to KLEE and DIVINE.

---

[4] This is true even in cases where such tools can work with partial programs – i.e. programs which use functions whose definitions are not available to the tool; however, this mode of operation negatively affects the precision of the analysis.

1.2   Related Work

A number of tools with related goals to `divcc` already exist. If we focus on LLVM-based tools, the most well-known tool which integrates white-box analysis into the standard build process is perhaps `scan-build` [7]. This tool shares the same fundamental technique of replacing the C/C++ compiler with a wrapper which, in this case, directly executes the `clang-analyzer` tool on each source file after compiling it using a standard compiler.

In the `scan-build` workflow, the compiler is only overridden temporarily, during the execution of `make` or another build tool – it is not in use during project configuration. This means that the compiler wrappers used by `scan-build` can be somewhat more lax about matching the behaviour of the underlying compiler perfectly. It is also simpler in the sense that it does not need to create persistent artefacts and bundle them with standard build products.

Another related tool, this time from the CBMC [8] toolkit is `goto-cc`, which is a `gcc`-compatible compiler which however does not produce executable binaries at all. For this reason, it rather heavily deviates from the behaviour of a standard compiler and as such can only work with comparatively simple build systems, which do not invoke external tools on their build products nor do they execute intermediate helper programs that were compiled as part of the build process.

An important source of inspiration in our effort was the *link time optimization* [12] (LTO) subsystem of LLVM, which uses a special section in object files[5] to store the bitcode which resulted from compiling the corresponding source unit. In this case, the goal is not program analysis as such, but late-stage program optimization: interprocedural optimization passes can operate more efficiently if they see the entire program at once, instead of just a single unit at a time.

A tool perhaps most closely related to `divcc` is known as `wllvm` (where the 'w' stands for whole-program). Like many of the previously mentioned tools, `wllvm` provides a wrapper for the compiler which performs additional work – in this case, in addition to compiling the unit in a standard way, it runs the compiler again but instructs it to produce bitcode instead of machine code. Unlike the link time optimization system, this bitcode is not stored in the object file – instead, it creates a hidden file next to the original object and embeds the absolute path to the bitcode file in a section of the object file. Subsequently, a special tool called `extract-bc` needs to be used to extract those paths from a build product (a library or an executable) and link it into a single bitcode unit.

The approach taken by `wllvm` has a number of downsides: first, the creation of hidden files deviates from standard compiler behaviour, and sometimes interferes with the operation of build configuration tools. Second, even after installation into a target location, the build products refer to files present in the original build directory which therefore cannot be cleaned up as would be usual, making builds of systems which consist of multiple independent packages more difficult and error-prone. The `wllvm` tool offers workarounds for both these problems, though

---

[5] And subsequently also in static libraries, which on POSIX systems are simply archives of object files.

they are not free of their drawbacks. Even then, integration into automated build orchestration systems which build and package individual components, often in a distributed computing environment without shared file systems, would be very difficult, if at all feasible. On the other hand, the `wllvm` approach has one major upside: there is no need to perform any additional work during the linking stage of the compilation, since the `wllvm`-specific sections are correctly merged by a standard linker, somewhat simplifying the implementation.

The whole problem is side-stepped by tools such as `valgrind` [9], which work directly with machine code and hence do not need any special tooling to integrate into build systems – at most, they re-use existing mechanisms to create *debug-enabled* builds. Finally, middle ground is occupied by the *clang sanitizers* family of dynamic analysis tools. Those tools are integrated in standard compilers (with support in both `clang` and `gcc`), but require special builds which differ from standard debug builds in the compiler flags passed to the compiler. They also require special versions of runtime libraries, which are usually shipped with the compiler in question.

1.3   Contribution

Our main contribution is an open-source tool, `divcc`,[6] which serves a similar purpose as `wllvm` but mitigates its problems by taking the LTO-like approach of embedding the entire bitcode in object, library and executable files. Additionally, unlike `wllvm`, our tool first translates the input C or C++ code into bitcode and then compiles that bitcode into native code, saving effort and reducing the chance of discrepancies between the bitcode and the corresponding machine code.

Moreover, our approach allows analysis tools to provide their own header files and bitcode libraries, overriding the host system. This is crucial in scenarios where strict verification is desired, ensuring that only the functionality fully covered by the verification tool is made available to the program during build configuration. Finally, we have evaluated the usability and performance of `divcc` on a number of software packages. We report the results of this evaluation in Sect. 4.

2   Preliminaries

In this section, we will explain the terms and concepts that are in more-or-less common use and which are directly relevant to the remainder of this paper, most prominently Sect. 3.

2.1   Storing Machine Code

On UNIX systems, the standard format for storing machine code (i.e. the binary code understood by the CPU) is ELF, short for Executable and Linkable Format. It is the common format for representing files that figure in the process of compilation, such as object files, executables, or libraries.

---

[6] Source code & supplementary material at https://divine.fi.muni.cz/2019/divcc.

During the process of building software, machine code exists in a number of related, but distinct forms. It is first generated by the compiler in the form of object code, which is usually stored in an object file. This form of the code is *relocatable*, meaning the routines and variables stored in the file have not been assigned their final addresses. A number of such object files can be bundled together, unaltered, to form a *static library* (also known as an *archive*), using a special program – `ar`. Finally, object files and archives can be linked into executables or shared libraries. This final step is performed by another program, a linker (often known as `ld`) and consists of resolving cross-references and performing relocations.

The data and code in an ELF file is split into multiple *sections*. There are several well-known sections that have special roles in ELF files, the most important of which are:

- `.text` - contains instructions (machine code) of the program,
- `.data` and `.rodata` - constant-initialized data, e.g. string literals,
- `.bss` - zero-initialized data (the zeroes are not stored in the file).

However, there are no significant restrictions on the number or the names of individual sections. In particular, operating systems or compiler toolchains can create or recognize additional sections with the semantics of their choosing.

2.2   Compiler Architecture

Most C and C++ compilers follow a fairly standard architecture, which is depicted in Fig. 2. The entire process is managed by a *driver*, which decides which stages and in what order need to be invoked. The responsibilities of the individual components are as follows:

1. the preprocessor reads the input source file and any header files it may refer to (via `#include` directives) and produces a single self-contained source file,
2. the frontend parses and analyses the source file produced by the preprocessor and generates an intermediate representation out of it,
3. the middle end performs transformations (mainly optimization) on the intermediate format, generating a new version thereof,
4. the backend, or code generator, translates the optimized intermediate representation into object code (i.e. relocatable machine code).

The linker is technically not a part of the compiler: in most cases, it is a separate program. However, it is usually the compiler driver that is responsible for executing the linker with the correct arguments – the linker then simply performs the tasks requested by the compiler. The selection and order of object files (including the system-specific components linked into every program, like `crt0.o`) and libraries (including system libraries like `libc`) to be linked is therefore the responsibility of the compiler driver.

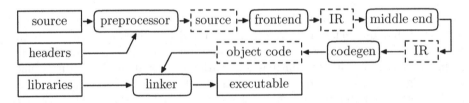

Fig. 2. The architecture of a typical compiler. The rounded boxes represent compiler components, the squares represent data. Dashed boxes only exist as internal objects within the compiler and will not be written into files unless requested by the user or by the build system. Out of the dashed boxes in the picture, typically only object code is written into a file.

Finally, an important consideration is the mechanics of archive linking: unlike shared libraries, which are indivisible and linked into each program in their entirety, or not at all, static libraries retain individual object files. By default, the linker will only include those object files from each archive that are required to provide symbols referenced by files already included. This optimization can influence program behaviour, because unlike shared libraries, global constructors which are defined in object files that are not referenced by the program (directly or indirectly) will not run. It is therefore important to replicate this behaviour in the bitcode linker component of `divcc`.

2.3 Build Systems

Non-trivial software tends to be composed of numerous source files and header files, which are often organized into multiple libraries and executables. In addition to the source code shipped with the software itself, there are usually dependencies on external libraries and header files, which may be either part of the operating system, or provided by third parties as separate software packages.

Not only is it repetitive and error-prone for the programmer to carry out this process manually, it is also vital to automate it if the software is expected to be built by third parties, who are not sufficiently familiar with it. It further gives a level of assurance that the build is deterministic and reproducible, which is undoubtedly valuable. Many build automation systems have been proposed and implemented. In most cases, the software package is accompanied by build instructions which are read and performed by the build system or build tool in question. For instance, the `make` build system reads a file called `Makefile` which describes the steps for compiling and linking source code. The build process carried out by a typical build system is split into 2 phases:

1. Build configuration is mainly concerned with inspecting the build platform.
   - i. The tool, taking into account the build instructions, examines the software installed in the system, to see what is available and whether it is possible to build the program at all.
   - ii. To this end, it may attempt to compile and sometimes run *feature tests* – essentially tiny test programs; if the compilation fails, the tool concludes

that the tested functionality is unavailable. Alternatively, it may contain a database of known systems and their properties.

iii. At the end of the build configuration phase, the build tool will store the configuration information (like compiler flags and feature macro definitions) in a form which can be used during compilation.

2. The build proper, in which the software is compiled and linked.[7] The build system performs the steps specified in the build instructions to produce libraries and executables which make up the package. The instructions are usually quite abstract and the particulars of tool orchestration are left to the build system.

3 Design and Implementation

In this section, we first summarize the functional requirements for a tool which would allow us to seamlessly integrate white-box dynamic analysis into existing build systems and workflows, then we spell out the specific design choices we made, describe the implementation, and discuss its limitations.

3.1 Functional Requirements

Our primary requirement when designing the tool was that it would serve as a drop-in replacement for a C (and C++) compiler. There are multiple issues that need to be considered, mainly to ensure compatibility with existing build systems. Our list of functional requirements for divcc is, therefore, as follows:

– compatible interface – avoiding the need to alter existing build instructions,
– compatible output – the build system expects that certain files are created, in a certain format so that it can work with them further,
– compilation – source code is compiled into intermediate and native code
– linking – both intermediate and native code is linked into executables and shared libraries,
– archive support – the handling of intermediate code in archives is semantically equivalent to the handling of object code therein,
– object bitcode – bitcode in object files needs to be stored in a format that can be linked to form shared libraries and executables,
– loadable bitcode – the final result must be in a format that the analysis tool can use as input, ideally with no changes to the tool
– single pass operation – no repeated front-end and middle end invocation, minimizing the overhead introduced by the tool into the build process.

Additionally, we have a few non-functional requirements:

– user-friendliness – this extends the functional requirement that the pre-existing build instructions do not need to be changed,
– re-use existing compiler code (CLang and LLVM),
– make it as easy as possible to keep up with changes in CLang and LLVM.

---

[7] Most build systems also attempt to speed up repeated builds by avoiding re-compiling files that are unchanged (and whose dependencies also remain up-to-date). This capability is important during development and testing, though of course it adds further complexity to the process.

```
$ wget http://ftp.gnu.org/gnu/gzip/gzip-1.8.tar.gz
$ tar xzf gzip-1.8.tar.gz
$ cd gzip-1.8 && ./configure CC=divcc && make
$ echo hello world | ./gzip - > hello.gz
$ divine check --stdin hello.gz ./gzip -f -d -
$ divcc-extract gzip gzip.bc
$ klee -exit-on-error gzip.bc hello.gz
```

Fig. 3. An example use of divcc to build and analyse gzip. We first retrieve the archive of the gzip project from the official site using wget. With the following commands, we unpack the archive, change to the project directory, run the configure script (passing divcc as the compiler to use) and run make to build the project. Next, we pass the traditional 'hello world' string to gzip to compress it into a file called hello.gz. We used DIVINE (a model checker mentioned in the motivation) to check the behaviour of the gzip executable, or rather the corresponding LLVM IR code. Running the model checker is demonstrated on the 5th line of the example – we run it in check mode on the gzip executable, taking standard input from the hello.gz file. The options are passed on to gzip and mean: decompress (-d), force decompression even if the input is a terminal (-f) and read the data to decompress from the standard input (-). The last two lines demonstrate use of divcc with KLEE, a tool which needs to work with the LLVM IR directly, so we first extract it from the executable using divcc-extract.

3.2 Intended Use

The expectation is that for the user, the only difference in building their programs is telling the build system to use divcc as the C compiler (and divc++ as the C++ compiler if the software contains C++ source code), for example:

- ./configure CC=divcc CXX=divc++ (with autotools-based builds)
- cmake -DCMAKE_C_COMPILER=divcc -DCMAKE_CXX_COMPILER=divc++
- make CC=divcc CXX=divc++ (with plain make-based builds)

The remainder of the build process should be unaffected. If the analysis tool supports loading of bitcode from executables, it can be directly used. Otherwise, the divcc-extract helper script can extract a standalone bitcode (.bc) file corresponding to the given executable. The entire process is illustrated in Fig. 3.

3.3 Design

To achieve our goals, we need to modify the flow of data through the compiler in a few places (the original data flow is illustrated in Fig. 2, the modifications are highlighted in Fig. 4). First, we need to obtain the intermediate representation after the middle end, so that we can store it alongside machine code in the object file. This also means that we need to alter the path on which the object file is written by the compiler, so that we can actually include the bitcode section[8]

---

[8] We use a section named .llvmbc, which is the same as the LTO subsystem. This section is recognized by some LLVM tools and is the closest there is to a 'standard' way to embed bitcode in object files.

in it. The implementation of these alterations in the data flow is explained in Sect. 3.4. The other component which needs to be modified is the part of the compiler driver which supervises the invocation of the linker.

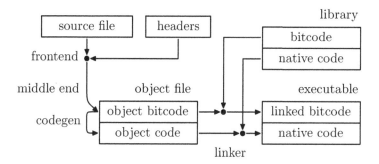

Fig. 4. The flow of the compiled code within divcc. The source code along with included header files is processed by the frontend and then middle end to generate LLVM IR. This IR is used by the code generator to produce object code, stored within the same object file. The linker then separately combines bitcode and machine code from object files and libraries to produce an executable which again contains both executable machine code and analysable bitcode.

1. Like with the changes in the compiler proper, we need to alter the data flow – this time, to extract the bitcode from constituent object files and libraries, and to include linked bitcode in the output of the linker.
2. We need to include a new component: a bitcode linker, which combines the input bitcode files into a single bitcode module which can be inserted into the output of the linker.

As noted in Sect. 2.2, the bitcode linker needs to follow the semantics of the native linker, specifically when dealing with archives. While a bitcode linker is part of LLVM, this linker can only combine individual modules and does not directly support linking bitcode archives, much less archives which consist of object files with embedded bitcode. There are essentially three options:

1. Re-use the LTO infrastructure, which uses linker plugins to perform bitcode linking of modules selected by the native linker. This approach has significant portability issues, since it requires the ability to extend the native linker.
2. Use an auxiliary section in a fashion similar to wllvm to learn which objects were included by the native linker and perform the link based on those.
3. Extend the existing module-based bitcode linker to handle archive linking semantics.

Even though not the simplest, we have taken option 3, since it has an important advantage of also working with archives which only contain bitcode which is not accompanied by any native code.[9]

3.4   Implementation

The implementation was done in C++ for the following reasons:

- to gain direct access to individual CLang components and utility functions,
- to allow distribution of divcc as a self-contained, statically linked binary,
- to avoid the overhead associated with fork-based wrappers.

Like upstream CLang, divcc will by default use fork and exec to invoke the system linker for the actual linking of object files. However, it also includes experimental support for using the lld linker as a library, avoiding the need to interface with external programs altogether. The construction of the correct linker command is delegated to the upstream CLang driver. Likewise, processing command-line switches is mainly done by existing CLang code (making interface compatibility a fairly straightforward matter), as is, obviously, all the heavy lifting of the compilation process itself.

A relatively minor but notable issue is that C++ programs need to link to additional libraries (the C++ runtime support library and the C++ standard library, and any system libraries these two language-specific libraries depend on – usually at least libpthread). For this reason, C++ compilers usually provide two binaries, one for compiling and linking C programs and another for C++ programs, the main difference being precisely the libraries which are linked into the program by default. A common solution, which divcc adopts as well, is to provide a single binary, which decides whether to use C or C++ mode based on the name it was executed with, so that divc++ can be made a link to divcc.

The final implementation issue is related to functions with variable arguments. LLVM provides a special instruction (va_arg) which implements access to arguments passed to a function through ellipsis. Unfortunately, current versions of CLang do not emit this instruction and instead produce an architecture-specific instruction sequence which directly reads the arguments from machine registers or the execution stack. In the context of program analysis, this is far from optimal – for this reason, we alter the behaviour of CLang so that divcc instead emits the va_arg LLVM instruction.

3.5   Library Substitutions

As mentioned in Sect. 1.1, it is sometimes desirable to provide alternate, bitcode-only versions of system libraries to make analysis of the resulting bitcode easier. We provide an alternate version of divcc, called dioscc, that links C programs

---

[9] This is important with e.g. libraries provided by DiOS, which are normally only compiled into bitcode and packaged into bitcode archives.

to the DiOS `libc` and C++ programs also to DiOS versions of `libc++` and `libc++abi`. Likewise, DiOS versions of header files which belong to those libraries are used during compilation. This is illustrated in Fig. 5. It is straightforward to build additional variants of `divcc` with different substitutions.

The most important issue which relates to library substitutions is ABI compatibility – the property that both libraries use the same in-memory layouts for data structures, same numeric values for various named constants and so on. If ABI (Application Binary Interface) compatibility is broken, either the bitcode or the native executable will misbehave. DiOS takes special precautions to make its `libc` binary compatible with the one provided by the host system.[10]

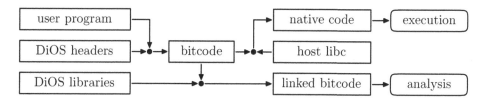

Fig. 5. The compilation process with library substitutions enabled.

Besides bitcode libraries, `dioscc` includes native versions of `libc++` and `libc++abi`, since different implementations of C++ libraries are usually not binary compatible with each other, and installing multiple versions of the C++ standard library is rather inconvenient. Finally, another native library bundled with `dioscc` is `libdios-host.a`, which contains native versions of functions which are present in the DiOS `libc` but may be missing from the system one.

Please note that unlike `dioscc`, `divcc` uses standard system headers, like any other compiler would, and does not supply bitcode definitions for functions from `libc`. It is up to the analysis tool in question to deal with the incomplete bitcode and the platform ABI defined in system headers.

3.6 Limitations

The main compromise in the current implementation is related to shared libraries. When a binary is linked to a shared library, the machine code version is linked in the usual way. However, we still link the bitcode statically, because no LLVM-based analysis tools can currently resolve dynamic dependencies and automatically load the bitcode from shared libraries.[11] The remaining limitations are mainly due to external causes:

---

[10] Unfortunately, `libpthread`, which is also provided by DiOS, is not yet ABI compatible with the host version – see also Sect. 4.2.

[11] This decision may be reversed in a later version, if the situation with support for shared libraries in analysis tools improves.

1. Inline assembly is compiled to machine code as normal, but the LLVM IR will simply retain the architecture-specific assembly instructions, compromising its usefulness for analysis.[12]
2. When used with DiOS, builds may fail due to missing API coverage or may produce crippled binaries due to ABI compatibility issues. These problems need to be addressed in DiOS.

Finally, a limitation of the implementation (i.e. not inherent in the design) is that `divcc` currently only supports systems which use the ELF format for storing executable code.

4   Evaluation

In this section, we introduce the projects selected for evaluation, report on our findings and note issues we encountered with the build processes. We also provide measurements of build time for each of the packages (shown in Table 1).

4.1   Summary

To evaluate our implementation, we have taken 7 existing C and C++ projects and built them from source using their respective build systems (which meant either CMake or configure, followed by make). Out of the tested projects, Eigen and zlib were built using CMake, the remaining projects used an autotools configure script which generates a `Makefile`.

Each project was built in 5 configurations: with `divcc`, `dioscc`, CLang version 8, GCC version 8.3 and `wllvm`. All tools have built all the projects successfully, with some caveats described in Sect. 4.2.

- `coreutils` 8.31 is a set of over 100 GNU core utilities and various helper programs for file and text manipulation (such as `cat` or `ls`) and shell utilities (`env`, `pwd`, and others),
- `gzip` 1.10 – a data compression and decompression utility,
- Eigen 3.3.7 [C++] is a header-only template library that provides linear algebra structures, such as matrices and vectors and operations on them,
- SQLite 3.28.0 – a widely used SQL database engine for database management
- BerkleyDB 4.6.21 – another database management library, more closely coupled with the application
- `libpng` 1.6.37 – a library for reading and writing PNG image files
- `zlib` 1.2.11 – a compression library, included because it is required by `libpng`

---

[12] In some cases, it may be possible to reconstruct platform-neutral LLVM IR using the Remill decompilation library. This is especially pertinent to legacy software which may use inline assembly in applications which would be better served with compiler built-in functions. We will investigate using Remill in this capacity as an option in the future.

Table 1. Total elapsed time for the configuration and compilation phases[a] of different software packages. The `clang` and `gcc` columns are baseline compilers which only produce native executables. The `divcc` and `dioscc` columns are variants of the tool proposed in this paper (`divcc` uses native system libraries with no bitcode, `dioscc` uses DiOS replacements for `libc` and `libc++`). We included `wllvm`, which is an existing tool with similar goals to `divcc`, as another reference point. The `make` command was run with 4 jobs in parallel using `-j4`.

	gcc	clang	divcc	dioscc	wllvm
coreutils	1:33 + 0:22	2:28 + 0:31	3:59 + 0:42	3:46 + 0:45	7:01 + 1:04
db	0:18 + 0:20	0:33 + 0:26	0:43 + 0:45	0:51 + 0:47	1:11 + 0:53
eigen	0:14 + 0:00	0:21 + 0:00	0:27 + 0:00	0:30 + 0:00	0:34 + 0:00
gzip	0:21 + 0:02	0:45 + 0:04	1:04 + 0:05	1:13 + 0:05	2:08 + 0:09
libpng	0:05 + 0:09	0:10 + 0:10	0:16 + 0:11	0:17 + 0:12	0:28 + 0:18
sqlite	0:05 + 1:23	0:11 + 2:03	0:17 + 2:08	0:20 + 2:12	0:27 + 3:24
zlib	0:02 + 0:01	0:03 + 0:02	0:05 + 0:03	0:05 + 0:03	0:06 + 0:04

[a]The times for the two phases are given as configuration time + compile time in the table columns.

The measurements (Table 1) show that the implementation is slightly slower than upstream CLang, in both configuration and building of the software, which is not surprising as bitcode manipulation incurs overhead. This is, however, not a significant cost when compared to `wllvm`, which compiles source code in two passes. The times for `wllvm` also exclude the additional time required to link the bitcode when `extract-bc` is executed and, when configuring Berkeley DB, `wllvm` had to be given the `WLLVM_CONFIGURE_ONLY=1` flag during configuration, as the bitcode files it otherwise produces were confusing the build system. Finally, GCC proved to be considerably faster than CLang and the remaining compilers (which are all based on CLang).

4.2 Package Details

Eigen. This was the only project of the selection which uses CMake exclusively. Since it is also a header-only library, the build instructions mainly exist to build tests (with `make buildtests`) or build and run them (`make check`).[13] As some of the tools we used did not manage to build all test files, we did not include compilation of the tests in the time measurements.

Berkeley DB. In this case, shared libraries have been disabled (using the `--disable-shared` configure flag), to include at least one statically-built library in the evaluation. In `dioscc`, several of the binaries result in a segmentation fault when run. This is due to the use of the `libpthread` library, as the system version is not ABI compatible with the DiOS `libpthread`.

---

[13] This is the reason for zero build time of Eigen for all compilers.

In this case, it was also necessary to run the `configure` script specially for wllvm, passing `WLLVM_CONFIGURE_ONLY=1` in the environment.

SQLite. This package was configured with `--disable-dynamic-extensions` because DiOS (and hence `dioscc`) does not currently support the `dlopen` family of functions. SQLite further exhibited the same problem as Berkeley DBD when built with `dioscc` due to ABI incompatibility of `libpthread`.

Libpng. This package was partly included in the evaluation since it has a dependency on a 3rd-party library, namely `zlib`. We built `zlib` version 1.2.11 using the same tool as `libpng` and provided the resulting `libz.so` or `libz.a` to `libpng` at configure time – in this case, we built both a static and a dynamic variant of `libpng` (along with a matching build of `zlib`).

5   Conclusions

We have designed and implemented a tool which makes integration of dynamic program analyses based on LLVM into the build and development processes significantly easier. Our design takes the best ideas from a number of related tools and combines them in a unique way to offer seamless integration into existing processes. Moreover, `divcc` optionally integrates with DiOS, making the resulting bitcode more analysis-friendly without compromising the guarantees stemming from the use of the same bitcode for native code generation and for analysis. Finally, we have evaluated `divcc` on a number of existing software packages, establishing its practicality and efficiency.

References

1. Abdulla, P.A., Aronis, S., Atig, M.F., Jonsson, B., Leonardsson, C., Sagonas, K.: Stateless model checking for TSO and PSO. Acta Informatica **54**(8), 789–818 (2016). https://doi.org/10.1007/s00236-016-0275-0
2. Baranová, Z., et al.: Model checking of C and C++ with DIVINE 4 (2017)
3. Cadar, C., Dunbar, D., Engler, D.R.: KLEE: unassisted and automatic generation of high-coverage tests for complex systems programs. In: OSDI, pp. 209–224. USENIX Association (2008)
4. Chalupa, M., Vitovská, M., Jonáš, M., Slaby, J., Strejček, J.: Symbiotic 4: beyond reachability. In: Legay, A., Margaria, T. (eds.) TACAS 2017. LNCS, vol. 10206, pp. 385–389. Springer, Heidelberg (2017). https://doi.org/10.1007/978-3-662-54580-5_28
5. Günther, H., Laarman, A., Weissenbacher, G.: Vienna verification tool: IC3 for parallel software (competition contribution). In: TACAS, pp. 954–957 (2016). https://doi.org/10.1007/978-3-662-49674-9_69
6. Kokologiannakis, M., Lahav, O., Sagonas, K., Vafeiadis, V.: Effective stateless model checking for C/C++ concurrency. Proc. ACM Program. Lang. **2**(POPL), 17:1–17:32 (2017). https://doi.org/10.1145/3158105
7. Kremenek, T., et al.: Scan-build (2009). https://clang-analyzer.llvm.org/scan-build.html

8. Kroening, D., Tautschnig, M.: CBMC – C bounded model checker. In: Ábrahám, E., Havelund, K. (eds.) TACAS 2014. LNCS, vol. 8413, pp. 389–391. Springer, Heidelberg (2014). https://doi.org/10.1007/978-3-642-54862-8_26

9. Nethercote, N., Seward, J.: Valgrind: a framework for heavyweight dynamic binary instrumentation. In: PLDI (2007)

10. Ročkai, P., Baranová, Z., Mrázek, J., Kejstová, K., Barnat, J.: Reproducible execution of POSIX programs with DiOS. In: Ölveczky, P.C., Salaün, G. (eds.) SEFM 2019. LNCS, vol. 11724, pp. 333–349. Springer, Cham (2019). https://doi.org/10.1007/978-3-030-30446-1_18

11. Sinz, C., Merz, F., Falke, S.: LLBMC: a bounded model checker for LLVM's intermediate representation. In: Flanagan, C., König, B. (eds.) TACAS 2012. LNCS, vol. 7214, pp. 542–544. Springer, Heidelberg (2012). https://doi.org/10.1007/978-3-642-28756-5_44

12. The LLVM Project. LLVM Link Time Optimization (2019). https://www.llvm.org/docs/LinkTimeOptimization.html

13. Thompson, S., Brat, G.: Verification of C++ flight software with the MCP model checker. In: 2008 IEEE Aerospace Conference, pp. 1–9 (2008). https://doi.org/10.1109/AERO.2008.4526577

Model Checking in a Development Workflow: A Study on a Concurrent C++ Hash Table

Petr Ročkai[✉]

Faculty of Informatics, Masaryk University, Brno, Czech Republic
xrockai@fi.muni.cz

Abstract. In this paper, we report on our effort to design a fast, concurrent-safe hash table and implement it in C++, correctly. It is especially the latter that is the focus of this paper: concurrent data structures are notoriously hard to implement, and C++ is not known to be a particularly safe language. It however does offer unparalleled performance for the level of programming comfort it offers, especially in our area of interest – parallel workloads with intense interaction.

For these reasons, we have enlisted the help of a software model checker (DIVINE) with the ability to directly check the C++ implementation. We discuss how such a heavyweight tool integrated with the engineering effort, what are the current limits of this approach and what kinds of assurances we obtained. Of course, we have applied the standard array of tools throughout the effort – unit testing, an interactive debugger, a memory error checker (`valgrind`) – in addition to the model checker, which puts us in an excellent position to weigh them against each other and point out where they complement each other.

1 Introduction

Designing correct software is hard and implementing it correctly is possibly even harder. This is especially true of 'plumbing' – low-level code which must be both robust and perform well. Of course, there are established libraries of such code in wide use and considered correct precisely because they are universally used and nobody has found a defect in them for a long time. However, for the same reason, those same libraries are somewhat dated and assimilate new functionality at a very slow rate.

A typical case would be data structures for representing sets and associative arrays. Until 2011, the only implementation available in standard C++ libraries were rebalancing binary search trees. Changes in computer hardware, however, have gradually made data structures based on pointers, like linked lists and search trees, less favourable when compared to more compact, array-like

---

This work has been partially supported by the Czech Science Foundation grant No. 18-02177S.

E. Sekerinski et al. (Eds.): FM 2019 Workshops, LNCS 12232, pp. 46–60, 2020.
https://doi.org/10.1007/978-3-030-54994-7_5

structures. In particular, it is often much better to implement sets and associative arrays using hash tables, even though search trees have, in theory, superior complexity. The 2011 revision of the C++ standard has seen the inclusion of `unsorted_set` and `unsorted_map` container classes, which are represented using a hash table. Unfortunately, the design of those container classes is such that a conforming implementation needs to use *open hashing* and must not invalidate references to items while rehashing the table, strongly suggesting chained buckets. None of these design choices are particularly suitable for modern processors, though they do make the hash table easier to use.[1]

The remainder of the paper is organized as follows: the rest of this section highlights the contributions of this paper and surveys the related work, while Sect. 2 outlines the basic premises of the paper, including the basic methodology and tools which we used. Section 3 then gives a high-level overview of design criteria and design choices we have made for the hash table. Section 4 describes the implementation and verification process in detail – one subsection for each development iteration, where each of the iterations constitute 2–3 person-days of combined programming, debugging and verification effort. Finally, Sect. 5 summarizes and concludes the paper.

1.1   Contribution

The main goal of this paper is to describe the experience of using a comparatively heavyweight model checker in an otherwise lightweight development process. The main takeaways are the following:

1. It is surprisingly easy to use model checking with self-contained C++ code.
2. While automated, exhaustive verification of source code seems quite remote, using a model checker has real, practical benefits in day-to-day development.

We also hope that the moderately detailed description of our development process can serve as a mostly positive example of applying formal methods in the trenches of rather low-level programming.

1.2   Related Work

Formal methods have been the subject of steady interest from both academia and industry, as evidenced by a substantial body of surveys on their applications, e.g. [4,16]. A number of case studies have been performed and published, in many instances with production software. Unlike the present work, most of the existing studies focus on specific mission-critical software – flight control [3], satellite control systems [5], particle accelerators [6,8] or real-time operating system kernels [10]. A unique effort in this area is seL4 [7], which is, however, based on heavyweight methods centred around theorem proving.

---

[1] In particular, they provide nicer iterator and reference invalidation semantics and are less susceptible to pathological behaviour when using sub-optimal user-supplied hash functions.

The most closely related study to ours is perhaps [8], since it involves directly applying model checking to a C++ implementation, and employs the same model checker – DIVINE – for this task as we do. The system examined, however, was quite different, and included a separate model for checking liveness (LTL) properties using SPIN.

2   Preliminaries

In this section, we first give a very brief overview of hash tables and their design criteria, then of testing and debugging, and finally of model checking software at the implementation level.

2.1   Hash Tables

A hash table is a data structure that represents an (unordered) set, in which *keys* can be *looked up* and into which new keys can be *inserted*. Besides encoding sets, hash tables can be straightforwardly extended to encode associative arrays though we will only discuss the simpler case of sets in this paper. Both the abovementioned operations are, on average, in $\mathcal{O}(1)$ – the average number of steps is a constant. Of course, this complexity depends on the properties of the *hash function* which the hash table uses and even with very good hash functions, it is always possible to construct a sequence of operations that will exhibit pathological behaviour (i.e. individual operations running in linear time). In the remainder of this paper, we assume that a suitable hash function is available.

An important aspect of modern data structure design is the safety of *concurrent access*,[2] which stems from properties of contemporary hardware: high computation throughput can only be achieved with specific designs which minimize *contention*. Luckily, in normal operation, hash tables naturally cause only minimal contention. Of course, this assumes that there are no global locks or some other heavyweight synchronization mechanism: either each cell, or at most a small segment of cells, needs to be protected from *race conditions* individually. Operations that access multiple cells of the hash table need to be carefully designed to not require additional communication to avoid races.

2.2   Testing and Debugging

Testing is the natural backbone of any validation or verification effort – examples are the most intuitive tool for understanding the behaviour of processes and systems. In the case of data structure design, the majority of testing is usually done at the unit level – the programmer writes down small example programs which exercise the data structure and inspects the results for conformance with their expectations.

---

[2] Here, concurrency means that multiple CPU cores perform operations on the same data structure without additional synchronization.

The most obvious and immediate problem that arises with (unit) testing is concurrency. A single (sequential) unit test is a very concrete entity and is easy to work with and argue about. Unfortunately, test scenarios that involve concurrency lack this concreteness: there is now an implicit quantifier over all possible reorderings of concurrent actions. Every time we execute the test scenario, we see a different ordering, and many types of problems will only appear in some such orderings, but not in all of them. Due to the nature of concurrent programming systems, it is usually also very hard to reproduce the exact ordering that led to an error. In our effort, we have used a software model checker to deal with the quantification over allowable event reorderings (for more details see Sect. 2.3).

Even with sequential test cases, the root cause of a failure is not always obvious: even short test cases can generate a fairly long sequence of steps, depending on the internal complexity of the operations under test. There are two basic techniques to clarify the sequence of steps that led to a failure, in addition to mere inspection. First, tracing statements can be inserted into the program under test, allowing the programmer to more easily follow the execution of the program. Information about which branches were taken and the values of key variables are usually included in such traces.

Second, the user can inspect the execution using an interactive *debugger*, such as gdb [14]. In this case, the execution can be stopped at various points, the user can instruct the debugger to only proceed with execution in small, incremental steps and can inspect values of the variables at any point in the execution. Usually, it is only possible to step or execute the program forward in time, though extensions exist to allow *reversible* debugging [9,15] – the ability to step back, to a point in the execution that was already visited once. While an interactive debugger is an invaluable tool, it is in some sense also the tool of last resort: it is the least amenable to automation, and modifications in the program require a possibly long sequence of interactions to be repeated.

2.3   Model Checking

There are few choices when it comes to applying formal methods to C++ implementations of concurrent data structures. Heavyweight formal methods often require the design to be 'implemented' in a special language (in addition to the C++ implementation). The special language in question might be a protocol modelling language (e.g. ProMeLa), or it might be a proof language (e.g. Coq), but in either case, there is non-trivial effort involved in the translation of the informal (working) description into this language.

Additionally, this special language is overwhelmingly likely to be unfamiliar and hence pose additional challenges, including an increased risk of mistakes. Even in proof languages, it is essential that the semantics of the theorems that are being proved are properly understood, otherwise it might easily happen that they do not correspond to the informal properties that we were interested in.

Finally, there would be no guarantee that the C++ version, which is what will be actually executed, corresponds to the one that has been verified in any meaningful way. While there has been an effort in the seL4 project to extend the proofs to cover machine code [11], anything of this sort is still extremely far-fetched for code that relies on the extensive C++ runtime libraries.

For these reasons, we are more interested in comparatively lightweight methods which can directly work with the implementation. There are, obviously, significant gaps: such tools tend to be more complex (especially when considering correctness-critical cores), their semantics are less rigorous and there is inevitably a disconnect between the assumed and the actual semantics of the underlying hardware.

In our case, model checking for safety properties appears to be the most appropriate choice. The technique is very similar to testing (among their other shared attributes, it is a dynamical method) but with efficient handling of universal quantification – either over inputs, over event reorderings or over possible interactions with the environment.

There is a wide selection of (safety) model checking tools based on LLVM or on CBMC which both have usable C++ frontends. Unfortunately, the latter does not support modern C++ features and the tools based on the former often lack support for concurrency (and exceptions). The one tool which fits all mentioned criteria is DIVINE [1], even though it also has a number of limitations. Verification of parallel programs with DIVINE is rather resource-intensive, since it enumerates the entire state space. Even though it employs various state space reductions [13], the state spaces for small programs with only 2 threads are rather large. In the verification tasks we have performed, we were limited to 100 GiB of RAM, an amount which unfortunately proved rather constraining.

Another limitation that we encountered in DIVINE is that enabling support for weak memory models causes an additional blowup in the size of the state space. However, our implementation only uses sequentially consistent atomic operations, which hopefully means that this is not a significant issue.

2.4   Assertions

Assertions are a programming aid where a statement in the source code describes a condition which the programmer expects to hold in every execution through the given source code location. The program then checks, at runtime, that this condition is indeed satisfied and aborts execution when the check fails. Assertion statements are commonly used in testing and are compiled out of the program in production builds. Depending on the number and quality of the assertion statements, they can range from a sporadic sanity check to comprehensive pre- and post-condition annotations reminiscent of inductive verification.

Besides testing, assertion annotations are also extremely useful in model checking, since the verifier can easily execute the runtime check and ensure that it holds true on every execution covered by the quantification provided by the model checker (whether it is over event reorderings or input values).

3   Design

The following points summarize our upfront design choices for the hash table (i.e. the choices were made before the implementation work started).

1. The hash table will be stored as a flat array of *cells*[3] using open addressing and will use a cache-friendly combination of linear and quadratic probing for collision resolution.
2. There will be multiple cell implementations for different scenarios and the table will be parametrized by the cell type:
   - a low-overhead cell for sequential programs,
   - lock-free cells for small keys based on atomic compare & exchange,
   - lock-based cells for medium-sized keys.
3. The table will employ on-demand, parallel rehashing, so that it can be used in scenarios where the number of distinct keys is not known upfront.
4. It will implement key removal based on tombstones. The ability to shrink the table (automatically or manually) is not a priority.

Our design was informed by the considerations outlined in Sect. 2.1 and by our past experience with hash table design [2]. To simplify our task, we assume that keys have a fixed size and are small (i.e. they are integers or pointers or that a single key consists of at most a few pointers) and expect the user to use indirection as appropriate to store larger or variable-sized keys. Together, these criteria naturally lead to *open addressing* in a flat array of cells. A hash table based on open addressing resolves the inevitable hash collisions by *probing*: computing a sequence of indices instead of just one, and trying each index in turn, until it either finds the correct key or an empty cell.

This immediately brings a few problems: the cell must be able to distinguish a special 'empty' state, which is distinct from all possible key values. In some circumstances, this could be a specific key picked by the user, but this approach is fragile and not very user-friendly. Additionally, another special state is required for tombstone-based key removal.

4   Development and Verification

The implementation and verification work was done in 4 iterations, each iteration including both programming and testing and/or model checking activities. Each iteration corresponds to 2–3 person-days of effort, adding up to approximately 2 weeks (10 days).

4.1   First Iteration

In this phase, we have done the programming equivalent of a 'first draft', knowingly omitting part of the expected functionality and using sub-optimal,

---

[3] Each cell can hold at most a single key. Basic operations on a cell include storing a key and comparing the content of the cell with a key.

but known-correct (or at least presumed correct) primitives from the standard library. We have also re-used pieces of code from previous hash table designs, especially for cell implementation. The main goal in this iteration was reduction of memory overhead associated with our previous design.

The implementation after the first iteration uses a per-thread object which only consists of a single std::shared_ptr (2 machine pointers) and a flat table with the cells and additional 5 machine words of metadata (the size, a rehashing counter, another std::shared_ptr and finally the reference count managed by std::shared_ptr). By the end of the fourth iteration, the per-thread object was reduced to a single machine pointer and the per-table metadata to 4 words.[4]

Initial Implementation. The code is split into 3 layers:

1. the top-level class template is hash_set[5] and uses a simpler, fixed-size hash_table to implement the actual storage, lookup and insertion of keys
2. hash_table is a compact structure (i.e. it is laid out contiguously in memory and does not use pointers or references) whose main part is an array of *cells*
3. there are multiple implementations of the *cell* concept and each can hold a single key and possibly a small amount of metadata

The hash_set class is responsible for providing an interface to the user and for managing the capacity of the hash table: when the hash_set runs out of space, a new, bigger hash_table is constructed and the content of the previous one is rehashed into the new one. The individual hash_table instances form a linked list – there might be an arbitrary number of them, since some threads may fall behind others and hence keep the old instances alive (see also Fig. 1).

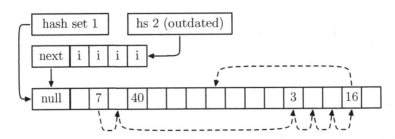

Fig. 1. Example of a pair of hash_set structures (each belonging to a different thread), sharing a single list of hash_table instances. The dashed arrows represent the lookup sequence for an item with the hash value 1. Cells marked 'i' are invalid.

---

[4] In comparison, the design from [2] uses 3 machine words per thread, 64 + 32 words of fixed overhead per a hash table instance and 11 words per cell vector. It also incurs 3 indirections compared to the single indirection in the current design.

[5] The class naming has changed during later development stages. We use the last iteration of the class names throughout the paper to avoid confusing the reader.

For efficiency reasons, the linked list must be lock-free and concurrent-safe: checking the existence of an item linked to the currently active `hash_table` instance is used to determine whether another thread has initiated rehashing. In this iteration, a standard reference-counted smart pointer (`std::shared_ptr`) was used for memory management. A standard atomic compare-and-swap operation on those pointers was then used to implement the linked list in a concurrent-safe fashion.

The rehashing is done in contiguous segments of the original `hash_table`,[6] each segment being rehashed as a single unit by a single thread. Allocation of segments to rehash to threads is coordinated using a pair of atomic counters, one counter in each `hash_table` instance involved in the rehashing.

Finally, a separate 'sequential' variant of the `hash_set` is included in the implementation. Since it does not need to provide safe concurrent access, it is somewhat simpler and also slightly faster.

The first iteration resulted in 820 lines of C++ (discounting unit tests), distributed as follows: the cell implementations took 220 lines, utility classes, shared interface code and other helpers 110 lines, the sequential implementation of `hash_set` was 170 lines and its concurrent counterpart was 280 lines (including `hash_table`). The remainder went to high-level comments and type alias declarations.

Verification (Round 1). The initial implementation was only subject to unit testing and to stress testing via concurrent application code (i.e. no model checking was performed in this iteration). No ill effects were observed during the initial testing run (though a number of problems were uncovered in later iterations). The hash function was more or less assumed correct (however, the only real requirement is that it is a function in the mathematical sense).

The implementation itself contains 7 consistency assertions which were checked during unit testing, in addition to the checks performed by the tests themselves. Those assertions were included for multiple reasons:

- first of all, they serve as machine-checked documentation, informing the reader about local pre- and post-conditions and about assumptions the author of the code has made,
- assertions make initial development easier, by quickly alerting the programmer about unwarranted assumptions and about mistakes in code composition (where e.g. a pre-condition of a subroutine is violated by a caller),
- finally, they are checked during unit tests and model checking, serving as additional checks of correctness.

We also include a few statistics about the unit tests:

- the unit testing code (written against the interface of the `hash_set` class template) consisted of approximately 250 lines of C++,
- there were 6 sequential test scenarios and 4 concurrent access scenarios,

---

[6] Clearly, the keys stored in a continuous segment of the smaller `hash_table` may end up distributed arbitrarily in the entire range of the bigger (target) instance.

- the sequential implementation was subjected to the sequential test cases with 2 sequential cell types,
- the concurrent implementation with 2 concurrent cell types were subjected to both the sequential and the concurrent test cases,
- this added up to 32 unit test cases; code coverage was not measured.

The concurrent test cases were mainly of the stress-testing type: they performed many operations in parallel in the hopes of more or less blindly hitting problems. This approach, while rather inelegant, tends to work for 'shallow' or high-probability bugs, but overall, it is not a very reliable method.

4.2   Second Iteration

The main driver of the second iteration was unification of the code between the sequential and concurrent-safe implementations of the hash_set class. The comparatively expensive rehashing protocol is statically disabled in the sequential variant.

Implementation Changes. The sequential implementation of hash_set has been made a special case of the concurrent variant, with certain paths through the code cut short: this change saved about 150 lines of code and a substantial amount of duplication, leading to cleaner and more maintainable code. Overall, by the end of this iteration, the implementation was down to 680 lines of code, a net reduction of 140 lines.

This iteration has also seen improvements to the initially crude interaction with the client code (especially in case of errors). In particular, a failure to rehash the table is now reported as an exception and does not abort the entire program. There are two reasons why rehashing may fail: either due to insufficient uniformity of the hash function (in which case, aborting the program might be appropriate, since it is really an implementation error in the client code) or due to adversarial inputs that cause excessive collisions. In the latter case, throwing an exception is much more appropriate, since the circumstance is likely outside the control of the client application.

Verification (Round 2). Due to the merge of the two hash_set implementations, one of the consistency assertions was removed (having become redundant), leaving 6. In addition to the assertions, tracing statements were added to the implementation to ease analysis of test failures and counterexamples from model checking: the trace output shows up in the counterexample traces from the model checker, which makes the said counterexamples much easier to understand, even without using the interactive simulator [12]. Like consistency assertions, the traces are kept in the code permanently, but compiled out in release builds.

The unit tests in this iteration were extended with cases of longer (68 byte long) keys, which uncovered errors in the sequential cell types, which were in turn fixed. Additionally, a problem was discovered through a combination of unit testing and the use of valgrind. In this case, the unit tests were executed on a different platform than usual and exhibited sporadic failures affecting test cases which used the atomic cell type, indicating a race condition or a memory error. Since the latter are easier to diagnose, the unit test code was first executed in valgrind, which quickly pinpointed the problem to a read of uninitialized memory. The problem turned out to be due to padding bytes which the compiler in some cases inserted into the implementation of the atomic cell. Because the entire cell was accessed using a single atomic compare & exchange operation, padding bytes were included in the comparison, leading to failures.

Besides the padding problem, a few edge cases were found in the implementation of the atomic cell which warranted a minor redesign of the metadata stored in the cell and the operations on them. In the new version, 2 bits are reserved to encode special cell states: empty, invalid,[7] tombstone and full.

This was also the first iteration to use model checking for verification, with a small initial set of scenarios to be considered. In each case, there are 2 threads,[8] both accessing a single hash table, with each thread performing a fixed sequence of operations (including fixed arguments), but arbitrary reorderings of those operations are considered by the model checker. The scenarios included in this iteration were following:

- a check for correctness of insertion concurrent with rehashing running in the other thread (without the insertion triggering another resize),
- a case running an erase concurrent with insertions in the other thread,
- same, but an insert also triggered a rehashing concurrent with the erase.

No new counterexamples were found at this time, but the effort helped to validate the fixes that were done in the atomic cell implementation based on problems uncovered via testing.

4.3   Third Iteration

The third iteration was comparatively minor, with focus on application-level testing and changes and improvements in the interface provided to the client code. Minor mistakes caused by rearranging the code were caught by existing unit tests and corrected.

Implementation Changes. This iteration included, besides a few small optimizations in the key lookup code, mainly changes to the outside class interface: the growth pattern (sequence of hash_table sizes to use) was made into a static (compile-time) parameter and the first iteration of the adaptor interface was added. Among other things, this change further reduced the memory overhead of hash_set in cases where the user-provided object which performs hash computation contains data members. At the end of this iteration, the code was 685 lines long (a net growth of only 5 lines).

---

[7] Cells are invalidated when they are rehashed, so that concurrent insertion will not accidentally use an empty cell that has already been 'moved' to the next generation leading to a loss of the inserted key.

[8] Unfortunately, model checking of scenarios with more than 2 threads does not seem to be realistic, at least not with the allocated budget of 100 GiB of RAM.

Verification (Round 3). The verification effort in this iteration was centred around a first major push in application-level testing: the hash table was used in an application which does a mix of key insertions with both new keys and with keys already present in the hash table. These keys are indirect – the hash table stores a pointer, and an adaptor is provided to compare the actual structured, variable-size keys stored behind the pointer. The application was then exercised in both single-threaded and in multi-threaded configurations.

During this testing, an error was discovered in the rehashing code, where rehashing failures were not properly detected (instead, the code went into an infinite loop making the hash table ever larger). Rehashing failures happen when the table is used with a poor hash function which cause collisions that do not get remapped as the hash table grows (i.e. they are collisions which are already present in the hash output and are not introduced by scaling the range of the hash function to the current size of the hash table). This was detected thanks to a bug in the custom hash function which was part of the application code.[9] Additionally, with the code path exposed to testing, a deadlock was discovered in a previously unreachable error path in the same area of code.

Both errors were tracked down with the help of tracing and `gdb` (which quite easily provided backtraces at the location of the deadlock once it could be reproduced). It is also worth noting that even if the path was covered in model checking scenarios (by using an intentionally conflict-prone hash function), the deadlock was caused by spin-based synchronization – a type of error which is rather hard to specify in current versions of DIVINE.[10]

Finally, no new test cases or model checking scenarios were introduced in this iteration, though in the manner of continuous integration, existing unit tests were executed after each self-contained change to the code.

4.4   Fourth Iteration

The last iteration reported in this paper brought a number of substantial changes in the internals of the hash table, even though only indirectly. The well-tested `std::shared_ptr` was replaced with an *intrusive pointer*[11] which did not yet support atomic compare & exchange. This operation was added along with more basic support for atomic access (atomic loads and stores of the pointer, and support for manipulating reference counts atomically). Neither unit testing nor application-level testing uncovered any problems in this code.

In addition to the changes in internals, the interface of the `hash_set` class was finalized in this iteration, providing the desired level of flexibility and ease of use. The verification part of the effort was focused on correctness in general and uncovering possible concurrency problems in particular.

---

[9] This incident also revealed a weakness in our testing methodology, where only 'good' hash functions were used during unit testing and model checking – cf. Sect. 4.1.

[10] Deadlocks involving `pthread` mutexes are detected, but these mutexes are too expensive to be used in concurrent data structures.

[11] A pointer which can only point at objects which manage their own reference counter.

Implementation Changes. As outlined above, there were two main avenues of change in this iteration. The first group of changes was directed at the hash_set interface:

1. the iterators which allow enumeration of values stored in the hash table were slightly simplified,
2. the adaptor now offers the capability to store data outside of the hash table proper, opening way to alternate collision resolution methods, which were validated by creating an experimental concurrent-safe linked-list bucket implementation.[12]

The other major change was the migration away from std::shared_ptr:

- unlike std::shared_ptr which is represented as a pair of machine pointers, the intrusive reference-counting pointer (refcount_ptr) only needs one, reducing the memory overhead
- refcount_ptr provides low-contention (even if not entirely atomic) compare & swap operation – the least-significant bit of the pointer itself is used as a lock while the reference counts are rearranged

Finally, it was noticed that in certain cases, the sequential cell types could contain uninitialized values – this defect was also corrected. The final implementation spans 730 lines of code, a net increase of 45 lines, mainly attributable to the changes in the adaptor interface.

Verification (Round 4). As mentioned above, the main focus of this iteration was model checking. We have mostly focused on three instances, which all allowed for runs, on which an insertion concurrent with rehashing could trigger another rehashing of the table. The variants were as follows:

1. only insertions, with exactly 1 concurrent insert on one of the threads
2. same as above but with a call to erase sequenced after the isolated insertion,
3. another insert-only scenario where both threads perform 5 fully concurrent insertions in opposite orders, exposing further arrangements of concurrent inserts triggering rehashing[13]

The main 'workhorse' of the model checking effort was the first scenario. In most cases, it took about 2 h to produce a counterexample, and consumed about 40 GiB of RAM. The second scenario did not differ substantially from the first, while the third took almost 4 h. We have uncovered a number of problems during this endeavour:

---

[12] The implementation was tested, but not model checked, and is not part of the hash table implementation (it was done in application-level code in an application-specific manner).

[13] All the scenarios used a hash_set with the growth pattern 2-4-8. The last scenario was however also attempted with the pattern 1-2-4, reducing the size of the state space and memory requirements considerably, from 85 GiB to about 15 GiB.

- the initial lock-free implementation of compare/exchange on refcount_ptr was wrong (it could cause one of the objects to be freed prematurely due to a race condition),
- the contended case of a helper function, `atomic_add_if_nonzero` was wrong, updating the pointer even if it was, in fact, zero (though the return value correctly indicated that the counter reached zero),
- a race condition in the rehashing protocol (during a concurrently triggered rehashing).

Interestingly, all three problems uncovered in model checking were caught by the same consistency assertion in the rehash protocol during model checking of the same scenario (the first one in the above list). Since the model checker only provides a single counterexample, the problems were detected sequentially: the first counterexample pointed at the reference count problem; after that was fixed, another counterexample cropped up due to the incorrect `atomic_add_if_nonzero`, and finally after this problem was also fixed, the race condition in the rehash protocol surfaced.

Finally, after the initial fix to the race condition passed model checking (i.e. no more counterexamples were reported), a deadlock was quickly found during application-level testing. After it was confirmed that the race fix introduced the deadlock, the problem was quickly analysed and corrected, partially because the change was in a single line. The final fix for the race (which no longer caused the deadlock) was confirmed by running the model checking scenarios again. No further problems were detected.

4.5   Discussion

From the point of validation and verification, the most useful way to split the code is along the sequential – concurrent axis. The sequential code is rather trivial – almost all bugs were quickly discovered via unit testing and fixed almost immediately after being introduced. The one exception to this rule was the uninitialized memory read that was discovered and fixed in iteration 2. What is noteworthy about this bug is that unit tests exercised this part of the code quite heavily, but since we execute each unit test in a new process, the test cases reliably encountered zeroed memory, which masked the problem. Automatically running the unit tests through `valgrind` would have alerted us to the problem earlier and we will consider altering our work flow to this effect in the future.

The concurrent case is very different, even though the code is still comparatively simple on its surface and some of the concurrent behaviours can still be tested with success: specifically, problems on paths that are commonly taken can be often uncovered with test cases that do not much differ from the sequential instances. However, concurrent code often contains paths which are only traversed under heavy contention (which is hard to trigger in traditional testing), illustrated e.g. in the `atomic_add_if_nonzero` problem. In this case, the detection was further hampered by the fact that the contention had to coincide with zeroing of a counter, which only happens at most once for each such counter.

The second source of hardness in concurrent code is 'interaction at a distance'. This was the case with the race condition in the rehashing protocol: two distinct synchronization handshakes on the same variable (number of segments to be rehashed) accidentally matched up. In testing, a thread never woke up at exactly the right moment to trigger the problem, even though unit tests triggered a number of concurrent rehash operations. Code inspection did not uncover this problem either – each handshake considered separately appears to be correct.

5 Conclusions

Like other authors, we have found that model checking can be a valuable tool despite its numerous limitations. Our use case was perhaps somewhat unique in the level of integration of model checking into the development process and in the low-level nature of the code to which it was applied. Our experience shows that testing and model checking nicely complement each other and that employing both can mitigate some of their individual drawbacks. One feature of the model checker which was essential in our endeavour was its ability to work with unrestricted and annotation-free C++ code – in this sense, model checking was entirely transparent. Preparing inputs was essentially the same as writing unit tests, the only difference being that the cases must be *small*: running only a few operations over small data structure instances. Fortunately, this 'smallness' does not seem to limit the ability of the model checker to uncover problems.

In our case, the most important weakness of model checking was, in agreement with previous accounts, its high resource consumption and substantial delay between asking a question and obtaining an answer. Sometimes, a simpler tool can do the job: for instance `valgrind` can often detect similar classes of programming errors. However, it only works well with deterministic, sequential programs where the universal quantification over event reordering provided by the model checker is not required.

Finally, interpretation of counterexamples was challenging, though not disproportionately so when compared to traditional debugging. The two tools we used the most in this context was ability to add text-based tracing (without having to worry about reproducing the problem at hand), and the interactive simulator, which allowed us to step through a single fixed counterexample.

References

1. Baranová, Z., et al.: Model checking of C and C++ with DIVINE 4 (2017)
2. Barnat, J., Ročkai, P., Štill, V., Weiser, J.: Fast, dynamically-sized concurrent hash table. In: Fischer, B., Geldenhuys, J. (eds.) SPIN 2015. LNCS, vol. 9232, pp. 49–65. Springer, Cham (2015). https://doi.org/10.1007/978-3-319-23404-5_5
3. Chen, Z., Gu, Y., Huang, Z., Zheng, J., Liu, C., Liu, Z.: Model checking aircraft controller software: a case study. Softw. Pract. Exp. **45**(7), 989–1017 (2015). https://doi.org/10.1002/spe.2242

4. Fitzgerald, J., Bicarregui, J., Larsen, P.G., Woodcock, J.: Industrial Deployment of Formal Methods: Trends and Challenges. Springer, Heidelberg (2013). https://doi.org/10.1007/978-3-642-33170-110. ISBN 978-3-642-33170-1

5. Gan, X., Dubrovin, J., Heljanko, K.: A symbolic model checking approach to verifying satellite onboard software. Sci. Comput. Program. **82**, 44–55 (2014). https://doi.org/10.1016/j.scico.2013.03.005

6. Hwong, Y.L., Keiren, J.J., Kusters, V.J., Leemans, S., Willemse, T.A.: Formalising and analysing the control software of the CMS experiment at the large hadron collider. Sci. Comput. Program. **78**(12), 2435–2452 (2013). https://doi.org/10.1016/j.scico.2012.11.009

7. Klein, G., et al.: seL4: formal verification of an OS kernel. In: SOSP, pp. 207–220. ACM (2009). https://doi.org/10.1145/1629575.1629596

8. Lång, J., Prasetya, I.S.W.B.: Model checking a C++ software framework, a case study (2019). https://doi.org/10.1145/3338906.3340453

9. O'Callahan, R., Jones, C., Froyd, N., Huey, K., Noll, A., Partush, N.: Engineering record and replay for deployability (2017). arXiv:1705.05937

10. Penix, J., Visser, W., Engstrom, E., Larson, A., Weininger, N.: Verification of time partitioning in the DEOS scheduler kernel. In: International Conference on Software Engineering, pp. 488–497. ACM Press (2000)

11. Potts, D., Bourquin, R., Andresen, L., Andronick, J., Klein, G., Heiser, G.: Mathematically verified software kernels: raising the bar for high assurance implementations. Technical report, NICTA, Sydney, Australia (2014)

12. Ročkai, P., Barnat, J.: A simulator for LLVM bitcode (2017). https://arxiv.org/abs/1704.05551. Preliminary version

13. Ročkai, P., Barnat, J., Brim, L.: Improved state space reductions for LTL model checking of C and C++ programs. In: Brat, G., Rungta, N., Venet, A. (eds.) NFM 2013. LNCS, vol. 7871, pp. 1–15. Springer, Heidelberg (2013). https://doi.org/10.1007/978-3-642-38088-4_1

14. Stallman, R., Pesch, R., Shebs, S.: Debugging with GDB (2010)

15. Visan, A.-M., Arya, K., Cooperman, G., Denniston, T.: URDB: a universal reversible debugger based on decomposing debugging histories. In: PLOS 2011 (2011)

16. Woodcock, J., Larsen, P.G., Bicarregui, J., Fitzgerald, J.: Formal methods: practice and experience. ACM Comput. Surv. **41**(4), 19:1–19:36 (2009). https://doi.org/10.1145/1592434.1592436

Addressing Usability in a Formal Development Environment

Paolo Arcaini[1]([✉]) [ID], Silvia Bonfanti[2] [ID] and Angelo Gargantini[2] [ID],
Elvinia Riccobene[3] [ID], and Patrizia Scandurra[2] [ID]

[1] National Institute of Informatics, Tokyo, Japan
`arcaini@nii.ac.jp`
[2] University of Bergamo, Bergamo, Italy
`{silvia.bonfanti,angelo.gargantini,patrizia.scandurra}@unibg.it`
[3] Università degli Studi di Milano, Milan, Italy
`elvinia.riccobene@unimi.it`

Abstract. Even though the formal method community tends to overlook the problem, formal methods are sometimes difficult to use and not accessible to average users. On one hand, this is due to the intrinsic complexity of the methods and, therefore, some level of required expertise is unavoidable. On the other hand, however, the methods are sometimes hard to use because of lack of a user-friendly tool support. In this paper, we present our experience in addressing usability when developing a framework for the Abstract State Machines (ASMs) formal method. In particular, we discuss how we enhanced modeling, validation, and verification activities of an ASM-based development process. We also provide a critical review of which of our efforts have been more successful as well as those that have not obtained the results we were expecting. Finally, we outline other directions that we believe could further lower the adoption barrier of the method.

Keywords: Abstract State Machines · ASMETA · Usability · Formal methods

1 Introduction

One of the seven myths that Hall listed in his well-known paper [27] is that "formal methods are unacceptable to users". Bowen and Hinchey discussed seven more myths [19] and, among these, they reported the lack of tool support as another myth. However, as formal method community, we have to admit that there is a part of truth in each myth: formal methods can be sometimes difficult to use and not accessible to average users. On one hand, this is due to the intrinsic complexity of the methods and, therefore, some level of required expertise is unavoidable.

P. Arcaini is supported by ERATO HASUO Metamathematics for Systems Design Project (No. JPMJER1603), JST. Funding Reference number: 10.13039/501100009024 ERATO.

© Springer Nature Switzerland AG 2020
E. Sekerinski et al. (Eds.): FM 2019 Workshops, LNCS 12232, pp. 61–76, 2020.
https://doi.org/10.1007/978-3-030-54994-7_6

On the other hand, however, the methods are hard to use because of lack of a user-friendly support. Hall himself, while dispelling the method, recognized that designers should "make the specification comprehensible to the user" [27], and Bowen and Hinchey recognized that more effort must be spent on tool support [19].

The Abstract State Machines (ASMs) formal method [18] is a state-based formal method that is usually claimed to be usable, since a practitioner can understand ASMs as pseudo-code or virtual machines working over abstract data structures. However, from our long time experience in using the method and in teaching it, we realized that there are some aspects of the method that can prevent from using it in the most fruitful way.

In 2006, we started developing the ASMETA framework, with the aim of building a set of tools around the ASM method. While developing validation and verification techniques for the method, we kept *usability* as one of our leading principles. This was also motivated by the fact that, in addition to us, the primary users of the framework are our students to which we teach ASMs. As most of them are not naturally attracted by formal methods, we wanted to build a framework that could assist them in using the ASM method and would lower the adoption barriers of the method. In particular, we declined usability in three more concrete driving principles:

- *smoothness*: the framework should be usable with as less effort as possible. The user should not care about technical details that can be hidden and automatized;
- *understandability*: the framework should help in understanding the model itself and the results of its validation and verification;
- *interoperability*: the different tools of the framework should be integrated as much as possible, such that the user can inspect the results of one tool with another tool without any effort. As an example, the counterexamples of a model checker should be re-executable by the simulator.

In this paper, we describe how the different tools/techniques of ASMETA try to fulfil these principles.

The paper is structured as follows. Section 2 briefly introduces the ASM method, and Sect. 3 gives a general overview of the ASMETA framework. Section 4 describes how we addressed usability at the modeling, validation, and verification levels. Then, Sect. 5 critically reviews our efforts and outlines other directions that could further increase the usability of the framework. Finally, Sect. 6 reviews some related work, and Sect. 7 concludes the paper.

2   Abstract State Machines

Abstract State Machines (ASMs) [18] are an extension of FSMs, where unstructured control states are replaced by states with arbitrary complex data.

ASM *states* are algebraic structures, i.e., domains of objects with functions and predicates defined on them. An ASM *location*, defined as the pair (*function-name*, *list-of-parameter-values*), represents the ASM concept of basic object

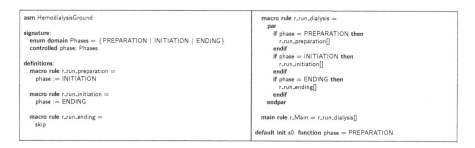

Fig. 1. Example of ASM model

container. The couple (*location, value*) represents a memory unit. Therefore, ASM states can be viewed as abstract memories.

Location values are changed by firing *transition rules*. They express the modification of functions interpretation from one state to the next one. Note that the algebra signature is fixed and that functions are total (by interpreting undefined locations $f(x)$ with value *undef*). Location *updates* are given as assignments of the form $loc := v$, where loc is a location and v its new value. They are the basic units of rules construction. There is a limited but powerful set of *rule constructors* to express: guarded actions (`if-then`, `switch-case`), simultaneous parallel actions (`par`), sequential actions (`seq`), nondeterminism (existential quantification `choose`), and unrestricted synchronous parallelism (universal quantification `forall`).

An ASM *computation* (or *run*) is, therefore, defined as a finite or infinite sequence $S_0, S_1, \ldots, S_n, \ldots$ of states of the machine, where S_0 is an initial state and each S_{n+1} is obtained from S_n by firing the unique *main rule* which in turn could fire other transitions rules. An ASM can have more than one *initial state*. It is also possible to specify state *invariants*.

During a machine computation, not all the locations can be updated. Indeed, functions are classified as *static* (never change during any run of the machine) or *dynamic* (may change as a consequence of agent actions or *updates*). Dynamic functions are distinguished between *monitored* (only read by the machine and modified by the environment) and *controlled* (read and written by the machine). A further classification is between *basic* and *derived* functions, i.e., those coming with a specification or computation mechanism given in terms of other functions.

ASMs allow modeling any kind of computational paradigm, from a *single* agent executing parallel actions, to distributed *multiple* agents interacting in a synchronous or asynchronous way. Moreover, an ASM can be nondeterministic due to the presence of monitored functions (external nondeterminism) and of choose rules (internal nondeterminism). Figure 1 shows a simple example of an ASM model (the ground model of the haemodialysis case study [4]).

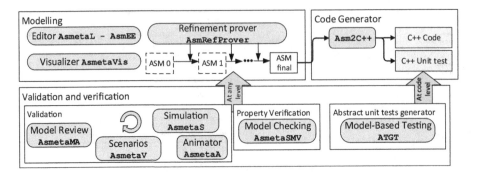

Fig. 2. The ASM development process powered by the ASMETA framework

3   ASMETA

The ASM method is applied along the entire life cycle of software development, i.e., from modeling to code generation. Figure 2 shows the development process based on ASMs.

The process is supported by the ASMETA (ASM mETAmodeling) framework[1] [11] which provides a set of tools to help the developer in various activities:

- **Modeling**: the system is modeled using the language AsmetaL. The user is supported by the editor AsmEE and by AsmetaVis, the ASMs visualizer which transforms the textual model into a graphical representation. The refinement process can be adopted in case the model is complex: the designer can start from the first model (also called the ground model) and can refine it through the refinement steps by adding details to the behavior of the ASM. The AsmRefProver tool checks whether the current ASM model is a correct refinement of the previous ASM model.
- **Validation**: the process is supported by the model simulator AsmetaS, the animator AsmetaA, the scenarios executor AsmetaV, and the model reviewer AsmetaMA. The simulator AsmetaS allows to perform two types of simulation: interactive simulation and random simulation. The difference between the two types of simulation is the way in which the monitored functions are chosen. During interactive simulation the user provides the value of functions, while in random simulation the tool randomly chooses the value of functions among those available. AsmetaA allows the same operation of AsmetaS, but the states are shown using tables. AsmetaV executes scenarios written using the Avalla language. Each scenario contains the expected system behavior and the tool checks whether the machine runs correctly. The model reviewer AsmetaMA performs static analysis in order to check model quality attributes like minimality, completeness, and consistency.

---

[1] http://asmeta.sourceforge.net/.

- **Verification**: properties are verified to check whether the behavior of the model complies with the intended behavior. The `AsmetaSMV` tool supports this process in terms of model checking.
- **Testing**: the tool `ATGT` generates abstract unit tests starting from the ASM specification by exploiting the counterexamples generation of a model checker.
- **Code generation**: given the final ASM specification, the `Asm2C++` automatically translates it into C++ code. Moreover, the abstract tests, generated by the `ATGT` tool, are translated to C++ unit tests.

The framework has been applied to the formal analysis of different kinds of systems: a landing gear system [9], a haemodialysis device [4], self-adaptive systems [14], cloud systems [12], etc.

4 How We Have Addressed Usability in ASMETA

In this section, we describe how we have targeted usability when developing the ASMETA framework. First of all, in order to obtain an integrated framework in which the different tools can be used together, we developed all the tools as eclipse plugins[2].

In the following, we overview the techniques of the framework that have improved it according to the three driving principles (i.e., *smoothness*, *understandability*, and *interoperability*), rather than purely improvements in terms of functionality of the framework. In the following sections, we focus on the three main phases of a formal development process: modeling, validation, and verification.

4.1 Modeling

The first step of the development process is model definition. On the top of the original parser and editor [26], we introduced a technique that provides a better visualization of the model (so improving the *understandability*), and another technique that automatically checks for common errors (so improving the *smoothness* of use).

Visualization. When a model is particularly complex, exploring it can become difficult, and so the developer does not have a proper understanding of the whole structure. In order to improve the exploration of the structure of an ASM model, in [5], we introduced the graphical visualizer `AsmetaVis`. The *basic visualization* permits to show the syntactical structure of the ASM in terms of a tree (similar to an AST); the notation is inspired by the classical flowchart notation, using green rhombuses for guards and grey rectangles for rules. The leaves of the tree are the update rules and the macro call rules. For each macro rule in the model,

---

[2] The update site is http://svn.code.sf.net/p/asmeta/code/code/stable/asmeta_upd ate/.

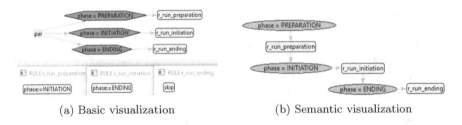

(a) Basic visualization   (b) Semantic visualization

Fig. 3. Visualizer `AsmetaA` – visualization of the ASM model shown in Fig. 1

there is a tree representing the definition of the rule; double-clicking on a macro call rule shows the tree of the corresponding macro rule. Figure 3a shows the basic visualization with `AsmetaVis` (starting from rule `r_run_dialysis`) of the ASM model shown in Fig. 1.

In this case, all the macro rules are shown (i.e., the user has selected all the call rules). Note that the visualization is particularly useful when the model is big, as the user can decide which rules to visualize.

Control states ASMs [18] are a particular class of ASMs in which there is a function (called *phase function*) that identifies the current *control state*; this can be understood as a *mode* of the system. A control state is an abstraction of a set of ASM states having the same value for the phase function. The main rule of a control state ASM is a parallel of conditional rules checking the value of the phase function: in this way, the evolution of the machine depends on the current mode. The model in Fig. 1 is an example of control state ASM. A control state ASM naturally induces an FSM-like representation, where each state corresponds to one value of the phase function. Since such class of ASMs occur quite frequently, we implemented in `AsmetaVis` also a *semantic visualizer* that is able to visualize the FSM-like representation of a control state ASM. The visualization consists in a graph where control states are shown using orange ellipses. The semantic visualization of the ground model is shown in Fig. 3b. The initial control state is identified by the `PREPARATION` phase; from there, the system moves to the `INITIATION` phase by executing rule `r_run_preparation`; then, it moves to the `ENDING` phase by executing rule `r_run_initiation`. In the `ENDING` phase, rule `r_run_ending` is executed, but this does not modify the phase. Note that this visualization turned out to be quite useful, as it allows to get an understanding of the system evolution without the need of simulating the model.

Automatic Model Review. Due to a low familiarity of the formal method, during the development of a formal model, the developer can introduce different types of errors: domain specific ones (i.e., a wrong implementation of the system requirements), and non-domain specific ones that depend on the wrong usage of the method. In order to capture the former category of errors, domain specific properties derived from the requirements need to be verified; for the latter category, instead, automatic techniques can be devised.

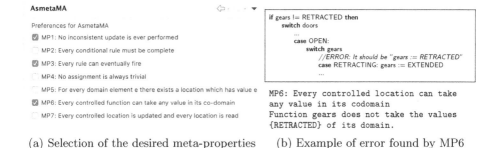

(a) Selection of the desired meta-properties   (b) Example of error found by MP6

Fig. 4. Model reviewer `AsmetaMA`

Based on our experience in modeling with the ASM method and in teaching it to students, we noticed that one of the main modelling (i.e., non-domain specific) errors is related to the computational model of the ASMs, which is based on parallel execution of function updates. If not properly guarded, they could lead to inconsistent results by simultaneously updating the same location to two different values (this is know as *inconsistent update* [18]). Such problem is usually difficult to observe by a manual review of the code, and it is usually only discovered during simulation.

Another problem that we observed frequently with our students is that, due to wrong rule guards, some transition rules can never be executed.

As a minor problem, we also observed that our students tend to write *over-specified* models containing unnecessary functions (that are never used); these could be either really unnecessary, and so removed, or they should be used in some rule that has not been implemented yet.

On the base of the previously described experience, in [7], we proposed the `AsmetaMA` tool that performs *automatic* review of ASMs. The tool checks whether the model contains typical errors that are usually done during the modeling activity using ASMs (suitable *meta-properties* specified in CTL are checked with the model checker `AsmetaSMV` [6]). Figure 4a shows the selection of the available meta-properties in the tool.

For example, MP1 checks that no inconsistent update ever happens, and MP7 that all the model locations are used somewhere in the model. Model reviewer has been extremely helpful also in our modeling of complex case studies. For example, Fig. 4b shows an error that we were able to automatically find when developing the model of a landing gear system [17]: function `gears` should become `RETRACTED` when it is `RETRACTING`, but we wrongly updated it to `EXTENDED`. The meta-property MP6, that checks that each location assumes any possible value, allowed to (indirectly) spot this error.

4.2 Validation

One of the first analysis activities that is performed while writing a formal model is *validation* to check that the model reflects the intended requirements. The

```
Insert a boolean constant for auto_test_end:
true
<State 0 (monitored)>
auto_test_end=true
</State 0 (monitored)>
<State 1 (controlled)>
alarm(DF_PREP)=false
alarm(SAD_ERR)=false
alarm(TEMP_HIGH)=false
dialyzer_connected_contr=false
error(DF_PREP)=false
error(SAD_ERR)=false
error(TEMP_HIGH)=false
phase=PREPARATION
prepPhase=CONNECT_CONCENTRATE
preparing_DF=false
signal_lamp=GREEN
</State 1 (controlled)>
Insert a boolean constant for conn_concentrate:
true
<State 1 (monitored)>
conn_concentrate=true
</State 1 (monitored)>
<State 2 (controlled)>
alarm(DF_PREP)=false
alarm(SAD_ERR)=false
alarm(TEMP_HIGH)=false
dialyzer_connected_contr=false
error(DF_PREP)=false
error(SAD_ERR)=false
error(TEMP_HIGH)=false
phase=PREPARATION
prepPhase=SET_RINSING_PARAM
preparing_DF=true
signal_lamp=GREEN
</State 2 (controlled)>
```

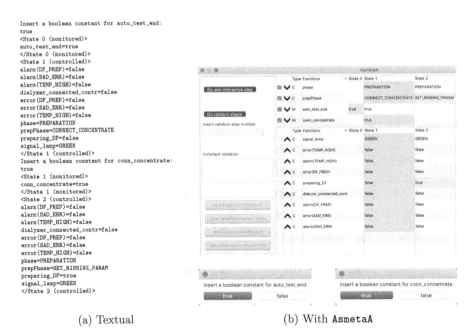

(a) Textual   (b) With `AsmetaA`

Fig. 5. Simulation

main validation technique of the ASMETA framework is simulation, in which inputs are interactively provided to the model by the user who can then check the produced state. Figure 5a shows two steps of the textual simulation (using the simulator `AsmetaS` [26]) of the second refined model of the haemodialysis case study [4].

In this case, the user sets the value of monitored functions `auto_test_end` and `conn_concentrate`; the main functions of interest that the user wants to observe are `phase` and `prepPhase`. However, as shown by this small example, at every step, the whole state is printed, and checking that the simulation is as expected may become difficult as the state size grows. In order to tackle this issue and improve the *understandability* of the simulation traces, we developed the graphical animator `AsmetaA` that allows to select which functions to show, provides dialog boxes to select the values of monitored functions, and highlights the functions that have changed value in the new state. Figure 5b shows the visual simulation of the previous example, in which only the functions of interest have been selected (in the top half of the window).

4.3   Verification

The framework supports verification by model checking with the `AsmetaSMV` tool [6]. The tool translates an AsmetaL model to a model of the model checker

-- specification AG ((gears = RETRACTING & handle = DOWN) -->
                                        AX gears = EXTENDING) is false
-- as demonstrated by the following execution sequence
Trace Description: CTL Counterexample
Trace Type: Counterexample
  --> State: 1.1 < --
    gears = EXTENDED
    handle = DOWN
    doors = CLOSED
  --> State: 1.2 < --
    handle = UP
  --> State: 1.3 < --
    doors = OPENING
  --> State: 1.4 < --
    doors = OPEN
  --> State: 1.5 < --
    gears = RETRACTING
    handle = DOWN
  --> State: 1.6 < --
    gears = EXTENDED
	scenario lgsGMfromCex.test
	
	load LGS_GM.asm
	
	set handle := UP;
	step
	check doors=OPENING;
	
	set handle := UP;
	step
	check doors=OPEN;
	
	set handle := UP;
	step
	check doors=OPEN;
	check gears=RETRACTING;
	
	set handle := DOWN;
	step
	check doors=OPEN; **check** gears=EXTENDED;

(a) Original counterexample	(b) Counterexample in `Avalla`

Fig. 6. Reproduction of `AsmetaSMV` counterexamples

NuSMV[3], performs the verification with NuSMV, and translates the output back in terms of AsmetaL locations. We tried to improve the usability of this tool in different directions.

Smoothness of Use. First of all, the model checker is transparent to the user who interacts with only one tool: (i) (s)he can specify the properties directly in the AsmetaL model using the AsmetaL syntax, (ii) the invocation of NuSMV is done directly only with the framework, (iii) and the output is captured and pretty-printed in terms of AsmetaL locations.

Reproducibility of Counterexamples. In model checking, when a property that should hold is falsified, the model must be fixed in order to satisfy the property (unless the property itself is wrong). To assist the developer in this activity, we developed a translator from the model checker counterexamples to `Avalla` *scenarios*. `Avalla` scenarios allow to describe simulation sequences by providing commands to **set** the values of monitored functions, to perform a **step** of simulation, and to **check** that the output is as expected; the `AsmetaV` tool is able to read `Avalla` scenarios and execute them using the simulator `AsmetaS`. By translating a counterexample in an `Avalla` scenario, the developer, while debugging the model, can rerun it as many times as needed, till the wrong behaviour is removed from the model. In this way, we achieved *interoperability* of the tools, and a better *understandability* of the verification results. Figure 6 shows the counterexample of a property for the landing gear system checking that when the gears are retracting and the handle is pushed down, the gears must start extending.

The violation occurred in a preliminary version of the model (as explained in Sect. 4.1). Figure 6b shows the `Avalla` translation of the counterexample.

---

[3] http://nusmv.fbk.eu/.

```
macro rule r_changeOrganization($c in Camera) =
  par
    let ($getMasterCameraOCself = getMaster($c)) in
      let ($prevGetMasterCameraOCself = prev($getMasterCameraOCself)) in
        par
          r_setMaster[$prevGetMasterCameraOCself]
          if not newSlave($prevGetMasterCameraOCself, $c) then
            newSlave($prevGetMasterCameraOCself, $c) := true
          endif
        endpar
      endlet
    endlet
    change_master($c) := false
  endpar
```

```
macro rule r_changeOrganization($c in Camera) =
  par
    r_setMaster[prev(getMaster($c))]
    if not newSlave(prev(getMaster($c)), $c) then
      newSlave(prev(getMaster($c)), $c) := true
    endif
    change_master($c) := false
  endpar
```

(a) Without flattener   (b) With flattener

Fig. 7. AsmetaSMV – models suitable for model checking

Supporting a Large Class of ASMs. ASMs can describe infinite state systems; however, for model checking, only finite state ASMs having finite domains are admissible. While this limitation is unavoidable, when we originally proposed the tool, we had to impose further restrictions on the class of ASMs that could be translated. Indeed, the AsmetaL language provides a powerful language that allows to describe complex systems in a concise way. While this is advantageous from a modeling point of view, it complicates the mapping to target languages such as NuSMV that have much simpler notations. Some constructs of the ASM formalism are indeed difficult to translate in the target notation, and, although possible, we did not implement such translations because too complex. For example, originally we did not support variable arguments in functions; if the user wanted to use them, (s)he had to write the model as shown in Fig. 7a (taken from [14] where we made the formalization of a self-adaptive system), where the function arguments are made explicit by means of a let rule.

This turned out to be a quite strong limitation; indeed, we noticed that our students were used to write quite compact and elegant models at first, but then this constituted a problem when they had to do model checking, as they had to refactor the ASM model in unnatural ways. Therefore, in [13] we introduced a tool that *flattens* the ASM before being translated to NuSMV; the flattened ASM is a kind of *normal form* that only contains parallel, update, and choose rules. Such kind of ASM is supported by AsmetaSMV; in this way, we have been able to enlarge the class of models supported by the tool, so allowing a *smoother* use of the model checker. Figure 7b shows a model equivalent to the one in Fig. 7a, in which functions are freely used as function arguments: this can be supported by the new version of AsmetaSMV extended with the flattener. Note that we could have achieved this also trying to modify directly the translation from ASM to NuSMV; however, not only this would have been difficult, but it would have improved only AsmetaSMV. The introduction of the flattener, instead, improved the capabilities of different other tools of the ASMETA framework that perform translations to other languages, namely a mapping to SPIN for test case generation [25], to SMT for proof of refinement correctness [8,10], and to C++ code [16].

5   Lessons Learned

We here provide a more critical overview of our efforts in targeting usability in the ASMETA framework. Before, we discuss which tools turned out to be useful and those that, instead, were not successful as expected. Then, we outline some of the ongoing and future efforts that should further increase the usability of the framework.

5.1   Critical Review of Previous Efforts

We should say that not all the techniques we applied for improving the usability of ASMETA have been equally successful. We started developing the visualizer `AsmetaVis` while we were developing the formal specification of a haemodialysis device [4]; indeed, the model was so big that we needed a better way to visualize its structure than the textual model. Although this was extremely helpful for us, it is not used very frequently by our students. The reasons could be different. First of all, the models they develop are not usually too big, and usually they can already have an overview of the model by scrolling once or twice the textual representation. Moreover, students are already used to code and it could be that they do not feel the need of such visualization facilities. We still believe that the visualizer has some potentials for communicating the model structure; however, we need further investigation with different stakeholders (other than students) less accustomed to code.

Among the tools that we introduced to improve the method usability, the animator `AsmetaA` has been one of the most successful. Indeed, reading long simulation traces has always been annoying both for us and our students; first, small models can already have tens of locations and their listing can be long; second, if the listing of a state is long, understanding what has changed between two states is not trivial. The animator solved these issues by allowing to customize which locations to show, and by highlighting those that have been changed.

As we discussed in Sect. 4.3, the introduction of the flattener allowed to enlarge the class of ASMs that could be model checked; the users can now write the ASM model as they wish, with any degree of nesting and compactness. While this is a clear improvement, it also introduced an unexpected drawback. Since the users have a lot of freedom in writing the model, they do not consider anymore that this will be translated for model checking and, therefore, often they write models so complicated that then their verification does not scale. From the experience with our students, we noticed that, when they were constrained by the limitation of the tool (e.g., they could not use functions as argument of other functions), they tended to write simpler models that scaled better. Our observation is that a too high-level notation could detach the user from the computational complexity of verification tasks; therefore, there is the need for some approaches that give the idea of the model complexity: these could be inspired by code metrics as cyclomatic complexity, cohesion, etc.

Being ASMETA an academic tool developed for research, most of the tools have been originally developed as complement of some research work. As such, the implementation usually reached the point in which the research result was evident and could be published; due to deadline pressure, the usability of the tool was sometimes sacrificed. This was the case for the `AsmetaSMV` tool for which we originally restricted the class of ASMs that could be translated. We believe that, as research community, we have to promote initiatives that incentive the production of tools not only innovative from the research point of view, but also usable. Artefacts evaluations, now applied by major conferences as CAV and TACAS, are good initiatives going in this direction.

5.2   Ongoing Efforts and Future Work

As explained before, the visualizer `AsmetaVis` is not used too much because some users (as our students) are accustomed to code. However, there are still problems in managing large models. One solution could be to improve the textual editor by allowing folding/unfolding facilities as those available in main IDEs for programming languages.

CoreASM is the other major framework for ASMs [24]; ASMETA and Core-ASM are somehow complementary, as CoreASM mainly provides support for model debugging, while ASMETA more focuses on simulation-based validation, and automated verification. Being able to write models that are compatible with both frameworks would highly increase the usability of the ASM method, as a user could use all the available tools. As an attempt in this direction, in [3] we proposed a uniform syntax that should be accepted by both frameworks, so that a designer can use all the available tools for ASMs. However, such integration (that is still ongoing) is not trivial, as there are different aspects that need to be merged (e.g., AsmetaL is typed, while CoreASM is not). We believe that the effort spent for this integration is worthy, as standard notations are usually beneficial for the tools that adopt them, as demonstrated by the DIMACS notation for SAT solvers and by SMT-LIB for SMT solvers.

Model refinement [1] is one of the principles of the ASM method [18], as of other methods as B [2] and Z [21]. It consists in developing models incrementally, from a high-level description of the system to more detailed ones, by adding, at each refinement step, design decisions and implementation details. The ASM notion of correct refinement is based on the correspondence of abstract and refined runs; in the framework, we provide an SMT-based tool [8] that is able to prove a particular kind of refinement correctness. However, the framework does not help the designer in deciding what to refine and does not provide support for documenting the refinement decisions; although doing a good refinement depends on the modelling skills of the developer, we believe that a proper tool support could help in obtaining more meaningful refinement steps. For example, we could allow the user to specify which abstract rule is refined in which refined rule(s); this would also help in performing more tailored refinement proofs, as we would exactly know what needs to be related in the SMT-based proof. Moreover, this would also improve incremental test generation techniques that combine refinement and conformance testing [15].

6   Related Work

Due to the lack of space, a complete survey on usability in formal methods is not possible. We only refer to some approaches that have achieved usability using approaches similar to those we proposed.

The formal method community seems to recognize the importance of having visualization techniques (similar to our visualizer `AsmetaVis`) [23,35,41], and there are positive success stories showing that the use of these visualization techniques makes the use of formal methods feasible also for non-experts [35], and also helps in teaching formal methods [34].

Some approaches perform *model visualization* [22,29] (similar to our basic visualization in `AsmetaVis`), while others provide a visual representation of the model execution (or *model animation*) [32,33]. Among these, ProB [32] is one of the most successful tools; it performs animation of B models, and can also be used for error and deadlock checking (similar to our model reviewer `AsmetaMA`), and test-case generation.

Other approaches use UML-like notation as modeling front-end. UML-B [39] uses the B notation as an action and constraint language for UML, and defines the semantics of UML entities via a translation into B. In a similar way, in [36], transforming rules are given from UML models to Object-Z constructs. In the method SPACE and its supporting tool Arctis [31], services are composed of collaborative building blocks that encapsulate behavioral patterns expressed as UML 2.0 collaborations and activities.

Regarding model review, different approaches have been proposed for different formal methods. They all automatize some checks that are usually performed manually by human reviewers; Parnas, in a report about the certification of a nuclear plant, observed that "reviewers spent too much of their time and energy checking for simple, application-independent properties which distracted them from the more difficult, safety-relevant issues" [37]. Approaches for automatic model review have been proposed, e.g., for Software Cost Reduction (SCR) models [28], software requirements specifications (SRS) [30], and UML [38].

7   Conclusions

The paper presented our efforts in addressing usability in the ASMETA framework, and a critical review of what has been more successful and what less.

Note that all our conclusions are only based on our experience; properly assessing the usability of a method/technique would need user studies that, however, are difficult and costly to conduct. Moreover, we defined *usability* according to our understanding, and not relying on notions of usability provided by the Human-Computer Interaction community [20,40]; as future work, it would be interesting to investigate which of those concepts also apply to our framework and which, instead, we are not targeting.

Moreover, all our observations come from the use of the framework by us and by our students; we do not know what would work and what wouldn't in an industrial context.

References

1. Abadi, M., Lamport, L.: The existence of refinement mappings. Theoret. Comput. Sci. **82**(2), 253–284 (1991). https://doi.org/10.1016/0304-3975(91)90224-P
2. Abrial, J.R., Hallerstede, S.: Refinement, decomposition, and instantiation of discrete models: application to Event-B. Fundam. Inform. **77**(1), 1–28 (2007)
3. Arcaini, P., et al.: Unified syntax for abstract state machines. In: Butler, M., Schewe, K.-D., Mashkoor, A., Biro, M. (eds.) ABZ 2016. LNCS, vol. 9675, pp. 231–236. Springer, Cham (2016). https://doi.org/10.1007/978-3-319-33600-8_14
4. Arcaini, P., Bonfanti, S., Gargantini, A., Mashkoor, A., Riccobene, E.: Integrating formal methods into medical software development: the ASM approach. Sci. Comput. Program. **158**, 148–167 (2018). https://doi.org/10.1016/j.scico.2017.07.003
5. Arcaini, P., Bonfanti, S., Gargantini, A., Riccobene, E.: Visual notation and patterns for abstract state machines. In: Milazzo, P., Varró, D., Wimmer, M. (eds.) STAF 2016. LNCS, vol. 9946, pp. 163–178. Springer, Cham (2016). https://doi.org/10.1007/978-3-319-50230-4_12
6. Arcaini, P., Gargantini, A., Riccobene, E.: AsmetaSMV: a way to link high-level ASM models to low-level NuSMV specifications. In: Frappier, M., Glässer, U., Khurshid, S., Laleau, R., Reeves, S. (eds.) ABZ 2010. LNCS, vol. 5977, pp. 61–74. Springer, Heidelberg (2010). https://doi.org/10.1007/978-3-642-11811-1_6
7. Arcaini, P., Gargantini, A., Riccobene, E.: Automatic review of Abstract State Machines by meta property verification. In: Muñoz, C. (ed.) Proceedings of the Second NASA Formal Methods Symposium (NFM 2010), NASA/CP-2010-216215, pp. 4–13. NASA, Langley Research Center, Hampton, April 2010
8. Arcaini, P., Gargantini, A., Riccobene, E.: SMT-based automatic proof of ASM model refinement. In: De Nicola, R., Kühn, E. (eds.) SEFM 2016. LNCS, vol. 9763, pp. 253–269. Springer, Cham (2016). https://doi.org/10.1007/978-3-319-41591-8_17
9. Arcaini, P., Gargantini, A., Riccobene, E.: Rigorous development process of a safety-critical system: from ASM models to Java code. Int. J. Softw. Tools Technol. Transfer **19**(2), 247–269 (2015). https://doi.org/10.1007/s10009-015-0394-x
10. Arcaini, P., Gargantini, A., Riccobene, E.: SMT for state-based formal methods: the ASM case study. In: Shankar, N., Dutertre, B. (eds.) Automated Formal Methods. Kalpa Publications in Computing, vol. 5, pp. 1–18. EasyChair (2018)
11. Arcaini, P., Gargantini, A., Riccobene, E., Scandurra, P.: A model-driven process for engineering a toolset for a formal method. Softw. Pract. Exp. **41**, 155–166 (2011). https://doi.org/10.1002/spe.1019
12. Arcaini, P., Holom, R.-M., Riccobene, E.: ASM-based formal design of an adaptivity component for a Cloud system. Formal Aspects Comput. **28**(4), 567–595 (2016). https://doi.org/10.1007/s00165-016-0371-5
13. Arcaini, P., Melioli, R., Riccobene, E.: AsmetaF: A flattener for the ASMETA framework. In: Masci, P., Monahan, R., Prevosto, V. (eds.) Proceedings 4th Workshop on Formal Integrated Development Environment, Oxford, England, 14 July 2018. Electronic Proceedings in Theoretical Computer Science, vol. 284, pp. 26–36. Open Publishing Association (2018). https://doi.org/10.4204/EPTCS.284.3
14. Arcaini, P., Riccobene, E., Scandurra, P.: Formal design and verification of self-adaptive systems with decentralized control. ACM Trans. Auton. Adapt. Syst. **11**(4), 251–2535 (2017). https://doi.org/10.1145/3019598

15. Bombarda, A., Bonfanti, S., Gargantini, A., Radavelli, M., Duan, F., Lei, Y.: Combining model refinement and test generation for conformance testing of the IEEE PHD protocol using Abstract State Machines. In: Gaston, C., Kosmatov, N., Le Gall, P. (eds.) ICTSS 2019. LNCS, vol. 11812, pp. 67–85. Springer, Cham (2019). https://doi.org/10.1007/978-3-030-31280-0_5

16. Bonfanti, S., Carissoni, M., Gargantini, A., Mashkoor, A.: Asm2C++: a tool for code generation from abstract state machines to Arduino. In: Barrett, C., Davies, M., Kahsai, T. (eds.) NFM 2017. LNCS, vol. 10227, pp. 295–301. Springer, Cham (2017). https://doi.org/10.1007/978-3-319-57288-8_21

17. Boniol, F., Wiels, V., Aït-Ameur, Y., Schewe, K.-D.: The landing gear case study: challenges and experiments. Int. J. Softw. Tools Technol. Transfer **19**(2), 133–140 (2016). https://doi.org/10.1007/s10009-016-0431-4

18. Börger, E., Raschke, A.: Modeling Companion for Software Practitioners. Springer, Heidelberg (2018). https://doi.org/10.1007/978-3-662-56641-1

19. Bowen, J.P., Hinchey, M.G.: Seven more myths of formal methods: Dispelling industrial prejudices. In: Naftalin, M., Denvir, T., Bertran, M. (eds.) FME 1994. LNCS, vol. 873, pp. 105–117. Springer, Heidelberg (1994). https://doi.org/10.1007/3-540-58555-9_91

20. Brooke, J.: SUS: a retrospective. J. Usability Stud. **8**(2), 29–40 (2013)

21. Derrick, J., Boiten, E.: Refinement in Z and object-Z: Foundations and Advanced Applications. Springer, London (2001). https://doi.org/10.1007/978-1-4471-5355-9

22. Dick, J., Loubersac, J.: Integrating structured and formal methods: a visual approach to VDM. In: van Lamsweerde, A., Fugetta, A. (eds.) ESEC 1991. LNCS, vol. 550, pp. 37–59. Springer, Heidelberg (1991). https://doi.org/10.1007/3540547428_42

23. Dulac, N., Viguier, T., Leveson, N., Storey, M.A.: On the use of visualization in formal requirements specification. In: 2012 IEEE Joint International Conference on Requirements Engineering. Proceedings, pp. 71–80. IEEE (2002)

24. Farahbod, R., Glässer, U.: The CoreASM modeling framework. Softw. Pract. Exp. **41**(2), 167–178 (2011). https://doi.org/10.1002/spe.1029

25. Gargantini, A., Riccobene, E., Rinzivillo, S.: Using spin to generate tests from ASM specifications. In: Börger, E., Gargantini, A., Riccobene, E. (eds.) ASM 2003. LNCS, vol. 2589, pp. 263–277. Springer, Heidelberg (2003). https://doi.org/10.1007/3-540-36498-6_15

26. Gargantini, A., Riccobene, E., Scandurra, P.: A metamodel-based language and a simulation engine for abstract state machines. J. UCS **14**(12), 1949–1983 (2008). https://doi.org/10.3217/jucs-014-12-1949

27. Hall, A.: Seven myths of formal methods. IEEE Softw. **7**(5), 11–19 (1990). https://doi.org/10.1109/52.57887

28. Heitmeyer, C.L., Jeffords, R.D., Labaw, B.G.: Automated consistency checking of requirements specifications. ACM Trans. Softw. Eng. Methodol. **5**(3), 231–261 (1996). https://doi.org/10.1145/234426.234431

29. Kim, S.K., Carrington, D.: Visualization of formal specifications. In: Proceedings of the Sixth Asia Pacific Software Engineering Conference, APSEC 1999, p. 102. IEEE Computer Society, Washington (1999). https://doi.org/10.1109/APSEC.1999.809590

30. Kim, T., Cha, S.: Automated structural analysis of SCR-style software requirements specifications using PVS. Softw. Test. Verif. Reliab. **11**(3), 143–163 (2001). https://doi.org/10.1002/stvr.218

31. Kraemer, F.A., Slåtten, V., Herrmann, P.: Tool support for the rapid composition, analysis and implementation of reactive services. J. Syst. Softw. **82**(12), 2068–2080 (2009). https://doi.org/10.1016/j.jss.2009.06.057
32. Ladenberger, L., Bendisposto, J., Leuschel, M.: Visualising event-B models with B-motion studio. In: Alpuente, M., Cook, B., Joubert, C. (eds.) FMICS 2009. LNCS, vol. 5825, pp. 202–204. Springer, Heidelberg (2009). https://doi.org/10.1007/978-3-642-04570-7_17
33. Leuschel, M., Bendisposto, J., Dobrikov, I., Krings, S., Plagge, D.: From Animation to Data Validation: The ProB Constraint Solver 10 Years On, pp. 427–446. Wiley (2014). https://doi.org/10.1002/9781119002727.ch14
34. Leuschel, M., Samia, M., Bendisposto, J.: Easy graphical animation and formula visualisation for teaching B. In: The B Method: From Research to Teaching (2008)
35. Margaria, T., Braun, V.: Formal methods and customized visualization: a fruitful symbiosis. In: Margaria, T., Steffen, B., Rückert, R., Posegga, J. (eds.) Services and Visualization Towards User-Friendly Design. LNCS, vol. 1385, pp. 190–207. Springer, Heidelberg (1998). https://doi.org/10.1007/BFb0053506
36. Miao, H., Liu, L., Li, L.: Formalizing UML models with object-Z. In: George, C., Miao, H. (eds.) ICFEM 2002. LNCS, vol. 2495, pp. 523–534. Springer, Heidelberg (2002). https://doi.org/10.1007/3-540-36103-0_53
37. Parnas, D.L.: Some theorems we should prove. In: Joyce, J.J., Seger, C.-J.H. (eds.) HUG 1993. LNCS, vol. 780, pp. 155–162. Springer, Heidelberg (1994). https://doi.org/10.1007/3-540-57826-9_132
38. Prochnow, S., Schaefer, G., Bell, K., von Hanxleden, R.: Analyzing robustness of UML state machines. In: Workshop on Modeling and Analysis of Real-Time and Embedded Systems (MARTES 2006) (2006)
39. Snook, C., Butler, M.: UML-B: formal modeling and design aided by UML. ACM Trans. Softw. Eng. Methodol. **15**(1), 92–122 (2006). https://doi.org/10.1145/1125808.1125811
40. Speicher, M.: What is usability? A characterization based on ISO 9241-11 and ISO/IEC 25010. CoRR abs/1502.06792 (2015)
41. Spichkova, M.: Human factors of formal methods. CoRR abs/1404.7247 (2014)

Formal Modelling and Verification as Rigorous Review Technology: An Inspiration from INSPEX

Richard Banach[1]([✉]), Joseph Razavi[1], Olivier Debicki[2], and Suzanne Lesecq[2]

[1] School of Computer Science, University of Manchester,
Oxford Road, Manchester M13 9PL, UK
{richard.banach,joseph.razavi}@manchester.ac.uk
[2] Commissariat à l'Énergie Atomique et aux Énergies Alternatives,
17 Rue des Martyrs, 38054 Grenoble Cedex, France
{olivier.debicki,suzanne.lesecq}@cea.fr

Abstract. Reviews of various kinds are an established part of system development, but rely on the vigilance and thoroughness of the human participants for their quality. The use of formal methods as part of the toolkit deployed during review can increase those elements of dependability that formal methods do best to support. A methodology that proposes that formal techniques are used alongside conventional system construction practices during review is introduced. These can reduce the human burden of ensuring review quality, even if the coupling between the formal and conventional strands is not itself formally enforced.

The approach advocated was inspired by experience of the use of formal methods in the INSPEX Project. This project targets the creation of a minaturised smart obstacle detection system, to be clipped onto a visually impaired or blind (VIB) person's white cane, that would give aural feedback to the user about obstacles in front of them. The increasing complexity of such systems itself invites the use of formal techniques during development, but the hardware challenges preclude the application of textbook top-down formal methods. The use of formal methods in INSPEX is *ad hoc*, and the methodology proposed is an abstraction from the practical experience.

1   Introduction

Reviews of various kinds have been part and parcel of system development methodologies since systems of more than a trivial size began to be conceived. To the extent that reviews and inspections engage with the details of system

The INSPEX Project has received funding from the European Union's Horizon 2020 research and innovation programme under grant agreement No 730953. The work was also supported in part by the Swiss Secretariat for Education, Research and Innovation (SERI) under Grant 16.0136 730953. We thank them for their support.

E. Sekerinski et al. (Eds.): FM 2019 Workshops, LNCS 12232, pp. 77–91, 2020.
https://doi.org/10.1007/978-3-030-54994-7_7

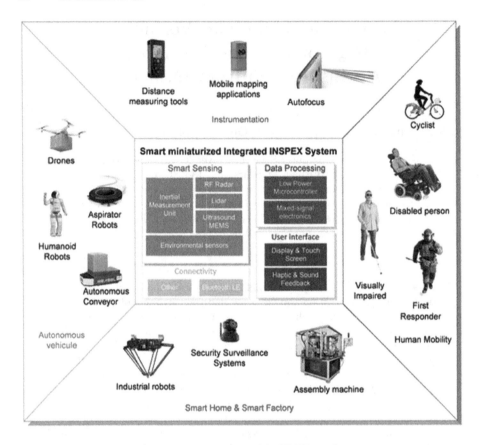

Fig. 1. A selection of potential INSPEX applications.

functionality, they rely on the vigilance and thoroughness of the human participants to ensure the quality of the review results in terms of delivering a reliable
outcome. But since human vigilance is a fallible attribute, while a good review
outcome encourages belief in the system's dependability, it does not guarantee
it. The use of formal methods as part of the toolkit deployed during reviews can
increase those elements of dependability that formal methods do best to support.

In this paper, a methodology that proposes that formal modelling and verification activities should take place alongside conventional system construction
practices is introduced. When this is done, the insights from the formal strand of
the work must be reconciled with the insights from the conventional strand. But
since formal techniques can enforce such aspects as consistency and completeness
very effectively, when this approach is pursued, the human burden of ensuring
these via reviews and inspections is reduced, even if the coupling between the
formal and conventional strands is not itself formally enforced.

The approach advocated was inspired by experience of the use of formal methods in the INSPEX Project. This project targets the creation of a minaturised

smart obstacle detection system, in turn, inspired by the sensor constellations and their supporting software that underpin the intelligence of contemporary automated vehicle driving systems. While such a system can have many potential applications—see Fig. 1, which illustrates a selection of potential use cases for an INSPEX-like system—the specific goal of INSPEX is the creation of a TRL4 prototype device to clip on to a visually impaired or blind (VIB) person's white cane. This would give aural feedback to the user about obstacles in front of them, in order that the risks of collisions, and of accidents, can be diminished. The increasing complexity of such multi-sensor systems creates challenges for ensuring their correct operation, inviting the introduction of formal techniques to help maximise system dependability. Still, the preponderant challenge to building such systems resides at the hardware end of the development, and this impedes the routine application of top-down formal methods, resulting in an *ad hoc* approach to the use of formal techniques in INSPEX. The methodology proposed in this paper is an abstraction from this practical experience.

The rest of this paper is as follows. The next two sections focus on INSPEX, illuminating the background to our proposal. Thus, Sect. 2 overviews the INSPEX VIB system, and Sect. 3 discusses the INSPEX design approach, and the areas in which formal techniques were deployed during the development. We concentrate on the issue that provided the inspiration for our proposed methodology, and on how formal modelling and verification evolved *de facto* into a rigorous code inspection technique. The abstract methodological framework we propose is described in Sect. 4, which may be read without reference to the earlier sections if desired. Sect. 5 concludes.

2   The INSPEX VIB System

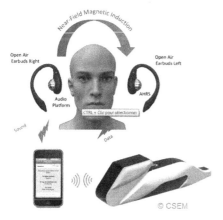

Fig. 2. The complete INSPEX system for the VIB use case.

Given the trend in sensors towards smaller, lighter and more power efficient devices, the INSPEX concept envisages a plethora of possible applications for a smart device that is truly capable of fine grained 3D spatial awareness. A range of these is indicated in Fig. 1.

As stated earlier, the INSPEX Project itself focuses on the VIB use case. Figure 2 shows the complete INSPEX system for this use case from the user's perspective. The complete system consists of three modules. There is the mobile detection device which contains the main sensors (of which more shortly). There is a pair of open air earbuds which transmit a binaural audio representation of the environment sensed by the detection unit to the user. And there is a smartphone. This receives the information from the detection unit, information about the user's head orientation from the earbuds, and other helpful signals from any relevant smart beacons that there might be in the surroundings, and computes an audio signal depicting this information to be presented to the user, which is then sent to the earbuds via Bluetooth.

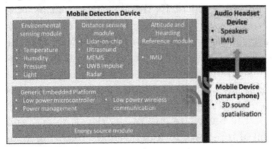

Fig. 3. The architecture of the INSPEX VIB system.

The detection unit is the module that is fixed to a VIB person's white cane. Its architecture is shown in the left part of Fig. 3. It contains the sensors that generate the data needed for the rest of the system. The chief among these comprise a short range LiDAR, a long range LiDAR, a wideband RADAR, and a MEMS ultrasound sensor.

Besides these there are the support services that they need, namely an energy source unit, environmental sensors for ambient light, temperature and humidity, an inertial measurement unit (IMU) and a generic embedded platform (GEP). The latter gathers all the data generated and performs all the computations needed to support all the other devices mentioned.

The main sensors are subject to significant development and minaturisation by a number of partners in the INSPEX Project. The short range LiDAR is developed by the Swiss Center for Electronics and Microtechnology (CSEM) and the French Alternative Energies and Atomic Energy Commission (CEA). The long range LiDAR is developed by the Tyndall National Institute Cork and SensL Technologies, while the wideband RADAR is also developed by CEA. The MEMS ultrasound sensor is from STMicroelectronics (STM). Cork Institute of Technology (CIT) design the containing enclosure and support services.

The smartphone that performs the processing needed to convert the geometrical information provided by the detection unit into an aural signal, needs to take into account the movement of the user's head, this being independent from the movement of the white cane. So the binaural earbuds contain an IMU sensor to detect movement, and this information is transmitted to the smartphone. The earbud system is designed by French SME GoSense. Similar remarks regarding movement apply to the main detection unit which also contains an IMU sensor. The smartphone takes all of this into account in computing an aural image which is stationary in 3D space, thus enabling meaningful perception of obstacle location by the user. Figure 3 shows all the contributing elements and the Bluetooth connections between modules.

Of course, the idea for the INSPEX VIB system did not come out of thin air. A number of white cane add-ons are already available on the market, for example [20, 23, 26]. The INSPEX system is more complex though, and utilises more sensors, in order to give users more complete and more precise information, and this is the source of the added complexity of INSPEX, compared with these earlier systems.

3   The INSPEX Design Approach and the Role of Formal Methods in INSPEX

INSPEX is, first and foremost, a hardware systems integration project. Without working hardware, the project achieves nothing. So the overwhelming emphasis in the project is on overcoming the physical challenges in bringing the equipment to life—everything from the detailed properties of the sensors and their physical signals, to the minaturisation of the constituent devices to the extent possible, to the movement of these signals and their mutual isolation, to the significant software challenges of a design of such complexity, to the properties of the main INSPEX device container, with its need for robustness and durability under a variety of weather conditions while at the same time permitting each sensor to transmit its signal and receive the corresponding reflection.

If formal approaches are to be used to help control the complexity of such an undertaking (a decision taken early in INSPEX), some methodological novelty is going to be unavoidable compared with the familiar way that such techniques are applied in practice [1,4,7,13]. One consequence of this was that it was not clear at the outset what the best strategies for applying formal techniques in INSPEX would be. In the end, the most useful approach turned out to be to use Event-B with its Rodin toolkit [2,22]. This conveniently supported formal modelling and verification. Some use was also made of Blast [6] and of PRISM [18]. Below, we outline the areas of the project upon which it was decided to focus the use of formal techniques, and we elaborate one area, the sensor reading pathway, which spurred the conception of a methodologically distinct use of formal technologies as a formalised contributor to development review.

3.1   Modelling INSPEX Power Management

Given that the main INSPEX device is intended for the maximum possible minaturisation and portability, striving for the minimum possible expenditure of power is a clear necessity. Accordingly, one strand of the INSPEX Project entailed the development of a power management strategy, in order to eke out the capacity of the power supply system to the greatest degree possible.

If we are candid, the sheer challenge of bringing the various not-off-the-shelf hardware components that form the core of the INSPEX prototype to an adequate level of development, is sufficiently taxing that switching everything on and having it working demonstrably is itself considered a resounding success. Nevertheless, as the system progresses towards a commercial product, sophisticated tuning of power use will become important, so design of a power management strategy was included as a strand of the INSPEX development.

In a complex system such as INSPEX, each sensor and subsystem has its own power consumption characteristics. But an exclusive focus on the individual subsystems risks paying too little attention to issues of global coordination. For this reason, a higher level perspective towards power management was adopted, which made it an ideal candidate for predicting power consumption behaviour using modelling via formal techniques.

The approach used for the modelling work centred on Event-B and its Rodin toolkit [2,22], the latter an being outcome of the RODIN [21], DEPLOY [9] and ADVANCE [3] projects. PRISM [18] was used to handle the quantitative aspects. Being targetted at future needs, the power management work was much closer to a textbook formal development, and thus of less interest for this paper.

3.2   Modelling and Verification of the Sensor Readings Pathway

In contrast to the power management work, the handling of the data from the sensors is not only mission critical (without it the hardware does not work at all), but complex (because of the optimisations used), and it also relies on preexisting code (because the relevant software is an outgrowth of code used in earlier projects, as well as containing portions for future deployment). The complexity of this subsystem warranted the employment of formal techniques to improve assurance. However, a pure top-down approach to formal modelling and verification was not practical.

The information from the sensors is gathered by the acquisition software. This accepts interrupts from the short and long range LiDARs, the RADAR, the MEMS (ultrasound) and the IMU (inertial measurement unit). These need to be timestamped so that the freshness of the data can later be taken into account. At regular intervals, the available fresh data is packaged and transmitted to the fusion software. The fusion software then uses an approach to fusion based on Bayesian estimation [15] to compute an *occupation grid*, which is an estimate of which sections of the 3D space in front of the user are occupied by obstacles. While conventional techniques for data fusion [14] are computationally too intensive for a minaturised application like INSPEX, in [10] there is a much more lightweight approach to the occupation grid problem that makes it suitable for adoption in INSPEX. The granularity of the estimate that is obtained is constrained by the quality of the information received, by the bandwidth of the Bluetooth connection to the smartphone, by many pragmatic hardware and architectural considerations, and by the computational power available. Moreover, the detailed operation of the data fusion algorithm is a tightly protected commercial secret of CEA,[1] so only the most basic information about its input interface is available.

Thus the sensor readings acquisition software is complex, it is concurrent (because all the sensors involved act concurrently and with varying levels of reliability), and it must cope with a wide range of timescales (the LiDARs and RADAR act almost instantaneously, while by comparison, the ultrasound takes orders of magnitude longer to respond). On the one hand, this makes it a prime candidate for scrutiny via formal techniques with the aim of reinforcing its dependability. On the other, it raises interesting methodological questions regarding quite how one might go about doing that.

---

[1] It remains a secret, not withstanding the IP protection provisions of the INSPEX Project's Grant Agreement, Consortium Agreement, and even bilateral software access and nondisclosure agreements between consortium partners.

The way this challenge was approached involved an eclectic mix of top-down and bottom-up elements. When the task was started, there was already in existence a large body of code, developed conventionally. It was clear that an understanding of this had to be gained before much progress could be made. So at the outset, there was a lot of informal discussion regarding the purpose of the code and its main constituents. This yielded enough information to enable some initial formal modelling to take place, but was not yet precise enough that detailed refinement would be productive in creating models that accurately reflected the reality of the code (as opposed to merely embodying the imagination of the model's creators regarding desirable lower level properties of the code).

To go further, the code itself had to be examined in detail. Facing up to a large body of C code that embodies the elements mentioned above is a considerable challenge. The implementation level code is replete with a large amount of low level detail that is not directly pertinent to the concerns of high level correctness. And quite apart from that, the scenario being described begs the question: *what exactly does high level correctness amount to?*

In a textbook style formal methods aware development milieu, there is some process that captures the requirements, sharpens the focus to a specification, after which a formal development proceeds in stages, eventually resulting in implementation code. Some of the earier phases of this are captured in documentation of one kind or another.

In a hardware centred project such as INSPEX, the focus being so much on the hardware has the following consequence. The hardware constrains (at a very low level of abstraction) what the software can do to such an extent that little documentation is produced. In essence, the low level code defines itself. And so, from a higher level viewpoint, correctness criteria have to be elicited from the code via a combination of: understanding the code, abstracting from relevant parts of the code, reflection about the code, and reconciling the conclusions evinced from this process with what 'makes sense' in the context of what is known about the application and its context. Not unnaturally, all of this takes quite some time.

The fruits of this activity can be summarised as follows. There are some relatively self-evident high level properties, stating for example that sensors have to be OFF before they can be switched ON, and *vice versa*. These are easy to model and verify without much deep investigation. Beyond that, comes the recognition that the software maintains a buffer in which sensor data is recorded. Saying that there is a buffer (a familiar notion) does not elaborate exactly how that buffer is used. In the INSPEX context, the following facts pertinent to the buffer have to be taken into account.

Messages from the various sensors (LiDARs, RADAR, MEMS US, IMU, etc.) arrive at the Generic Embedded Processor (GEP) and are inserted into the buffer. To be useful in terms of the 3D objective of the application, they have to be associated with a time and orientation. Timing can be handled by the real time clock of the GEP, while orientation is inferred from the IMU. But the IMU is a separate sensor, sending its data at time points different from those at which the other sensors send. To mitigate this, a consecutive pair of IMU data messages are used as brackets, within which the data messages which arrive from other sensors and which are timestamped with values between the timestamps of the two IMU brackets are aggregated into a 'frame', and this frame is the basic unit which is passed to the fusion software. Obviously, what has just been described goes well beyond what is one's first thought on hearing the word 'buffer', and presents a non-trivial undertaking for the formal modelling and verification activity, especially considering that the devices involved are subject to failures of various kinds and the system has to be robust against these.

It should be clear already that what was involved in adding the assurance obtainable via verification to the sensor readings acquisition software entailed a deep analysis of the existing code, and contemplation of how its high level purpose could be formalised. Thus, the formal modelling and verification amounted *de facto* to a sophisticated kind of code inspection, and this is what has inspired us to make the more abstract methological proposal in the remainder of this paper.

4   Formal Modelling and Verification as Rigorous Review Technology

In this section we abstract from, and extrapolate, our experience with INSPEX described in the preceding sections, and we present an approach to the use of formal modelling and verification as an adjunct to conventional approaches to system development with an emphasis on the use of formal techniques as a review technology. The latter aspect intersects with existing ideas on reviews, both formal and less formal, that have been around for a number of decades.

The first point to note is that we are aiming at development methodologies that do not wish to, or do not have the resources to, or are unwilling to, adapt their main development path to accommodate the exigencies of a fully formalised development strategy. Nevertheless they recognise that formal approaches can yield benefits in terms of improved dependability, and wish to gain what benefits they can from a cooperative relationship with formal techniques.[2] In this context, we must assume that the formal work that is to take place is supported by resources separate from those that support the existing practices.

The fact that we are concerned with development practices that are specifically *not* led by formal development considerations, implies that we cannot be too prescriptive about how the formal and conventional practices might work together. Therefore, a considerable degree of flexibility is needed in how formal techniques might fit alongside existing conventional techniques. However, we can infer the following.

---

[2] In the case of INSPEX, it was the lack of resources that prevented a greater integration with formal techniques. It would have necessitated a considerable investment of time and manpower, far beyond the resources of the project, to evolve the existing practices of firmware and hardware development to bring them closer to formal approaches.

Since the conventional techniques are specifically *not* formal, the connection between the formal and conventional sides must be human mediated. For this to be possible, the formal side must replicate some of what the conventional side does; otherwise, there would be no sensible point of comparison, no bridge, between the two sides.

The latter point is the focus of costs and benefits. The costs are obvious: the additional resources that must be found to support the formal work. The benefits are to be found in the independent scrutiny that a formal reappraisal of the relevant elements of the conventional work brings. Independent scrutiny of any kind is widely recognised as being beneficial, even if its benefits are often hard to quantify, and that, far beyond purely technical considerations.

The approach outlined has its strengths and weaknesses too. An obvious strength is the much greater control over consistency and completeness that a formal, mechanically checked definition of a system possesses, when compared with a purely conventionally developed counterpart. An equally obvious weakness though, lies in the fact that the formally defined model is the translation of a human interpretation of some conventionally developed counterpart, and therefore, its reliability is wholly dependent on the reliability of the human interpretation. Part and parcel of our proposal then, is that the human interpretation of the conventional system model is likely to be more reliable than human performed consistency and completeness checking of the same conventional system model, based on the presumption that consistency and completeness checking are detailed, bureaucratic activities, better done by machines, whereas reinterpretation of a system model from a different technical perspective suits the abilities of the human imagination better. This observation has the potential to turn what is a perceived weakness, partly at least, into a strength also.

4.1 Reviews

The role of formal techniques within conventional development, as suggested heretofore, is to reappraise the conventional development, casting a diverse perspective on it, with the aim of improving its overall integrity. This brings it close to the traditional role played by reviews of one kind or another. We turn to this issue now.

No activity of any scale can come to a successful conclusion without an appropriate degree of oversight as it proceeds. The construction of a complex artifact such as a digital system is no exception, and for the oversight to be effective, it has to engage sufficiently with the actual technical details of the project.[3] Thus reviewing of technical progress has always been around, one way or another.

---

[3] The hazards of not engaging with the technical details sufficiently are well illustrated in [25], which describes how the original management of the Crossrail Project in the UK failed to stay in close touch with the technical progress (and problems), resulting in sudden announcements of delays of two or more years, and budget overruns of billions of GBP.

The idea of formalising the structure of reviews, especially reviews of the code in large software projects, was pioneered by Fagan [11,12], whose proposals aimed to maximise the effectiveness of the reviewing process by formalising the process in a way that made the best use of the review's human participants, in particular, paying attention to the limitations of human attention span, etc. Fagan's ideas gained widespread traction in the mainstream [8,16,17,24], and different kinds of review were developed to suit different stages of development and different kinds of project: e.g. requirements reviews, design reviews, as well as code reviews. Different levels of rigour for the reviewing process also emerged, ranging from a structured discussion with a wide range of stakeholders in an informal walkthrough, to much more formalised processes involving a strictly defined team of participants each of which engages in a precisely defined role within the review, which itself takes place within tightly constrained time limits and procedural norms. The article [19] contains an interesting discussion about the world of reviews of different kinds.

Since the use of formal techniques as described above is intended to bring increased dependability to an otherwise conventional development process via the oversight that a formal reformulation can bring, and the use of formally structured reviews has the same aim via the oversight that the review process imposes, it is natural to try to blend the two approaches. That is the aim of the proposal of this paper.

To blend the two ideas, for the sake of definiteness, we have in mind a relatively formally structured review process, but in fact, this is not obligatory. The essence of our proposal is that formal techniques be used to reappraise the appropriateness of the conventionally developed system—reviews are a convenient means of crystalising the conclusions of such a process.[4]

A relatively formally structured review will have a number of formal roles, with at minimum the following. There is a moderator who ensures that when the review meeting is convened, it flows smoothly, and does not get stalled, or distracted by side issues. There is a recorder who focuses on ensuring that an accurate record of the review process is maintained, but who takes no active part in the proceedings. After that there are a number of technical personnel concerned with different perspectives on the system being developed, as suits the situation. In the next sections, we look at how this plays out at the requirements, design, and implementation levels. However, in keeping with allowing the approach to be adaptable to different kinds of development scenarios, we do not assume, at the lower levels, that the corresponding higher level activities have necessarily taken place.

4.2   The Requirements Level Process

At a high level requirements review, the technical personnel will range from stakeholder representatives to high level designers. The fact that a requirements

---

[4] In INSPEX, formal reviews of this kind were not constituted as such. Instead the conclusions of the modelling and verification work were captured in reports that were delivered to the conventional developers.

level review is conceivable, implies that a significant amount of requirements level documentation is envisaged to exist. In this context, we can propose a process incorporating formal technical elements as follows:

- As well as the stated technical personnel, there is an individual competent in formal modelling and verification technologies, referred to below as the FM-tech.
- Part way though the requirements definition process, preliminary requirements documents are released to the FM-tech, who begins building high level models. These may be built in any suitable formalism. Model based approaches are often closest to design and implementation paradigms, but if the requirements are mostly of a behavioural type, then temporal logic formalisms may be more useful.
- If inconsistencies or omissions are detected during model building by the FM-tech, these are queried and resolved as they arise.
- At the completion of the requirements definition process, the final set of requirements documents are released to the FM-tech, who completes model building and summarises findings in a report.
- The requirements review takes place in the standard manner. During this, the FM-tech reports findings resulting from the formal model building. Issues to be resolved are documented, for followup post-review. A criterion for satisfactory resolution is consistency between the final requirements documents and the formal models (insofar as the informal nature of the former permits).

Following the above process encourages achieving as much completeness at the requirements level at the earliest possible opportunity, yet without abandoning traditional requirements activities completely. Lack of precision in requirements is often bewailed in commentary on the system development activity as a major source of system defects. In [1,2], as well as many other places (especially works discussing the deployment of the B-Method), the necessity of completely rewriting the requirements documents before any formal development can begin is ruefully repeated. But even if formal development from the requirements is not envisaged, requirements documentation that enjoys a demonstrable level of consistency and completeness will help to ensure a smooth development process.

4.3   The Design Level Process

After the requirements definition process (or even without there having been such a process, if the requirements are intuitively well enough understood by the system designers), system design can proceed with some precision. As before, the fact that a design review is envisaged at all, implies the creation of appropriate amount of design level documentation. Focusing on the review process again, the technical personnel involved will cover a range of concerns, but probably will not include stakeholders in the same way. A process incorporating formal technical elements can then be proposed as follows:

- As before, there is an FM-tech (or perhaps more than one) involved.
- Part way though the design definition process, preliminary documentation is released to the FM-tech who begins building intermediate level models. These ought to be characterised as refinements of the corresponding high level models (provided such high level models have been created earlier). However, due to possible lack of precision at a higher level, refinement might only become possible after some alteration of the high level models. In such cases reconsideration of consistency with high level requirements should take place, and the relevant issues should be documented.
- At the completion of the design process, the final set of design documents are released to FM-tech, who completes model building and refinement, and summarises findings in a report.
- The design review takes place in the standard manner. During this, the FM-tech reports findings resulting from the formal modelling and refinement. Issues to be resolved are documented, for followup post-review. A criterion for satisfactory resolution is thoroughgoing consistency, top to bottom.

For many system types, where there have been well understood precursor systems developed by the same teams, design is the most likely starting point for development. For such systems the design stage is the earliest stage at which the kind of formal scrutiny proposed in this paper becomes possible.

4.4 The Implementation Level

Regardless of whether the activities at requirements or design level have, or have not taken place, the corresponding review processes at implementation level are always possible in principle. This is because the implementation level definition of any system is always a formal one, irrespective of whether it is one that is easily amenable to formal analysis, or whether it addresses the system requirements (whether clearly articulated or intuitively understood) either appropriately or correctly. Thus, following on from design is coding and other implementation activity, and we make a proposal in sympathy with those above, for reviewing the code that results from the implementation process.

- As before, there is an FM-tech (or perhaps more than one) involved.
- Part way though coding, some relatively complete portions of the code are released to the FM-tech who begins to assess consistency with earlier models, and begins application of source code analysis tools. Issues germane to eventual consistency are documented for resolution as work progresses.
- At the completion of coding, the final code is released to the FM-tech, who completes analysis (both human level and tool based), and summarises findings in a report.
- The code review takes place. During this, as well as the usual commentary arising from human inspection of the code, the FM-tech reports findings resulting from reconciling the refined formal models with the code, and the outputs from source code analysis tools. As always, issues to be resolved are documented, for followup post-review. A criterion for satisfactory resolution is thoroughgoing consistency, top to bottom.

4.5   Development Processes and the Involvement of Formalism

The above proposals might easily be seen as an elaboration of a process that is both a traditionally based waterfall process, and one that is rather costly. We address these two points in turn.

Regarding cost, it is true that introducing formal techniques into the development process raises costs early on. However, this has to be weighed against cost savings later down the line when faults discovered in the field have to be remedied, usually at a much higher cost. It is by now relatively well known that, done in a judicious manner, formally assisted development need not cost more, overall, than traditional development, when total system lifetime costs are properly accounted.

Furthermore, in the review scheme we proposed above, we advocated the involvement of the FM-tech from a relatively early stage. Although the maximum degree of independence of the FM-tech maximises also the diversity of perspective that the FM-tech brings to the appraisal of the system, the maximum degree of ignorance about its details maximises also the time taken—and thus the cost—of achieving a comprehensive and accurate review. We have advocated a middle way: the FM-tech should have *some* familiarity—but not too much—with the subject of the development, so that a healthy (but not unhealthy) degree of skepticism can be brought to the FM-tech's involvement.

Regarding the waterfall basis of the description, its main purpose was pedagogical, in that the clean separations of the various phases of development facilitated the explanation of our proposal. We claim that our proposal can be adapted to more agile methodologies without too much modification. In such a more agile process, successive iterations, or sprints, could be embellished with a lightweight review process gleaned from the above account. Perhaps the main apparent obstacle to doing so, though, is the ill-adaptedness of formal refinement technologies in general, to modifications of a given level of abstraction after it is once completed—such modifications can seldom be expressed as refinements. One approach to this is to simply redo the formal development after each such modification—with good tool support this is unlikely to be too burdensome in developments of modest size. An alternative approach comes through enlarging the range of processes that a formal system model can undergo, to include the increments of functionality typified in successive sprints. In [5] there is a proposal for precisely such an enhancement to formal development processes, intended for iterative development, and adapted to Event-B.

5   Conclusions

This paper takes the experience of using formal methods in the context of the INSPEX Project, and abstracts that experience to propose an approach to the use of formal techniques as an adjunct to conventional development processes. In particular, is it proposed to use formal techniques as a more rigorous version of review techniques that might form an element of conventional development processes anyway.

Thus the preceding sections overviewed the inspiration for INSPEX arising from within the autonomous automotive domain, and how the potential for minaturisation and low power consumption in the sensor families used for automotive autonomous navigation opens the door for a host of novel applications. Prime among these is one that targets the desire to assist the visually impaired and blind to navigate more safely in their environment, by providing information about the whole of the 3D space in front of the user via an aural information feed that can be comprehended by the VIB user.[5]

The adoption of formal techniques by the INSPEX Project was a consequence of the recognition that increasing complexity of such integrated multi-sensor systems as foreseen in INSPEX, creates an increasing risk that errors in the design and implementation may survive into production systems undetected. This spurs the adoption of more disciplined techniques for the development of such systems, and one of the most robust approaches of this type involves the introduction of formal approaches during the development process.

The fact that as a primarily hardware led project, the development route would need to be grounded in conventional hardware design techniques to yield results on time and within cost, entailed considerable creativity in aligning the usual practice in the embedded field with the usual practice in the formal domain. This enforced novelty in the application of formal technologies in INSPEX was paramount in inspiring the idea that salient aspects of this experience could be generalised to make them applicable more widely.

We thus outlined the use of formal techniques in INSPEX. On the one hand, there was a basically top-down approach for the power management strategy modelling exercise, which proceeded in a manner relatively recognisable as a top-down methodology. On the other hand there was a much more bottom-up approach for the verification of the sensor readings pathway, the discovery of the relevant correctness criteria there, and their reconciliation with the existing implementation.

The latter led to the main novel contribution of this paper, namely the proposal that formal modelling and verification can be used to form a significant addition to the power of review approaches in conventional system development. When the unavoidably unforgiving nature of formal systems is brought into the review process, primarily as a consistency and completeness enforcement tool, the successful completion of the modelling and verification task confirms that nothing essential has been left out at the given level of abstraction. This is something that is left to the vigilance of the human reviewer in the conventional review process, and is much harder to achieve there, given that it involves recognising what has been erroneously left out, as well as recognising what might be wrong with what has been put in.

---

[5] The 'first responder' use case, shown in Fig. 1, refers especially to firefighters who often have to work in smoke-filled environments, and thus experience issues similar to VIB persons. It thus forms a natural follow-up to the VIB use case.

References

1. Abrial, J.R.: Formal methods in industry: achievements. problems future. In: Proceedings of the ACM/IEEE ICSE 2006, pp. 761–768 (2006)
2. Abrial, J.R.: Modeling in Event-B: System and Software Engineering. CUP (2010)
3. ADVANCE: European Project ADVANCE. IST-287563 (2011). http://www.advance-ict.eu/
4. Banach, R. (ed.): Special issue on the state of the art in formal methods. J. Univers. Comput. Sci. **13**(5) (2007)
5. Banach, R.: Retrenchment for Event-B: usecase-wise development and Rodin integration. Form. Asp. Comp. **23**, 113–131 (2011)
6. BLAST Tool (2011). https://forge.ispras.ru/projects/blast/
7. Bowen, J., Hinchey, M.: Seven more myths of formal methods. IEEE Softw. **12**, 34–41 (1995)
8. Braude, E., Bernstein, M.: Software Engineering: Modern Approaches. Wiley, Hoboken (2011)
9. DEPLOY: European Project DEPLOY. IST-2007.1.2 No. 214158 (2008). http://www.deploy-project.eu/
10. Dia, R., Mottin, J., Rakotavao, T., Puschini, D., Lesecq, S.: Evaluation of occupancy grid resolution through a novel approach for inverse sensor modeling. In: Proceedings of the IFAC World Congress, FAC-PapersOnLine, vol. 50, pp. 13841–13847 (2017)
11. Fagan, M.: Design and code inspections to reduce errors in program development. IBM Syst. J. **15**, 182–211 (1976)
12. Fagan, M.: Advances in software inspections. IEEE Trans. Softw. Eng. **SE-12**, 744–751 (1986)
13. Hall, A.: Seven myths of formal methods. IEEE Softw. **7**, 11–19 (1990)
14. Hall, D.: Mathematical Techniques in Multisensor Data Fusion. Artech House, Norwood (2004)
15. Kedem, B., De Oliveira, V., Sverchkov, M.: Statistical Data Fusion. World Scientific, Singapore (2017)
16. Pfleeger, S., Atlee, J.: Software Engineering. Pearson, London (2010)
17. Pressman, R.: Software Engineering: A Practitioner's Approach. McGraw Hill, New York (2005)
18. PRISM Tool. https://www.prismmodelchecker.org/
19. Radice, R.: Software Inspections (2002). http://www.methodsandtools.com/archive/archive.php?id=29
20. Rango (2018). http://www.gosense.com/rango/
21. RODIN: European Project RODIN. IST-511599 (2005). http://rodin.cs.ncl.ac.uk/
22. RODIN Tool (2018). http://www.event-b.org/
23. Smartcane (2017). https://www.phoenixmedicalsystems.com/assistive-technology/smartcane/
24. Sommerville, I.: Software Engineering. Pearson, London (2015)
25. UK Terrestrial TV Channel 5: Crossrail: Where Did It All Go Wrong? 3 August 2019
26. Ultracane (2017). https://www.ultracane.com/

DataMod 2019 - 8th International Symposium From Data to Models and Back

DataMod 2019 Organizers' Message

The 8th International Symposium From Data to Models and Back (DataMod 2019) was held in Porto, Portugal, during 7–8 October 2019. The symposium aimed at bringing together practitioners and researchers from academia, industry, government and non-government organizations to present research results and exchange experiences, ideas, and solutions for modeling and analyzing complex systems and using knowledge management strategies, technology, and systems in various domain areas such as ecology, biology, medicine, climate, governance, education, and social software engineering. The Symposium received a total of 13 submissions. After a careful review process, which involved at least three peer reviewers per submission, the Program Committee accepted all of them, eight as regular papers for presentation at the symposium and inclusion in the post-proceedings, and three as short presentation reports. The program of DataMod 2019 was also enriched by two keynote speeches: the first, held by Mieke Massink, entitled "Verification of Data in Space and Time"; the second, by Ana Cavalcanti, entitled "Diagrammatic physical robot models in RoboSim".

DataMod 2019 was a successful event thanks to the contribution of several people involved in its organization at different levels. In particular, we are grateful to the whole Steering Committee, and to the Organizing Committee, formed by Oana Andrei, Antonio Cerone and Paolo Milazzo, for their assistance in the organization of the event. We would like to thank the organizers of FM'19, and in particular the Workshop and Tutorial Chairs, Emil Sekerinski and Nelma Moreira. We would also like to thank the Program Committee and the additional reviewers for their work in reviewing the papers. The process of reviewing and selecting papers was supported by EasyChair. We thank all attendees of the symposium and hope that this event helped in sharing ideas and establishing new collaborations.

December 2019

Vashti Galpin
Riccardo Guidotti
Mirco Nanni

Organization

DataMod 2019 - Steering Commmittee

Antonio Cerone	Nazarbayev University, Kazakhstan
Jane Hillston	University of Edinburgh, UK
Marijn Janssen	Delft University of Technology, The Netherlands
Stan Matwin	University of Ottawa, Canada
Paolo Milazzo	University of Pisa, Italy
Anna Monreale	University of Pisa, Italy

DataMod 2019 - Program Committee

Oana Andrei	University of Glasgow, UK
Luís Barbosa	United Nations University, UNU-EGOV, Portugal
Giovanna Broccia	ISTI-CNR, Italy
Antonio Cerone	Nazarbayev University, Kazakhstan
Vittorio Cuculo	Université degli Studi di Milano, Italy
Ricardo Czekster	University of Santa Cruz do Sul, Brazil
Giuditta Franco	University of Verona, Italy
Cheng Fu	University of Zurich, Switzerland
Vashti Galpin (Co-chair)	University of Edinburgh, UK
Rocio Gonzalez-Diaz	University of Seville, Spain
Riccardo Guidotti (Co-chair)	ISTI-CNR, Italy
Tias Guns	Vrije Universiteit Brussel, Belgium
Haosheng Huang	University of Zurich, Switzerland
Juliana Kuster Filipe Bowles	University of St Andrews, UK
Martin Lukac	Nazarbayev University, Kazakhstan
Paolo Milazzo	University of Pisa, Italy
Anna Monreale	University of Pisa, Italy
Mirco Musolesi	University College London, UK
Mirco Nanni (Co-chair)	ISTI-CNR, Italy
Amedeo Napoli	LORIA Nancy, CNRS, France
Laura Nenzi	TU Wien, Austria
Nicola Paoletti	Stony Brook University, USA
Nikos Pelekis	University of Piraeus, Greece
Roberto Pellungrini	ISTI-CNR, Italy
Carla Piazza	University of Udine, Italy
Giuseppe Pirrò	University of Rome, Italy
Gwen Salaün	University of Grenoble Alpes, France
Mark Sterling	Nazarbayev University, Kazakhstan
Andrea Tagarelli	University of Calabria, Italy
Luca Tesei	University of Camerino, Italy
Evgenij Thorstensen	University of Oslo, Norway
Ludovica Luisa Vissat	University of Edinburgh, UK

DataMod 2019 - Organizing Committee

Oana Andrei	University of Glasgow, UK
Antonio Cerone	Nazarbayev University, Kazakhstan
Paolo Milazzo	University of Pisa, Italy

Keynote Talks

Verification of Data in Space and Time

Mieke Massink

Consiglio Nazionale delle Ricerche - Istituto di Scienza e Tecnologie
dell'Informazione 'A. Faedo', CNR, Pisai, Italy

Abstract. Research data can take very many forms, but in many cases there are
interesting relations between elements of data. Such relations could be of various
nature, for example causal relations, temporal relations, spatial relations or
any combination thereof, to mention a few. Reasoning about time and space and
their combination has a long history. Only more recently, reasoning about
spatial aspects of systems, that is, the properties of entities that relate to their
position, distance, connectivity and reachability in space, have received
increasing attention in computer science. We present recent results in spatial and
spatio-temporal logic, that have their origin in Modal logic and early work
dating back to McKinsey and Tarksi, and their evolution into efficient spatial
and spatio-temporal model checking methods. We illustrate these methods by
their application to various domains ranging from smart public transportation to
medical imaging. In the latter domain, data-analysis techniques, such as machine
learning, provide a popular new area of research too, opening the way for an
interesting discussion on how various methods could be used profitable in a
complementary way.

Diagrammatic Physical Robot Models in Robosim

Ana Cavalcanti

Department of Computer Science, University of York, York, UK

Abstract. Simulation is a favoured technique for analysis of robotic systems. Lack of standardisation and portability between simulators, however, has impact on usability and cost of simulations. We present RoboSim, a diagrammatic tool-independent domain-specific language to model robotic platforms and their controllers. It can be regarded as a profile of UML/SysML enriched with time primitives, differential equations, and a formal process algebraic semantics. In RoboSim, a robotic platform is specified by a block diagram, which can be linked to a data model to characterise how events, variables, and operations of the software controller map to inputs and outputs of sensors and actuators. The behaviours of inputs, outputs, and joints are specified by systems of differential algebraic equations. Simulations and mathematical models for proof can be generated automatically from RoboSim models.

Validation of a Simulation Algorithm for Safety-Critical Human Multitasking

Giovanna Broccia[1(⊠)], Paolo Milazzo[1], Cristina Belviso[2],
and Carmen Berrocal Montiel[2]

[1] Department of Computer Science, University of Pisa, Pisa, Italy
{giovanna.broccia,milazzo}@di.unipi.it
[2] Dipartimento di Patologia Chirurgica, Medica, Molecolare e dell'Area Critica,
University of Pisa, Pisa, Italy
belvcristina@gmail.com, carmen.berrocalmontiel@med.unipi.it

Abstract. Multitasking has become surprisingly present in our life. This is mostly due to the fact that nowadays most of our activities involve the interaction with one or more devices. In such a context the brain mechanism of *selective attention* plays a key role in determining the success of a human's interaction with a device. Indeed, it is a resource to be shared among the concurrent tasks to be performed, and the sharing of attention turns out to be a process similar to process scheduling in operating systems. In order to study human multitasking situations in which a user interacts with more than one device at the same time, we proposed in a previous work an algorithm for simulating human selective attention. Our algorithm focuses, in particular, on safety-critical human multitasking, namely situations in which some of the tasks the user is involved in may lead to dangerous consequences if not executed properly. In this paper, we present the validation of such an algorithm against data gathered from an experimental study performed with real users involved concurrently in a "main" task perceived as safety-critical and in a series of "distractor" tasks having different levels of cognitive load.

Keywords: Validation · Simulation algorithm · Human-computer interaction · Safety-critical · Multitasking · Experimental study

1 Introduction

Nowadays we often interact with multiple devices or with a single device performing multiple tasks concurrently: keeping up several instant message conversations at once, answering an e-mail while listening to a talk at a conference, hanging out with social network while watching television, just to give some examples. However, despite what most of us could believe, the multitasking performance takes a toll on productivity and psychologists who study the mental processes involved in multitasking have found that the human mind and brain are not designed for doing more than one task at a time [23,25]. We cannot focus on

E. Sekerinski et al. (Eds.): FM 2019 Workshops, LNCS 12232, pp. 99–113, 2020.
https://doi.org/10.1007/978-3-030-54994-7_8

more than one thing at a time, what we can do is to switch from one task to another with incredible speed, since all these tasks use the same part of the brain [20].

One of the main resources to be shared in such multitasking contexts is the *human selective attention* – a selective activity whose purpose is to focus on one element of the environment while ignoring the others: several studies show how attentional limitations could cause troubles while performing multitasking [22, 24, 28]. According to [15], the *cognitive load* of each task (i.e., the amount of cognitive resources required by each task) influences the activity of the attentional mechanisms. In particular, focusing attention on a "main" task may be impeded by a secondary "distractor" task with a high cognitive load.

Moreover, in a multitasking context, another factor influencing the attentional mechanism is the fact that some tasks might be more critical than others. If the user is performing concurrent tasks, one of which is safety-critical and the others non-critical but characterised by a high cognitive load, such a cognitive load could cause users to draw away their attention from the safety-critical task.

To study such kinds of problems we proposed a model of safety-critical human multitasking (SCHM model), which describes the cognitive processes involved in a multitasking interaction with safety-critical systems [5].

Although the proposed model is designed according with psychological literature and results from experimental psychological studies, we conducted an experimental study with real users involved in a multitasking interaction on a web application with a "main" critical task and a secondary "distractor" task. Essentially, the main question we wanted to answer is:

Does the SCHM model "mirror" the task prioritisation that real users perform in a safety-critical multitasking context?

The experiment and the analysis of the experimental data, together with the development of a simulator in Java, allowed us to fine-tune the proposed model and to validate it.

We will present the model and its Java implementation in Sect. 2, the experimental study in Sect. 3, the design of the simulation experiments in Sect. 4 and the results we obtained in Sect. 5.

2 Safety-Critical Human Multitasking Model

The SCHM model is a mathematical model of human selective attention used to study situations where users concurrently interact with multiple devices and they have to voluntary choose which task to execute next.

The model is an extension and modification of the cognitive framework proposed by Cerone for the analysis of interactive systems [9]. Other related models of human multitasking are ACT-R [1], SEEV [30], STOM [29] and the models proposed in [19, 21] (see [6] for a deeper discussion about related work).

As in that work, we describe the cognitive processes involved in HCI and the human working memory. However, we focus on multitasking and not on the analysis of the interaction with single device as in [9]. Moreover, our model also describes the limitations of the working memory, enabling us to reason about memory overload, and includes timing features, enabling us to reason about hazards caused by distractions.

We implemented a simplified version of the model as a Java simulator based on the algorithm proposed in [3] in order to have quick feedback about whether users can successfully and safely complete a given group of tasks at the same time. The simulator models human multitasking where users are allowed to perform a single task on each interface, we then decide not to model the interfaces.

Moreover, we implemented the multitasking model in Real-Time Maude, which is a rewriting logic language and tool which supports the formal specification and analysis of real-time systems [4,6]. The Real-Time Maude framework enables us to analyse safety-critical human multitasking through simulation and reachability analysis.

Within the model, each task is defined as a sequence of subtasks, which in turn are defined as a sequence of basic tasks (i.e. atomic action composing the task which cannot further decomposed). Between two basic tasks, it is possible to have some time, which could correspond to the time necessary to switch from one basic task to the next, but also to the time required by the device to process the received input and to enable the execution of the next basic task; we call such a time *delay*. Moreover, each basic task is characterised by a duration and a measure of how much it is difficult. By using such information we can compute the cognitive load of each task, starting from the definition of the cognitive load presented in [2]. Moreover, each task is characterised by a measure of how much the user perceives it to be safety-critical.

We define basic tasks as follows:

$$j \mid p \implies a \mid k \textbf{ duration } t \textbf{ difficulty } d \textbf{ delay } \delta$$

where j, k are information items, p is a perception (from the user viewpoint) about the device (interface) state, and a is an action to be performed on the device interface.

The basic task indicates that when the interface is on state p and the user has inside his/her working memory the information j, he/she can perform the action a and replace the information j with the information k in his/her working memory; such a basic task has duration t and difficulty d and it is enabled – and thus it can be executed – if and only if the delay δ is elapsed.

For each task we compute an α-factor representing the likelihood the task will attract the user's attention. At each step of the interaction the user chooses the task to be executed with a probability proportional to its α-factor. The α-factor of a task T is described as the product of three parameters: the cognitive load of the task (computed over the current subtask), the criticality level of the task, and the time elapsed since the last time the task has been executed:

$$\alpha_T = CogLoad_T \times c \times (waitTime_T + 1) \tag{1}$$

where:

- $CogLoad_T$ denotes the cognitive load of the task T;
- c denotes the criticality of the task T;
- $waitTime_T$ denotes the time the task T has not been executed.

As already mentioned, we implemented a Java simulator whose full specification is available at http://www.di.unipi.it/msvbio/software/AttentionSim.html.

We implemented a Java class for each element of the SCHM model:

- a `BasicTask` class;
- a `Subtask` class, containing a list of `BasicTasks`;
- a `Task` class, containing a list of `Subtaskss` and the criticality parameter c;
- a `WorkingMemory` class, modeling a (limited) working memory of a user;
- a `Configuration` class, which models the state of the simulation. An object of this class contains
  - a vector of `Task` objects, representing the concurrent tasks
  - a `WorkingMemory` object
  - variable `globalClock` of type `Integer` measuring the time elapsed from the beginning of the execution of the tasks
- a `Simulator` class, where the algorithm for simulating selective attention is specified.

The algorithm performs a main loop that essentially executes one basic task in each iteration. The basic task to be executed is the first basic task of one of the enabled tasks. For each of such enabled tasks, the α-factor is computed. These α-factors are then normalized in order to obtain a probability distribution used for the choice of the task. The first basic task of the chosen task is then executed as follows:

- the global clock is updated with the duration of the executed basic task;
- the chosen task is marked with a timestamp tracking the last time the task has been executed;
- the working memory is updated as specified by the executed basic task;
- the executed basic task is removed from the configuration.

If the algorithm reaches a configuration where no task is enabled, the main loop performs an iteration where only the global clock is updated with the minimum value needed to reach a configuration where at least one task is enabled.

The simulation terminates when all of the tasks in its configuration are completed.

3   Experimental Study

The development of the web application for the experimental study is part of a collaboration between computer scientists and psychologists from the University of Pisa (authors of this paper), which led to the definition of a set of appropriate tasks for the validation of the proposed algorithm. We defined two separate tests: one for evaluating the working memory (WM) performances of the participants, and one called *shared attention test* where users were asked to interact with two tasks concurrently.

3.1   Working Memory Span Tasks

Before the shared attention test, we administrate to the participants two different *working memory span tasks* (WMST) – standard tasks used to measure the performance of the working memory – in order to identify different inclinations to multitasking.

WMST are widely used in cognitive psychology [13] since WM plays an important role in a wide range of complex cognitive behaviours, such as comprehension, reasoning, and problem solving [18], and it is an important individual variable in general intellectual ability [11,12,17].

WMST were created to require not only information maintenance, but also the concurrent processing of additional information [8,14,27]. Such tasks involve performing two sequential activities: one mnemonic activity which imposes the memorisation and recall of a set of elements (such as digits or words); and one secondary activity which imposes a processing operation (e.g. comprehending sentences, verifying equations, or enumerating an array of shapes). Participants are asked to see or hear a sequence of elements spaced by a processing operation. At the end of each trial they have to recall the sequence correctly (which means recall the correct elements and in the correct order), with increasingly longer sequences being tested in each trial (from two to five elements per trial).

We administrate two different WM span tasks: the reading span task (RST) [14], and the operation span task (OST) [27][1]. In both, a sequence of numbers of variable length (from 2 to 5 numbers) is presented on the screen; each number is spaced by a sentence (RST) or an equation (OST) to evaluate. When all numbers are presented to the users, they have to recall the numbers in the exact order they were presented. We administrate 3 test repetitions for each sequence length: in total 12 repetitions for both RST and OST.

As regards the procedure for measuring the WM capacity, different scoring procedures are available in the literature [13]; we use the partial-credit unit scoring (PCU), namely the mean proportion of elements within a test that were recalled correctly. The PCU for each user is computed as follows:

$$PCU = \frac{\sum_{i=1}^{N} \frac{b_i}{a_i}}{N}$$

where N is the number of items, b_i the number of elements correctly recalled, and a_i the number of elements to recall.

---

[1] Available at http://pages.di.unipi.it/milazzo/AppSpans/.

3.2 Shared Attention Test

As regards the shared attention test[2], we defined two tasks, (i) a main and critical one, and (ii) a secondary distracting task (with different levels of cognitive load):

i As shown in Fig. 1, in the main task users visualise on the screen a chain of 9 rings and a black pellet which randomly moves left and right along the chain. Every time the task starts, the black pellet is on the central green ring and moves randomly every second. Users are asked to avoid that the black pellet reaches one of the red rings at the two ends of the chain, by pushing two buttons on the screen which move the pellet in the two directions: if they do not succeed, the task fails.

ii In the secondary distracting task (shown in Fig. 2), users visualise on the screen a sequence of boxes and a keyboard. At cyclic intervals, a letter appears inside a box; letters appear one by one until all boxes are full.

Users have to find and push on the keyboard the letter corresponding to the one inside the box indicated by the arrow, until all the letters are inserted in the same order they were presented. Every time they have to insert a new letter (i.e. the previous letter has been successfully inserted and the next one has appeared) the keyboard changes.

Such activity has a total duration expressed through a timeout, visualised by a decreasing number and a black progress bar. Once the timeout expires the task is concluded: if the user did not succeed in inserting all the letters, the task is considered failed, otherwise the task succeeds.

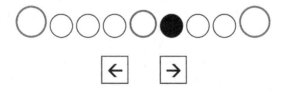

Fig. 1. Main critical task. (Color figure online)

Fig. 2. Secondary distracting task.

---

[2] Available at http://pages.di.unipi.it/milazzo/AppSpans2/.

The tasks are presented on two separate tabs of the same window: users can see only one of the two tabs at a time, and they can switch from one to another by pushing the space bar. So, the user has to perform the two tasks concurrently by interleaving them. Both tasks have to be completed successfully.

The secondary task is instantiated with different levels of cognitive load. In order to do this, three different parameters of the secondary task are varied: the number of letters to insert (*letters*), the number of keys composing the keyboard (*keys*), and the total duration of the task (*duration*). As regards the letters, we define three kinds of task where users have to insert 2 letters, 4 letters, and 8 letters, respectively; as regards the keys, we define a task where users should search for the right letter in a *single* keyboard (i.e. the number of keys composing the keyboard is equal to the number of letters to be inserted), and a kind of task where they have to search for the letter in a *double* keyboard (i.e. the number of keys is twice as the number of letters to be inserted); as regards the duration, it can be either 18, 22, or 26 s.

Summing up, we have 18 different levels of CL for the secondary task, and the web application administrates 3 test repetitions for each level (presented randomly). In total, users have to perform 54 test repetitions. Accordingly to the definition of the α-factor (see Eq. 1) each task has a different α value depending on its cognitive load, its criticality and the time the task has not been chosen by the user.

3.3 Participants

The definition of the experimental study has been submitted to the ethical committee of the University of Pisa, which authorised the administration of the test. To take part in the experimental study, participants were asked to sign an informed consent form and a consent for the processing of personal data.

We performed two test sessions taking care that the environment, the provided equipment, and the test timetable were the same in both sessions. Exclusion criteria for the participants were cognitive functions disorders and drug consumption with an effect on such functions. Participation has been voluntary and without any incentive; participants were free to abandon the test at any time.

In total, 26 participants took part in the experimental study: mother-tongue Italian, of both sexes (60% men, 40% women), aged between 18 and 40 years, and with a normal visual acuity (or corrected by lenses).

3.4 Data Collection

WM Span Tasks. The web application is able to collect users' answers for both WM span tasks for each item, and it is thus able to compute the PCU for the OST task and for the RST task. From such data, we can compute the total PCU score for each participant, calculated as the mean of the scores of both tasks. Total PCU values go from a minimum of 0.35 to a maximum of 0.97.

Shared Attention Test. For the shared attention test, the web application is able to track every user action, and it is thus able to compute the number of errors for the main task and for the secondary task, as well as the time users pass on the main task and on the secondary task.

In order to explore correlations between the users' PCU and their multitasking performance – which would be consistent with the relevant psychological literature – we divide PCU values into 3 intervals and we divide participants into 3 different groups:

1. *lowPCU*: user total PCU ≤ 0.80;
2. *mediumPCU*: $0.80 <$ user total PCU ≥ 0.90;
3. *highPCU*: user total PCU > 0.90;

In Table 1 we show, for all users whose PCU is in a given interval, the average time to find and push the right letter on the keyboard for each level of cognitive load (number of letters to find and keybord size). We notice that the higher the PCU, the faster participants find and push the correct letter. On the other hand, from the collected data the total duration of the secondary task seems to have no influence on the time required by the user to find and push the letter on the keyboard. Hence, we didn't group users on this parameter while computing the average times shown in Table 1.

Table 1. Average time to find and push the correct letter for each PCU group and each combination of number of letters (nL) and number of keys (nK) in the keyboard.

	2L 2K	2L 4K	4L 4K	4L 8K	8L 8K	8L 16K
lowPCU	1.257	1.4	1.528	1.843	1.538	1.931
mediumPCU	1.197	1.262	1.466	1.711	1.421	1.665
highPCU	1.042	1.175	1.2	1.471	1.291	1.572

As regards the time spent on the main task and on the secondary task, from data we can deduce how much each participant perceives as critical the main task with respect to the secondary task. We call *criticality* the percentage of time a user stays on the main task with respect to the secondary task. In order to check if the less a user perceives the main task as critical (i.e. the criticality is lower), the more he/she fails in such task, we divide the criticality values (which vary from 48% to 66%) into 2 groups: the first groups values up to 57%, the second groups values higher than 58%. We then compute the average number of errors for each of these groups, and we find that the more the main task is perceived as critical, the less the users fail in it: 3,36 errors on average for the low criticality group and 1,8 errors on average for high criticality group. Since we observed this correlation, we decided to keep these two groups of users separated in the analysis, by identifying 2 additional subgroups that we call *lowCriticality* and *highCriticality*.

Therefore, we consider, overall, 6 different groups of users, by considering the 3 PCU groups and the 2 criticality subgroups, that are:

1. $lowPCU - lowCriticality$
2. $lowPCU - highCriticality$
3. $mediumPCU - lowCriticality$
4. $mediumPCU - highCriticality$
5. $highPCU - lowCriticality$
6. $highPCU - highCriticality$

4 Simulation Experiments

For each group devised above, and for each level of cognitive load of the secondary task, we implement a different simulation experiment. Parameters of these simulations have been estimated through data fitting.

Main Task. As regards the main critical task (i.e. the one where users are asked to avoid that the black pellet reaches one of the two red rings), we implement it as a sequence of basic tasks, whose duration is set to 1 and difficulty is set to 0.1. We implement the same task for each PCU group, and two variants of the task for each criticality subgroup: for $highCriticality$ we set the criticality of the task to 40, for $lowCriticality$ we set it to 4.

Secondary Task. As explained in Sect. 3.2, in the secondary task, a letter appears inside the white boxes at a specific time: the total duration of the task is divided by the number of letters to insert, and such measure gives us the interval of time between the appearance of a letter and the next one. Therefore, the secondary task could be defined as follows:

$noinfo \mid letter_1 \Rightarrow findL_1 \mid noInfo$ **duration** t **difficulty** d **delay** δ_1

$\vdots$

$noinfo \mid letter_n \Rightarrow findL_n \mid noInfo$ **duration** t **difficulty** d **delay** δ_n

where:

- n is the number of letters to insert, and thus the number of basic tasks composing the secondary task;
- $findL_i$ represent the action of finding and pushing in the keybord the $i - th$ letter appeared;
- t_i is the duration of the action $findL_i$, set as the average duration for a given combination of number of letters and keys, according to the duration presented in Table 1;
- d_i is the difficulty of the action $findL_i$, which we set to 6;
- δ_i denotes the time which has to elapse so that the letter appears, namely the interval of time between the appearance of two letters minus the duration t_i.

Actually, the appearance of a letter in the secondary task is independent of the previous letter, which means that each letter in a sequence appears as soon as the given time interval has passed, whether the previous letter has been correctly inserted or not. Instead, the task presented above, implies that the delay δ_i of each basic task (namely of each letter) starts elapsing as soon as the basic task becomes the first one of the current subtask, which means that by modelling the secondary task in that way, the appearance of a letter would wait for the correct insertion of the previous letter.

We thus decided to model a different task for each letter to be inserted in the secondary task, namely to divide the *unique* task presented above into n different tasks:

$$info_i \mid letter_i \Rightarrow findL_i \mid info_{i+1} \textbf{ duration } t \textbf{ difficulty } d' \textbf{ delay } \delta_i'$$

In this way, each delay of each task represents the time which has to elapse from the beginning of the simulation of the interaction with the secondary task in order that the letter appears.

Each task composing the secondary task shares a memory. In this way it is possible to ensure that all tasks are executed in the right order: each task has to put inside the memory the information to be retrieved by the next task to be executed so that a task cannot be carried out until the previous task has not been accomplished (i.e. letters have to be inserted in the correct order).

Moreover, the difficulties of each task are computed in order to ensure that the cognitive load of each task is equal to the one of the unique task presented above.

Simulation Settings. In total, we implemented 108 different tests for each combination of PCU levels (3), levels of cognitive load (18), and level of criticality (2). For each of these combinations, we performed 1000 simulations and we computed the average value for the time to complete the simulated secondary task and the maximum time the simulated main task is ignored.

It is worth to note that the simulated tests are approximation of the real users performance. For instance, by modelling the secondary task as a single basic task where the user finds and push the right letter in the keyboard, we cannot simulate the case where a user goes backward and forward from the main task to the secondary task, just to check if the next letter appeared. Hence, in the real data we subtracted such time from the time passed on the secondary task, and we added it to the time passed on the main task.

5   Results

We performed 1000 simulations for each of the 6 groups presented above. Namely during a simulation are executed 18 different tests (one for each level of cognitive load of the secondary task), where the main task has a given criticality according to which of the 2 criticality subgroups we are simulating, and the secondary task has precise durations and difficulties according to which of the 3 PCU groups we are simulating. We performed each simulation in order to check if the "simulated users" behave as the real users. In particular, we observed:

1. If the time passed on the main task with respect to the time passed on the secondary task is equal to that observed in the data;
2. If the number of errors in the main task follows the same distribution of the one observed in the data;
3. If the number of errors in the secondary task follows the same distribution of the one observed in the data.

The time passed on the main task respect to the time passed on the secondary task is what we called criticality in Sect. 3.4.

As regard the main task, we know that it fails as soon as the black pellet reaches one of the red rings, and we know that the minimum number of steps for the pellet to reach a red ring (starting from the green one) is 4 steps; the longer such a task is ignored by the user, the higher is the probability to fail it. We thus consider the maximum wait time of the main task – namely the longest time it has been ignored – as a measure of the probability to fail it: the higher is the maximum wait time, the higher is the probability.

On the other hand, for the secondary task we consider the time its last basic task has been executed and we compare such time with the total duration of the task: the higher is the difference between such two values (i.e. the former is greater than the latter), the higher is the probability that the secondary task has failed.

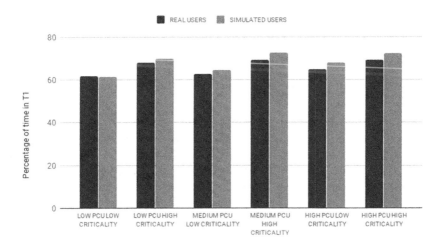

Fig. 3. Time on task T1 for simulated and real users.

Regarding the number of errors observed from data, it is worth to note that it is particularly low and it can be subject to statistical noise. Therefore, we concentrate more on the criticality and as regards the errors (for both the main task and the secondary task) we analyse if the simulated trend is similar to the real trend.

Criticality. As regards the criticality, we compute the percentage of time the simulated test has passed on the main task. We compute the average of such measures for the entire simulation, for each of the six groups.

As shown in Fig. 3, the time the simulated users pass on the main task is very close to the time real users pass on the main task: the level of approximation varies from -0.2% to $+3.3\%$.

Tasks Fails. As regards the errors on the main task, we compute the average of the maximum wait time for the main task of the entire simulation, for each of the six groups, and we compare such measures with the average number of errors for each of the six group.

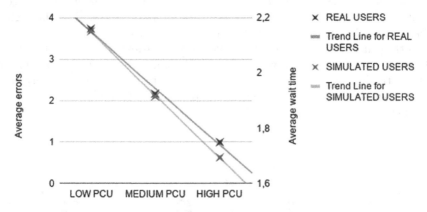

Fig. 4. Average number of errors for the main task (T1) and average wait time when varying PCU.

As shown in Fig. 4 the probability to fail the main task decreases as the level of PCU increases, as well as the number of errors which decreases as the users' PCU increases. The probability to fail the main task decreases as well as the criticality increases, and such trend is observed also in the data. Finally, as shown in Fig. 5, the probability of fail and the average number of errors decrease for each of the six groups as the PCU decreases and the criticality passes from low to high.

Regarding the errors on the secondary task, we subtract the final duration of the secondary simulated task to the total duration of the task and we compute the average of such measures for the entire simulation, for each of the six groups.

Also in this case, we notice a decrease of the probability of errors in the secondary task when the PCU level increases, and a growth in the probability of errors when the criticality increases. We observe the same trend in the data.

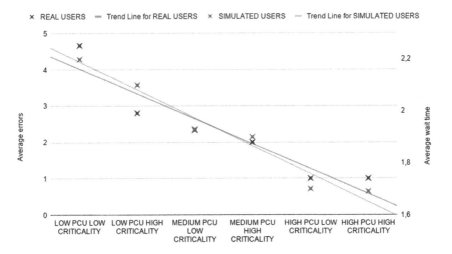

Fig. 5. Average number of errors for the main task (T1) for each group and average wait time for simulated tasks for each group.

Concluding, it is worth to note that the small sample size and the approximation of the simulation are factors to be taken into account when analysing the results obtained. However, such results agree with the data gathered from the experimental study, for both the probability of fails in both tasks and the time passed on the main task. We, thus, consider our algorithm and, in particular, SCHM model capable to produce relevant results, according to the behaviour of real users in a safety-critical human multitasking context.

References

1. Anderson, J.R., Matessa, M., Lebiere, C.: ACT-R: a theory of higher level cognition and its relation to visual attention. Hum. Comput. Interact. **12**(4), 439–462 (1997)
2. Barrouillet, P., Camos, V.: The time-based resource-sharing model of working memory. Cogn. Neurosci. Work. Mem. **455**, 59–80 (2007)
3. Broccia, G., Milazzo, P., Ölveczky, P.C.: An algorithm for simulating human selective attention. In: Cerone, A., Roveri, M. (eds.) SEFM 2017. LNCS, vol. 10729, pp. 48–55. Springer, Cham (2018). https://doi.org/10.1007/978-3-319-74781-1_4
4. Broccia, G., Milazzo, P., Ölveczky, P.C.: An executable formal framework for safety-critical human multitasking. In: Dutle, A., Muñoz, C., Narkawicz, A. (eds.) NFM 2018. LNCS, vol. 10811, pp. 54–69. Springer, Cham (2018). https://doi.org/10.1007/978-3-319-77935-5_4
5. Broccia, G.: A formal framework for modelling and analysing safety-critical human multitasking. Ph.D. Thesis. University of Pisa, Department of Computer Science (2019)
6. Broccia, G., Milazzo, P., Ölveczky, P. C. Formal modeling and analysis of safety-critical human multitasking. Innov. Syst. Softw. Eng., 1–22 (2019)
7. Dangerous distraction: Safety Investigation Report B2004/0324. Australian Transport Safety Bureau (2005). https://www.atsb.gov.au/media/36244/distraction_report.pdf

8. Case, R., Kurland, D.M., Goldberg, J.: Operational efficiency and the growth of short-term memory span. J. Exp. Child Psychol. **33**(3), 386–404 (1982)

9. Cerone, A.: A cognitive framework based on rewriting logic for the analysis of interactive systems. In: De Nicola, R., Kühn, E. (eds.) SEFM 2016. LNCS, vol. 9763, pp. 287–303. Springer, Cham (2016). https://doi.org/10.1007/978-3-319-41591-8_20

10. Clark, T., David, Y.: Impact of clinical alarms on patient safety. American College of Clinical Engineering Healthcare Technology Foundation Web site (2009)

11. Conway, A.R.A., Cowan, N., Bunting, M.F., Therriault, D.J., Minkoff, S.R.B.: A latent variable analysis of working memory capacity, short-term memory capacity, processing speed, and general fluid intelligence. Intelligence **30**(2), 163–183 (2002)

12. Conway, A.R.A., Kane, M.J., Engle, R.W.: Working memory capacity and its relation to general intelligence. Trends Cogn. Sci. **7**(12), 547–552 (2003)

13. Conway, A.R.A., Kane, M.J., Bunting, M.F., Hambrick, D.Z., Wilhelm, O., Engle, R.W.: Working memory span tasks: a methodological review and user's guide. Psychon. Bull. Rev. **12**(5), 769–786 (2005). https://doi.org/10.3758/BF03196772

14. Daneman, M., Carpenter, P.A.: Individual differences in working memory and reading. J. Verbal Learn. Verbal Behav. **19**(4), 450–466 (1980)

15. de Fockert, J.W., Rees, G., Frith, C.D., Lavie, N.: The role of working memory in visual selective attention. Science **291**(5509), 1803–1806 (2001)

16. Dingus, T.A., Guo, F., Lee, S., Antin, J.F., Perez, M., Buchanan-King, M., Hankey, J.: Driver crash risk factors and prevalence evaluation using naturalistic driving data. Proc. Natl. Acad. Sci. **113**(10), 2636–2641 (2016)

17. Engle, R.W., Tuholski, S.W., Laughlin, J.E., Conway, A.R.A.: Working memory, short-term memory, and general fluid intelligence: a latent-variable approach. J. Exp. Psychol. Gen. **128**(3), 309 (1999)

18. Engle, R.W.: Working memory capacity as executive attention. Curr. Dir. Psychol. Sci. **11**(1), 19–23 (2002)

19. Gelman, G., Feigh, K.M., Rushby, J.M.: Example of a complementary use of model checking and human performance simulation. IEEE Trans. Hum. Mach. Syst. **44**(5), 576–590 (2014)

20. Hamilton, J.: Think you're multitasking? Think again. Morning Edition (2008). https://www.npr.org/templates/story/story.php?storyId=95256794&t=1566830957675

21. Houser, A., Ma, L.M., Feigh, K., Bolton, M.L.: A formal approach to modeling and analyzing human taskload in simulated air traffic scenarios. In: Complex Systems Engineering (ICCSE), pp. 1–6. IEEE (2015)

22. Lavie, N., Hirst, A., De Fockert, J.W., Viding, E.: Load theory of selective attention and cognitive control. J. Exp. Psychol. Gen. **133**(3), 339 (2004)

23. Mittelstädt, V., Miller, J.: Separating limits on preparation versus online processing in multitasking paradigms: evidence for resource models. J. Exp. Psychol. Hum. Percept. Perform. **43**(1), 89 (2017)

24. Pashler, H.: Dual-task interference in simple tasks: data and theory. Psychol. Bull. **116**(2), 220 (1994)

25. Redick, T.S., et al.: Cognitive predictors of a common multitasking ability: contributions from working memory, attention control, and fluid intelligence. J. Exp. Psychol. Gen. **145**(11), 1473 (2016)

26. Shorrock, S.T.: Errors of memory in air traffic control. Saf. Sci. **43**(8), 571–588 (2005)

27. Turner, M.L., Engle, R.W.: Is working memory capacity task dependent? J. Mem. Lang. **28**(2), 127–154 (1989)

28. Wickens, C.D.: Processing resources and attention. Mult. Task Perform., 3–34 (1991)
29. Wickens, C.D., Gutzwiller, R.S., Santamaria, A.: Discrete task switching in overload: a meta-analyses and a model. Int. J. Hum. Comput. Stud. **79**, 79–84 (2015)
30. Wickens, C.D., Sebok, A., Li, H., Sarter, N., Gacy, A.M.: Using modeling and simulation to predict operator performance and automation-induced complacency with robotic automation: a case study and empirical validation. Hum. Factors **57**(6), 959–975 (2015)

An Ontology-Based Approach to Support Formal Verification of Concurrent Systems

Natalia Garanina[1,2,3]([✉]), Igor Anureev[1,2], Elena Sidorova[1,3], Dmitry Koznov[4],
Vladimir Zyubin[2,3], and Sergei Gorlatch[5]

[1] A.P. Ershov Institute of Informatics Systems, Novosibirsk, Russia
{garanina,anureev,lena}@iis.nsk.su
[2] Institute of Automation and Electrometry, Novosibirsk, Russia
[3] Novosibirsk State University, Novosibirsk, Russia
zyubin@iae.nsk.su
[4] St. Petersburg University, Saint Petersburg, Russia
d.koznov@spbu.ru
[5] University of Muenster, Münster, Germany
gorlatch@uni-muenster.de

Abstract. Formal verification ensures the absence of design errors in a system with respect to system's requirements. This is especially important for the control software of critical systems, ranging from automatic components of avionics and spacecrafts to modules of distributed banking transactions. In this paper, we present a verification support framework that enables automatic extraction of a concurrent system's requirements from the technical documentation and formal verification of the system design using an external or built-in verification tool that checks whether the system meets the extracted requirements. Our support approach also provides visualization and editing options for both the system model and requirements. The key data components of our framework are ontological descriptions of the verified system and its requirements. We describe the methods used in our support framework and we illustrate their work for the use case of an automatic control system.

Keywords: Ontology · Information extraction · Formal verification · Requirement engineering · Formal semantics

1 Introduction

Our long-term goal is a comprehensive approach to support practical formal verification of safety-critical concurrent systems. Such approach should include understandable representations of both concurrent systems and their requirements (graphical and in a limited natural language), as well as tools for editing these representations and navigating over them. Also a support for information extraction is necessary because of large volumes of technical documentation,

© Springer Nature Switzerland AG 2020
E. Sekerinski et al. (Eds.): FM 2019 Workshops, LNCS 12232, pp. 114–130, 2020.
https://doi.org/10.1007/978-3-030-54994-7_9

especially for legacy software systems. The use of practical formal verification methods should greatly improve quality assurance for safety-critical systems.

Various tools for specification and verification support have been suggested for different kinds of safety-critical systems. A commercial requirement engineering tool for embedded systems Argosim [25] allows software engineers to test the systems and perform inconsistency checking for requirements, but formal verification and information extraction are not supported. Software Cost Reduction toolset [32], Model Based Systems Engineering [27], RoboTool [14] are used for development, simulation and formal verification in avionics, space-crafts, robots and other control systems, but they do not use information extraction. SEVA [13] extracts information from natural language queries and can reason about system requirements, but no formal verification is offered. An approach to both information extraction and formal verification is suggested in [20], but it is restricted to a very special application field.

Our approach to supporting formal verification is based on patterns, because many requirements on real-world systems have recurring formulations with similar properties. Systems for supporting the development and verification of requirements based on patterns are an active topic of research [1,15,17,19,21,22]. Patterns are parameterized expressions in natural language that describe typical requirements for the behaviour of a system. Usually, parameters of patterns are system events or their combinations. For example, in pattern "The event *Restart* will occur", *Restart* is a parameter. The key property of patterns is that they have precisely-defined formal semantics. Patterns make it easier for developers to specify and verify typical system requirements. The drawback of the current support systems is that they offer only manual formulation of requirements and description of its formal semantics, sometimes with visualization. The first approach to employ an ontology as a knowledge organization method for patterns [22] does not yet use all benefits of the ontological knowledge representation.

Our envisaged advantage over the state-of-the-art approaches is that our framework supports a user-friendly, integrated strategy for the quality assurance of concurrent systems using a flexible tool that supports model extraction, correction, and verification, together with textual explanation and visualization of requirements. In particular, our support framework offers the following functionality: 1) constructing the model of a concurrent system and the system requirements by extracting information about them from technical documentation and/or using development tools and/or using information from experts via questionnaires, 2) generating typical requirements from the internal description of this extracted/constructed model, 3) representing the extracted/constructed requirements in a mathematical, linguistic and graphical manner, and editing these representations, 5) checking the integrity and consistency of the model's and requirements' representations, 6) translating the model representation into the input language of a suitable verifier. A special feature in our framework is automatic generation of requirements both from technical documentation and from the internal description of the concurrent system model, which considerably simplifies the work of requirement engineers. However, due to the linguistic ambiguities in technical documentation, a correction of extracted requirements and models is usually required; it is accomplished using the editors of our system.

In comparison to the state-of-the-art support systems, we suggest flexible customization of system components in four aspects. This flexibility is based on the intensive use of ontologies for representing knowledge about concurrent systems and their requirements, and especially on the formal semantics of these ontologies. First, due to the formal semantics, we can apply various methods of model/requirements extraction and construction taking into account various methods of formal verification. Second, it is possible to address various kinds of concurrent systems: from telecommunication protocols to cyber-physical systems, by defining the corresponding formal semantics for system models: finite/abstract state machines, hybrid systems, probabilistic automata [2,11], etc. Third, to specialize system descriptions for a particular subject domain we can use ontology axioms and rules. Forth, the requirements semantics also can be customised by choosing appropriate logics: LTL, CTL, PLTL [2], etc. The ontological representations allows us to check the integrity and consistency of a model and requirements' descriptions; it also naturally supports the term consistency between them.

The current configuration of our support framework uses an ontology-driven, rule-based approach to information extraction [5], labelled transition systems as formal semantics for concurrent models [9], and logics LTL, CTL and their real-time extensions as formal semantics for requirements [7].

The following Sect. 2 outlines our framework for supporting practical formal verification as a whole. Section 3 describes our ontology-driven methods used for information extraction, and illustrates them with a use case of a bottle-filling system. Section 4 defines the Requirement and Process Ontologies used for the internal representation of systems and their requirements. Sections 5–7 describe the methods used for processing requirements. Section 8 discusses our current framework's limitations that we plan to address in future work.

2   The Framework for Supporting Formal Verification

Figure 1 shows an overview of our framework for supporting formal verification of concurrent systems that automatically extracts and generates system requirements. The key components of the framework are the Process Ontology [9] and the Requirement Ontology based on patterns [7]. We use ontologies for an internal representation of concurrent systems and their requirements, because ontologies are convenient for systematizing knowledge, and they facilitate formulating and checking non-trivial consistency properties. Moreover, there are several well-developed tools for creating, editing and checking ontologies [26, 29]. In our case, the contents of ontologies are descriptions of a particular concurrent system model and the requirements it must meet. These data must be acquired by Data Acquisition modules and then verified by Data Verification modules. After expert analysis of verification result, we can make corrections to particular development artefacts, such as high-level requirements and specifications, design specifications, software code, etc.

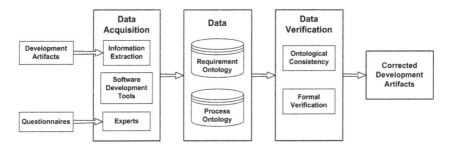

Fig. 1. The framework for supporting formal verification

Data Acquisition. System and requirement descriptions can be extracted from technical documentation containing development artifacts or constructed using concurrent software development tools (e.g. IBM Rhapsody [30]). These descriptions can be refined by domain experts via answering questions from ontology-based questionnaires. For populating the ontologies, we use our Information Extraction System [4–6] described in Sect. 3. The extracted requirements can be extended with typical requirements, automatically generated from the ontological description of the system (see Sect. 5). The descriptions of the system model and the requirements are the basis for formal verification.

Data Verification. The extracted description of the system model and its requirements may be incomplete or incorrectly constructed due to insufficiency of information presented in technical documentation or incorrect software development process. The Ontological Consistency procedure verifies the integrity and consistency of the constructed instances of the Process and Requirement Ontologies. In addition, as a rule, a large number of requirements are formulated for concurrent systems. Therefore, for the Requirement Ontology, it is also reasonable to check the semantic consistency of a requirement set using standard ontological methods. The output of these checking procedures are sets of incorrectly constructed entities of the considered concurrent system, as well as incorrectly formulated or inconsistent requirements. This procedure, described in Sect. 6, executes a simple pre-checking, before time-consuming formal verification. To formally verify a system, we choose a suitable verifier taking into account the formal semantics of the ontology-based requirement representation. If such a verifier is available, we translate the ontological description of the system into the model specification input language of the verifier, and the requirements' description is translated into the input language of the verifier (usually, this language is some temporal logic). If no suitable verifier is available, then our framework exploits the special verification algorithms for specific patterns.

Requirement Processing. Let us sketch the ontology processing activities necessary for the framework operation described in Sect. 7. Dealing with requirements involves representing them in three ways. The mathematical representation as formulas of some logic enables formal verification. The current formal representation is LTL and CTL with real-time extensions. The language and graphical representations both help a requirement engineer to understand formal representations. Due to the ambiguity of the natural language, it is possible that the extracted and generated requirements may not meet the engineer's expectations, and manual corrections are required. These corrections can use the editors for ontology representations, as well as the editors for formal, language and graphical representations.

In this paper, we do not consider methods for the formal verification module and ontology-based questionnaires. In the following sections, we describe in more detail the main ontologies and other parts of our framework.

3   The Information Extraction System

Figure 2 shows the general scheme of our information extraction system that takes technical documentation as input and searches for concepts and relations to populate the Process and Requirement Ontologies as described below. We use a rule-based, multi-agent approach to implement this system [5].

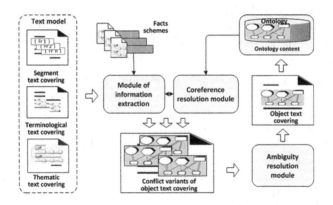

Fig. 2. The information extraction and ontology population system

The process of information extraction includes the preliminary (lexical) step and the main (ontological) step. At the lexical step, the system constructs a text model that includes the terminological, thematic, and segment coverings of the input text. The terminological covering is the result of lexical text analysis that extracts the terms of a subject domain from the text and forms lexical objects using semantic vocabularies. The segment text covering is a division of the input text into formal fragments (clauses, sentences, paragraphs, headlines, etc.) and genre fragments (document title, annotation, glossary, etc.). The thematic covering selects text fragments of a particular topic. The construction of a thematic covering is based on the thematic classification methods. At the lexical step, the system constructs objects that represent instances of concepts and relations of the domain ontology from the lexical objects. Our system uses the ontology population rules which are automatically generated from lexico-syntactic patterns formulated by experts taking into account the ontology and language of a subject domain. Each lexico-syntactic pattern describes a typical situation for the subject area in terms of specific subject types of objects in the situation. These lexico-syntactic patterns constrain morphological, syntactic, genre, lexical, and semantic characteristics of the objects. The outputs of modules of disambiguation [4] and co-reference resolution [6] are used to choose the best version of text analysis for populating the ontology with a consistent set of instances of subject domain concepts and relations found in the input text.

To implement the described extraction technology for analyzing concurrent systems and their requirements, we create a knowledge base that includes: 1) a genre model of the input text for constructing segments, 2) a semantic dictionary, and 3) lexico-syntactic patterns for the subject domain. We illustrate this approach below, using the subject domain of automatic control systems (ACS).

We consider Technical Documentation (TD) as a set of documents used for the design, creation and use of any technical objects. TDs have strong genre features: they do not contain figurative expressions, evaluative adjectives, almost no adverbs, the natural language ambiguity is compensated by the use of previously defined terms, etc. For this genre, we mark out sub-genre *Purpose* (the description of the system and its elements with respect to goals and functions) and sub-genre *Scenario* (the description of sequences of actions of automatic processes and the corresponding input and output states of the system). The detection of these genre fragments is based on a set of lexical markers which indicate that these sub-genres are located in the headings of the text.

The main component of the knowledge base of our information extraction system is a semantic dictionary. The system of lexico-semantic characteristics in the dictionary provides the connection of subject vocabulary with the ontology elements. For the ACS subject domain, we define the following lexical-semantic classes of lexical units in the dictionary:

- the vocabulary for the names of entities (objects, substances, technical devices and their parts, software products and their components);
- the vocabulary for naming situations:
  - state predicates (absence, be, contain),
  - event predicates for representing automatic processes and actions (move, rotate, feed, warm up, turn on, stop),
  - functional predicates (used for, provide),
  - mental predicates (control, measure, monitor, determine);
- the parametric vocabulary:
  - the names of qualitative/quantitative parameters (e.g., level, position),
  - the numbers and units of measurement, lexical names of reference scores (e.g., low/high, given position),
  - the predicates of quantitative change (e.g., fall, grow, normalize, etc.);
- the reference designation:
  - as proper names (e.g., Large Solar Vacuum Telescope – LSVT),
  - as unique numeric identifiers for designating referents of objects (e.g., temperature is measured by sensor (12)).

For constructing the lexico-syntactic patterns for descriptions of technological processes, we define the following types of situations: 1) actions leading the system or its components into enabled/disabled state; 2) activity characteristics for the functionality of the system or its components; 3) states of the values of quantitative or qualitative parameters; 4) processes for changing the parameters of system elements; and 5) information transfer processes. Most of situations and lexical names described in the TD texts are universal. Therefore, the generated lexico-syntactic patterns can be used for a large class of technical objects. Our developed methods are focused on the analysis of a linear text, however, after small changes, they can be applied to tables or TD schemas with language labels.

Illustrative Example. Let us illustrate our ontology-based approach to support formal verification with a system documentation text taken from [18]. This technical documentation describes the work of a bottle-filling system and includes several requirements on the system. We use two lexico-syntactic patterns shown in Fig. 3 to extract an ontology object corresponding to a sensor from the following text: "Two sensors^{arg1} are also attached to the tank to read^{arg2} the fluid level^{arg3} information." With terms and ontology objects **arg1**, **arg2**, and **arg3**, satisfying the syntactical **Condition**, the Sensor-Construct1-pattern creates an object of class *Process* with predefined attribute values following the ACS-ontology structure, as explained in the next section. The SensorFeatures pattern evaluates the attribute values of this sensor object using only the ACS-ontology structure without the input text.

```
Scheme SensorConstruct1:                        Scheme SensorFeatures
    genre_segment System_description segment Clause     arg1: Object:: PROCESS(type: Sensor)
    arg1: Term::Sensor()                                arg2: Object::Controller()
    arg2: Term::Measuring()                       → create x = Channel::(from: arg1, to: arg2)
    arg3: Object::Parameter()                        create y = ComAction::(from: arg1, to: x,
    Condition CGov(arg2, arg1, arg3),                             message: arg1.shared, when: true)
        preposition(arg1, arg2), preposition (arg2, arg3)   edit arg1(channels: add(x), comacts: add(y))
→ create PROCESS::(type: arg1::sem, shared: arg3)
```

Fig. 3. Example: the lexico-syntactic patterns for extracting objects for "sensors"

4   The Ontologies

We consider an ontology as a structure that includes the following elements: (1) a finite, non-empty set of classes, (2) a finite, non-empty set of data attributes and relation attributes, and (3) a finite, non-empty set of domains of data attributes. Each class is defined by a set of attributes. Data attributes take values from domains, and relation attributes' values are instances of classes. An information content of an ontology is a set of instances of its classes formed by taking particular values of their attributes. In our case, the input data for populating the Process and Requirement Ontologies is technical documentation.

We represent the classes of our ontologies, their properties and axioms using the system Protégé [29] with the OWL language [28] and the SWRL language

[31]. These properties and axioms define the rules for checking the correctness of attribute values. Using the SWRL rules, we define the conditions used in Protégé for checking the correctness and consistency of ontological descriptions by the Hermit inference engine [26].

The Process Ontology. The Process Ontology [9] is used for an ontological description of a concurrent system by a set of its instances. We consider a concurrent system as a set of communicating processes that are described by the class *Process* and are characterized by: 1) their type for a subject-domain description (e.g. sensor, controller); 2) sets of local and shared variables; 3) a list of actions on these variables which change their values; 4) a list of channels for the process communication; and 5) a list of communication actions for sending messages. The process variables (class *Variable*) and constants (class *Constant*) take values in domains from a set consisting of basic types (Booleans, finite subsets of integers or strings for enumeration types) and finite derived types. Initial conditions of the variable values can be defined by comparison with constants. The actions of the processes (class *Action*) include operations over variables' values. The enabling condition for each action is a guard condition (class *Condition*) for the variable values and the contents of the sent messages. The processes can send messages via channels (class *Channel*) under the guard conditions. The communication channels are characterized by the type of reading messages, capacity, and modes of writing and reading. Currently, we define the Process Ontology formal semantics as a labelled transition system [9].

The classes of the Process Ontology are universal: they do not take into account the features of a subject domain. In order to describe specific-domain process ontology, we use ontology axioms and SWRL-rules. In the next subsection, we give an example of an SWRL-rule which restricts the Process Ontology for typical elements of automatic control systems (ACS), such as simple and complex sensors, controllers, actuators and the controlled object.

The ACS Process Ontology. The SWRL-rules impose the following restrictions on sensors. Sensors must read the observed values from the variables shared with the controlled object and they cannot change it. They have outgoing channels connecting them with controllers and communication actions for sending messages to the controllers. There is at least one controller and a shared variable associated with each sensor. Simple sensors have no local variables and actions: they can observe exactly one variable shared with the controlled object and send the observed value unchanged to controllers. Complex sensors can process observable and local variables to produce output for controllers.

Controllers, actuators and controlled objects are also restricted by the corresponding SWRL-rules. Controllers and actuators must not have shared variables. Controllers must have output channels connecting them with other controllers and actuators, and input channels connecting them with sensors and actuators. Actuators must have output channels connecting them with controllers and the controlled object, and input channels connecting them with controllers. There must be at least one sensor and at least one actuator connected with a controller via input and output channels, respectively. There must be at least one controller and controlled object connected with an actuator through input and output channels, respectively. A controlled object must be connected with actuators by input channels. There must be at least one shared variable, one sensor and one actuator associated with a controlled object.

The following SWRL rule establishes the existence of a connection between a sensor and a single controller in an automatic control system:

```
Process(?p)^Process(?q)^type(?p,Sensor)^type(?q,Controller) ->
Channel(?c)^channels(?p, ?c)^channels(?q, ?c)
```

In [8], we describe ontology axioms and SWRL-rules for ACS in detail.

The lexico-syntactic patterns that extract information have to follow the restrictions mentioned above. In particular, for the bottle-filling system from [18] the patterns in Fig. 3 generate the sensor-process with name *id1* shown in Fig. 4 that has to send the observable value of the fluid level to the controller-process named *Cont* via channel *Cont_id1*. The attribute values in bold capital letters correspond to particular words in the input text, and other attribute values are generated automatically using the subject domain restrictions without direct text correspondence. For our text, a single controller-process is created at the beginning of model extraction automatically. Other lexico-syntactic patterns produce the actuator-process *id2* for the bottom valve that must be closed when the fluid level is low. This closing action is controlled by the controller-process that sends to *id2* the *Off*-message when the sensor *id1* reports the low fluid level. Sending communication actions are in ComActs-attributes and receiving communication actions are in Actions-attributes.

Name	id1
Type	SENSOR
Local	-
Shared	fluid level
Actions	-
Channels	Cont_id1
ComActs	when true : Con_id1 ! fluid level

Name	Cont
Type	controller
Local	Sens_1; Do_1: {On, Off}, ...
Shared	-
Actions	when true: Cont_id1 ? Sens_1; ...
Channels	Cont_id1, Cont_id2, ...
ComActs	when Sens_1 < EMPTY : Cont_id2 ! Off; ...

Name	id2
Type	ACTUATOR
Local	On, Off:Bool; Cont...
Shared	-
Actions	when true: Cont_id2 ? Cont; when Cont=Off : Off=true; ...
Channels	Cont_id2, Obj_id2, ...
ComActs	when Off : Obj_id2 ! Stop; ...

Fig. 4. Example: the processes of the bottle-filling system

The Requirement Ontology. Let us define how requirements are described by specification patterns. Requirements are expressed using standard Boolean connections of five basic patterns defining the appearance of certain events which can be considered as a particular combination of parameter values of the model. These patterns are: *Universality* (the event always takes place), *Existence* (the event will occur sometime), *Absence* (the event will never occur), *Precedence* (one event surely precedes another), and *Response* (one event always causes another). The patterns and their events can be constrained by eventual, time, and quantitative restrictions. Requirements expressed by these patterns have formal semantics as formulas of temporal logics LTL, CTL and their real-time variants [2] with temporal operators over events specified as Boolean combinations of propositions. These semantics unambiguously express requirements, and they precisely define the corresponding verification method.

Using ontologies for organizing a set of system requirements makes it possible to accurately systematize knowledge about them due to a hierarchical structure of concepts and relations. With our approach to the system requirements' presentation, the user can rely on a small set of class attributes to describe a wide range of properties of concurrent systems. This variability in expressing requirements is important, because for the same system it is necessary to specify both simple, easily verifiable properties (e.g. reachability), and complex properties that depend on the execution time of the system components. The possibility to formulate such different properties within a single formalism increases the quality of support for the development of complex systems as it covers the entire picture of the system requirements. Moreover, the ontological representation of a set of requirements enables its consistency checking. The output of our system of information extraction is a content of a certain ontology of a subject domain.

Our Requirement Ontology [7] organizes the existing systems of specification patterns [3,12] into unified structure and contains 12 classes and 17 relations between them. This ontology is designed to specify the requirements of system models described by the Process Ontology. Events of such systems occur in discrete time and the processes are completely dependent on the observed system states (including the current time), but may be non-deterministic.

In Fig. 5, the instance *id1* of the Requirement Ontology is produced by our IE-system from the following text fragment: ``Both the bottle-filling and the heating operations are prohibited when the fluid is pumped to the filler tank'' [18]. The formal semantic of this requirement are given by the LTL formula $\mathbf{G}(id3.Local.On \rightarrow id2.Local.Off \wedge id4.Local.Off)$, where *id3* and *id4* are identifiers for the inlet valve and the heating steam valve, respectively. The other requirement *gen_id1* is automatically generated by the Requirement Extraction Module described in the next section.

Name	id1
Kind	universality
Time type	linear
Sub1	id3.Local.On → id2.Local.Off & id4.Local.Off
...	...

Name	gen_id1
Kind	existence
Time type	branch
Sub1	id2.Local.Off
...	...

Fig. 5. Example: the requirements for the bottle-filling system

5   The Requirement Extraction

The task of the requirement extraction is to prompt the requirement engineer to formulate requirements expressed by patterns, because important requirements expressing the correct behavior of the system are not always explicitly defined in the technical documentation using the actions and variables of the system processes. The generated requirements use variables and events of the extracted (constructed) system; the process ontology is the input of the extraction procedure. This procedure explores the ontological description of the processes to find in the attribute values the events of interest whose satisfiability and appearance order can affect correctness. Such events are: changing the values of shared variables, sending/receiving messages, etc. The requirements may be subject-independent or subject-dependent. In any concurrent system, the following communication properties can be formulated:

- every sent message will be read (or overwritten) (*Response*);
- every message that has been read was sent before (*Precedence*);
- every guard condition for actions and communication actions must be satisfied in some system execution (*Existence* with Branching time).

For example, in Fig. 5, the right requirement for the bottle filling system *gen_id1* says that there is at least one point in at least one system execution when the bottom valve is open. Its formal semantic is CTL formula **EF***id2.Local.Off*.

The subject-specific requirements deal with the specifics entities of the subject domain, hence the extraction method must be customized to the subject area. For example, the typical requirements for ACS are as follows:

- the controller will send a control signal to the actuator (*Existence*);
- the actuator will send a modifying signal to the controlled object (*Existence*);
- the values captured by the sensor do not exceed its range (*Universality*).

Based on the found events, the requirements are formed as specially marked instances to populate the Requirement ontology. After population, the requirement engineer can change these instance requirements by adding eventual, time and quantitative restrictions, using the editors, or remove these requirements.

6   The Ontological Consistency

The extracted descriptions of concurrent processes and requirements may be incomplete due to insufficient information in the technical documentation. The integrity and consistency checking procedures inspect the correctness of the constructed ontology instances, i.e., the integrity of the Process and Requirement Ontologies, taking into account the default attribute values. Both ontologies are described in the OWL language of the Protégé system, with the ontology constraints formulated by axioms and SWRL-rules, hence, it is possible to use standard tools for inference ontology processing, e.g., Hermit.

For the Process Ontology, we can check the general integrity properties: definiteness of variables in processes, manipulation of only visible variables and channels, mandatory execution of any actions, the interaction with the environment through channels or shared variables, etc. For ontologies of subject domain systems, specific constraints described by axioms and SWRL-rules must also be checked. Some constraints for the ACS ontology are described in Sect. 4.

The integrity of the Requirement Ontology mainly concerns the definiteness of all attribute values for class instances. For example, an instance of class *Order* must contain two events as the values of the attributes of the ordered events. Besides the descriptive integrity, it is also necessary to check semantic integrity, since a large number of requirements are usually formulated for concurrent systems, both from technical documentation and by the Extract Requirement procedure. Formal verification of these requirements is a rather time-consuming process. The Ontological Consistency procedure executes pre-checking the simple consistency of these requirements. Since an ontology is just a declarative description of a subject domain, it is only possible to check the compatibility of requirements whose semantics do not have nested temporal operators. For more complex requirements, including, e.g., time restrictions, it is reasonable to leave consistency checking for standard formal verification tools. The following SWRL-rule restricts the inconsistent pair of requirements:

Proposition p holds always (*Universality*) vs.
                    Proposition p will be false sometime (*Existence*):
Occurence(?f) ˆ kindPat(?f,Univ) ˆ Prop(?p) ˆ PatS1(?f,?p)ˆ
Occurence(?g) ˆ kindPat(?f,Exis) ˆ Prop(?q) ˆ PatS1(?f,?q)ˆ
ProOp(?q,Neg) ˆ ProSub1(?q,p)   -> Answ(?a)ˆ res(?a,Error1)

In [10], we describe the approach to checking requirement in detail. The Ontological Consistency procedure reports to the requirement engineer about the instances that do not satisfy the ontology constraints.

7   The Representation Modules and Editors

This section describes three ways of requirement representation in our system.

The Formal Semantic Representation. For using formal verification methods, requirements for concurrent systems must be presented as logic formulas. Since currently we focus on model checking, the formal semantics for instances of the Requirement ontology are expressed by formulas of temporal logics. The FSR-procedure translates the requirement instances into LTL or CTL formulas.
    The translation takes several steps for determination:

1) determine whether time is branching or linear;
2) determine the requirement pattern;
3) determine the temporal/quantitative restrictions of the requirement/events;
4) compute the formula using the results of the previous steps, such that the resulting formula corresponds to the requirement without eventual constraints;
5) determine the eventual constraints;
6) compute the formula using the results of the previous steps, such that the resulting formula corresponds to the requirement with eventual constraints.

The translation grammar is highly context-sensitive. Hence, for calculating formulas, the procedure uses mainly the tables of formulas' dependence

T_p	T_q	D_w	P_w	Q_w	D_p	P_p	Q_p	D_q	P_q	Q_q	Meaning
0	0	0	0	0	0	0	0	0	0	0	|--.-----,.--.--.---,.--------.----,.----,.--------> p induces q $G(p\text{->}\mathbf{F}q)$
0	0	0	0	0	0	0	0	0	0	z	|--.---,-,-.---.--.---.--,--,-,.--,----,---,--------> p induces zQ repetitions of q $G(p\text{->}\mathbf{F}^{zQ}q)$
0	0	0	0	0	0	0	0	0	z	0	|--.---,.----,.----,.----,.---,-,-,-,-,-,-,-,-,-,-,-> p induces appearance q with period zP $G(p \text{->} \mathbf{F}(q \wedge \mathbf{G}(q \text{->} \neg q\ \mathbf{U}_{zP}q)))$

Fig. 6. A fragment of the translation table for *Response* requirements

on the restrictions and several analytic rules. The fragment of the table for *Order* requirements on Fig. 6 illustrates three variants of formal semantics of the *Response* requirement. The first columns of the table characterize the presence of duration D, periodic P, and quantitative Q restrictions on the requirement pattern itself (subscript $_w$), p-event (subscript $_p$), and q-event (subscript $_q$). The time delay of the first occurrence of p or q events using T_p or T_q, respectively, can be taken into account. The last column contains a graphical, language, and formal presentation of the *Responce* requirement for the following combination of restrictions: 1) an absence of restrictions (zero in each column), 2) the restriction on the number of repetitions of proposition q (number z in column Q_q), and 3) the restriction on the periodicity of proposition q (number z in column P_q).

The Language Representation. The requirements represented as instances of the Requirement Ontology or logic formulas are usually difficult to understand. The LR-procedure provides a natural language description of requirements. It translates instances of the Requirement Ontology into statements in natural language using a limited set of terms (e.g., "always", "never", "repetitions", etc.). The translation grammar for this procedure is low context-sensitive. Hence, for formulating language expressions, the procedure uses mainly analytic rules. The language statements for the *Response* requirement are shown in Fig. 6.

The Graphical Representation. Due to the ambiguity of natural language, the language representations of requirements may be poly-semantic, and, at the same time, their unambiguous formal semantics may be hard to read. For smoothing the ambiguity of the first representation and the low readability of the second, the GR-procedure translates a requirement instance into a graphical representation which is a representative segment of a linear path (for linear time) or a fragment of a computation tree (for branching time) with the depicted events of the requirement. For this visualization, the procedure uses the tables of formulas with the restrictions and analytic rules equally. We develop a method for translating the requirements with linear time into a graphical representation in ASCII format. Examples of the translation are shown in the table in Fig. 6.

Due to the incomplete formalization of technical documentation, the correct extraction of a concurrent system and its requirements cannot be fully automatic. The requirement engineers must be provided with the editors for the data components of the verification process. For the Process and Requirement Ontologies written in the OWL-language, there exist editors, in particular, Protégé. However, for getting more visibility for the Process Ontology, we plan to develop an editor based on the semantic markup ontology [8]. It will present the processes in a tabular form as instances of classes with the corresponding constraints of the domain, and it will visualize the scheme of data flows between processes.

The instances of the Requirement Ontology can be modified by the editor that combines four editing methods depending on the representation type:

- Ontology: changing the values of class attributes within axiomatic constraints.
- Formulas: changing the syntax elements of a formula within the given patterns.
- Language: the limited natural language is used.
- Graphic: the set of patterns for events ordering on a line or in a tree is provided.

All representations should be visible in the same window (the formula and the text are usually not long). Changes in one of the representations affect the others.

8   Conclusion

In this paper, we propose an ontology-based support framework for verification of safety-critical concurrent systems. Our approach has the following advantages. First, a flexible customizing extraction/construction for systems and requirements with respect to various methods of formal verification is provided by formal semantics of ontological representation of concurrent systems and requirements. Second, a variability of verification methods becomes possible due to the customization of formal semantics defined both for the ontological representation of systems and ontological representation of requirements. Third, these formal semantics give the base for checking the integrity and consistency of systems and requirements. Simple requirement consistency checking makes applying formal verification methods easier. Fourth, comprehensible formulation of requirements in our framework is provided by using several requirement representations: the ontological representation, the formal representation as logic formulas, the representation in a limited natural language, and the graphic representation. The customizable tools for viewing, editing, and navigating over these representations help the requirement engineers to deal with requirements. Currently, we use a rule-based, ontology-driven information extraction approach [5], labelled transition systems as formal semantics for concurrent models [9], and logics LTL, CTL and their real-time extensions as formal semantics for requirements [7].

There are two main directions for future work: improving and implementing the internal components of our support framework, and customizing the variable external components.

Internal Components. Extending the Process and Requirement Ontologies with new classes will allow us to capture a wider set of formal semantics, including semantics with real numbers and probabilities. For the Requirement Ontology, we plan to introduce the dependability relation and automatic methods for detecting it. We will extend the set of requirement patterns that can be generated from the Process Ontology with possible general correctness requirements. We will study the possibilities to enrich the set of requirement patterns that can be checked for consistency with ontology means. We also will develop a semantic markup of classes of the Process Ontology for customizing it to a specific subject domain. The Requirement Extraction, Integrity and Consistence, and Representation procedures will also be implemented.

External Components. We will develop new semantics for the Process Ontology, in particular, hyperprocesses [23], abstract state machines [11], and Markov decision processes [16]. We work on designing new methods of translation to the Process Ontology from various formalisms of concurrent system descriptions (e.g., Reflex [24]), to improve our approach. We will customize our information extraction methods for important concurrent systems' subject domains, in particular, for automatic control systems. These methods will also be adopted for tables and diagrams in technical documentation.

Acknowledgment. This research has been supported by Russian Foundation for Basic Research (grant 17-07-01600), Funding State budget of the Russian Federation (IAE project No. AAAA-A17-11706061006-6), and by the BMBF project HPC2SE at WWU Muenster (Germany).

References

1. Autili, M., Grunske, L., Lumpe, M., Pelliccione, P., Tang, A.: Aligning qualitative, real-time, and probabilistic property specification patterns using a structured English grammar. IEEE Trans. Softw. Eng. **41**(7), 620–638 (2015)
2. Clarke, E.M., Henzinger, Th.A., Veith, H., Bloem, R. (eds.): Handbook of Model Checking. Springer, Heidelberg (2018). https://doi.org/10.1007/978-3-319-10575-8
3. Dwyer, M., Avrunin, G., Corbett, J.: Patterns in property specifications for finite-state verification. In: Proceedings of the 21st International Conference on Software Engineering (ICSE-99), pp. 411–420. ACM, New York (1999)
4. Garanina, N., Sidorova, E.: Context-dependent lexical and syntactic disambiguation in ontology population. In: Proceedings of the 25th International Workshop on Concurrency, Specification and Programming (CS&P-16), pp. 101–112. Humboldt-Universitat zu Berlin, Berlin (2016)
5. Garanina, N., Sidorova, E., Bodin, E.: A multi-agent text analysis based on ontology of subject domain. In: Voronkov, A., Virbitskaite, I. (eds.) PSI 2014. LNCS, vol. 8974, pp. 102–110. Springer, Heidelberg (2015). https://doi.org/10.1007/978-3-662-46823-4_9
6. Garanina, N., Sidorova, E., Kononenko, I., Gorlatch, S.: Using multiple semantic measures for coreference resolution in ontology population. Int. J. Comput. **16**(3), 166–176 (2017)
7. Garanina, N., Zubin, V., Lyakh, T., Gorlatch, S.: An ontology of specification patterns for verification of concurrent systems. In: Proceedings of the 17th International Conference on Intelligent Software Methodology Tools, and Techniques (SoMeT_18), pp. 515–528. IOS Press, Amsterdam (2018)

8. Garanina, N., Anureev, I., Zyubin, V.: Constructing verification-oriented domain-specific process ontologies. Syst. Inform. **14**, 19–30 (2019)

9. Garanina, N., Anureev, I., Borovikova, O.: Verification oriented process ontology. Autom. Control. Comput. Sci. **53**(7), 584–594 (2019). https://doi.org/10.3103/S0146411619070058

10. Garanina, N., Borovikova, O.: Ontological approach to checking event consistency for a set of temporal requirements. In: Proceedings of 5th International Conference on Engineering, Computer and Information Sciences, Novosibirsk, Russia. IEEE (2019)

11. Gurevich, Y.: Evolving algebras 1993: Lipari guide. In: Böorger, E. (ed.) Specification and Validation Methods. Oxford University Press, Oxford (1995)

12. Konrad, S., Cheng, B.: Real-time specification patterns. In: Proceedings of 27th International Conference on Software Engineering, pp. 372–381. ACM, New York (2005)

13. Krishnan J., Coronado P., Reed T.: SEVA: a systems engineer's virtual assistant. In: Proceedings of the AAAI 2019 Spring Symposium on Combining Machine Learning with Knowledge Engineering (AAAI-MAKE-19), Palo Alto, California, USA. CEUR-WS (2019). http://ceur-ws.org/Vol-2350/paper3.pdf

14. Miyazawa, A., Ribeiro, P., Li, W., Cavalcanti, A., Timmis, J., Woodcock, J.: RoboChart: modelling and verification of the functional behaviour of robotic applications. Softw. Syst. Model. **18**(5), 3097–3149 (2019). https://doi.org/10.1007/s10270-018-00710-z

15. Mondragón, O., Gates, A., Roach, S.: Prospec: support for elicitation and formal specification of software properties. Electron. Notes Theor. Comput. Sci. **89**(2), 67–88 (2003)

16. Puterman, M.: Markov Decision Processes: Discrete Stochastic Dynamic Programming. Wiley, New York (1994)

17. Salamah, S., Gates, A., Kreinovich, V.: Validated templates for specification of complex LTL formulas. J. Syst. Softw. **85**(8), 1915–1929 (2012)

18. Shanmugham, S., Roberts, C.: Application of graphical specification methodologies to manufacturing control logic development: a classification and comparison. Int. J. Comput. Integr. Manuf. **11**(2), 142–152 (2010)

19. Smith, M., Holzmann, G., Etessami, K.: Events and constraints: a graphical editor for capturing logic requirements of programs. In: Proceedings of 5th IEEE International Symposium on Requirements Engineering, Toronto, Canada, pp. 14–22. IEEE (2001)

20. Vu, A.V., Ogawa, M.: Formal semantics extraction from natural language specifications for ARM. In: ter Beek, M.H., McIver, A., Oliveira, J.N. (eds.) FM 2019. LNCS, vol. 11800, pp. 465–483. Springer, Cham (2019). https://doi.org/10.1007/978-3-030-30942-8_28

21. Wong, P.Y.H., Gibbons, J.: Property specifications for workflow modelling. In: Leuschel, M., Wehrheim, H. (eds.) IFM 2009. LNCS, vol. 5423, pp. 56–71. Springer, Heidelberg (2009). https://doi.org/10.1007/978-3-642-00255-7_5

22. Yu, J., Manh, T.P., Han, J., Jin, Y., Han, Y., Wang, J.: Pattern based property specification and verification for service composition. In: Aberer, K., Peng, Z., Rundensteiner, E.A., Zhang, Y., Li, X. (eds.) WISE 2006. LNCS, vol. 4255, pp. 156–168. Springer, Heidelberg (2006). https://doi.org/10.1007/11912873_18

23. Zyubin, V.: Hyper-automaton: a model of control algorithms. In: Proceedings of Siberian Conference on Control and Communications, Tomsk, Russia, pp. 51–57. IEEE (2007)

24. Zyubin, V., Liakh, T., Rozov, A.: Reflex language: a practical notation for cyber-physical systems. Syst. Inform. **12**, 85–104 (2018)
25. Argosim. www.argosim.com. Accessed 27 Nov 2019
26. HermiT OWL Reasoner. www.hermit-reasoner.com. Accessed 27 Nov 2019
27. Model Based Systems Engineering. www.nasa.gov/consortium/ModelBasedSystems. Accessed 27 Nov 2019
28. Web Ontology Language. www.w3.org/OWL. Accessed 27 Nov 2019
29. Editor Protégé. protege.stanford.edu. Accessed 27 Nov 2019
30. IBM Rhapsody. https://www.ibm.com/se-en/marketplace/systems-design-rhapsody. Accessed 27 Nov 2019
31. SWRL: a Semantic Web Rule Language combining OWL and RuleML. www.w3.org/Submission/SWRL. Accessed 27 Nov 2019
32. Software Cost Reduction. www.nrl.navy.mil/itd/chacs/5546/SCR. Accessed 27 Nov 2019

How to Look Next? A Data-Driven Approach for Scanpath Prediction

Giuseppe Boccignone⬤, Vittorio Cuculo$^{(\boxtimes)}$⬤, and Alessandro D'Amelio⬤

PHuSe Lab - Dipartimento di Informatica, University of Milan, Milan, Italy
{giuseppe.boccignone,vittorio.cuculo,alessandro.damelio}@unimi.it

Abstract. By and large, current visual attention models mostly rely, when considering static stimuli, on the following procedure. Given an image, a saliency map is computed, which, in turn, might serve the purpose of predicting a sequence of gaze shifts, namely a scanpath instantiating the dynamics of visual attention deployment. The temporal pattern of attention unfolding is thus confined to the scanpath generation stage, whilst salience is conceived as a static map, at best conflating a number of factors (bottom-up information, top-down, spatial biases, etc.).

In this note we propose a novel sequential scheme that consists of a three-stage processing relying on a center-bias model, a context/layout model, and an object-based model, respectively. Each stage contributes, at different times, to the sequential sampling of the final scanpath. We compare the method against classic scanpath generation that exploits state-of-the-art static saliency model. Results show that accounting for the structure of the temporal unfolding leads to gaze dynamics close to human gaze behaviour.

Keywords: Saliency model · Visual attention · Gaze deployment · Scanpath prediction

1 Introduction

Background. The unfolding of visual attention deployment in time can be captured at the *data level* by eye-tracking the observer while scrutinising for a time T a scene, either static or dynamic, under a given task or goal. Figure 1 (left panel) summarises the process.

The raw gaze trajectories can be subsequently parsed in a discrete sequence of time-stamped gaze locations or fixations $(\mathbf{r}_{F_1}, t_1), (\mathbf{r}_{F_2}, t_2), \cdots$, a scanpath, where the displacement from one fixation to the next might occur as a quick jump/flight (saccade) or through the smooth pursuit of a moving item in the scene. Further, by collecting the fixations of S subjects on the i-th stimulus, an attention map or heat map can be computed in the form of a 2D empirical fixation distribution map, say $\mathcal{M}_T^{D(i)}$. At the *model level*, given a stimulus and an initial gaze point, attentive eye guidance entails answering the question: *Where to Look Next?* In a nutshell, the "Where" part concerns choosing *what* to gaze at

© Springer Nature Switzerland AG 2020
E. Sekerinski et al. (Eds.): FM 2019 Workshops, LNCS 12232, pp. 131–145, 2020.
https://doi.org/10.1007/978-3-030-54994-7_10

- features, objects, actions - and their location; the "Next" part involves *how* we gaze at what we have chosen to gaze, that is directly affected by factors such as context [36], spatial biases [34], affect and personality [17] and crucially brings in the unfolding dynamics of gaze deployment.

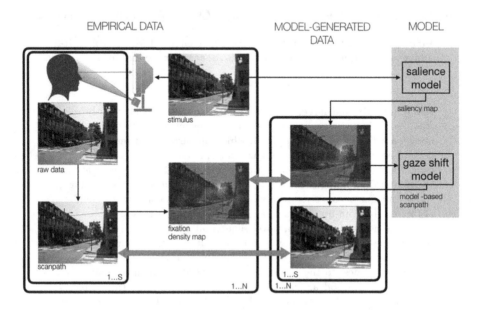

Fig. 1. Gaze data recording via eye-tracking and modelling. Given a stimulus (image **I**), the observer's gaze trajectory is sampled and recorded. Raw data are parsed and classified in fixations sequences (scanpaths). Collecting fixations from all subjects the 2D empirical fixation distribution $\mathcal{M}^D$ is estimated. On the model side, for the same stimulus a saliency map $\mathcal{S}$ is derived; if available, a gaze shift model can be exploited for sampling scanpaths based on $\mathcal{S}$. The overall model performance is routinely evaluated by comparing either the model-generated saliency map $\mathcal{S}$ with the empirical $\mathcal{M}^D$ map (light blue two-head arrows) and/or, albeit less commonly, by confronting the model-generated scanpaths $\{\widetilde{\mathbf{r}}_F(1), \widetilde{\mathbf{r}}_F(2), \cdots\}$, with the actual ones $\{\mathbf{r}_F(1), \mathbf{r}_F(2), \cdots\}$.

More formally, a computational model of visual attention deployment should account for the mapping from visual data of a natural scene, say **I** (raw image data, either a static picture or a stream of images), to the scanpath

$$\mathbf{I} \mapsto \{\mathbf{r}_{F_1}, t_1; \mathbf{r}_{F_2}, t_2; \cdots\}. \tag{1}$$

When dealing with static stimuli (images) such mapping boils down to the following (cfr. Fig.1, right panel)

1. Compute a saliency map $\mathcal{S}$, i.e.,

$$\mathbf{I} \mapsto \mathcal{S}; \tag{2}$$

2. Use $\mathcal{S}$ to generate the scanpath,

$$\mathcal{S} \mapsto \{\mathbf{r}_F(1), \mathbf{r}_F(2), \cdots\}, \tag{3}$$

where we have adopted the compact notation $(\mathbf{r}_{F_n}, t_n) = \mathbf{r}_F(n)$.

In its original formulation [21], the "saliency map" $\mathcal{S}$ is a topographic representation indicating *where* one is likely to look within the viewed scene, that is $\mathcal{S}(\mathbf{r}) \approx P(\mathbf{r} \mid \mathbf{F}(\mathbf{I}))$, where $\mathbf{F}(\mathbf{I})$ are low-level features computed from image $\mathbf{I}$. In a sense, it can be considered the modelling counterpart of the fixation density map $\mathcal{M}_T^{D(i)}$. Notice that, in recent years, computer vision efforts to achieve benchmarking performance have resulted in the heuristic addition of high-level processing capabilities to attention models, which are still referred to as salience models [9–13]. As a matter of fact, the term "saliency" now stands for any image-based prediction of which locations are likely to be fixated by subject guided by either low- or high-level cues [29].

Challenges. Despite of the original purpose behind steps 1 and 2, i.e. computing the mapping in Eq. 1, it is easily recognised by overviewing the field [9–11,33], that computational modelling of visual attention has been mainly concerned with stage 1, that is calculating salience $\mathcal{S}$. As to stage 2, it is seldom taken into account: as a matter of fact, it is surmised that $\mathcal{S}$ is *per se* predictive of human fixations. Thus, saliency models to predict where we look have gained currency for a variety of applications in computer vision, image and video processing and compression, quality assessment.

Under such circumstances, a crucial and often overlooked problem arises: saliency maps do not account for temporal dynamics. In current practice, saliency models are learned and/or evaluated by simply exploiting the fixation map on an image as "frozen" at the end of the viewing process (i.e, after having collected all fixations on stimulus along an eye-tracking session). The temporal pattern of attention unfolding, whether considered, is thus confined to the scanpath generation stage (Eq. 3), whilst salience $\mathcal{S}$ is conceived as a static map, at best simultaneously conflating a number of factors (bottom-up information, top-down, spatial biases, etc.) In simple terms, the unfolding of visual attention does not unfold.

Our Approach. In an earlier communication [7], it has been shown that the evolution of the empirical fixation density $\mathcal{M}_t^{D(i)}$ within the time interval $[t_0, T]$ from the onset of the stimulus i up to time T, provides a source of information which is richer than that derived by simply considering its cumulative distribution function $\int_{t_0}^{T} \mathcal{M}_t^{D(i)} dt$. By resorting to a simulation of scanpath generation from empirical fixation densities collected at different stages of attention unfolding, it was possible to show that:

(i) the scanpaths sampled in such way considerably differ from those generated by a static attention map;

(ii) "time-aware" scanpaths exhibit a dynamics akin to that of actual scanpaths recorded from human observers.

More precisely, those analyses [7] were based on sequentially computing, from empirical data, three different fixation density maps $\mathcal{M}_{t_k}^{D(i)}$, within the time interval $[t_0, T]$, $k = 1, 2, 3$ with $t_k < t_j$, for $k < j$, thus with time delays $D_k = t_k - t_0$. Each map was used to sample the partial scanpath related to that specific time window.

In the work presented here, we operationally take into account such temporal aspects of attention deployment (Sect. 2). In brief, we provide a "time-aware" model that addresses the three stages described above by exploiting a center bias model, a context model and an object model whose output maps are sequentially used to sample gaze shifts contributing to the final scanpath (cfr. Fig. 2, below)

We show (Sect. 3) that in such way the model-based sampling of gaze shifts, which simulates *how* human observers actually allocate visual resources onto the scene (i.e., the scanpath), departs from that achieved by classic modelling relying on a unique static saliency map (Eqs. 2 and 3), and it exhibits the features noticed in preliminary analyses based on empirical data [7].

2   A Model for Time-Aware Scanpath Generation

Recent work by Schutt *et al.* [32] has considered the temporal evolution of the fixation density in the free viewing of static scenes. They have provided evidence for a fixation dynamics which unfolds into three stages:

1. An initial orienting response towards the image center;
2. A brief exploration, which is characterized by a gradual broadening of the fixation density, the observers looking at all parts of the image they are interested in;
3. A final equilibrium state, in which the fixation density has converged, and subjects preferentially return to the same fixation locations they visited during the main exploration.

In [7] it has been shown that by estimating from eye-tracking data the empirical fixation distribution $\mathcal{M}_k^{D(i)}$ at each temporal stage described above and using it to sample a partial scanpath $\mathcal{R}t_k^{(s,i)}$, $k = 1, 2, 3$, eventually the "time-aware" scanpath $\mathcal{R}t^{(s,i)} = \{\mathcal{R}t_1^{(s,i)}, \mathcal{R}t_2^{(s,i)}, \mathcal{R}t_3^{(s,i)}\}$ more closely resembles human scanpaths than scanpaths classically obtained from the final attention map.

The main goal of this note is thus to outline a model to substantiate such results. In brief, the scheme we propose consists of a three-stage processing where the dynamics described by Schutt *et al.* [32] basically relies on: 1) a center-bias model for initial focusing; 2) a context/layout model accounting for the broad exploration to get the gist of the scene; an object-based model, to scrutinise objects that are likely to be located in such context. The output of each model is a specific map, guiding, at a that specific stage, the sequential sampling of a partial scanpath via the gaze shift model. The three-stage model is outlined at a glance in Fig. 2. The overall model dynamics can be described as follows. Given the i-th image stimulus at onset time t_0:

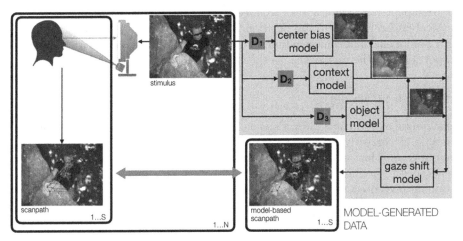

Fig. 2. The proposed three-stage model. The "time-aware" scanpath $\mathcal{R}t^{(s,i)} = \{\mathcal{R}t_1^{(s,i)}, \mathcal{R}t_2^{(s,i)}, \mathcal{R}t_3^{(s,i)}\}$, for each "artificial observer" s viewing the i-th stimulus, is obtained from the three partial scanpaths. These are sampled by relying on the three maps computed via the center bias, context and object models, respectively. Each model m is activated at a delay time D_m, while inhibiting the output of model $m-1$, so that the gaze model operates sequentially in time on one and only map. Empirical data collection is organised as outlined in Fig. 1. Here, the overall model performance is assessed by comparing the model-generated scanpaths $\{\widetilde{\mathbf{r}}_F(1), \widetilde{\mathbf{r}}_F(2), \cdots\}$, with the actual ones $\{\mathbf{r}_F(1), \mathbf{r}_F(2), \cdots\}$.

For all stages $k = 1, 2, 3$

    Step 1. At time delay D_k, compute the model-based map $\mathcal{M}_k^{(i)}$

    Step 2. Based on $\mathcal{M}_k^{(i)}$, generate "subject" fixations via the gaze shift model $\mathbf{r}_F^{(s,i)}(n) = f(\mathbf{r}_F^{(s,i)}(n-1), \mathcal{M}_k^{(i)})$:

$$\mathcal{M}_k^{(i)} \mapsto \{\widetilde{\mathbf{r}}_F^{(s,i)}(m_{k-1}+1), \cdots, \widetilde{\mathbf{r}}_F^{(s,i)}(m_k)\} = \mathcal{R}t_k^{(s,i)}, \qquad (4)$$

Eventually, collect the "time-aware" scanpath $\mathcal{R}t^{(s,i)} = \{\mathcal{R}t_1^{(s,i)}, \mathcal{R}t_2^{(s,i)}, \mathcal{R}t_3^{(s,i)}\}$.

For what concerns scanpath sampling, as proposed in [7], we exploit the Constrained Levy Exploration (CLE [3]) model, that has also been widely used for evaluation purposes, e.g., [24,38].

More specifically we consider the following model components to compute the maps $\mathcal{M}_k^{(i)}, k = 1, 2, 3$.

2.1   Center Bias

Many studies [31,37] of attentional selection in natural scenes have observed that the density of the first fixation shows a pronounced initial center bias caused by a number of possible factors: displacement bias of an image content (known as photographer bias), motor bias (related to the experiment protocol) as well as physical preferences in orbital position. In this study the center bias is modelled with a bidimensional Gaussian function located at the screen center with variance proportional to the image size, as shown in the first column of Fig. 5.

2.2   Context Model

Behavioural experiments [30] on scene understanding demonstrated that humans are able to correctly identify the semantic category of most real-world scenes even in case of fast and blurred presentations. Therefore, objects in a scene are not needed to be identified to understand the meaning of a complex scene. The rationale presented in [30], where a formal approach to the representation of scene *gist* understanding is presented, was further developed in [42] addressing scene classification via CNNs. The models were trained on the novel Places database consisting of 10 million scene photographs labelled with environment categories. In particular, we exploited the WideResNet [39] model fine-tuned on a subset of the database consisting of 365 different scene categories. The context map, therefore, is the result of the top-1 predicted category Class Activation Map (CAM) [41]. CAM indicates the discriminative image regions used by the network to identify a particular category and, in this work, simulates the exploration phase during which observers look at those portions of the image which are supposed to convey the relevant information for the scene context understanding.

In Fig. 3 is shown an example extracted from the dataset adopted in Sect. 3, where a bowling alley is correctly identified by the network when focusing on the bowling lanes.

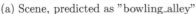

(a) Scene, predicted as "bowling_alley"   (b) Context map

Fig. 3. Components of the context map. In (a) is shown the Class Activation Map of a scene correctly identified as "bowling alley", while in (b) the corresponding considered context map

2.3   Object Model

The last stage to the realisation of the final scanpath accounts for the convergence of fixations on relevant objects.

It is worth noting that the relevance of an object is in principle strictly related to a given task [33]. The study presented here relies on eye-tracking data collected from subjects along a free-viewing (no external task) experiment and the sub-model design reflects such scenario. However, even under free-viewing conditions, it has been shown that at least faces and text significantly capture the attention of an observer [14]. Clearly, when these kinds of object are missing, other common objects that might be present within the scene become relevant.

In order to obtain a realistic object map we exploited three different sub-frameworks implementing face detection, text detection and generic object segmentation, respectively. The output of each detector contributes, with different weight, to the final object map.

More specifically, the face detection module relies on the HR-ResNet101 network [20] that achieves state-of-the-art performance even in presence of very small faces. This extracts canonical bounding box shapes that identify the regions containing a face. An example of the face detection phase is provided in Fig. 4a.

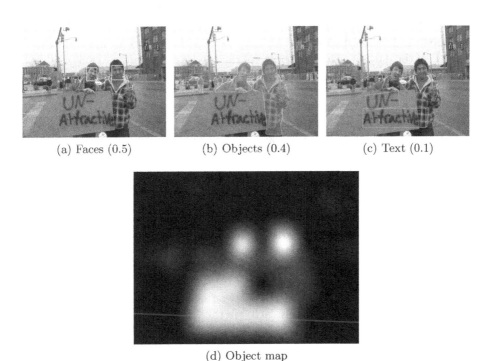

(a) Faces (0.5)   (b) Objects (0.4)   (c) Text (0.1)

(d) Object map

Fig. 4. Components of the object map: (a) shows the result of the face detector module; (b) the result of the object segmentation; (c) text detection result. In brackets, the weights of each component, in terms of contribution to the final object map (d).

The generic object detection component is implemented via Mask R-CNN [18,19]. The latter capture objects in an image, while simultaneously generating a high-quality segmentation mask for each instance. The CNN is trained on the COCO dataset [27], that consists of natural images that reflect everyday scene and provides contextual information. Multiple objects in the same image are annotated with different labels, among a set of 80 possible object categories, and segmented properly. Figure 4b shows an example, where all persons present in the image, as well as traffic lights and cars are precisely identified and segmented. The text detection component is represented by a novel Progressive Scale Expansion Network (PSENet) [26], which can spot text with arbitrary shapes even in presence of closely adjacent text instances. An example of text detection result is shown in Fig. 4c.

3   Simulation

Dataset. The adopted dataset is the well-known MIT1003 [22], that consists of eye tracking data (240 Hz) recorded from $N_S = 15$ viewers during a free-viewing experiment involving 1003 natural images. The stimuli were presented at full resolution for 3 s. The raw eye tracking data were classified in fixations and saccades by adopting an acceleration threshold algorithm [22].

Evaluation. As described in Sect. 2, we generated four different maps for each image $\mathbf{I}^i$ of the dataset. Three of these are the results of the adopted sub-models: center bias, context and object. The latter is obtained by combining the outputs of the three detectors: faces, text and common objects. The first two are the most relevant cues [14] and we empirically assigned weights 0.5 and 0.4, respectively, while weighting 0.1 the object segmentation result. The final object map is later normalised to deal with possible lacks of any of the three components.

The comparison was carried out with the state-of-the-art static saliency model DeepGaze II [23]. This is based on deep neural network features pre-trained for object recognition. The model is later fine-tuned on the MIT1003 dataset and the center bias is explicitly modelled as a prior distribution that is added to the network output. The prior distribution is the result of a Gaussian kernel density estimation over all fixations from the training dataset.

All the considered saliency maps are convolved with a Gaussian kernel with $\sigma = 35$ px (corresponding to 1dva for the MIT1003 dataset). Figure 5 shows examples of the generated maps.

These were used to support the generation of $N_S = 15$ scanpaths for both the proposed and DeepGaze II approach, via the CLE gaze shift model[1] [3]. The number of fixations generated for each subject is sampled from the empirical distribution of the number of fixations performed by the human observer over each stimulus. Furthermore, in the proposed model, the switching time from the center bias map to the context map is set to 500 ms, while the permanence of the second map is equal to 1000 ms and the sampling of fixations from the object

---

[1] Code available at https://github.com/phuselab/CLE.

map is done for 1500 ms. In terms of delay time D_m, each model m is activated at $D_m = \{0, 500, 1000\}$ ms, while inhibiting the output of model $m - 1$.

Figure 6 shows CLE generated scanpaths, compared against the actual set of human scanpaths. The examples show how considering the context in the exploration of a scene and the precise detection of salient high-level objects, leads to scanpaths that are closer to those resulting from human gaze behaviour, than scanpaths generated via the classic saliency map. In particular, the first two rows of Fig. 6 show how the contribution of the context map reflects the human exploration of the background, rather than focusing only on faces. The third row shows an example where DeepGaze II gives high relevance to low-level features that are not salient for human observers. In the following row it can be noticed how during the exploration phase all the faces are relevant, even when these are

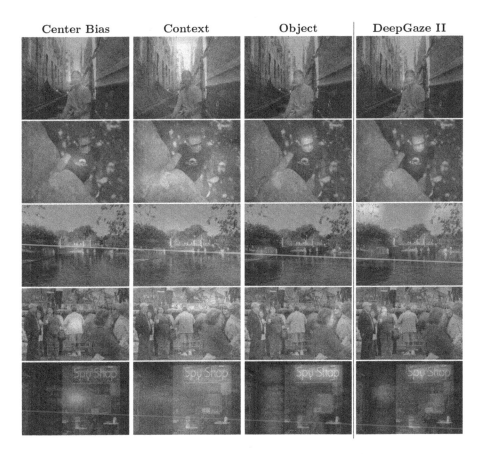

Fig. 5. Example of different maps generated for five images extracted from MIT1003 dataset. From left to right: the center bias, the context map and the object map, superimposed on the original stimulus; the saliency map resulting from saliency model DeepGaze II.

Ours   DeepGaze II   Ground truth

Fig. 6. Examples of scanpaths for the images considered in Fig. 5. Left to right: 15 model-generated scanpaths, from the proposed method, 15 model-generated scanpaths from the DeepGaze II saliency map, 15 scanpaths from actual human fixation sequences (ground-truth). Different colours encode different "observers", either artificial or human.

not faced towards the observer. Finally, as regards text, the last example shows how the whole text region is relevant and not just individual portions of it.

To quantitatively support such insights, the generated scanpaths have been evaluated on each image of the dataset by adopting metrics based on Scan-Match [16] and recurrence quantification analysis (RQA, [2])[2].

ScanMatch is a generalised scanpath comparison method that overcomes the lack of flexibility of the well-known Levenshtein distance (or string edit method) [25]. A similarity score of 1 indicates that the sequences are identical while a score of 0 indicates no similarity. One of the strengths of this method is the ability to take into account spatial, temporal, and sequential similarity between scanpaths; however, as any measure that relies on regions of interest or on a regular grid, it suffers from issues due to quantisation.

Differently, RQA is typically exploited to describe complex dynamical systems. Recently [2] it has been adopted to quantify the similarity of a pair of fixation sequences by relying on a series of measures that are found to be useful for characterizing cross-recurrent patterns [1]. Since we are interested in whether two scanpaths are similar in terms of their fixations sequence, we adopted the determinism and center of recurrence mass (CORM) figures of merit. The determinism provides a measure of the overlap for a sequence of fixations considering the sequential information. The CORM is defined as the distance of the center of gravity of recurrences from the main diagonal in a recurrence plot; small values indicate that the same fixations from the two scanpaths tend to occur close in time.

Results. All the generated scanpaths belonging to our approach and DeepGaze II have been evaluated against human scanpaths for each image. Table 1 reports the average values over all the "observers" related to the same images in the dataset. To quantify the intra-human similarity, an additional measure resulting from the comparison of ground truth scanpaths with themselves is provided.

It must be noted that, in case of DeepGaze II, the adopted model is fine-tuned exactly on the same dataset adopted for testing. Although this clearly introduces bias on the results, it can be seen how the proposed approach outperforms the model without center bias in all three considered metrics. When comparing with the "center bias-aware" model, the ScanMatch result of our approach is worse. In this case, the DeepGaze II output benefits from the addition of a prior distribution estimated over all fixations from the test dataset.

Table 1. Average values (standard deviations) of the considered metrics evaluated over all the artificial and human "observers" related to the same images in the dataset.

	ScanMatch	Determinism	CORM
DeepGazeII w/o CB	0.34 (0.10)	41.16 (16.23)	19.09 (6.21)
DeepGazeII w/ CB	**0.41** (0.07)	50.34 (13.04)	16.39 (4.22)
Ours	0.36 (0.06)	**54.47** (6.54)	**13.75** (2.65)
Ground truth	0.45 (0.05)	59.72 (7.64)	10.02 (2.11)

---

[2] An implementation is provided at https://github.com/phuselab/RQAscanpath.

4   Conclusive Remarks

Preliminary results show that the "time-aware" scanpaths sampled by taking into account the underlying process of visual attention as unfolding in time considerably differ from those generated by a static attention map; further, they exhibit a dynamics akin to that of scanpaths recorded from human observers.

The model presented here and results so far achieved, albeit simple and preliminary, respectively, bear some consequences. On the one hand, it may suggest a more principled design of visual attention models. A similar perspective has been taken, for instance, in video salience modelling, e.g. [8,15]; nevertheless, static image processing and recognition task could benefit from resorting to dynamics [35]. It is worth noting that the embedding of explicit gaze shift generation is an essential constituent of the model. Too often the design of visual attention models boils down to that of a saliency model. There are of course exceptions to such questionable approach. Le Meur and colleagues [24] have proposed saccadic models as a framework to predict visual scanpaths of observers, where the visual fixations are inferred from bottom-up saliency and oculomotor biases incorporated by gaze shift dynamics are modeled using eye tracking data (cfr. Fig. 1). Yet, there is a limited number of saccadic models available, see [24] for a comprehensive review; generalisation to dynamic scenes have been presented for instance in [6,28]. Also, a "salience free" approach is feasible [40], where steps 2 and 3 can be performed without resorting to an initial salience representation, In [40] generic visual features are exploited via variational techniques under optimality constraints. In this case too a salience map can be obtained *a posteriori* from model-generated fixations [40], but it is just instrumental for comparison purposes [40]. In a similar vein, the maps at the heart of our method do not rely on the concept of saliency as classically conceived. Here, to keep things simple, we have relied on the baseline CLE gaze shift model [3]; yet, one could resort to more complex models, e.g. [4,5].

On the other hand, our approach suggests that fine-grained assessment and benchmarking of models, as surmised in [32], needs to be aware that a static saliency map might not be as predictive of overt attention as it is deemed to be. It is clear that the temporal evolution of the empirical fixation density [7], or its modelling counterpart as proposed here, provides a source of information that is richer than that derived by simply considering its cumulative distribution function at the end of the process.

References

1. Anderson, N.C., Anderson, F., Kingstone, A., Bischof, W.F.: A comparison of scanpath comparison methods. Behav. Res. Methods **47**(4), 1377–1392 (2014). https://doi.org/10.3758/s13428-014-0550-3

2. Anderson, N.C., Bischof, W.F., Laidlaw, K.E.W., Risko, E.F., Kingstone, A.: Recurrence quantification analysis of eye movements. Behav. Res. Methods **45**(3), 842–856 (2013). https://doi.org/10.3758/s13428-012-0299-5

3. Boccignone, G., Ferraro, M.: Modelling gaze shift as a constrained random walk. Phys. A: Stat. Mech. Appl. **331**(1–2), 207–218 (2004)

4. Boccignone, G., Ferraro, M.: Gaze shifts as dynamical random sampling. In: Proceedings of 2nd European Workshop on Visual Information Processing (EUVIP 2010), pp. 29–34. IEEE Press (2010)

5. Boccignone, G., Ferraro, M.: Feed and fly control of visual scanpaths for foveation image processing. Ann. Telecommun. annales des télécommunications **68**(3–4), 201–217 (2013)

6. Boccignone, G., Ferraro, M.: Ecological sampling of gaze shifts. IEEE Trans. Cybern. **44**(2), 266–279 (2014)

7. Boccignone, G., Cuculo, V., D'Amelio, A.: Problems with saliency maps. In: Ricci, E., Rota Bulò, S., Snoek, C., Lanz, O., Messelodi, S., Sebe, N. (eds.) ICIAP 2019. LNCS, vol. 11752, pp. 35–46. Springer, Cham (2019). https://doi.org/10.1007/978-3-030-30645-8_4

8. Boccignone, G., Cuculo, V., D'Amelio, A., Grossi, G., Lanzarotti, R.: Give ear to my face: modelling multimodal attention to social interactions. In: Leal-Taixé, L., Roth, S. (eds.) ECCV 2018. LNCS, vol. 11130, pp. 331–345. Springer, Cham (2019). https://doi.org/10.1007/978-3-030-11012-3_27

9. Borji, A., Itti, L.: State-of-the-art in visual attention modeling. IEEE Trans. Pattern Anal. Mach. Intell. **35**(1), 185–207 (2013)

10. Bruce, N.D., Wloka, C., Frosst, N., Rahman, S., Tsotsos, J.K.: On computational modeling of visual saliency: examining what's right, and what's left. Vis. Res. **116**, 95–112 (2015)

11. Bylinskii, Z., DeGennaro, E., Rajalingham, R., Ruda, H., Zhang, J., Tsotsos, J.: Towards the quantitative evaluation of visual attention models. Vis. Res. **116**, 258–268 (2015)

12. Bylinskii, Z., Judd, T., Oliva, A., Torralba, A., Durand, F.: What do different evaluation metrics tell us about saliency models? IEEE Trans. Pattern Anal. Mach. Intell. **41**(3), 740–757 (2019)

13. Bylinskii, Z., Recasens, A., Borji, A., Oliva, A., Torralba, A., Durand, F.: Where should saliency models look next? In: Leibe, B., Matas, J., Sebe, N., Welling, M. (eds.) ECCV 2016. LNCS, vol. 9909, pp. 809–824. Springer, Cham (2016). https://doi.org/10.1007/978-3-319-46454-1_49

14. Cerf, M., Frady, E.P., Koch, C.: Faces and text attract gaze independent of the task: experimental data and computer model. J. Vis. **9**(12), 1–15 (2009)

15. Coutrot, A., Guyader, N.: An audiovisual attention model for natural conversation scenes. In: Proceedings of the IEEE International Conference on Image Processing (ICIP), pp. 1100–1104. IEEE (2014)

16. Cristino, F., Mathôt, S., Theeuwes, J., Gilchrist, I.D.: ScanMatch: a novel method for comparing fixation sequences. Behav. Res. Methods **42**(3), 692–700 (2010)

17. Cuculo, V., D'Amelio, A., Lanzarotti, R., Boccignone, G.: Personality gaze patterns unveiled via automatic relevance determination. In: Mazzara, M., Ober, I., Salaün, G. (eds.) STAF 2018. LNCS, vol. 11176, pp. 171–184. Springer, Cham (2018). https://doi.org/10.1007/978-3-030-04771-9_14

18. Girshick, R., Radosavovic, I., Gkioxari, G., Dollár, P., He, K.: Detectron (2018). https://github.com/facebookresearch/detectron
19. He, K., Gkioxari, G., Dollár, P., Girshick, R.: Mask R-CNN. In: Proceedings of the IEEE International Conference on Computer Vision, pp. 2961–2969 (2017)
20. Hu, P., Ramanan, D.: Finding tiny faces. In: 2017 IEEE Conference on Computer Vision and Pattern Recognition (CVPR), pp. 1522–1530. IEEE (2017)
21. Itti, L., Koch, C., Niebur, E.: A model of saliency-based visual attention for rapid scene analysis. IEEE Trans. Pattern Anal. Mach. Intell. **20**, 1254–1259 (1998)
22. Judd, T., Ehinger, K., Durand, F., Torralba, A.: Learning to predict where humans look. In: IEEE 12th International Conference on Computer Vision, pp. 2106–2113. IEEE (2009)
23. Kummerer, M., Wallis, T.S., Gatys, L.A., Bethge, M.: Understanding low-and high-level contributions to fixation prediction. In: Proceedings of the IEEE International Conference on Computer Vision, pp. 4789–4798 (2017)
24. Le Meur, O., Coutrot, A.: Introducing context-dependent and spatially-variant viewing biases in saccadic models. Vis. Res. **121**, 72–84 (2016)
25. Levenshtein, V.I.: Binary codes capable of correcting deletions, insertions, and reversals. Sov. Phys. Dokl. **10**, 707–710 (1966)
26. Li, X., Wang, W., Hou, W., Liu, R.Z., Lu, T., Yang, J.: Shape robust text detection with progressive scale expansion network. arXiv preprint arXiv:1806.02559 (2018)
27. Lin, T.-Y., et al.: Microsoft COCO: common objects in context. In: Fleet, D., Pajdla, T., Schiele, B., Tuytelaars, T. (eds.) ECCV 2014. LNCS, vol. 8693, pp. 740–755. Springer, Cham (2014). https://doi.org/10.1007/978-3-319-10602-1_48
28. Napoletano, P., Boccignone, G., Tisato, F.: Attentive monitoring of multiple video streams driven by a Bayesian foraging strategy. IEEE Trans. Image Process. **24**(11), 3266–3281 (2015)
29. Nguyen, T.V., Zhao, Q., Yan, S.: Attentive systems: a survey. Int. J. Comput. Vis. **126**(1), 86–110 (2018)
30. Oliva, A., Torralba, A.: Building the gist of a scene: the role of global image features in recognition. Prog. Brain Res. **155**, 23–36 (2006)
31. Rothkegel, L.O., Trukenbrod, H.A., Schütt, H.H., Wichmann, F.A., Engbert, R.: Temporal evolution of the central fixation bias in scene viewing. J. Vis. **17**(13), 3 (2017)
32. Schütt, H.H., Rothkegel, L.O., Trukenbrod, H.A., Engbert, R., Wichmann, F.A.: Disentangling bottom-up versus top-down and low-level versus high-level influences on eye movements over time. J. Vis. **19**(3), 1 (2019)
33. Tatler, B.W., Hayhoe, M.M., Land, M.F., Ballard, D.H.: Eye guidance in natural scenes: reinterpreting salience. J. Vis. **11**(5), 1–23 (2011)
34. Tatler, B., Vincent, B.: The prominence of behavioural biases in eye guidance. Vis. Cogn. **17**(6–7), 1029–1054 (2009)
35. Tavakoli, H.R., Borji, A., Anwer, R.M., Rahtu, E., Kannala, J.: Bottom-up attention guidance for recurrent image recognition. In: 2018 25th IEEE International Conference on Image Processing (ICIP), pp. 3004–3008. IEEE (2018)
36. Torralba, A., Oliva, A., Castelhano, M., Henderson, J.: Contextual guidance of eye movements and attention in real-world scenes: the role of global features in object search. Psychol. Rev. **113**(4), 766 (2006)

37. Tseng, P.H., Carmi, R., Cameron, I.G., Munoz, D.P., Itti, L.: Quantifying center bias of observers in free viewing of dynamic natural scenes. J. Vis. **9**(7), 4 (2009)
38. Xia, C., Han, J., Qi, F., Shi, G.: Predicting human saccadic scanpaths based on iterative representation learning. IEEE Trans. Image Process. **28**(7), 3502–3515 (2019)
39. Zagoruyko, S., Komodakis, N.: Wide residual networks. arXiv preprint arXiv:1605.07146 (2016)
40. Zanca, D., Gori, M.: Variational laws of visual attention for dynamic scenes. In: Advances in Neural Information Processing Systems, pp. 3823–3832 (2017)
41. Zhou, B., Khosla, A., Lapedriza, A., Oliva, A., Torralba, A.: Learning deep features for discriminative localization. In: Proceedings of the IEEE Conference on Computer Vision and Pattern Recognition, pp. 2921–2929 (2016)
42. Zhou, B., Lapedriza, A., Khosla, A., Oliva, A., Torralba, A.: Places: a 10 million image database for scene recognition. IEEE Trans. Pattern Anal. Mach. Intell. **40**(6), 1452–1464 (2017)

"Know Thyself" How Personal Music Tastes Shape the Last.Fm Online Social Network

Riccardo Guidotti[1,2(✉)] and Giulio Rossetti[1]

[1] ISTI-CNR, Via G. Moruzzi, Pisa, Italy
{riccardo.guidotti,giulio.rossetti}@isti.cnr.it
[2] University of Pisa, Largo B. Pontecorvo, Pisa, Italy
riccardo.guidotti@unipi.it

Abstract. As Nietzsche once wrote *"Without music, life would be a mistake"* (Twilight of the Idols, 1889.). The music we listen to reflects our personality, our way to approach life. In order to enforce self-awareness, we devised a Personal Listening Data Model that allows for capturing individual music preferences and patterns of music consumption. We applied our model to 30k users of Last.Fm for which we collected both friendship ties and multiple listening. Starting from such rich data we performed an analysis whose final aim was twofold: *(i)* capture, and characterize, the individual dimension of music consumption in order to identify clusters of like-minded Last.Fm users; *(ii)* analyze if, and how, such clusters relate to the social structure expressed by the users in the service. Do there exist individuals having *similar* Personal Listening Data Models? If so, are they directly connected in the social graph or belong to the same community?.

Keywords: Personal data model · Online social network · Music

1 Introduction

Music consumption is one of the activities that better reflects human personality: each one of us has her own tastes and habits when talking about music. In recent history, the World Wide Web revolution has deeply changed the way music enters in our daily routine. Online giants like Spotify, iTunes, SoundCloud have made huge accessible catalogs of music products to everybody everywhere.

We propose a *Personal Listening Data Model* (*PLDM*) able to capture the characteristics and systematic patterns describing music listening behavior. PLDM is built on a set of personal listening: a listening is formed by the song listened, the author of the song, the album, the genre and by the listening time. PLDM summarizes each listener behavior, explains her music tastes and pursues the goal of providing *self-awareness* so as to fulfill the Delphic maxim *"know thyself"*.

© Springer Nature Switzerland AG 2020
E. Sekerinski et al. (Eds.): FM 2019 Workshops, LNCS 12232, pp. 146–161, 2020.
https://doi.org/10.1007/978-3-030-54994-7_11

However, listening music is not only an individual act but also a social one. This second nature of music consumption is the stone on which several online services pose their grounds. Among them, one of the most famous is *Last.Fm*. On such platform, users can build social ties by following peer listeners. The social network that arises from such a process represents highly valuable information. On such structure, artists/tracks/album adoptions give birth to a social-based recommender system in which each user is exposed to the listening of her friends.

It has been widely observed how homophily [19, 26] often drives implicitly the rising of social structures encouraging individuals to establish ties with like-minded ones. Does music taste play the role of social glue in the online world? To answer such a question, we combine individual and group analysis, and we propose a way to characterize communities of music listeners by their preferences and behaviors.

The paper is organized as follows. Section 2 surveys works related to personal data model and Last.Fm online social network. Section 3 describes our model for analyzing musical listening and the relationship with friends. In Sect. 4 are presented the individual and social analysis performed on a dataset of 30k Last.Fm users. Finally, Sect. 5 summarizes conclusion and future works.

2   Related Work

The analysis of music listening is becoming increasingly valuable due to the increasing attention the music world is receiving from the scientific community. Several works have analyzed data regarding online listening in order to model diffusion of new music genres/artists, as well as to analyze the behaviors and tastes of users. In [24] the authors identified through factor analysis three patterns of preference associated with liking for most types of *Rock Music*, general *Breadth of Musical Preference*, and liking for *Popular Music*. Also [25] examined individual differences in music preferences, and preferences for distinct music dimensions were related to various personality dimensions. In [6] was proposed a music recommendation algorithm by using multiple social media information and music acoustic-based content. In [4], the authors, studied the topology of the Last.Fm social graph asking for similarities in taste as well as on demographic attributes and local network structure. Their results suggest that users connect to "online" friends, but also indicate the presence of strong "real-life" friendship ties identifiable by the multiple co-attendance of the same concerts. The authors of [22] measured different dimensions of social prominence on a social graph built upon 70k Last.Fm users whose listening were observed for 2 years. In [23] was analyzed the cross-cultural gender differences in the adoption and usage of Last.Fm. Using social media data, the authors of [21] designed a measure describing the diversity of musical tastes and explored its relationship with variables that capture socioeconomic, demographics, and traits such as openness and degree of interest in music. In [32] is shown how to define statistical models to describe patterns of song listening in an online music community. In [13] is shown how the usage of a personal listening data model (also exploited in this work) can provide a high level of self-awareness and to enable the development of a wide range of analysis exploited here with social network analysis measures.

The access to this huge amount of data generates novel challenges. Among them, the need to handle efficiently individual data is leading to the development of personal models able to deal and summarize human behavior.

These data models can be generic or specific with respect to the type of data. In [20] is described *openPDS*, a personal metadata management framework that allows individuals to collect, store, and give fine-grained access to their metadata to third parties. [31] described *My Data Store* a tool that enables people to control and share their personal data. My Data Store has been integrated in [30] into a framework enabling the development of trusted and transparent services. Finally, in [1] is proposed that each user can select which applications have to be run on which data enabling in this way diversified services on a personal server. The majority of works in the literature focus their attention on the architecture of the personal data store and on how to treat data sharing and privacy issues. The main difference between the personal data model proposed and those present in the literature is that our model focuses in obtaining an added value from the personal data through the application of data mining techniques.

In this work, we propose to apply the methodological framework introduced in [16] for mobility data to analyze personal musical preferences. An application of this approach in mobility data and transactional data can be found in [11,17, 29]. Moreover, in [14] is shown haw the network component becomes fundamental to leverage the power of the analysis from the personal level to the collective ones. User experience in online social media services, however, is composed not only of individual activities but also of interactions with other peers. The role of social communities and friendship ties is, for sure important to understand the factors that drive the users' engagement toward an artist/product. In order to assess the strength of social influence measures based on *homphily* [19] and on common interests have long been applied in social networks. For instance, the structure of ego-networks and homophily on Twitter was studied in [3] where the authors investigated the relations between homophily and topological features discovering a high homophily w.r.t. topics of interest. The authors of [2] exploited homophily in latent attributes to augment the users' features with information derived from Twitter profiles and from friends' posts. Their results suggest that the neighborhood context carries a substantial improvement to the information describing a user. To the best of our knowledge, this work is the first attempt to define a data model able to capture musical listening behavior and to use it to analyze the relationships in the social network.

3   Personal Listening Data Model

In this section, we formally describe the *Personal Listening Data Model*. By applying the following definitions and functions, it is possible to build for each user a listening profile giving a picture of her habits in terms of listening.

Definition 1 (Listening). *Given a user u we define $L_u = \{\langle time\text{-}stamp, song, artist, album, genre\rangle\}$ as the set of listening performed by u.*

$$\text{♫} = \langle \text{🕐}, \text{♫}, \text{👤}, \text{◉}, \text{♫} \rangle$$

Fig. 1. A listening $l = \{\langle time\text{-}stamp, song, artist, album, genre\rangle\}$ is a tuple formed by the *time-stamp* indicating when the listening was performed, the *song* listened, the *artist* which played the song, the *album* the song belongs to and the *genre* of the artist.

Each listening l (see Fig. 1) is an abstraction of a real listening since a song can belong to more than a genre and can be played by more than an artist[1]. However, we can assume this abstraction without losing in generality.

From the set of listening L_u we can extract the set of songs S_u, artists A_u, albums B_u and genres G_u for each user. More formally we have:

- $S_u = \{song | \langle \cdot, song, \cdot, \cdot, \cdot \rangle \in L_u\}$
- $A_u = \{artist | \langle \cdot, \cdot, artist, \cdot, \cdot \rangle \in L_u\}$
- $B_u = \{album | \langle \cdot, \cdot, \cdot, album, \cdot \rangle \in L_u\}$
- $G_u = \{genre | \langle \cdot, \cdot, \cdot, \cdot, genre \rangle \in L_u\}$

Besides the sizes of these sets, a valuable summary of the user behavior can be realized through frequencies dictionary indicating the support (i.e. the relative number of occurrences) of each feature of the listening.

Definition 2 (Support). *The* support *function returns the frequency dictionary of (item, support) where the support of an item is obtained as the number of occurring items on the number of listening.*

$$sup(X, L) = \{(x, |Y|/|L|) | x \in X \wedge Y \subseteq L s.t. \forall l \in Y, x \in l\}$$

We define the following frequency dictionaries: $s_u = sup(S_u, L_u)$, $a_u = sup(A_u, L_u)$, $b_u = sup(B_u, L_u)$, $g_u = sup(G_u, L_u)$, $d_u = sup(D, L_u)$ and $t_u = sup(T, L_u)$ where $D = \{mon, tue, wed, thu, fri, sat, sun\}$ contains the days of weeks, and $T = \{(2\text{-}8], (8\text{-}12], (12\text{-}15], (15\text{-}18], (18\text{-}22], (22\text{-}2]\}$ contains the time slots of the day (i.e. early and late morning, early and late afternoon, early and late night).

These dictionaries can be exploited to extract indicators.

Definition 3 (Entropy). *The* entropy *function returns the normalized entropy in $[0, 1]$ of a dictionary x. It is defined as:*

$$entropy(X) = -\sum_{i=1}^{n} P(x_i) \log_b P(x_i) / \log_b n$$

---

[1] The choice of describing a listening with these attributes is related to the case study. Additional attributes can be used when available from the data. We highlight that listening means that the song was played and not necessarily entirely listened.

The entropy tends to 0 when the user behavior with respect to the observed variable is systematic, tends to 1 when the behavior is not predictable. These indicators are similar to those related to shopping behavior described in [10,12]. We define the entropy for songs, artists, albums, genres, days and time-slots as $e_{s_u} = entropy(g_u)$, $e_{a_u} = entropy(a_u)$, $e_{b_u} = entropy(b_u)$, $e_{g_u} = entropy(g_u)$, $e_{d_u} = entropy(d_u)$ and $e_{t_u} = entropy(t_u)$.

A pattern we consider is the top listened artist, genre, etc.

Definition 4 (Top). *The* top *function returns the most supported item in a dictionary. It is defined as:*

$$top(X) = \underset{(x,y)\in X}{argmax}(y)$$

We define the top for songs, artists, albums and genres as $\hat{s}_u = top(s_u)$, $\hat{a}_u = top(a_u)$, $\hat{b}_u = top(b_u)$ and $\hat{g}_u = top(g_u)$.

Moreover, we want to consider for each user the set of representatives, i.e. significantly most listened, subsets of artists, albums, and genres.

Definition 5 (Repr). *The* repr *function returns the most representative supported items in a dictionary. It is defined as:*

$$repr(X) = \underset{(x,y)\in X}{knee}(y)$$

The result of $repr(X)$ contains a set of preferences such that their support is higher than the support of most of the listening done with respect to other artists, albums, and genres. For example if user u has $g_u = \{(rock, 0.4), (pop, 0.3), (folk, 0.1), (classic, 0.1), (house, 0.1)\}$. Then the result of $repr(g_u)$ will bet $\{(rock, 0.4), (pop, 0.3)\}$. This result is achieved by employing a technique known as "knee method" [28] represented by the function $knee(\cdot)$. It sorts the vector according to the supports, and it returns as most representative the couples with support greater or equal than the support corresponding to the *knee* in the curve of the ordered frequencies. We define the most representative for songs, artists, albums and genres as $\tilde{s}_u = repr(s_u)$, $\tilde{a}_u = repr(a_u)$, $\tilde{b}_u = repr(b_u)$ and $\tilde{g}_u = repr(g_u)$. Obviously we have $\hat{g}_u \subseteq \tilde{g}_u \subseteq g_u$ that holds also for songs, albums and artists.

Finally, in order to understand how each user is related with her *friends* in terms of preferences we define the set of friends of a user u as $f_u = \{v_1, \ldots, v_n\}$ where $\forall v_i \in U$, $v_i \in f_u$. The ego-network of each user u is modeled by f_u.

By applying the definitions and the functions described above on the user listening L_u we can turn the raw listening data of a user into a complex personal data structure that we call *Personal Listening Data Model* (PLDM). The PMDL characterizes the listening behavior of a user by means of its *indicators*, *frequencies* and *patterns*.

Definition 6 (Personal Listening Data Model). *Given the listening L_u we define the personal listening data model as*

$$P_u = \langle |L_u|, |S_u|, |A_u|, |B_u|, |G_u|, \qquad\qquad indicators$$
$$e_{s_u}, e_{a_u}, e_{b_u}, e_{g_u}, e_{d_u}, e_{t_u}, \qquad\qquad indicators$$
$$s_u, a_u, b_u, g_u, d_u, t_u, \qquad\qquad frequencies$$
$$\hat{s}_u, \hat{a}_u, \hat{b}_u, \hat{g}_u, \qquad\qquad patterns$$
$$\tilde{s}_u, \tilde{a}_u, \tilde{b}_u, \tilde{g}_u, \qquad\qquad patterns$$
$$f_u \rangle \qquad\qquad friends$$

It is worth to notice that, that according to the procedures followed in [15,18], the PLDM can be extracted by following a parameter-free approach.

4 LastFM Case Study

In this section, we discuss the benefits derivable from using PLDM while analyzing the data extracted from a famous music-related online social network: *Last.Fm*. In Last.Fm people can share their own music tastes and discover new artists and genres on the bases of what they, or their friends, like. In such a service, each user produces is characterized by two elements: the social structure it is embedded in and her own listening. Through each listening, a user expresses a preference for a certain song, artist, album, genre, and take place in a certain time. Using Last.Fm APIs[2] we retrieved the last 200 listening, as well as the social graph $G = (U, E)$, of about $30,000$ users resident in the UK[3]. For each user $u \in U$, given the listening L_u we calculated her PLDM P_u. Using such individual model, we then performed a two-stage analysis aimed at: *(a)* describing how Last.Fm users can be characterized, Sect. 4.1, and *(b)* analyzing if, and how, the Last.Fm social structure reflects homophily behaviors, Sect. 4.2.

4.1 Who I Am? PLDM Analysis

The first analysis we report is related to the *indicators* of the PLDMs $\{P_u\}$ extracted. In Fig. 2 are reported the distributions of the number of users which have listened a certain number of songs $|S_u|$, artists $|A_u|$, albums $|B_u|$ and genres $|G_u|$. The first distribution is right-skewed with most of the users who have listened to about 140 songs (this implies that some tracks have been listened more than once). On the other hand, the other distributions are left-skewed: a typical user listened to about 60 artists, 70 albums and 10 genres.

Figure 3 depicts the distributions of the entropy. It emerges that users are much more systematic with respect to the listening time (day of week and time of

---

[2] http://www.last.fm/api/, retrieval date 2016-04-04.
[3] The code, along with the ids of seed users used in this study, is available at https://github.com/GiulioRossetti/LastfmProfiler. The complete dataset is not released to comply with Last.fm TOS.

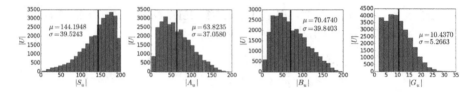

Fig. 2. Distributions of the number of songs $|S_u|$, artists $|A_u|$, albums $|B_u|$ and genres $|G_u|$ respectively. The black vertical lines highlight the means.

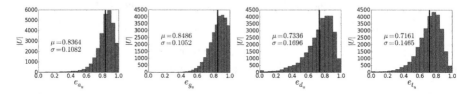

Fig. 3. Distributions of entropy for artists e_{a_u}, genre e_{g_u}, day of week e_{d_u} and time of day e_{t_u} respectively. The black vertical lines highlight the means.

the day) than with respect to what they listen to. This behavior is in opposition to what happens in shopping [10]. Apparently, since the artist and genre entropy are right-skewed, it seems that most of the users are not very systematic with respect to the genre or to the artist. This can indicate that it is very unlikely that it exists a unique prevalence towards a certain artist or genre.

In Fig. 4 (left), we observe the heat-map of the correlations among the indicators. Some of them like $|A_u|$, $|B_u|$, $|G_u|$ are highly correlated[4] ($cor(|A_u|, |B_u|) = 0.8569, cor(|G_u|, |B_u| = 0.6358)$): the higher the number of artists or genres, the higher the number of albums listened. Other interesting correlations are $cor(|B_u|, e_{g_u}) = -0.3275$ and $cor(|B_u|, e_{a_u}) = 0.5483$. Their density scatter plots are reported in Fig. 4 *(center, right)*: the higher the number of albums listened, the lower the variability with respect to the genre and the higher the variability with respect to the artists. From this result, we understand that a user listening to many different albums narrows its musical preferences toward a restricted set of genres and that it explores these genres by listening to various artists of this genre and not having a clear preference among these artists.

A user can get benefit from a smart visualization of the PLDM *indicators* obtaining a novel level of *self-awareness* of her listening behavior. For instance, a user could discover that is listening to a great variety of artists but that they all belong to the same genre and that she always listens to them following the same pattern of songs. A possible reaction could be to start her new listening with an unknown artist belonging to a different genre to enlarge her musical knowledge and discover if she really dislikes certain genres or just had never the occasion to listen to them. Moreover, due to the continuously growing size of the personal

---

[4] The *p-value* is zero (or smaller than 0.000001) for all the correlations.

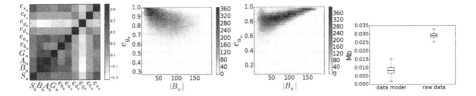

Fig. 4. (*left*) Correlation matrix; (*center-left*) Scatter density plots of number of albums $|B_u|$ versus genre entropy e_{g_u} and (*center-right*) versus artists entropy e_{a_u}; (*right*) Storage for the model.

raw listening dataset, the PLDM can be recalculated in different time windows so that the user can observe changes and/or stability in the listening profile.

PLDM Efficiency, Storage Analysis. We report in Fig. 4(right) the box-plots of the storage occupancy of the data model PLDMs (left) and for the raw listening (right). The storage required by the data model is typically one third of the storage required by the raw data. Moreover, the storage space of the data model will not grow very much when storing more listening because the number of possible genres, artists, albums, songs is limited, while the number of listening grows continuously. Thus, an average storage of $0.01Mb$ together with a computational time of max 5 s per user guarantees that the PLDM could be calculated and stored individually without the need for central service.

Frequency and Patterns Analysis. When dealing with music listening data, it is common to identify users by looking only to their most listened genre/artist. In order to prove that this assumption does not represent the users' preferences properly, we exploit the knowledge coming from the frequency vectors. We analyze the frequency vectors a_u, g_u, the top listened $\hat{a}_u$, $\hat{g}_u$, and the most representative $\tilde{a}_u$, $\tilde{g}_u$. In order to simplify the following discussion, we will refer to the sets $\tilde{a}_u$ and $\tilde{g}_u$ equivalently as $\tilde{x}$ and to the artists and genres contained in such sets as *preferences*. In Fig. 5 is depicted the result of this analysis for the genre (top row) and artist (bottom row)[5].

The first column shows the distribution of the number of users with respect to the number of representative genres $|\tilde{g}_u|$ and artists $|\tilde{a}_u|$. In both cases, the smallest value is larger than 1, indicating that each user has more than a preference. On the other hand, a large part of all the genres and artists listened are removed when passing from x to $\tilde{x}$. Indeed, the mean for the genres passes from 10 to 3, the mean for the artist passes from 60 to 10.

The second column in Fig. 5 illustrates the distribution of the number of users with respect to the maximum difference in frequencies between the listening preference obtained as $max(\tilde{x}) - min(\tilde{x})$. Both for genres and artists, the mode

---

[5] The analysis of b_u have similar results (not reported due to lack of space).

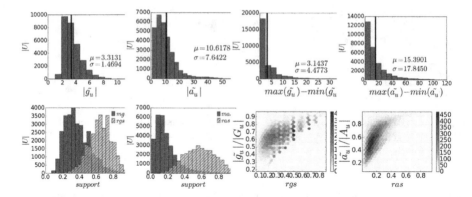

Fig. 5. Frequencies analysis for genre (left) and artist (right). *First row*: distribution of number of users w.r.t the number of representative preferences. *Second row*: distribution of number of users w.r.t the maximum difference in frequencies between the listening preference. *Third row*: distribution of number of users w.r.t the support given by the representative preferences. *Last row*: density scatter plot between the representative preferences support and the ratio of their number on the number of all the possible artists or genres.

of this value is close to zero. This proofs that the highest preferences are similar in terms of listening for the majority of the users.

The third column shows the distributions of the users with respect to the most listened artist support mas and most listened genre support mgs given by $mas = v|(a,v) = \hat{a}_u$ and $mgs = v|(g,v) = \hat{g}_u$ respectively, versus the representative artist support ras and representative genre support rgs given by $ras = sum(v|(a,v) \in \tilde{a}_u)$ and $rgs = sum(v|(g,v) \in \tilde{g}_u)$. From these distributions is evident the increase of the support when are considered, not only the preferred, but also all the representative preferences.

The last column reports a density scatter plot between the representative preferences support (rgs and the ras) and the ratio of their number on the number of all the artists or genres listened, i.e. $|\tilde{a}_u|/|A_u|$ and $|\tilde{g}_u|/|G_u|$ respectively. Since the higher concentration of the points is tends to be around 0.2 with respect to the x-axis and around 0.5 with respect to the y-axis we have that for most of the users it is sufficient a limited number of preferences (but more than one) to reach a very high level of support. This concludes that each user can be described by a few preferences that highly characterize her.

Finally, it is interesting to observe how the total support of the users and consequently the ranks of the top ten artists and genres change when the preferences in $|\tilde{g}_u|$ and $|\tilde{a}_u|$ are considered instead of those in $|\hat{g}_u|$ and $|\hat{a}_u|$. We report in Table 1 the top ten of the top listened genres and artists and the top ten of the most representative genres and artists with the users support, i.e., the percentage of users having that genre or artist as $\hat{g}_u$ or $\hat{a}_u$, and $\tilde{g}_u$ or $\tilde{a}_u$. We can notice how for the two most listened genres (rock and pop) there is a significant drop in the total support, vice-versa the other genres gain levels of support. The overall rank in the genre top ten is not modified very much. On the other hand, a completely new rank appears for the artists with a clear redistribution of the support out of the top ten. This last result is another proof that the user's preferences are systematic, but they are not towards a unique genre or artist, while they are towards groups of preferences.

Table 1. Top ten of the top listened ($\{\hat{g}_u\}$, $\{\hat{a}_u\}$) and most representative ($\{\tilde{g}_u\}$, $\{\tilde{a}_u\}$) genres and artists with corresponding support.

	$\{\hat{g}_u\}$	sup	$\{\hat{a}_u\}$	sup	$\{\tilde{g}_u\}$	sup	$\{\tilde{a}_u\}$	sup
1	Rock	53.86	The Beatles	0.75	Rock	13.41	David Bowie	0.29
2	Pop	19.64	David Bowie	0.72	Pop	9.73	Arctic Monkeys	0.26
3	Hip Hop	5.05	Kanye West	0.56	Hip Hop	5.16	Radiohead	0.24
4	Electronic	2.21	Arctic Monkeys	0.54	Inide Rock	4.39	Rihanna	0.24
5	Folk	2.03	Rihanna	0.51	Folk	4.31	Coldplay	0.23
6	Punk	1.74	Lady Gaga	0.48	Electronic	4.26	The Beatles	0.22
7	Inide Rock	1.65	Taylor Swift	0.47	Punk	4.07	Kanye West	0.21
8	Dubstep	0.90	Radiohead	0.43	House	2.63	Muse	0.19
9	House	0.85	Muse	0.38	R&B	2.53	Florence	0.19
10	Metal	0.84	Daft Punk	0.37	Emo	2.11	Lady Gaga	0.19

4.2   Who Are My Friends? PLDM, Network and Homophily

So far, we focused on describing how individual users can be characterized by their listening patterns; however, sometimes self-awareness by itself is not sufficient to realize *who we are*. In order to understand *where we are* positioned with respect to the mass or with respect to our friends, we need to compare ourselves with them and to calculate the degree of the differences.

Given two users $u, v \in U$ it is possible to calculate the similarity between them by comparing their PLDMs P_u and P_v. By exploiting the previous result, we decided to compute two distinct families of similarities:

- *music-taste* similarity: computed on the most representative music preferences, e.g. $\tilde{g}_u$, instead of complete frequency dictionaries for artist, album and genre;
- *temporal* similarity computed on the day/timeslot frequency dictionaries.

We can analyze the similarity among two users by using the *cosine similarity function* among their frequency dictionaries: for example given $\tilde{g}_u$ and $\tilde{g}_v$ for u and v, we measure their similarity as $cos(g_u, g_v) = \frac{g_u * g_v}{||g_u|| ||g_v||}$.

To understand if, and how, friendship ties affect the listening behavior and users' homophily we calculated the similarities among all the pairs of users in U (we call this set A), and we compared these distributions with the ones obtained by filtering out the nodes that are not directly connected in the social graph. Figure 6 reports the distribution between pairs of users for artist, album, genre, day, and time-slot. Quite surprisingly, we can observe nearly exactly the same distributions[6] when considering all the pairs in A or just the friends (F). This means that users' ties in Last.Fm social network are not driven by a special listening behavior: the friends in the users' ego-networks are a sample of all the users inscribed to the system. Another interesting result is that genre, day and time-slot distributions are "reverse tilde" $\sim$-shaped. There is a peak of pairs which are not similar at all (similarity equals to zero), and a growing trend of pairs of users which are more and more similar up to another peak of quite similar use: just a few couples are identical. On the other hand, the distributions for artists are long-tailed, while those for album are U-shaped with a peak between most similar and a peak between most different.

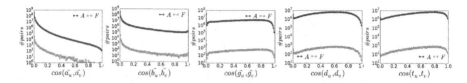

Fig. 6. Distributions between all the pairs of users A and between users which are friends F for artists, albums, genres, days and time-slots (from left to right).

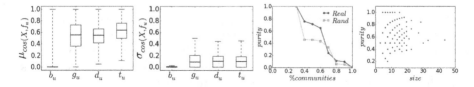

Fig. 7. (left) Boxplots of ego-network indicators μ and σ for album, genre, day and time-slots; (right) Community Discovery results.

Ego-Networks and Homophily. According to [2,9], we decided to characterize each user with respect to her listening behavior and the listening behavior of her friends. We described the ego-network and the homophily of each user (for each analyzed feature) through two additional *indicators* μ and σ. We indicate with μ the inter-quartile mean and with σ the standard deviation of the cosine similarity calculated on the Last.Fm friends f_u of a given user u. The higher is μ, the more homophilous is u with her friends w.r.t. a certain variable X (where

---

[6] The Pearson correlations ranges in $[0.96, 0.99]$, p-value $\ll 1.0e^{-60}$.

X can be the genre, album, etc.). The higher is σ, the more various is the similarity between u and her friends f_u w.r.t. a certain variable X. Figure 7 depicts the boxplots of μ (left) and σ (right) for album, genre, day and time-slot. We indicate with $cos(X, f_u)$ the cosine of a certain variable X calculated between user u and her friends f_u. Most of the users have a low μ indicator for the album, but many users have quite high μ indicators for the genre, day and time-slot. The variability σ is in line with the previous indicator: the higher the similarity, the higher the variability of the features.

Segmentation Analysis. By exploiting the previous indicators μ and σ we investigate the existence of different groups of listeners with respect to their listening taste compared with those of their friends. We applied the clustering algorithm K-Means [28] by varying the number of clusters $k \in [2, 50]$. By observing the sum of squared error [8] we decided to select 8 as the number of clusters. In Fig. 8 are described the normalized radar charts representing the centroids and the size of the clusters.

Cluster D is the cluster with the lowest indicators. It contains the users who are not very similar to their friends. If we observe the left part of the radars representing clusters B and G, we can notice that they are comparably pronounced in terms of users having friends with similar listening behavior (time-slot, day and genre). However, cluster G has also a great variety with respect to these features. On the contrary, cluster C contains only users having a great variability but not significant similarity in preferences with their friends. Clusters E, F and H have variability very low and are complementary in terms of μs. The first one contains users similar w.r.t. time-slot and genre, the second one users similar w.r.t. day and time-slot, the last one users similar w.r.t genre and day.

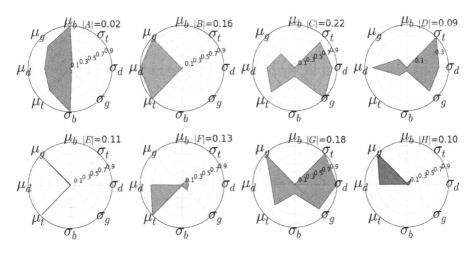

Fig. 8. Radar charts for the centroids of the clusters extracted on the indicators of friendship homophily based on PMDLs.

Finally, cluster A, the smallest one, contains users who are similar w.r.t album besides genre, day and time.

Once identified clusters of similar users, we analyzed if their characterization reflects on the network structure: are community formed by users belonging to the same cluster? To achieve this goal we design a three-step approach:

1. *partitioning* of the social graph $G = (U, E)$ in mesoscale topologies by applying a community discovery;
2. *labeling* of each node within a community with the identifier of the cluster it belongs to;
3. *evaluating* the level of *purity* of each community as the relative support of the most shared node label.

Among various community discovery algorithms, we decided to adopt a state-of-art bottom-up approach: Demon [7]. Demon works on the assumption that, in a social scenario, communities emerge from the choices of individuals: each Last.Fm user directly chooses her friends, and the community she belongs to is implicitly described by this bottom-up wiring pattern. Demon extract micro-communities starting from the ego-network graph of each user and then recombines them in order to identify stable and dense mesoscale structures without suffering the so-called "scale problem" that affects other approaches based on modularity (e.g., Louvain [5]). Moreover, the chosen algorithm has proven to be one of the best solutions while the final task was to identify network substructures able to bound homophilic behaviors [27].

By applying Demon we obtained 2160 communities. Most of the communities are pure with respect to the clustering labels. Indeed 30% of the communities are perfectly pure and 60% of the communities have a purity higher than the 0.67 (see Fig. 7 *(center-right)*). We compared this result against a random model obtained through 100 random permutations of the clustering labeling in the communities. The line represents the average of these simulations. Even though the shape of the distribution is similar, high levels of purity are not reached for a considerable portion of the communities. Thus, in general, the users in a community tend to belong to the same cluster. This result lets us conclude that, even if each user has its own peculiar profile, it tends to be surrounded by peers that share similar behavior with respect to the listening tastes compared with those of her friends. Communities are not composed by users that necessarily listen to the same artist/album/genre or that use the service during the same day/time-slot. Conversely, they group together users having the same degree of erratic behaviors. What emerges is that service usage drives people to connect. For example, users that like to listen to various genres tend to surround themselves with people with high music preference entropy (maybe to maximize the exposure to novelty). Vice-versa, users that like to listen to few genres tend to surround themselves with friends with music taste narrowed towards specific genres (maybe to deeply explore various artists of those genres) As highlighted by Fig. 7 *(right)* this result is not affected by the size of the community even though it seems that for larger communities the purity tends to 0.5.

5   Conclusion

The endless growth of individual data is requiring efficient models able to store information and tools for automatically transforming this knowledge into a personal benefit. In this paper, we have presented the Personal Listening Data Model (PLDM). The PLDM is designed to deal with musical preferences and can be employed for many applications. By employing the PLDM on a set of 30k Last.Fm users we endorsed the potentiality of this data structure. We have shown how our modeling approaches can be used to increase the self-awareness of Last.Fm users enabling for a succinct description of music tastes as well as service usage habits. We have discussed how the indicators composing the PLDM can be exploited to produce a user segmentation able to discriminate between different groups of listeners. Finally, we studied the correlations among the segments identified and the modular structure of the Last.Fm social graph. From this last analysis clearly emerges that Last.Fm users tend to cluster, in the network sense, with peers having a similar degree of music entropy and/or similar temporal listening behaviors. In the future, we would like to implement a real web service where a user can provide his Last.Fm username and a personal dashboard exploiting all the features contained in the PLDM, as well as her similarity to her friends, is shown. The dashboard would allow self-awareness and self-comparison with other users, with similar users or with the user's friends. In this way, a user could enlarge his musical experience, try novel tracks, and increase her musical education because knowledge comes from listening.

Acknowledgment. This work is partially supported by the European Community H2020 programme under the funding schemes: INFRAIA-1-2014-2015: Research Infrastructures G.A. 654024 *SoBigData* (http://www.sobigdata.eu), G.A. 78835 *Pro-Res* (http://prores-project.eu/), and G.A. 825619 *AI4EU* (https://www.ai4eu.eu/), and G.A. 780754 *Track & Know* (https://trackandknowproject.eu/).

References

1. Abiteboul, S., André, B., Kaplan, D.: Managing your digital life. Commun. ACM **58**(5), 32–35 (2015)
2. Al Zamal, F., Liu, W., Ruths, D.: Homophily and latent attribute inference: inferring latent attributes of twitter users from neighbors. In: ICWSM, vol. 270 (2012)
3. Arnaboldi, V., Conti, M., Passarella, A., Pezzoni, F.: Analysis of ego network structure in online social networks. In: Privacy, security, risk and trust (PASSAT), 2012 International Conference on and 2012 International Confernece on Social Computing (SocialCom), pp. 31–40. IEEE (2012)
4. Bischoff, K.: We love rock 'n' roll: analyzing and predicting friendship links in last.fm. In: Web Science 2012, WebSci 2012, Evanston, IL, USA - 22–24 June 2012, pp. 47–56 (2012)
5. Blondel, V.D., Guillaume, J.L., Lambiotte, R., Lefebvre, E.: Fast unfolding of communities in large networks. J. Stat. Mech: Theory Exp. **2008**(10), P10008 (2008)

6. Bu, J., et al.: Music recommendation by unified hypergraph: combining social media information and music content. In: International conference on Multimedia, pp. 391–400. ACM (2010)

7. Coscia, M., Rossetti, G., Giannotti, F., Pedreschi, D.: Uncovering hierarchical and overlapping communities with a local-first approach. ACM Trans. Knowl. Discovery Data (TKDD) 9(1), 1–27 (2014)

8. Draper, N.R., Smith, H., Pownell, E.: Applied regression analysis, vol. 3. Wiley, New York (1966)

9. Guidotti, R., Berlingerio, M.: Where is my next friend? Recommending enjoyable profiles in location based services. In: Cherifi, H., Gonçalves, B., Menezes, R., Sinatra, R. (eds.) Complex Networks VII. SCI, vol. 644, pp. 65–78. Springer, Cham (2016). https://doi.org/10.1007/978-3-319-30569-1_5

10. Guidotti, R., Coscia, M., Pedreschi, D., Pennacchioli, D.: Behavioral entropy and profitability in retail. In: International Conference on Data Science and Advanced Analytics (DSAA), pp. 1–10. IEEE (2015)

11. Guidotti, R., Monreale, A., Nanni, M., et al.: Clustering individual transactional data for masses of users. In: SIGKDD, pp. 195–204. ACM (2017)

12. Guidotti, R., Rossetti, G., Pappalardo, L., et al.: Market basket prediction using user-centric temporal annotated recurring sequences. In: 2017 International Conference on Data Mining (ICDM), pp. 895–900. IEEE (2017)

13. Guidotti, R., Rossetti, G., Pedreschi, D.: AUDIO ERGO SUM. In: Milazzo, P., Varró, D., Wimmer, M. (eds.) STAF 2016. LNCS, vol. 9946, pp. 51–66. Springer, Cham (2016). https://doi.org/10.1007/978-3-319-50230-4_5

14. Guidotti, R., Sassi, A., Berlingerio, M., Pascale, A., Ghaddar, B.: Social or green? A data-driven approach for more enjoyable carpooling. In: 2015 18th International Conference on Intelligent Transportation Systems, pp. 842–847. IEEE (2015)

15. Guidotti, R., Trasarti, R., Nanni, M.: TOSCA: two-steps clustering algorithm for personal locations detection. In: International Conference on Advances in Geographic Information Systems (SIGSPATIAL). ACM (2015)

16. Guidotti, R., Trasarti, R., Nanni, M.: Towards user-centric data management: individual mobility analytics for collective services. In: SIGSPATIAL. ACM (2015)

17. Guidotti, R., Trasarti, R., et al.: There's a path for everyone: a data-driven personal model reproducing mobility agendas. In: DSAA, pp. 303–312. IEEE (2017)

18. Keogh, E., Lonardi, S., Ratanamahatana, C.A.: Towards parameter-free data mining. In: International Conference on Knowledge Discovery and Data Mining (SIGKDD), pp. 206–215. ACM (2004)

19. McPherson, M., Smith-Lovin, L., Cook, J.M.: Birds of a feather: homophily in social networks. Ann. Rev. Sociol. 27(1), 415–444 (2001)

20. de Montjoye, Y.A., Shmueli, E., Wang, S.S., Pentland, A.S.: openPDS: protecting the privacy of metadata through safeanswers. PLoS ONE 9(7), e98790 (2014)

21. Park, M., Weber, I., Naaman, M., Vieweg, S.: Understanding musical diversity via online social media. In: AAAI Conference on Web and Social Media (2015)

22. Pennacchioli, D., Rossetti, G., Pappalardo, L., Pedreschi, D., Giannotti, F., Coscia, M.: The three dimensions of social prominence. In: Jatowt, A., et al. (eds.) SocInfo 2013. LNCS, vol. 8238, pp. 319–332. Springer, Cham (2013). https://doi.org/10.1007/978-3-319-03260-3_28

23. Putzke, J., Fischbach, K., Schoder, D., Gloor, P.A.: Cross-cultural gender differences in the adoption and usage of social media platforms - an exploratory study of last.fm. Comput. Netw. 75, 519–530 (2014)

24. Rawlings, D., Ciancarelli, V.: Music preference and the five-factor model of the neo personality inventory. Psychol. Music 25(2), 120–132 (1997)

25. Rentfrow, P.J., Gosling, S.D.: The do re mi's of everyday life: the structure and personality correlates of music preferences. J. Pers. Soc. Psychol. **84**(6), 1236 (2003)
26. Rossetti, G., Guidotti, R., Miliou, I., Pedreschi, D., Giannotti, F.: A supervised approach for intra-/inter-community interaction prediction in dynamic social networks. Soc. Netw. Anal. Min. **6**(1), 1–20 (2016). https://doi.org/10.1007/s13278-016-0397-y
27. Rossetti, G., Pappalardo, L., Kikas, R., Pedreschi, D., Giannotti, F., Dumas, M.: Community-centric analysis of user engagement in skype social network. In: ASONAM, pp. 547–552. IEEE (2015)
28. Tan, P.N., Steinbach, M., Kumar, V., et al.: Introduction to Data Mining, vol. 1. Pearson Addison Wesley, Boston (2006)
29. Trasarti, R., Guidotti, R., Monreale, A., Giannotti, F.: Myway: location prediction via mobility profiling. Inf. Syst. **64**, 350–367 (2015)
30. Vescovi, M., Moiso, C., Pasolli, M., Cordin, L., Antonelli, F.: Building an ecosystem of trusted services via user control and transparency on personal data. In: Damsgaard Jensen, C., Marsh, S., Dimitrakos, T., Murayama, Y. (eds.) IFIPTM 2015. IAICT, vol. 454, pp. 240–250. Springer, Cham (2015). https://doi.org/10.1007/978-3-319-18491-3_20
31. Vescovi, M., Perentis, C., Leonardi, C., Lepri, B., Moiso, C.: My data store: toward user awareness and control on personal data. In: International Joint Conference on Pervasive and Ubiquitous Computing, pp. 179–182. ACM (2014)
32. Zheleva, E., Guiver, J., Mendes Rodrigues, E., Milić-Frayling, N.: Statistical models of music-listening sessions in social media. In: Proceedings of the 19th International Conference on World Wide Web, pp. 1019–1028. ACM (2010)

Gender Recognition in the Wild with Small Sample Size - A Dictionary Learning Approach

Alessandro D'Amelio$^{(\boxtimes)}$ [ID], Vittorio Cuculo [ID], and Sathya Bursic [ID]

Dipartimento di Informatica, University of Milan, Milan, Italy
{alessandro.damelio,vittorio.cuculo,sathya.bursic}@unimi.it

Abstract. In this work we address the problem of gender recognition from facial images acquired in the wild. This problem is particularly difficult due to the presence of variations in pose, ethnicity, age and image quality. Moreover, we consider the special case in which only a small sample size is available for the training phase. We rely on a feature representation obtained from the well known VGG-Face Deep Convolutional Neural Network (DCNN) and exploit the effectiveness of a sparse-driven sub-dictionary learning strategy which has proven to be able to represent both local and global characteristics of the train and probe faces. Results on the publicly available LFW dataset are provided in order to demonstrate the effectiveness of the proposed method.

Keywords: Facial gender recognition · Sparse dictionary learning · Deep features · Soft biometrics

1 Introduction

Human gender recognition is a problem of soft biometrics that has gained a lot of attention in the recent years. In particular the problem of recognizing gender from human faces is typically used in applications like human computer interaction, image retrieval, surveillance, market analysis or for the improvement of traditional biometric recognition systems, moreover, has gained popularity due to large availability of face datasets. In the past few years a lot of research has been carried on, mainly focusing on the problem of gender recognition from faces in a constrained setting (e.g. frontal images, controlled lighting conditions, absence of occlusions). However in order to produce applications that can be used in every day situations (e.g. web pages, webcam, mobile devices) it's necessary to build models which are able to deal with face images in an unconstrained setting; this includes images with occlusions, facial expressions, variation of pose and lighting condition and low resolution images. In the most recent literature, this problems have been addressed using both hand crafted features and Deep Learning and in particular Deep Convolutional Neural Networks (DCNN). In this work we propose a method for the classification of gender from facial images

© Springer Nature Switzerland AG 2020
E. Sekerinski et al. (Eds.): FM 2019 Workshops, LNCS 12232, pp. 162–169, 2020.
https://doi.org/10.1007/978-3-030-54994-7_12

acquired in an unconstrained setting and when only few examples are available for the training phase. The paper is organized as follows: in the next section we give a brief review of the related work and the state of the art. In Sect. 3 a detailed description of the proposed algorithm is provided. In Sect. 4 experimental results of the proposed method on a benchmark dataset are presented with related discussion.

2 Related Work

The problem of gender recognition from face images has been addressed in many works in the recent literature [12], however most of those focus on datasets acquired in a controlled environment, that is out of the scope of the present investigation. To a first approximation, the methods for gender recognition in the wild follow two distinct paths: in one case, a standard classification pipeline is adopted and the dataset is divided in training and test sets. For each image a feature extraction procedure is implemented followed by a machine learning method stated as a binary classification model, eventually preceded by a dimensionality reduction or feature selection module. In this category falls the work of Dago-Casas et al. [7] in which Gabor features are extracted and the classification step is carried out using a linear SVM. In order to deal with the imbalance of classes a weighted SVM model is adopted for classification. Shan [16] used Boosted Locally Binary Pattern as features for the classification with a SVM with RBF kernel, while Tapia et al. [17] adopted a feature selection algorithm based on mutual information and fusion of intensity, shape and texture features as input for an SVM classifier. However, both used a subset of the LFW dataset [10] composed of 4500 males and 2943 females, excluding images that did not contain near frontal faces. The second group of methods concerns those who exploit the deep learning for the classification of gender. In [2], Afifi et al. rely on the combination of isolated and holistic facial features used to train deep convolutional neural networks followed by an AdaBoost-based score fusion to infer the final gender class. In [15] a Deep Multi-Task Learning Framework called HyperFace is proposed; gender recognition is presented as one of the tasks and is carried out by fusion of different DCNN features (each of which has been trained for a specific task) via a multi-task learning algorithm which exploits the synergy among the tasks to boost up the performances.

3 Proposed Method

The proposed method relies on the construction of highly discriminative dictionaries of deep features. Each training (gallery) or test image is first processed using standard image augmentation techniques. For each of those images, the feature characterization from the VGG-Face Net is computed. In the training step only a small subset of images is retained to build the gallery. A sparse-driven sub-dictionary learning strategy is then adopted to build the dictionary. Probe faces are classified via sparse recovery on the learnt dictionary. The overall schema of the model is sketched in Fig. 1. At training stage (red route), each augmented face image (Sect. 3.1) is passed through the VGG-Face DCNN and according to the associated label, the obtained feature may be selected to initialize the corresponding sub-dictionary (male or female) prior to the learning stage (Sect. 3.3). At testing stage (blue route) the probe face image, after augmentation and feature extraction, is classified through sparse recovery on the learnt dictionary (Sect. 3.4).

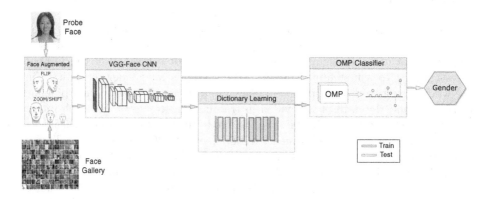

Fig. 1. Pipeline of the model.

3.1   Augmented DCNN Features

In order to build a dictionary we need to find a feature representation that can be suitable for the discrimination of certain characteristics of human faces. In this work we decided to exploit the effectiveness of Deep Convolutional Neural Networks and in particular the popular architecture VGG-Face Net [13]. Given that we set up the problem to have a small sample size approach, it would be impossible to train a DCNN from scratch; conversely we use a pre-trained network as feature extractor by feeding images into the VGG-Face and taking the output of the network truncated at the last fully connected layer. It is worth noticing that original VGG-Face architecture was trained to recognize face identities with no explicit information about the gender. Moreover there is no overlap between the test dataset and the one used to train the VGG-Net. As pointed out in [5], an augmentation stage which relies on standard image transformations (e.g. flipping, random crops, rescalings) is beneficial for the recognition accuracy. Moreover, adopting augmentation techniques delivers some advantages: first by cropping, scaling and flipping faces at different levels we are able to extract both local and global characteristics for the problem at hand. Secondly, this leads to an increase of the number of training images, thus allowing to have a smaller sample size for the gallery. The augmented feature extraction procedure is carried out by applying to each image the same set of transformations (9 crops, 4 scales, 2 flips), thus producing $L = 72$ transformations. For each "augmented" image, a feature characterization is extracted using the VGG-Face Net, which delivers a 4096 dimensional feature vector.

3.2   Sparse Representation of DCNN Features

It is assumed that every feature representation of each augmented face image from class i can be recovered from the linear combination of the training data from that class: $\mathbf{y}_{i,j} = x_{i,1}\mathbf{v}_{i,1} + x_{i,2}\mathbf{v}_{i,2} + ... + x_{i,n_i}\mathbf{v}_{i,n_i}$, where $\mathbf{y}_{i,j} \in \mathbb{R}^m$ is the j-th feature vector for the generic augmented face image and x values are the coefficients corresponding to the training data samples for class i. In other words we assume that the feature representation of a given face image with a certain gender can be approximated by linearly combining the features belonging to other images of the same gender. Following this idea, we can represent every generic feature vector $\mathbf{y}_j$ associated to a new test image as:

$$\mathbf{y}_j = \mathbf{D}\mathbf{x}_j \tag{1}$$

Here $\mathbf{D}$ is commonly referred to as the *dictionary* which is, in general, a matrix where each column is a feature vector associated to a training example. From now on, j index will be omitted unless needed. Assume to select n_i training data samples for the i-th class, where each data sample is represented by a vector $\mathbf{v}_{i,j}$ of m elements. These vectors are then used to construct the columns of matrix A_i:

$$\mathbf{A}_i = [\mathbf{v}_{i,1}, \mathbf{v}_{i,2}, ..., \mathbf{v}_{i,n_i}] \tag{2}$$

In the specific scenario adopted here, we have two classes, so $i \in \{\male, \female\}$, $n_i = q_i * K$ where q_i is the number of images from the i-th class selected to join the gallery (this number is chosen to be reasonably small and equal for both classes, so $q_\male = q_\female$) and $K << L$ is the number of augmented features to keep in the dictionary for every training image. Each feature vector of 4096 elements is reduced dimensionally using Principal Component Analysis (PCA) in order to retain 95% of the variance. The concatenation of the $\mathbf{A}_i$ matrices yields the dictionary:

$$\mathbf{D} = [\mathbf{A}_\male, \mathbf{A}_\female] \in \mathbb{R}^{m \times n} \tag{3}$$

Where m is the result of the dimensionality reduction step and $n = n_\male + n_\female$. The solution of the linear equation (1) boils down to the problem of solving an under determined system given that the matrix $\mathbf{D}$ is a $m \times n$ matrix with $m < n$. The "common way" of solving this kind of systems is by defining an optimization problem of the form: $\min_\mathbf{x} \mathbf{J}(\mathbf{x})$ *s.t.* $\mathbf{y} = \mathbf{D}\mathbf{x}$.

The form of $\mathbf{J}(\mathbf{x})$ governs the kind of solutions we may obtain. If we choose $\mathbf{J}(\mathbf{x})$ to be the squared Euclidean norm $\|\mathbf{x}\|_2^2$, then the solution to the optimization problem can be obtained in closed form by $\mathbf{x} = \mathbf{D}^\dagger \mathbf{y}$ which is the standard least-squares solution, where $\mathbf{D}^\dagger$ is the pseudo-inverse of the matrix $\mathbf{D}$. However this kind of solution is not suitable for the problem of recognition. In fact, we wish to obtain the sparsest solution in order to "select" only those atoms of the matrix $\mathbf{D}$ that correspond to the correct class at hand. In practice, if we have a probe image containing, say, a female face, we (ideally) wish to recover a solution for the vector $\mathbf{x}$ in which the support of $\mathbf{x}$ is non-zero only at the columns of $\mathbf{D}$ that belong to $\mathbf{A}_{\female}$.

In order to yield the sparsest solution for $\mathbf{x}$, an $\mathcal{L}_0$ norm is chosen for $J(x)$: $\min_{\mathbf{x}} \|\mathbf{x}\|_0$ *s.t.* $\mathbf{y} = \mathbf{Dx}$. Moreover, when at most k atoms are sufficient to represent the sample $\mathbf{y}$, the previous problem can be rewritten as in the following:

$$\mathbf{y} = \mathbf{Dx} \quad s.t. \quad \|\mathbf{x}\|_0 \leq k \tag{4}$$

Since data in real applications often contains noise, the model appearing in the previous equation is somewhat unrealistic. Thus, it is reasonable to revise such exact model introducing a noise assumption:

$$\min_{\mathbf{x}} \|\mathbf{Dx} - \mathbf{y}\|_2^2 \quad s.t. \quad \|\mathbf{x}\|_0 \leq k \tag{5}$$

Finding a solution to this optimization problem is an NP-Hard problem, but approximations can be found using approximate algorithms [18].

3.3 Sparse Sub-dictionary Learning

In this section we aim at building class specific sub-dictionaries of the form of Eq. 2 able to capture the sparsity patterns for the gender classification problem. In the vein of [6], this can be achieved by learning such sub-dictionaries to well represent face characteristics through the sparse vectors $\mathbf{x}$. To this end the *sparse dictionary learning problem* can be defined as follows:

$$\min_{\mathbf{X},\mathbf{D}} \|\mathbf{DX} - \mathbf{Y}\|_F^2 \quad s.t. \quad \|\mathbf{x}_u\|_0 \leq k, \quad \|\mathbf{d}_u\|_2 = 1 \tag{6}$$

where $\mathbf{Y} = [\mathbf{y}_1, ..., \mathbf{y}_q] \in \mathbb{R}^{m \times q}$ is the data matrix obtained by concatenating column-wise all the $q = (q_{\male} + q_{\female}) \times L$ training feature vectors and similarly, $\mathbf{X} = [\mathbf{x}_1, ..., \mathbf{x}_q] \in \mathbb{R}^{n \times q}$ is the matrix of the corresponding sparse representations. There is no closed form solution for the problem defined by Eq. 6 in the same way as there isn't for the problem of Eq. 5. However, this can be heuristically solved by adopting the well-established alternating optimization scheme consisting in repeatedly executing these two steps until a stop condition is met:

- *Sparse coding:* solve problem (6) for $\mathbf{X}$, fixing the dictionary $\mathbf{D}$
- *Dictionary update:* solve (6) for each $\mathbf{A}_i$ separately, fixing $\mathbf{X}_i$, then build the new dictionary as in Eq. 3

At the very first step, the dictionary $\mathbf{D}$ may be initialized by randomly selecting training feature vectors; the sparse coding step can then be solved resorting to standard sparse approximation algorithms like [1] or [14] as well as for the dictionary update rule that can be casted into different forms (e.g. [3,8,9]).

In this work we exploit the well established Orthogonal Matching Pursuit (OMP) [14] and K-SVD [3] algorithm for the sparse coding and dictionary update steps, respectively.

3.4   Classification via Sparse Recovery

The problem of recognizing the gender of a new probe subject can be casted to the recovery of the sparsest solution of a linear system. In particular, given a dictionary $\mathbf{D}$, of the form of Eq. 3, and a new probe image I, the augmentation step is computed yielding L transformed images (I_l). The feature extraction is then performed via the VGG-Face DCNN. For each augmented feature vector, the PCA projection computed in the dictionary learning phase is applied, thus obtaining $L = 72$ (9 crops $\times$ 4 scales $\times$ 2 flips) feature vectors $(\mathbf{y}_l)$. For each of the obtained $\mathbf{y}_l$, the sparse recovery on the learnt dictionary $\mathbf{D}$ is computed using OMP, following Eq. 5. The solutions have the following form: $\mathbf{x}_l = \left[\mathbf{x}_{l,\sigma'}; \mathbf{x}_{l,\varphi} \right]$; for each $\mathbf{x}_l$ vector $(l \in \{1, ..., 72\})$, the number of non-zero elements in $\mathbf{x}_{l,\sigma'}$ and $\mathbf{x}_{l,\varphi}$ is counted and classification is performed by majority voting.

4   Experimental Results

The effectiveness of the method is assessed on the Labeled Faces in the Wild (LFW) dataset [10]. This dataset contains more than 13000 images of 5749 different subjects acquired in uncontrolled conditions. The pose, illumination, and expression variations, together with the possible presence of partial occlusions and disguised faces make the gender recognition problem challenging.

The original release of the LFW dataset does not contain gender labels, however Afifi et al. [2] used an estimation method for the gender label based on the first name of the subjects; the obtained labels where then reviewed three times to completely eliminate any incorrect labels. Besides the difficulties outlined in the previous paragraph, the LFW dataset adds another hitch to the gender recognition problem, namely a huge imbalance between the two classes. In particular the dataset is composed by 10268 examples for the male category and only 2966 for the female one. For what concerns the cardinality of the gallery, we conducted 3 experiments using $q_{\sigma'} = q_{\varphi} = [50, 100, 200]$, in order to asses the importance of the size of the gallery on the classification accuracy. In other words, among the 13234 images of the dataset, only, 50, 100 or 200 are in turn selected from the male and female category respectively and used for training, while all the others are used for test. We experimentally set $K = 5$, that is for every gallery image, 5 feature vectors out of the 72 are randomly chosen to join the appropriate subdictionary, prior to the learning phase. All the three experiments are repeated 10 times each. In each trial the set of images to be put in gallery is selected by uniformly sampling 50, 100 or 200 images from both classes. This ensures that in each trial the model potentially has a different set of images, identities, occlusions and ethinicities in gallery, while maintaining the distribution of males and females constant. For each trial a learning and testing phase is executed and the results are averaged. In Table 1 mean results are displayed alongside comparison with state of the art methods on LFW proposed in literature. Precision, recall and F1-measure are reported if available.

As shown in the table, the method proposed here yields comparable results with other models in the literature. Notably, by augmenting the size of the

Table 1. Experiments on LFW dataset and comparisons. For each method we report the accuracy, precision, recall and F1 measure. The cardinality of the two classes is shown in brackets. For the proposed method the number of images per class that compose the gallery is put in curly brackets

Method	Accuracy	Precision	Recall	F1-measure
Our {50} (10268 m 2966f)	91.73	80.57	91.23	85.57
Our {100} (10268 m 2966f)	94.43	84.71	95.10	89.60
Our {200} (10268 m 2966f)	95.13	86.10	94.42	90.06
Gabor+W-SVM (10129m 2959f) [7]	92.96	94.10	89.05	91.50
Boosted LBP+SVM (4500 m 2943f) [16]	94.81	–	–	–
LBP+SVM (4500 m 2943f) [17]	98.01	–	–	–
$AFIF^4$ [2]	95.98	–	–	–
HyperFace [15]	94.00	–	–	–

gallery, both the accuracy and the F1-measure increase, reaching results that sensibly outperform those in [7] in terms of accuracy. Among the other methods outlined, [7] is the method that uses the biggest subset of LFW; in fact, many of the analyzed models act on a subset of the LFW dataset by rejecting images for which face detection fails; we believe that this would lead to exclude from the analysis the most challenging images. Moreover in some works the most numerous class is sub-sampled in order to obtain a class balanced dataset. To the best of our knowledge, the method proposed in [7] is the only one that clearly provides results for the whole LFW dataset on the gender recognition problem.

5   Conclusions

In this work a method for the classification of gender from facial images in the wild is proposed. The method exploits the effectiveness of the sparse-driven sub-dictionary learning strategy on DCNN features formerly presented in [6]. The experimental results show that the proposed method is able to deal with variations in pose, lighting, occlusions, facial expressions and ethnicity while using a training set (gallery) with a small sample size. The results obtained are comparable with the state of the art on the LFW dataset, despite the huge difference in the cardinality of both the training set and the test set used. In future work, we plan to explicitly inquire the impact of specific hurdles (facial expressions, occlusions, etc.) by relying on appropriate datasets [4,11].

References

1. Adamo, A., Grossi, G., Lanzarotti, R., Lin, J.: Sparse decomposition by iterating lipschitzian-type mappings. Theoret. Comput. Sci. **664**, 12–28 (2017)
2. Afifi, M., Abdelhamed, A.: Afif4: Deep gender classification based on adaboost-based fusion of isolated facial features and foggy faces. arXiv preprint arXiv:1706.04277 (2017)

3. Aharon, M., Elad, M., Bruckstein, A., et al.: K-SVD: an algorithm for designing overcomplete dictionaries for sparse representation. IEEE Trans. Signal Process. **54**(11), 4311 (2006)
4. Boccignone, G., Conte, D., Cuculo, V., Lanzarotti, R.: Amhuse: a multimodal dataset for humour sensing. In: Proceedings of the 19th ACM International Conference on Multimodal Interaction, pp. 438–445. ACM (2017)
5. Bodini, M., D'Amelio, A., Grossi, G., Lanzarotti, R., Lin, J.: Single sample face recognition by sparse recovery of deep-learned LDA features. In: Blanc-Talon, J., Helbert, D., Philips, W., Popescu, D., Scheunders, P. (eds.) ACIVS 2018. LNCS, vol. 11182, pp. 297–308. Springer, Cham (2018). https://doi.org/10.1007/978-3-030-01449-0_25
6. Cuculo, V., D'Amelio, A., Grossi, G., Lanzarotti, R., Lin, J.: Robust single-sample face recognition by sparsity-driven sub-dictionary learning using deep features. Sensors **19**(1), 146 (2019)
7. Dago-Casas, P., González-Jiménez, D., Yu, L.L., Alba-Castro, J.L.: Single-and cross-database benchmarks for gender classification under unconstrained settings. In: 2011 IEEE International Conference on Computer Vision Workshops (ICCV Workshops), pp. 2152–2159. IEEE (2011)
8. Engan, K., Aase, S.O., Husoy, J.H.: Method of optimal directions for frame design. In: 1999 IEEE International Conference on Acoustics, Speech, and Signal Processing. Proceedings. ICASSP99 (Cat. No. 99CH36258), vol. 5, pp. 2443–2446. IEEE (1999)
9. Grossi, G., Lanzarotti, R., Lin, J.: Orthogonal procrustes analysis for dictionary learning in sparse linear representation. PLoS ONE **12**(1), e0169663 (2017)
10. Huang, G.B., Mattar, M., Berg, T., Learned-Miller, E.: Labeled faces in the wild: a database for studying face recognition in unconstrained environments. In: Workshop on faces in 'Real-Life' Images: Detection, Alignment and Recognition (2008)
11. Martinez, A.M.: The AR face database. CVC Technical Report 24 (1998)
12. Ng, C.-B., Tay, Y.-H., Goi, B.-M.: A review of facial gender recognition. Pattern Anal. Appl. **18**(4), 739–755 (2015). https://doi.org/10.1007/s10044-015-0499-6
13. Parkhi, O.M., Vedaldi, A., Zisserman, A., et al.: Deep face recognition. In: BMVC, vol. 1, no. 6 (2015)
14. Pati, Y.C., Rezaiifar, R., Krishnaprasad, P.S.: Orthogonal matching pursuit: recursive function approximation with applications to wavelet decomposition. In: Proceedings of 27th Asilomar Conference on Signals, Systems and Computers, pp. 40–44. IEEE (1993)
15. Ranjan, R., Patel, V.M., Chellappa, R.: Hyperface: a deep multi-task learning framework for face detection, landmark localization, pose estimation, and gender recognition. IEEE Trans. Pattern Anal. Mach. Intell. **41**(1), 121–135 (2019)
16. Shan, C.: Learning local binary patterns for gender classification on real-world face images. Pattern Recogn. Lett. **33**(4), 431–437 (2012)
17. Tapia, J.E., Perez, C.A.: Gender classification based on fusion of different spatial scale features selected by mutual information from histogram of LBP, intensity, and shape. IEEE Trans. Inf. Forensics Secur. **8**(3), 488–499 (2013)
18. Zhang, Z., Xu, Y., Yang, J., Li, X., Zhang, D.: A survey of sparse representation: algorithms and applications. IEEE access **3**, 490–530 (2015)

An Instrumented Mobile Language Learning Application for the Analysis of Usability and Learning

Aigerim Aibassova, Antonio Cerone[(⊠)], and Mukhtar Tashkenbayev

Department of Computer Science, Nazarbayev University, Nur-Sultan, Kazakhstan
{aigerim.aibassova,antonio.cerone,mukhtar.tashkenbayev}@nu.edu.kz

Abstract. Mobile applications for language learning (MALL) is a field that is at large dominated by translation-based learning approaches. Moreover, MALL feature a number of common practices that may not effectively address learning or may even increase the number of user errors. In this tool paper, we introduce a language learning application equipped with instrumentation code to collect data about user behavior and use such data in different ways. The most obvious use is to provide statistics and patterns of learning of the users, which can be used by users to adjust their learning approaches and by researchers to study learning processes and attitudes. For the benefit of the user collected data can be also exploited to drive the synthesis of exercises that best suit the user's language level and learning approach and are not likely to cause usability errors.

The main use of the application is, however, as a tool for research purposes. In fact, it is a tool for testing new forms of exercises and their combination on samples of users, thus providing valuable information for research in language learning as well as supporting the software development process of new MALL. Finally, an additional feature of the tool is the conversion of the collected data into a formal description of the user's behaviour to be used for formal verification and validation purposes.

Keywords: Mobile applications · Language learning · Usability · Instrumentation code

1 Introduction

A large variety of mobile applications for language learning (MALL) has been developed during the last years. Such applications are very appealing to the large public and mostly inexpensive, at least in their freeware and shareware versions. Since they can be easily used anytime and anywhere in very short sessions of just a few minutes, they appear to many users as a panacea to learn new languages effortlessly.

Work partly funded by Seed Funding Grant, Project SFG 1447 "Formal Analysis and Verification of Accidents", University of Geneva, Switzerland.

E. Sekerinski et al. (Eds.): FM 2019 Workshops, LNCS 12232, pp. 170–185, 2020.
https://doi.org/10.1007/978-3-030-54994-7_13

However, although the effectiveness of such applications has not been studied systematically, the sparse studies on their usability and learning effectiveness seem to agree on the following issues:

- these applications can only be used as a secondary tool in learning a new language, i.e. the user cannot gain a reasonable fluency in a new language using only MALL tools [10];
- the opportunity to learn more new languages simultaneously using MALL creates its own unique set of challenges, that are not present in traditional learning, e.g. increased rate of confusion of grammar and/or vocabulary among the languages [3];
- the core issue is the translation-based learning approach, which provides little grammatical support [6, 9, 10].

However, since most research is based on self-reported user feedback, it could potentially be unreliable [5].

The main aim of our work is to empirically identify best linguistic and application design approaches that lead to learning effectiveness of language learning applications. For this purpose we have developed a MALL tool that includes instrumentation code to collect data on user behaviour and performance as well as analysis features for the visualisation and exploitation of such data. All examples in this paper refer to an English speaker learning the Kazakh language.

Data exploitation is carried out with two aims. First the way lessons are delivered is adapted to the characteristics and the progresses of the user. This is achieved by the data-driven synthesis and sequentialisation of exercises that best foster the user's language level and learning approach. The aim is to avoid the usability errors that have been found to be a commonplace for the considered user. Second, by collecting data on the effectiveness of exercises and different exercise sequences, in terms of the number and type of errors made by the user, the application will be able to provide valuable information for research and software development purposes. This includes information on usability and learning-related errors. In terms of data exploitation, an important feature of our application is the automatic conversion of collected data into a formal description of the user's behaviour to be used for verification and validation purposes.

In terms of data visualisation, the application can provide statistics and patterns of learning of the users. Some of these forms of visualisation can be observed by the users with the aim of adjusting their learning approaches. Other can be observed by researchers to study learning processes and attitudes.

The rest of the paper is structured as follows. Section 2 illustrates some of the review work carried out to compare various MALL as well as to analyse in depth some of the most popular MALL. Contextually, the section also provides a general background on MALL. Section 3 presents the architecture of our instrumented MALL. Sections 4, 5 and 6 illustrate the implementation components: database, web interface and mobile application, respectively. Section 7 evaluates mobile applications in terms of usability and their functionalities for analysing learning effectiveness. Finally, Sect. 8 presents the current implementation status and concludes the paper, also proposing possible future work.

2   MALL Literature Review

Gangaiamaran and Pasupathi [6] review a wide range of different applications. They partition them into three main categories, depending on the addressed learners:

- *primary learners*, i.e. children 3–11 years old;
- *secondary learners*, i.e. teenagers 12–17 years old;
- *tertiary learners*, i.e. university students and adults.

For each category, the authors select a number of applications that they have considered the best, and list them in a comparative table together with basic information, such as the name and a description.

Although Gangaiamaran and Pasupathi's work is merely descriptive, with little or no exploratory attempts, some general information can be gathered from the tables. Devices running on iOS, such as iPhone and iPad have a larger number of high-quality apps in comparison with Android devices. This is especially noticeable in the primary learners category, which is quite diverse in terms of the study topics. Vocabulary and speaking skills are widely represented in the secondary learners category. However, only one of the considered applications focuses on grammar. The tertiary learners category adds focus on pronunciation, but still seems to lack applications that work on grammar intensively. The obvious conclusion of this work is that listening is the only skill that can be best developed via the use of mobile applications.

Lai and Zheng [8] provide the results of a survey and interview study held in Hong Kong on a sample size of 256 people. All participants were of Chinese descent, and 77% of them were females. The study focuses on the way students use their mobile devices for studying in their free time, and draw a number of important conclusions:

- Mobile devices can significantly improve the personalisation of the study, but are not necessarily as good in terms of *authenticity*, e.g increasing participation in target language communities, and *connectivity*, e.g connection with native speakers or peer learners.
- Social interaction appears to be a big obstacle for both authenticity and connectivity measures, with participants reporting uncertainty when using unknown languages both in personal or public spaces.
- Smart-phones are mostly considered to be leisure devices, unlike laptops or personal computers, but are used effectively to fill in "pockets of time" with activities such as watching short videos, studying during travel, or conversations on-the-go. Therefore, participants did tend to choose specific tools for different tasks.
- Time of device usage for language learning averaged between 1 and 3 hours per week.

Nushi and Eqbali [9] focus on the features of the most popular language application, Duolingo [1]. Duolingo is an application that actively uses the translation aspect of learning, with most exercises focusing on this aspect. Although such an approach can be effective, it actually has a major limitation. It addresses effectively only those people who are fluent in the supposedly known language for which the course is designed. For example, English users have a selection of 16 languages to learn, while Spanish ones have only 6. Duolingo provides five types of exercises for its users:

- *translation* exercises, either writing the translation or choosing words among a given set to compose the translation;
- *matching* exercises, selecting the appropriate figure and associated word to learn for a given word in the known language;
- *pairing* exercises, pairing words from a list of mixed words belonging to the two languages;
- *speaking* exercises, orally repeating a sentence presented in the language to learn;
- *listening* exercises, either writing or composing the sentence heard in the language to learn.

Only the last type of exercise does not involve translation.

One major aspect of the Duolingo is "gamifying" the experience through a system of rewards for completing daily goals, and inclusion of competition via XP points gained when finishing each lesson. Duolingo has social-media features, such as connecting with friends and competing with them, which can be encouraged by receiving notifications when some of the friends scores more points than the user. Notifications are a major part of the application, being sent also when users do not meet their daily goals. Such notification tend to use coercive language.

Nushi and Eqbali point out multiple problems with the application in terms of its teaching techniques, mostly in terms of limitations:

- users are not provided with grammar explanations, and have to figure them out by themselves;
- many words are introduced without information about their meanings or without pronunciation;
- a lot of sample sentences and the synthetic voice that is used to read them can be off-putting and unnatural.

They conclude that the application does not provide a complete learning experience by itself, although it can be helpful to a certain extent.

Nushi and Eqbali conducted a similar study for 50Languages, another popular application in the MALL category [10].

3   System Architecture

Our MALL tool supports the synthesis of exercises and their delivery modalities, as featured by various existing MALL, including the ones considered in Sect. 2. In this way approaches used by distinct MALL can be emulated and compared in terms of their usability and learning effectiveness.

The system we have developed consists of two parts:

- a *front-end* comprising
  - an *Android application*, and
  - a *web interface*.
- a *back-end* comprising a database and the APIs for data collection, storage, data analytics, data presentation, client control and data exploitation.

The interaction between such components is shown by the UML sequence diagram in Fig. 1.

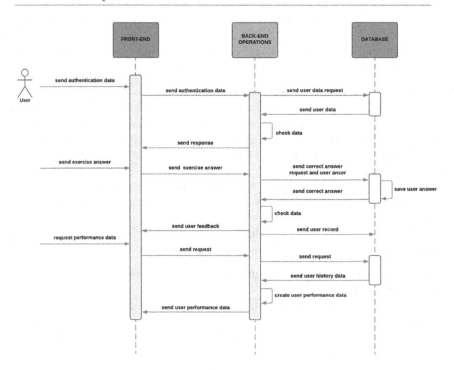

Fig. 1. Application sequence diagram.

The development of the front-end has been carried out using Android NDK for the Android app and HTML/CSS/JS web tools for the web interface. The back-end part of the system comprises a NoSQL Firebase realtime database to store all data necessary for the application.

The Android application serves the purpose of teaching the language as well as recording the data. The web interface is used for designing the delivery of exercises and the display of analytic data. The types of the exercises that are illustrated in this paper are chosen from the most popular language learning applications such as Duolingo and Rosetta Stone. The web interface supports the possibility of choosing from different variants in the exercise presentation. For example, Duolingo matching exercises consist always in the selection of a figure and the associated word to learn to be matched with a given word in the known language. Our application can provide several variants of this exercise. One variant is given in Fig. 5(c), where the choice is between words in the language to learn to be matched with just one figure with no word in the known language. The design of such variants is carried out using the web interface.

Section 4 describes in details the kind of data that can be stored and collected. Sections 4, 5 and 6 highlight the system functionalities, including exercise classification, user functionality and data analytics and exploitation.

4 Database and Analytics

The system uses the Firebase NoSQL realtime database. This choice was motivated by several factors. First, it is easy to integrate Firebase with the Android application. Second, NoSQL provides a more flexible framework, which was crucial during the development process, when there were frequent changes to the specification of the overall system and its functionality. Third, Firebase offers unique tools like authentication and database manipulation through the usage of additional functions. This was essential in developing the research-oriented features of the tool.

The database stores:

- exercises, as shown in Fig. 2(a);
- personal user data;
- user exercise history, as shown in Fig. 2(b);
- analytical data, as shown in Fig. 2(c).

Figure 2(a) contains the information of two exercises of the same type (BS, i.e. fill in the Blank Space as type field) in which the user has to choose the right, among four possible alternatives, to insert in the missing part of a sentence (question). The subject field defines the grammatical topics covered, i.e. the language skills this exercise is aimed at training. Values for this field in the example considered in this paper are V for 'Vocabulary', P for 'Pronouns' and N for 'Number' (i.e. singular vs. plural).

All data used for data analytics are stored in the database in the form of user exercise history. For example, the information in Fig. 2(b), contains: correctness of the given exercise answer (value 0 in the example means that the answer was wrong), subject of the exercise (P for pronouns), type (TS, i.e. Translate Sentence), and time taken to complete the exercise (4848 ms).

This data is then analysed using Firebase cloud functions, which allow developers to host any custom JavaScript functions on Firebase servers. These functions retrieve and transform data to create new statistical data then stored back in the database. Three category of *statistical data* are stored in the database:

Individual user data comprise success/failure rate of exercises (`SFRate`), number of total exercises completed (`allExCount`), number of exercises completed with mistakes (`mistOverall`) and number of mistakes for each subject. An example is given in Fig. 2(c).

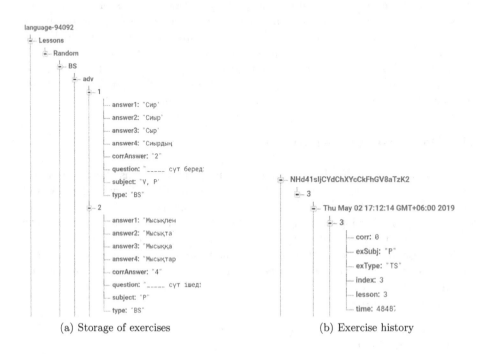

(a) Storage of exercises   (b) Exercise history

(c) User statistics

Fig. 2. Database contents

Population data comprise the same kinds of data as for individual user data, but for the entire population of users.

Exercise data comprise success/failure rate for every type of exercise and for every subject on which the exercises focus.

5   Web Application and Research-Oriented Functionalities

The web application has a limited use for language learners (whom we call users). They may use it just to view their own individual statistics (individual user data).

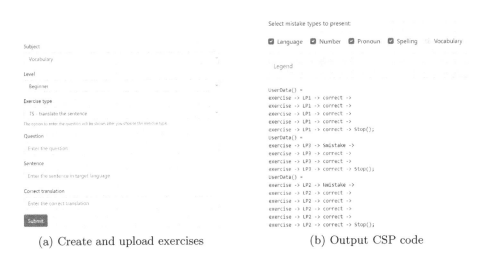

(a) Create and upload exercises   (b) Output CSP code

Fig. 3. Database input ad output

It is instead an essential interface for the researcher. It implements the following functionalities:

- creation and upload of exercises, as shown in Fig. 3(a);
- generation of a formal specification format from the user's exercise history, as shown in Fig. 3(b);
- presentation of statistical data in form of charts and diagrams as shown in Fig. 4;
- set the strategy for delivering the exercises.

Setting appropriate strategies for delivering the exercises is an essential functionality for the researcher. The simplest setting is a *random* sequentialisation of the exercises. The researcher can also manually *control* the presentation and sequentialisation of the exercises

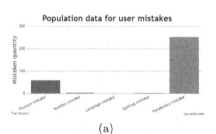

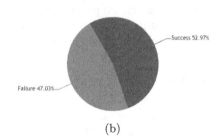

Fig. 4. Visual data display

- by choosing the presentation form, for example whether or not to add the word to learn to the figure in a matching exercise;
- by forcing or preventing a pair of exercise types to occur consecutively.

This first control may be used to empirically evaluate which presentation form may lead to more mistakes in general or with specific users. The second control allows the researcher to emulate approaches used by a specific, existing MALL, in order to compare them, or to analyse the learning process in general terms, for example by identifying interferences between questions.

5.1 Formal Analysis

Our tool may also generate a formal specification from the user's exercise history to be used for formal verification and validation purposes. Following the approach by one of the authors [4], the tool generates *CSP (Communicating Sequential Processes)* [7] code to be used within the *PAT (Process Analysis Toolkit)* [2]. For example, the web page in Fig. 3(b) produces a CSP representation of data on user interaction, in which we consider all errors apart from vocabulary mistakes ('Vocabulary' is the only unchecked type of mistake). The generated CSP code shown in Fig. 3(b) concerns three users: the first does not make any mistake of the selected types, the second makes one 'Spelling' mistake (`Smistake`) and the third a 'Number' mistake (`Nmistake`).

Users perceive, focus and act in different ways while interacting with a MALL. For example, considering Duolingo, in translation exercises to the known language the sentence in the language to learn is presented simultaneously in written and audio modality. In this case, there are two alternative categories of users with two distinct cognitive profiles: focussing on the audio modality and focussing on the written modality. It would be interesting to understand whether, in general, such a user's cognitive profile has a correlation with the level reached by the user in the learning language. Although the user's level can be assessed by our MALL tool, assessing the cognitive profile is challenging. Interviewing user is not helping since focussing on a specific modality is a form of implicit attention, of which the user is normally unaware. Moreover, using special technologies, such as an eye-tracking system, does not provide a definite answer: the user may actually read the sentence while the attention mechanism selects the audio information and discharges the written information, so that only the read information progresses to mental processing.

Both the MALL system and user's cognitive profiles may be formally specified using CSP [4] and composed in parallel to produce a constrained model of the system. The CSP process that fomalises real data on the interaction of user at a specific level in the language to learn (i.e. beginners or advanced), which is automatically generated by our tool, can be then composed with the constrained system model. The formal verification of a temporal logic property that characterises the MALL system functional correctness against such a further constrained CSP model may then be used to validate a research hypothesis such as "A learner at an advanced level in the foreign language always focuses on the hearing modality."

6 Mobile Application

The mobile application runs on Android NDK and implements different lesson functionalities, several types of exercises and data collection features. Although the full plan is to cover written sentence construction and comprehension, listening comprehension and spoken sentence construction, the current implementation does not include any audio functionalities. Therefore lessons and exercises are restricted to the written form.

Researchers are registered through the system setting and have special access rights, which allow them to use the full functionality of the web interface. Users, instead, have to register through the authentication page of the mobile application and they can only access their own individual statistical data using the web interface. Researchers may also register as users through the mobile interface.

When users first register in the system, using their email addresses, a unique token and entry in the database are created to be used in order to match the data that is being sent by the application from this specific account. Authentication through Firebase creates learner profiles that are used to track their progress, using encrypted email-password pairs. At registration, users are also asked to self-rate themselves in the language they intend to learn. This rating is recorded in the system and used to assign a beginner, intermediate or advanced level to the user, in order to present the user with exercises appropriate for that level.

Depending on the setting, *random* or *controlled*, defined by the researcher as explained in Sect. 5, *lessons* can be

adaptive users are presented with exercises appropriate for their levels, which are chosen at random from the pool in the database, and their performance is tracked and contributes to change their ratings and, as a result, their levels;

controlled the exercise sequences are controlled by the researcher, but the user's performance does not affect rating and level.

The current implementation of our tool features one kind of *learning practice*

word learning in which the user is presented with a number of pictures of objects or a concept representations together the words that express them in the language to learn (grouped in lessons characterised by topics of increasing difficulties), as shown in Fig. 5(b) where the Kazakh word means 'mother';

and the following kinds of *exercises*:

word matching whose purpose is to recall the words learned previously, reinforce them and verify whether the user knows them, as shown in Fig. 5(c);
filling in the blank space whose purpose is to recall words in context;
sentence translation whose purpose is to test the user's ability to build full sentences and which may be skipped if the user does not feel confident.

Learning practice and exercises are normally combined together in lessons but, for research purposes, may also be used as stand-alone.

All lesson practices and exercises are stored in the database as the user progresses. Information on user performance is recorded by the application, and is stored in the database following the structure shown in Fig. 2(b). The application requires internet connection to function properly.

7 Evaluation

The tool was evaluated in terms of usability and in terms of its functionalities for analysing learning effectiveness. We have evaluated our application using convenience samples of university students as users.

7.1 Usability

The sample consisted of 15 subjects with the following levels in Kazakh language: 6 native/advanced speakers, 3 intermediate level speakers, and 6 beginner level speakers. The users were asked to test the application for around 10 min, going through most of the functionalities, starting from the registration process and ending with language lessons. The whole process was monitored and the interview process was carried out in an informal manner with the addition of some guiding questions. Moreover, the respondents were given a chance to request clarifications about questions.

All subjects in the sample underwent *adaptive lessons*, finished multiple lessons, and were further interviewed by one of the researchers. The interview process consisted of ranking questions and a free feedback part. Ranking questions aimed at evaluating the application's usability, intuitiveness, and overall design on a scale from 1 to 10. Questions were as follows:

1. How easy it is for you to use the language learning application?
2. Does the visual presentation of the application have any distracting details that, while not confusing you, might create a distraction?
3. How do you rate the visual appeal of the application?

Users found the application to be both usable and useful. Average ratings for the three questions were 8.27, 8.67 and 7.00, respectively. Standard deviations were 0.80, 1.29 and 1.07, respectively.

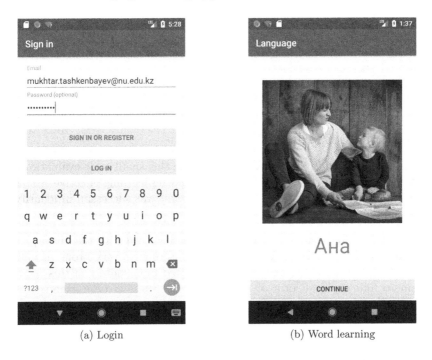

(a) Login   (b) Word learning

(c) Matching exercise   (d) Translation exercise

Fig. 5. Mobile application screenshots

Common critiques from the feedback part included:

- loading time issues and minor bugs;
- repeated and easy questions;
- poor exercise input checking, e.g. accepting only one of the possible correct answers in translation exercises.

7.2 Learning Effectiveness

The sample consisted of 20 subjects. Purpose of this small scale evaluation was to test the approach of using the tool for evaluating learning effectiveness. This evaluation made use of *controlled lessons*. The test was successful in identifying some common patterns in the user's behaviour:

1. immediately after matching the correct singular word with the given picture (vocabulary-type exercise, as in Fig. 6(a)), users were very prone to make a mistake in the matching exercise that followed immediately, if this required them to find a plural form of the same word (number-type exercise, as in Fig. 6(b)).
2. translation exercises have gathered significantly more mistakes than any other type of exercise;

(a) Vocabulary

(b) Plural

Fig. 6. Matching exercises

3. after learning a new word through a learning practice, some users still made mistakes while testing the same word.

We can interpret such common patterns respectively as follows:

1. users tended to click on the singular form as soon as they saw it, without actually trying to discern the difference between exercises.
2. translation exercises should be presented only when the learner has acquired sufficient confidence, with the granted option of skipping the exercise, without this affecting the performance score;
3. users did not focus enough during learning practice and this shows that learning practice needs to be more engaging.

8   Conclusion and Future Work

We have introduced a tool capable to emulate a variety of MALL approaches, collect data on the user interaction and performance, present the collected data in a visual format, convert such data into a formal representation to be used in formal analysis, and exploit the data to drive the synthesis and sequentialisation of exercises. The tool is not just another MALL. In fact, it is not intended for teaching languages but, instead, as a research tool. In this respect, it can emulate approaches used by distinct MALL in order to compare their learning effectiveness.

More generally, the tool may contribute to learning theory through the analysis of learning processes. In Sect. 5.1 we have seen how the tool may be used to validate a research hypothesis on cognitive approaches to learning. Finally, in Sect. 7.2 we have illustrated the use of the tool to identify interferences between questions.

In the current implementation of the system

- audio functionalities are not included and lessons and exercises are restricted to the written form;
- adaptive lessons are limited to changing the user's rating and levels.

Concerning the implementation, our proposals for future work in the *short term* include:

1. add audio functionalities in order to analyse interference between audio and written presentation either when they are merged through a multimodal presentation or when they occur in sequence;
2. perform the analysis proposed at Item 1 using a formal methods approach as the one described in the previous work of one of the authors [4];
3. exploit the collected data on the user's performance not only to adapt the delivered exercises to the user's rating and level but also to automatically adjust the presentation of the exercises and their sequentialisation in such a way to prevent the errors that are a commonplace for that user and maximise learning effectiveness.

The future work proposed at Item 3 involves the definition of appropriate measures to characterise learning effectiveness. This is a non-trivial task due to the difficulty in detecting the underlying causes of user errors. For instance, if a users is prone to do mistakes with a specific exercise, this may be due either to the fact that the user is weak in the subject of that exercise or that the exercise is inappropriate for the user's attitude or learning approach. In the former case learning effectiveness may improve by intensifying the use of that exercise. In the latter case, instead, removing that exercise would be the best strategy.

If we consider again the sequence of the two exercises in Fig. 6(a) and 6(b), the error might be actually due to the fact that the user has not masterised the rule to form the plural of nouns. In our testing, the recurrence of such a mistake was frequent only when the two exercises were in a sequence. This suggests that the error was caused by an interference between the two exercises. Although this is likely to be true in most cases, such a sequence of exercises would actually be beneficial during the stage when the user has not masterised the formation of plural yet. In such a situation, the automatic control of the sequentialisation could force the sequentialsation during the learning phase of plural formation and could prevent it during the reinforcement phase. In this context, the use of our MALL tool would be twofold: first to realise the automatic control described above, then to collect and analyse data on the effectiveness of such a strategy.

Currently the database is populated only with lessons and exercises for teaching the Kazakh language with the Cyrilic writing systems to English speakers. Considering other language is just a matter of further populating the database. This is obviously a time-consuming task, which requires a lot of human resources and high expertise in linguistic, languages and language learning. This future work is therefore part of our *long term* plans.

Finally, a more extensive evaluation of the system is needed, both in terms of usability and learning effectiveness. In particular, it is essential to test our MALL tool on a large number of real users of various demographic groups.

References

1. Duolingo. https://www.duolingo.com
2. PAT: Process Analysis Toolkit. pat.comp.nus.edu.sg
3. Ahmed, H.B.E.: Duolingo as a bilingual learning app: a case study. Arab World English J. **7**(2), 256–267 (2016)
4. Cerone, A., Zhexenbayeva, A.: Using formal methods to validate research hypotheses: the duolingo case study. In: Mazzara, M., Ober, I., Salaün, G. (eds.) STAF 2018. LNCS, vol. 11176, pp. 163–170. Springer, Cham (2018). https://doi.org/10.1007/978-3-030-04771-9_13
5. Gafni, R., Achituv, D.B., Rahmani, G.: Learning foreign languages using mobile applications. J. Inf. Technol. Educ. Res. **16**, 301–317 (2017)
6. Gangaiamaran, R., Pasupathi, M.: Review on use of mobile apps for language learning. Int. J. Appl. Eng. Res. **12**(21), 11242–11251 (2017)
7. Hoare, C.A.R.: Communication Sequential Processes. Prentice All Int., Upper Saddle River (2004)

8. Lai, C., Zheng, D.: Self-directed use of mobile devices for language learning beyond the classroom. ReCALL **30**(3), 299–318 (2017)
9. Nushi, M., Eqbali, M.H.: Duolingo: a mobile application to assist second language learning. Teach. English Technol. **17**(1), 89–98 (2017)
10. Nushi, M., Eqbali, M.H.: 50languages: a mobile language learning application. Teach. English Technol. **18**(1), 93–104 (2018)

Analysis and Visualization of Performance Indicators in University Admission Tests

Michela Natilli[1,2], Daniele Fadda[1,2], Salvatore Rinzivillo[2(✉)], Dino Pedreschi[1], and Federica Licari[3]

[1] Computer Science Department, University of Pisa, Pisa, Italy
{michela.natilli,daniele.fadda,dino.pedreschi}@di.unipi.it
[2] KDDLab, ISTI-CNR Pisa, Pisa, Italy
{michela.natilli,daniele.fadda,salvatore.rinzivillo}@isti.cnr.it
[3] CISIA - Consorzio Interuniversitario Sistemi Integrati per l'Accesso, Pisa, Italy
federica.licari@cisiaonline.it

Abstract. This paper presents an analytical platform for evaluation of the performance and anomaly detection of tests for admission to public universities in Italy. Each test is personalized for each student and is composed of a series of questions, classified on different domains (e.g. maths, science, logic, etc.). Since each test is unique for composition, it is crucial to guarantee a similar level of difficulty for all the tests in a session. For this reason, to each question, it is assigned a level of difficulty from a domain expert. Thus, the general difficultness of a test depends on the correct classification of each item. We propose two approaches to detect outliers. A visualization-based approach using dynamic filter and responsive visual widgets. A data mining approach to evaluate the performance of the different questions for five years. We used clustering to group the questions according to a set of performance indicators to provide labeling of the data-driven level of difficulty. The measured level is compared with the *a priori* assigned by experts. The misclassifications are then highlighted to the expert, who will be able to refine the question or the classification. Sequential pattern mining is used to check if biases are present in the composition of the tests and their performance. This analysis is meant to exclude overlaps or direct dependencies among questions. Analyzing co-occurrences we are able to state that the composition of each test is fair and uniform for all the students, even on several sessions. The analytical results are presented to the expert through a visual web application that loads the analytical data and indicators and composes an interactive dashboard. The user may explore the patterns and models extracted by filtering and changing thresholds and analytical parameters.

Keywords: Performance evaluation · University entrance tests · Cluster analysis

E. Sekerinski et al. (Eds.): FM 2019 Workshops, LNCS 12232, pp. 186–199, 2020.
https://doi.org/10.1007/978-3-030-54994-7_14

1   Introduction

In this paper we present an analytical process to explore the performances of questions included in the tests submitted to the students applying to several Italian Universities.

We evaluate the performance of each question based on the outcomes of the answers it received within the tests. From these performances we want to highlight outliers and anomalies. We followed two approaches:

- **Visualization-based approach**:
    - Analysis of the distributions of the proportion of right answers for each question in relation to the level of difficulty provided by the domain experts.
    - Analysis of the joint distributions of the proportions of correct, wrong and not given answers in relation to the corresponding difficulty level.
- **Data-mining approach**:
    - Cluster analysis on performance indicators, compared with the rule-based approach.
    - Market basket analysis on co-occurrences of questions within the tests

The analytical tasks listed above were implemented and integrated within a system that supports the users in the exploration of the performance of each question and the detection of anomalous performances of questions. We have designed a process that, starting from every single answer to each question in each test, evaluate a series of indicators (described in Sect. 4.2), performs unsupervised analysis on such aggregations, and visualizes the results on a user-friendly web-based dashboard. The analyst can browse the analytical results by filtering on different dimensions: year, period of the year, topic of the test, discipline of the test. Items classified as anomalies are highlighted and flagged, and they can also be downloaded as *.csv* file for external analysis.

The data is provided by CISIA[1] (Consorzio Interuniversitario Sistemi Integrati per l'Accesso), a non-profit consortium formed by public universities. Currently, CISIA consortium counts 45 Universities and the Conferences of Engineering, Architecture and Sciences, CUIA - the Italian University Architecture Conference, the CopI - Conference for Engineering and Con.Scienze - National Conference of Presidents and Structure Directors University of Science and Technology.

The Consortium is open to the participation of all Italian universities; among the different statutory purposes, the main is to organize and coordinate the orientation activities for the access to the universities. CISIA organizes and provides access to admittance entry tests for students in many universities of the Consortium. For those faculties with a restricted number of admitted students, these tests are used as selection and ranking tools. These tests have two main purposes:

---

[1] http://www.cisiaonline.it.

- for students enrolling the test, they provide a self-assessment of their preparation and aptitude to undertake the chosen discipline of studies;
- for the faculties and departments, the tests give a view of the actual skills and preparation of the students, allowing the management to prepare specific orientation and integrative training activities.

CISIA tests are currently available for six areas: Engineering, Economics, Pharmacy, Sciences, Humanities, and Agriculture.

The analytical tool is already deployed within CISIA consortium and it improved the inspection on the questions by enabling new detection mechanism, both the visual-based and the data-driven one.

2   Related Work

The measurement and assessment of individual or collective performances are the starting steps to improve the quality of offered services, to enhance professional skills, to assess responsibility for results, integrity and transparency of the actions carried out.

Proper assessment requires a variety of methods; no single approach can test the whole of the performance. Designing assessment programs and selecting the best instruments for each purpose is not easy [1].

Many approaches can be used to design methods for evaluating performance and detecting anomalies [2], starting from *a-priori* defined indicators or using a completely data-driven approach, or a combination of the two. The advantage of the latter is that using one or more indicators it is possible to:

- Overcome personal judgment on measuring the performance
- Create a system that allows confrontation over time
- Construct a system that scales on large numbers

The measures and the approaches to measure performance are, obviously, strictly related to the field of evaluation: when evaluating scientific productivity the focus is on the metric $h - index$ also with all the limitation that this index has [3] or when measuring performance in sports (like soccer) measures like Pass Shot Value (PSV) or PlayeRank [4] have been used.

In the field of performance evaluation using tests, the focus has mainly been on the results of the test (students for an exam, Student Test Scores to Measure Teacher Performance [5]), but for those who build the tools there is the need to evaluate how the test performs or better how the single items composing the test perform.

In this work, we propose two approaches for identifying anomalies in the behaviors of the different items composing a test.

The first method (the visualization-based approach) has been used as a starting point using simple proportions, and to give also to a non-expert audience the possibility to immediately understand the results. As stated in [6] "The basic idea of visual data exploration is to present the data in some visual form, allowing the human to get insight into the data, draw conclusions, and directly interact with the data". The advantage of this technique is to create a meaningful abstraction of the data, rather than trying to visualize it all at once [7].

The second method, a data-driven approach, using clustering analysis has been chosen to group data into classes with very similar characteristics (i.e. performances), with the scope of identifying homogeneous groups of questions and pinpointing groups with anomalous behavior. An implementation of the k-means algorithm (optimized for one-dimensional space) has been chosen given its ability to group items with the same performance in homogeneous groups [8,9,16].

At the same time, the possibility of having combinations of questions with the same outcome was tested using a market basket analysis algorithm. The intuition behind this choice is that if two or more questions compare together and have the same result (right, wrong or not answered question), they probably measure the same "skill": the extraction of these rules can also help in identifying strange behaviors in the questions. Generally, this algorithm is mainly used for transactional data (i.e. the supermarket register) to identify set(s) of items purchased together [10], but it can be successfully used also on different kind of data (i.e. crash data [11]).

The results deriving from these analyzes have all been reported on a visual dashboard, to obtain an exhaustive and quick overview of the results obtained, simplify the interpretative work by parts of the domain experts and allow comparisons between different areas and different years. Through visualization, in fact, the results of data processing are made more accessible, straightforward, and user-friendly [12]. The choice of a dashboard is supported by the fact that, as stated in [13], "compared to visualization modalities for presentation and exploration, dashboards bring together challenges of at-a-glance reading, coordinated views, tracking data and both private and shared awareness". Furthermore, the integration of data mining and information visualization techniques has received a lot of attention, given its ability to filter and extract valuable patterns and to provide a better understanding of the final results [14].

3   Problem Statement

CISIA Online Test (acronym TOLC) is a tool for orientation and assessment of the knowledge required for access to the Study Programs of Italian Universities, which can be used to select students for access. TOLC is an individual test, different from student to student, automatically composed for each student by a software. The software follows a set of *rules* (defined *a priori* by CISIA experts) to guarantee that all the tests generated are equivalent in terms of the level of difficulty. This means that in each TOLC there are a series of questions on different subjects with different level of difficulty. Thus it is crucial to have tests with comparable difficulties. CISIA has developed a methodology to provide a human-based classification of difficulty levels for each question and they exploit such labeling to compose equivalent individual tests.

The objective of our system is to provide an inspection platform where analysts may evaluate the labeling and the behavior of each question. The performance of a question is the outcomes of the answers of the students in terms of the number of correct or wrong answers. When a student has doubts for a specific question, she can decide to provide no solution: a missing answer has a small penalty in the final grade, but there is a higher penalty in case of a wrong answer.

The basic strategy consists in the exploitation of the *a priori* level of difficulty of a question to define an expected performance: questions classified as "easy" should have a high proportion of right answers, while questions labeled as "difficult" should have a higher proportion of wrong answers.

The analytical system should automatically ingest the answers of the students and evaluate the classification of the level of difficulty of each question. The results of this analysis are made available with a visual interface to explore the performances of every single question during the time.

4   Analytical Process

The analytical process is organized in two macro steps (see Fig. 1): first, data is collected, aggregated and analyzed; secondly, the results are organized and optimized for fast interaction and visualization.

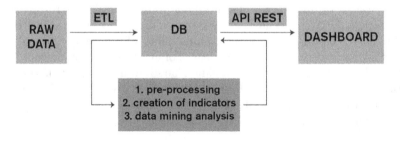

Fig. 1. The schema of the process.

4.1   Data Loading and Indicators Extraction

The ETL (Extraction, Transformation, Load) phase is designed to incrementally update the performance indicators described below. Starting from the raw data (first box in Fig. 1), the answers to each question in each test are collected and saved in a "working database". These data do not arrive in real-time since CISIA performs internal checks and assessment. Regularly, we can consider an update every week. The results of the tests are saved into a working area within a DBMS, where the analytical process is executed.

In analyzing the data, the robustness of the calculated indicators is taken into account. For instance, if a new question appears, results in terms of performance are calculated (and shown) only if the new question was administered a sufficient number of times.

At the moment of writing, data are related to the last six years (2014–2018). Table 1 reports the number of tests taken by students in different disciplines.

Table 1. Number of tests administered online.

	2014	2015	2016	2017	2018
Biology					7,259
Economics	5,144	10,382	14,365	21,463	33,184
Pharmacy				3,871	6,706
Engineering	16,526	30,048	35,981	51,013	55,449
Science					13,748

4.2 Performance Indicators

To have a data-driven criterion to measure the performance of every single question, we defined a series of indicators that summarized the performance of the questions in terms of correct, incorrect and not given answers. To represent the three possible outcomes for each question, we defined a new attribute, namely $R3$, which get values -1, 1, or 0, respectively for a wrong answer, a right answer, a not-given answer. From this attribute, we derive three new indicators: PR, the proportion of correct answers[2]; PW, the proportion of wrong answers[3]; PNA, the proportion of not answered questions[4]. The attributes have been calculated for each year and for each type of TOLC (e.g. engineering, economics, etc.).

We also define a series of derivative indicator, computed based on the previous ones. The first indicator *Perf1* provides a measure of the performance of the answers given, ignoring the cases when no answer was given.

$$Perf1 = \frac{sum(R3)}{count(R3 = -1) + count(R3 = 1)}$$

The second performance indicator *Perf2*, instead, takes into account the answers not given. This value is always less than or equal to *Perf1*.

$$Perf2 = \frac{sum(R3)}{count(R3)}$$

---

[2] $PR = count(R3 = 1)/count(R3)$.
[3] $PW = count(R3 = -1)/count(R3)$.
[4] $PNA = count(R3 = 0)/count(R3)$.

By introducing a simplification of the R3 attribute into two levels (naming it R2, where $R2 = 1$ if the answer is correct, while $R2 = 0$ if the answer is wrong or not given) it is possible to obtain an additional performance indicator.

$$PerfR2 = \frac{sum(R2)}{count(R2)}$$

The last performance indicator gives equal weight both to wrong and to not given answer, namely zero.

5   Performance Evaluation Through Anomaly Detection

Two different methods have been developed to highlight anomalous performance behaviors. The first method exploits visualization technique to compare outliers with the expected performance of questions on the basis of the level of difficulty, such that, easy questions should have a more significant proportion of right answers, while a higher level of wrong answers is expected for difficult questions. The second method uses data mining methods to identify groups of questions with similar performance and then compare these with the classification applied by the experts. In both approaches, the objective is to highlight those question whose classification needs to be revised.

5.1   Visualization-Based Anomaly Detection

The visual approach we propose is based on the visualization of the expected behavior of each question based on the level of difficulty. We implemented two possible strategies.

With the first one, in collaboration with the domain experts, we have identified a set of intervals for each level of difficulty. Figure 2 shows the values of PR for which an anomalous behavior should be highlighted. For example, an easy question with a low value of PR should be inspected to check if it should be classified as more difficult.

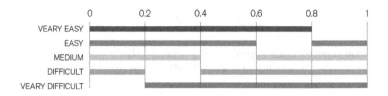

Fig. 2. Anomaly detection using the values of the PR indicator

This approach has a significant limitation: it considers only the PR indicator. However, difficult questions may produce two different behaviors: a high proportion of wrong answers and not-answers.

To overcome this problem, we introduce second strategy, a visualization based on *Ternary Plots*. This visualization allows a very effective representation of the behavior of each question, with a concurrent comparison of three indicators. This is a visual chart used mainly in geology to present proportions of soils or terrains.

This visualization is based on visual space determined by three axes: we map our indicators (PW, PR, PNA) to each axis. The triangle that is defined by these axes contains those points whose sum of values is constant (in our case 1). Each attribute interval is represented on one side of the triangle. Figure 3(a) shows an example of a visual representation of a set of questions. Each point is located accordingly to its indicator values and its color represents the level of difficulty assigned *a priori*. The vertexes of the triangle are annotated with the label of the three indicators: those points closer to one vertex have a high value of the corresponding indicator. In details:

- the attribute PR decreases from the top vertex (value=1) in the direction that goes from that vertex to the bottom left corner (value=0);
- the attribute PW decreases from the lower-left corner (value=1) in the direction that goes from that vertex to the opposite side, the lower right corner (value=0);
- the attribute PNA decreases from the bottom right corner (value=1) in the direction that goes from that vertex to the top vertex.

In the example in Fig. 3(a), we can notice a dark red point (meaning a difficult question) with a very high proportion of right answers (it is close to vertex PR): this question should be checked to verify the correct classification.

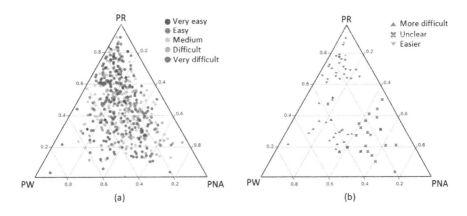

Fig. 3. Joint distribution of PR, PW and PNA (a) and anomaly detection (b) using a ternary plot

Each vertex, therefore, corresponds to the value 1 of a variable and the 0 of the other variables. To know the values of "Correct", "Wrong" and "Not given" relating to any point of the ternary diagram, it is necessary to draw from this point 3 lines that are parallel to the 3 sides of the triangle: the intersections of these lines with the sides of the triangle provide the values sought for each of the three variables, as shown in Fig. 4.

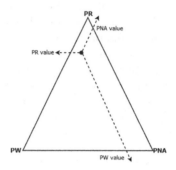

Fig. 4. Reading a ternary plot

When the number of questions is high, it may be difficult to identify anomalous points based on the color and position. Thus, we have developed a filter interface to visually highlight relevant points on the basis of a set of rules. These rules take into account the distribution of the three indicators for all the questions. For example, Fig. 3(b) shows an example of detection that follows the following rules:

1. If the question was classified as "very easy" or "easy" and the value of the PW (wrong) is greater than the value corresponding to 75th percentile of the distribution of the PW (right-tail of the distribution) then the question could be more difficult;
2. If the question was classified as "very easy" or "easy" and the value of the PNA is greater than the value corresponding to the 75th percentile of the distribution of the PNAs (right-tail of distribution) then the question may be unclear;
3. If the application was classified as "very difficult" or "difficult" and the PR value is greater than the value corresponding to the 75th percentile of the PR distribution (right-tail distribution) then the question could be easier

The visual interface allows to dynamically change the value of the percentile threshold (as described in details in Sect. 7). The result of the filter is represented visually with the same color schema (mapping the level of difficulty) and with a new set of symbols:

   ↑ up-arrow: the question probably should be classified as more difficult;
   ↓ down-arrow: the question probably should be classified as more easier;
   × cross: the question is not very clear.

5.2   Data Mining Anomaly Detection

In this section, we present a data-driven approach to explore the whole dataset of answers, without relying on the definition of thresholds from the analysts or domain experts.

Cluster Analysis. We exploit cluster analysis to group questions with similar performance into clusters. We adopt *k-means* [15], a partitioning cluster algorithm that allows subdividing a set of objects into k groups based on their attributes. A centroid or midpoint identify each cluster. The algorithm follows an iterative procedure. Initially, it creates k partitions and assigns the entry points to each partition either randomly or using some heuristic information. Then calculate the centroid of each group. It then constructs a new partition by associating each entry point with the cluster whose centroid is closest to it. Then the centroids for the new clusters are recalculated and so on until the algorithm converges. Each question within the clustering is represented as a combination of the *Perf* indicators defined in Sect. 4.2. Given the possibility to the analyst to focus on one of the indicators at a time, we used an optimized implementation of *k-means* for uni-dimensional points: *ck-means* [16]. This algorithm performs better in the case in which each object has a single attribute[5]. We tested both algorithms and we stated that their performances are comparable for our case study. In our final implementation we adopted the *ck-means* algorithm. The k was chosen using the elbow method: a series of clustering runs on the dataset for a range of values of k (k from 1 to 20), and for each value of k the sum of squared errors (SSE) was calculated. According to the SSE distribution, we set $k = 5$. This number of clustering also allows an indirect comparison with the level of difficulties of the questions (see Sect. 7 for an example). The basic idea here it that grouping data data into classes with very similar characteristics (i.e. performances) allows the identification of similar groups of questions and permits to pinpoint groups with anomalous behavior.

Pattern Mining Analysis. Pattern mining analysis is a technique of analysis used primarily in marketing that analyzes the buying habits of customers in retail sales, finding associations on different products purchased, to obtain rules of association between products purchased together. In our domain, we use frequent items analysis [10] to verify how frequently questions with similar behavior in terms of answers occur together. We want to check if in the composition of each test there is bias and two different questions repeatedly occur in many tests.

In the proposed application, a test can be seen as a transaction (a basket of goods) composed of many items (questions) and it would be analyzed to search if a particular combination tends to co-exist. We are interested only in the extraction of the frequent itemsets and in the verification that their support is below a statistical expected probability of co-occurrence. From the analysis,

---

[5] We used the Python implementation published in https://github.com/llimllib/ckmeans.

we assessed that there no itemset overly represented. Thus the construction of the tests (in terms of the composition of questions) is done in a fair manner.

6   Visual Dashboard

All the analytical processes were organized into a visual dashboard, where the domain experts can formulate a hypothesis and dynamically explore the dataset through a set of filters, to be able to identify anomalies in the performance of the questions. The filter allows selecting specific subdimensions according to year, the period of the year, disciplines, topics. Figure 5 shows a schematic organization of the section with a description of the actual web application.

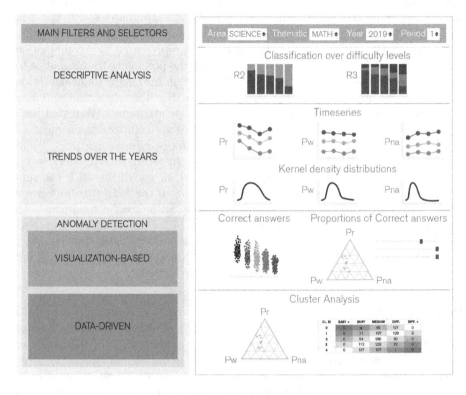

Fig. 5. The web-page schema.

The filters are organized in the top of the window and they are always visible to show the current active selection. A first section presents the various distribution of the data (performance indicators, distributions over year, trends of indicators, etc.)

The second part of the dashboard presents the interface for the outlier analysis, using both the visualization-based approach or the data-driven approach.

The data-driven approach contains a cross-table to compare the results from the clustering analysis with the labels assigned *a priori* to the questions: in the diagonal of the matrix there are the questions that have a behavior similar to the expected one, while in the corners of the matrix the anomalies are present. It is possible to select, from a drop-down menu, the performance indicator to be used for the cluster analysis. For both sections, a selection of a set of outliers also produces an analytical table with all the attributes of the selected questions, with the possibility to download a *.csv* table for further investigations.

7   Test Case

We describe here a typical analytical task that can be performed on the platform. We omit the discussion of the visual exploration of the distributions and trends and focus on the outlier detection task.

The second section of the dashboard has two tools dedicated to this analysis: a visual-based approach and a cluster-based method. We present here a case study using both methods. Figure 6 shows the resulting ternary plots after the commit of a filter. On the right, we selected three percentile thresholds for PR, PW, and PNA: the value of the 75th percentile of PR is used as a threshold to select those on the right side of the distribution. Since these questions are classified as easy (green color of the markers) and they have a large proportion of correct answers, the system suggests to check these questions to increase their level of difficulty. In the example, the question with ID 1234 (the id as been obfuscated to protect the original data, the indicators are real) has a PR value very low: this question should be classified as difficult, for example.

We repeat a similar analysis using cluster analysis. Figure 6 (left) shows the result of the selection of the cell in the cross table corresponding to cluster *0* and level of difficulty *very easy*. The selection highlight six questions. Among these six questions, there is the same question with ID 1234 that we discovered before.

It worth noting how the two approaches yield to different (but comparable) results. By comparing the two groups of points in the two charts, there is a subset of questions (4 questions in the central part of each ternary plot) that are in common in the two selections, but there are different questions in the remaining parts of the two charts. This is due to the fact that the first method (on the right) takes into account only the PR indicator, while the other method (on the left) exploit the *Perf2* indicator.

The choice between the two methods depends on the specific need of the experts: using the visual approach the performance of a question is seen through an index at a time (PR, PW or PNA) while, using cluster analysis, we work on a composite indicator that takes into account the three proportions together.

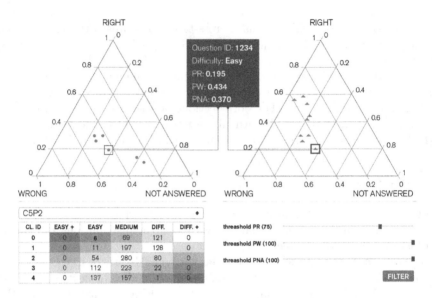

Fig. 6. An example of outlier detection using cluster analysis (left) and visualization-based approach (right).

8　Conclusion

In this paper we presented an analytical platform to evaluate the performance and anomaly detection of tests for admission to public universities in Italy. The process of analysis followed two different approaches: a visualization-based approach, where a set of rules provided by the domain experts are represented to create a visual highlight of candidate outliers; a data-driven approach where a clustering-based method is used to partition the set of questions into groups to be compared with the *a priori* classification of the level of difficulties.

The analytical results are made available to the users through a dynamic dashboard, where the user may set a filter to explore subdimension of the data, accordingly to the values of the year, the period of the year, the discipline and the topic.

The analytical tool is already deployed within CISIA consortium and it improved the inspection on the questions by enabling new detection mechanism, both the visual-based and the data-driven one. The system is being extended with specific analysis on the subtopics (for example considering "physics of fluid" rather than the general topic "physics").

References

1. Schuwirth, L.W., van der Vleuten, C.P.: How to design a useful test: the principles of assessment. In: Understanding Medical Education: Evidence, Theory, and Practice, pp. 275–289 (2018)

2. Agrawal, S., Agrawal, J.: Survey on anomaly detection using data mining techniques. Procedia Comput. Sci. **60**, 708–713 (2015)
3. Dorogovtsev, S., Mendes, J.F.: Ranking scientists. Nat. Phys. **11**, 882–883 (2015). 10.1038
4. Pappalardo, L., Cintia, P., Ferragina, P., Massucco, E., Pedreschi, D., Giannotti, F.: PlayeRank: data-driven performance evaluation and player ranking in soccer via a machine learning approach (2018)
5. Ballou, D., Springer, M.G.: Using student test scores to measure teacher performance: some problems in the design and implementation of evaluation systems. Educ. Res. **44**(2), 77–86 (2015)
6. Keim, D.A.: Information visualization and visual data mining. IEEE Trans. Visual Comput. Graphics **8**(1), 1–8 (2002)
7. Paul, C.L., Rohrer, R., Nebesh, B.: A "Design First" approach to visualization innovation. IEEE Comput. Graphics Appl. **35**(1), 12–18 (2015)
8. Sarker, A., Shamim, S.M., Zama, M.S., Rahman, M.M.: Employee's performance analysis and prediction using K-means clustering & decision tree algorithm. Global J. Comput. Sci. Technol. (2018)
9. Lakshmi, T.M., Martin, A., Begum, R.M., Venkatesan, V.P.: An analysis on performance of decision tree algorithms using student's qualitative data. Int. J. Modern Educ. Comput. Sci. **5**(5), 18 (2013)
10. Agrawal, R., Imieliński, T., Swami, A.: Mining association rules between sets of items in large databases. In: ACM SIGMOD Record, vol. 22, no. 2, pp. 207–216. ACM (1993)
11. Pande, A., Abdel-Aty, M.: Market basket analysis of crash data from large jurisdictions and its potential as a decision support tool. Saf. Sci. **47**(1), 145–154 (2009)
12. Tao, F., Qi, Q., Liu, A., Kusiak, A.: Data-driven smart manufacturing. J. Manuf. Syst. **48**, 157–169 (2018)
13. Sarikaya, A., Correll, M., Bartram, L., Tory, M., Fisher, D.: What do we talk about when we talk about dashboards? IEEE Trans. Visual Comput. Graphics **25**(1), 682–692 (2019)
14. Shneiderman, B.: Inventing discovery tools: combining information visualization with data mining. Inf. Visual. **1**(1), 5–12 (2002)
15. Rokach, L., Maimon, O.: Clustering methods. In: Maimon, O., Rokach, L. (eds.) Data Mining and Knowledge Discovery Handbook, pp. 321–352. Springer, Boston (2005). https://doi.org/10.1007/0-387-25465-X_15
16. Wang, H., Song, M.: Ckmeans. 1D. DP: optimal k-means clustering in one dimension by dynamic programming. R J. **3**(2), 29 (2011)

Anomaly Detection from Log Files Using Unsupervised Deep Learning

Sathya Bursic$^{(\boxtimes)}$ ⓘ, Vittorio Cuculo ⓘ, and Alessandro D'Amelio ⓘ

Dipartimento di Informatica, University of Milan, Milan, Italy
{sathya.bursic,vittorio.cuculo,alessandro.damelio}@unimi.it

Abstract. Computer systems have grown in complexity to the point where manual inspection of system behaviour for purposes of malfunction detection have become unfeasible. As these systems output voluminous logs of their activity, machine led analysis of them is a growing need with already several existing solutions. These largely depend on having hand-crafted features, require raw log preprocessing and feature extraction or use supervised learning necessitating having a labeled log dataset not always easily procurable. We propose a two part deep autoencoder model with LSTM units that requires no hand-crafted features, no preprocessing of data as it works on raw text and outputs an anomaly score for each log entry. This anomaly score represents the rarity of a log event both in terms of its content and temporal context. The model was trained and tested on a dataset of HDFS logs containing 2 million raw lines of which half was used for training and half for testing. While this model cannot match the performance of a supervised binary classifier, it could be a useful tool as a coarse filter for manual inspection of log files where a labeled dataset is unavailable.

Keywords: Deep learning · Anomaly detection · Log file

1 Introduction

Today's computer systems in commercial environments are frequently complex and distributed and work on large data throughput. For any part of such a system, be it networking, program execution, machine performance, etc., there is the occurrence of process anomalies and most of these systems generate and keep logs which are intended to be analysed for detecting malfunctions. The commercial systems usually are intended to operate incessantly and reliably with failure to do so having potential to incur costs for the organization. The process of analyzing them has been historically manually done. However, given the scale of these systems the problems that present are that system behaviour may be too complex for a single human to understand and that the systems may generate logs on the order of gigabytes per hour making it infeasible for human comprehension and human anomaly detection [5].

This gave rise to demand for automated log anomaly detection. The problem has been addressed in literature by first performing feature extraction and then

© Springer Nature Switzerland AG 2020
E. Sekerinski et al. (Eds.): FM 2019 Workshops, LNCS 12232, pp. 200–207, 2020.
https://doi.org/10.1007/978-3-030-54994-7_15

applying a linear machine learning model such as PCA, logistic regression or a linear SVM. In this project we propose a two-part model of deep autoencoders that require minimal raw log file preprocessing and detect both anomalous log content and anomalous temporal evolution of logs. The paper is organised as follows: in the next section we review recent approaches to the problem, in Sect. 3 we present in detail our approach, following which the experiment and results are presented and discussed.

2 Related Work

Traditionally log anomaly detection has had three basic steps: log parsing, which turns unstructured text into structured data; feature extraction, where the text is transformed into a numerical feature vector; and anomaly detection, where a machine learning algorithm is applied to classify log events as anomalous or normal execution [5].

The approaches to the log parsing step can loosely be divided into *clustering based* and *heuristic based*. The clustering based approach parts from calculating distances between logs first and then clustering them into groups using the calculated distance. Heuristic based instead count word occurrences in logs for each position and then frequent words in the positions are selected as event candidates. As an example of clustering based parsing, in [3] the authors separate the changing and constant parts of log messages by first using empirical rules (eg. a regular expression to identify IP addresses), and then by token clustering. A different approach for log message clustering as described in [7] is called the IPLoM Algorithm and pertains to the class of heuristic approaches which are said to perform better than clustering based.

Among the machine learning algorithms that have been applied to the problem are logistic regression, decision tree and SVM of supervised models, and clustering, PCA and invariant mining of unsupervised models. Results indicate that supervised methods achieve performance levels not reachable with unsupervised methods. Also, the performance of the supervised methods are mostly similar with SVM giving greatest and decision tree giving lowest performance, while among unsupervised methods invariant mining gives notably superior performance to other unsupervised methods [5].

Recently, deep learning has been also applied to the problem. Du et al. [2] proposed an LSTM deep neural network to model system logs as a natural language sequence with the purpose of allowing the model to automatically learn log patterns from normal execution, and detect anomalies when log patterns deviate from the model trained on log data under normal execution. For parsing the logs from unstructured text into log keys they used a method similar to [3], ie. a clustering based approach. The results reported outperform all other anomaly detection methods not based on deep learning models. In parallel with supervised deep learning, unsupervised deep learning methods have started being used for anomaly detection. Thus, Tuor et al. [9] developed an online unsupervised deep learning approach to detect anomalous network activity from system logs in real time outperforming PCA, SVM and isolation forest models. They use a deep neural network (DNN) composed of LSTM units trained to predict the following event in a sequence of events, similar to [2]. Finally, in [1] and [11] the authors used deep autoencoders to detect anomalies by looking at input reconstruction errors. In the former [1], they applied it to assessing the behaviour of high performance computing systems while in the latter [11], they used it for finding anomalies in multivariate time series data such as those encountered in industrial production systems.

3   Proposed Method

3.1   Model Architecture

The goal of this work is to develop a model requiring minimal raw log preprocessing that is capable of detecting both anomalous message content and anomalous temporal evolution of log messages. We follow the work of [8] in developing a deep autoencoder for text. They used a multilayer LSTM to map input sequences to a vector of fixed dimensionality, after which another multilayered LSTM to decode the target sequence from the vector. They achieve then state of the art on English to French translation tasks and furthermore introduce using bidirectional models to counter the problems of performance on long sequences.

A property of this model is that it learns to map an input sequence of variable length to a fixed length vector in an embedding space. In this work, the approach of [8] provides an opportunity to not have to preprocess log files in any elaborate manner, thus making the model suitable to any type of log file with the only cost being that of training the model. The second part of the model is another LSTM autoencoder that has the purpose of detecting anomalies. Following the work of [1] and [11], we suppose that after training an autoencoder is able to reconstruct better those inputs of which it has been exposed to more during training and vice versa. Finally, using a numerical measure of the distance between the inputs to the second part of the model and their reconstruction at its output an anomaly score is obtained.

The full definition of the model is the following, also represented in Fig. 1: first the autoencoder embedding log messages is trained on log text (without timestamp) to learn a fixed dimensional embedding of the log messages. After training the decoder is discarded and the autoencoder for detecting anomalies is trained taking as input the embeddings of the message and the numerical timestamp of the message. Finally, a distance measure between the inputs and outputs is calculated and an input is considered anomalous if its distance measure lies above an appropriately chosen threshold. While the anomaly detection autoencoder is the same approach that [1] and [11] had, and the message embedding autoencoder comes from the work of [8], the innovation of this work comes from the model not imposing requirements on the log message structure and not requiring preprocessing of the log messages which ensures generality and applicability to any type of logs.

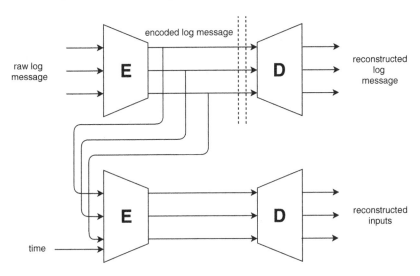

Fig. 1. Schema of the model architecture

3.2 Implementation and Model Training

The dataset used to train and evaluate the proposed model came out of a work of Xu et al. [10] where they mined console logs to detect system runtime problems by parsing them. Combining source code analysis based on C *printf* statements with information retrieval and after extracting features from the parsed logs, they detect operational problems using machine learning. The dataset contains 11 million lines of Hadoop File System logs and is furthermore labeled which will provide a measure of performance for the model. An example of a log entry from the dataset would be:

081109 204453 34 INFO dfs.FSNamesystem: BLOCK*
NameSystem.addStoredBlock: blockMap updated: 10.250.11.85:50010 is added to blk_2377150260128098806 size 67108864

The date and time format is "$DDMMYYhhmmss$" with D representing day, M month, Y year, h hour, m minute and s second, respectively.

After separating the date and time, all non-alphanumeric characters are replaced by whitespace and whitespace is inserted between single digit numbers. Furthermore, all multi digit numbers are considered as separate tokens, eg. the number "67108864" from the previous example becomes "6 7 1 0 8 8 6 4". This is done because it is not practical that all numbers, which are frequently variable for a type of log message, be a part of the vocabulary for the text autoencoder. As per how the network encoding text is constructed, all words in the dataset during preprocessing are put into a vocabulary and assigned a numerical value. Making multi digit numbers that are a log variable part of the vocabulary would constrain the model only to those numbers seen during training. Separating the numbers by whitespace makes the model consider them as separate tokens and allows the model to easily encode numerical values in log messages.

Only a subset of the dataset has been considered, totaling 2 million lines which was further divided into 50% of training data and 50% of test data. The peculiarity of this problem in general and the dataset at hand is the strongly uneven class distribution where there approximately 3% of anoumalous data in the dataset.

The text encoder network is trained with the hyperparameters shown in Table 1. These values have been found experimentally. The vectors output by

Table 1. Log message embedding network parameters

Parameter	Value
Word embedding size	200
LSTM units	100
Initial learning rate	0.01
Batch size	64
Dropout keep probability	0.75
Training epochs	4

Table 2. Anomaly detection network parameters

Parameter	Value
LSTM units	64
Batch size	64
Dropout keep probability	0.8
Training epochs	4

the text encoder are then fed as input into the anomaly detection network for training that takes also the cosine transform of the percentage of the seconds passed for that day. The expression transforming the time is thus

$$f(t) = \cos\left(2\pi \frac{t}{86400}\right) \tag{1}$$

with t being the seconds from midnight at which the log event occurred. The aim here is of normalizing the data around zero as deep neural network training has been shown to behave better when inputs are normalized around zero [6]. This transformation of time removes any possibility of detecting inter-day seasonal patterns in the data and hence the model is geared toward detecting short-term anomalies. There are other ways of transforming inputs of cyclical nature to feed into a neural network. Most notably, the corresponding cosine transform could have also been included which would have provided more precise information of the time of day. Also, the same transform could have been included for the day of month and month. However, given that the frequency of log message generation is high, all other temporal information is considered less relevant and discarded for simplicity. The cost function used for training is the MSE function and the experimentally found training parameters for the anomaly detection network can be found in Table 2. The reconstruction error on the anomaly detection network is calculated using an L_1 distance of the inputs and their reconstruction.

4 Experimental Results

On Fig. 2 anomaly values for 1 million lines of the test dataset are plotted. Several outliers where the anomaly value is strongly above the mean are particularly interesting. However, most of the values lie within a particular band which could potentially necessitate careful choice of threshold. If the threshold were chosen too low there could be a lot of false positives, and if chosen too high there could be a lot of false negatives.

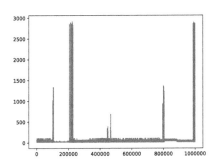

Fig. 2. Test anomaly scores

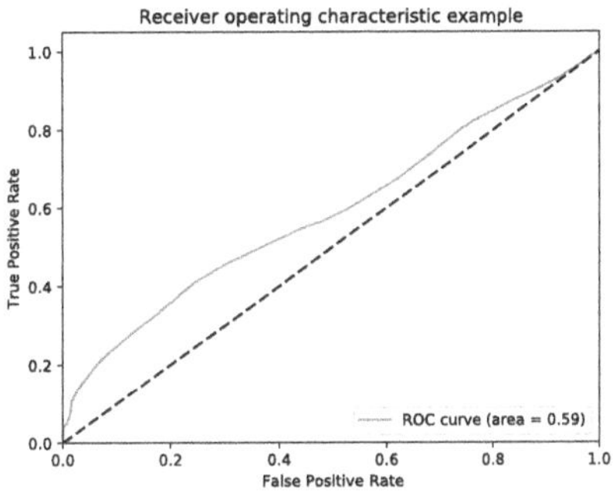

Fig. 3. ROC curve for the test dataset

As the dataset is labeled the problem can be considered a binary classification problem with the classes being *anomalous* and *not anomalous* for any log message. For this reason we can consider techniques usually applied for evaluating binary classifier performance.

The ROC curve for the test dataset can be seen in Fig. 3 with AUC equal to 0.59. The value isn't high indicating that the classifier doesn't perform well. This can be supported by visual inspection of the curve showing poor class separation, especially at higher values of FPR and TPR. Regardless, the importance of precision and recall relative one to another can be considered inherent to the problem at hand. This has been considered a critique of the F-measure as a commonly used binary classifier quality indicator [4].

A plot of precision, recall and F-score for the test dataset can be seen in Fig. 4. The plot shows the maximum of F-score at a threshold level of 62, after which precision rises rapidly and recall falls rapidly.

The values of true positives, true negatives, false positives and false negatives at eight different threshold values are presented in Table 3. A consistently high level of false negatives can be noticed meaning that the largest part of anomalies will be left out by the model. This is also supported by the recall curve parting from a value of around 0.6 for a low threshold value with the precision being low. This could possibly indicate that certain erroneous events are indeed fairly common. However, at higher threshold values the false positives fall faster than the true positives which is also supported by the rapidly rising precision in Fig. 4.

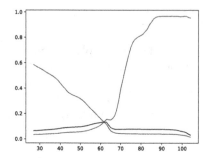

Fig. 4. A plot of precision (red), recall (green) and F-measure (blue) on the test dataset for threshold values between 25 and 106 (Color figure online)

Table 3. True positives, true negatives, false positives and false negatives for eight different threshold values.

Thresh	TP	TN	FP	FN
27	17279	473614	493378	12244
37	14395	630785	336207	15128
47	10035	789325	177667	19488
57	6185	899853	67139	23338
67	1435	960561	6431	28088
77	1195	966663	329	28328
87	1169	966940	52	28354
97	1083	966955	37	28440

This is in line with what can be seen on Fig. 2 as there are outliers which have an anomaly score vastly higher than the average. As supported by the values in Table 3 most of these outliers seem to be anomalies. Given the above, a potential use for this kind of model is as a coarse filter for human inspection of log files of high enough frequency such that human inspection of the whole stream is infeasible. By choosing higher threshold values (for example at 77), while most anomalies won't be detected, the anomalies with the highest anomaly values will, and the precision will be high. This means that if all values which the model will classify as anomalous are given to a human for inspection most of them indeed will be. One might consider that optimizing for recall rather than precision might be more adapt for application as a filter for manual inspection, but the fundamental ceiling on recall of the approach is that the definition of anomalous here is that which occurs rarely. While the choice of optimal threshold isn't directly addressed here, in potential applications several approaches might be taken depending on the problem at hand. Firstly, a validation dataset could be used with manual choice of threshold. Secondly, the threshold can be dynamically changed and optimized by the user based on experience and circumstances. Thirdly, any number of statistical measures can be adopted as a threshold, such as the mean plus n standard deviations.

5   Conclusions

In this work we proposed a two-part unsupervised deep learning model for detecting anomalies in system log files. The model is composed of two autoencoders with LSTM units of which one is applied to text as per the work of [8], and the other that takes the text embeddings and a temporal value as input and serves to detect anomalies. Using a publicly available labeled dataset of HDFS logs, experimental results show that at most thresholds recall is low but at higher thresholds precision is high showing that most errors aren't detected by the model at higher thresholds, but those detected are mostly errors. The properties of the model being it doesn't require any log preprocessing or feature extraction and works on generic log data, a potential use could be as a filter for human inspection for anomaly detection in systems generating logs with high frequency. The results presented in this note represent a preliminary proof of concept and in future work we plan to provide a more exhaustive experimental part.

References

1. Borghesi, A., Bartolini, A., Lombardi, M., Milano, M., Benini, L.: Anomaly detection using autoencoders in high performance computing systems. arXiv preprint arXiv:1811.05269 (2018)
2. Du, M., Li, F., Zheng, G., Srikumar, V.: DeepLog: anomaly detection and diagnosis from system logs through deep learning. In: Proceedings of the 2017 ACM SIGSAC Conference on Computer and Communications Security, pp. 1285–1298. ACM (2017)
3. Fu, Q., Lou, J.G., Wang, Y., Li, J.: Execution anomaly detection in distributed systems through unstructured log analysis. In: 2009 Ninth IEEE International Conference on Data Mining, pp. 149–158. IEEE (2009)
4. Hand, D., Christen, P.: A note on using the f-measure for evaluating record linkage algorithms. Stat. Comput. **28**(3), 539–547 (2018)
5. He, S., Zhu, J., He, P., Lyu, M.R.: Experience report: system log analysis for anomaly detection. In: 2016 IEEE 27th International Symposium on Software Reliability Engineering (ISSRE), pp. 207–218. IEEE (2016)
6. LeCun, Y.A., Bottou, L., Orr, G.B., Müller, K.-R.: Efficient BackProp. In: Montavon, G., Orr, G.B., Müller, K.-R. (eds.) Neural Networks: Tricks of the Trade. LNCS, vol. 7700, pp. 9–48. Springer, Heidelberg (2012). https://doi.org/10.1007/978-3-642-35289-8_3
7. Makanju, A.A., Zincir-Heywood, A.N., Milios, E.E.: Clustering event logs using iterative partitioning. In: Proceedings of the 15th ACM SIGKDD International Conference on Knowledge Discovery and Data Mining, pp. 1255–1264. ACM (2009)
8. Sutskever, I., Vinyals, O., Le, Q.V.: Sequence to sequence learning with neural networks. In: Advances in Neural Information Processing Systems, pp. 3104–3112 (2014)
9. Tuor, A., Kaplan, S., Hutchinson, B., Nichols, N., Robinson, S.: Deep learning for unsupervised insider threat detection in structured cybersecurity data streams. In: Workshops at the Thirty-First AAAI Conference on Artificial Intelligence (2017)
10. Xu, W., Huang, L., Fox, A., Patterson, D., Jordan, M.: Largescale system problem detection by mining console logs. In: Proceedings of SOSP 2009 (2009)
11. Zhang, C., et al.: A deep neural network for unsupervised anomaly detection and diagnosis in multivariate time series data. arXiv preprint arXiv:1811.08055 (2018)

FMAS 2019 - 1st Formal Methods for Autonomous Systems Workshop

FMAS 2019 Organizers' Message

The first Formal Methods for Autonomous Systems (FMAS) workshop was held as a satellite event at the 3rd World Congress on Formal Methods, on the 11th of October 2019 in Porto. Autonomous systems are highly complex and they present unique challenges for formal methods. They can act without human intervention, and are often embedded in a robotic system, so they can interact with the real world. As such, they can be described as safety-critical, cyber-physical, hybrid, and real-time systems.

The aim of FMAS was to bring together leading researchers, who are tackling the unique challenges of autonomous systems using formal methods, to present recent and ongoing work. We were interested in the use of formal methods to specify, model, or verify autonomous or robotic systems; in whole or in part. We were also interested in hearing about successful industrial applications and potential future directions for this emerging application of formal methods.

FMAS 2019 encouraged submission of both long and short papers. We received six long papers and one short paper, by authors in Australia, Brazil, Czech Republic, France, Germany, and the UK. After a thorough reviewing process, we accepted four long papers, and one short paper, for presentation at the workshop. After the workshop, the presented papers underwent a second round of reviewing for acceptance into this LNCS proceedings.

In addition to the paper presentations, FMAS hosted two invited speakers and a discussion session. Claudio Menghi was invited to talk about his collaborations with industrial partners, which involved developing approaches for specification and verification of missions. Kristin Y. Rozier was invited to talk about her work on developing on-board runtime verification for a variety of resource-constrained autonomous systems, including aerial and space systems. The workshop's final session was a panel discussion, featuring the invited speakers and Michael Fisher as panellists. This session was well-received and involved participation from the entire audience.

We would like to thank our invited speakers, Claudio Menghi and Kristin Y. Rozier; the authors of the submitted papers; our programme committee, for their reviews; and all of the attendees of FMAS 2019. Our thanks are also owed to the wonderful conference volunteers, who helped us throughout the workshop; and the friendly staff of the Vincci hotel, our hosts.

November 2019

Marie Farrell
Matt Luckcuck
Michael Fishe

Organization

Workshop Chairs

Marie Farrell	University of Liverpool, UK
Matt Luckcuck	University of Liverpool, UK
Michael Fisher	University of Liverpool, UK

Program Committee

Mikael Asplund	Linkoping University, Sweden
Matthew Bradbury	University of Warwick, UK
Rafael C. Cardoso	University of Liverpool, UK
Marie Farrell (Chair)	University of Liverpool, UK
Angelo Ferrando	University of Liverpool, UK
Jérémie Guiochet	University of Toulouse, France
Rob Hierons	University of Sheffield, UK
Taylor Johnson	University of Illinois at Urbana-Champaign, USA
Bruno Lacerda	University of Oxford, UK
Sven Linker	University of Liverpool, UK
Matt Luckcuck (Chair)	University of Liverpool, UK
Tiziana Margaria	University of Limerick, Ireland
Dominique Mery	Université de Lorraine, France
Alice Miller	University of Glasgow, UK
Alvaro Miyazawa	University of York, UK
Kristin Yvonne Rozier	University of Iowa, USA
Marija Slavkovik	University of Bergen, Norway
James Stovold	Swansea University, UK
Silvia Lizeth Tapia Tarifa	University of Oslo, Norway
Hao Wu	Maynooth University, Ireland

Invited Talks

Formal Methods Meet Autonomous Systems: A Journey on A Two-Year Research Collaboration with Industry

Claudio Menghi[ID]

SnT Centre, University of Luxembourg, Luxembourg
claudio.menghi@uni.lu

Autonomous — and Robotic — Systems are made of collaborating computational elements that adapt their behaviors and take autonomous decisions depending on the physical environment in which they are deployed. Formal methods provide mathematically-based techniques for the specification and development of software and hardware systems. The adoption of formal methods by the industry developing autonomous and robotic systems is, however, still slow.

This talk reports on a two-year research collaboration with industry focused on applying formal method techniques in the development of autonomous systems. First, it discusses the main challenges and results achieved in the definition of specification patterns for robotic missions [5, 7], a project in collaboration with PAL Robotics [3] and BOSCH [1]. Mission specification patterns provide logic-based solutions for recurrent specification problems where developers have to define the desired behavior of a robotic application (a.k.a missions). Then, it discusses a procedure for generating online test oracles from logic-based formulations of functional requirements of autonomous systems [6], a project in collaboration with Luxspace [2] and QRA Corp [4]. The procedure has been evaluated on an industrial satellite system model. Finally, the talk presents a set of challenges and opportunities that emerged from the two-year journey of collaboration with industry.

Reference

1. BOSCH (2018). https://www.bosch.com/
2. Luxspace (2019). http://luxspace.lu/
3. PAL Robotics (2019). http://pal-robotics.com/
4. QRA corp (2019). https://qracorp.com/

This work has received funding from the European Research Council under the European Union's Horizon 2020 research and innovation programme (grant agreement No. 731869 and No. 694277), from QRA Corp, and from the University of Luxembourg (grant "ReACP").

5. Menghi, C., Tsigkanos, C., Pelliccione, P., Ghezzi, C., Berger, T.:Specification patterns for robotic missions. Trans. Softw. Eng. (2019). https://doi.org/10.1109/TSE.2019.2945329
6. Menghi, C., Nejati, S., Gaaloul, K., Briand, L.C.: Generating automated and online test oracles for simulink models with continuous and uncertain behaviors. In: Foundations of Software Engineering. ESEC/FSE, ACM (2019)
7. Menghi, C., Tsigkanos, C., Berger, T., Pelliccione, P.: PsALM: Specification of Dependable Robotic Missions. In: ICSE: Companion Proceedings (2019)

Runtime Reasoning that Really Flies

Kristin Y. Rozier

Iowa State University, USA

Real-time, on-board runtime reasoning about system safety and security is required for autonomous systems, including most everything that flies: aircraft, spacecraft, satellites, and the robotic systems therein. The field of runtime verification (RV) is vast, and quickly growing, yet when it comes to real-life autonomous systems, current RV capabilities just don't fly. There is a dearth of RV tools that can operate within the constraints of real-life embedded operations that limit the system instrumentation, space, timing, power, weight, cost, operating conditions, and other resources. Even when we devise tools for embedded operation, RV must first clear the tall hurdles of input specifications, validation, verification, and flight certification. We highlight case studies where RV has recently risen to the occasion of reasoning on-board real-life autonomous systems, such as Unmanned Aerial Systems and NASA's Robonaut2, and examine the way up from here. What will it take for RV to really take off?

Formalisation and Implementation of Road Junction Rules on an Autonomous Vehicle Modelled as an Agent

Gleifer Vaz Alves[1]($\boxtimes$)(ID), Louise Dennis[2](ID), and Michael Fisher[2](ID)

[1] UTFPR - Universidade Tecnológica Federal do Paraná, Ponta Grossa, Brazil
gleifer@utfpr.edu.br
[2] Department of Computer Science, University of Liverpool, Liverpool, UK
{L.A.Dennis,MFisher}@liverpool.ac.uk

Abstract. The design of autonomous vehicles includes obstacle detection and avoidance, route planning, speed control, etc. However, there is a lack of an explicitly representation of the rules of the road on an autonomous vehicle. Additionally, it is necessary to understand the behaviour of an autonomous vehicle in order to check whether or not it works according to the rules of the road. Here, we propose an agent-based architecture to embed the rules of the road into an agent representing the behaviour of an autonomous vehicle. We use temporal logic to formally represent the rules of the road in a way it should be possible to capture when and how a given rule of the road can be applied. Our contributions include: i. suggestion of changes in the rules of the road; ii. representation of rules in a suitable way for an autonomous vehicle agent; iii. dealing with indeterminate terms in the Highway Code.

Keywords: Agent · Autonomous vehicles · Temporal logic · Rules of the road

1 Introduction

Usually, the design of current control software in autonomous vehicle does not explicitly implement the rules of the road. Here, we propose an architecture, where an agent represents the behaviour of an autonomous vehicle and temporal logic is used to formally specify a subset from the rules of the road. With this, we aim to formally verify that an agent endowed with the rules of the road actually respects the flow of traffic without any sort of conflicts, inconsistency or redundancies in the use of the rules.

Autonomous Vehicles and the Rules of the Road: One can easily enumerate possible advantages the deployment of autonomous vehicles may bring to cities, e.g. reduce indices of traffic congestion, driver inactivity, and also the number of accidents [11]. With this in mind, several companies have been working towards the goal of launching (fully) autonomous vehicles on our roads on a daily basis.

© Springer Nature Switzerland AG 2020
E. Sekerinski et al. (Eds.): FM 2019 Workshops, LNCS 12232, pp. 217–232, 2020.
https://doi.org/10.1007/978-3-030-54994-7_16

Predictions as to when (fully) autonomous vehicles will appear on our roads vary (e.g., [2] and [16]), but it expected to be within the next 5 years. However, there are plenty of questions which should be addressed in order to have these vehicles driving safely on the roads. The design of an autonomous vehicle must consider obstacle detection and avoidance, route planning, safety, speed control, etc. But, how about the road rules: is an autonomous vehicle behaviour adapted to the road rules? Prakken mentions in [15], that his work seems one of the first towards the comprehension of how an autonomous vehicle design should be established in accordance with the road rules. Nevertheless, Prakken's approach is a conceptual approach without addressing either implementation or formal verification. Previously [1], we have presented the first steps towards the formalisation of the rules of the road. In [17], Vellinga also discusses the necessity to understand how the road rules should be adapted into an autonomous vehicle. The author presents road rules from California (USA), the UK and the Netherlands.

In the UK, the government has also shown concern about the regulation of autonomous vehicles. That is why the Law Commission in the UK has released (Nov. 2018) a consultation paper in order to review the regulatory framework for the safe deployment of autonomous vehicles [12]. In this review, different topics are addressed, including the Highway code which is responsible for determining the so-called Rules of the Road in the UK. This set of rules establishes how one should use the road for overtaking, road junctions, pedestrian crossing, and so on [8]. Moreover, in June 2019, the Law Commission made available a summary of the responses concerning the aforementioned consultation paper [12]. Among the presented topics we highlight the adaption of the road rules, which according to the document should address the following issues (among others):

1. Apply analogue driving rules into a digital highway code (Sect. 6.1 in [12]).
2. Struggle to determine a digital highway code that sets precise rules for every instance. In the document, it is mentioned that: *"is impossible to predict all future scenarios in advance... it is not desirable nor realistic to ask developers to deterministically prescribe the behaviour of automated driving systems in advance for every scenario"* (Sect. 6.5 in [12]).
3. Establish a forum on the application of road rules to autonomous vehicles, some possible scenarios which should be considered are (Sect. 6.7 in [12]):
   (a) interpretation of indeterminate terms in legislation and in the Highway code, e.g., *road users should take extra care*, or *there is a safe gap large enough*.
   (b) identify possible additions to the Highway code to resolve conflicts involving autonomous vehicles. As mentioned in [12] (footnote 7 on page 12), usually conflicts are resolved through human communication. As an example, a human driver may use hand and arm gestures to give way for another human driver in a road junction.

Autonomy, Agents and Formal Verification: According to Herrmann et al. [11] an automated vehicle includes several stages of automation, where there is a person in the loop, at least in order to handle specific traffic scenarios, e.g. an emergency situation. On the other hand, in an autonomous vehicle, a person is out of the loop and the system is responsible for all driving tasks everywhere and at all times. For the sake of clarity, in our paper we use the term *autonomous vehicle* to represent the vehicle modelled in our system, which indeed is described by means of an intelligent agent [18]. An intelligent agent can be easily used to represent the behaviour of an autonomous vehicle, as we have previously presented in [9], where an agent is endowed with strategies to avoid obstacles in a simulated environment.

Agent-based modelling is a suitable approach to represent high-level decisions of an autonomous system. As illustrated by Marks, in [13], there are several layers in an autonomous vehicle stack. Here we are mainly concerned with the Reasoning and Decision Layer. As a result, the low-level layers, like Sensor, Localization and Control layers are out of our scope. Moreover, an agent programming approach is indeed a reasonable technique when we take into account the code complexity for vehicles. In 2010, some vehicles had ten million software lines of code (SLOC). In 2016, the SLOC number has increased to around 150 million [4]. Thus, agent-oriented programming could be seen as a suitable approach for the high-level decisions of an autonomous vehicle. Usually, a program written in an agent programming language has fewer lines than (the same program written) in other general-purpose languages and also an agent language is a good choice for prototyping.

In our work we use the GWENDOLEN agent programming language [6] in order to implement a BDI (*Belief-Desire-Intention*) agent [3] to capture the behaviour of an autonomous vehicle. By using GWENDOLEN, we can also take advantage of the *Model Checking Agent Programming Language* (MCAPL) framework [7], where the *Agent Java Path Finder* (AJPF) model checker can be used to formally verify the behaviour of an intelligent agent. When comparing to other techniques, like machine learning, by using a model checking agent-based architecture, we intend to avoid the so-called *black box* problem [5], i.e. the lack of transparency to control and understand the decision-making process. Notice that by doing the formal verification of a GWENDOLEN agent is possible to give the explicit reasons that the agent has used to select a given decision.

BDI Agent: An agent program language which implements a BDI agent usually has the following structure for an agent plan:

```
trigger_event : guard <- body
```

Where a given agent may have different plans in order to achieve a certain goal. Using our translation we may establish the following mapping:

- Goal is determined by the specific road junction rule.
- The `trigger_event` is given by a new belief or a goal.
- The `guard` is defined by a set of beliefs.
- The `body` is represented as a set of actions.

Contributions: Our major goal is the proposal of an agent-based architecture in order to embed the rules of the road in an agent representing the high-level decisions of an autonomous vehicle. With this in mind, we point out the following questions: **i.** How can we handle the use of ambiguous terms in the road rules, when embedding these rules into an autonomous vehicle? **ii.** How can we formally verify the behaviour of an autonomous system endowed with the rules of the road? **iii.** By having a simple and direct mapping of the Highway code into a digital highway code, can we say it is enough to have an autonomous vehicle driving safely on the roads? Notice that here we only address the first question.

In this paper, we extend the formalisation proposed in [1] by setting up a language and a grammar for the road junction rules together with an agent-based architecture capable of capturing the behaviour of an autonomous vehicle in an urban traffic environment. Moreover, we establish a translation of road junction rules written in Temporal logic into a BDI agent plan. As an instance of our architecture, we present the formalisation and implementation of a given road rule from the UK Highway Code.

2   Road Junction Rules: Language and Grammar

In this section we present the so-called RoR language and grammar created to represent the Rules of the Road. The RoR language is used in the next section to formalise the Rules of the Road. We intend that our language should be expressive enough to represent the rules of the road (specifically the road junction rules), but also as simple as possible. As it follows we present the operators, terms, and actions from the RoR language, which is based on Linear Temporal Logic (LTL) [10].

2.1   Operators and Constants

- Operators from LTL:
- $\land$, $\lor$, $\rightarrow$, $\neg$.
- $\Box$, $\Diamond$, $\circ$, $\cup$.
- where:
    - $\Box$: *always*
    - $\Diamond$: *eventually*
    - $\circ$: *next*
    - $\cup$: *until*
- Constants: `True, False`.

2.2   Terms: Agent and Objects

Terms in the RoR language are used together with actions. We have two kinds of terms: Agent and Objects.

- Agent (Ag) defines the agent who has an active role in a given action (and road junction rule).

– Objects (*Obj*) represents the different objects that can be used in an action to represent the elements of a given road junction rule. There are four different kinds of objects. The first three concrete and the last is an abstract object:

Space: establishes the environment where a given road rule occurs.

Dynamic: determines the dynamic objects used in a rule that are situated in an environment.

Static: defines the static objects used in a rule that are situated in an environment.

Abstract: represents the abstract notions which are related to a road rule.

As it follows, we present the Agent and Objects in the RoR language.

Agent

– Autonomous Vehicle: represents an intelligent agent conducting the vehicle. Abbreviation: AV.

Objects

– Concrete Space Objects

Junction: a junction between two or more roads. Abbreviation: JC.

Road: a road that usually has a single traffic direction. Abbreviation: RO.

Main Road: the main road has both traffic directions. Abbreviation: MR.

Lane: a road or the main road may be divided by two or more lanes. Abbreviation: LA.

Filter Lane: a filter lane is a special lane used to guide the driver to turn in a road. Abbreviation: FL.

Central Reservation: a central reservation on a dual carriageway is used by a car to wait for the safe moment to cross a road. Abbreviation: CR.

Box Junction: a box junction has criss-cross yellow lines painted on the road. Abbreviation: BJ.

Box Junction at Signalled Roundabouts: Similar to Box Junctions, but with signalled roundabouts. Abbreviation: BJS.

– Concrete Dynamic Objects

Road User: a road user can be any of the following, another vehicle, pedestrians, cyclists, motorcyclists, powered wheelchairs, mobility scooters or horse rider. Abbreviation: RU.

Long Vehicles: a long vehicle can be a bus, a lorry or a truck. Abbreviation: LV.

– Concrete Static Objects

Stop sign or Solid white line across the road: both are signs which means that you should stop at a junction. Abbreviation: ST.

Give way sign or Triangle marked on the road: both are signs which means you should give way to traffic. Abbreviation: GW.

Broken white lines across the road: also means to give way traffic, but when you are emerging from a junction on the main road. Abbreviation: BWL.

Traffic light: a Traffic light which may have a Green, Red or Amber light. Abbreviation: TL.

Green Light: on a traffic light. Abbreviation: GL.

Amber Light: on a traffic light. Abbreviation: AL.

Red Light: on a traffic light. Abbreviation: RL.

Advanced stop line: some signal-controlled junctions have advanced stop lines to allow cycles to be positioned ahead of other traffic. Additionally, an Advanced stop line has two lines marking its area, the so-called: First White Line and Second White Line. Abbreviation: AD.

First White Line. Abbreviation: FWL.

Second White Line. Abbreviation: SWL.

Mirrors: a driver is supposed to use the mirrors of his vehicle to observe the traffic. Abbreviation: MI.

– Abstract Objects

Safe Gap: usually when turning on a junction a driver is supposed to verify if there is a Safe Gap for the vehicle on the road. Abbreviation: SG.

* NB: for the sake of simplicity of RoR language, it is used SG to represent not only the previous description, but also any situation where the AV needs to take extra care when turning on any kind of junction, crossing roads, crossing a box junction, waiting in a lane for turning right or left, among others. That is why SG is used in several road junction rules.

Blind Spot: when waiting to cross the main road it may be necessary to check for blind spots. Abbreviation: BS.

Possible Collision: in some very specific rules some exceptions are allowed but if and only if a collision may occur in a given road junction environment. Abbreviation: PC.

Oncoming Traffic: in some scenarios, it might be necessary to look for oncoming traffic in a corresponding environment. Abbreviation: OT.

Behind: when preparing to turn into a junction it is necessary to look behind (possibly using the mirrors) for oncoming traffic. Or the driver can also be turning right behind another vehicle which is also turning right in the same junction. Abbreviation: BH.

Front: the driver can turn right in front of another vehicle which is also turning right at the same junction. Abbreviation: FR.

Both Directions: when waiting to cross the main road it may be necessary to watch out for traffic in both directions on the main road. Abbreviation: BD.

2.3 Actions

Definition 1 (Action). *An Action is given by an action name followed by one of two different tuples (with three or two elements) and optional pre and post-conditions:*

$$\texttt{<pre>}\ action\_name\ (t_1, t_2, t_3)\ \texttt{<post>}$$

– *where,*

t_1 *is an Agent.*

t_2 *is a Concrete Space Object.*

t_3 *can be a Concrete Static or Dynamic Object; or an Abstract Object; or it can be empty.*

$\texttt{<pre>}$ *some actions require the so-called pre-conditions which should be satisfied for a given action to be applied. We use flags (*True *or* False*) to represent a given pre-condition from an action,* True *means the action can be applied,* False *means the action should not be applied.*

$\texttt{<post>}$ *similarly there are the so-called post-conditions which represent the application result from a given action.* True *means the action has been successfully achieved,* False *means the action has not been successfully achieved.*

Notice pre and post-conditions are both optional since not every rule demands this sort of additional context related to the effect of a rule application.

$$\texttt{<pre>}\ action\_name\ (t_1, t_2)\ \texttt{<post>}$$

– *where,*

t_1 *can be a Concrete Static or Dynamic Object; or an Abstract Object.*

t_2 *is a Concrete Space Object.*

List of Actions. We have defined the following list of action names:

```
stop, wait, give-way, cross, enter, exit,
turn-right, turn-left, give-right-signal, give-left-signal,
exists, overtake, turn-keep-left-lane, watch.
```

Example of Actions. We present four examples of different kinds of actions.

```
enter(AV,JC)
```
- the action **enter** is given by a tuple with two elements: AV represents an Autonomous Vehicle Agent and JC represents a Concrete Space Object, the Junction. This action can be read as: "*an AV is supposed to enter when it is at the Junction*".

```
watch(AV,JC,RU)
```
- the action **watch** is given by a tuple with three elements: AV and JC represent the same elements from previous action, and RU represents a Concrete Dynamic Object, the Road User. This action can be read as: "*an AV is supposed to watch out for Road Users, when it is at the Junction*".

```
cross(RU,JC) <False>
```

- the action cross is given by a tuple with two elements and a post-condition: RU represents a Concrete Dynamic Object, the Road User; and JC a Concrete Space Object, the Junction. The flag "False" is used as a post-condition. This action can be read as: *"A Road User is supposed to cross, when it is at a Junction. According to the post-condition, there is no Road User crossing at the Junction"*.

exists(SG,JC) <True>

- the action exists is also given by a tuple with two elements and a post-condition: SG represents an Abstract Object, the Safe Gap; and JC represents the Junction. The flag "True" is used as a post-condition. This action can be read as: *"A Safe Gap is supposed to exist, and it is at the Junction. According to the post-condition, there is indeed a Safe Gap at the Junction"*.

2.4 Grammar

As it follows we present the grammar for RoR language. The grammar is defined to represent the road junction rules and it is presented using Extended Backus-Naur Form (EBNF) style [14].

```
road_junction_rule = context"->" result ;
context = "□" [op_unary] action { op_binary [op_unary] action } ;
result = ["◊"] [op_unary] action |
  ["◊"] [op_unary] action op_binary [op_unary] ["◊"] action ;
op_binary = "∧" | "∨" | "∪" ;
op_unary = "¬" | "○" ;
action =   ["<"pre">"] action_name tuple ["<"post">"] ;
```

- Notice that in this EBNF style grammar the following notation is used:
  = represents definition.
  ; represents termination.
  [...] represents optional.
  { ... } represents repetition.
  " ... " represents terminal string.

The grammar determines that a road junction rule has a context, followed by the "→" operator and terminated by a result. A context always starts with the operator "□" followed by at least one action. While a result may have the "◊" operator with a single action, or a pair of actions.

3 Formalising the Road Junction Rules

The UK Highway code presents the road rules [8]. Here, we address a subset representing the road junction rules. This subset comprises 14 rules which deal with stop signs, traffic lights, turning right and left, crossroads and also watching out for a road user. As an example, we show `rule 170`[1], which establishes the requirements for a driver to enter or wait at a road junction. As it follows, a fragment of `rule 170` is described as seen in [8]. Next, a formal representation is given using LTL.

– `Rule 170` from Road Junction Highway Code:
   • You Should watch out for road users (`RU`) (cyclists, motorcyclists, powered wheelchairs/mobility scooters and pedestrians).
   • watch out for pedestrians crossing a road junction (`JC`) into which you are turning.
   • look all around before emerging[2]. Do not cross or join a road until there is a safe gap (`SG`) large enough for you to do so safely.
– `Rule 170`: represented in LTL, when the autonomous vehicle (`AV`) may **enter** the junction (`JC`):

$$\Box \; (\texttt{watch(AV, JC, RU)} \cup \texttt{cross(RU, JC)} \; \texttt{<False>} \land$$
$$\texttt{exists(SG, JC)} \; \texttt{<True>}) \rightarrow \Diamond \texttt{enter(AV, JC)}$$

   • `Rule 170` – description: *it is always the case that the* `AV` *is supposed to watch for any road users (*`RU`*) at the junction (*`JC`*) until there are no road users crossing the junction (*`JC`*) and also there is a safe gap (*`SG`*). As a result, at some time the* `AV` *may enter the junction.*

4   From a Road Junction Rule Towards a BDI Agent Plan

In this section, we describe how the formalisation presented in Sect. 3 can be used in the translation towards BDI agent plans. Through such a translation, we intend to better bridge the gap between the rules of the road and the agent implementation. Additionally, this translation could be used as a first step in the implementation of these rules in a BDI agent programming language different from GWENDOLEN.

Our translation process is executed through different cases according to the possible actions used to describe the road junction rules.

Here `<pre>` and `<post>` are used as an effect on the given action. In the case of a pre-condition it indicates there is a previous belief that should be satisfied for the given action to be applied. In the case of a post-condition, the application of the action will result in a new belief. Thus, both pre and post-conditions represent beliefs when translated into BDI plans, as shown in the following definitions.

`<pre> action_name` (t_1, t_2, t_3) `<post>`

---

[1] LTL representation of road junction rules: https://github.com/laca-is/SAE-RoR.

[2] For the sake of clarity of the rules of the road language, we choose to use the term **enter** as an action which represents not only a driver entering a road junction, but also emerging from a road junction to another road.

`<pre>` `action_name`: the action becomes a belief for the agent.

t_1 as an Agent is translated as an agent.

t_2 as a Space Object is translated as a belief from the environment.

t_3 as an Abstract or Static or Dynamic Object is translated as a belief from the environment.

`<post>` `action_name`: the action result becomes a belief for the agent.

`action_name`: is the own action which should be part of the body plan in the agent.

`<pre>` `action_name` (t_1, t_2) `<post>`

`<pre>` and `<post>` will be translated in the same way of the previous case.

t_1 as an Abstract or Static or a Dynamic Object is translated as belief from the environment.

t_2 as a Space Object is translated as a belief from the environment.

`action_name`: is the own action which should be part of the body plan in the agent.

Now, to illustrate the translation, we show an example using the Rule 170, previously seen in Sect. 3.

- The Goal is given by Rule 170, which is to *enter at the junction*.
- From the four actions written in the formalisation of Rule 170, we extract the following elements, which will be used to create different agent plans with the corresponding trigger events, guards, and body plans.
- We consider that a LTL rules of the road is a flow of actions when translated into agent plans:
  • The flow of action starts with those actions from the "Context" (see Grammar at Subsect. 2.4), *action-1* will obtain new beliefs (from the agent environment) that will be used as guards for *action-2*; *action-2* will obtain new beliefs used as guards for *action-3*; this goes on until the "Result" action, which can use all beliefs obtained by previous actions.
- Our translation target is the BDI structure (trigger event, guards, body) previously seen in Sect. 1.

- First action (from the Context):
  `watch(AV, JC, RU)`

  AV is the Agent.
  JC is a belief at Junction from the environment.
  RU is a belief there is a road user.
  `watch` is the action watch implemented in the environment.

• Translation target:

$$\texttt{enter-junction : (empty) <- watch}$$

the trigger event is named `enter-junction`, this is the AV-agent goal (this same trigger event is used for all plans).

since this is the first action (in the flow of actions), there is no beliefs obtained from the environment, that is the reason the guards are empty.

`watch` is the action used in the body of agent plan (all following actions will be used similarly).

- Second action (from the Context):
  `cross(RU, JC) <False>`

    RU is a belief there is a road user.

    JC is a belief at Junction from the environment.

    `cross(RU, JC) <False>` is a belief related to *RU* and *JC* that there is no road user crossing at the junction.

    `cross` is the action cross implemented in the environment.

  • Translation target:

    `enter-junction : JC <- cross`

    now, the second action (`cross`) has obtained a belief (`JC` - Junction) from the environment, which is used as guard in the plan.

- Third action (from the Context):
  `exists(SG, JC) <True>`

    SG is a belief on safe gap from the environment.

    JC is a belief at Junction from the environment.

    `exists(SG, JC) <True>` this flag has effect in the action and in both elements from the tuple, thus we say: *"there is a new belief that exists a Safe Gap at the Junction."*

    `exists` is the action exists implemented in the environment

  • Translation target:

    `enter-junction : JC, RU <- exists`

    next, the third action (`exists`) still has the same previous guard (`JC`) and obtains a new belief (`RU`, there is no road user), used as a second guard in the agent plan.

- Fourth action (from the Result):
  `enter(AV, JC)`

    AV is the Agent.

    JC is a belief at Junction from the environment.

    `enter` is the action enter implemented in the environment.

  • Translation target:

    `enter-junction : JC, RU, SG <- enter`

    at last, the "Result" action (`enter`) keeps the previous guards and adds a third one, `SG` (Safe Gap), obtained from the third action application.

Notice that when implementing the agent plans in GWENDOLEN (as next section will present), we have changed some details in the code, but only to have a clear BDI syntax code. The main target objects obtained from the translation are all used in the agent BDI plans.

5   Simulated Automotive Environment for the Rules of the Road

Our proposed architecture (see Fig. 1) is named SAE-RoR (*Simulated Automotive Environment for the Rules of the Road*).

In Fig. 1, the semantics of the arrows represent data. The road junction rules are formally represented using a grammar. With this representation we are able to embed the rules into a GWENDOLEN agent and also formally verify related properties written in LTL using AJPF. Moreover, the agent updates its beliefs from perceptions obtained from the Urban Traffic Environment. This will determine the set of plans that should be executed and sends back to the environment the corresponding actions, e.g. watch and enter (a road junction).

As an example of a property that could be formally verified is given below (in natural language):

> "*It is always the case that when there is a road user crossing a road junction and/or there is no safe gap at the junction, then the AV-agent will not enter the junction.*"

Notice that our intention is not simply checking this property considering the rule 170, but also verify it according to the whole set of road junction rules. In a way we could check if there is any conflict, inconsistency or redundancies among the road junction rules.

Code 1.1 presents a fragment of our AV-agent, which implements a subset of plans from rule 170, and is responsible for achieving the goal of entering a road junction (as seen in Sect. 3).

Listing 1.1. AV-agent plans for Rule 170

```
: Initial  Goals:

want_enter_junction  [achieve]

: Plans:

+!want_enter_junction  [achieve]  :  { B to_watch(X,Y) } <-
watch(X,Y);
+!want_enter_junction  [achieve]  :  { B junction } <-
check_cross(X,Y);
+!want_enter_junction  [achieve]  :  { B junction ,
B road_user(X,Y) } <- wait, give_way, check_cross(X,Y);
+!want_enter_junction  [achieve]  :  { B junction ,
B no_road_user(X,Y) } <- check_safe_gap(X,Y);
+!want_enter_junction  [achieve]  :  { B junction ,
B no_road_user(X,Y), B safe_gap(X,Y) } <- enter;
```

Notice the AV-agent has a sequence of five plans representing the stages of rule 170.

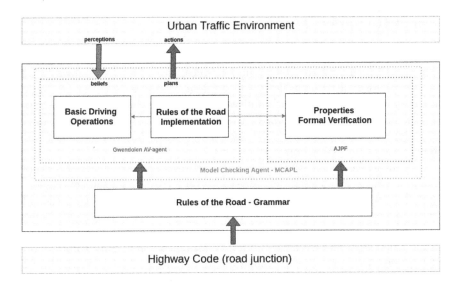

Fig. 1. SAE-RoR Architecture

1. When the agent believes that it should watch for something in the environment (*represented by* (X, Y)), then it should watch out for road users.
   - `want-enter-junction` is the agent goal it should be achieved.
   - `(X,Y)` represents a position in the environment; the agent receives per-
     ceptions placed at this position.
   - `B` in GWENDOLEN stands for an agent Belief.
   - `watch(X,Y)` is an action taken by the agent, which has an effect in the
     environment (*notice that all actions have some effect in the environment*).
2. When the agent believes that it is at the junction, it should check if there is
   a road user crossing the junction.
   - `check-cross(X,Y)` is an action taken by the agent.
3. When the agent believes that it is at the junction and there is a road user
   crossing it, then it shoud wait, give way and check the junction again.
   - `wait`, `give-way` are actions taken by the agent.
4. When the agent believes that it is at the junction and there is no road user
   crossing it, then it needs to check for a safe gap.
   - `check-safe-gap(X,Y)` is an action taken by the agent.
5. When the agent believes that it is at the junction, there is no road user
   crossing it, and there is a safe gap, then it may enter the junction.
   - `enter` is an action taken by the agent.

6 Final Remarks

We have proposed an agent-based architecture which represents the rules of the road (a subset including the road junction rules) from the UK Highway Code. The rules are formalised using LTL and implemented in a GWENDOLEN agent. Notice that it is an ongoing work and we intend to produce a complete implementation and formal verification of the road junction rules in a forthcoming work, where we will use the MCAPL model checker in order to formally verify the behaviour of the AV-agent.

The Highway Code uses different terms to represent the same sort of concepts. An example can be given with the Safe Gap term (an Abstract Object as seen in Subsect. 2.2), which indeed is used as a meaning for different terms in the rules of the road. This sort of abstraction is necessary to create a language simple enough and suitable for an AV-agent.

Some rules from the Highway Code overlap each other. An example is the rules 175 and 176, both of which handle traffic lights scenarios. With the LTL formalisation it is possible to analyse such rules and find out that the desired outcome for a digital highway code should include a new rule which combines the main elements from rules 175 and 176. This is suggested because an AV-agent requires consistent and non-ambiguous information in order to build the agent plans (which includes beliefs and actions).

With the SAE-RoR architecture we shall be able to answer the three questions previously presented in the first section: **i.** Use a (formal) grammar and LTL to represent the objects and actions from the Highway Code in order to deal with ambiguity issues. **ii.** Apply model checking with AJPF in order to formally verify the behaviour of the AV-agent, in a way one can check the agent acts according to the expected flow of traffic without conflicts, inconsistency or redundancies when using the rules of the road. **iii.** The direct mapping of the Highway code into a digital version of it does not seem to be enough because some rules may overlap (e.g., rules 175 and 176) and also the AV-agent requires (in some scenarios) additional road context in order to implement a decision-making process. (Notice that we intend to properly answer questions **ii** and **iii** in a forthcoming work.) Indeed, as mentioned in [13], the road context can be used, for example, to determine when a vehicle is nearby a school at a specific time, then it should watch out for children. As future work, we aim to include in our architecture a component responsible for perceiving and extracting the relevant road context in a way that the AV-agent can obtain a new set of beliefs from the road junction rules plus a given road context.

Acknowledgements. Work partially supported through EPSRC research project Verifiable Autonomy [EP/L024845].

The authors kindly thank the anonymous reviewers for the insightful suggestions which have considerably improved the quality of our paper.

References

1. Alves, G.V., Dennis, L., Fisher, M.: Formalisation of the rules of the road for embedding into an autonomous vehicle agent. In: International Workshop on Verification and Validation of Autonomous Systems, Oxford, UK, pp. 1–2, July 2018. https://sites.google.com/site/wsvavas2018/home/proceedings
2. BBC News: UK wants fully autonomous cars on road, February 2019. https://www.bbc.com/news/technology-47144449
3. Bratman, M.E.: Intentions, Plans, and Practical Reason. Harvard University Press, Cambridge (1987)
4. Burkacky, O., Deichmann, J., Doll, G., Knochenhauer, C.: Rethinking car software and electronics architecture — McKinsey. https://www.mckinsey.com/industries/automotive-and-assembly/our-insights/rethinking-car-software-and-electronics-architecture
5. Davey, T.: Towards a code of ethics in artificial intelligence with Paula Boddington, July 2017. https://futureoflife.org/2017/07/31/towards-a-code-of-ethics-in-artificial-intelligence/
6. Dennis, L.A.: Gwendolen semantics: 2017. Technical report ULCS-17-001, University of Liverpool, Department of Computer Science (2017)
7. Dennis, L.A., Fisher, M., Webster, M.P., Bordini, R.H.: Model checking agent programming languages. Autom. Softw. Eng. **19**(1), 5–63 (2012). https://doi.org/10.1007/s10515-011-0088-x
8. Department for Transport: Using the road (159 to 203) - The Highway Code - Guidance - GOV.UK (2017). https://www.gov.uk/guidance/the-highway-code/using-the-road-159-to-203
9. Fernandes, L.E.R., Custodio, V., Alves, G.V., Fisher, M.: A rational agent controlling an autonomous vehicle: implementation and formal verification. In: Bulwahn, L., Kamali, M., Linker, S. (eds.) Proceedings First Workshop on Formal Verification of Autonomous Vehicles. Electronic Proceedings in Theoretical Computer Science, vol. 257, pp. 35–42 (2017). https://doi.org/10.4204/EPTCS.257.5
10. Fisher, M.: An Introduction to Practical Formal Methods Using Temporal Logic. Wiley, Hoboken (2011). https://doi.org/10.1002/9781119991472, http://eu.wiley.com/WileyCDA/WileyTitle/productCd-0470027886.html
11. Herrmann, A., Brenner, W., Stadler, R.: Autonomous Driving: How the Driverless Revolution will Change the World, 1st edn. Emerald Publishing, Bingley (2018)
12. Law Commission - UK: Automated Vehicles: Summary of the Analysis of Responses to the Preliminary Consultation Paper, June 2019. https://www.lawcom.gov.uk/project/automated-vehicles/
13. Marks, J.: How to ensure the safety of self-driving cars: Part 1/5, June 2018. https://medium.com/@olley_io/how-to-ensure-the-safety-of-self-driving-cars-part-1-5-2fcc891ea90b
14. Pattis, R.E.: Teaching EBNF first in CS 1. In: Proceedings of the Twenty-Fifth SIGCSE Symposium on Computer Science Education, Phoenix, Arizona, USA, pp. 300–303. SIGCSE 1994. ACM, New York (1994). https://doi.org/10.1145/191029.191155
15. Prakken, H.: On the problem of making autonomous vehicles conform to traffic law. Artif. Intell. Law **25**(3), 341–363 (2017). https://doi.org/10.1007/s10506-017-9210-0, https://doi.org/10.1007/s10506-017-9210-0
16. Southworth, P.: Driverless cars to be on Britain's roads by the end of the year, government reveals. The Telegraph, February 2019. https://www.telegraph.co.uk/news/2019/02/06/driverless-cars-britains-roads-end-year-government-reveals/

17. Vellinga, N.E.: From the testing to the deployment of self-driving cars: legal challenges to policymakers on the road ahead. Comput. Law Secur. Rev. **33**(6), 847–863 (2017). https://doi.org/10.1016/j.clsr.2017.05.006, http://www.sciencedirect.com/science/article/pii/S0267364917301334
18. Wooldridge, M., Rao, A.: Foundations of Rational Agency, Applied Logic Series, vol. 14. Springer, Netherlands (1999). https://doi.org/10.1007/978-94-015-9204-8, http://www.springer.com/gp/book/9780792356011

CriSGen: Constraint-Based Generation of Critical Scenarios for Autonomous Vehicles

Andreas Nonnengart$^{(\boxtimes)}$, Matthias Klusch, and Christian Müller

German Research Center for Artificial Intelligence, Saarbrücken, Germany
{andreas.nonnengart,matthias.klusch,christian.mueller}@dfki.de

Abstract. Ensuring pedestrian-safety is paramount to the acceptance and success of autonomous cars. The scenario-based training and testing of such self-driving vehicles in virtual driving simulation environments has increasingly gained attention in the past years. A key challenge is the automated generation of critical traffic scenarios which usually are rare in real-world traffic, while computing and testing all possible scenarios is infeasible in practice. In this paper, we present a formal method-based approach **CriSGen** for an automated and complete generation of critical traffic scenarios for virtual training of self-driving cars. These scenarios are determined as close variants of given but uncritical and formally abstracted scenarios via reasoning on their non-linear arithmetic constraint formulas, such that the original maneuver of the self-driving car in them will not be pedestrian-safe anymore, enforcing it to further adapt the behavior during training.

Keywords: Autonomous driving · Formal methods · Critical scenarios

1 Introduction

Scenario-based training and testing of autonomous vehicles in driving simulators gained quite some attention recently. In fact, from an ethical perspective, synthesizing critical traffic scenarios in order to virtually train self-driving cars to perform pedestrian-safe (pedestrian collision avoiding) navigation suggests itself. Such scenarios are usually rare in real-world traffic and computing all possible scenarios for extracting unsafe ones is infeasible in practice. This challenge is addressed by various approaches to automated traffic scenario generation based on formal methods [1,4,8,13] or evolutionary and deep learning methods [14,19]. However, none of these generation approaches take known safe maneuvers of the self-driving car in given scenarios into account in order to determine critical traffic scenarios.

To this end, we developed a novel formal method-based approach **CriSGen** for an automated, complete generation of critical traffic scenarios for virtual training of self-driving cars. Critical scenarios are determined as close variants of given but uncritical maneuver and scenario abstraction via formal reasoning

© Springer Nature Switzerland AG 2020
E. Sekerinski et al. (Eds.): FM 2019 Workshops, LNCS 12232, pp. 233–248, 2020.
https://doi.org/10.1007/978-3-030-54994-7_17

on non-linear arithmetic constraint formulas with free parameters, such that the original maneuver of the self-driving car in them will not be pedestrian-safe anymore.

The remainder of the paper is structured as follows. A brief overview of the approach is given in Sect. 2, while its formal analysis techniques are described in more detail in Sect. 3. An illustrative example is provided in Sect. 4, and related work is summarized in Sect. 5 before we conclude in Sect. 6.

2   CriSGen Overview

The overall approach of **CriSGen** is illustrated in Fig. 1. An autonomous car operates in a virtual driving simulation environment such as OpenDS [5] and utilizes some learning technique for pedestrian-safe maneuver training. In each simulated traffic scenario, the adaptive car control determines its maneuver actions in terms of acceleration and steering, and is supposed to update its action policy based on feedback from the simulation environment such as whether it nearly misses or even hits a pedestrian. The automated generation of critical traffic scenarios by **CriSGen** can be triggered at any time, in particular in cases where the self-driving car appears to behave pedestrian-safe for some time period. The **CriSGen** process starts with transforming both the car maneuver action in the considered (uncritical) traffic scenario into a formal model and the scenario itself into a formal abstraction by replacing some of its concrete values with free parameters such that it represents a whole range of variants of the original scenario. These formal models together with a suitable unsafe-property (cf. Sect. 3.1) are then automatically analyzed (cf. Sect. 3.2) to obtain a non-linear arithmetic constraint formula which reflects all those scenario variants that must be considered *critical* for the given maneuver of the car. Geometrically, what we obtain this way is a collection of regions in n-dimensional space (where n is

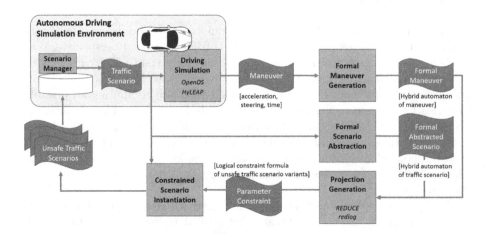

Fig. 1. Overview of the CriSGen approach for critical scene generation

the number of free parameters) such that each point in any of these regions represents a valuation of the parameters that makes the maneuver unsafe. The original scenario is represented as a single point in this n-dimensional space and lies outside any of the unsafe regions. **CriSGen** then selects points in the unsafe regions that are as close as possible, i.e. geometrically near to the original scenario (cf. Sect. 3.3). In other words, we translate and compose the abstracted scenario together with the original maneuver into some sort of hybrid automaton. A forward reachability analysis with respect to some suitable unsafety property ("hitting pedestrians") ends up in a constraint formula whose solutions are exactly the representatives of critical scenarios. In the final instantiation steps, a whole bunch of critical scenarios are obtained which are returned to the scenario manager of the driving simulator for challenging the car.

Our implementation setting for **CriSGen** employs OpenDS [5] as a virtual driving simulator and HyLEAP [17] for adaptive maneuver training of the car in OpenDS. For reachability analysis one might adapt systems like PVS [12] or TLA+ [15]. Instead, **CriSGen** makes utilizes the general-purpose computer algebra system REDUCE, in particular, its module **redlog** [6], to perform quantifier elimination on non-linear arithmetic constraint formulas. For instance, given that $a > 0$, the quantifier-free equivalent of $\exists x\ ax^2 + bx + c \leq 0$ is $b^2 \geq 4ac$ [7]; **redlog** determines the projections of complex constraint formulas onto the set of variables of interest, for example the parameters introduced by traffic scenario abstractions. In the remainder of this paper, whenever we speak of the quantifier-free equivalent of a (quantified) constraint formula we mean **redlog**'s quantifier elimination output when called with this constraint formula.

3   CriSGen: Formal Models and Analysis

3.1   Formal Models of Maneuver and Scenario

The formal analyses by **CriSGen** require formal models of car maneuvers, (abstracted) traffic scenarios, the composition of these models and an unsafe-property to be analyzed. In the following, we assume traffic scenarios with a single pedestrian, though the approach is not restricted to that.

Abstracted Scenario. We assume a two-dimensional grid upon which the pedestrian and the autonomous vehicle move. Each point on this grid is called a *position*, and the movements of pedestrians are described in sequences of positions together with a scalar velocity as[1]

$$(x_0, y_0) \xrightarrow{v_0} (x_1, y_1) \longrightarrow \cdots \longrightarrow (x_i, y_i) \xrightarrow{v_i} (x_{i+1}, y_{i+1}) \longrightarrow \cdots$$

In the original scenario all the x's, y's, and v's are concrete numbers, while in the next step we relax this and produce abstracted variants of this scenario with

---

[1] OpenDS scenarios are described in specific XML files from which such behaviors can be extracted.

the help of what we called *Abstraction Modifiers*. These are operators that can be applied to a given scenario (that may be already partially abstracted):

1. Replace a waypoint component with a (fresh) parameter (with or without propagation)
2. Replace a segment velocity with a (fresh) parameter
3. Split a segment (thus adding a waypoint and a parameter)
4. Double a waypoint

The application of an Abstraction Modifier has an instance, i.e. an instantiation of the free parameters, that is behavior equivalent to the original behavior. Regarding propagation, let us consider the simple scenario $(0,0) \xrightarrow{1} (0,1) \xrightarrow{1} (10,1)$, and suppose that we want to replace the y-component of the second waypoint with parameter c. Without propagation this ends up with the result $(0,0) \xrightarrow{1} (0,c) \xrightarrow{1} (10,1)$ as one might have expected. *With* propagation, however, would consider the y-component of the third waypoint as a function of the abstracted one. In the example this means that the two y-components should remain equal, i.e. we end up with $(0,0) \xrightarrow{1} (0,c) \xrightarrow{1} (10,c)$.

Splitting of a segment can be formulated in terms of quantifier elimination. For instance, to split a segment $(1,2) \xrightarrow{1} (2,5)$ we determine the quantifier-free equivalent of $\exists \lambda \ (0 \le \lambda \le 1 \wedge a = 1+\lambda \wedge b = 2+3\lambda)$ which is $1 \le a \le 2 \wedge b = 3a-1$. The split segment therefore is $(1,2) \xrightarrow{1} (a, 3a-1) \xrightarrow{1} (2,5)$, where $1 \le a \le 2$. Of course, this also works in cases where parameters have already been introduced. For example, splitting the segment $(1,2) \xrightarrow{1} (3,p)$, where p is a parameter, results in the split segment $(1,2) \xrightarrow{1} (a, \frac{1}{2}(ap - 2a - p + 6)) \xrightarrow{1} (3,p)$ with $1 \le a \le 3$. A scenario modification is then defined as the successive application of several such Abstraction Modifiers.

Formal Model of Abstracted Scenario. Let (p_x, p_y) denote the pedestrian's position (x and y component) with both values being functions over time, such that the respective velocity components are the first derivatives of p_x and p_y denoted by $\dot{p}_x$ and $\dot{p}_y$. These components have to be specified in order to be able to describe the reachable positions of the pedestrian within a phase of the scenario. Since the pedestrian walks from (x_i, y_i) to (x_{i+1}, y_{i+1}) with velocity v_i (a scalar), we have that $v_i^2 = \dot{p}_x^2 + \dot{p}_y^2$. Besides, the pedestrian takes the same time to cross the distance $x_{i+1} - x_i$ as the distance $y_{i+1} - y_i$: the ratio $(x_{i+1} - x_i)/(y_{i+1} - y_i)$ is the same as the ratio $\dot{p}_x/\dot{p}_y$, and so $\dot{p}_y\,(x_{i+1} - x_i) = \dot{p}_x\,(y_{i+1} - y_i)$ holds. This does not yet uniquely describe the velocity components. In order to make sure that the velocities have the correct sign we also add $\dot{p}_x\,(x_{i+1} - x_i) \ge 0$ and $\dot{p}_y\,(y_{i+1} - y_i) \ge 0$. Together, all these (in)equations fully describe the pedestrian's continuous dynamics.

Next, we have to make sure that the pedestrian completes the current segment as soon as she reaches (x_{i+1}, y_{i+1}), and that she passes through each point of the line segment while walking. This gives rise to the following segment invariant: If $x_{i+1} \ge x_i$ it suffices to add the invariant $p_x \le x_{i+1}$

(and analogously for the y-component). Similarly, if $x_{i+1} \leq x_i$ then the invariant $p_x \geq x_{i+1}$ would do. However, we can avoid such a case distinction if we declare $p_x (x_{i+1} - x_i) \leq x_{i+1} (x_{i+1} - x_i)$ and $p_y (y_{i+1} - y_i) \leq y_{i+1} (y_{i+1} - y_i)$ as our phase invariant. Obviously, if the distance is positive then the differences cancel out and if it is negative they cancel out but also reverse the inequality sign. The two lower implications capture the marginal cases where the pedestrian moves straight in the y-direction (x-direction respectively).

Definition 1 (Specification of pedestrian dynamics and invariant for segment i). *Let segment i of an abstracted scenario be $(x_i, y_i) \xrightarrow{v_i} (x_{i+1}, y_{i+1})$. Let $\Delta x = x_{i+1} - x_i$ and $\Delta y = y_{i+1} - y_i$ We define pedestrian p dynamics dyn_i^p and invariant inv_i^p for segment i as follows:*

$$
\text{dyn}_i^p = \begin{bmatrix} v_i^2 = \dot{p}_x^2 + \dot{p}_y^2 \wedge v_i \geq 0 & \wedge \\ \dot{p}_x \, \Delta x \geq 0 & \wedge \\ \dot{p}_y \, \Delta y \geq 0 & \wedge \\ \Delta x \, \dot{p}_y = \Delta y \, \dot{p}_x \end{bmatrix}
\qquad
\text{inv}_i^p = \begin{bmatrix} p_x' \, \Delta x \leq x_{i+1} \, \Delta x & \wedge \\ p_y' \, \Delta y \leq y_{i+1} \, \Delta y & \wedge \\ x_{i+1} = x_i \rightarrow p_x' = p_x & \wedge \\ y_{i+1} = y_i \rightarrow p_y' = p_y \end{bmatrix}
$$

With these definitions we can imagine an (hybrid) automaton-like representation of the translation of an abstracted scenario as a sequence of nodes each representing one segment Seg_i with continuous dynamics dyn_i^p, invariant inv_i^p and transition guards $p_x = x_{i+1}, p_y = y_{i+1}$. Informally, the reachability semantics defines the set of reachable states, in this case the pedestrian's positions, for each of the segments (cf. Sect. 3.2).

Formal Model of Maneuver. The virtually simulated autonomous car outputs a maneuver description that starts with an initial position (α, β) together with an initial x, y-velocity (μ_0, ν_0) followed by a sequence of maneuver events each accompanied with a τ that expresses the duration of the current state of movement. A typical maneuver would thus be:

$$
((\alpha, \beta), (\mu_0, \nu_0)) \xrightarrow{\tau_0} e_1(n_1) \xrightarrow{\tau_1} e_2(n_2) \xrightarrow{\tau_2} e_3(n_3) \xrightarrow{\tau_3} \dots
$$

where each $e_i(n_i)$ denotes one of the maneuver events from below

`de-/accelerate by` n: De-/Increase velocity while keeping the direction
`steer left/right by` ϕ: ϕ might be in degrees or radians, velocity remains
    constant

In the course of driving these car dynamics change from (μ_j, ν_j) to (μ_{j+1}, ν_{j+1}) depending on the current maneuver event. Thus, for modelling the maneuver, we determine the – as we call it – velocity sequence as follows:

$$
(\mu_0, \nu_0), (\mu_1, \nu_1), (\mu_2, \nu_2), (\mu_3, \nu_3), \dots
$$

(μ_0, ν_0) is already given in the maneuver description. Having (μ_j, ν_j), the next velocity vector (μ_{j+1}, ν_{j+1}) depends on the maneuver event $e_{j+1}(n_{j+1})$. In case of a steering event, we simply multiply by the rotation matrix, i e.,

$$
\begin{pmatrix} \mu_{j+1} \\ \nu_{j+1} \end{pmatrix} = \begin{pmatrix} \cos(\phi) & -\sin(\phi) \\ \sin(\phi) & \cos(\phi) \end{pmatrix} \begin{pmatrix} \mu_j \\ \nu_j \end{pmatrix}
$$

Otherwise, $e_{j+1}(n_{j+1})$ is a de-/acceleration event. In this case, (μ_{j+1}, ν_{j+1}) is uniquely characterized by the quantifier-free equivalent of

$$\exists\, \texttt{old}, \texttt{new} \begin{bmatrix} \texttt{old}^2 = \mu_j^2 + \nu_j^2 \wedge \texttt{old} \geq 0 \quad \wedge \\ \texttt{new}^2 = \mu_{j+1}^2 + \nu_{j+1}^2 \wedge \texttt{new} = \texttt{old} + n_{j+1} \quad \wedge \\ \mu_j\, \nu_{j+1} = \mu_{j+1}\, \nu_j \quad \wedge \\ \mu_j\, \mu_{j+1} \geq 0 \wedge \nu_j\, \nu_{j+1} \geq 0 \end{bmatrix}$$

The top four in-/equations express the change in velocity, the fifth guarantees that the absolute value of the direction is kept constant, and the final two equations make sure that the velocities are not reversed[2]. With these definitions the characterization of the car's continuous dynamics and invariant for phase j – in the sequel denoted by Ph_j – becomes

$$\texttt{dyn}_j^c = \left[\dot{c}_x = \mu_j \wedge \dot{c}_y = \nu_j \wedge \dot{t} = 1\right] \qquad \texttt{inv}_j^c = \left[t' \leq \tau_j\right]$$

In terms of hybrid automata, we obtain again a sequence of nodes, each responsible for a maneuver phase with continuous dynamics $\texttt{dyn}_j^c$, invariant $\texttt{inv}_j^c$ and transition annotations $t = \tau_j, t' = 0$. The formal model of a maneuver in terms of hybrid automata (with reachable state semantics defined in Sect. 3.2) can therefore be described as in Fig. 2.

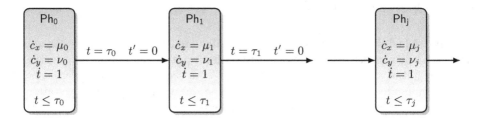

Fig. 2. Hybrid automaton for maneuvers.

Composition of Formal Models of Scenario and Maneuver. Given an abstracted scenario $(x_0, y_0) \xrightarrow{v_0} (x_1, y_1) \xrightarrow{v_1} \ldots$ and a maneuver $((\alpha, \beta), (\mu_0, \nu_0)) \xrightarrow{\tau_0} e_1(n_1) \xrightarrow{v_0} \ldots$ with velocity sequence $(\mu_0, \nu_0), (\mu_1, \nu_1), \ldots$, we obtain the pedestrian's (hybrid) automaton and the car's maneuver (hybrid) automaton as described above. There are no synchronization labels involved, nor are there any cycles. The composition of these two hybrid automata is therefore straightforward: Its nodes are the cross-products $(Seg_i \times Ph_j)$ of the scenario and the maneuver nodes, the continuous dynamics and the invariants are the

---

[2] This disallows maneuvers in which a car drives slowly by, say, 1 m/s, and decelerates by 2 m/s, thus reversing its motion direction. Reversing the sense of direction should be described by decelerating to a stop and a further deceleration for driving backwards.

conjunction of the local dynamics and invariants, and the transitions are the local transitions from the local automata, i. e. two outgoing transitions for each node.

Safety Property. Pedestrian avoidance serves as a unique safety property to be satisfied by the self-driving car. To this end, the pedestrian hit area of the car is defined in terms of the car's position and direction. A maneuver is called **safe** if there is no point in time where a pedestrian's position lies within the car's hit area. Let the car's position and velocity vector be (c_x, c_y) and $(\dot{c}_x, \dot{c}_y)$, respectively. One vector perpendicular to the sense of direction is $(\dot{c}_y, -\dot{c}_x)$ and the car's speed is $\sqrt{\dot{c}_x^2 + \dot{c}_y^2}$, which we abbreviate to α. For checking the safety of the pedestrian's position, we extend the car's position (c_x, c_y) by at most ± 3 (meters, say)[3] in the sense of direction, which is normalized to $(\dot{c}_x, \dot{c}_y)/\alpha$, and at most ± 1 perpendicular to the sense of direction, which is normalized to $(\dot{c}_y, -\dot{c}_x)/\alpha$. After minor simplifications, we finally end up with: The position (p_x, p_y) is inside the car's hit area (during node $Seg_i \times Ph_j$) iff $(p_x, p_y, c_x, c_y) \in$ $\mathtt{Hit}_{(i \times j)}$ where

$$\mathtt{Hit}_{(i \times j)} = \exists \lambda_1, \lambda_2, \alpha \begin{bmatrix} \alpha^2 = \dot{c}_x^2 + \dot{c}_y^2 \ \wedge \ \alpha \geq 0 \quad \wedge \\ -1 \leq \lambda_1 \leq 1 \ \wedge \ -3 \leq \lambda_2 \leq 3 \quad \wedge \\ \alpha\, c_x - \alpha\, p_x = \lambda_1\, \dot{c}_y + \lambda_2\, \dot{c}_x \quad \wedge \\ \alpha\, c_y - \alpha\, p_y = \lambda_2\, \dot{c}_y - \lambda_1\, \dot{c}_x \end{bmatrix}$$

with $\dot{c}_x = \mu_j$ and $\dot{c}_y = \nu_j$. Obviously, this safety property changes from phase to phase of the composed automaton, since velocities and directions of participants vary from phase to phase, and the safety property depends on these values.

3.2   Formal Analysis of Abstracted Scenarios and Maneuvers

For the formal assessment of given maneuvers with respect to abstracted scenarios we define what we understand by the set of reachable states and how these are represented. Therefore let us assume that we have an abstracted scenario

$$(x_0, y_0) \xrightarrow{v_0} (x_1, y_1) \xrightarrow{v_1} \ldots \xrightarrow{v_{i-1}} (x_i, y_i) \xrightarrow{v_i} (x_{i+1}, y_{i+1}) \xrightarrow{v_{i+1}} \ldots$$

and a maneuver

$$((\alpha, \beta), (\mu, \nu)) \xrightarrow{\tau_0} \mathsf{e}_1(\mathsf{n}_1) \xrightarrow{\tau_1} \mathsf{e}_2(\mathsf{n}_2) \xrightarrow{\tau_2} \mathsf{e}_3(\mathsf{n}_3) \xrightarrow{\tau_3} \ldots$$

Since the continuous dynamics change from node to node in the composition we consider the set of reachable states as the union of the sets of reachable states

---

[3] The units do not really matter as long as they are kept consistent throughout the specification.

for the various composed nodes. In each such node the respective velocities are considered constant, therefore let

$$\texttt{Reach} = \begin{bmatrix} \delta \geq 0 \wedge t' = t + \delta \quad \wedge \\ p'_x = p_x + \delta \, \dot{p}_x \wedge p'_y = p_y + \delta \, \dot{p}_y \quad \wedge \\ c'_x = c_x + \delta \, \dot{c}_x \wedge c'_y = c_y + \delta \, \dot{c}_y \end{bmatrix}$$

This together with the local continuous dynamics and invariant gives rise to the following definition of the set of reachable states.

Definition 2 (Reachable States for Node $Seg_i \times Ph_j$). *Let* $vars = \{p_x, p_y,$ $\dot{p}_x, \dot{p}_y, c_x, c_y, \dot{c}_x, \dot{c}_y, t, \delta\}$. *Then the set of reachable states in node* $Seg_i \times Ph_j$, $\texttt{States}_{(i \times j)}$, *is uniquely determined by (the quantifier-free equivalent of)*

$$\texttt{States}_{(i \times j)} = \exists \, vars \, \Big[\texttt{Init}_{(i \times j)} \wedge \texttt{Dyn}_{(i \times j)} \wedge \texttt{Reach} \wedge \texttt{Inv}_{(i \times j)} \Big]$$

where $\texttt{Dyn}_{(i \times j)} = dyn_i^p \wedge dyn_j^c$ *and* $\texttt{Inv}_{(i \times j)} = inv_i^p \wedge inv_j^c$. *For* $\texttt{Init}_{(i \times j)}$ *see below.*

In fact, according to the definitions of $\texttt{Dyn}_{(i \times j)}$, $\texttt{Inv}_{(i \times j)}$, and $\texttt{Reach}$ the constraint $\texttt{States}_{(i \times j)}$ talks about parameters and primed variables only. For convenience, we rename these variables to their unprimed versions[4].

$$\texttt{States}_{(i \times j)} = \texttt{States}_{(i \times j)}[p_x/p'_x][p_y/p'_y][c_x/c'_x][c_y/c'_y][t/t']$$

The above definition requires $\texttt{Init}_{(i \times j)}$, the constraint that describes the initial states for node $Seg_i \times Ph_j$. These depend on the reachable states of "earlier" nodes where the transition guards hold.

Definition 3 (Initial States for Node $Seg_i \times Ph_j$). *Given an abstracted scenario* $(x_0, y_0) \xrightarrow{v_0} (x_1, y_1) \xrightarrow{v_1} \ldots \xrightarrow{v_{i-1}} (x_i, y_i) \xrightarrow{v_i} (x_{i+1}, y_{i+1}) \xrightarrow{v_{i+1}} \ldots$ *and a maneuver* $((\alpha, \beta), (\mu, \nu)) \xrightarrow{\tau_0} e_1(n_1) \xrightarrow{\tau_1} e_2(n_2) \xrightarrow{\tau_2} e_3(n_3) \xrightarrow{\tau_3} \ldots$ *with derived velocity sequence* $(\mu_0, \nu_0), (\mu_1, \nu_1), (\mu_2, \nu_2), (\mu_3, \nu_3), \ldots$ *we define*

$$\texttt{Init}_{(0 \times 0)} = [p_x = x_0 \wedge p_y = y_0 \wedge c_x = \alpha \wedge c_y = \beta \wedge t = 0]$$

$$\texttt{Init}_{(0 \times (j+1))} = \Big[\exists t \, \{\texttt{States}_{(0 \times j)} \wedge t = \tau_j\} \wedge t = 0 \Big]$$

$$\texttt{Init}_{((i+1) \times 0)} = \Big[\texttt{States}_{(i \times 0)} \wedge p_x = x_{i+1} \wedge p_y = y_{i+1} \Big]$$

$$\texttt{Init}_{((i+1) \times (j+1))} = \begin{bmatrix} \texttt{States}_{(i \times (j+1))} \wedge p_x = x_{i+1} \wedge p_y = y_{i+1} \\ \vee \\ \exists t \, \{\texttt{States}_{((i+1) \times j)} \wedge t = \tau_j\} \wedge t = 0 \end{bmatrix}$$

Finally, after having determined the reachable states (for node $Seg_i \times Ph_j$) and having found the hit area (also for node $Seg_i \times Ph_j$), the constraint describing unsafe states is as follows.

---

[4] This can trivially be described as a quantifier elimination problem.

Definition 4 (Unsafe States for Node $Seg_i \times Ph_j$). *Given* $\text{States}_{(i \times j)}$ *and* $\text{Hit}_{(i \times j)}$, *the unsafe states for node* $Seg_i \times Ph_j$ *are defined as the quantifier-free equivalent of*

$$\text{Unsafe}_{(i \times j)} = \exists p_x, p_y, c_x, c_y, t \ \left[\text{States}_{(i \times j)} \wedge \text{Hit}_{(i \times j)} \right]$$

Each of the Unsafe-constraints contains no variable at all, and not all of them are simply true or false. In general, they still contain constraints over the parameters that had been introduced by Abstraction Modifiers. Algorithm 3.1 summarizes the forward-reachability mechanism defined above. Note that the nested for-loop guarantees that the constraint predicates are determined just-in-time.

Algorithm 3.1: FORWARDREACHABILITY(*Abstr.Scenario, Maneuver*)

$\text{Critical} \leftarrow \textbf{false}$

$\textbf{for } i \leftarrow 0, 1, 2, \ldots$

$\textbf{do} \begin{cases} \textbf{for } j \leftarrow 0 \textbf{ to } i \\ \\ \textbf{do} \begin{cases} \text{Init}[j][i-j] \leftarrow \text{see Definition 3} \\ \text{Dyn}[j][i-j] \leftarrow \text{see Definition 1} \\ \text{Inv}[j][i-j] \leftarrow \text{see Definition 1} \\ \text{States}[j][i-j] \leftarrow \text{see Definition 2} \\ \text{Hit}[j][i-j] \leftarrow \text{see Section 3.1} \\ \text{Unsafe}[j][i-j] \leftarrow \text{see Definition 4} \\ \text{Critical} \leftarrow \text{Critical} \vee \text{Unsafe}[j][i-j] \end{cases} \end{cases}$

$\textbf{return } (\text{Critical})$

3.3 Generating Critical Scenarios

Suppose that the scenario abstraction introduced the parameters $\{p_1, \ldots, p_n\}$. Now consider an n-dimensional grid with axes $p_1, \ldots, p_n$. Each point in this grid represents a variant of the abstracted scenario. The closer two such points are, the more similar are the variants that they represent. Some of these variants are behavior equivalent to the original scenario by definition (of the Abstraction Modifiers). Let O denote the area within this grid of the variants that are behavior equivalent to the original scenario. Algorithm 3.1 provides us with the constraint Critical that describes the variants that are unsafe with respect to the original maneuver. We determine the distance between the areas O and Critical by solving an optimization problem along the lines of [7] : The distance between any point $(a_1, \ldots, a_n)$ that satisfies O and any other point $(b_1, \ldots, b_n)$ that satisfies Critical is greater than or equal to the minimal distance between the two areas. Thus the quantifier-free equivalent of

$$\forall a_1, \ldots, a_n, b_1, \ldots b_n \; O[a_i/p_i] \wedge \texttt{Critical}[b_i/p_i] \rightarrow \sqrt{\sum_{i=1}^{n}(a_i^2 - b_i^2)} \geq d$$

is some constraint $d \leq \texttt{min}$ from which we can read $\texttt{min}$ as the minimal distance that we are interested in. With the computation of witnesses for the e_i in

$$\exists c_1, \ldots, c_n, e_1, \ldots e_n \; O[c_i/p_i] \wedge \texttt{Critical}[e_i/p_i] \wedge \texttt{min} \leq \sqrt{\sum_{i=1}^{n}(c_i^2 - e_i^2)} \leq \texttt{min} + \epsilon$$

(where ϵ is a small non-negative constant[5]) we have finally found the most appropriate candidates for instantiation.

4   An Illustrative Example

Scenario and Maneuver. As an illustrative example of our formal method-based approach to the generation of critical scenarios suppose that the simulation engine provides **CriSGen** with the traffic scenario and maneuver as depicted in Fig. 3. In this scenario, a pedestrian starts with velocity 1 (m/sec, say) at position $(0,0)$ goes straight to $(0,1)$, and crosses the street for point $(10,1)$. The car's maneuver simultaneously starts at $(3,70)$ while driving downwards with velocity 0 in x-direction and velocity -10 in y-direction. Both scenario and maneuver is summarized as follows:

$$(0,0) \xrightarrow{1} (0,1) \xrightarrow{1} (10,1) \qquad ((3,70),(0,-10)) \xrightarrow{\infty}$$

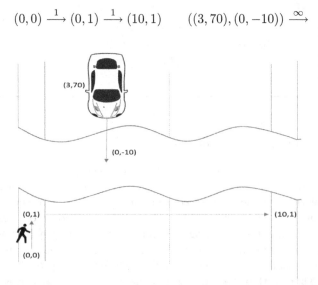

Fig. 3. Original (non-critical) scenario: the autonomous car drives too slow to jeopardize the pedestrian.

---

[5] ϵ compensates minor differences between the computed reachable states and the driving simulator's behavior.

One-Dimensional Abstraction. Consider a single abstraction, namely replacing the y-component of the second waypoint by a parameter c (unrestricted) *with propagation*, which ends up in the abstracted scenario

$$(0,0) \xrightarrow{1} (0,c) \xrightarrow{1} (10,c)$$

By applying Algorithm 3.1 to this abstraction, we obtain two Unsafe-constraints: $\text{Unsafe}_{(0 \times 0)} = \texttt{false}$ as expected; the pedestrian's behavior in the initial phase is certainly not critical (yet). The other Unsafe-constraint is more interesting:

$$\text{Unsafe}_{(1 \times 0)} = 27 \le 11c \le 53 \ \lor \ -53 \le 9c \le -27$$

Accordingly, the critical region consists of two parts: One where the pedestrian walks towards the car for some distance and then crosses the street, and another one, where the pedestrian actually walks away from the car before crossing the street (see Fig. 4). The ultimate goal of **CriSGen** is to synthesize critical scenarios that are possibly near the (non-critical) original traffic scenario (the circle at position 1 in Fig. 4). For this example, values 2.5 and -3.5 are reasonable.

Fig. 4. Unsafe (red rectangles) and original (green circle) scenarios. (Color figure online)

As a consequence, in this simple example, **CriSGen** ends up with several critical scenarios, e.g. for the values from above:

$$(0,0) \xrightarrow{1} (0,2.5) \xrightarrow{1} (10,2.5) \quad \text{and} \quad (0,0) \xrightarrow{1} (0,-3.5) \xrightarrow{1} (10,-3.5)$$

Two-Dimensional Abstraction. Suppose that the following abstractions are performed: a split of the second segment, and a doubling of the (new) fourth waypoint together with an abstraction of the x-component of the newest waypoint. This yields the abstracted scenario

$$(0,0) \xrightarrow{1} (0,1) \xrightarrow{1} (c,1) \xrightarrow{1} (a,1) \xrightarrow{1} (10,1)$$

where a,c are restricted to $0 \le c,a \le 10$. For this abstracted scenario (and maneuver) the Algorithm 3.1 returns within about $70 \, \text{m/sec}$

$$\texttt{Critical} = \text{Unsafe}_{(0 \times 0)} \lor \text{Unsafe}_{(1 \times 0)} \lor \text{Unsafe}_{(2 \times 0)} \lor \text{Unsafe}_{(3 \times 0)}$$

where $\text{Unsafe}_{(0 \times 0)}$ and $\text{Unsafe}_{(1 \times 0)}$ are both `false` and

$$\text{Unsafe}_{(2 \times 0)} = 38 \le 10c \le 51 \land 0 \le a \le 4 \land 5a - 10c + 28 \le 0$$
$$\text{Unsafe}_{(3 \times 0)} = 0 \le a \le 4 \land -5a + 10c - 31 \le 0 \land 8 \le 10c - 10a \le 21$$

These computed constraint formulas are illustrated in Fig. 5 where the lambda-shaped red area represents the unsafe scenarios and the top left green triangle represents the original scenario[6]. Note that the red area consists of two parts: The vertical part is responsible for phase (2×0), i.e. situations where the pedestrian is heading towards the other side of the street, but decides fairly late to return. The more diagonal part illustrates the critical a, c-pairs for phase (3×0). Here again, the pedestrian first tries to cross the street, decides pretty early to turn but finally nevertheless returns again for the other side.

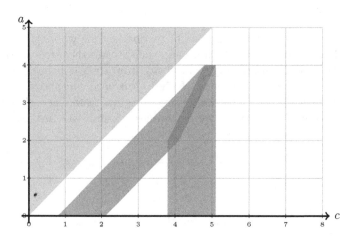

Fig. 5. Unsafe (red λ-shaped) and original (green triangle) scenarios. (Color figure online)

There are several interesting points in this region that can serve as candidates for (c, a), like $(5, 3.5), (4, 3), (3, 2), (2, 1), (1, 0)$. For instance, the pairs $(5, 3.5)$ and $(1, 0)$ result in the critical scenarios

$$(0,0) \xrightarrow{1} (0,1) \xrightarrow{1} (5,1) \xrightarrow{1} (3.5,1) \xrightarrow{1} (10,1)$$
$$(0,0) \xrightarrow{1} (0,1) \xrightarrow{1} (1,1) \xrightarrow{1} (0,1) \xrightarrow{1} (10,1)$$

Three-Dimensional Abstraction. Finally, let us perform some further abstraction by replacing the pedestrian's velocity in the final segment with a parameter b. This leads to the abstracted scenario

$$(0,0) \xrightarrow{1} (0,1) \xrightarrow{1} (c,1) \xrightarrow{1} (a,1) \xrightarrow{b} (10,1)$$

---

[6] Evidently, for any $0 \leq c \leq a \leq 10$ the corresponding instantiation is behavior equivalent to the original scenario. Therefore the safe (green) variants form the top-left triangle instead of a single point.

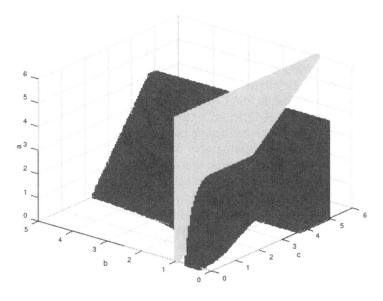

Fig. 6. Unsafe region (red) and original region (green). (Color figure online)

After determining the various constraint formulas and after computing all the necessary projections, **CriSGen** produces after about 250 m/sec the constraint formula for `Critical`, which, in this example, consists of five disjunctions:

`Critical` =
$38 \leq 10c \leq 51 \wedge 0 \leq a \leq 4 \wedge 5a - 10c + 28 \leq 0$ $\vee$
$b > 0 \wedge b < 1 \wedge 5bc - 31b - 5c + 10 \leq 0 \wedge 5bc - 28b - 5c + 20 \geq 0 \wedge a = c$ $\vee$
$a \leq 4 \wedge a < c \wedge 5a - 10c + 31 \geq 0 \wedge b > 0 \wedge 5ab + 5a - 10bc + 28b \leq 20$ $\wedge$
$\qquad\qquad\qquad\qquad\qquad\qquad 5ab + 5a - 10bc + 31b - 10 \geq 0$ $\vee$
$a \leq 4 \wedge a < c \wedge 5a - 10c + 31 \geq 0 \wedge b > 0$ $\wedge$
$\qquad\qquad\qquad\qquad 10 + 10bc - 31b \leq 5ab + 5a \leq 20 + 10bc - 28b$ $\vee$
$0 < b < 1 \wedge 5ab - 5a - 31b + 10 \leq 0 \wedge 5ab - 5a - 28b + 20 \geq 0 \wedge c \leq a$

Since there are three parameters involved, the corresponding unsafe region can be illustrated in a 3D graphic as shown in Fig. 6[7]. There are lots of additional interesting points in these unsafe-regions. For instance, $(a, b, c) = (2.5, 0.4, 1)$ and $(a, b, c) = (2.4, 0.5, 2)$, which instantiate the abstracted scenario to the critical scenarios

$$(0,0) \xrightarrow{1} (0,1) \xrightarrow{1} (1,1) \xrightarrow{1} (2.5,1) \xrightarrow{0.4} (10,1)$$

and

$$(0,0) \xrightarrow{1} (0,1) \xrightarrow{1} (2,1) \xrightarrow{1} (2.4,1) \xrightarrow{0.5} (10,1)$$

respectively.

---

[7] Note that in this illustration the unsafe region and the original region do not intersect, since cutting the area with the plane at $b = 1$ produces exactly Fig. 5.

5   Related Work

To our knowledge the **CriSGen** approach is the first that utilizes formal reasoning on non-linear arithmetic constraint formulas with free parameters to synthesize critical scenarios for self-driving cars from previous, similar traffic scenarios and maneuvers. Nevertheless, there exist various alternative, related approaches for scenario generation [2, 8–11, 13, 14, 19, 20].

In [8] Eggers et al. derive constraint problem classes to be solved for their synthesis, however without showing how to solve them. Their underlying language is based on the graphic representation of Damm et al. [4]. The graphic components get their semantics by a translation into a first-order sorted linear temporal logic which is interpreted in terms of the trajectories of the hybrid automata that represent the vehicles and pedestrians. Althoff and Lutz [1] propose yet another way to automatically generate critical scenarios with the help of formal methods. Whereas we consider a fixed maneuver in a traffic scenario to be challenged, they try to reduce the solution space for maneuvers of the car.

For systematic testing, Frassinelli et al. [9] propose a rule-based mechanism which confronts the autonomous car online while driving with just-in-time generated but not necessarily critical road extensions. Groh et al. [11] discuss transferring the test space into a scenario-depending representation which enables the comparison of scenarios across test domains. Aréchiga [2] use signal temporal logic and Bouton et al. [3] employ reinforcement learning together with a model checker to ensure safety guarantees. In fact, using evolutionary computing or deep learning methods for the generation of critical scenarios is becoming interesting recently such as in Wachi [14, 19]. Other related work focuses on extraction and representation of scenarios. For example, Queiroz et al. [18] propose OpenDSL for scenario representations and Menzel et al. [16] introduce a method to automatically generate executable scenario representations from keyword-based descriptions. Fremont et al. [10] introduce SCENIC, a scenario specification language that allows the modeler to mutate scenarios and Yaghoubi and Fainekos [20] determine adversaries for neural network inputs with a gradient descent approach.

6   Conclusion

In this paper, we presented a novel formal method-based approach **CriSGen** for an automated and complete generation of critical traffic scenarios for virtual training of self-driving cars. These scenarios are determined as close variants of given but uncritical and formally abstracted scenarios via reasoning on their non-linear arithmetic constraint formulas, such that the original maneuver of the self-driving car in them will not be pedestrian-safe anymore, hence enforcing it to further adapt the maneuver behavior. The approach is *complete* for the considered scenario abstraction in the sense that, unlike other related methods, it can guarantee to not overlook any of the possible scenario instances that are critical for the original maneuver.

Acknowledgement. This research was supported by the German Federal Ministry for Education and Research (BMB+F) in the project REACT.

References

1. Althoff, M., Lutz, S.: automatic generation of safety-critical test scenarios for collision avoidance of road vehicles. In: Proceedings of the 29th IEEE Intelligent Vehicles Symposium (IV) (2018)
2. Aréchiga, N.: Specifying safety of autonomous vehicles in signal temporal logic. In: Proceedings of the 30th IEEE Intelligent Vehicles Symposium (IV) (2019)
3. Bouton, M., Nakhaei, A., Fujimura, K., Kochenderfer, M.J.: Safe reinforcement learning with scene decomposition for navigating complex urban environments. In: Proceedings of the 30th IEEE Intelligent Vehicles Symposium (IV) (2019)
4. Damm, W., Kemper, S., Möhlmann, E., Peikenkamp, T., Rakow, A.: Traffic sequence charts - from visualization to semantics. Technical report, AVACS (2017)
5. DFKI: OpenDS. https://opends.dfki.de/
6. Dolzmann, A., Sturm, T.: Redlog. http://www.redlog.eu
7. Dolzmann, A., Sturm, T., Weispfenning, V.: Real quantifier elimination in practice. In: Matzat, B.H., Greuel, G.M., Hiss, G. (eds.) Algorithmic Algebra and Number Theory. Springer, Heidelberg (1999). https://doi.org/10.1007/978-3-642-59932-3_11
8. Eggers, A., Stasch, M., Teige, T., Bienmüller, T., Brockmeyer, U.: Constraint systems from traffic scenarios for the validation of autonomous driving. In: Proceedings of Symbolic Computation and Satisfiability Checking (2018)
9. Frassinelli, D., Gambi, A., Nürnberger, S., Park, S.: DRiVERSITY - synthetic torture testing to find limits of autonomous driving algorithms. In: Proceedings of the 2nd ACM Computer Science in Cars Symposium (CSCS) (2018)
10. Fremont, D.J., Dreossi, T., Ghosh, S., Yue, X., Sangiovanni-Vincentelli, A.L., Seshia, S.A.: Scenic: a language for scenario specification and scene generation. In: Proceedings of the 40th ACM SIGPLAN Conference on Programming Language Design and Implementation (PLDI). ACM (2019)
11. Groh, K., Kuehbeck, T., Fleischmann, B., Schiementz, M., Chibelushi, C.C.: Towards a scenario-based assessment method for highly automated driving functions. In: Proceedings of the 8th Conference on Driver Assistance (2017)
12. Henzinger, T.A., Rusu, V.: Reachability verification for hybrid automata. In: Henzinger, T.A., Sastry, S. (eds.) HSCC 1998. LNCS, vol. 1386, pp. 190–204. Springer, Heidelberg (1998). https://doi.org/10.1007/3-540-64358-3_40
13. Jesenski, S., Stellet, J.E., Schiegg, F., Zöllner, J.M.: Generation of scenes in intersections for the validation of highly automated driving functions. In: Proceedings of the 30th IEEE Intelligent Vehicles Symposium (IV) (2019)
14. Klischat, M., Althoff, M.: Generating critical test scenarios for automated vehicles with evolutionary algorithms. In: Proceedings of the 30th IEEE Intelligent Vehicles Symposium (IV) (2019)
15. Lamport, L.: Hybrid systems in TLA+. In: Grossman, R.L., Nerode, A., Ravn, A.P., Rischel, H. (eds.) HS 1991-1992. LNCS, vol. 736, pp. 77–102. Springer, Heidelberg (1993). https://doi.org/10.1007/3-540-57318-6_25
16. Menzel, T., Bagschik, G., Isensee, L., Schomburg, A., Maurer, M.: From functional to logical scenarios: detailing a keyword-based scenario description for execution in a simulation environment. In: Proceedings of the 30th IEEE Intelligent Vehicles Symposium (IV) (2019)

17. Pusse, F., Klusch, M.: Hybrid online POMDP planning and deep reinforcement learning for safer self-driving cars. In: Proceedings of the 30th IEEE Intelligent Vehicles Symposium (IV). IEEE (2019)
18. Queiroz, R., Berger, T., Czarnecki, K.: GeoScenario: an open DSL for autonomous driving scenario representation. In: Proceedings of the 30th IEEE Intelligent Vehicles Symposium (IV) (2019)
19. Wachi, A.: Failure-scenario maker for rule-based agent using multi-agent adversarial reinforcement learning and its application to autonomous driving. In: Proceedings of International Joint Conference on Artificial Intelligence (IJCAI) (2019)
20. Yaghoubi, S., Fainekos, G.: Gray-box adversarial testing for control systems with machine learning components. In: Proceedings of the 22nd ACM International Conference on Hybrid Systems: Computation and Control (HSCC) (2019)

Verification of Fair Controllers for Urban Traffic Manoeuvres at Intersections

Christopher Bischopink$^{(\boxtimes)}$ and Maike Schwammberger$^{(\boxtimes)}$

Department of Computing Science, University of Oldenburg, Oldenburg, Germany
{bischopink,schwammberger}@informatik.uni-oldenburg.de

Abstract. Autonomous crossing manoeuvres at intersections are especially challenging. In related work, a crossing controller for provably safe autonomous urban traffic manoeuvres was introduced. We extend this controller by a decentralised communication procedure that ensures fair behaviour of the controller and also guarantees bounded liveness. We verify the correctness of our extension by an implementation and analysis with UPPAAL Stratego.

Keywords: MLSL · Autonomous cars · Urban traffic manoeuvres · Fairness · Distributed controllers · Timed automata · UPPAAL Stratego

1 Introduction

For autonomous cars, functional properties are of the utmost importance, as e.g. in case of *safety*, human life is endangered. We consider the Multi-lane Spatial Logic (MLSL) approach, where in the first paper [1], safety of autonomous highway lane change manoeuvres was considered. Equally focusing on safety, there exist MLSL extensions for country roads with opposing traffic [2] and urban traffic with intersecting roads [3]. While safety is an important property, other functional properties for autonomous cars are of interest but have received less attention from the research community. As e.g., safety could be achieved if the cars do not drive at all, *liveness* is of interest. Liveness here means that something good, e.g. a lane change or a crossing manoeuvre, happens *finally*. The first liveness approach for the MLSL approach was presented for the highway traffic case in [4]. There, an implementation of the highway traffic controller from [1] in UPPAAL [5] was used to certify safety, show absence of liveness in the original controller and to introduce a live controller.

In this paper, we transfer the liveness result of [4] to the urban traffic crossing controller in [3]. However, liveness means that something good *finally* happens, which means that our crossing controller is live, even if it potentially needs a significant amount of time for a crossing manoeuvre. Thus, we introduce *fairness* into the crossing controller by simultaneously implementing a cooperative

This research was partially supported by the German Research Council (DFG) in the Research Training Group GRK 1765 SCARE.

E. Sekerinski et al. (Eds.): FM 2019 Workshops, LNCS 12232, pp. 249–264, 2020.
https://doi.org/10.1007/978-3-030-54994-7_18

crossing procedure where the *priorities* of cars are communicated over broadcast channels. With that, our controller commits crossing manoeuvres not only live, but also within some time bound and with a fair behaviour w.r.t. other cars. As an extension motivated by reality, we take probabilistic failures of message sending into account. We implement the extended controller protocol in UPPAAL Stratego [6] and verify correctness of the fair behaviour of our controllers.

Related work. There exist several approaches on centralised *cooperative intersection management* (CIM), where a road-side unit, e.g. a traffic light, acts as a centralised scheduler (cf. [7,8]). These approaches are limited to signalised intersections, whereas we use a *decentralised* CIM approach in this paper, where the cars negotiate their passage through the intersection amongst each other. Thus, we also discuss related work for decentralised CIM in the following.

A prior approach using distributed reservation was proposed based on Petri-Net models [9]. For implementing fairness, the authors also propose priorities depending on waiting time and velocity, and support their claims by simulation results. However, only one car at a moment has a send-token and may thus communicate with the other cars. Furthermore, time is not explicitly considered with the Petri-Net models. Other approaches on traffic control without road-side units introduce a *virtual traffic light* (VTL) [10,11]. For this, one of the vehicles approaching an intersection is cooperatively selected to be the VTL leader. This leader then again acts as a central scheduler for all cars approaching the crossing. However, [12] points out that a problem with VTL is the leader selection, as this a) takes some time and b) possible communication failure during the negotiation phase may lead to a disagreement in the leader selection.

In [13], a constraint solver is used to prove the correctness of a vehicle coordination protocol for intersections. They focus on the effect of parameters for longitudinal movement, whereas we focus more on the effect of time and the choice of probabilities for communication failure. Although uncertain communication is also possible in [13], there are no quantitative statements regarding the choice of such parameters.

The structure of this paper is as follows. In Sect. 2, we introduce the preliminaries for the urban traffic approach. Next, in Sect. 3, we give an overview over our implementation of the crossing controller in UPPAAL Stratego and describe our protocol for fair behaviour of the controllers, followed by UPPAAL Stratego analysis results. We extend our approach in Sect. 4 by probabilities for message sending failures. We conclude with an outlook on future work and a short summary of the key contributions of our approach in Sect. 5.

2   Preliminaries

In this section, we give a brief overview of the necessary concepts from [3] and give the formal details for the key concepts. We start with an introduction of the model and logic for urban traffic manoeuvres in Sect. 2.1, give an overview over the crossing controller in Sect. 2.2 and conclude with the introduction of the underlying automaton type of the controller, automotive-controlling timed automata (ACTA), in Sect. 2.3.

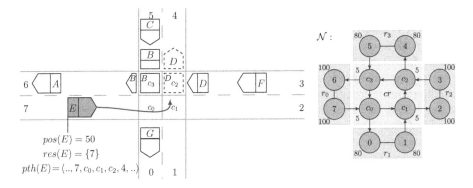

Fig. 1. Abstract model for a 2-by-2 intersection to the left with cars A to G visible, where *ego* car E plans on turning left. Car D plans to enter the intersection, as indicated by its dashed *claim* on segment c_2 and some part of lane 4 after the crossing. The related graph topology describing the connections of segments is depicted to the right.

2.1 An Abstract Model for Urban Traffic Manoeuvres

To formally reason about urban traffic manoeuvres, we abstract from the real world with an *abstract model*, for which we briefly explain concepts in the following paragraphs. A picture of a running example for our model for urban traffic which we use throughout this paper is depicted in Fig. 1.

As our model is tailored to handle traffic situations at intersections, it contains a set $\mathbb{CS}$ of *crossing segments* $c_0, c_1, \ldots$, where all adjacent crossing segments are grouped into *intersections/crossings* cr from the set $\mathcal{P}(\mathbb{CS})$ such that we have the intersection $cr := \{c_0, c_1, c_2, c_3\}$ in the example. To connect different intersections with each other, we introduce the set $\mathbb{L}$ of *lane segments* $0, 1, \ldots$. Each crossing segment and each lane segment has a finite length.

To each car, we assign a unique *car identifier* $A, B, \ldots$ from the set $\mathbb{I}$ of all car identifiers and a real value for the *position pos* of its rear on a lane or crossing segment. We use car E as the car under consideration with valuation $\nu(ego) = E$ to refer to this car. When we are talking about an arbitrary car, we use the identifier C. We distinguish between the *reservation res*(C) of a car, meaning the space the car is actually occupying, and the *claim clm*(C) of a car, indicating the space a car plans to drive on in the future. To allow for uncertain sensors, both reservations and claims might be seen as over-approximations of the actual space occupied by the cars. A claim is thus comparable to setting the turn signal, e.g. see car D in Fig. 1 claiming crossing segment c_2 and some space on lane 4 behind cr, as indicated by the dashed lines.

Connections of lane and crossing segments are formalised by a directed graph topology called *urban road network* $\mathcal{N}$ with set of nodes $\mathcal{V}$ built from the respective sets of lane and crossing segments: $\mathcal{V} = \mathbb{L} \cup \mathbb{CS}$. We consider continuous movement on lane segments and discrete crossing segments, whereas a crossing segment is either fully occupied by one car or empty. We only permit undirected edges $e \in E_u$ between lane segments, e.g. see the undirectedly connected lanes 6 and 7 in Fig. 1, to allow for bi-directional overtaking manoeuvres between intersections. All other types of edges in $\mathcal{N}$ are directed ($e \in E_d$), whereby a driving direction for our continuous lane segments is specified. Thus, a car is allowed to drive from lane 7 onto crossing segment c_0, but not vice versa. For each car C, we assign an *infinite path* $pth(C)$ with $pth : \mathbb{I} \to (\mathbb{Z} \to \mathcal{V})$, resembling its travelling route through the urban road network. In Fig. 1, the path of car E for turning left at the depicted crossing is given by $pth(E) = \langle \ldots 7, c_0, c_1, c_2, 4, \ldots \rangle$.

Information like reservations, claims, positions $pos(C)$ and paths $pth(C)$ for each car are collected in a global *traffic snapshot* $\mathcal{TS}$. One traffic snapshot can be considered as one snapshot of the overall traffic in $\mathcal{N}$ at one moment. For instance, whenever time passes or a car claims or reserves a new lane or crossing segment, the traffic snapshot is modified with the respective changes. However, for reasoning about traffic manoeuvres of the ego car E, it is unrealistic and moreover unnecessary to consider the complete traffic snapshot $\mathcal{TS}$. Instead, we only consider a finite excerpt of $\mathcal{TS}$ called *virtual view* $V(E)$ containing the surroundings of *ego* car E up to a specified horizon.

For reasoning about traffic situations in such a virtual view $V(E)$, we use our two-dimensional logic *Urban Multi-lane Spatial Logic (UMLSL)*, which is an extension of the highway logic MLSL. With a spatial formula $\phi = re(E) \frown free$, we can state that there is free space in front of the reservation of our ego car E. We have atoms cs for representing crossing segments, $re(c)$ (resp. $cl(c)$) for a reservation (resp. claim) and $u = v$ to compare the values of two variables $u, v \in Var$. Further on, with $\ell = r$, we can compare the length ℓ of a space interval with a real value r. For instance, this is used for checking the distance of a car to an upcoming intersection. Note that while we write $res(E)$ for the set of reserved segments of car E stored in the traffic snapshot $\mathcal{TS}$ (cf. Fig. 1), we use $re(c)$ as an atom in our logic UMLSL to distinguish both concepts.

Definition 1 (Syntax of UMLSL).   *Consider a car variable $c \in$ CVar, a real variable $r \in$ RVar and general variables $u, v \in Var$. The syntax of atomic UMLSL formulae is defined by* $\mathsf{a} ::= cs \mid true \mid u = v \mid \ell = r \mid free \mid re(c) \mid cl(c)$, *whereas an arbitrary UMLSL formula ϕ_U is formalised by*

$$\phi_U ::= \mathsf{a} \mid \neg\phi \mid \phi_1 \wedge \phi_2 \mid \exists c \colon \phi_1 \mid \phi_1 \frown \phi_2 \mid {}^{\phi_2}_{\phi_1}.$$

We denote the set of all UMLSL formulae by Φ_U.

The semantics of UMLSL formulae is evaluated over a traffic snapshot $\mathcal{TS}$, a virtual view $V(E)$ and a variable valuation ν. For reasons of brevity, we omit a formal semantics definition at this point.

2.2   Crossing Controller Protocol

The idea for this crossing controller goes back to the lane change controller from [1]. Thus, we first *claim* an area that we want to enter (here: a part of the intersection) and *reserve* it only if no potential collision is detected. An overview over our crossing controller protocol is depicted in Fig. 2. Note that in

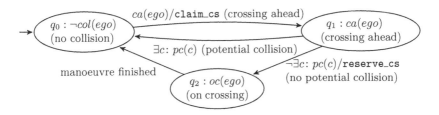

Fig. 2. Overview over crossing controller protocol.

this overview a lot of details, e.g. time and data constraints, are omitted. For the detailed original controller, see [3]. Also, in Sect. 3, we discuss our extension of adding fairness to the controller in more detail. We construct the crossing controller from the perspective of our ego car E. Initially, we start in a safe state c_0, thus the *collision check* formula

$$col(ego) \equiv \exists c : c \neq ego \land \langle re(ego) \land re(c) \rangle \tag{1}$$

does *not* hold initially, where $\langle \varphi \rangle$ is an abbreviation for "somewhere" in the view $V(E)$ of ego car E holds φ. Whenever an intersection comes within a distance less than d_c, our *crossing ahead check*

$$ca(ego) \equiv \langle re(ego) \frown free^{<d_c} \land \neg \langle cs \rangle \frown cs \rangle \tag{2}$$

holds and with $cc()$ the needed crossing segments of the path $pth(E)$ are claimed. In formula (2), the subformula $free^{<d_c}$ is an abbreviation for the UMLSL formula $free \land \ell < d_c$, which measures that the free space between the reservation of car E and the intersection has a size of less than d_c. After changing to the new location c_1, the controller checks whether its new claim for the intersection overlaps with an existing claim or reservation of another car with the *potential collision check*

$$pc(c) \equiv c \neq ego \land \langle cl(ego) \land (re(c) \lor cl(c)) \rangle. \tag{3}$$

Only if there exists no potential collision, our controller may change its crossing claim into a reservation with $rc(ego)$ and thus enter the intersection. With that, the *on crossing check* holds:

$$oc(ego) \equiv \langle re(ego) \land cs \rangle \tag{4}$$

Note that we do not allow lane change manoeuvres near to and on crossings.

2.3 Automotive-Controlling Timed Automata

We introduce the underlying automaton type of our controllers, *automotive-controlling timed automata (ACTA)*, for a better understanding of the translation of our crossing controller to an UPPAAL automaton we present in Sect. 3. ACTA extends the widely used timed automata (TA) from [14] and moreover the extended version of TA UPPAAL which is described in [5].

Equally as for timed automata, a core concept of ACTA is using time, i.e. *clock variables* $x \in \mathbb{X}$ ranging over the continuous time domain $Time = \mathbb{R}_{\geq 0}$. Additionally, we use *data variables* from the set $\mathbb{D}$ ranging over the sets of lane segments $\mathbb{L}$, crossing segments $\mathbb{CS}$ and car identifiers $\mathbb{I}$. We use *data constraints* $\varphi_{\mathbb{D}}$, similar to the clock constraints from timed automata, where with a data constraint $\varphi_{\mathbb{D}} \equiv l = n + 1$ for $l, n \in \mathbb{D}$, we can check for the equality of two lanes. Data variables may be set to a type respecting value with *data modifications*. With these data constraints, we now introduce the possible *guards* and *invariants* that we allow for ACTA.

Definition 2 (Guards and Invariants). *With data constraints $\varphi_{\mathbb{D}} \in \Phi_{\mathbb{D}}$, clock constraints $\varphi_{\mathbb{X}} \in \Phi_{\mathbb{X}}$ and UMLSL formulae $\varphi_{\mathbb{U}} \in \Phi_{\mathbb{U}}$ from of Definition 1, a guard or invariant φ is defined by $\varphi ::= \varphi_{\mathbb{D}} \mid \varphi_{\mathbb{X}} \mid \varphi_{\mathbb{U}} \mid \varphi_1 \wedge \varphi_2 \mid true$. The set of all guards and invariants is denoted by Φ.*

An example for a guard of an ACTA is $x > 0 \wedge \langle re(ego) \frown free \rangle$, meaning that the valuation of a clock x is bigger than 0 and that somewhere there is free space ahead of the reservation of the ego car.

On introducing the traffic snapshot in Sect. 2.1, we hinted that the traffic snapshot changes, whenever new claims or reservations occur or when they are withdrawn. These claims or reservations for lane or crossing segments are set (resp. withdrawn) by our controllers using *controller actions*. We only allow for one single controller action on each transition of an ACTA.

For instance, with the controller action $cc(ego)$, the ego car claims all those crossing segments it needs to pass an upcoming intersection according to its path. With $wd\,c(c)$, this crossing claim is again withdrawn, while with $rc(ego)$, it is converted into a crossing reservation. In all cases, the controller action also changes the respective traffic snapshot.

An example for an ACTA is provided in Fig. 3. Note that we adapt the broadcast communication from UPPAAL by adding data that may be sent over the channels. For instance, with the output action *finished!c* depicted on the transition from q_1 to q_0, the value of the variable c is sent over the channel *finished*. With that, other controllers synchronising with *finished!c* can check the identifier of the sending controller.

The semantics of an ACTA $\mathcal{A}$, as for networks of ACTA, is given by a *transition system* $\mathcal{T}(\mathcal{A})$. For details on this, we refer to [3] and to Sect. 4, where we introduce our extension of *probabilistic automotive-controlling timed automata* (PACTA), including an example of their semantics.

3   Introducing Fairness into the Protocol

We now describe our adaption of the controller from [3] to a fair crossing controller. By the term *fairness*, we mean a stronger property than liveness, where a desirable behaviour not only happens *finally*, but within a reasonable time bound t. Moreover, we require that a car waiting longer in front of an intersection gets access to it earlier than a newly arriving car. To implement our notion of fairness, we introduce *priorities* to the crossing controller protocol from Sect. 2.2.

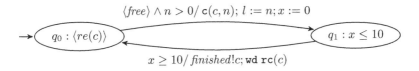

$$\langle \mathit{free} \rangle \wedge n > 0/\, \mathtt{c}(c,n);\, l := n;\, x := 0$$

$q_0 : \langle re(c) \rangle$ $q_1 : x \leq 10$

$$x \geq 10/\, \mathit{finished}!c;\, \mathtt{wd}\ \mathtt{rc}(c)$$

Fig. 3. A basic example for an ACTA. If the guard $\langle \mathit{free} \rangle \wedge n > 0$ is satisfied, a change from q_0 to q_1 is possible, while executing $\mathtt{c}(c,n)$, $l := n$ and resetting the clock x. Location q_1 is left after exactly 10 time units, together with sending the value of c via channel $\mathit{finished}$ and executing $\mathtt{wd}\ \mathtt{rc}(c)$.

In this section, we first describe how we implement our abstract model in UPPAAL in Sect. 3.1, followed by a description of the adapted UPPAAL controller and a *helper concept* we use for the decentralised negotiation procedure using priorities in Sect. 3.2. Lastly, we present the queries that we use to analyse the fairness of our controller and give details on our verification results in Sect. 3.3.

3.1   An Urban Traffic Model in UPPAAL

For our UPPAAL model[1] we implement a generic 2-by-2 intersection cr consisting of road segments with each two lane segments (cf. Fig. 1). We choose this model, as it is a common type of intersection in urban areas and as our implementation of the crossing protocol is generalisable to bigger intersections (cf. Sect. 3.2). Also, UPPAAL can only verify a limited number of extended timed automata in parallel within reasonably short time. We thus consider only those cars that are of interest for our analysis with UPPAAL. For example cars approaching cr, where the crossing ahead check formula $ca(ego)$ (2)

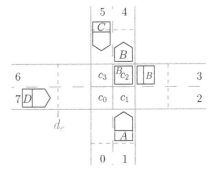

Fig. 4. Reduced model for UPPAAL implementation.

holds, or cars already on cr (cf. on crossing check $oc(ego)$) as those potentially block some crossing segments for other cars. Cars driving away from cr are not interesting, equally cars driving behind cars for which $ca(ego)$ holds, as those are not already allowed to claim or reserve crossing segments.

This dramatically reduces the amount of cars to be considered in our model, whereas we consider only 4 cars, one car approaching from each of the four roads leading to cr, see Fig. 4. We consider the following three states for our cars: a) Away from the intersection (cf. car D in Fig. 4), b) In the crossing ahead state, where $ca(ego)$ holds and thus the threshold d_c is crossed over (cf. cars A and C

---

[1] Implementation available at https://doi.org/10.6084/m9.figshare.c.4649534.v2.

in Fig. 4) and c) On the crossing, where $oc(ego)$ holds and possibly some other cars have to wait until a car leaves certain crossing segments (cf. car B in Fig. 4).

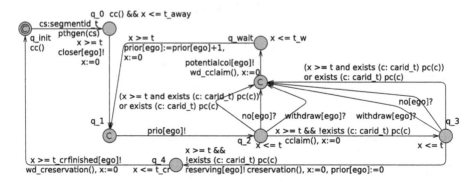

Fig. 5. The crossing controller $CRP_F(ego)$ that sends its priority on the transition from q_1 to q_2. In q_2 and q_3, the controller waits for potential collisions or notifications of helper controllers. If no potential collision exists, crossing segments are reserved and location q_4 is entered. Always, a new path through the intersection is generated in the beginning (transition from q_init to q_0).

We allow for arbitrary turn manoeuvres through the intersection for each car, by non-deterministically generating a path for the cars on arriving at the intersection (right-turn, straightforward, left-turn, u-turn). Whenever one car successfully has finished its manoeuvre, it is newly spawned in front of the intersection with a newly generated path through the intersection.

To implement our collision check $col(ego)$ and potential collision $pc(ego)$ UMLSL formulae in UPPAAL, we simply check for intersection of claims or reservations on the discrete crossing segments, which are represented by global structure arrays, which fits, as our traffic snapshot $\mathcal{TS}$ is also a global construct. In the next Sect. 3.2, we check for path intersection. Our implementation of the checks crossing ahead $ca(ego)$ and on crossing $oc(ego)$ were motivated in the previous paragraph with the cars' states.

3.2   Implementation of the Controller and Helper Protocol

One of the major extensions of the crossing controller from [3] is that our new crossing controller sends its priority for claiming its crossing segments to all other cars on approaching an intersection via a broadcast channel. On receiving such a message, the other cars determine whether the priority of the sender is big enough to enter the requested crossing segments, or if their own car has a a bigger priority for entering the intersection. For deciding this, a *helper controller* is used. If a car's request to enter a crossing was rejected, it waits for some time before incrementing and sending its priority again.

We describe both the new crossing controller and the helper controller in the following again from the perspective of our *ego* car and depict their respective

UPPAAL automata CRP_F(ego) and HP_F(ego) in Figs. 5 and 6. Note that the depicted automata comply with the UPPAAL colour coding.

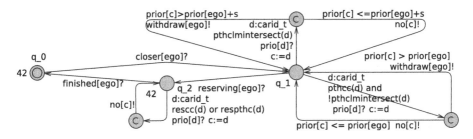

Fig. 6. The helper controller HP_F(ego) for priority evaluation. In q_1, two possible actions exist: Deny or allow other cars to enter the intersection, if their respective priority is (significantly) larger, depending on whether the own car already has an own claim. In q_2, HP_F(ego) denies requests, as its car is already on the crossing.

Crossing Controller (cf. Fig. 5). After the non-deterministic choice of a path through the intersection on the transition from q_init to q_0 and some waiting time up to t_away in q_0, CRP_F(ego)'s priority is communicated via $prio[ego]$! on the transition from q_1 to q_2. In q_2, CRP_F(ego) waits for t time units before claiming the needed crossing segments with the function $cclaim()$. This is only allowed if no potential collision exists. Otherwise, the controller withdraws its claim, waits for some time in location q_wait and only after that increments its priority and proceeds to q_1 again. Location q_2 is also left for location q_wait if a message $withdraw[ego]$? is sent from CRP_F(ego)'s own helper controller HP_F(ego) or a message $no[ego]$? is sent by some other cars' helper controller. After claiming the needed crossing segments and entering location q_3, it is again checked whether a potential collision occurs or whether an incoming message forbids CRP_F(ego) from reserving crossing segments. Similarly as for location q_2, CRP_F(ego) then proceeds to location q_{wait}. If no potential collision occurs within t time units, CRP_F(ego) reserves the previously claimed crossing segments and enters the intersection. After the crossing manoeuvre is finished after t_cr time units, CRP_F(ego) is in its initial location again, ready to spawn as a new car with a new path in front of the intersection.

Note that on some transitions of HP_F(ego) we add the internal messages $closer[ego]$!, $reserving[ego]$! and $finished[ego]$! to enable it to synchronise with CRP_F(ego). This is needed, as HP_F(ego) evaluates other cars' priorities based on the location that CRP_F(ego) is in.

Helper Controller (cf. Fig. 6). If the helper controller HP_F(ego) is in its initial location, the *ego* car is far away from the crossing and therefore does not need to react to other cars' priorities. On receiving a message via the channel *closer*, HP_F(ego) changes to location q_1 and must react whenever a message is received via the channel *prio*. We distinguish two cases: In the first case, only the paths of the car sending its priority and the *ego* car intersect (lower-right transition). In this case, $HP_F(ego)$ only compares its own priority with the received priority. If the own priority is lower, *withdraw*[*ego*]! is sent, otherwise *no*[*c*]! is sent and the car related to the variable *c* has to withdraw its claim. The second case (upper transition) is that the *ego* car already has a claim on some crossing segments that intersect with the path of the car that just sent its priority. In this case, it is compared if the *ego* car's priority is significantly (*s*) smaller than the received priority. The intuition for this is that a claim is "worth" more than a path, as it was set before the other car arrived. With this, only a new car with a very high priority is allowed to enter the intersection faster than the *ego* car, e.g. an emergency vehicle.

If $HP_F(ego)$ receives the message *reserving*[*ego*], meaning the *ego* car has changed its claim into a reservation, it proceeds to location *q_2*. In this location, $HP_F(ego)$ rejects all demands from other cars *c* for claiming some of *ego*'s reserved crossing segments via *no*[*c*]!. If $HP_F(ego)$ receives the notification that the crossing manoeuvre is finished, it again changes to the initial location.

3.3　Fairness Analysis of the Protocol

We use UPPAAL Stratego to examine two different types of queries. Firstly, we use the "standard" UPPAAL queries asking whether some property is satisfied on some (E)/ all (A) runs of the system always ([])/ eventually (<>). Secondly, we use queries for examining the probability that some property is satisfied among random runs of the system within some time bound.

The queries are analysed for an arbitrary car $i \in \{A, B, C, D\}$. We use the following two queries; Firstly, we analyse liveness, where with the query

$$A <> (Observer(i).success)$$

with one observer automaton $Observer(i)$ for each car i, it is determined whether within all runs of the system the car i finally finishes a crossing manoeuvre.

With the second query, we analyse fairness with

$$E <> (\bigvee_{i \in \{A,B,C,D\}} Observer2(i).bad).$$

Now with the help of multiple observer automata $Observer2(i)$, we determine whether there exists a path on which a car with a (significantly) lower priority intersecting with another car finishes its crossing manoeuvre first. As desired, the first query is satisfied and the second is not. Please note that we only use 3 cars for the model checking queries (using approximately 1.3–6.3 GB of DDR4-RAM within 19–25 min on an i7-8550U CPU), as the verification using 4 cars was not computable in a reasonable time (using approximately 85 GB of RAM, including 54 GB SWAP, within nearly 48 h on the same computer before aborting). For the constants of the crossing controller we set $s = 2$ and the timing constants are set to $t = 1$, $t\_w = t\_cr = 2$, and $t\_away = 3$.

For the second type of queries computing the probability with which a property is satisfied, we first give values for some of the statistical parameters in

UPPAAL Stratego. For the probability parameter for false negatives α we use $\alpha = 0.01$ and $\epsilon = 0.01$ for the probability uncertainty parameter ϵ. This results in slim confidence intervals $[p - \epsilon, p + \epsilon]$ that contain the "true" probability p for the property with a confidence of $1 - \alpha$. The remaining parameters are UPPAAL Stratego's default ones, and we refer the reader to [6] for more information.

Table 1. Evaluation of the query $Pr[<= b_t](<> (Observer(C).success))$ with different upper time bounds b_t.

Time bound	Computed interval
$b_t = 5$	$[0.31857, 0.33857]$
$b_t = 10$	$[0.618562, 0.638561]$
$b_t = 15$	$[0.865901, 0.885899]$
$b_t = 20$	$[0.980005, 1]$

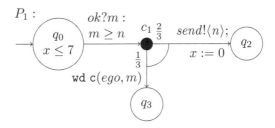

Fig. 7. A PACTA P_1. If the location c_1 is reached, the automaton proceeds to q_2 with probability $\frac{2}{3}$ and to q_3 with probability $\frac{1}{3}$.

The results for time-bounded liveness for an arbitrary car C are depicted in Table 1, where different values for the upper time bound b_t are used. We use 4 cars (computable in seconds), as this type of queries only simulates the system multiple times, which is easily computable, compared to model checking. From Table 1, we conclude that the system becomes more live the longer we observe it.

4 Introducing Uncertainty to the Controller Protocol

One assumption of our approach regarding the communication of ACTA is that the communication via channels never fails. This is a very strong assumption. In this section, we therefore relax it and introduce uncertainty to the ACTA model from Sect. 2.3 and to the protocol described in Sect. 3. We thus describe *Probabilistic* ACTA (PACTA) in Sect. 4.1, extend the protocol in Sect. 4.2 and analyse the probabilistic extension of the protocol in Sect. 4.3.

4.1   Probabilistic ACTA

For brevity, we omit a formal definition of the syntax of PACTA and instead introduce it using the example depicted in Fig. 7.

PACTA shares basic concepts with ACTA, such as locations and most of the components of the transitions. Differing from ACTA are probabilistic transitions. An example for such a transition is the transition from c_1 to q_2 in Fig. 7, which is chosen with a probability of $\frac{2}{3}$. Additionally, the value of n is sent and the clock x is reset. Such probabilistic transitions are only allowed to have a committed location as their source and the sum of all probabilities on outgoing edges of such a committed location must equal 1. Sending of broadcast messages, controller actions and data modifications are still allowed on probabilistic transitions, whereas guards and receiving a message are not allowed.

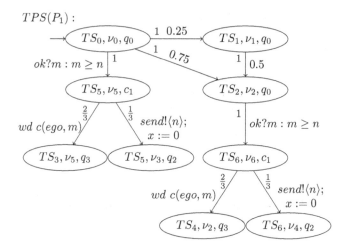

Fig. 8. Excerpt of the TPS (extended labelled transition system) for P_1 from Fig. 7.

For the semantics of PACTA, we use a *Timed-Probabilistic-System (TPS)* [15]. We depict (an excerpt of) the (infinite) TPS that is the semantic model of the PACTA P_1 from Fig. 7 in Fig. 8. Using this semantics, we are now able to reason about properties such as (timed) reachability of certain locations in such a PACTA. We refer to [15] for more details on that topic.

4.2   Implementation with Uncertainties

As all transitions of ACTA are also possible in PACTA, we can use both certain and uncertain communication in them. We decided to make the communication channels *prio* and *no* uncertain and let the remaining channels remain unchanged. The reason for this is that all other channels are for inner-vehicle communication. We therefore assume that these communication channels are wired and have a failure rate near zero. In contrast to that the two channels *prio* and *no* are for the communication between different cars, are therefore unwired and have a significantly larger rate of failure.

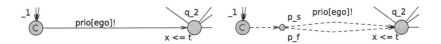

Fig. 9. Original transition from Fig. 5 to the left and transition with uncertain communication to the right.

Table 2. Results of the query $Pr[<= b_t](<> Observer(C).success)$ with different parameters for b_t and p_s.

b_t	$p_s = 0.99,\ p_f = 0.01$	$p_s = 0.95,\ p_f = 0.05$	$p_s = 0.8,\ p_f = 0.2$
$b_t = 5$	$[0.316353, 0.336352]$	$[0.315686, 0.335685]$	$[0.31465, 0.334649]$
$b_t = 10$	$[0.615449, 0.635449]$	$[0.613901, 0.633901]$	$[0.611239, 0.631239]$
$b_t = 15$	$[0.861585, 0.881584]$	$[0.855226, 0.875223]$	$[0.836026, 0.856025]$
$b_t = 20$	$[0.980005, 1]$	$[0.979366, 0.999359]$	$[0.95156, 0.971557]$

We omit to depict the entire controllers again, as their basic behaviour remains unchanged. Only transitions with output actions on the channels *no* and *prio* change and are shown in Fig. 9. As we assume that these channels use the same communication medium, we use the same probabilities for communication success and failure (p_s resp. p_f) for both channels.

4.3 Fairness Analysis with Uncertainties

Given the probabilistic extension of the protocol, we are interested in the question of how the properties of the protocol change. As expected, the system is neither live nor fair anymore if message sending can fail (queries evaluated using 3 cars again). To determine the impact of lossy channels, we evaluate two queries with different probabilities for the communication success (p_s) and failure (p_f) for different time bounds b_t (using 4 cars again).

The results of the query for time-bounded liveness are depicted in Table 2, the results of the query for non-fairness in Table 3. The following two observations from Tables 2 and 3 are especially remarkable: Firstly, and unsurprisingly, the system becomes less live and fair the more lossy the channels used for broadcasting are. Secondly, the system becomes also less live and fair the longer the time b_t we observe it (compared to the system without uncertainties). The reason for this is that at the very start of the system run, the priorities are all 0 and it is not that likely that one car's priority increases much more than another car's priority, thus communication is not that important. This observation changes over time when cars finish their crossing manoeuvres and start from the beginning again, leading to more significant differences in their priorities.

Although the system becomes less live the more lossy the channels are, the differences are not very significant compared to the fairness query. The reason for this is that the fairness property is easier to violate: It is sufficient that a single priority message fails to violate the fairness property. For a violation of the liveness property, each communication for the car under consideration within the time bound b_t must fail, which is less likely than the failure of a single communication.

Despite losing liveness and fairness on allowing lossy broadcast communication, the system still remains safe, i.e. there are never two intersecting reservations of two different cars. Thus the safety result from [3] is still preserved in our extended crossing controller protocol. For the verification of this property in UPPAAL, an additional upper bound on the priorities is added.

Table 3. Results of the query $Pr[<= b_t](<> \bigvee_{i \in \{A,B,C,D\}} Observer2(i).bad$ with different parameters for b_t and p_s.

b_t	$p_s = 0.99,\ p_f = 0.01$	$p_s = 0.95,\ p_f = 0.05$	$p_s = 0.8,\ p_f = 0.2$
$b_t = 5$	$[0, 0.0199955]$	$[0, 0.0199955]$	$[0, 0.0199955]$
$b_t = 10$	$[0, 0.0199955]$	$[0.00219789, 0.0221855]$	$[0.0108718, 0.0308586]$
$b_t = 15$	$[0.0027273, 0.0227209]$	$[0.0182431, 0.0382385]$	$[0.0838251, 0.103823]$
$b_t = 20$	$[0.00324724, 0.0232427]$	$[0.0443753, 0.0643705]$	$[0.17867, 0.19867]$

5   Conclusion

Contribution. We extended the UMLSL approach for urban traffic [3] with three key features; Liveness, fairness and communication failure. Using UPPAAL Stratego, we implemented and analysed the extended crossing controller protocol, showing that a system using our controllers behaves safe, live and fair in every situation and examined probabilities for which a car might pass an intersection within a given time bound. We furthermore showed how these probabilities change if we allow communication channels to be lossy. As in our case communication is not strictly necessary for safety, we still preserve the proven safety property from [3].

Future Work. We could apply our PACTA to more traffic scenarios. For instance, in the country roads approach [2], communication with a helper car is used. Here we could analyse how the system properties change with uncertain communication channels. Also, we could use PACTA not only for introducing uncertainty to communication channels in the MLSL approach, but also for other uncertainties, e.g. sensor uncertainty. Whenever an autonomous car detects uncertain sensor information, it could e.g. ask an appropriate *sensor helper controller* for additional information to complete a driving manoeuvre.

In our approach, we have several strong assumptions for the considered abstract model to allow for purely formal reasoning. In this paper, we already weakened the strong assumption of having completely reliable communication by introducing uncertainty to our communication channels. A second strong assumption, we consider that all cars are autonomous and capable of communicating with each other. However, in recent work [16] we examined possibilities for our autonomous cars to cope with human controlled vehicles for the highway traffic approach from [1]. In this case safety can no longer be fully guaranteed, as some actions of the human driver may only be guessed.

It is also of interest to compare our approach with other approaches regarding its efficiency. An implementation allowing more complex intersections than the 2-by-2 crossing used for our UPPAAL model in Sect. 3.1 might be helpful. A more complex priority system where cars can increase their priority even if they are not directly in front of the crossing might help to increase the efficiency further. Using such a system, it might also be reasonable to examine the efficiency of urban road networks instead of single crossings. Another point for future work is an optimisation of our controllers, to allow for more than 3 cars in the case of verification without probabilities (cf. Sect. 3.3).

Acknowledgements. We thank the anonymous reviewers for their helpful comments with which we were able to improve our paper.

References

1. Hilscher, M., Linker, S., Olderog, E.-R., Ravn, A.P.: An abstract model for proving safety of multi-lane traffic manoeuvres. In: Qin, S., Qiu, Z. (eds.) ICFEM 2011. LNCS, vol. 6991, pp. 404–419. Springer, Heidelberg (2011). https://doi.org/10.1007/978-3-642-24559-6_28

2. Hilscher, M., Linker, S., Olderog, E.-R.: Proving safety of traffic manoeuvres on country roads. In: Liu, Z., Woodcock, J., Zhu, H. (eds.) Theories of Programming and Formal Methods. LNCS, vol. 8051, pp. 196–212. Springer, Heidelberg (2013). https://doi.org/10.1007/978-3-642-39698-4_12

3. Schwammberger, M.: An abstract model for proving safety of autonomous urban traffic. Theor. Comput. Sci. **744**, 143–169 (2018)

4. Schwammberger, M.: Introducing liveness into multi-lane spatial logic lane change controllers using UPPAAL. In: Gleirscher, M., Kugele, S., Linker, S. (eds.) Proceedings 2nd International Workshop on Safe Control of Autonomous Vehicles, SCAV@CPSWeek 2018. Volume 269 of EPTCS, pp. 17–31 (2018)

5. Behrmann, G., David, A., Larsen, K.G.: A tutorial on UPPAAL. In: Bernardo, M., Corradini, F. (eds.) SFM-RT 2004. LNCS, vol. 3185, pp. 200–236. Springer, Heidelberg (2004). https://doi.org/10.1007/978-3-540-30080-9_7

6. David, A., Jensen, P.G., Larsen, K.G., Mikučionis, M., Taankvist, J.H.: UPPAAL STRATEGO. In: Baier, C., Tinelli, C. (eds.) TACAS 2015. LNCS, vol. 9035, pp. 206–211. Springer, Heidelberg (2015). https://doi.org/10.1007/978-3-662-46681-0_16

7. Loos, S.M., Platzer, A.: Safe intersections: at the crossing of hybrid systems and verification. In: Yi, K. (ed.) Intelligent Transportation Systems, pp. 1181–1186 (2011)

8. Dresner, K., Stone, P.: A multiagent approach to autonomous intersection management. J. Artif. Intell. Res. **31**, 591–656 (2008)
9. Naumann, R., Rasche, R., Tacken, J., Tahedl, C.: Validation and simulation of a decentralized intersection collision avoidance algorithm. In: Proceedings of Conference on Intelligent Transportation Systems, pp. 818–823. IEEE (1997)
10. Ferreira, M., Fernandes, R., Conceição, H., Viriyasitavat, W., Tonguz, O.K.: Self-organized traffic control. In: Proceedings of the Seventh ACM International Workshop on VehiculAr InterNETworking. VANET 2010, pp. 85–90. ACM (2010)
11. Li, L., Wang, F.: Cooperative driving at blind crossings using intervehicle communication. IEEE Trans. Veh. Technol. **55**, 1712–1724 (2006)
12. Fathollahnejad, N., Villani, E., Pathan, R., Barbosa, R., Karlsson, J.: On reliability analysis of leader election protocols for virtual traffic lights. In: 43rd IEEE/IFIP Conference on Dependable Systems and Networks Workshop, pp. 1–12 (2013)
13. Asplund, M.: Automatically proving the correctness of vehicle coordination. ICT Express **4**, 51–54 (2018)
14. Alur, R., Dill, D.L.: A theory of timed automata. Theor. Comput. Sci. **126**, 183–235 (1994)
15. Kwiatkowska, M., Norman, G., Parker, D., Sproston, J.: Performance analysis of probabilistic timed automata using digital clocks. In: Larsen, K.G., Niebert, P. (eds.) FORMATS 2003. LNCS, vol. 2791, pp. 105–120. Springer, Heidelberg (2004). https://doi.org/10.1007/978-3-540-40903-8_9
16. Bischopink, C.: Moving hazards - reasoning about humand drivers in autonomous traffic. Master's thesis, University of Oldenburg, Oldenburg (2018)

Temporal Logic Semantics for Teleo-Reactive Robotic Agent Programs

Keith Clark[1], Brijesh Dongol[2(✉)], and Peter Robinson[3]

[1] Imperial College London, London, UK
k.clark@imperial.ac.uk
[2] University of Surrey, Guildford, UK
b.dongol@surrey.ac.uk
[3] University of Queensland, Brisbane, Australia
pjr@itee.uq.edu.au

Abstract. Teleo-Reactive (TR) robotic agent programs comprise sequences of guarded action rules clustered into named parameterised procedures. Their ancestry goes back to the first cognitive robot, Shakey. Like Shakey, a TR programmed robotic agent has a deductive *Belief Store* comprising constantly changing predicate logic *percept* facts, and *knowledge* facts and rules for querying the percepts. In this paper we introduce TR programming using a simple example expressed in the teleo-reactive programming language TeleoR, which is a syntactic extension of QuLog, a typed logic programming language used for the agent's *Belief Store*. We give a formal definition of the *regression* property that rules of TeleoR procedures should satisfy, and an informal operational semantics of the evaluation of a TeleoR procedure call. We then formally express key features of the evaluation in LTL. Finally we show how this LTL formalisation can be used to prove that a procedure's rules satisfy the regression property by proving it holds for one rule of the example TeleoR program. The proof requires us: to formally link a TeleoR agent's percept beliefs with sensed configurations of the external environment; to link the agent's robotic device *action intentions* with actual robot actions; to specify the eventual physical effects of the robot's actions on the environment state.

1 Introduction

A Teleo-Reactive (TR) programmed robotic agent has a deductive *Belief Store* comprising constantly changing predicate logic *percept* facts generated from the latest sensor readings. The facts are updated using fresh sensor readings at an application dependent frequency, which may be several times a second. The percept facts are the agent's current *beliefs* about the state of the robotic device or devices it controls, and the state of the physical environment in which the devices operate.

Dongol is supported by EPSRC Grants EP/R019045/2, EP/R032556/1 and EP/R025134/2.

E. Sekerinski et al. (Eds.): FM 2019 Workshops, LNCS 12232, pp. 265–280, 2020.
https://doi.org/10.1007/978-3-030-54994-7_19

Augmenting these dynamic percept facts are fixed facts about the robotic devices and their environment, Prolog-style rules for non-percept relations, allowing higher level interpretations of the percept facts. The fixed facts and rules are the robot's *knowledge*.

In this paper we introduce TR programming using a simple example expressed in the TR subset of TeleoR [1]. TeleoR is a syntactic extension of QuLog [2], a typed logic and functional programming language used for the agent's percept beliefs and knowledge.

A TeleoR procedure named p comprises a parameterised *sequence* of *guarded action rules* rules of the form:

```
p(X₁,..,Xₖ){
    G₁ ~> A₁
    .
    .
    Gₙ ~> Aₙ
    }
```

proceeded by a type definition giving the required types of the parameters $X_1, .., X_k$. The parameters can appear in any rule of the procedure body.

A rule may contain variables other than $X_1, .., X_k$. These are the local variables of the rule. All local variables in A_i must also appear in G_i.

Each G_i rule *guard* is a *Belief Store* query. Each A_i is either a call to a TeleoR procedure, including a recursive call, or a tuple comprising one or more actions for robotic devices to be executed concurrently.

When the p procedure is called, the parameter values must be *ground* (fully instantiated) values. These values partially instantiate the sequence of guarded rules of the procedure body, giving the modified rule sequence:

$$G'_1 \rightsquigarrow A'_1$$
$$\cdots$$
$$G'_i \rightsquigarrow A'_i$$
$$\cdots$$
$$G'_j \rightsquigarrow A'_j$$
$$\cdots$$
$$G'_n \rightsquigarrow A'_n$$

In before/after order, the partly instantiated guard queries are evaluated one by one against the current state of the agent's *Belief Store*. This is in order to find the *first* rule with a guard G'_j that is inferable from the *Belief Store*. This typically further instantiates remaining variables in G'_j, and always results in a ground A''_j action of the rule, should A'_j not be ground.

Rule j is *fired* and action A''_j is invoked. If it is a TeleoR procedure call the first fireable rule of this new call is found and, in turn, its fully instantiated action invoked. Eventually a procedure will be called in which the fired rule for the current *Belief Store* has robotic device actions. The *Belief Store* is unchanged during the evaluation of this sequence of calls. The determined robotic device actions are dispatched to the robotic devices. They typically result in changes

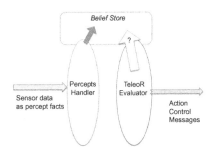

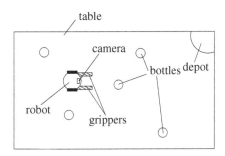

Fig. 1. Two thread agent architecture

Fig. 2. Top-down view of bottle collecting robot

in the position of the robotic devices, and/or cause changes in their physical environment that can detected by the sensor devices.

A two-thread robotic agent architecture is depicted in Figure 1[1] The percepts handler atomically updates the *Belief Store* when a new batch of percept facts arrives from the sensor interpretation routines. They may be batched so that each new set of percepts gives a comprehensive view of the state of the robotic devices and their environment.

The `TeleoR` evaluator thread executes some initial call to a `TeleoR` procedure, this is the *task procedure call*. The existential closure of the partly instantiated guard of the first rule of this procedure call is the *task goal*. This first rule usually has the empty action tuple (). When such a rule is fired all currently executing robotic actions are terminated (Fig. 2).

After each percept thread update the task call is re-evaluated to determine if new robotic device actions need to be dispatched to the robotic devices. If the re-evaluation results in the same robotic actions as were determined on the last percepts update, these actions are allowed to continue.

However, the hope is that after a repetition of some initial sequence of the same procedure calls and rule firings, eventually a call C will be fire a rule *earlier* than the rule that was previously fired for C. Almost certainly the new rule firing will result in different robotic actions being determined.

Suppose that rule i was fired last time in C. Further suppose that the robotic actions that were executed directly or indirectly as a result of firing this rule have brought about their intended environment changes, resulting in new sensor readings and changed percept facts. Querying the agent's updated *Belief Store* an earlier rule j of C is now fired. `TeleoR` programs are written so that this normally, eventually happens for every procedure call. The existential closure of guard G_i' is viewed as a direct sub-goal of the existential closure of the earlier guard G_j'. More generally, the existential closure of every rule guard of a called procedure,

---

[1] `QuLog` actually has another rule type, imperative action rules for defining multi-threaded agent behaviour. They can call primitive actions for forking threads, updating *Belief Store* facts and message communication. The two thread architecture is implemented using these action rules.

except that of the first rule, should be a *direct* sub-goal of the existential closure of the partly instantiated guard of some *earlier* rule in the call's rule sequence. This is its *regression* property.

Example 1. Here are two `TeleoR` procedures, with associated type definitions and type declarations. The goal of the first procedure is to get a mobile robot close to something, `Th`. It uses of independent `move` and `turn` action names, and a `see` percept name. We use the Prolog convention that variables begin with an upper case letter or underscore.

```
def thing ::= bottle | drop | ...
def dir ::= left | centre | right
def dist ::= close | near | far
percept see(thing,dist,dir)
durative move(num), turn(dir,num)

tel get_close_to(thing)
get_close_to(Th){
    see(Th,close,_) ~> ()  % Empty tuple of actions
    see(Th,near,_) ~>  approach_until(close,Th,3.0,1.0)
    see(Th,far,_) ~> approach_until(near,Th,4.5,0.5)
    true ~> turn(right,0.5)   % Singleton tuple of actions
    }
tel approach_until(dist,thing,num,num)
approach_until(Dist,Th,Fs,Ts){
    see(Th,Dist,_) ~> ()  % Th being approached is now Dist away
    see(Th,_,centre) ~> move(Fs)
    see(Th,_,Dir) ~> move(Fs),turn(Dir,Ts)   % tuple of 2 actions
    % Dir is left or right. move forward turning Dir to bring back into centre view.
    }
```

The underscores in the `see` conditions of the first procedure, and the first rule of the second procedure, indicate that the orientation of the seen `Th` is not relevant for the action of the rule. Those in the last two rules of the second procedure indicate that the distance is not relevant.

An example of a percept fact is `see(bottle,near,centre)`, reporting that the analysis of the image from a forward pointing camera of a mobile robot has determined that a bottle of known size is near to the camera, more or less in centre view.

The `see` percept gives a qualitative measure of its distance from the robot's on-board camera, as `close`, `near` or `far`, and indicates whether the seen `thing` is within, or to the left or right of a central area of the camera's field of view.

An example of a primitive action is `move(3.0)` which causes both drive wheels of a mobile robot to turn at the same speed so that normally the robot will move forward, more or less in a straight line, at the specified speed of 15 centimetres per second.

Suppose that a task is started with a call `get_close_to(bottle)`. Before the call, let us assume that the robot is stationary near to and facing a bottle. Analysis of the image of its forward pointing camera has resulted in the percept `see(bottle,near,centre)` being in the agent's *Belief Store*.

The second rule of call `get_close_to(bottle)` will be fired with action the procedure call `approach_until(close,bottle,3.0,1.0)`. The second rule of this auxiliary procedure call will be fired because its guard `see(bottle,_,centre)` matches the percept `see(bottle,near,centre)`. The rule's action will be `move(3.0)`. The control action `start(move(3.0))` will be sent to the mobile robot.

The durative action `move(3.0)` should *normally, eventually* result in the mobile robot getting close to the bottle. But before that, because of wheel slip, or because the bottle is moved, percept updates may record that the bottle is still seen as near, but to the left or right of the camera image. When that happens, the last rule of the `approach_until(close,bottle,3.0,1.0)` will be fired resulting in a control message to turn towards the bottle to bring it back into centre view, the turn to be done in parallel with the continuing forward move. Eventually, analysis of the robot's camera image should result in a percept `see(bottle,close,Dir)`, for some direction `Dir`, being received by the agent, replacing any other `see` percept in its *Belief Store*. When this happens the first rule of the call `get_close_to(bottle)`, with action () will be fired, pre-empting the firing of the first rule of the call `approach_until(close,bottle,3.0,1.0)`. Control messages to stop the forward `move`, and any accompanying `turn` action, will be sent to the robot. The goal of the task call `get_close_to(bottle)` has been achieved.

In another scenario, before the goal of getting near to the seen `bottle` is achieved, the `bottle` may be moved by the interfering person to be `far` from the robot but still in view. Suppose that immediately after this interference, the percept `see(bottle,far,right)` is received, replacing `see(bottle,near,centre)`. Re-evaluation of guards of rules of the task call `get_close_to(bottle)` will result in its rule 4 being fired with action `approach_until(near,bottle,4.5,0.5)`.

As the percept fact `see(bottle,far,right)` will still be the *Belief Store*, the last rule of the new `approach_until` call will be fired and control actions

$$\text{start}(\text{turn}(0.5, \text{right})) \, \text{mod}(\text{move}(3.0), \text{move}(4.5))$$

will be sent to the robot. The result is that the robot will move forward more quickly at a speed of 4.5, with a correctional turn to the right at speed 0.5. This is in order to get `near` to the bottle again, and to bring it into centre view.

Finally, suppose that whilst the robot is moving more speedily towards the seen bottle, the bottle is moved to be near to the robot in centre view. Immediately the percept `see(bottle, near, centre)` is received the task call will switch to firing its second rule slowing the robot down and terminating any correctional turn.

The above scenario descriptions illustrate another positive feature of `TR` and `TeleoR` procedures. Not only are they declarative, with the goals and sub-goals of tasks given as rule guards, they also automatically recover from setbacks and take advantage of any help. The program control jumps up and down the tree of guard goals of active procedures in response to helping or hindering exogenous events.

However, the main aim of this paper is to enable reasoning about the evaluation of `TeleoR` procedure calls in a modular manner. Our contributions are: **(1)** the use of linear temporal logic (LTL) to give a declarative semantics to `TeleoR` procedure call evaluations and the desired regression property; **(2)** the explicit decoupling of agent *Belief Store* state from the state of the external environment, with the consequent need to be explicit about the mapping of properties of the environment into partial and approximate sensor data encoded as percept facts, the need to explicitly map the agent's robotic device action intentions into external device actions, and the need to be explicit about the physics of the device actions for particular environment states; **(3)** the illustration of the use of **(1)** and **(2)** to verify regression properties.

The paper builds on existing work on logic programming [7] and robot behavioural programming [5,8]. We were motivated to explore the use of LTL for `TeleoR` semantics and verification by [6].

2   Key Properties of `TeleoR` Procedures

We now introduce the key properties of `TeleoR` procedures, including the structural properties, compile time-guarantees on both actions and guards, and transition semantics to enable smooth control of robotic agents.

Sub-goal Structure and Regression. The existential closures of the partially instantiated guards, in which each local variable is existentially quantified, lie on an implicit sub-goal tree rooted at the existential closure of the guard of the first rule.

Definition 2. *An action* A_j *satisfies* regression *iff whenever it is started when its guard is the first inferable guard, and continued whilst this is the case, it will eventually result in progression up the sub-goal tree of guards.*

That is, eventually the guard of an earlier rule G_i, $i < j$, should become the first inferable guard. Nilsson calls G_j the *regression* of G_i through A_j.

Guarantee of Ground Actions. When a guard query is successfully evaluated against the *Belief Store* (which uses a Prolog-style evaluation) its local variables will be given values. Compile time analysis of each guarded rule ensures that should the guard query succeed, the rule's action will be ground with arguments of the required type. This is why we use typed `QuLog` [2] for the agent's *Belief Store* rather than `Prolog`. So every `TeleoR` procedure call action will be ground and correctly typed, consequently any actions sent to the robotic devices, perhaps via ROS [9], will also be fully instantiated and type correct.

Covering All Eventualities. The partially instantiated guards of a procedure call should also be such that for every *Belief Store* state in which the call may be active there will be at least one inferable guard. Nilsson calls this the *completeness* property of a procedure. This property holds for both of our example procedures. For the first it trivially holds since the last rule will always be fired if no earlier rule can be fired. It holds for the second procedure given the two guard contexts from which it is called in the first procedure, both of which require a see percept to be in the *Belief Store* while the call is active.

Smooth Transitions Between Primitive Actions. When each new batch of percepts arrives this process of finding and firing the first rule of each call with an inferable guard is restarted. This is in order to determine, as quickly as possible, the appropriate tuple of robotic actions in response to the new percepts. Thus,

1. actions that were in the last tuple of actions are allowed to continue, perhaps modified,
2. other actions of the last tuple are stopped, and
3. new actions are started.

For example, if the last tuple of actions was move(4.5), turn(left,0.5) and the new tuple is just move(3), the turn action is stopped and the move action argument is modified to 3.

Elasticity of Complete Procedure Programs. This reactive operational semantics means that each TeleoR procedure is not only a universal conditional plan for its call goals, it is also a plan that recovers from setbacks and immediately responds to opportunities. If, after a *Belief Store* update a higher rule of some procedure call C can unexpectedly be fired, perhaps because of a helping exogenous event, that rule will immediately be fired *jumping* upwards in the task's sub-goal tree. Conversely, an unexpected result of some robotic action, or an interfering exogenous event, then the climb up the sub-goal tree of C's rule guards will be restarted from a sub-goal guard of C as all eventualities are covered.

From Deliberation to Reaction. Although not the case for our example procedures initially called TeleoR procedures typically query the percept facts through several levels of defined relations. Via procedure call actions, they eventually call a TeleoR procedure that directly queries the percept facts and mostly has non-procedure call actions. So, for TeleoR, the interface between deliberation about what sub-plans to invoke to achieve a task goal, to the invoking of a sensor reactive behaviour to directly control robotic resources, is a sequence of procedure calls.

3   Temporal Logic Semantics for TeleoR Procedures

The core of our semantics is that it decouples the controller (agent program) from the environment (see Fig. 3). This is achieved using two coupling relations that describe how closely the internal state of an agent matches the real world. Any actions that a robot performs are interpreted through the coupling relation that in turn produces some physical change. In turn, the physical changes are sampled by the robot to potentially update the *Belief Store*.

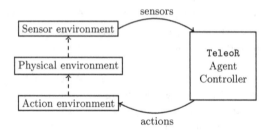

Fig. 3. Decomposed environment and `TeleoR` controller

The *agent controller* is defined with respect to the agent's *Belief Store*, whereas the *physical environment* describes how object properties change in the real world as a result of robot actions. We typically do not model the actual physics of any component (e.g., via differential equations). Instead, the behaviour of the physical world is formalised as abstract assertions. This section focuses on the agent controller; we formalise its interaction with the environment in Sect. 4.

Our formal model for the agent controller assumes that each agent generates traces of the form:

$$\beta_0\,\beta_1\,\beta_2\,\beta_3\,\dots$$

where each β_i is a *Belief Store* that describes the agent's view of the world. For any of these traces, it is possible to interpret standard LTL formulae, with predicates that support beliefs and intentions. In particular, we admit formulae of the form

$$\varphi ::= P \mid \neg\varphi \mid \varphi_1 \oplus \varphi_2 \mid \mathbf{X}\varphi \mid \mathbf{G}\varphi \mid \mathbf{F}\varphi \mid \varphi_1\mathbf{U}\varphi_2 \mid \varphi_1\mathbf{W}\varphi_2$$

where P is a *Belief Store* predicate and $\mathbf{X}$, $\mathbf{G}$, $\mathbf{F}$, $\mathbf{U}$ and $\mathbf{W}$ denote the standard next, globally, finally, until and unless modalities of linear temporal logic and $\oplus$ is a binary boolean operator. Examples of belief store states over which P is evaluated are given in Sect. 4; the traces these induce are made more precise in Definition 3. In particular, it is worth noting that they may include first-order quantifiers.

In order to give the semantics of TR procedures we need to keep track of which actions (both TR procedure calls and intended robot actions) are currently being active, and which guards are currently true (and what instantiations of variables make a given guard true). To simplify the semantics we assume the *Belief Store* contains facts of the form do A to indicate that the action A is currently active. For a given goal G, we write bel $G\theta$, where θ is a substitution (instantiation of variables in G), that makes $G\theta$ the first inferable instance of G.

Each ground instance, C, of a TR procedure call is defined as a sequence of guarded actions instances $\mathsf{G}_1 \leadsto \mathsf{A}_1, \mathsf{G}_2 \leadsto \mathsf{A}_2, \dots, \mathsf{G}_n \leadsto \mathsf{A}_n$.

3.1 Evaluation Semantics

The following two LTL formulae give the semantics of the evaluation of call C.

$$\mathbf{G}(\forall 1 \leq i \leq n, \theta_i. \text{ do } C \wedge \text{bel } G_i\theta_i \wedge$$
$$(\forall 1 \leq j < i. \, \neg\exists\text{bel } G_j) \Rightarrow \textit{fired}(C, i, \theta_i)) \qquad\qquad (\textit{Fire})$$

$$\mathbf{G}(\forall 1 \leq i \leq n, \theta_i. \, \textit{fired}(C, i, \theta_i) \Rightarrow \text{do } A_i\theta_i) \qquad\qquad (\textit{Action})$$

Informally, if we are executing C and the i'th rule is the active (fired) rule (because some instance of its guard is inferable from the *Belief Store* and no instance of an earlier guard is inferable) then we will be executing the action A_i with the instantiation of all of the variables in A_i determined by the inferred instantiation θ_i of the rule guard.

Note that we only need to consider ground TR procedure calls as the top-level TR procedure that we call will be ground and the θ_i in the above formulae will ground the action (which may be another TR procedure call).

In general, because TR programs allow hierarchical nesting, we typically need to repeatedly apply the above formula to determine what primitive robotic actions will be intended for a given *Belief Store*. For example, if we are executing `get_close_to(bottle)`, and the *Belief Store* contains only the belief `see(bottle,far,left)`, then applying both (*Fire*), (*Action*) with

$$C = \texttt{get\_close\_to(bottle)}$$

will tell us that call `approach_until(near,bottle,4.5, 0.5)` will become active. Applying (*Fire*), (*Action*) to this procedure call then tells us that the primitive actions `move(4.5)` and `turn(left,0.5)` will be the intended actions.

Repeated application of formulae (*Fire*), (*Action*) generates the "call stack" starting with the initial call T and ending with a set of primitive actions. For a given state of the *Belief Store* the generated call stack is unique and, in particular, the tuple of primitive actions is unique.

3.2 Only the Latest Inferred Robotic Actions Are Intended for Execution

As part of the semantics of TR programs we insist that the primitive actions generated by the application of (*Fire*), (*Action*) are the only intended actions. We formalise this with the following, where *primitive_actions* is the set of all possible ground primitive actions terms for some `TeleoR` program, and A is the current tuple of intended actions.

$$\mathbf{G}(\text{do } A \Rightarrow \forall A'(A' \in \textit{primitive\_actions} \wedge A' \notin A \Rightarrow \neg\text{do } A')) \qquad (\textit{RoboticActs})$$

Here $\in$ is being used for both set and tuple membership.

3.3   Regression Property

Suppose that the action A_i, where $i > 1$ of rule i of call C is intended to bring about a future state of the environment E such that an instance $G_j\theta_j$ for $j < i$ of one of the guards prior to rule i can be inferred from E's sense data percepts.

This is captured in the LTL statement:

$$\mathbf{G}(\forall 1 < i \leq n.\ \mathsf{do}\ C \wedge \mathit{fired}(C, i, \_) \Rightarrow \mathbf{F}(\exists 1 \leq j < i.\ \exists \mathsf{bel}\ G_j)) \qquad (\textit{Regression})$$

4   TeleoR Environment

As depicted in Fig. 3, the `TeleoR` controller only forms part of the overall system. More work is required to ensure that (1) intended actions have an effect on the real-time environment; (2) that the action's effects in the environment bring about some physical changes; and (3) these physical changes are sensed and mapped into new percepts for the agent. This inter-dependency between a controller and its environment has long been studied in the control systems and cyber-physical domains. We treat the three requirements above as environment assumptions and express the assumptions as abstractly as possible. We model separate assumptions that cover intended actions to robotic device actions (outputs), physics of effects of device actions, and sensor readings to percepts (inputs). In the context of autonomous systems, a decoupled approach has recently been proposed by Kamali et al. [6], who describe a separation of concerns between physical and discrete assumptions.

We describe environment assumptions in Sect. 4.1, which we formalise in terms of `TeleoR` traces in Sect. 4.2. An example verification is provided in Sect. 4.3.

4.1   Environment Assumptions

Consider, for example, an intended `turn(right,0.5)` action. This becomes the robotic action to rotate the robot at a velocity of $+0.5/s$. Agent `turn` intentions are mapped into robot rotation actions by the two rules:

$$\forall x.\ \mathsf{do}\ \mathtt{turn(right},x) \vdash \mathit{rot\_spd} = x \qquad (1)$$

$$\forall x.\ \mathsf{do}\ \mathtt{turn(left},x) \vdash \mathit{rot\_spd} = -x \qquad (2)$$

Here, $\mathit{rot\_spd}$ is an *environment* variable recording the actual physical rotational speed of the robot. On the other hand, do $\mathtt{turn(right},x)$ is a belief store assertion, stating that the robot control agent believes and intends that the controlled robot turns to the right a speed of x. Of course, one might have environments in which the rotational speed is less accurate (e.g., due to slippage of the wheels). Such phenomena can be modelled by an equation of the form $\forall x.\ \mathsf{do}\ \mathtt{turn(right},x) \vdash \mathit{rot\_spd} = x \pm x * 0.1$ which states that the turn right agent intention translates to an actual rotational velocity within some tolerance bounds.

Recall that the semantics of a `TeleoR` procedure guarantees that actions are not agent intentions unless they are the actions of the last fired rule, and that it is possible to perform more than one action in parallel. In Example ex:aux-proc, the second rule of `approach_until` only determines a `move`. On the other hand, the third rule determines that a `move` and `turn` should be executed together. Our mapping of action intentions to robotic actions should also tell us what happens when an action intention is not determined:

$$\neg(\exists x.\ \mathsf{do\ move}(x)) \vdash \mathit{fwd\_spd} = 0 \tag{3}$$

Thus, by Eq. 3, if a `move` action is not intended by the agent, then the robot will not be moving forward. In Example 1, assumptions (1) and (3) together ensure that firing of the last rule of `get_close_to` causes the robot to spin on its axis.

Note that there is a difference between (3) and $\forall x.\ \mathsf{do\ move}(x) \vdash \mathit{fwd\_spd} = x$, which for $x = 0$ gives

$$\mathsf{do\ move}(0) \vdash \mathit{fwd\_spd} = 0. \tag{4}$$

The antecedent of (3) states that there is no percept fact $\mathsf{do\ move}(x)$ recorded in the agent's *Belief Store*, for any value of x, whereas the antecedent of (4) states that the value recorded for a `move` intention is $\mathsf{do\ move}(0)$. In other words, for (3), we assume the *Belief Store* query $\mathsf{do\ move}(X)$ returns false, whereas in (4), the *Belief Store* query returns a value 0 for X. In both cases, the (physical) value of $\mathit{fwd\_spd}$ is required to be 0.

Given that there is a stationary bottle on the table, we require that the `turn` action is such that it eventually causes the bottle to be seen. This first of all requires a physical assumption that turning on its axis at a rate of $\mathit{rot\_spd} = 0.5$ is adequate for the robot to be pointing towards a bottle. We state a bottle being in front of the robot using a predicate $\mathit{bot\_in\_front}$, which we assume holds precisely when there is some bottle in front of the robot. An implementation may guarantee $\mathit{bot\_in\_front}$ in more than one way, e.g., as with $\mathit{rot\_spd}$ above, may be within certain tolerance bounds calculated using the angle of vision of the robot's camera, the robot's current position and the bottle's current position. Thus $\mathit{bot\_in\_front}$ may mean that a bottle is directly in front of the robot, or slightly to the right or left of centre. Such details can be described by the logic, but are ignored for the purposes of this paper.

Formally, we assume that the environment ensures the following.

$$\mathbf{G}(((\mathit{rot\_spd} = 0.5 \wedge \mathit{fwd\_spd} = 0)\mathbf{W}\,\mathit{bot\_in\_front}) \Rightarrow \mathbf{F}\,\mathit{bot\_in\_front}) \tag{5}$$

The antecedent, i.e., $(\mathit{rot\_spd} = 0.5 \wedge \mathit{fwd\_spd} = 0)\mathbf{W}\,\mathit{bot\_in\_front}$, states that the robot continues to rotate on its axis unless there is a bottle in front of the robot. This alone does not guarantee progress (i.e., that $\mathit{bot\_in\_front}$ holds). However, the consequent of 5 ensures that a bottle will eventually be seen.

We note that 5 is an abstract property that encompasses a number of different scenarios. For example, it guarantees that if there is only one bottle on the table, then this bottle will eventually be seen, provided the robot continues to rotate at a velocity of $0.5\pi/s$. This means that we assume the bottle is not moved away by the environment (unless another bottle is placed on the table as a replacement). If there are multiple bottles on the table, then the environment guarantees that the robot will eventually rotate towards at least one of these (e.g., the bottles will not all be removed from the table). Condition 5 also guarantees that if there are no bottles on the table, then the environment eventually places at least one bottle on the table, and given that the robot continues to spin on its axis, then some bottle will be in front of the robot.

Finally, we require that a *bot_in_front* predicate triggers a new *Belief Store* update. In particular, if there is a bottle in front of the robot, then the guard see(bottle, _, _) must become true in the *Belief Store*. This is formalised by the assertions

$$bot\_in\_front \vdash \exists x, y. \text{ bel see}(\texttt{bottle},x,y) \tag{6}$$

$$\neg bot\_in\_front \vdash \neg\exists x, y. \text{ bel see}(\texttt{bottle},x,y) \tag{7}$$

Again, there are different levels of detail one can apply in modelling reality when making sensor assumptions, e.g., sensor inaccuracies, timing delays etc.

Putting these together, from assumption 1, we have that the turn action with value 0.5 induces a physical rotation; from assumption 5, we have that a physical rotation induces that the bottle is in front of the robot; and from assumption 6 the fact that the bottle is in front of the robot can be sensed. Moreover, this guarantees regression, i.e., that turn causes the higher priority guard see to become true.

4.2   TeleoR Traces

We now provide a formalisation of the ideas above for a given TeleoR program (and its environment). First, we define an *environment state* to be a function mapping from (physical) variables to values. We let *Init* be the set of all possible initial environment states. A *sensor assertion* is a predicate of the form $E \vdash P$, where E is a ground predicate on the environment state and P is a ground predicate on the belief store. Given an environment state ϵ and belief store β, we say $E \vdash P$ holds in (ϵ, β), denoted $E \vdash_{\epsilon,\beta}$ bel P iff $(\epsilon \models E) \Rightarrow (\beta \models P)$. Similarly, an *action assertion* is a predicate of the form do $A_i \vdash E$, where A_i is an ground action. We say do $A_i \vdash E$ holds in (β, ϵ), denoted do $A_i \vdash_{\beta,\epsilon} E$ iff $(\beta \models$ do $A_i) \Rightarrow (\epsilon \models E)$.

A TeleoR *state* is triple $(\epsilon, \beta, \epsilon')$, where ϵ is the environment being sensed, β is the belief store that results from sensing ϵ, which includes the firing of a new action, and ϵ' is the new environment that results from firing this action.

Consistency of a TeleoR state is judged with respect to the set of sensor and action assertions that are assumed for the program. In particular, given a set of sensor assertions S and a set of action assertions Z, we say the TeleoR state $(\epsilon, \beta, \epsilon')$ is *consistent* with respect to S and Z iff

1. for each $(E \vdash P) \in S$, we have $E \vdash_{\epsilon, \beta} P$,
2. for each $(\mathbf{do}\ \mathsf{A}_i \vdash E) \in Z$, we have $\mathbf{do}\ \mathsf{A}_i \vdash_{\beta, \epsilon'} E$, and
3. ϵ and ϵ' are identical except for the environment variables that are changed as a result of the updated action in β.

Definition 3. *A* TeleoR *trace is a sequence*

$$\tau = (\epsilon_0, \beta_0, \epsilon_0'), (\epsilon_1, \beta_1, \epsilon_1'), (\epsilon_2, \beta_2, \epsilon_2'), \dots$$

of TeleoR *states such that* $\epsilon_0 \in Init$, *and each* $(\epsilon_i, \beta_i, \epsilon_i')$ *is consistent.*

We define two projection functions π_p and π_e that restrict a given TeleoR trace to the belief stores and environment states, respectively. For τ above:

$$\pi_p(\tau) = \beta_0, \beta_1, \beta_2, \beta_3, \dots \qquad \pi_e(\tau) = \epsilon_0, \epsilon_0', \epsilon_1, \epsilon_1', \epsilon_2, \epsilon_2', \dots$$

Note that above we are considering the TeleoR trace obtained from the execution of a top-level ground TR procedure call C and so for each β_i in $\pi_p(\tau)$ we have a corresponding set of primitive actions which are determined by repeated uses of (*Fire*).

Finally, we must introduce *system assumptions*, which are assumptions over TeleoR traces. Such assumptions can be used to state that environment variables under the control of the robot are not arbitrarily modified by the environment. System assumptions are formalised as temporal formulae over TeleoR traces. This requires that we define predicates over TeleoR states (of the form $(\epsilon, \beta, \epsilon')$); LTL operators over TeleoR traces can be readily defined by extending predicates over TeleoR states and recursively defining the each of the LTL operators over these predicates (as done in Sect. 3 for belief store traces). When defining predicates over TeleoR states, we use unprimed and primed variables to distinguish environment variables in ϵ and ϵ', respectively.

4.3   Example Verification

For our running example, we use system assumptions to limit the scope of the environment that we consider. For example, we assume that the environment does not impede a robot's (physical) rotation.[2] Thus, for each consecutive pair of TeleoR states in τ, i.e., τ_i, τ_{i+1}, the value of *rot_spd* in the post-environment state of τ_i is the same as the value of *rot_spd* in the pre-environment state of τ_{i+1}. This is formalised as:

$$\forall k, l.\ \mathbf{G}(rot\_spd' = k \wedge fwd\_spd' = l \Rightarrow \mathbf{X}(rot\_spd = k \wedge fwd\_spd = l)) \qquad (8)$$

---

[2] Of course, in reality, there are environments that could impede a robot's motion—we do not make any claims about correctness of our implementation for such environments. In a full development, one would need to make sure that the physical environment in which a verified robot operates does indeed conform to any assumptions made in the proof.

We now return to the the procedure call `get_close_to(bottle)` in Example 1 and describe how it can be shown to satisfy the regression property when it is executing the lowest priority rule 4 with intended action `turn(right, 0.5)`. We need to show that eventually a bottle will be seen in the robot environment, i.e. *bot_in_front*, resulting in $\exists x, y$ bel `see(bottle,x,y)` by 6.

Suppose

$$\tau = (\epsilon_0, \beta_0, \epsilon_0'), (\epsilon_1, \beta_1, \epsilon_1'), (\epsilon_2, \beta_2, \epsilon_2'), \ldots$$

is a `TeleoR` trace of the program.

Consider an arbitrary index i. Assume for each belief store up to and including β_i we have bel $\neg \exists x, y.$`see(bottle,`$x, y)$. From this assumption, using equation (*Fire*) and (*RoboticActs*), we obtain

$$\beta_i \models \text{do turn(right}, 0.5) \wedge \neg \exists x.\text{do move}(x).$$

Now, by assumptions (1) and (3) we have $\epsilon_i' \models (rot\_spd = 0.5 \wedge fwd\_spd = 0)$.

We now argue as follows by case analysis.

– If for some $j > i$, we have $\tau_j \models bot\_in\_front$, then we trivially have regression, since condition (6) ensures that this triggers the required belief store update in τ_j.

– So suppose that for all $j > i$, $\tau_j \models \neg bot\_in\_front$. Then by (7), for all $j > i$, we have

$$\beta_j \models \neg \exists x, y.\text{sees(bottle,}x, y).$$

This also means (by the semantics of the program) that

$$\beta_j \models \text{do turn(right}, 0.5) .$$

Hence, by (1) and (3), for each $j > i$, we have

$$\epsilon_j' \models (rot\_spd = 0.5 \wedge fwd\_spd = 0).$$

Now, since we also have $\epsilon_i' \models (rot\_spd = 0.5 \wedge fwd\_spd = 0)$, by (8), we have that for all $j > i$, $\epsilon_j \models (rot\_spd = 0.5 \wedge fwd\_spd = 0)$. Thus, the antecedent of 5 is satisfied, and hence we must have $\tau_j \models bot\_in\_front$ for some j, which contradicts our initial assumption.

This completes the proof and gives us the required regression result:

$$\text{do get\_close\_to(bottle)} \wedge \textit{fired}(\text{get\_close\_to(bottle)}, 4, \{\}) \Rightarrow \\ \mathbf{F} \ \exists x, y.\text{bel see(bottle}, x, y) \tag{9}$$

This is an instance of the (*Regression*), repeated below:

$$\mathbf{G}(\forall 1 < i \leq n. \text{ do } C \wedge \textit{fired}(C, i, \_) \Rightarrow \mathbf{F}(\exists 1 \leq j < i. \exists \text{bel } G_j))$$

5 Conclusions

This paper develops an adaptation of LTL to reason about `TeleoR` programs that enables reasoning over belief stores in a decoupled manner. Actions (having an effect on the environment) and sensors (taking readings from the environment) are modelled as assumptions linking the belief store and the environment, which are subsequently used in system proofs. The logic also enables modelling of purely physical assumptions and those pertaining to the system as a whole in a straightforward manner. We apply this logic to show regression of a `TeleoR` program.

This separation of concerns enables less idealised sensor information (inputs) and robotic movements (outputs) to be modelled more easily. Such information may also be provided by domain experts, and further refined at different stages of development. Of course, to cater for a wider range of implementations (without requiring proofs to be replayed), one must use specifications that are as abstract as possible. Precisely what this entails, however, is a subject of further study.

Our ultimate aim for this work is to encode the framework in a verification tool within a theorem proving environment. Hence, we do not consider questions such as decidability of the logic. However, for several of the example programs we have developed, it is possible to develop controllers that operate over discretised approximations that result in finitely many possibilities of the belief store. For example, for our bottle collecting robot, it is possible to record `high` and `low` values instead of precise speeds, and record `far`, `near` and `very near` instead of precise distances.

Prior work on `TeleoR` has focussed on addressing real-time properties [3,4] using an interval temporal logic. The focus there has been to cope with timing issues, including those that lead to sampling errors. Although the formalism enables separation of properties into those of the environment (formalised by a rely) and those of the agent (formalised by a guarantee), both are asserted over a monolithic state containing all system variables. In contrast, this paper presents a separation of concerns, whereby the inputs and outputs to the `TeleoR` program are linked in a separate step.

Acknowledgements. We thank our anonymous FMAS reviewers for their careful readings of this paper and comments, which have helped improve quality overall.

References

1. Clark, K.L., Robinson, P.J.: Robotic agent programming in TeleoR. In: Proceedings of International Conference of Robotics and Automation. IEEE (2015)
2. Clark, K.L., Robinson, P.J.: Chapter 3: introduction to QuLog. In: Programming Communicating Robotic Agents: A Multi-tasking Teleo-Reactive Approach. Springer (2020). (To appear)
3. Dongol, B., Hayes, I.J.: Rely/Guarantee reasoning for teleo-reactive programs over multiple time bands. In: Derrick, J., Gnesi, S., Latella, D., Treharne, H. (eds.) IFM 2012. LNCS, vol. 7321, pp. 39–53. Springer, Heidelberg (2012). https://doi.org/10.1007/978-3-642-30729-4_4

4. Dongol, B., Hayes, I.J., Robinson, P.J.: Reasoning about goal-directed real-time teleo-reactive programs. Formal Asp. Comput. **26**(3), 563–589 (2014). https://doi.org/10.1007/s00165-012-0272-1
5. Jones, J., Roth, D.: Robot Programming: A Practical Guide to Behavior-based Robotics. McGraw-Hill, New York (2004)
6. Kamali, M., Linker, S., Fisher, M.: Modular verification of vehicle platooning with respect to decisions, space and time. In: Artho, C., Ölveczky, P.C. (eds.) FTSCS 2018. CCIS, vol. 1008, pp. 18–36. Springer, Cham (2019). https://doi.org/10.1007/978-3-030-12988-0_2
7. Levesque, H.: Thinking as Computation. MIT Press, Cambridge (2012)
8. Mataric, M.J.: The Robotics Primer. MIT Press, Cambridge (2007)
9. Quigley, M., et al.: ROS: an open-source Robot Operating System (2009). www.robotics.stanford.edu/~ang/papers/icraoss09-ROS.pdf

A Mission Definition, Verification and Validation Architecture

Louis Viard[(⊠)] [iD], Laurent Ciarletta, and Pierre-Etienne Moreau

Université de Lorraine LORIA, UMR 7503, 54600 Villers-lès-Nancy, France
{louis.viard,laurent.ciarletta,pierre-etienne.moreau}@loria.fr

Abstract. Safe operation of Cyber-Physical Systems such as Unmanned Aircraft Systems requires guarantees not only on the system, but also on the mission. Following approaches that are used to produce robust Cyber-Physical Controllers, we present the architecture of a mission definition, verification and validation toolchain. We conclude by reporting on the current state of the authors' implementation of this framework.

1 Introduction

A large part of current Cyber-Physical System (CPS) development focuses on greater automation. Systems such as heaters have sensors to enable autonomous actions based on environment awareness, and this interaction promotes them to CPS. The disappearance – at least, the new role – of humans in this control loop raises questions about the dependability of these systems: critical software must yet give guarantees in order to replace humans who are deemed error-prone. Confidence in critical systems can be given by using formal methods and extensive testing. Much work has already been done on verifying and validating CPS design. It includes the verification of modules such as detect-and-avoid devices or collision avoidance systems for aircrafts [6,10]. Formal methods play a pivotal role in building such robust systems by giving strong guarantees about their control.

To achieve complex operation such as Unmanned Aircraft (UA) inspections, missions are built by composing atomic actions of the CPS. They quickly become critical as the consequences of an ill-defined mission for systems evolving in open areas are severe. Thus, there is a need for integrated frameworks to define these CPS operations, that include formal verification and validation of missions. A thorny problem of verifying and validating CPS is the physical environment. Physical models fall short of the real environment, such as wind gusts of an unexpected magnitude tossing a small aircraft around. Such hazards occurs sporadically, and the CPS should be equipped for these situations to the extent that it makes sense (probability of occurence, reaction capacity, physical integrity, cost, *etc.*). The discrepency between models and actual behaviours must consequently be monitored at runtime, potentially leading to fallback missions execution (*e.g.* safely leaving a no-fly area).

© Springer Nature Switzerland AG 2020
E. Sekerinski et al. (Eds.): FM 2019 Workshops, LNCS 12232, pp. 281–287, 2020.
https://doi.org/10.1007/978-3-030-54994-7_20

We report on an architecture to define, verify, and validate missions for CPS. It is build around an intermediate representation of the CPS and of its mission. This toolchain is currently being developed by the authors, and was partially demonstrated for the definition of missions with monitoring by design [13]. To illustrate the proposed architecture, the current state of this implementation is described in conclusion.

2   Background

Prior works exists on formal verification of CPS missions. It goes back to at least 1997, with the `Maestro` language [7] that was developed for the `Orccad` robotic framework. `Orccad` [3] (not maintained anymore) revolved a around two key structures, *Robot-Tasks* and *Robot-Procedures*, that are analogous to what we refer to as, respectively, actions and missions. *Robot-Tasks* are atomic control laws, using continuous times and discrete events that occur at execution. *Robot-Procedures* are logical composition of *Robot-Tasks* (sequential, loop, parallel, and preemption). On a conceptual level, these key elements are roughly equivalent to what we refer to as, respectively, actions and missions. The resulting robot controllers were compiled in `Esterel` [1], formal verification was performed on the resulting automata, and the framework offered possibilities for logical simulation of the controller. Our approach differs as we stress the discrepancy between the real and ideal execution: *Robot-Tasks* produce dynamics whereas *actions* describe it.

Several works have introduced Model-Driven Engineering for design and operation of CPS. They often place emphasis on having non-programmers or non-experts as users. Verification and validation of the mission, when considered at all, is often done through simulation [5,8]. Formal verification benefits Cyber-Physical Controllers design [11]. Unmanned Aircrafts often embed formally verified *geofencing* devices to keep them in their assigned flying area [9,12]. Code that integrates formally verified model monitoring may be generated from hybrid programs [2]. These works act at the V&V CPS design phase, but were not developed for mission definition.

3   Concepts for Mission Verification

We illustrate some of the concepts needed for mission verification, using a generic UA operating on a mission to take photos. The mission has three properties being monitored: mission-related (proper camera angle), safety-related (no-fly areas) *geofencing*, and power management. *Geofencing* constrains the motion of the aircraft, and power management involves ensuring that the UA will finish the mission before it runs out of power.

We abstract a CPS as a tuple of state variables, which represent the current state of a system, and actions. Actions are atomic behaviours of the CPS, such as arming (powering the vehicle), taking off, setting the velocity, *etc.* They are given as hybrid programs that, assuming prerequisites, define an *ideal* continuous evolution of the state using differential systems ($\sigma' = f(\sigma, \sigma')$) and implicit functions ($f(\sigma) = 0$). Their interpretation is twofold, depending on the posture we adopt. The formal model uses actions as descriptions of the dynamics of the system whereas the runtime posture considers them as fallible: the execution may not follow the specification. For instance, the aircraft may depart from its assigned trajectory due to wind gusts or GPS noise. These kinematics descriptions are used at runtime to observe the agreement between the real execution and the model.

A mission is built from sequential actions and monitoring control structures. Figure 1 sums up the latter. A monitoring control structures involves a guard and two missions. The main mission, the sequence of actions n and $n + 1$, is executed as long as the guard (φ) is satisfied. As soon as the guard evaluates to `False`, the fallback mission is triggered. This mission acts as a temporary measure to reach a safe(r) state. In our example, the UA moves if it does not have a good camera angle, returns to its landing point when the power level falls below a threshold, and releases the parachute when entering a no-fly area. A fallback mission finishes with one of the three following behaviours:

- *resumes*: the main mission execution carries on from where it was interrupted, which would be the case for the camera angle adjustment scenario
- *roll back*: the mission execution rolls back to a previously labelled
- *abort*: the mission escapes the current control structure. The fallback for power management would be followed by a landing manoeuvre, and releasing the parachute would have no follow-up action.

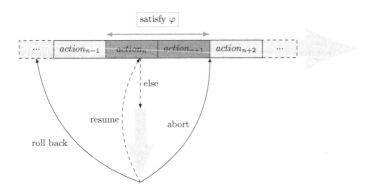

Fig. 1. Three classes of monitors depending on the fallback return point.

4   Mission Definition, Verification and Validation Architecture

This section presents the architecture that we envision for mission definition, verification, and validation. The architecture shown is by no means an exhaustive

view, it focuses on the direct writing of the mission, its verification and validation, and how it translates into the executed code on the real CPS. Extensions
are mentioned in Sect. 4.2.

4.1 Core Architecture

The proposed architecture is presented in Fig. 2; it revolves around an intermediate representation of the CPS and of its operation, which we call the Mission
Language. This modelling language enables the definition of the system and missions as introduced in Sect. 3. When the CPS is Verified and Validated, each
action has a formal specification. These specifications may be reused when defining the system in the Mission Language, or weakened: although we would first
think of them as being exactly the same, the reachable state space of an action
may be loosened, considering that some uncertainties that were neglected during the CPS design validation must be included due to operation conditions that
were previously disregarded.

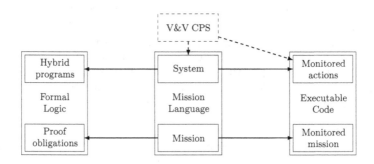

Fig. 2. Core architecture of a verified and validated mission definition toolchain.

The Mission Language descriptions are translated into: *(i)* formal models,
with proof obligations to verify and validate the mission; *(ii)* executable code,
which is generated to ensure its correctness. In this paper, we focus on the formal
models.

Actions are translated into hybrid programs (of the corresponding logic *e.g.*
differential dynamic logic) that describe the evolution of the state variables.
The first step is to check that the mission is executable, by checking that each
action prerequisite will be satisfied (*viz.* that the UA will be armed and landed
when calling `takeoff`) and by ensuring termination (finite looping). The second
step is to verify properties (relating to safety, mission objective, *etc.*) that were
defined as monitor guards. For instance, we have to prove that the *ideal* mission
execution won't breach the *geofencing* and power management constraints.

In addition to checking the correctness of the model, other proof obligations
arise such as verifying that fallback missions restore their associated guards. This
rule especially applies to the mission-related guards: the fallback movement must

ensure a correct camera angle. Likewise, fallback missions must be verified to not lead to greater complications by breaching higher guards. When the power level drops lower than the threshold, the path taken to return to the home station must still satisfy the safe *geofencing*.

As is usual, automatic generation of executable code from the Mission Language models should be developed to avoid new errors being introduced at this stage. As mentioned previously, actions are translated into monitors (*cf* Sect. 3). The *dynamics* of the action is given by the real CPS implementation. From the point of view of the generated action, this roughly corresponds to calling an API function. For instance, if the flight stack of a UA implements a `takeoff` service, the corresponding monitored action calls it while keeping a check on the state evolution.

4.2 Extension and Contextualisation

We have presented the core of a V&V mission definition system, but many add-ons would prove to be useful and to nicely complement this first raw architecture. Here we present two illustrative examples: simulation and visualisation.

Complete formal verfication of complex systems rapidly becomes intractable. To be fully comprehensive, it requires *e.g.* a complete formal model of the hardware. Even then, there is no guarantee that a proof can be derived. Thus, to contribute to the verification and validation process, tests in various simulation environments (software in the loop, hardware in the loop, with fault injection) are resorted to. Simulation integrates into the V&V mission definition architecture without any hurdle as it builds on top of the executable code.

Practical operations generally involve many different players. Expertise in various fields for not only the system and its validation (*e.g.* networks, formal proof, multi-agent, control theory) but also for the use case (such as the operator that has been doing the work that is being automated) need to interact with the legislator, customers, and occasionally citizens. In these situations, having supports that facilitate the communication around the mission, at the cost of the ease to develop with these representations, comes in handy. Simulated missions with physically-based renderering is a first natural way to have non-experts involved. Another recurrent feature are high-level graphical languages that enable non-experts users to define missions (*e.g.* [4]). Other avenues of research should be investigated, such as graphical rendering of the reachable states, or immersive simulators, and remote monitoring of the mission being executed.

5   Conclusion and Perspectives

Safe CPS operations require tools as rigorous as those used to design the system. Following approaches that are currently under development for Cyber-Physical Controllers, we have outlined the architecture for a mission definition and V&V toolchain. The authors are currently building such a framework around a Domain-Specific Language for mission definition, Sophrosyne.

Its usage has been showcased on inspection missions [13]. Monitors were hierarchically composed to stop the mission should too many breaches occur. The system and its mission were compiled into *(i)* executable code, that was run in a Software in the Loop simulation; *(ii)* a symbolic system, that produces a graph of reachable states, exemplifying both core parts and extensions of the presented architecture. However, missions were not formally verified. Achieving a formal description of the rules is part of our ongoing research effort, together with the automatic generation of corresponding hybrid programs and proof obligations.

References

1. Berry, G., Gonthier, G.: The Esterel synchronous programming language: design, semantics, implementation. Sci. Comput. Program. **19**, 87–152 (1992)
2. Bohrer, B., Tan, Y.K., Mitsch, S., Myreen, M.O., Platzer, A.: VeriPhy: verified controller executables from verified cyber-physical system models. In: 39th ACM SIGPLAN Conference on Programming Language Design and Implementation, pp. 617–630 (2018)
3. Borelly, J.J., et al.: The orccad architecture. Int. J. Robot. Res. **17**(4), 338–359 (1998)
4. Bozhinoski, D., Di Ruscio, D., Malavolta, I., Pelliccione, P., Tivoli, M.: FLYAQ: enabling non-expert users to specify and generate missions of autonomous multicopters. In: 30th IEEE/ACM International Conference on Automated Software Engineering, pp. 801–806 (2015). https://doi.org/10.1109/ASE.2015.104
5. Ciccozzi, F., Di Ruscio, D., Malavolta, I., Pelliccione, P.: Adopting MDE for specifying and executing civilian missions of mobile multi-robot systems. IEEE Access **4**, 6451–6466 (2016). https://doi.org/10.1109/ACCESS.2016.2613642
6. Consiglio, M., Muñoz, C., Hagen, G., Narkawicz, A., Balachandran, S.: ICAROUS integrated configurable algorithms for reliable operations of unmanned systems. In: 35th Digital Avionics Systems Conference, pp. 1–5 (2016)
7. Coste-Maniere, E., Turro, N.: The MAESTRO language and its environment: specification, validation and control of robotic missions. In: IEEE/RSJ International Conference on Intelligent Robots and Systems, pp. 836–841 (1997). https://doi.org/10.1109/IROS.1997.655107
8. Dhouib, S., Kchir, S., Stinckwich, S., Ziadi, T., Ziane, M.: RobotML, a domain-specific language to design, simulate and deploy robotic applications. In: 3rd International Conference on Simulation, Modeling, and Programming for Autonomous Robots, pp. 149–160 (2012)
9. Dill, E.T., Young, S.D., Hayhurst, K.J.: SAFEGUARD: an assured safety net technology for UAS. In: AIAA/IEEE Digital Avionics Systems Conference - Proceedings, pp. 1–10 (2016). https://doi.org/10.1109/DASC.2016.7778009
10. Jeannin, J.B., Ghorbal, K., Kouskoulas, Y., Schmidt, A., Gardner, R., Mitsch, S.: A formally verified hybrid system for safe advisories in the next-generation airborne collision avoidance system. Int. J. Softw. Tools Technol. Transfer **19**, 717–741 (2017). https://doi.org/10.1007/s10009-016-0434-1
11. Mitsch, S., Passmore, G.O., Platzer, A.: Collaborative verification-driven engineering of hybrid systems. Math. Comput. Sci. **8**(1), 71–97 (2014). https://doi.org/10.1007/s11786-014-0176-y

12. Ricketts, D., Malecha, G., Alvarez, M.M., Gowda, V., Lerner, S.: Towards verification of hybrid systems in a foundational proof assistant. In: International Conference on Formal Methods and Models for Codesign, pp. 248–257. IEEE (2015)
13. Viard, L., Ciarletta, L., Moreau, P.E.: Monitor-centric mission definition with sophrosyne. In: 2019 International Conference on Unmanned Aircraft Systems (ICUAS), pp. 111–119 (2019)

FMBC 2019 - 1st Workshop on Formal Methods for Blockchains

FMBC 2019 Organizers' Message

The 1st Workshop on Formal Methods for Blockchains (FMBC) was held on October 11, 2019 in Porto, Portugal, as part of FM'19, the 3rd World Congress on Formal Methods. Its purpose was to be a forum to identify theoretical and practical approaches applying formal methods to blockchain technology.

This very first edition of FMBC attracted 20 submissions (11 long papers and 9 short papers) on topics such as verification of smart contracts or analysis of consensus protocols. Each paper was reviewed by at least three program committee members or appointed external reviewers. This led to a selection of 10 articles (8 long and 2 short) that were presented at the workshop as regular talks, as well as two articles that were presented as lightning talks. Additionally, we were very pleased to have an invited keynote by Ilya Sergey (Yale-NUS College and NUS).

This volume contains the papers selected for regular talks, as well as the abstract of the invited talk. Before inclusion, the papers were reviewed a second time after the workshop by the program committee.

We thank all the authors that submitted a paper, as well as the program committee members and external reviewers for their immense work. We are grateful to José Nuno Oliveira, General Chair of FM'19, and to Emil Sekerinski and Nelma Moreira, Workshop and Tutorial Chairs of FM'19, for their support and guidance. Finally, we would like to express our gratitude to our sponsor Nomadic Labs for its generous support.

December 2019

Bruno Bernardo
Néstor Cataño
Diego Marmsoler

Organization

Program Committee

Pietro Abate	Nomadic Labs, France
Ijaz Ahmed	University of Madeira, Portugal
Jonathan Aldrich	Carnegie Mellon University, USA
Bernhard Beckert	Karlsruhe Institute of Technology, Germany
Bruno Bernardo	Nomadic Labs, France
Sukriti Bhattacharya	LIST, Luxembourg
Néstor Cataño	Innopolis University, Russia

Maria Christakis	MPI-SWS, Germany
Zaynah Dargaye	Nomadic Labs, France
Georges Gonthier	Inria, France
Neville Grech	University of Athens, Greece/University of Malta, Malta
Davide Grossi	University of Groningen, Netherlands
Sorren Hanvey	Liverpool John Moores University, UK
Andreas Lochbihler	Digital Asset, Switzerland
Diego Marmsoler	Technical University of Munich, Germany
Anastasia Mavridou	NASA Ames, USA
Simão Melo de Sousa	Universidade da Beira Interior, Portugal
Fabio Mogavero	University of Naples Federico II, Italy
Peter Ölveczky	University of Oslo, Norway
Karl G Palmskog	KTH Royal Institute of Technology, Sweden
Vincent Rahli	University of Birmingham, UK
Steve Reeves	University of Waikato, New Zealand
Camilo Rueda	PUJ, Colombia
Claudio Russo	Dfinity, USA
Jorge Sousa Pinto	Universidade do Minho, Portugal
Bas Spitters	Aarhus University, Denmark
Christoph Sprenger	ETH Zurich, Switzerland
Mark Staples	Data61, Australia
Philip Wadler	University of Edinburgh, UK
Xi Wu	University of Sydney, Australia
Santiago Zanella-Béguelin	Microsoft Research, UK

Additional Reviewers

Cláudio Belo Lourenço
Luis Horta
Carlos Olarte
Mário Pereira
João Reis
Valentin Wüstholz

The Scilla Journey: From Proof General to Thousands of Nodes (Invited Talk)

Ilya Sergey

Yale-NUS College, Singapore and National University of Singapore, Singapore
ilya.sergey@yale-nus.edu.sg

Abstract. The Scilla project has started in late 2017 as a 100-lines-of-code prototype implemented in Coq proof assistant. Learning from the mistakes of Ethereum, which had pioneered the area of blockchain-based applications (aka smart contracts), the aim of Scilla was to provide a smart contract language, which is expressive enough to accommodate most of the reasonable use-cases, while allowing for scalable and tractable formal verification and analysis. As such, Scilla has been positioned as an intermediate-level language, suitable to serve as a compilation target and also as an independent programming framework. Two years later, Scilla is now powering the application layer of Zilliqa, the world's first publicly deployed sharded blockchain system. Since its public launch less than a year ago, dozens of unique smart contracts implemented in Scilla have been deployed, including custom tokens, collectibles, auctions, multiplayer games, name registries, atomic token swaps, and many others. In my talk, I will describe the motivation, design principles, and semantics of Scilla, and outline the main use cases and the tools provided by the developer community. I will also present a framework for lightweight verification of Scilla programs, and showcase it with two automated domain-specific analyses. Finally, I will discuss the pragmatic pitfalls of designing a new smart contract language from scratch, and present the future exciting research directions that are enabled by Scilla's take on smart contract design.

Smart Contracts: Application Scenarios for Deductive Program Verification

Bernhard Beckert, Jonas Schiffl[✉], and Mattias Ulbrich

Karlsruhe Institute of Technology, Karlsruhe, Germany
{bernhard.beckert,jonas.schiffl,mattias.ulbrich}@kit.edu

Abstract. Smart contracts are programs that run on a distributed ledger platform. They usually manage resources representing valuable assets. Moreover, their source code is visible to potential attackers, they are distributed, and bugs are hard to fix. Thus, they are susceptible to attacks exploiting programming errors. Their vulnerability makes a rigorous formal analysis of the functional correctness of smart contracts highly desirable.

In this short paper, we show that the architecture of smart contract platforms offers a computation model for smart contracts that yields itself naturally to deductive program verification. We discuss different classes of correctness properties of distributed ledger applications, and show that design-by-contract verification tools are suitable to prove these properties. We present experiments where we apply the KeY verification tool to smart contracts in the Hyperledger Fabric framework which are implemented in Java and specified using the Java Modeling Language.

1 Introduction

Smart contracts are programs that work in conjunction with a distributed ledger. They automatically manage resources on that ledger. Multiple distributed ledger platforms supporting smart contracts have been developed, most prominently the public Ethereum blockchain. Smart contracts manage resources representing virtual or real-world assets. Their source code is visible to potential attackers. Therefore, they are susceptible to attacks exploiting errors in the program source code. Furthermore, smart contracts cannot be easily changed after deployment. They need to be correct upon deployment, and formal methods should be used for ensuring their correctness [3].

In this paper, we describe the computational model of smart contracts, which makes them an ideal target for deductive program verification. We discuss different notions of smart contract correctness, and the implications for formal verification.

We focus on the Hyperledger Fabric [4] architecture. Fabric is a framework for the operation of private, permission-based distributed ledger networks. Smart contracts in Fabric can currently be written in Go, Java, and Javascript. While our concrete verification efforts target Fabric smart contracts written in Java,

© Springer Nature Switzerland AG 2020
E. Sekerinski et al. (Eds.): FM 2019 Workshops, LNCS 12232, pp. 293–298, 2020.
https://doi.org/10.1007/978-3-030-54994-7_21

much of the concepts can be generalized to other programming languages, and also to other smart contract platforms.

The KeY system [1], which we used for experiments, is a deductive program verification tool for verifying Java programs w.r.t. a formal specification. KeY follows the principle of design-by-contract, i.e., system properties are broken down into method specifications called *contracts* that must be individually proven correct. Specifications for KeY are written in the Java Modeling Language [7], the de-facto standard language for formal specification of Java programs. For verification, KeY uses a deductive component operating on a sequent calculus for JavaDL, a program logic for Java.

In Sect. 2, we describe an abstract computational model for applications in a distributed ledger architecture. In Sect. 3, we discuss different notions and classes of smart contract correctness w.r.t. that model. Then, in Sect. 4, we describe how properties from these classes can be verified in the KeY tool. Finally, we draw some conclusions and discuss future work in Sect. 5.

2   Distributed Ledger Infrastructure and the Computational Model

Smart contract platforms are complex systems. Their functionality is spread across several layers and components. Some components are by necessity part of every smart contract platform, other components are unique to certain types of smart contract systems.

The correct behavior of a smart contract depends on all components of the distributed ledger architecture. This includes: the implementation of the blockchain data structure, which ensures that the shared history cannot be changed; the consensus and ordering algorithms for creating a single view of the system state; the cryptography modules for chain integrity and the public key infrastructure; and the network layer, which ensures correct distribution of transaction requests and new blocks.

If all these components work correctly, they provide an abstract computational model for the execution of smart contract applications in a distributed ledger system. This computational model can be described as follows: a distributed ledger platform behaves like a (non-distributed) single-core machine which takes requests (in the form of function calls) from clients. The execution of a request (a transaction) is atomic and sequential. The machine's storage is a key-value database in which serialized objects are stored at unique addresses. The storage can only be modified through client requests. The overall state of the storage is determined entirely by the order in which requests are taken. No assumptions can be made about the relationship between the order of requests made by the clients and the actual order of execution. However, it can be assumed that every request is eventually executed. All requests are recorded, even if they do not modify the state or are malformed.

3   Correctness of Smart Contracts

In the previous section, we have described the abstraction provided by smart contract architectures: it behaves like a single-core machine operating on a database storage and taking requests from clients. In this section, we discuss how this abstraction is useful for applying program verification techniques and tools. We give an overview of different classes of smart contract correctness properties and characterize the requirements and challenges for formal analysis that each class entails. The properties are roughly ordered by the effort required to prove them. Existing approaches to verification of smart contracts are given as examples for each class.

3.1   Generic Properties

Generic properties are independent of the concrete smart contract application and its functionality, i.e., there is no need to write property specifications for individual contracts. Typical examples of generic properties are termination for all inputs and absence of exceptions such as null-pointer dereference.

Program properties such as termination are undecidable in general, and proofs may be non-trivial and require heavy-weight verification tools. Nevertheless, many generic properties can be validated by syntactical methods like type checking or simple static analysis. They are less precise than program verification and produce false alarms in case of doubt, but are still very useful in practice. Especially in the context of Ethereum, there is a wide variety of static analysis tools, e.g. [8,9], that can show the absence of known anti-patterns or vulnerabilities, like the notorious reentrance vulnerability, or inaccessible funds. For Hyperledger Fabric, there exists a tool which statically checks a smart contract for anti-patterns like non-determinism or local state.[1]

3.2   Specific Correctness Properties of Single Transactions

Correctness of a smart contract applications cannot be captured by generic properties alone: there has to be some formal specification which expresses the expected resp. required behavior of a program. Smart contract functions, which are atomic and deterministic in our computational model, are the basic modules of smart contracts (much like methods are basic components of programs), and therefore also the basic targets for correctness verification. The specification of a function consists of a precondition, which states what conditions the caller of the function has to satisfy, and a postcondition expressing what conditions are guaranteed to hold after the transaction (i.e., the function execution). In case of smart contracts, the specification should generally treat public ledger state and function call parameters as potentially malicious; therefore, the precondition should make no assumptions about them, as correctness properties must hold for all possible values.

---

[1] https://chaincode.chainsecurity.com/.

Examples of specific properties of a single transaction include functional correctness statements (e.g., "the specified amount is deducted from the account if sufficient funds are available, otherwise the account remains unchanged") and statements about what locations on the ledger a transaction is allowed to modify.

An approach to verification of single transaction correctness using the Why3 verification platform has been proposed [6]; our own approach using the KeY tool is discussed in Sect. 4.

3.3   Correctness of Distributed Ledger Applications

While transactions are equivalent to individual program functions, a *distributed ledger application* (DLA) is equivalent to a reactive program whose functions can be called by external agents. Informally, a DLA is a part of a smart contract network concerned with one specific task, like running an auction or providing a bank service. More precisely, a DLA is the set of all transactions that can affect a given set of storage locations (including transactions that cannot access a storage location but are used in the calculation of the values being written).

While correctness of the component transactions is a necessary pre-requisite for the correctness of the DLA, there are properties which inherently are properties of transaction traces. They cannot be readily expressed as correctness properties of single transactions. To break them down into a set of single-transaction properties is a non-trivial process. Examples for this class of properties include invariants (e.g., "the overall amount of funds stays the same" for a banking application) and liveness properties giving the guarantee that some condition will eventually be fulfilled. Complex properties of this kind typically are expressed in temporal logic.

4   Verification of Smart Contracts Using the KeY Tool

In this section, we discuss verification of smart contract correctness using the KeY tool. The abstract computational model devised in Sect. 2 is an excellent fit for KeY because, in this setting, a distributed ledger application can be viewed as the equivalent of a Java program where single transactions correspond to Java methods. Thus, the KeY tool, which is designed for verifying Java programs, can be utilized for DLA verification, requiring only minor adaptations. These adaptations mostly concern the nature of the storage, since KeY operates on a heap with object references, while the distributed ledger application's storage is a database of serialized objects. Furthermore, due to the unknown order of execution and the fact that different agents operate within the shared program, there cannot be any assumptions as to the contents of the storage or order of transaction execution.

4.1   Generic Properties

The KeY tool can be used to verify any generic property. As a heavy-weight verification tool, it is particularly useful for properties that cannot be handled by light-weight tools resp. that require KeY's higher precision to avoid too many false alarms. Examples are program termination and the absence of exceptional behavior (the Java Modeling Language keyword `normal_behavior` can be used to specify that a method terminates without exception).

While constructing proofs for such properties is a non-trivial task in general, typical smart contracts are compact and lack complex control flows. In such settings, proofs of termination and absence of exceptions can be expected to be found automatically by KeY, requiring none or minimal auxiliary specifications.

4.2 Chaincode Transaction Correctness

Verification of Hyperledger Fabric chaincode functions, if written in Java, is possible in KeY. The difference between a normal Java program and our computational model is in the storage: while Java programs operate on a heap, a Fabric Smart Contract operates on an (abstracted) key-value database storing serialized objects. In a case study [5] demonstrating how to use KeY to prove the correctness of Hyperledger Fabric chaincode functions, this difference was addressed by an extension of the KeY tool,[2] including an axiomatisation of the read/write interface of the Fabric ledger, a model of the ledger on a logical level, and the introduction of abstract data types for each type of object that is managed by the smart contract.

In the auction example, one might want to specify the `closeAuction()` method as follows:

```
/*@ ensures read(ID) != null ==> read(ID).closed;
  @ ensures (\forall Item i \in read(ID).items;
  @         i.owner_id == read(ID).highestBidderID);@*/
void closeAuction(int ID) { ... }
```

This JML specification is somewhat simplified for readability; the `read` function is an abstraction for accessing the ledger, i.e., reading and deserializing the object at the given location. The specification states that, if the auction object at `ID` is not null, then after execution of the `closeAuction()` method the `closed` flag must be correctly set; furthermore all items in the auction must belong to the highest bidder (as indicated by the `owner_id` attribute). For the correctness proof in KeY, the logical rules necessary for handling the data types stored on the ledger (in this case, auctions, items, and participants) are created automatically. The proof requires some user interaction, since the new rules have not yet been included in the automation mechanism of the prover.

There exists a comparable approach for using KeY to verify Ethereum smart contracts [2].

4.3 Correctness of Distributed Ledger Applications

More complex properties can be reasoned about in KeY using class invariants, two-state invariants, and counters, thereby reducing complex properties of transaction traces (including temporal logic properties) to KeY's method-modular

---

[2] Available at https://key-project.org/chaincode.

approach. For example, the specification of the auction application could state that, as long an auction is open, the items that are offered still belong to the auctioneer:

```
//@ invariant (\forall Auction a; !a.closed;
        (\forall item i \in a.items; i.owner_id == a.auctioneer_id));
```

If every bidder has to deposit the funds for their bid in the auction, the specification could state that as long as the auction remains open, the sum of the funds in the auction remains the same or increases, but never decreases. This can be expressed with a history constraint:

```
//@ constraint \forall Auction a; !a.closed; \old(a.funds) <= a.funds;
```

Though this constraint can easily be expressed in the Java Modeling Language, proving in KeY that a smart contract conforms to this specification is currently infeasible due to the large amount of user interactions that is necessary to close the proof, and due to the inefficiencies of our current approach regarding the handling of reading from and writing to the ledger.

5   Conclusion and Future Work

We have outlined the setting in which deductive program verification of distributed ledger applications takes place and shown that the KeY verification tool is suitable to prove different classes of correctness properties which are interesting in smart contract platforms.

The extensions to KeY which enable verification of Hyperledger Fabric smart contracts are still in a prototypical state. Further improvements are necessary to improve scalability and enable proofs of more complex properties.

References

1. Ahrendt, W., Beckert, B., Bubel, R., Hähnle, R., Schmitt, P.H., Ulbrich, M.: Deductive Software Verification - The KeY Book. Springer, Cham (2016). https://doi.org/10.1007/978-3-319-49812-6
2. Ahrendt, W., et al.: Verification of smart contract business logic. In: Hojjat, H., Massink, M. (eds.) FSEN 2019. LNCS, vol. 11761, pp. 228–243. Springer, Cham (2019). https://doi.org/10.1007/978-3-030-31517-7_16
3. Ahrendt, W., Pace, G.J., Schneider, G.: Smart contracts: a killer application for deductive source code verification. In: Principled Software Development (2018)
4. Androulaki, E., Vukolić, M., et al.: Hyperledger fabric: a distributed operating system for permissioned blockchains. In: EuroSys 2018. ACM (2018)
5. Beckert, B., Herda, M., Kirsten, M., Schiffl, J.: Formal specification and verification of hyperledger fabric chaincode. In: SDLT (2018)
6. Bhargavan, K., et al.: Formal verification of smart contracts: short paper. In: PLAS 2016, Vienna, Austria. ACM Press (2016)
7. Leavens, G.T., et al.: JML Reference Manual (2013)
8. Nikolić, I., Kolluri, A., Sergey, I., Saxena, P., Hobor, A.: Finding the greedy, prodigal, and suicidal contracts at scale. In: ACSAC 2018. ACM (2018)
9. Tsankov, P., Dan, A., Drachsler-Cohen, D., Gervais, A., Buenzli, F., Vechev, M.: Securify: practical security analysis of smart contracts. In: ACM SIGSAC (2018)

Deductive Proof of Industrial Smart Contracts Using Why3

Zeinab Nehaï[1,2(✉)] and François Bobot[2]

[1] Université Paris Diderot, Paris, France
[2] CEA LIST, Palaiseau, France
{zeinab.nehai,francois.bobot}@cea.fr

Abstract. In this paper, we use a formal tool that performs deductive verification on industrial smart contracts, which are self-executing digital programs. Because smart contracts manipulate cryptocurrency and transaction information, if a bug occurs in such programs, serious consequences can happen, such as a loss of money. This paper aims to show that a language dedicated to deductive verification, called *WhyML*, can be a suitable language to write correct and proven contracts. We first encode existing contracts, using the *Why3* tool, into *WhyML* program; next, we formulate specifications to be proven as the absence of Run-Time Error and functional properties, then we verify the behaviour of the program using the *Why3* system. Finally, we compile the *WhyML* contracts to the Ethereum Virtual Machine (EVM). Moreover, our approach estimates the cost of gas, which is a unit that measures the amount of computational effort during a transaction.

Keywords: Deductive verification · Why3 · Smart contracts · Solidity

1 Introduction

Smart Contracts [20] are sequential and executable programs that run on Blockchains [16]. They permit trusted transactions and agreements to be carried out among parties without the need for a central authority while keeping transactions traceable, transparent, and irreversible. These contracts are increasingly confronted with various attacks exploiting their execution vulnerabilities. Attacks lead to significant malicious scenarios, such as the infamous *DAO* attack [7], resulting in a loss of ~$60M. In this paper, we use formal methods on smart contracts from an existing Blockchain application. Our motivation is to ensure safe and correct contracts, avoiding the presence of computer bugs, by using a deductive verification language to write, verify and compile such programs. The chosen language is *WhyML* provided by an automated tool called *Why3* [12], which is a complete tool to perform deductive program verification, based on Hoare logic. A first approach using *Why3* on *Solidity* contracts (the Ethereum smart contracts language) has already been undertaken [2].

© Springer Nature Switzerland AG 2020
E. Sekerinski et al. (Eds.): FM 2019 Workshops, LNCS 12232, pp. 299–311, 2020.
https://doi.org/10.1007/978-3-030-54994-7_22

The author uses *Why3* to formally verify *Solidity* contracts based on code annotation. Unfortunately, that work remained at the prototype level. We describe our research approach through a use case that has already been the subject of previous work, namely the Blockchain Energy Market Place (BEMP) application [18]. In summary, the contributions of this paper are as follows:

1. Showing the adaptability of *WhyML* as a formal language for writing, checking and compiling smart contracts.
2. Detailing a formal and verified *Trading* contract, an example of a more complicated contract than the majority of existing contracts.
3. Providing a way to prove the quantity of *gas* (fraction of an Ethereum token needed for each transaction) used by a smart contract.

The paper is organized as follows. Section 2 describes the approach from a theoretical and formal point of view by explaining the choices made in the study, and Sect. 3 is the proof-of-concept of compiling *WhyML* contracts. A state-of-the-art review of existing work concerning the formal verification of smart contracts is described in Sect. 4. Finally, Sect. 5 summarizes conclusions.

2   A New Approach to Verifying Smart Contracts

2.1   Background of the Study

Deductive Approach & Why3 Tool. A previous work aimed to verify smart contracts using an abstraction method, model-checking [18]. Despite interesting results from this modelling method, the approach to property verification was not satisfactory. Indeed, it is well-known that model-checking confronts us either with limitations on combinatorial explosion, or limitations with invariant generation (most frequently implicit). Thus, proving properties involving a large number of states was impossible to achieve. This conclusion led us to consider applying another formal method technique, deductive verification, which has the advantage of being less dependent on the size of the state space. In this approach, the user is asked to write the invariants. We chose the automated *Why3* tool [12] as our platform. It provides a rich language for specification and programming, called *WhyML*, and relies on well-known external theorem provers such as Alt-ergo [10] (Alt-ergo is the only prover used throughout our study), Z3 [15], and CVC4 [8]. *Why3* comes with a standard library[1] of logical theories and programming data structures. The logic of *Why3* is a first-order logic with polymorphic types and several extensions: recursive definitions, algebraic data types and inductive predicates.

Case Study: Blockchain Energy Market Place. We have applied our approach to a case study provided by industry [18]. It is an Ethereum Blockchain application (BEMP) based on *Solidity* smart contracts language. Briefly, this Blockchain application aims to manage energy exchanges in a peer-to-peer way among the

---

[1] http://why3.lri.fr/.

inhabitants of a district as shown in Figure 1. The figure illustrates (1) & (1')
respectively energy production (Alice) and consumption (Bob). (2) & (2') Smart
meters provide production/consumption data to Ethereum. (3) Bob pays Alice in
ether (Ethereum's cryptocurrency) for his energy consumption. For more details
about the application, please refer to [18].

In our initial work, we applied
our method on a simplified version
of the application, that is, a one-to-
one exchange (1 producer and 1 consumer), with a fixed price for each
kilowatt-hour. This first test allowed
us to identify and prove RTE properties (Runtime Error, e.g., *integer overflow, division by zero, ..*). The simplicity of the unidirectional exchange
model did not allow the definition of
complex functional properties to show
the importance and utility of *Why3*. In

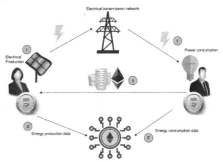

Fig. 1. BEMP process

a second step, we extended the application under study to an indefinite number
of users, and then enriched our specifications. The use of *Why3* is quite suitable
for this order of magnitude. In this second version, we have a set of consumers
and producers willing to buy or to sell energy. Accordingly, we introduced a
simple trading algorithm that matches consumers with producers. In addition
to transferring *ether*, users transfer crypto-Kilowatthours to reward consumers
that consume energy locally produced. Hence, the system needs to formulate and
prove predicates and properties of functions handling various data other than
cryptocurrency. For a first trading approach, we adopted, to our case study, an
order book matching algorithm [11]. Please refer to [17], the technical report,
for the complete BEMP application.

2.2   Why3 Features Intended for Smart Contracts

Library Modelling.   *Solidity* is an imperative object-oriented programming
language, characterized by static typing[2]. It provides several elementary types
that can be combined to form complex types such as booleans, signed, unsigned,
and domain-specific types like addresses. Moreover, the address type has primitive functions able to transfer *ether* (e.g., **send()**) or manipulate cryptocurrency balances (**.balance**). *Solidity* contains elements that are not part of the
WhyML language. One could model these as additional types or primitive features.
Examples of such types are **uint256** and **address**. For machine integers, we use
the range feature of *Why3*: `type uint256 = <range 0 0x7FFFFFFFFFFFFFFFFFFFFFFFFFFFFFFF...>`
because it represents exactly the set of values we want to represent. Thus, *Why3*
firstly checks that constants written by the user are inside the bounds (machine

---

[2] Ethereum foundation: Solidity, the contract-oriented programming language. https://
github.com/ethereum/solidity.

integers constants) and secondly automatically generates conversion functions from machine integers to mathematical integers. Indeed it is a lot more natural and clearer to express specifications with mathematical integers, for example with wrap-around semantic `account = old account - transfer` does not express that the account loses money (if the account was empty it could now have the maximum quantity of money).

Based on the same reasoning, we have modelled the type `Int160`, `Uint160` (which characterizes type `uint` in *Solidity*). We also model the `address` type and its members. We choose to encode the private storage (`balance`) by a Hashtable having as a key value an address, and the associated value a `uint256` value. The current value of the balance of addresses would be `balance[address]`. In addition, the `send` function is translated by a `val` function, which performs operations on the `balance` hashtable. Moreover, we model primitive features such as the `modifier` function, whose role is to restrict access to a function; it can be used to model the states and guard against incorrect usage of the contract. In *WhyML* this feature would be either an exception to raise or a precondition to verify, depending on the function type. This notion of function type will be explained in more detail later (see *Oracle notions*). Finally, we give a model of *gas*, in order to specify the maximum amount of *gas* needed in any case. We introduce a new type: `type gas = int`. The quantity of *gas* is modelled as a mathematical integer because it is never manipulated directly by the program. This part is detailed later.

It is important to note that the purpose of our work is not to achieve a complete encoding of *Solidity*. The interest is rather to rely on the case study in our possession (which turns out to be written in *Solidity*), and from its contracts, we build our own *WhyML* contracts. Some primitives of *Solidity* seems interesting to keep, so we chose to encode them in *WhyML*. Therefore, throughout the article, we have chosen to encode only *Solidity* features encountered through our case study. Consequently, notions like `revert` or `delegatecall` are not treated. Conversely, we introduce additional types such as `order` and `order_trading`, which are specific to the BEMP application. The `order` type is a record that contains `orderAddress` which can be a seller or a buyer, `tokens` that express the crypto-Kilowatthours (wiling to buy or to sell), and `price_order`. The `order_trading` type is a record that contains seller ID; `seller_index`, buyer ID; `buyer_index`, the transferred amount `amount_t`, and the trading price `price_t`.

Remark: In our methodology, we choose to encode some primitives of *Solidity* but not all. For example, the `send()` function in *Solidity* can fail (return `False`) due to an out-of-gas, e.g. an overrun of 2300 units of *gas*. The reason is that in certain cases the transfer of *ether* to a contract involves the execution of the contract fallback, therefore the function might consume more *gas* than expected. A fallback function is a function without a signature (no name, no parameters), it is executed if a contract is called and no other function matches the specified function identifier, or if no data is supplied. As we chose a *private* blockchain type, all users can be identified and we have control on who can write or read from the blockchain. Thus, the *WhyML* `send()` function does not need a fallback

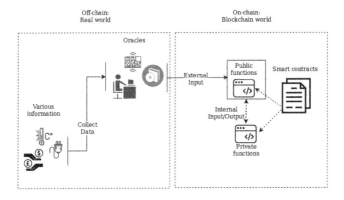

Fig. 2. Link between on-chain and off-chain

execution, it only transfers *ether* from one address to another. The *WhyML* **send()** function does not return a boolean, because we require that the transfer is possible (enough *ether* in the sending contract and not too much in the receiving) and we want to avoid DoS attack [3]. Indeed, if we allow to propagate errors and accept to send to untrusted contracts, it could always make our contract fail and revert. So we cannot prove any property of progress of our contract. In *Tezos* blockchain [13], call to other contracts is postponed to after the execution of the current contract. So another contract should not be able to make the calling contract fail.

Encoding and Verifying Functions from the BEMP Application

Oracle Notions. Developing smart contracts often relies on the concept of *Oracles* [1]. An oracle can be seen as the link between the blockchain and the "real world". Some smart contracts functions have arguments that are external to the blockchain. However, the blockchain does not have access to information from an off-chain data source which is untrusted. Accordingly, the oracle provides a service responsible for entering external data into the blockchain, having the role of a trusted third party. However, questions arise about the reliability of such oracles and accuracy of information. Oracles can have unpredictable behaviour, e.g. a sensor that measures the temperature might be an oracle, but might be faulty; thus one must account for invalid information from oracles. Figure 2 illustrates the three communication stages between various systems in the real world with the blockchain: *(1)* the collection of off-chain raw data; *(2)* this data is collected by oracles; and finally, *(3)* oracles provide information to the blockchain (via smart contracts). Based on this distinction, we defined two types of functions involved in contracts. We noted that some functions are called internally by other smart contracts functions *"Private functions"*, while others are called externally by oracles *"Public functions"*. The proof approach of the two types is different. For the *private* functions one defines pre-conditions and post-conditions, and then we prove that no error can occur and that the function behaves as it should. It is thus not necessary to define exceptions to be raised throughout the program; they are proved to never occur. Conversely, the *public* functions are called by oracles, the behaviour of the function must take into account any input values and it is not possible to require conditions upstream of the call. In contrast, exceptions are necessary; we use so-called *defensive proof* to protect ourselves from errors that can be generated by oracles. No constraints are applied on post-conditions. Thus, valid data (which does not raise exceptions) received by a *public* function will satisfy the pre-conditions of the *public* function that uses it, because pre-conditions are proven.

Methodology of Proving BEMP Functions. To illustrate our methodology, we take an example from BEMP.

```
1   function transferFromMarket (address _to, uint _val) onlyMarket returns (bool
        success) {
2     if (exportBalanceOf[market] >= _val){/*Transfer _val from market to _to*/}
3     else {success = false; Error("Tokens couldn't be transferred");}}
```

The function allows transferring _val (expressing cryptokwh) from the **market** to _to address. The mapping **exportBalanceOf[]** stores balances corresponding to addresses that export tokens. The function can be executed solely by the market (the modifier function **onlyMarket**). The program checks if the market has enough tokens to send to _to. If this condition is verified, the transfer is done. If the condition is not verified, the function returns **false** and triggers an **Error** event (a feature that allows writing logs in the blockchain)[3]. This process is internal to the blockchain, there is no external exchange, hence the function is qualified as *private*. According to the modelling approach, we define complete pre-conditions and post-conditions to verify and prove the function. The corresponding *WhyML* function is:

```
1   let transferFromMarket (_to : address) (_val : uint) : bool
2     requires {!onlymarket ∧ _val > 0} requires {marketBalanceOf[market] ≥ _val}
3     requires {importBalanceOf[_to] ≤ max_uint - _val}
4     ensures {(old marketBalanceOf[market]) + (old importBalanceOf[_to]) = marketBalanceOf[
        market] + importBalanceOf[_to]}
5   = (* The program *)
```

The pre-condition in line 2 expresses the **modifier onlyMarket** function. Note that **marketBalanceOf** is the hashtable that records crypto-Kilowatthours balances associated with market addresses, and **importBalanceOf** is the hashtable that records the amount of crypto-Kilowatthours intended for the buyer addresses. From the specification, we understand the behaviour of the function without referencing to the program. To be executed, **transferFromMarket** must respect RTE and functional properties:

---

[3] https://media.consensys.net/technical-introduction-to-events-and-logs-in-ethere-um-a074d65dd61e.

– RTE properties: *(1) Positive values*; a valid amount of crypto-Kilowatthours to transfer is a positive amount (Line 2). *(2) Integer overflow*; no overflow will occur when _to receives _val (Line 3).
– Functional properties: *(1) Acceptable transfer*; the transfer can be done, if the market has enough crypto-Kilowatthours to send (Line 2). *(2) Successful transfer*; the transaction is completed successfully if the sum of the sender and the receiver balances before and after the execution does not change (Line 4). *(3)* modifier *function*; the function can be executed only by the market (Line 2).

The following function illustrates a *Solidity public* function.

```
1  function registerSmartMeter (string m_Id, address ownerAddress) onlyOwner
          {addressOf[m_Id] = ownerAddress; MeterRegistered(ownerAddress,
      m_Id);}
```

The function registerSmartMeter() is identified by a meter ID (m_ID) and an owner (ownerAddress). Note that all meter owners are recorded in a hashtable addressOf associated with a key value m_ID. The main potential bug in this function is possibly registering a meter twice. When a meter is registered, the function broadcasts an event MeterRegistered. Following the modelling rules, there are no pre-conditions, instead, we define exceptions. The corresponding *WhyML* function is:

```
1  Exception OnlyOwner, ExistingSmartMeter
2  let registerSmartMeter (m_ID : string) (ownerAddress : address)
3    raises {OnlyOwner→ !onlyOwner = False} raises {ExistingSmartMeter→ mem addressOf m_ID}
4    ensures {(size addressOf) = (size (old addressOf) + 1 )} ensures {mem addressOf m_ID}
5  = (*The program*)
```

The exception OnlyOwner represents the modifier function which restricts the function execution to the owner, the caller function. It is not possible to pre-condition inputs of the function, so we manage exceptional conditions during the execution of the program. To be executed, registerSmartMeter must respect RTE and functional properties:

– RTE properties: *Duplicate record*; if a smart meter and its owner is recorded twice, raise an exception ExistingSmartMeter (Line 3)
– Functional properties: *(1)* modifier *function*; the function can be executed only by the owner, thus we raise OnlyOwner when the caller of the function is not the owner (Line 3). *(2) Successful record*; at the end of the function execution, we ensure (Line 4) that a smart meter has been recorded. *(3) Existing record*; the registered smart meter has been properly recorded in the hashtable addressOf (Line 4) using mem function.

The set of specifications of both functions are necessary and sufficient to prove the expected behaviour of each function since we understand what each function does without a look to the program. Moreover, this set represents the only proof effort to verify a *WhyML* contract.

Trading Contract. The trading algorithm allows matching a potential consumer with a potential seller, recorded in two arrays buy_order and sell_order taken as parameters of the algorithm. To obtain an expected result at the end of the algorithm, properties must be respected. We define specifications that make it possible throughout the trading process. The algorithm is a *private* function. The Trading contract has no *Solidity* equivalent because it is a function added to the original BEMP project. Below is the set of properties of the function:

```
1   let trading (buy_order : array order) (sell_order : array order) : list order_trading
2       requires {length buy_order > 0 ∧ length sell_order > 0}
3       requires {sorted_order buy_order} requires {sorted_order sell_order}
4       requires {forall j:int. 0 ≤ j < length buy_order → 0 < buy_order[j].tokens}
5       requires {forall j:int. 0 ≤ j < length sell_order → 0 < sell_order[j].tokens}
6       ensures {correct result (old buy_order) (old sell_order)}
7       ensures {forall l. correct l (old buy_order) (old sell_order) → nb_token l ≤
            nb_token result}
8       ensures {!gas ≤ old !gas + 374 + (length buy_order + length sell_order) * 928}
9       ensures {!alloc ≤ old !alloc + 35 + (length buy_order + length sell_order) * 384}
10  = (* The program *)
```

- RTE properties: *positive values*; parameters of the functions must not be empty (empty array) (Line 2), and a trade cannot be done with null or negative tokens (Lines 4, 5).
- Functional requirements: *sorted orders*; both orders array need to be sorted in a decreasing way according to the price of energy (Lines 3).
- Functional properties: *(1) correct trading* (Lines 6); for a trading to be qualified as correct, it must satisfy two properties:
  - the conservation of buyer and seller tokens that states no loss of tokens during the trading process: forall i:uint. 0 ≤ i < length sell_order → sum_seller (list_trading) i ≤ sell_order[i].tokens. For the buyer it is equivalent by replacing seller by buyer.
  - a successful matching; a match between a seller and a buyer is qualified as correct if the price offered by the seller is less than or equal to that of the buyer, and that the sellers and buyers are valid indices in the array.

(2) Best tokens exchange; we choose to qualify a trade as being one of the best if it maximizes the total number of tokens exchanged. Line 7 ensures that no correct trading list can have more tokens exchanged than the one resulting from the function. The criteria could be refined by adding the desire to maximize or minimize the total amount to pay for a trade. *(3) Gas consumption*; line 8 ensures that the **trading** function will consume exactly or less than "374 + (length buy_order + length sell_order) * 928". 374 corresponds to the quantity of gas consumed by parts of the code that are not dependent on parameters, and 928 parts that depends on it. The estimation of gas consumption depends on memory allocation (line 9). As the quantity of gas, 35 is the quantity of allocated memory for parts of the code that are not dependent on parameters, and 384 that depends on it (see Sect. 3 for more details on memory allocation).

Proving the optimality of an algorithm is always challenging (even on paper), and we needed all the proof features of *Why3* such as ghost code and lemma function. It is an important property that users of a smart contract will desire to prove. So we believe it is worth the effort.

Gas Consumption Proof. Overconsumption of *gas* can be avoided by the *gas* model. Instructions in EVM consume an amount of *gas*, and they are categorized by level of difficulty; e.g., for the set $W_{verylow} = \{ADD, SUB, ...\}$, the amount to pay is $G_{verylow} = 3$ *units of gas*, and for a create operation the amount to pay is $G_{create} = 32000$ *units of gas* [20]. The price of an operation is proportional to its difficulty. Accordingly, we fix for each *WhyML* function, the appropriate amount of *gas* needed to execute it. Thus, at the end of the function instructions, a variable `gas` expresses the total quantity of *gas* consumed during the process. We introduce a `val ghost` function that adds to the variable `gas` the amount of *gas* consumed by each function calling `add_gas`.

```
1   val ghost add_gas (used : gas) (allocation: int): unit
2     requires {0 ≤ used ∧ 0 ≤ allocation}  ensures {!gas = (old !gas) + used}
3     ensures {!alloc = (old !alloc) + allocation} writes {gas, alloc}
```

The specifications of the function above require *positive values* (Line 2). Moreover, at the end of the function, we ensure that there is no extra *gas* consumption (Lines 2), and no extra allocation of memory (Line 3). `writes` specifies the changing variables. In the trading algorithm, we can see that a lot of allocations are performed, they are not necessary and we could change our code to only allocate a fixed quantity of memory.

3   Compilation and Proof of Gas Consumption

The final step of the approach is the deployment of *WhyML* contracts. EVM is designed to be the runtime environment for the smart contracts on the Ethereum blockchain [20]. The EVM is a stack-based machine (word of 256 bits) and uses a set of instructions (called opcodes)[4] to execute specific tasks. The EVM features two memories, one volatile that does not survive the current transaction and a second for storage that does survive but is a lot more expensive to modify. The goal of this section is to describe the approach of compiling *WhyML* contracts into EVM code and proving the cost of functions. The compilation[5] is done in three phases: *(1)* compiling to an EVM that uses symbolic labels for jump destination and macro instructions. *(2)* computing the absolute address of the labels, it must be done inside a fixpoint because the size of the jump addresses has an impact on the size of the instruction. Finally, *(3)* translating the assembly code to pure EVM assembly and printed it. Most of *WhyML* can be translated, the proof-of-concept compiler (an extraction module of *Why3*) allows using algebraic datatypes, without nesting pattern-matching, mutable records, recursive

---

[4] https://ethervm.io.
[5] The implementation can be found at http://francois.bobot.eu/fmbc2019/.

functions, while loops, integer bounded arithmetic (32, 64,128, 256 bits). Global variables are restricted to mutable records with fields of integers. It could be extended to hashtables using the hashing technique of the keys used in *Solidity*. Without using specific instructions, like for C, *WhyML* is extracted to garbage collected language, here all the allocations are done in the volatile memory, so the memory is reclaimed only at the end of the transaction. We have not formally proved yet the correction of the compilation, we only tested the compiler on function examples using reference interpreter[6] and by asserting some invariants during the transformation (*WhyML* code to EVM). However, we could list the following arguments for the correction: *(1)* the compilation of *WhyML* is straightforward to stack machine. *(2)* The precondition on all the arithmetic operations (always bounded) ensures arithmetic operations could directly use 256 bit operations. *(3)* Raising exceptions are accepted only in *public* function before any mutation so the fact they are translated into *REVERT* opcode does not change their semantics. *(4)* Only immutable datatypes can be stored in the permanent store. Currently, only integers can be stored, it could be extended to other immutable datatypes by copying the data to and from the store. *(5)* The send function in *WhyML* only modifies the state of balance of the contracts, requires that the transfer is acceptable and never fails, as discussed previously. So it is compiled similarly to the *Solidity* function send function with a gas limit small enough to disallow modification of the store. Additionally, we discard the result. *(6)* The *public* functions are differentiated from *private* ones using the attribute [@ evm:external]. The *private* functions do not appear in the dispatching code at the contract entry point so they can be called only internally.

The execution of each bytecode instruction has an associated cost. One must pay some *gas* when sending a transaction; if there is not enough *gas* to execute the transaction, the execution stops and the state is rolled back. So it is important to be sure that at any later date the execution of a smart contract will not require an unreasonable quantity of *gas*. The computation of WCET is facilitated in EVM by the absence of cache. So we could use techniques of [6] which annotate in the source code the quantity of *gas* used, here using a function "add_gas". The number of allocations is important because the real *gas* consumption of EVM integrates the maximum quantity of volatile memory used. The compilation checks that all the paths of the function have a cost smaller than the sum of the "add_gas" on it. Paths of a function are defined on the EVM code by starting at the function-entry and loop-head and going through the code following jumps that are not going back to loop-head. The following code is a function that takes as parameter the size of the list to build and returns it. Through this example, we want to show the different *gas* consumption and memory allocation according to the path taken by the function (if path no dependent on i, or else path dependent on i). Since it is a recursive function, we need to add a variant (line 2) to prove the termination.

---

[6] https://github.com/ethereum/go-ethereum.

```
1  let rec mk_list [@ evm:gas_checking] (i:int32) : list int32
2    requires {0 ≤ i}  ensures {i = length result}  variant {i}
3    ensures {!gas - old !gas ≤ i * 185 + 113} ensures {!alloc - old !alloc ≤ i * 96 + 32}
4  = if i ≤ 0 then (add_gas 113 32; Nil)
5    else (let l = mk_list (i-1) in add_gas 185 96; Cons (0x42:int32) l)
```

Currently, the cost of the modification of storage is over-approximated; using specific contract for the functions that modify it we could specify that it is less expensive to use a memory cell already used.

4 Related Work

Since the *DAO* attack, the introduction of formal methods at the level of smart contracts has increased. Static analysis tools are very common to achieve this task. There exist several frameworks, and one of them is called *Raziel*. It is a framework to prove the validity of smart contracts to third parties before their execution in a private way [19]. In that paper, the authors also use a deductive proof approach, but their concept is based on Proof-Carrying Code (PCC) infrastructure, which consists of annotating the source code, thus proofs can be checked before contract execution to verify their validity. Our method does not consist in annotating the *Solidity* source code but in writing the contract in a language designed for program verification in order to tackle harder properties. With a slightly different approach, we have *Oyente*. It has been developed to analyze Ethereum smart contracts to detect bugs. In the corresponding paper [14], the authors were able to run *Oyente* on 19,366 existing Ethereum contracts, and as a result, the tool flagged 8,833 of them as vulnerable. Although that work provides interesting conclusions, it uses symbolic execution, analyzing paths, so it does not allow to prove functional properties. We can also mention the work undertaken by the F^* community [9] where they use their functional programming language to translate *Solidity* contracts to shallow-embedded F^* programs. Just like [5] where the authors perform static analysis by translating *Solidity* contracts into Java using *KeY* [4]. We believe it is easier for the user to be as close as possible to the proof tool, if possible, and in the case of smart contract the current paper showed it is possible. The initiative of the current paper is directly related to a previous work [18], which dealt with formally verifying BEMP's smart contracts by using model-checking. However, because of the limitation of the model-checker used, ambitious verification could not be achieved (e.g., a model for m consumers and n producers).

5 Conclusions

In this paper, we applied concepts of deductive verification to a computer protocol intended to enforce some transaction rules within an Ethereum blockchain application. The aim is to avoid errors that could have serious consequences. Reproducing, with *Why3*, the behaviour of *Solidity* functions showed that *Why3* is suitable for writing and verifying smart contracts programs. The presented method was applied to a use case that describes an energy market place allowing local energy trading among inhabitants of a neighbourhood. The resulting modelling allows establishing a trading contract, in order to match consumers with producers willing to make a transaction. In addition, this last point demonstrates that with a deductive approach it is possible to model and prove the operation of the BEMP application at realistic scale (e.g. matching m consumers with n producers), contrary to model-checking in [18], thus allowing the verifying of more realistic functional properties.

References

1. Ethereum foundation: Ethereum and oracles. https://blog.ethereum.org/2014/07/22/ethereum-and-oracles/
2. Formal verification for solidity contracts. https://forum.ethereum.org/discussion/3779/formal-verification-for-solidity-contracts
3. Solidity hacks and vulnerabilities. https://hackernoon.com/hackpedia-16-solidity-hacks-vulnerabilities-their-fixes-and-real-world-examples-f3210eba5148
4. Ahrendt, W., Beckert, B., Bubel, R., Hähnle, R., Schmitt, P.H., Ulbrich, M.: Deductive software verification-the key book, vol. 10001. Springer, Cham (2016). https://doi.org/10.1007/978-3-319-49812-6
5. Ahrendt, W., et al.: Verification of smart contract business logic. In: Hojjat, H., Massink, M. (eds.) FSEN 2019. LNCS, vol. 11761, pp. 228–243. Springer, Cham (2019). https://doi.org/10.1007/978-3-030-31517-7_16
6. Amadio, R.M., et al.: Certified complexity (CerCo). In: Dal Lago, U., Peña, R. (eds.) FOPARA 2013. LNCS, vol. 8552, pp. 1–18. Springer, Cham (2014). https://doi.org/10.1007/978-3-319-12466-7_1
7. Atzei, N., Bartoletti, M., Cimoli, T.: A survey of attacks on ethereum smart contracts (SoK). In: Maffei, M., Ryan, M. (eds.) POST 2017. LNCS, vol. 10204, pp. 164–186. Springer, Heidelberg (2017). https://doi.org/10.1007/978-3-662-54455-6_8
8. Barrett, C., et al.: CVC4. In: Gopalakrishnan, G., Qadeer, S. (eds.) CAV 2011. LNCS, vol. 6806, pp. 171–177. Springer, Heidelberg (2011). https://doi.org/10.1007/978-3-642-22110-1_14
9. Bhargavan, K., et al.: Short paper: formal verification of smart contracts (2016)
10. Bobot, F., Conchon, S., Contejean, E., Iguernelala, M., Lescuyer, S., Mebsout, A.: The alt-ergo automated theorem prover (2008). http://alt-ergo.lri.fr/
11. Domowitz, I.: A taxonomy of automated trade execution systems. J. Int. Money Finance 12, 607–631 (1993)
12. Filliâtre, J.-C., Paskevich, A.: Why3 — where programs meet provers. In: Felleisen, M., Gardner, P. (eds.) ESOP 2013. LNCS, vol. 7792, pp. 125–128. Springer, Heidelberg (2013). https://doi.org/10.1007/978-3-642-37036-6_8
13. Goodman, L.: Tezos: a self-amending crypto-ledger position paper (2014)
14. Luu, L., Chu, D.H., Olickel, H., Saxena, P., Hobor, A.: Making smart contracts smarter. In: Proceedings of the 2016 ACM SIGSAC Conference on Computer and Communications Security, pp. 254–269. ACM (2016)
15. de Moura, L., Bjørner, N.: Z3, an efficient SMT solver. http://research.microsoft.com/projects/z3/
16. Nakamoto, S.: Bitcoin: a peer-to-peer electronic cash system (2008)

17. Nehaï, Z., Bobot, F.: Deductive Proof of Ethereum Smart Contracts Using Why3. Research report, CEA DILS, April 2019. https://hal.archives-ouvertes.fr/hal-02108987
18. Nehaï, Z., Piriou, P.Y., Daumas, F.: Model-checking of smart contracts. In: The 2018 IEEE International Conference on Blockchain. IEEE (2018)
19. Sánchez, D.C.: Raziel: Private and verifiable smart contracts on blockchains. Cryptology ePrint Archive, Report 2017/878 (2017). http://eprint.iacr.org/2017/878.pdf. Accessed 26 Sept 2017
20. Wood, G.: Ethereum: a secure decentralised generalised transaction ledger. Ethereum Proj. Yellow Pap. **151**, 1–32 (2014)

Verifying Smart Contracts with Cubicle

Sylvain Conchon[1,2]($\boxtimes$), Alexandrina Korneva[1], and Fatiha Zaïdi[1]

[1] LRI (CNRS & Univ. Paris-Sud), Université Paris-Saclay, 91405 Orsay, France
Conchon@lri.fr
[2] Inria, Université Paris-Saclay, 91120 Palaiseau, France

Abstract. Smart contracts are usually conceived for an unkonwn (and potentially varying) number of users. From a theoretical point of view, they can be seen as parameterized state machines with multiple entry points, shared variables, and a message passing mechanism. To help in their design and verification, we propose in this paper to use Cubicle, a model checker for parameterized systems based on SMT. Our approach is a two-layer framework where the first part consists of a blockchain transactional model, while the second layer is a model of the smart contract itself. We illustrate our technique through the simple yet prime example of an auction. This preliminary result is very promising and lays the foundations for a complete and automatized framework for the design and certification of smart contracts.

Keywords: Blockchain · Smart-contracts · Model checking · MCMT

1 Introduction

The number of decentralized applications (DApps) running on top of blockchain networks is growing very fast. According to [3], there are now more than 3,000 DApps available on the Ethereum and EOS platforms which generate over 600 thousand transactions per day for a volume of 17 million USD. These DApps interact with the blockchain through around 4,700 smart contracts.

A smart contract is a stateful program stored in the blockchain with which a user (human or computer) can interact. From a legal perspective, a smart contract is an agreement whose execution is automated. As such, its revocation or modification is not always possible and worse than that, what the code of a smart contract does is *the law*... no matter what it may end up doing. Unfortunately, like any program, smart contracts may have bugs. Given the potential financial risks, finding these bugs before the origination of the contracts in the blockchain is an important challenge, both from economic and scientific points of view.

Various formal methods have been used to verify smart contracts. In [5], the authors present a shallow embedding of Solidity within F*, a programming language aimed at verification. Other similar approaches are based on deductive verification platforms like Why3 [10,12]. Interactive proof assistants (*e.g.* Isabelle/HOL or Coq) have also been used for modeling and proving properties about Ethereum and Tezos smart contracts [1,4].

© Springer Nature Switzerland AG 2020
E. Sekerinski et al. (Eds.): FM 2019 Workshops, LNCS 12232, pp. 312–324, 2020.
https://doi.org/10.1007/978-3-030-54994-7_23

A common thread here is the use of general-purpose frameworks based on sequential modeling languages. However, smart contracts can be considered as state machines [2, 9] whose execution model, according to [13], is closer to that of a concurrent programming language rather than a sequential one. In this context, the use of model checking techniques becomes highly appropriate [6, 11].

An important aspect of blockchains is that they are completely open. As a consequence, smart contracts are state machines that need to be conceived for an unknown (and potentially varying) number of users. This parameterized side of blockchains has not previously been taken into account.

In this paper, we propose a first ad-hoc attempt to model smart contracts into the declarative input language of Cubicle, a model checker for parameterized systems based on Satisfiability Modulo Theories (SMT) techniques. In our approach, smart contracts, as well as the transactional model of the blockchain, are encoded as a state machine on which safety properties of interest are encoded and verified. Our contributions are as follows:

- A two-layer framework for smart contract verification in Cubicle (Sect. 3). The first layer is a model of the blockchain transaction mechanism. The second layer models the smart contract itself.
- A description of how to express smart contract properties as Cubicle safety properties using both ghost variables and model instrumentation (Sect. 4)
- A way of interpreting Cubicle error traces as part of the smart contract development cycle (Sect. 5)

2   A Motivating Example

We illustrate our work with the example of an auction contract. The behavior of each client i is given by the automaton $\mathcal{A}(i)$ in Fig. 1.

Every client starts off in state $S1$ where they can either bid a certain value v and go to state $S2$, or close the auction and stay in $S1$. In $S2$, a client can either withdraw their bid and end up back in $S1$, close the auction and stay in $S2$, or try to win the auction and go to $S3$.

Each state transition is guarded by certain conditions to ensure that the auction works correctly. To implement these conditions, each automaton needs to share some variables with the other automata and be able to send or receive messages through communication channels. The shared variables are:

- HBidder: the current highest bidder (winner)
- HBid: the above's bid amount
- Ended: a boolean variable for whether or not an auction is over
- Owner: the person who owns the contract
- PR_i: the amount a client i can withdraw,

while channels for message passing are bid, withdraw, end, win, and refund$_i$ (a refund channel for each client i). These messages are synchronous and can have parameters. Sending a message with parameter c on channel ch is denoted by ch!(c), and the reception is written ch?(v).

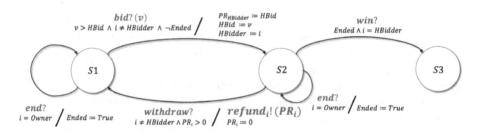

Fig. 1. Auction automaton $\mathcal{A}(i)$

In order to better explain how the automaton works, we'll look at states $S1$ and $S2$, and the transitions between them.

The condition to trigger the transition from $S1$ to $S2$ is given by the formula $\text{bid}?(v) \wedge v > \text{HBid} \wedge i \neq \text{HBidder} \wedge \neg\text{Ended}$, which should be read as follows:

- a message on channel bid is received with a value v superior to the current HBid ($v > \text{HBid}$);
- the client isn't the current winner ($i \neq \text{HBidder}$);
- the auction is still open ($\neg\text{Ended}$).

If these requirements are fulfilled, the transition is triggered, the client goes to $S2$ and the state variables are modified in the following manner:

- $\text{PR}_{\text{HBidder}} := \text{HBid}$ sets the pending returns for the old winner to their old winning bid;
- $\text{HBid} := v$ sets the new top bid to v;
- $\text{HBidder} := i$ sets the new winner to the client i.

Going from $S2$ back to $S1$ works the same way. The transition can be triggered when the condition $\text{withdraw}? \wedge i \neq \text{HBidder} \wedge \text{PR}_i > 0$ is true, that is when a message on `withdraw` is received and the client i is not the highest bidder and has some amount to withdraw. When moving to $S2$, the variable PR_i is reset and a message $\text{refund}_i!(\text{PR}_i)$ is sent. The corresponding reception $\text{refund}_i?(v)$ is part of a refund automaton $\mathcal{R}(i)$ run by each client, as seen in Fig. 2. The role of this one state automaton is to accept that kind of mes-

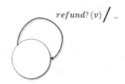

Fig. 2. Refund automaton $\mathcal{R}(i)$

sage and do whatever necessary to accept the refunded value v.

Finally, the global system of the auction and the clients it interacts with can be expressed as a product of the auction automata and the refund automata

$$\Pi_i \mathcal{A}(i) \times \Pi_i \mathcal{R}(i)$$

A client of this contract, aka the automaton, needs to be sure that certain properties hold. These properties can be simple and visible in the transition requirements, or they can be more complex to the point where you can't prove them through the requirements alone. Consider two properties:

(a) "Each new winning bid is superior to the old winning bid"
(b) "I do not lose money"

Property (a) is easy to see as it's the requirement $v >$ HBid of Fig. 1. Property (b) is less obvious as it requires not only a model of the contract itself, but also of the underlying blockchain semantics.

3   Modeling a Smart Contract with Cubicle

Anything done by a smart contract can be traced back to its blockchain. If HBidder is modified, that means that there was a message on channel bid with a sufficiently large value. Not being able to trace an action back to the blockchain implies a problem. Therefore, modeling a smart contract requires an accompanying model of the blockchain. We do this with the help of Cubicle, briefly introduced in the next subsection.

3.1   Cubicle

Cubicle is an SMT-based model checker for parameterized transition systems. For a more in-depth and thorough explanation, we refer the reader to [7,8]. In this section, we give a quick overview of the necessary aspects of Cubicle.

Cubicle input programs represent transition systems described by: (1) a set of type, variable and array declarations; (2) a formula for the initial states; and (3) a set of guarded commands (transitions).

Type, Variable and Array Declarations. Cubicle has several built-in data types, among which are integers (int), booleans (bool), and process identifiers (proc). Additionally, the user can define enumerations. For instance, the code

```
type location = L1 | L2 | L3
var W : location
var X : int
array Z[proc] : bool
```

defines a type location with three constructors (L1, L2, and L3), two global variables W and X of types location and int, respectively, and a proc-indexed array Z. The type proc is a key ingredient here as it is used to parameterize the system: given a process identifier i, the value $Z[i]$ represents somehow the *local* variable Z of i.

Initial States. The content of a system state is fully characterized by the value of its global variables and arrays. The initial states are defined by an **init** formula given as a universal conjunction of literals. For example, the following declaration

```
init (i) { Z[i] = False && W = L1 }
```

should be read as: "initially, for all process i, Z[i] is equal to False and W contains
L1". (Note that the content of variable X is unspecified, and can thus contain
any value)

Transitions. The execution of a parameterized system is defined by a
set of guard/action transitions. It consists of an infinite loop which non-
deterministically triggers at each iteration a transition whose guard is true and
whose action is to update state variables. Each transition can take one or several
process identifiers as arguments. A guard is a conjunction of literals (equations,
disequations or inequations) and an action is a set of variable assignments or
array updates. For instance, the following transition

```
transition  tr_1  ( i )
requires  {  Z[ i ]  =  False  }
{  W  :=  L2;
   X  :=  1;  }
```

should be read as follows: "if there exists a process i such that Z[i] equals False,
then atomically assign W to L2 and X to 1".

Unsafe States. The safety properties to be verified are expressed in their
negated form and characterize unsafe states. They are given by existentially-
quantified formulas. For instance, the following unsafe formula

```
unsafe  ( i )  {  Z[ i ]  =  False  && X  =  1  }
```

should be read as follows: "a state is unsafe if there exists a process i such that
Z[i] is equal to False and X equals 1".

Error Traces. All of the above allows Cubicle to verify a model. If it finds a
way to reach an unsafe state, an error trace is printed, such as the following

```
Error  trace:  Init  ->  t2(#1)  ->  t3(#3)  ->  unsafe [1]
```

This lets the user check which sequence of transitions led to the unsafe state. A
number preceded by # is a process identifier. This means that t2(#1) stands for
process 1 activating that transition. If you have multiple unsafe states declared,
the index next to **unsafe** lets you know which one was reached.

3.2 Blockchain Model

To model the blockchain we first need to model the elements that will constitute
transactions seen in the blockchain. Consider the transactions as the message
passing mechanism from Sect. 2.

```
type  call  =  Bid  |  Withdraw  |  Send  |  Finish  |  None

var  Cmd  :  call
var  Value  :  int
var  Sender  :  proc
var  Recv  :  proc
```

The constructors of type call represent calls to smart contract entry points (message channels). Bid, Withdraw, Finish, Send correspond to the channels bid, withdraw, end, and refund, while None means *absence of transactions*. The elements of a transaction are defined by four variables:

- Cmd, the calls to an entry point;
- Value, the amount of money attached to a transaction;
- Sender, who calls the contract;
- Recv; the receiver, used in the case of Withdraw, where the contract calls a client.

Once the elements of a transaction are declared, the next step is to model the transaction mechanism of the blockchain. For that, we define three transitions to simulate transactions to the three smart contract entry points.

```
transition  call_bid ( i )
requires  { Cmd = None }
{
  Cmd  :=  Bid ;
  Value  :=  Rand . Int ( );
  Sender  :=  i ;
}

transition  call_withdraw ( i )
requires  { Cmd = None }
{
  Cmd  :=  Withdraw ;
  Sender  :=  i ;
}

transition  call_finish ( i )
requires  { Cmd = None }
{
  Cmd  :=  Finish ;
  Sender  :=  i ;
}
```

Each transaction has a parameter i which represents the client who called the corresponding entry point. The only requirement indicates that the contract can't be doing something else simultaneously (Cmd = None). The effects of these transitions are simple: Cmd is set to the corresponding constructor (Bid, Withdraw, or Finish, respectively) and the variable Sender is assigned to i. In call_bid, the variable Value is set to a (positive) random integer corresponding to the amount bid by i.

Once the blockchain has been modeled, we can move on to modeling the contract itself.

3.3 Smart Contract Model

To model the actual contract, we need to model its variables and its functions. These correspond to the state variables and the transitions from Sect. 2, respectively.

```
var HBidder : proc
var HBid : int
var Ended : bool
var Owner : proc
array PR[proc] : int
```

The transitions from state $S1$ to $S2$ and back are modeled as Cubicle transitions. These transitions serve as entry points for our contract.

```
transition bid(i)
requires { Ended = False && Cmd = Bid && i = Sender
           && i <> HBidder && PR[i] = 0 && Value > HBid }
{
  HBid := Value;
  HBidder := i;
  PR[HBidder] := HBid;
  Cmd := None;
}

transition withdraw(i)
requires { Cmd = Withdraw && i = Sender && PR[i] > 0 }
{ PR[i] := 0;
  Cmd := Send;
  Value := PR[i];
  Recv := i;
}
```

Transition bid is called by one process, i, who has to be the Sender, but not the current HBidder. The other requirements should be read as follows:

Ended = False: the auction is open
Cmd = Bid: the transaction in the blockchain is Bid
PR[i] = 0: the new bidder hasn't previously bid
Value > HBid: the new bid is bigger than the old winning bid

The effects are simple, HBidder and HBid are set to the new values, PR for the old winner who has now been outbid is set to his old bid value, and Cmd is reset to None to indicate that the contract is no longer occupied.

Similarly, the requirements of transition withdraw are the following:

Cmd = Withdraw: the transaction in the blockchain is a call to withdraw
i = Sender: the process i is the one that called the function
PR[i] > 0: the person previously bid and was outbid by someone

The effects of transition withdraw are slightly different since withdraw goes on to send money to whoever called the method. The receiver is now set to i (Recv := i), and the value that will accompany the transaction is set to the amount of money to be returned (Value := PR[i]). The pending return PR[i] is reset globally for client i (PR[i] = 0) and Cmd is set to Send, to indicate that the contract is calling the client's method. The transition which Send corresponds to can be seen below:

```
transition value(i)
requires { Cmd = Send && Recv = i }
{ Cmd := None; }
```

This transition checks that Send was in fact called (Cmd = Send), as well as the fact that the receiver is the currently active process (Recv = i). It then resets Cmd to None to free the contract.

4   Defining and Verifying Properties

Recall that we want to be sure of certain properties:

(a) "Each new winning bid is superior to the old winning bid"
(b) "I do not lose money"

Once defined informally, the properties need to be converted into safety properties. This is not always straightforward and might require additional information. It is done via a two-step process consisting of (i) defining extra logical formulas (*ghost* variables) and (ii) instrumenting the model with these formulas.

4.1   Ghost Variables and Model Instrumentation

Ghost variables, introduced below, do not appear in the contract's state variables, nor do they impact the Cubicle model outside of property verification.

```
array Out[proc] : int
array In[proc] : int
var Old_HBid : int
```

The variables Out and In are for property (b). In is an array storing how much each client (aka process) bids, and Out stores how much they get back if/when they call withdraw. Old_HBid tracks the old highest bid for property (a). The code below is the instrumented model. Transition withdraw has been omitted since it is not instrumented.

```
transition bid(i)
requires { Ended = False && Cmd = Bid && i = Sender
           && i <> HBidder && PR[i] = 0 && Value > HBid}
{
   HBid := Value;
   HBidder := i;
```

```
    PR[HBidder] := HBid;
    Cmd := None;
    Old_HBid := HBid;
    In[i] := In[i] + Value;
}
transition value(i)
requires { Cmd = Send && Recv = i }
{ Cmd := None;
    Out[i] := Out[i] + Value;
}
```

The *ghost* variables appear only in the action parts of the transitions. The bid transition updates HBid to set a new highest bid value. To keep track of what the old value was, Old_HBid is set to HBid's value. In is updated for the new bidder with their bid value. The transition value is instrumented instead of withdraw, since the most important action, giving the client back their money, happens during value. It uses Out to keep track of the money that's been returned.

The ghost variables are also part of the initial state declaration.

```
init (i) { Ended = False && HBid = 0 && Cmd = None
           && PR[i] = 0 && In[i] = 0 && Out[i] = 0
           && Old_HBid = 0 }
```

That is to say, the auction hasn't ended, there is no winning bid, the contract isn't doing anything, and no one has bid and subsequently withdrawn money.

4.2 Defining Properties

Once the code is instrumented, we can introduce the safety properties we want Cubicle to check.

Property (a): New bids are higher

The first property is *"Each new winning bid is superior to the old winning bid"*. This property can be easily defined by the following unsafe formula which uses only the ghost variables Old_HBid and HBid.

```
unsafe () { Old_HBid > HBid }
```

Checking property (a) with the above formula simply means declaring Old_HBid being superior to HBid as unsafe, but only if the model was correctly instrumented with these variables.

Property (b): Do I lose money?

Defining this property is less obvious. While ghost variables have been introduced to keep track of money exchanges between users and the contract, another problem is the lack of precision of the sentence. When should we check that a user did not lose money? At the end of the auction? If so, when do we consider the auction to *really* be over?

We will make these issues more concrete in the next section. In particular, we shall explain how we arrived at the following formulation of property (b):

```
unsafe (i) { Ended = True && i <> HBidder && PR[i] = 0
             && Cmd = None && Out[i] < In[i] }
```

5   Interpreting Cubicle Error Traces

As stated previously, the tricky property is *"I do not lose money"*. The logical implication is that if the auction is over, (Ended = True), then your Out isn't less than your In.

```
unsafe (i) { Ended = True && Out[i] < In[i] }
```

Except Cubicle prints the following error trace:

```
Error trace: Init -> call_bid(#1) -> bid(#1) ->
             call_finish(#1) -> finish_auction() -> unsafe
UNSAFE !
```

Upon further inspection, it becomes obvious why this state is reached. This is true for every client, even the winner, who technically does *lose* money, so to speak. We modify our unsafe state to the following by adding that the process cannot be the winner (HBidder <> i).

```
unsafe (i) { Ended = True && i <> HBidder &&
             Out[i] < In[i] }
```

However, Cubicle still says

```
Error trace: Init -> call_bid(#1) -> bid(#1) ->
             call_bid(#2) ->  bid(#2) ->
             call_finish(#1) -> finish_auction() -> unsafe
UNSAFE !
```

as what's missing is checking whether or not a client withdrew their bid. We incorporate that check below.

```
unsafe (i) { Ended = True && i <> HBidder &&
             PR[i] = 0 && Out[i] < In[i] }
```

but Cubicle can still reach that state:

```
Error trace: Init -> call_bid(#1) -> bid(#1) ->
             call_bid(#2) ->  bid(#2) ->
             call_finish(#1) -> finish_auction() ->
             call_withdraw(#1) -> withdraw(#1) -> unsafe
UNSAFE !
```

Once the smart contract has completely finished every action associated with a function (i.e. transition), it resets Cmd to None, which we haven't checked for. We add that to our unsafe state.

```
unsafe (i) { Ended = True && i <> HBidder && PR[i] = 0
             && Cmd = None && Out[i] < In[i] }
```

The above is the correct implementation of "I do not lose money". This time Cubicle replies **Safe**

But error traces aren't always the result of incorrectly written unsafe states. The automaton in Fig. 1 is incorrect. Modeling its bid requirements in Cubicle gives the following model and subsequent error trace:

```
transition  bid(i)
requires  { Ended = False && Cmd = Bid && i = Sender
            && i <> HBidder && Value > HBid}
. . .
```

```
Unsafe trace:  call_bid(#1) -> bid(#1) -> call_bid(#3) ->
               bid(#3) -> call_bid(#1) -> bid(#1) ->
               call_bid(#2) -> bid(#2) -> call_finish(#2) ->
               finish_auction() -> call_withdraw(#1)->
               withdraw(#1) -> value(#1) -> unsafe
```
        UNSAFE !

This is due to the requirements in Fig. 1 for bid not matching bid's effects on the state variables. When a client is outbid, they can't bid again without first having withdrawn their old bid. This is seen in Fig. 1 when bid sets PR_i to v with = instead of +=. This means that if an old bid wasn't withdrawn, its value will be overwritten and the client will lose that amount. The way to fix this is to add $PR_i = 0$ to bid's requirements in Fig. 1

6   Related Work

By their nature, smart contracts lend themselves well to formal verification. Numerous approaches have been used to verify smart contracts. In [11], the authors create a three-fold model of Ethereum smart contracts and apply model checking in order to verify them. The authors of [9] introduce a finite-state machine model of smart contracts along with predefined design patterns, allowing developers to conceive smart contracts as finite-state machines, which can then be translated to Solidity. Deductive verification platforms like Why3 are used to verify specific properties of smart contracts. The authors of [10] use Why3 to verify RTE properties like integer overflow and functional properties, like the success of a transaction. Interactive proof assistants are also used in smart contract verification, such as Isabelle/HOL in [4] in order to check Ethereum bytecode. A major trend is the focus on a specific language, most notably Solidity, whereas we propose a more general framework, not tied to any concrete language. Our application of parameterized model-checking allows us to address the parametric aspects of smart contracts and treat them as concurrent programs.

7   Conclusion and Future Work

In this paper we proposed a two-layer framework for smart contract verification with the model checker Cubicle. This method implements a model of the smart contract itself and the blockchain transaction mechanism behind it. Our method introduces a way of verifying various types of functional properties linked to a smart contract as Cubicle safety properties. Since this is done through ghost variables and model instrumentation, it has no impact on the original smart contract itself, meaning it is independent of any particular smart contract language, and is therefore generalizable and usable for multiple smart contract languages. We also describe a way of interpreting potential error traces generated by Cubicle, and how they can aid in the development of a smart contract. An immediate line of future work is to automate this stepwise process. We need to define an abstract high-level language to express the properties to be checked by Cubicle. From this language, the ghost variables will be automatically generated to instrument the Cubicle code. Furthermore, we would also like to consider automatic translation of Solidity or Michelson code to Cubicle.

References

1. Mi-Cho-Coq: formalisation of the Michelson language using the Coq proof assistant. https://gitlab.com/nomadic-labs/mi-cho-coq
2. Solidity Common Patterns. https://solidity.readthedocs.io/en/v0.5.10/common-patterns.html#state-machine
3. State of DApps website. https://www.stateofthedapps.com/stats
4. Amani, S., Bégel, M., Bortin, M., Staples, M.: Towards verifying ethereum smart contract bytecode in Isabelle/HOL. In: Proceedings of the 7th ACM SIGPLAN International Conference on Certified Programs and Proofs, pp. 66–77. ACM (2018)
5. Bhargavan, K., et al.: Formal verification of smart contracts: short paper. In: Proceedings of the 2016 ACM Workshop on Programming Languages and Analysis for Security, pp. 91–96. ACM (2016)
6. Bigi, G., Bracciali, A., Meacci, G., Tuosto, E.: Validation of decentralised smart contracts through game theory and formal methods. In: Bodei, C., Ferrari, G.-L., Priami, C. (eds.) Programming Languages with Applications to Biology and Security. LNCS, vol. 9465, pp. 142–161. Springer, Cham (2015). https://doi.org/10.1007/978-3-319-25527-9_11
7. Conchon, S., Goel, A., Krstić, S., Mebsout, A., Zaïdi, F.: Cubicle: a parallel SMT-based model checker for parameterized systems. In: Madhusudan, P., Seshia, S.A. (eds.) CAV 2012. LNCS, vol. 7358, pp. 718–724. Springer, Heidelberg (2012). https://doi.org/10.1007/978-3-642-31424-7_55
8. Conchon, S., Mebsout, A., Zaïdi, F.: Vérification de systèmes paramétrés avec Cubicle. In: JFLA, Aussois, France, February 2013
9. Mavridou, A., Laszka, A.: Designing secure ethereum smart contracts: a finite state machine based approach. In: Meiklejohn, S., Sako, K. (eds.) FC 2018. LNCS, vol. 10957, pp. 523–540. Springer, Heidelberg (2018). https://doi.org/10.1007/978-3-662-58387-6_28

10. Nehai, Z., Bobot, F.: Deductive proof of ethereum smart contracts using Why3. arXiv preprint arXiv:1904.11281 (2019)
11. Nehai, Z., Piriou, P.-Y., Daumas, F.: Model-checking of smart contracts. In: IEEE International Conference on Blockchain, pp. 980–987 (2018)
12. Reitwiessner, C.: Formal verification for solidity contracts
13. Sergey, I., Hobor, A.: A concurrent perspective on smart contracts. In: Brenner, M., Rohloff, K., Bonneau, J., Miller, A., Ryan, P.Y.A., Teague, V., Bracciali, A., Sala, M., Pintore, F., Jakobsson, M. (eds.) FC 2017. LNCS, vol. 10323, pp. 478–493. Springer, Cham (2017). https://doi.org/10.1007/978-3-319-70278-0_30

Call Me Back, I Have a Type Invariant

M. Anthony Aiello[1], Johannes Kanig[1(✉)], and Taro Kurita[2]

[1] AdaCore Inc., New York, USA
{aiello,kanig}@adacore.com
[2] Sony Corporation, Tokyo, Japan
taro.kurita@sony.com

Abstract. Callbacks in Smart Contracts on blockchain-based distributed ledgers are a potential source of security vulnerabilities: callbacks may lead to reentrancy, which has been previously exploited to steal large sums of money. Unfortunately, analysis tools for Smart Contracts either fail to support callbacks or simply detect and disallow patterns of callbacks that may lead to reentrancy. As a result, many authors of Smart Contracts avoid callbacks altogether, and some Smart Contract programming languages, including Solidity, recommend using primitives that avoid callbacks. Nevertheless, reentrancy remains a threat, due to the utility of and frequent reliance on callbacks in Smart Contracts.

In this paper, we propose the use of *type invariants*, a feature of some languages supporting formal verification, to enable proof of correctness for Smart Contracts, including Smart Contracts that permit or rely on callbacks. Our result improves upon existing research because it neither forbids reentrancy nor relies on informal, meta-arguments to prove correctness of reentrant Smart Contracts. We demonstrate our approach using the SPARK programming language, which supports type invariants and moreover can be compiled to relevant blockchains.

Keywords: Callbacks · Invariants · Formal verification · Smart contracts

1 Introduction

Smart contracts [18] are protocols that are intended to facilitate, verify or enforce the negotiation or performance of a contract. Within a blockchain-based distributed ledger [16], smart contracts are realized by autonomous agents that always execute specific functionality in response to defined events, such as the receipt of a message or transaction [7]. Smart contracts make their behavior available through public interfaces, are typically small, and have no global state. However, their composition, especially through callbacks, leads to complex and difficult-to-predict behavior—behavior that may be malicious, as illustrated in the high-profile attack on the Ethereum DAO [5].

Callbacks arise when one or more of the parties interacting with a smart contract is another smart contract: a message or transaction sent to a public

© Springer Nature Switzerland AG 2020
E. Sekerinski et al. (Eds.): FM 2019 Workshops, LNCS 12232, pp. 325–336, 2020.
https://doi.org/10.1007/978-3-030-54994-7_24

interface of the first smart contract, S1, may result in the sending of a message or transaction to a public interface of the second smart contract, S2, and so on. Callbacks are useful and quite common [9], but may also lead to reentrancy: a public interface of S1 may send a message to the public interface of S2, which may send a message back to S1 through the same public interface.

Reentrancy may lead to data-integrity violations. Data local to S1 may be in an inconsistent state when control flow is transferred to S2. S2 then calls S1. Upon reentry to S1, the data remains in an inconsistent state, likely violating the assumptions under which the smart contract was judged to be correct. The attack on the Ethereum DAO was essentially an attack based on reentrancy that exploited inconsistent data. The chain of callbacks leading to reentrancy may be arbitrarily long. Moreover, new smart contracts may be added to the blockchain at any time. Thus, in general, authors of smart contracts must assume that any potential callback may result in reentrancy. Current approaches that address this problem focus on identifying potential callbacks with static analysis [10], use gas limits to restrict the computation of a callback and limit recursion depth [7], or rely on meta-arguments to prove correctness of smart contracts with external calls [9].

However, the threat to data integrity posed by reentrancy from callbacks or by recursion is not new and has received considerable attention by the formal verification community, although not in the context of smart contracts. In object-oriented languages, for example, callbacks are ubiquitous and play an important role in many design patterns [8]. Likewise in procedural languages, if the entirety of the code cannot be assumed to be available for analysis, any call to unknown code may result in recursion. The answer presented by the formal-verification community to address this issue is the use of invariants on critical state. Invariants ensure that, outside of specifically identified sections of code, data-integrity properties are always enforced.

In this paper, we apply invariants to critical data local to smart contracts and thus derive a means to prove the correctness of smart contracts, even in the presence of callbacks and potential reentrancy. We demonstrate our approach using the SPARK programming language and also show that our method can be applied in other languages that support formal verification.

2   Context

2.1   The Token Contract

A typical smart contract is the token contract. It allows sharing money or other tokens accessed by several accounts. At its heart the token contract is a map from accounts (identified by addresses) to the amount of tokens they have access to:

```
type Balances_Type is array (Address) of Natural;
Balances : Balances_Type;
```

There are functions to transfer tokens between users, adding tokens to one's allowance, and getting tokens paid out. In the simplest case, tokens are just ether. But note that the map above is only the contract's view of reality and of how many ether every user has access to. Bugs in the smart contract can cause a deviation between the reality and the token contract's vision of reality. For example, it is implicit in the above definition that the token contract (which is itself an account) holds at least as much money as the sum of the balances for all users. If there is a bug in the smart contract, this may not actually be the case.

2.2   Reentrancy, the Problem

A possible version of the token contract's payout procedure looks like this:

```
Procedure Payout (Sender : Address; Amount : Natural) is
begin
  if Balance (Sender) >= Amount then
  Send (Sender, Amount);
  Balance (Sender) := Balance (Sender) - Amount;
  end if;
end Payout;
```

The Sender object is automatically filled out by the calling mechanism of the language and corresponds to the invoking entity. We assume here that the sender is also a smart contract, because that is the interesting case. The Send procedure is also a primitive of the smart contract infrastructure. In the solidity language, there are several ways to send ether, we assume here that Send sends the money in such a way that the fallback function of the receiving contract is triggered. We ignore discussions of gas limits here and assume that the fallback function has as much gas available as required.

This version of the program is vulnerable to a reentrancy attack. In detail, it works this way. The attacker creates another smart contract as follows:

1. The attacking contract first puts some small amount of money inside the token contract using a Deposit functionality (not shown here).
2. The attacking contract calls the Payout procedure of the token contract, setting the Sender object to the smart contract itself, using an Amount which is less or equal to the deposited value.
3. This causes the condition in the Payout procedure to succeed and the token contract to send money to the attacking contract;
4. Sending money triggers the fallback code of the attacking contract. The fallback code simply calls Payout again, with the same amount.
5. As Payout has not yet updated the internal state of the token contract, the if- condition is still true and the token contract sends money again.
6. This again triggers the fallback code of the attacking contract.

The recursion continues until the transaction chain runs out of gas or the token contract doesn't have any ether any more.

A fix for the token contract is to update the internal state before sending any money:

```
Procedure Payout (Sender : Address; Amount : Natural) is
begin
  if Balance (Sender) >= Amount then
  Balance (Sender) := Balance (Sender) - Amount;
  Send (Sender, Amount);
  end if;
end Payout;
```

Reentrancy can still occur, but now the attacker cannot circumvent the protecting condition, so he will be able only to withdraw his own balance. Of course the Token contract is just one example of a contract that may be vulnerable to a reentrancy attack. Any contract that calls code of unknown other contracts is potentially vulnerable.

3   Existing Protections and Related Work

Reentrancy attacks in the Ethereum network are real and have cost a lot of money for the victims in the past. So measures have been taken to avoid the problem. To the best of our knowledge, these measures mostly consist of excluding reentrancy altogether (see also the section concerning related work). For example, the most commonly used functions for transferring ether now have a gas limit, so that the receiving contract can do only very few actions (in particular not call other contracts). However, as Grossman et al [9] show, callbacks are used in a large number of contracts and cannot be completely avoided.

3.1   Related Work

There is a vast body of work related to data invariants in object-oriented programming [2,13], which lead to the formulation of class invariants in JML [12]. Our work is also based on this existing research and applies it to callbacks in smart contracts. Existing formal methods for smart contracts that address this vulnerability simply forbid all reentrancy. This is usually achieved by only supporting transfers of ether that do not trigger the fallback code of the recipient (or specify a very small gas limit that does not allow much code execution), or excluding the problem from the analysis. This is the case for the ZEUS system [10], where a warning is signaled for any code that may contain reentrancy. Bhargavan et al. [3] present an F*-based method to apply formal verification to smart contracts. They discuss reentrancy and show that their system detects reentrancy, but do not present any solution to the issue. Grossman et al. [9] present the theoretical notion of effectively callback free contracts, whose state changes, even in the presence of callbacks (or reentrancy) happen in an order that can also be achieved by a callback-free sequence of calls. Such callbacks are harmless wrt. the type of reentrancy attack discussed here. Their paper mainly concentrates on online detection of violations of this property, but they also have a section of formal verification of a contract using Dafny [14]. However, Dafny does not support object or class invariants, so their Dafny-verification uses a meta-argument to remove some effects from calls that might contain callbacks. Our method can be seen as an in-language way to show that a contract is effectively callback free, which does not rely on meta-arguments.

4 Using SPARK Type Invariants to Deal with Callbacks

4.1 Quick Overview over SPARK

SPARK [15] is a subset of Ada [1] and targets mainly embedded applications. It has strong support for formal verification.

Basic Annotations for Proof. SPARK has built-in support for formal verification. One basic feature is pre- and postconditions, as well as global annotations that can be attached to a procedure declaration:

```
procedure Add_In_Z (X, Y : Integer)
with Global    => (In_Out => Z),
     Post      => (Z = Z'Old + X + Y);
```

Extra information can be attached to a procedure using the with keyword. This is used to attach the information Global, which says that this procedure reads and writes the global variable Z. Also, we attached the information Post, which says that the new value of this variable Z is the sum of the old value of Z and the values of X and Y (we ignore concerns of arithmetic overflow in this example). SPARK can formally verify that functions indeed respect the attached information such as Global and Post, similar to e.g. Dafny or Why3; in fact the formal verification engine in SPARK is based on Why3.

Private Types. SPARK allows the user to separate a project into packages, each package having a package specification, visible by others, and an implementation which is private to this package. The package specification can contain so-called private types, or abstract types in other languages, where clients of the package cannot see the actual implementation of the type, only that the type exists:

```
type T is private;
...
type T is new Integer;
```

Type Invariants. In SPARK, one can attach to type invariants to the implementation of a private type, for example as follows:

```
type T is private;
...
type T is record
   A : Integer;
   B : Integer;
End record
With Type_Invariant => T.A < T.B;
```

The idea is that type invariants must be maintained by the package. The package is allowed to assume the type invariant on input of any of its procedures or functions, and is allowed to temporarily break the invariant. However, it has to reestablish the invariant whenever an object leaves the scope of the package. This can be either by returning such an object to the caller, or by passing the object to a procedure or function that belongs to another package. The SPARK tool can prove that type invariants are correctly used and enforced by the package. SPARK type invariants have many restrictions; we mostly ignore these restrictions in the paper to keep a natural flow to the paper, but a dedicated section explains how we circumvented them to be able to actually use the SPARK tool.

Ghost Code. Any declaration in SPARK (e.g. a type, object or procedure) can be annotated as ghost. This means that the declaration is only used for the purposes of verification, and does not contribute to the functionality of the code. This property is checked by the compiler and SPARK tools. A well-defined set of statements, such as assignments to ghost objects and calls to ghost procedures, are considered ghost code by the compiler and removed when compiling the program[1]. The following code example makes sure that the procedure `Do_Some_Work` is called after calling `Initialize` first.

```
Initialized : Boolean := False with Ghost;

procedure Initialize with
   Post => Initialized;

procedure Do_Some_Work with
  Pre => Initialized;

procedure Initialize is
begin
   ...  Do some initialization here ...
   Initialized := True;
end Initialize;
```

---

[1] The compiler can also be configured to compile the application with ghost code enabled, which can be useful for dynamic checking of properties e.g. during unit testing.

4.2   Adding Annotations to the Payout Procedure

The first step to apply formal verification would be to add pre- and postconditions to the payout procedure. Here is a first attempt:

```
Procedure Payout (Sender : Address; Amount : Natural)
with Post =>
 (for all Addr of Address =>
 if Addr = Sender and then Balance'Old (Addr) >= Amount
 then Balance (Addr) = Balance'Old (Addr) - Amount
 else Balance (Addr) = Balance'Old (Addr));
```

This postcondition summarizes the naive understanding of what `Payout` does: it sends a fixed amount of money to Sender, updating the `Balance` variable as well. As is common in systems that are based on deductive verification, one needs to specify also what remains unchanged. Here, `Balance` is only changed for the Sender, and only when the amount is actually sent (that is, actually available to be paid out). To prove this postcondition, we also need to explain what `Send` is doing. In SPARK terms this means writing pre- and postconditions for the `Send` procedure, and Global annotations. Global annotations are frame conditions, a fundamental element of proof tools for imperative languages. They say what global state can potentially be modified by the procedure. It turns out `Send` can have quite a large effect, given that it can execute completely unknown code. The `Payout` procedure might well attempt to send money to some smart contract that was added to the blockchain at a later stage. Also we have seen that via reentrancy, `Send` can even modify our own state. We don't really care about the state of any other smart contract here, but we do care about the state of our own contract. So we have no choice but to annotate `Send` with this global annotation:

```
Procedure Send (Addr : Address; Amount : Natural)
with Global => (In_Out => Balance);
```

At this stage, we can't really add any information to `Send` in the form of a postcondition on how it changes the state. After all, `Send` may call any procedure of the token contract, via any of the public procedures or functions of the contract.

However, now there is no chance that we can prove the postcondition of `Payout`, because `Send` can change our own state, and in an unknown way! Moreover, looking at the postcondition we wrote for `Payout`, it is wrong anyway, even for the corrected code. Via reentrancy, the sender can transfer more money than just Amount, though in the corrected version the attacker cannot exceed his balance. We need to go back to the basics and understand the difference between the original version of `Payout` and the corrected one.

4.3 Why the Fix Works

For the following, we now assume that Send contains two actions, that are executed in this order:

1. The actual sending of ether from the sender to the recipient;
2. The execution of the fallback code of the recipient.

The issue with the original version of Payout was that in the second step, the global state of the token contract was in an inconsistent state. The money was already sent, but the Balance map hadn't been updated yet. The fallback code can be executed in this inconsistent state, and that's why the if-condition in Payout becomes useless. Now it is easy to see why the fix works: both the update to the token state as well as the ether transfer have been done when calling the fallback code. When the fallback code is executed, the state of the token contract is consistent. While the fallback code can still cause reentrancy, there should be no more "urprises" Grossman et al. [9] call the corrected version effectively callback free, because the state changes happen in such a way that they could also be achieved by a sequential series of calls to the interface of the object, without any reentrancy. This is not the case in the incorrect version, where the inconsistent sequence of state changes can only be achieved via reentrancy. In SPARK, we can model the two steps of Send as follows. We introduce ghost state for sent tokens and wrap the Send procedure as follows:

```
Sent : Balances_Type with Ghost;

procedure Wrap_Send (Addr : Address; Amount : Natural) is
begin
 Sent (Addr) := Sent (Addr) + Amount;
 Send (Addr, Amount);
end Send;
```

This also requires to update the global effect of Send to include Sent. Here is the a summary of the changes:

```
procedure Send (Addr : Address; Amount : Natural)
With Global => (In_Out => (Balance, Sent));

procedure Wrap_Send ... -- as above

procedure Payout (Sender : Address; Amount : Natural) is
begin
 if Balance (Sender) >= Amount then
 Balance (Sender) := Balance (Sender) - Amount;
 Wrap_Send (Sender, Amount);
 end if;
end Payout;
```

4.4   The Solution in SPARK

So to prove the correctness of the corrected version, we need to:

1. Come up with a criterion for the data to be consistent;
2. Prove that the data is consistent whenever the control flow leaves the token contract, either via a regular return statement, or via a call to other code.

For (1), concentrating only on the Payout procedure, it is enough to say that for each address, the sum of the money sent and the balance should remain constant. A way of saying that it stays constant is to say that it is equal to some other quantity which stays unmodified during the whole computation. Let's represent this quantity by a new array K:

```
K : Balances_Type with Ghost;
```

For (2), luckily, the SPARK language already has a construct that does exactly that. It is called a type invariant, that is a property attached to a type, that should hold at certain points. Simply expressing the property of (1) as a type invariant and attaching it to the right type will do exactly what we need. We can express our invariant of the relevant data like this:

```
(for all A of Address => K (A) = Balance (A) + Sent (A))
```

That is all. We can now remove the postcondition of Payout[2]. The final version can be proved by SPARK in a few seconds; the incorrect version (by switching the two statements in the if-block) is correctly not proved, because the type invariant cannot be established before calling Send.

4.5   Some Limitations of SPARK and Their Workarounds

As mentioned, we have described a solution which uses some features that SPARK doesn't actually support (but could). First, type invariants are attached to types, while we would like to attach them to objects, or maybe to the package itself. Then, type invariants can't mention global objects, while the invariant we showed mentions the three global objects Balance, Sent, and K. We can work around these two annoyances simply by creating a record type which contains these three variables as fields. We attach the type invariant to this type:

```
Type Data_Type is private;
...
type Data_Type is record
   Balance : Balance_Type;
   Sent    : Balance_Type;
   K       : Balance_Type;
```

---

[2] We can't really express anything useful in the postcondition here. Any public function of the Token contract might be called via reentrancy, updating the state in a consistent but unknown way.

```
end record
with Type_Invariant =>
   (for all A of Address => K (A) = Balance (A) + Sent (A));
```

This works well. One further limitation is that we now cannot specify the Ghost status of Sent and K anymore, because currently Ghost status cannot be set for individual fields of a record. But the entire record cannot be ghost, because the Balance data is required to be present during execution. The last limitation is that we cannot create global variables of a type which has a type invariant. So we need to add a parameter of type Data_Type to all relevant procedures, including the Send wand Wrap_Send procedures.

Reasoning in SPARK is strict on a per-procedure basis; this means that adding a wrapper such as Wrap_Send potentially increases the verification effort, as the wrapper would need annotations and separate proofs. However, local procedures with no annotations are automatically inlined by SPARK. So we deliberately do not add any pre- and postconditions to Wrap_Send.

4.6   Compilation of SPARK to Blockchain Virtual Machines

SPARK is a subset of Ada, so if we can compile Ada to a blockchain, we are good. A direct compiler from Ada to (say) EVM does not exist, but various indirect ways are possible. The easiest way is to use go from Ada to LLVM via the gnat-llvm [4] tool. The LLVM intermediate representation can then be translated to Solidity using Solidify, a tool that can generate Solidity code from LLVM [11]. Finally, we can use the Solidity compiler to translate to EVM byte-code citeEthereumFoundation.

5   Other Languages that Support Reasoning About Callbacks

SPARK is not the only tool to have both type invariants and ghost code. We give a non-exhaustive overview over other languages and tools that would also support this style of reasoning. Why3 [6] is a well-known research tool for formal verification. There is ongoing work to support compilation to the EVM byte-code [17]. Also, Why3 has support for type invariants and ghost code, although the rules are a bit different from the ones in SPARK. One main difference is that Why3 has no notion package encapsulation of abstract types, that is, a type in Why3 is either abstract for everybody, or the definition of the type fully visible to everybody. So there is no notion of scope for a type invariant, and type invariants are checked at every function boundary. We suspect that this is a bit too restrictive for realistic contracts. Our example, if the Wrap_Send function is inlined, should work in the same way in Why3. Similar to SPARK, the type invariant has to be attached to a single type, so one has to introduce a record type that holds all relevant data. The Java modeling language JML [12] has support for class invariants and ghost code, so the code shown in this paper should be easy to translate to JML and should work there, too. In addition, the JML language allows to specify an effect called "everything", which is a convenient way to say that a call may write "any" visible object. In SPARK and Why3, the user has to manually deduce the relevant set of objects, and annotate Send correctly. This style of verification using type or class invariants could be simulated in a language without type invariants (such as Dafny) by repeating the invariant as appropriate in pre- and postconditions and intermediate assertions. But this would require a meta-argument to show that the reasoning is correct; also it would be very error-prone. An intermediate assertion, for example, could be omitted by accident, and the tool would not be able to detect the error.

6   Conclusion

Research in deductive verification has already tackled the issue of callbacks and reentrancy, but to our knowledge this research had never been applied to smart contracts. We have shown that the language feature of type invariants enables deductive verification of smart contracts even in the presence of callbacks, including reentrancy. This result improves upon existing research, that either excludes callbacks, or requires a meta-argument to remove effects. Our paper has used SPARK to illustrate the running example, but Why3 and JML have similar language features and could also support this style of reasoning. Our conclusion is that a language for formal verification of smart contracts should have support for type, object or class invariants to efficiently deal with callbacks and reentrancy issues.

References

1. Barnes, J.: Ada 2012 rationale (2012). https://www.adacore.com/papers/ada-2012-rationale/
2. Barnett, M., DeLine, R., Fähndrich, M., Leino, K.R.M., Schulte, W.: Verification of object-oriented programs with invariants. J. Object Technol. **3**, 2004 (2004)
3. Bhargavan, K., et al.: Formal verification of smart contracts: short paper. In: Proceedings of the 2016 ACM Workshop on Programming Languages and Analysis for Security, PLAS 2016, pp. 91–96. ACM, New York (2016)
4. Charlet, A.: Adacore techdays - GNAT pro update (2018). https://www.adacore.com/uploads/page_content/presentations/TechDaysParis2018-2-GNAT-Pro-Update-Tech-Days-2018-Paris.pptx
5. Daian, P.: Analysis of the DAO exploit (2016). http://hackingdistributed.com/2016/06/18/analysis-of-the-dao-exploit/
6. Filliâtre, J.-C., Paskevich, A.: Why3 — where programs meet provers. In: Felleisen, M., Gardner, P. (eds.) ESOP 2013. LNCS, vol. 7792, pp. 125–128. Springer, Heidelberg (2013). https://doi.org/10.1007/978-3-642-37036-6_8
7. Foundation, E.: Solidity (2019). https://solidity.readthedocs.io/en/develop/
8. Gamma, E., Helm, R., Johnson, R., Vlissides, J.M.: Design Patterns: Elements of Reusable Object-Oriented Software, 1st edn. Addison-Wesley Professional, Boston (1994)

9. Grossman, S., et al.: Online detection of effectively callback free objects with applications to smart contracts. Proc. ACM Program. Lang. **2**(POPL), 48:1–48:28 (2017)

10. Kalra, S., Goel, S., Dhawan, M., Sharma, S.: ZEUS: analyzing safety of smart contracts. In: 25th Annual Network and Distributed System Security Symposium, NDSS 2018, San Diego, California, USA, 18–21 February 2018. The Internet Society (2018). http://wp.internetsociety.org/ndss/wp-content/uploads/sites/25/2018/02/ndss2018_09-1_Kalra_paper.pdf

11. Kothapalli, A.: Solidify, an LLVM pass to compile LLVM IR into solidity, version 00, July 2017. https://www.osti.gov//servlets/purl/1369636

12. Leavens, G.T.: JML reference manual (2019). http://www.eecs.ucf.edu/~leavens/JML/jmlrefman/jmlrefman_toc.html

13. Leino, K.R.M., Müller, P.: Modular verification of static class invariants. In: Fitzgerald, J., Hayes, I.J., Tarlecki, A. (eds.) FM 2005. LNCS, vol. 3582, pp. 26–42. Springer, Heidelberg (2005). https://doi.org/10.1007/11526841_4

14. Leino, K.R.M.: Dafny: an automatic program verifier for functional correctness. In: Clarke, Edmund M., Voronkov, Andrei (eds.) LPAR 2010. LNCS (LNAI), vol. 6355, pp. 348–370. Springer, Heidelberg (2010). https://doi.org/10.1007/978-3-642-17511-4_20. https://www.microsoft.com/en-us/research/publication/dafny-automatic-program-verifier-functional-correctness-2/

15. McCormick, J.W., Chapin, P.C.: Building High Integrity Applications with SPARK. Cambridge University Press, Cambridge (2015)

16. Nakamoto, S.: Bitcoin: a peer-to-peer electronic cash system (2008). https://bitcoin.org/bitcoin.pdf

17. Nehai, Z., Bobot, F.: Deductive Proof of Ethereum Smart Contracts Using Why3. Research report, CEA DILS, April 2019. https://hal.archives-ouvertes.fr/hal-02108987

18. Szabo, N.: Formalizing and securing relationships on public networks. First Monday **2**(9) (1997)

Statistical Model Checking of RANDAO's Resilience to Pre-computed Reveal Strategies

Musab A. Alturki[1,2(✉)] and Grigore Roşu[1,3]

[1] Runtime Verification Inc., Urbana, IL 61801, USA
[2] King Fahd University of Petroleum and Minerals, Dhahran, Saudi Arabia
musab.alturki@kfupm.edu.sa
[3] University of Illinois at Urbana-Champaign, Urbana, IL 61801, USA
grosu@illinois.edu

Abstract. RANDAO is a commit-reveal scheme for generating pseudo-random numbers in a decentralized fashion. The scheme is used in emerging blockchain systems as it is widely believed to provide randomness that is unpredictable and hard to manipulate by maliciously behaving nodes. However, RANDAO may still be susceptible to look-ahead attacks, in which an attacker (controlling a subset of nodes in the network) may attempt to pre-compute the outcomes of (possibly many) reveal strategies, and thus may bias the generated random number to his advantage. In this work, we formally evaluate resilience of RANDAO against such attacks. We first develop a probabilistic model in rewriting logic of RANDAO, and then apply statistical model checking and quantitative verification algorithms (using MAUDE and PVESTA) to analyze two different properties that provide different measures of bias that the attacker could potentially achieve using pre-computed strategies. We show through this analysis that unless the attacker is already controlling a sizable percentage of nodes while aggressively attempting to maximize control of the nodes selected to participate in the process, the expected achievable bias is quite limited.

Keywords: RANDAO · Rewriting logic · Maude · Statistical model checking · Blockchain

1 Introduction

Decentralized pseudo-random value generation is a process in which participants in a network, who do not necessarily trust each other, collaborate to produce a random value that is unpredictable to any individual participant. It is a core process of many emerging distributed autonomous systems, most prominently proof-of-stake (PoS) consensus protocols, which include the upcoming Ethereum 2.0 (a.k.a. Serenity) protocol [8,11]. A commonly accepted implementation scheme for decentralized random value generation is a commit-reveal scheme, known as

© Springer Nature Switzerland AG 2020
E. Sekerinski et al. (Eds.): FM 2019 Workshops, LNCS 12232, pp. 337–349, 2020.
https://doi.org/10.1007/978-3-030-54994-7_25

RANDAO (due to Youcai Qian [16]), in which participants first make commitments by sharing hash values of seeds, and then, at a later stage, they reveal their seeds, which can then be used for generating the random value. In a PoS protocol, and in particular in Serenity [11], the scheme is used repeatedly in a sequence of rounds in such a way that the outcome of a round is used as a seed for generating the random value of the following round. Moreover, the scheme is usually coupled with a reward system that incentivizes successful participation and discourages deviations from the protocol. Several other distributed protocols have also adopted this scheme primarily for its simplicity and flexibility.

However, this approach may still be susceptible to *look-ahead* attacks, in which a malicious participant may choose to refrain from revealing his seed if skipping results in randomness that is more favorable to him. In general, a powerful attacker may attempt to pre-compute the outcomes of (possibly many) reveal strategies, which are sequences of reveal-or-skip decisions, and thus may anticipate the effects of his contribution to the process and bias the generated random number to his advantage.

While this potential vulnerability is known and has been pointed to in several works in the literature (e.g. [4, 6, 7]), the extent to which it may be exploited by an attacker and how effective the attack could be in an actual system, such as a PoS system like Serenity, have not yet been thoroughly investigated, besides the exploitability arguments made in [7] and [6], which were based on abstract analytical models. While the high-level analysis given there is useful for gaining a foundational understanding of the vulnerability and the potential of the attack, a lower-level formalization that captures the interactions of the different components of the RANDAO process and the environment could provide deeper insights into how realizable the attack is in an actual system.

In this work, we develop a computational model of the RANDAO scheme as a probabilistic rewrite theory [1, 12] in rewriting logic [13] to formally evaluate resilience of RANDAO to pre-computed reveal strategies. The model gives a formal, yet natural, description of (possibly different designs of) the RANDAO process and the environment. Furthermore, the model is both *timed*, capturing timing of events in the process, and *probabilistic*, modeling randomized protocol behaviors and environment uncertainties. Being executable, the model facilitates automated formal analysis of *quantitative properties*, specified as real-valued formulas in QUATEX (Quantitative Temporal Expressions Logic) [1], through efficient statistical model checking and quantitative analysis algorithms using both MAUDE [9] (a high-performance rewriting system) and PVESTA [2] (a statistical verification tool that interfaces with MAUDE). Using the model, we analyze two properties that provide different measures of bias that the attacker could potentially achieve using pre-computed strategies: (1) the *matching score*, which is the expected number of proposers that the attacker controls, and (2) the *last-word score*, which is the length of the longest tail of the proposers list that the attacker controls.

We show through this analysis that unless the attacker is already controlling a sizable portion of validators and is aggressively attempting to maximize the number of last compromised proposers in the proposers list, or what we call the *compromised tail* of the list, the expected achievable bias of randomness of the RANDAO scheme is quite limited. However, an aggressive attacker who can afford to make repeated skips for very extended periods of time (e.g. in thousands of rounds), or an attacker who already controls a fairly large percentage (e.g. more than 30%) of participants in the network will have higher chances of success.

The rest of the paper is organized as follows. In Section 2, we quickly review rewriting logic and statistical model checking. In Sect. 3, we introduce in some detail the RANDAO scheme. This is followed in Sect. 4 by a description of our model of RANDAO in rewriting logic. Section 5 the analysis properties and results. The paper concludes with a discussion of future work in Sect. 6.

2   Background

Rewriting logic [14] is a general logical and semantic framework in which systems can be formally specified and analyzed. A unit of specification in rewriting logic is a *rewrite theory* $\mathcal{R}$, which formally describes a concurrent system including its static structure and dynamic behavior. It is a tuple $(\Sigma, E \cup A, R)$ consisting of: (1) a membership equational logic (MEL) [15] signature Σ that declares the kinds, sorts and operators to be used in the specification; (2) a set E of Σ-sentences, which are universally quantified Horn clauses with atoms that are either equations $(t = t')$ or memberships $(t : s)$; (3) A a set of equational axioms, such as commutativity, associativity and/or identity axioms; and (4) a set R of rewrite rules $t \longrightarrow t'$ if C specifying the computational behavior of the system (where C is a conjunction of equational or rewrite conditions). Operationally, if there exists a substitution θ such that $\theta(t)$ matches a subterm s in the state of the system, and $\theta(C)$ is satisfied, then s may rewrite to $\theta(t')$. While the MEL sub-theory $(\Sigma, E \cup A)$ specifies the user-defined syntax and equational axioms defining the system's state structure, a rewrite rule in R specifies a *parametric transition*, where each instantiation of the rule's variables that satisfies its conditions yields an actual transition (see [5] for a detailed account of generalized rewrite theories).

Probabilistic rewrite theories extend regular rewrite theories with probabilistic rules [1,17]. A probabilistic rule $(t \longrightarrow t'$ if C with probability $\pi)$ specifies a transition that can be taken with a probability that may depend on a probability distribution function π parametrized by a t-matching substitution satisfying C. Probabilistic rewrite theories unify many different probabilistic models and can express systems involving both probabilistic and nondeterministic features.

MAUDE [9] is a high-performance rewriting logic implementation. An equational theory $(\Sigma, E \cup A)$ is specified in MAUDE as a functional module, which may consist of sort and subsort declarations for defining type hierarchies, operator declarations, and unconditional and conditional equations and memberships. Operator declarations specify the operator's syntax (in mixfix notation), the number and sorts of the arguments and the sort of its resulting expression. Furthermore, equational attributes such as associativity and commutativity axioms may be specified in brackets after declaring the input and output sorts. A rewrite theory is specified as a *system module*, which may additionally contain rewrite rules declared with the `rl` keyword (`crl` for conditional rules).

Furthermore, probabilistic rewrite theories, specified as system modules in MAUDE [9], can be simulated by sampling from probability distributions. Using PVESTA [2], randomized simulations generated in this fashion can be used to statistically model check quantitative properties of the system. These properties are specified in a rich, quantitative temporal logic, QUATEX [1], in which real-valued state and path functions are used instead of boolean state and path predicates to quantitatively specify properties about probabilistic models. QUATEX supports parameterized recursive function declarations, a standard conditional construct, and a *next* modal operator $\bigcirc$, allowing for an expressive language for real-valued temporal properties (Example QUATEX expressions appear in Sect. 5). Given a QUATEX path expression and a MAUDE module specifying a probabilistic rewrite theory, statistical quantitative analysis is performed by estimating the *expected value* of the path expression against computation paths obtained by Monte Carlo simulations. More details can be found in [1].

3 The RANDAO Scheme

The RANDAO scheme [16] is a commit-reveal scheme consisting of two stages: (1) the commit stage, in which a participant p_i first commits to a seed s_i (by announcing the hash of the seed h_{s_i}), and then (2) the reveal stage, in which the participant p_i reveals the seed s_i. The sequence of revealed seeds $s_0, s_1, \cdots, s_{n-1}$ (assuming n participants) are then used to compute a new seed s (e.g. by taking the XOR of all s_i), which is then used to generate a random number.

In the context of the Serenity protocol [11], the RANDAO scheme proceeds in rounds corresponding to epochs in the protocol. At the start of an epoch i, the random number r_{i-1} generated in the previous round (in epoch $i-1$) is used for sampling from a large set of validators participating in the protocol an ordered list of block proposers $p_0, p_1, \cdots p_{k-1}$, where k is the cycle length of the protocol (a fixed number of time slots constituting one epoch in the protocol). Each proposer p_i is assigned the time slot i of the current round (epoch). During time slot i, the proposer p_i is expected to submit the pair (c_{p_i}, s_{p_i}), with c_{p_i} a commitment on a seed to be used for the next participation in the game (in some future round when p_i is selected again as a proposer), and s_{p_i} the seed to which p_i had previously committed in the last participation in the game (or when p_i first joined the protocol's validator set). The RANDAO contract keeps track of successful reveals in the game, which are those reveals that arrive in time and that pass the commitment verification step. Towards the end of an epoch i, the RANDAO contract combines the revealed seeds in this round by computing their XOR s_i, which is used as the seed for the next random number r_{i+1} to be used in the next round $i+1$. To discourage deviations from the protocol and encourage proper participation, the RANDAO contract penalizes proposers who did not successfully reveal (by discounting their Ether deposits) and rewards those proposers who have been able to successfully reveal their seeds (by distributing dividends in Ether).

4   A Rewriting Model of RANDAO

We use rewriting logic [14], and its probabilistic extensions [1,12], to build a generic and executable model of the RANDAO scheme. The model is specified as a probabilistic rewrite theory $\mathcal{R} = (\Sigma_\mathcal{R}, E_\mathcal{R} \cup A_\mathcal{R}, R_\mathcal{R})$, implemented in MAUDE as a system module. By utilizing different facilities provided by its underlying formalism, the model $\mathcal{R}$ is both (purely) *probabilistic*, specifying randomized behaviors and environment uncertainties, and *real-time*, capturing (dense) time clocks and message transmission delays. Furthermore, the model is *parametric* to a number of parameters, such as the attack probability, the size of the validator set and the network latency, to enable capturing different attack scenarios.

In this section, we describe generally the most fundamental parts of the model. A more detailed description of the model can be found in [3].

4.1   Protocol State Structure

The structure of the model, specified by the MEL sub-theory $(\Sigma_\mathcal{R}, E_\mathcal{R} \cup A_\mathcal{R})$ of $\mathcal{R}$, is based on a representation of actors in rewriting logic, which builds on its underlying object-based modeling facilities. In this model, the state of the protocol is a *configuration* consisting of a multiset of actor objects and messages in transit. Objects communicate asynchronously by message passing. An object is a term of the form <name: O | A >, with O the actor object's unique name (of the sort ActorName) and A its set of attributes, constructed by an associative and commutative comma operator _,_ (with mt as its identity element). Each attribute is a name-value pair of the form attr : value. A message destined for object O with payload C is represented by a term of the form O <- C, where the payload C is a term of the sort Content.

Objects. The three most important objects in the model are: (1) the blockchain object, (2) the RANDAO contract object, and (3) the attacker object.

The Blockchain Object. This object, identified by the actor name operator bc, models abstractly the public data maintained in a blockchain:

```
<name : bc  |  vapproved :  VHL ,    vapproved - size :  N ,
               vpending :    VHL ',  vpending - size :   N ',
               seed : S >
```

The object maintains a list of validator records of all approved and participating validators in the system in an attribute vapproved, with its current length in the vapproved-size attribute. As new validators arrive and request to join the system, the blockchain object accumulates these incoming requests as a growing list of validator records in its attribute vpending, along with its current size in the attribute vpending-size. Finally, this object maintains the seed value that was last computed by the previous round of the game in its seed attribute.

The RANDAO object. This object, identified by the operator r, models a RAN-DAO contract managing the RANDAO process:

```
<name: r | status:     U, balance:    N,  precords: PL,
          prop-size: M, prop-ilist: IL, pnext: I >
```

It maintains a status attribute, indicating its current state of processing, and a balance attribute, keeping track of the total contract balance. Moreover, the object manages the proposers list for the current round of the game using the attributes prop-ilist, a list of indices identifying the proposers, and precords, a list of proposer records of the form [v(I), B] with B a Boolean flag indicating whether the proposer v(I) has successfully revealed. Additionally, the size of the proposers list is stored in prop-size. Finally, the object also keeps track of the next time slot (in the current round) to be processed in the attribute pnext.

The Attacker Object. The attacker is modeled by the attacker object, identified by the operator a:

```
<name: a | vcomp:     CVL,  vcomp-ilist: IL, vcomp-size: N,
          strategy:  G >
```

The full list of the compromised validator indices is maintained by the attacker object in the attribute vcomp-ilist. This list is always a sublist of the active validators maintained by the blockchain object above. Its length is maintained in the attribute vcomp-size. Since in every round of the game, a portion of validators selected as proposers may be compromised, the attacker object creates compromised validator records for all such validators to assign them roles for the round and maintains these records in its attribute vcomp. If any one of these compromised validators is at the head of the longest compromised tail of the proposers list, the computed reveal strategy (whenever it becomes ready during the current round) is recorded in the attribute strategy.

The Scheduler. In addition to objects and messages, the state (configuration) includes a *scheduler*, which is responsible for managing the time domain, modeled by the real numbers, and the scheduling of message delivery. The scheduler is a term of the form {T | L}, with T the current global clock value and L a time-ordered list of scheduled messages, where each such message is of the form [T,M], representing a message M scheduled for processing at time T. As time advances, scheduled messages in L are delivered (in time-order) to their target objects, and newly produced messages by objects are appropriately scheduled into L. The scheduler is key in ensuring absence of any unquantified non-determinism in the model, which is a necessary condition for soundness of statistical analysis [3].

4.2 Protocol Transitions

The protocol's state transitions are modeled using the (possibly conditional and/or probabilistic) rewrite rules $R_{\mathcal{R}}$ of the rewrite theory $\mathcal{R} = (\Sigma_{\mathcal{R}}, E_{\mathcal{R}} \cup$

$A_\mathcal{R}, R_\mathcal{R}$). The rules specify: (1) the actions of the RANDAO contract, which are advancing the time slot, advancing the round and processing validator reveals, and (2) the behaviors of both honest and compromised validators. For space consideration, we only list and describe the rule for advancing the time slot below, while omitting some of the details. Complete descriptions of all the rules can be found in the extended report [3].

The transition for advancing the time slot specifies the mechanism with which the RANDAO contract object checks if a successful reveal was made by the proposer assigned for the current time slot:

```
rl [RAdvanceSlot] :
<name: bc | vapproved-size: N, vpending-size: N',
            seed: S, AS >
<name: r | status: ready, precords: ([ VID , B ] ; CL),
            prop-ilist: IL, pnext: K, AS' >
{ TG | SL } (RID <- nextSlot(L)) ...
=>
<name: bc | vapproved-size: N, vpending-size: N',
            seed: S, AS >
if L > #CYCLE-LENGTH then
  <name: r | status: processing,
              precords: ([ VID , B ] ; CL),
              prop-ilist:
              sampleIndexList(N + N', #CYCLE-LENGTH, S, nilIL),
              pnext: 1, AS' >
  { TG | SL } (RID <- nextRound)
else
  if L == K then
    <name: r | status: ready,
                precords: ([ VID , B ] ; CL),
                prop-ilist: IL, pnext: K, AS' >
  else
    <name: r | status: ready,
                precords: (CL ; [ VID , false ]),
                prop-ilist: IL, pnext: s(K), AS' >
  fi
  insert({ TG | SL }, [TG + 1.0, (RID <- nextSlot(s(L)))])
fi ... .
```

When the current time slot L is about to end, the message nextSlot(L) becomes ready for the RANDAO object to consume, which initiates the process of advancing the state of the protocol to the next slot. There are three cases that need to be considered depending on the value of L:

1. L > #CYCLE-LENGTH, meaning that the message's time slot number exceeds the number of slots in a round (slot numbering begins at 1), and thus, the protocol has already processed all slots of the current round, and progressing to the next slot would require advancing the current round of the game first. Therefore, the RANDAO contract object changes its status to processing

and samples a new list of proposers for the next round using the seed S that was computed in the current round. The object resets the time slot count to 1 and emits a self-addressed, zero-delay `nextRound` message.

2. `L == K`, where K is the next-slot number stored in the RANDAO object, which means that the slot number K was already advanced by successfully processing a reveal some time earlier during this slot's time window. In this case, the state is not changed and a `nextSlot(s(L))` message (with s the successor function) is scheduled to repeat this process for the next time slot.

3. Otherwise, the slot number K stored in the object has not been advanced before and, thus, either a reveal for the current time slot L was attempted and failed or that a reveal was never received. In both cases, the RANDAO object records that as a failure in the proposers record list, advances the slot number K and schedules a `nextSlot(s(L))` message in preparation for the next time slot.

These cases are specified by the nested conditional structure shown in the rule.

5　Statistical Verification

We use the model $\mathcal{R}$ to formally and quantitatively evaluate how much an attacker can bias randomness of the RANDAO process assuming various attacker models and protocol parameters. In the analysis presented below, we assume a 95% confidence interval with size at most 0.02. We also assume no message drops and random message transmission delays in the range [0.0, 0.1] time units (so reveals, if made, are guaranteed to arrive on time).

5.1　Matching Score (MS)

The *Matching score* (MS) is the number of attacker-controlled validators selected as proposers in a round of the RANDAO process. The baseline value for MS (assuming no attack) is given by the expectation of a binomial random variable X with success probability p (the probability of a validator being compromised) in k repeated trials (k is the length of the proposers list), which is:

$$EX[X] = kp \tag{1}$$

As a *temporal* formula in QuaTEx, the property MS is expressed as:

$$
\begin{aligned}
ms(t) = \ &\textbf{if } time() > t \textbf{ then } countCompromised() \\
&\textbf{else } \bigcirc ms(t) \textbf{ fi}; \\
&\textbf{eval } \mathbf{E}[ms(t_0)]
\end{aligned}
\tag{2}
$$

$ms(t)$ is a recursively defined path expression that uses two state functions: (1) $time()$, which evaluates to the time value of the current state of the protocol (given by the scheduler object), and (2) $countCompromised()$, which evaluates to the number of compromised proposers in the current state of the RANDAO object. Therefore, given an execution path, the path expression $ms(t)$ evaluates to $countCompromised()$ in the current state if the protocol run is complete (reached the time limit); otherwise, it returns the result of evaluating itself in the next state, denoted by the next-state temporal operator $\bigcirc$. The number of compromised proposers that an attacker achieves (on average) within the time limit specified can be approximated by estimating the expected value of the formula over random runs of the protocol, denoted by the query **eval** $\mathbf{E}[ms(t_0)]$.

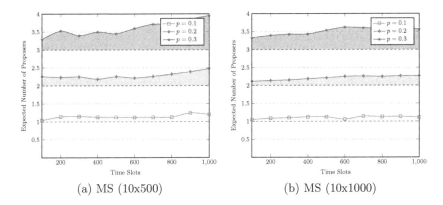

(a) MS (10x500)   (b) MS (10x1000)

Fig. 1. The expected number of attacker-controlled proposers in the proposers list against execution time in time slots, assuming the attacker is attempting to maximize the number of compromised proposers. The dashed lines represent the base values (with no active attack) computed using Eq. (1). The shaded areas visualize the expected bias achievable by the attacker for the three different attack probabilities plotted. We assume a proposers list of size 10, and a validator set of size (a) 10×500 and (b) 10×1000.

The analysis results for MS are plotted in the charts of Fig. 1. We use the notation $a \times b$ to denote the fact that the length of the proposers list (CYCLE-LENGTH) is a and that there are a total of $a \times b$ participating validators in the configuration[1]. The dashed lines in the charts represent the base values (with no active attack) computed using Eq. (1) for different attack probabilities p, while the plotted data points are the model's estimates.

As the charts show, the attacker can reliably but minimally bias randomness with this strategy. This, however, assumes that the attacker is able to afford all the skips that will have to be made in the process, since only after about 80

---

[1] The specific values for a and b used in this section and Sect. 5.2 are chosen so that the total size of the validator set $a \cdot b$ is large enough relative to the length of the proposers list a so that the probability of picking a compromised proposer stays the same (recall that the attack probability is fixed), while not too large to allow efficient analysis. This has the important consequence that the analysis results obtained are representative of actual setups (where the set of validators is much larger than that of the proposers), regardless of the exact proportion of proposers to validators.

rounds or so, the attacker is able to gain an advantage of about 20% (over the baseline). Nevertheless, an attacker that already controls a significant portion of the validators can capitalize on that to speed up his gains, as can be seen from the $p = 0.3$ attacker at around 100 rounds, compared with the weaker attackers. Furthermore, by comparing the charts in Fig. 1, we note that results obtained for different proportions of proposers to validators are generally similar.

5.2 Last-Word Score (LWS)

This is the length of the longest attacker-controlled tail of the proposers list in a round of the RANDAO process. We first compute a baseline value for LWS (assuming no attack). Let a be the event of picking an attacker-controlled validator, which has probability p, and b the event of picking an honest validator b, having probability $(1 - p)$. Let the length of the proposers list be k. A compromised tail in the proposers list corresponds to either a sequence of events a of length $j < k$ followed immediately by exactly one occurrence of event b, or a sequence of events a of length exactly k (the whole list is controlled by the attacker). Therefore, letting X be a random variable corresponding to the length of the longest compromised tail, we have:

$$Pr[X = i] = \begin{cases} p^i(1 - p) & i < k \\ p^i & i = k \end{cases}$$

Therefore, the expected value of X is

$$EX[X] = \sum_{i=0}^{k-1} i \cdot p^i(1 - p) + k \cdot p^k \tag{3}$$

We then specify the property LWS using the following formula:

$$lws(t) = \textbf{if } time() > t \textbf{ then } countCompromisedTail()$$
$$\textbf{else } \bigcirc lws(t) \textbf{ fi};\tag{4}$$
$$\textbf{eval } \mathbf{E}[lws(t_0)]$$

The formula uses the state function $countCompromisedTail()$, which counts the number of proposers in the longest compromised tail in the proposers list of the current state of the RANDAO object. As before, estimating the expectation expression $\mathbf{E}[lws(t_0)]$ gives an approximation of the expected length of the longest compromised tail that an attacker can achieve within the specified time limit.

The results are plotted in the charts of Fig. 2. As Fig. 2 shows, maximizing the length of the compromised tail can result in a steady and reliable effect on the proposers list. As the attack probability increases, the bias achieved can be greater within shorter periods of time. For example, at around 60 rounds, the bias achieved by a 0.1 attacker is negligible, while a 0.2 attacker is expected to achieve 20% gains over the baseline (at around 0.32 compared with 0.25), and a

0.3 attacker achieves 60% gains (at around 0.7 compared with 0.43). Nevertheless, even at high attack rates, the charts do not show strong increasing trends, suggesting that any gains more significant than those would require applying reveal strategies for very extended periods of time.

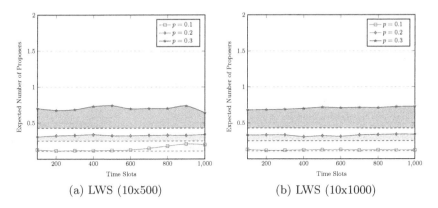

(a) LWS (10x500)   (b) LWS (10x1000)

Fig. 2. The expected number of attacker-controlled proposers in the proposers list against execution time in time slots, assuming the attacker is attempting to maximize the length of the compromised tail. The dashed lines represent the base values (with no active attack) computed using Eq. (3). The shaded areas visualize the expected bias achievable by the attacker for the three different attack probabilities plotted. We assume a proposers list of size 10, and a validator set of size (a) 10×500 and (b) 10×1000.

6   Conclusion

We presented an executable formalization of the commit-reveal RANDAO scheme as a probabilistic rewrite theory in rewriting logic. Through its specification in MAUDE, we used the model to analyze resilience of RANDAO against pre-computed reveal strategies by defining two quantitative measures of achievable bias: the matching score (MS) and the last-word score (LWS), specified as temporal properties in QuaTEx and analyzed using statistical model checking and quantitative analysis with PVESTA. Further analysis could consider other scenarios with dynamic validator sets, unreliable communication media and extended network latency. Furthermore, the analysis presented does not explicitly quantify the costs to the attacker, which can be an important economic defense against mounting these reveal strategies. An extension of the model could keep track of the number of skips, or specify a limit on these skips, so that the success of an attack strategy can be made relative to the cost of executing it. Finally, a holistic approach to analyzing quantitative properties of Serenity looking into availability and attack resilience properties makes for an interesting longer-term research direction.

Acknowledgements. We thank Danny Ryan and Justin Drake from the Ethereum Foundation for their very helpful comments. This work was performed under the first Ethereum Foundation security grant "Casper formal verification" [10].

References

1. Agha, G., Meseguer, J., Sen, K.: PMaude: rewrite-based specification language for probabilistic object systems. Electron. Notes Theor. Comput. Sci. **153**(2), 213–239 (2006)
2. AlTurki, M., Meseguer, J.: PVESTA: a parallel statistical model checking and quantitative analysis tool. In: Corradini, A., Klin, B., Cîrstea, C. (eds.) CALCO 2011. LNCS, vol. 6859, pp. 386–392. Springer, Heidelberg (2011). https://doi.org/10.1007/978-3-642-22944-2_28
3. Alturki, M.A., Roşu, G.: Statistical model checking of RANDAO's resilience against pre-computed reveal strategies. Technical report, The University of Illinois at Urbana-Champaign, November 2018. http://hdl.handle.net/2142/102076
4. Boneh, D., Bonneau, J., Bünz, B., Fisch, B.: Verifiable delay functions. Proc. Crypto **2018**, 757–788 (2018)
5. Bruni, R., Meseguer, J.: Semantic foundations for generalized rewrite theories. Theor. Comput. Sci. **360**(1–3), 386–414 (2006)
6. Buterin, V.: RANDAO Beacon exploitability analysis, round 2, November 2018. https://ethresear.ch/t/randao-beacon-exploitability-analysis-round-2/1980
7. Buterin, V.: RNG exploitability analysis assuming pure RANDAO-based main chain, November 2018. https://ethresear.ch/t/rng-exploitability-analysis-assuming-pure-randao-based-main-chain/1825
8. Buterin, V.: Validator ordering and randomness in PoS, November 2018. https://vitalik.ca/files/randomness.html
9. Clavel, M., et al.: All About Maude - A High-Performance Logical Framework. LNCS, vol. 4350. Springer, Heidelberg (2007). https://doi.org/10.1007/978-3-540-71999-1
10. Ethereum Foundation: Announcing beneficiaries of the Ethereum Foundation grants, November 2018. https://blog.ethereum.org/2018/03/07/announcing-beneficiaries-ethereum-foundation-grants
11. Ethereum Foundation: Ethereum 2.0 spec - Casper and Sharding, November 2018. https://github.com/ethereum/eth2.0-specs/blob/master/specs/beacon-chain.md
12. Kumar, N., Sen, K., Meseguer, J., Agha, G.: A rewriting based model for probabilistic distributed object systems. In: Najm, E., Nestmann, U., Stevens, P. (eds.) FMOODS 2003. LNCS, vol. 2884, pp. 32–46. Springer, Heidelberg (2003). https://doi.org/10.1007/978-3-540-39958-2_3
13. Meseguer, J.: Rewriting as a unified model of concurrency. In: Baeten, J.C.M., Klop, J.W. (eds.) CONCUR 1990. LNCS, vol. 458, pp. 384–400. Springer, Heidelberg (1990). https://doi.org/10.1007/BFb0039072
14. Meseguer, J.: Conditional rewriting logic as a unified model of concurrency. Theor. Comput. Sci. **96**(1), 73–155 (1992). https://doi.org/10.1016/0304-3975(92)90182-F

15. Meseguer, J.: Membership algebra as a logical framework for equational specification. In: Presicce, F.P. (ed.) WADT 1997. LNCS, vol. 1376, pp. 18–61. Springer, Heidelberg (1998). https://doi.org/10.1007/3-540-64299-4_26
16. Qian, Y.: RANDAO: A DAO working as RNG of Ethereum, November 2018. https://github.com/randao/randao/
17. Sen, K., Kumar, N., Meseguer, J., Agha, G.: Probabilistic rewrite theories: unifying models, logics and tools. Technical report, UIUCDCS-R-2003-2347, University of Illinois at Urbana Champaign, May 2003

A Distributed Blockchain Model
of Selfish Mining

Dennis Eijkel and Ansgar Fehnker[✉]

University of Twente, P.O. Box 217, 7500AE Enschede, The Netherlands
d.j.eijkel@student.utwente.nl, ansgar.fehnker@utwente.nl

Abstract. Bitcoin, still the most widely used cryptocurrency maintains
a distributed ledger for transactions known as the blockchain. Miners
should expect a reward proportional to the computational power they
provide to the network. Eyal and Sirer introduced *seflish mining*, a strategy gives a significant edge in profits. This paper models the behaviour
of honest and selfish mining pools in UPPAAL. Unlike earlier models in
literature, it does not assume a single view of the blockchain but does
include the presence of network delay.

Results for our model show the effects of selfish mining on the share
of profits, but more importantly the outwards observable effect on the
number of orphaned blocks. This paper compares the analysis results to
known results from literature and real-world data.

Keywords: Bitcoin · Bitcoin mining · Selfish mining · UPPAAL

1 Introduction

Bitcoin [3,12] is at the time of writing the most used cryptocurrency [5] by
market capitalisation. Miners in the Bitcoin network are incentivised by the
reward that they receive for validating new blocks of transactions. Miners expect
to receive their fair share of said reward, proportional to their computational
share of the network. The Bitcoin protocol does not specify when miners must
publish their newly found blocks. The most basic strategy is to publish them
immediately after the miner finds them. This is referred to as the *honest* strategy.

Eyal and Sirer introduced a strategy for publishing newly found blocks called
selfish mining [9], which strategically responds to what other miners in the network find and publish. They found that this strategy forces honest miners to
waste computational power.

The contribution of this paper are a UPPAAL-SMC model for selfish mining.
It models a blockchain network as a network of nodes, each with their own copy of
the blockchain, and includes stochastic network delays. These aspects are absent
from the Eyal and Sirer's models. UPPAAL-SMC can then analyse the behaviour
of the network and the evolution of the blockchain over the simulation time – one
day – and compare this with historical data obtained from the real blockchain.

© Springer Nature Switzerland AG 2020
E. Sekerinski et al. (Eds.): FM 2019 Workshops, LNCS 12232, pp. 350–361, 2020.
https://doi.org/10.1007/978-3-030-54994-7_26

In particular, how selfish mining affects the number of expected forks. This all is achieved with a single modelling artifact.

The next section describes related work, followed by a section on *selfish mining*. Section 4 describes the UPPAAL-SMC model, and Sect. 5 the results of the analysis. Sect. 6 will conclude with a discussion of future work.

2   Related Work

Eyal and Sirer provide in [9] pseudo-code for selfish mining, along with a mathematical model of the forking behaviour of the blockchain, and an additional model for the rewards. They compute the expected rewards in the steady-state, i.e. in the long run, using a Monto-Carlo Simulation model. For this, they computed a threshold for which selfish mining will increase the profit of the miner. Below this threshold, selfish mining will incur a penalty for the selfish miner. In contrast to this paper the use multiple modelling artifacts, assume a single view on the public blockchain, disregards network delays, and do not consider the number of observable forks.

Chaudary et al. used UPPAAL in [8] to model majority attacks. Their paper focuses on blockchain forking and included a detailed model of the blockchain. In [10] the same authors present a simplified version of the model presented in this paper to analyse a particular type of majority attack, intended to enforce a new Bitcoin standard. UPPAAL was also used by Andrychowicz et al. to verify the security of Bitcoin contracts, and to repair several issues in the protocol [6]. These consider other type of attacks than this paper.

Sapirshtein et al. mathematically investigate bounds for which selfish mining is profitable and optimize the original strategy [14]. They show that selfish mining can be optimized, such that the threshold above which the strategy is profitable is lower than described in the original paper [9]. Heilman et al. used Monte-Carlo simulation to investigate eclipse attacks and proposed countermeasures that will reduce the chances of such attacks to succeed [11]. Neudecker presents a full-scale simulation model of Bitcoin to study partition attacks [13]. While these paper study variations of a selfish mining, they do not discuss the observable behavior over a day, or a comparison with real world data.

3   The Bitcoin Mining Process and Selfish Mining

Bitcoin is a distributed and decentralized cryptocurrency [3,12] with a shared ledger of transactions which is stored in an append-only chain of *blocks* called the *blockchain*. A block contains a group of transactions, the hash of the preceding block, and a nonce. Since the block also includes the hash of the preceding block it defines a chain of blocks.

Nodes in the peer-to-peer Bitcoin network run a process, known as *mining*, to validate blocks of transactions, as well as to induce an order on transactions. Validation entails finding random nonce such that the hash value of the block falls below a certain threshold. Finding such a nonce can be considered to be

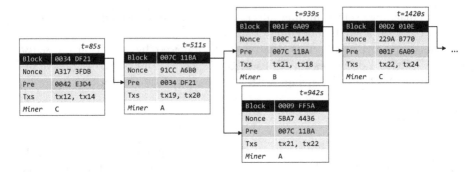

Fig. 1. Illustration of the Blockchain as hash-chain of blocks of transactions. For simplicity each block contains only two transactions.

a stochastic process with an exponential distribution, and is called the *proof-of-work challenge*. The threshold is regularly updated and agreed upon by the entire network such that a new block will be found on average every 10 min.

Figure 1 illustrates a blockchain. It starts with a block found by Miner C at t=85s, followed by a successor found by Miner A at t=511s. Due to the distributed nature of the network two pools may find a block at about the same time: in the example Miner B at t=939s, and Miner A at t=942s. If Miner A would have received the block of Miner B before it found its own, it would have abandoned its effort and switched to the `Block 001F 6A09`. The example assumes instead that Miner A found its own block first.

At this point, both blocks have been successfully mined as potential successors of `Block 007C 11BA`. Miners will continue with the block they receive first, and due to the distributed nature of the network, different pools may continue with mining different blocks, giving rise to so-called *forks*. It could take some time to resolve a fork and during that time, different views of the blockchain will exist. Blocks that fall outside of this longest chain are called *orphaned* blocks.

The race in Fig. 1 is resolved as soon as the next block is found; here Block `001F 6A09`. Once this happens the protocol stipulates that the blocks in the longest chain become part of the authoritative blockchain. Only miners of blocks in the longest chain will receive the rewards attached to mining. This incentivises miners to adopt the longest chain, and achieve consensus.

The Bitcoin protocol [3,12] does not specify when miners must publish their newly found blocks. The most basic strategy is to publish them immediately after they are mined. This is referred to as the *honest* strategy. Eyal and Sirer introduced a strategy for publishing newly found blocks called *selfish mining* [9].

Figure 2 illustrates one of the basic steps of selfish mining, intended to increase the number of forks. In this example, Miner C finds a block at t=7s. This block will be received by Miner A at t=8s, and by Miner B at t=11s[1]. All three miners will continue mining with this block. At t=99s Miner B finds

---

[1] Note, that in general, the network does not have access to a shared global time.

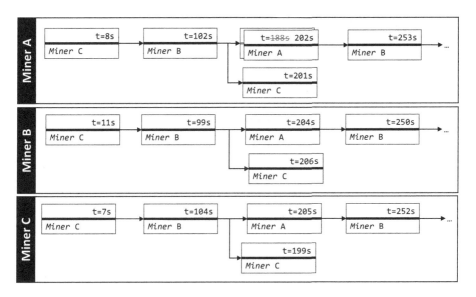

Fig. 2. Illustration of forks as races between different blockchains in a distributed network. Pool A is selfish miner, and postpones publication of a block found at t=188s until t=202s. This example omits for simplicity the hash values, nonces, and transactions.

a block and publishes it. It will be received by Miner A and C at t=102s and t=104s, respectively. Again all three miners will continue with this block. Up to this point, all miners employ honest mining.

Assume that Miner A employs the selfish strategy. If it finds a block at t=188s, it will not publish it immediately, but wait. If it receives a block by one of the other miners – in the example a block of Miner C at t=201s – it will publish its own block immediately, which intentionally creates a fork. The gamble is that its own block arrives at the others miners before the block of Miner C. In the example Miner B receives the block of Miner A before the block of Miner C, and thus continues mining the block of Miner A. If Miner B then finds a new block at time t=250s it will orphan the block Miner C found previously. Miner C's computational power from t=104s until t=252s – when it received the block of Miner B – was effectively wasted.

The question is if this can actually be beneficial for the selfish miner. In the example, Miner A forwent a certain reward for the block it found at t=188s to enter a race with pool C at t=202s. This looks superficially like a disadvantageous strategy. However, Fig. 2 describes only one step of selfish mining, namely the step that intentionally introduces forks.

The following gives a full list of steps for the selfish miners. It assumes that the selfish miner always mines at the end of its own private chain.

1. **The selfish miner finds a block.**
   (a) **There is a fork, and both branches have length 1.** In this case, the selfish miner found a block to decide the race in its favour. The selfish miner appends the block to its private chain and publishes it. The selfish miner intends to orphan the single block in the public branch, and secure the rewards of its own branch.
   (b) **Otherwise.** The new block will be appended to its private chain, without publishing it. This includes cases where the private chain is two or more blocks ahead of the public chain.
2. **The selfish miner receives a block.** Provided that it actually increases the height of the public chain, the selfish miner will proceed as follows:
   (a) **If there is no fork.** This means the public and private chains are identical. The received block is appended to the public chain, and the public chain is adopted as the private chain. The other miner will receive the rewards.
   (b) **There is one unpublished block in the private branch.** The received block is appended to the public chain. The unpublished block is published. This is the scenario depicted in Fig. 5.
   (c) **There are two unpublished blocks in the private branch.** The private chain is published. Since the public chain should still be one block behind, this would secure all rewards in the private branch for the selfish miner. After this, there is no fork.
   (d) **Otherwise.** This is the case when the selfish miner is more than two blocks in the lead. The selfish miner will publish the first unpublished block. While the private chain is at least two blocks ahead, the public branch and the portion of the private branch that has been published have the same height. To other miners, a race is ongoing, even though the selfish miner already has the blocks to decide the race in its favour.

To implement this strategy the selfish miner needs to maintain a record of the head of the public chain, of the head of the private chain, the head of the portion of the private chain that has been published, and the block where the private and public chain fork. It should be noted that the *public* chain is the local view that the selfish miner has of the blockchain. As discussed previously, in general, different miners may have different views.

Eyal and Sirer have shown that a miner using selfish mining will gain more rewards than would be proportional to their computational power, under the assumption that the other miners use the honest strategy. This result depends on the share α of computational power the selfish miner has in the network and the fraction γ of miners that adopt the block of the selfish miner in case of a fork. They discovered that selfish mining gives an increased reward if $(1 - \gamma)/(3 - 2\gamma) < \alpha$. This means, for example, that if a quarter of the other nodes adopt the block of the selfish miner, i.e. $\gamma = 0.25$, then the selfish mining strategy will pay off if the network share satisfies $\alpha > 0.3$.

4   Uppaal Model

UPPAAL-SMC is an extension of the model-checker UPPAAL, and adds stochastic delays and probabilistic choice to the timed automata of [7]. It provides a specification language for probability estimation, hypothesis testing, and value estimation.

Our UPPAAL-SMC model consists of three templates: one for modelling the behaviour of an honest miner, one for a selfish miner, and one the propagation delay between miners. A fourth template observes the blockchain but does not take part in the protocol. It is omitted here, but included in the published model.

Global Variables and Constants. The model includes two arrays of broadcast channels, sendBlock[POOLS] and recvBlock[POOLS], for miners to send and receive blocks, where POOLS is the number of miners. A block is defined as a struct of the height, a bounded integer BlockIndex, and array rewards[POOLS]. If a miner with ID id mines a new block, it increments height and rewards[id].

Global variable syncBlock is used as an auxiliary to copy blocks between processes. Important constants are integer PDELAY for the expected network delay, and integer array POOL_RATES[POOLS], which contains for each miner the rate at which it finds blocks. The model uses as basic time unit 1 s; a rate of 1200 means that a miner finds on average one block every 1200 s.

Network Links. The network link between any two miners is modelled as a one-place buffer with delay. For any pair of IDs in and out, the model includes one instance of the link template, depicted in Fig. 3. From the initial state it synchronizes on channel sendBlock[in] with Pool in and copy the received block in global variable syncBlock to its local variable blockBuffer. It then enters the location to the right, where it synchronizes on channel recvBlock[out] with Miner out at a rate of 1 in PDELAY seconds. This transition copies the value of the buffer to syncBlock. If it receives another block from Miner in, it stores that block in the buffer. Note, that the model includes for any pair of miners one link, i.e. for a network with 10 miners, 100 links, each with its own buffer.

Honest Mining. Figure 4 shows an honest miner with ID id. It has a single location with two edges. The first edge models mining a block. It calls method outputBlock which increments the height of its private chain and the rewards for itself. The other edge models receiving a block which calls method updateBlock. It adopts the new block if it improves the height of its private chain.

Selfish Mining. The selfish miner keeps a record of four blocks: the head of the private chain privateBlock, the head of the public chain publicBlock, the most recently published block publishedBlock, and the block where the public and the private chain fork, forkBlock. In addition, it uses a local Boolean publishBlock to encodes if a block should be published.

The top-most edge models mining a block (case 1 on Page 5). It calls method mineBlock() at a rate of 1 in POOL_RATE[id] seconds, and decides whether to publish (part of) its private chain.

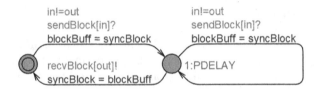

Fig. 3. Parameters of the link template are the ID of sender in and receiver out.

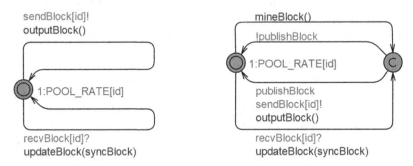

Fig. 4. The honest mining template has as parameter the id of the miner.

Fig. 5. The selfish mining template has as parameter the id of the miner.

The bottom-most edge models receiving a block (case 2 on Page 5). It synchronizes on recvBlock[id], and calls updateBlock which decides whether to append it to the private chain, or whether to publish a part of the private chain. It sets Boolean publishBlock to true if a block should be published.

The committed location in the mining template in Fig. 5 completes the process. If mineBlock() or updateBlock set publishBlock to false, the selfish miner returns silently to the initial location. If publishBlock is true, outputBlock copies the block to be published to syncBlock, and to publishedBlock and publicBlock. Listing 1 gives the code for mineBlock() and updateBlock.

Limitations. UPPAAL-SMC only facilitates exponential distributions, i.e. memoryless delays. In absence of a validated network model we assumed a uniform network with identical links. However, real or pathological networks such as a Sybil attacks could be analysed by adjusting the individual delays, or removing links altogether. A uniform network is not a necessity.

System Composition. The analysis in Sect. 5 uses 10 miners and 100 links. It considers the 6 sets of network shares, as given in Table 1. The selfish miner would be Miner A. Miner B has a share of 20% in all experiments to make the results comparable. A share of 20% would correspond to finding a block once every 3000 s, assuming a network rate of one block every 600 s. These rates are simplified but still largely similar to the distribution of hash rates in the real world [4]. UPPAAL-SMC simulated each scenario 1000 times for one day of simulation time, i.e. for 86400 s. The simulation of one single scenario takes about 80 s on an Intel Core i5-5200 with 2 cores at 2.2 GHz.

```
1   void mineBlock() {//case 1
2       if (privateBlock.height == publicBlock.height &&
3           privateBlock.height-forkBlock.height == 1) {//case 1.(a)
4           privateBlock.height++;
5           privateBlock.rewards[id]++;
6           outputBuffer    = privateBlock;
7           forkBlock       = privateBlock;
8           publishBlock    = true;
9       }
10      else{                                          //case 1.(b)
11          privateBlock.height++;
12          privateBlock.rewards[id]++;
13          publishBlock    = false;
14      }
15  }
16
17  void updateBlock(Block newBlock) {                 //case 2
18      if (newBlock.height>publicBlock.height) {
19          if(newBlock.height>privateBlock.height){   //case 2.(a)
20              privateBlock    = newBlock;
21              forkBlock       = newBlock;
22              publishedBlock  = newBlock;
23              publicBlock     = newBlock;
24              publishBlock    = false;
25          }
26          else
27          if(newBlock.height == privateBlock.height) {//case 2.(b)
28              outputBuffer    = privateBlock;
29              publishBlock    = true;
30          }else                                      //case 2.(c)
31          if(newBlock.height == privateBlock.height-1) {
32              outputBuffer    = privateBlock;
33              forkBlock       = privateBlock;
34              publishBlock    = true;
35          }
36          else {                                     //case 2.(d)
37              publishedBlock.height++;
38              publishedBlock.rewards[id]++;
39              outputBuffer    = publishedBlock;
40              publishBlock    = true;
41          }
42      }
43  }
```

Listing 1. Essential methods of the selfish miner.

Table 1. Network shares for different scenarios. Miner **A** may be selfish, Miner **B** is the reference miner.

Scenario	A	B	C	D	E	F	G	H	I	J
#1	1%	20%	20%	15%	15%	10%	10%	5%	2%	2%
#2	10%	20%	20%	15%	15%	10%	5%	2%	2%	1%
#3	20%	20%	15%	15%	10%	10%	5%	2%	2%	1%
#4	30%	20%	15%	10%	10%	5%	5%	2%	2%	1%
#5	40%	20%	10%	10%	5%	5%	5%	2%	2%	1%
#6	50%	20%	10%	5%	5%	2%	2%	2%	2%	2%

5   Analysis Results

This section presents for a 24 h period the expected mining rewards and the expected number of orphaned blocks. The former allows a comparison with results by Eyal and Sirer, the latter with data obtained from the publicly available Bitcoin blockchain.

Mining Rewards. Figure 6 depicts the height and rewards for different miners. First is the number of *blocks mined* over the 24 h period. It is around 144 blocks, as expected for a network that finds on average one block every 10 min.

Not all of these blocks will become part of the longest chain. Figure 6 gives the blockchain height and the reward of the selfish and first honest miner, reward selfish and reward honest, respectively. Each of these three come in two versions depending on whether it is part of the private chain of the selfish miner, or the chain as known by the network.

These results show that as the network share of the selfish miner increases, it decreases the height of the blockchain, and increases the rewards for the selfish miner. For a 50% share the height is 89.4 and the reward 68.9, in the private blockchain of the selfish miner. In the blockchain of the first honest miner – Miner B in Table 1 – the height is only 81.7 and the reward of the selfish miner is only 57.7. The difference is partly due to network delay, but mostly because the selfish miner has a buffer of 7.6 unpublished blocks in its private chain.

Figure 7 translates these numbers to shares in the rewards. It also includes the nominal share these miners should achieve; the selfish miner proportionally to its network share, and the honest miner 20%. The results show that selfish mining becomes profitable once the network share of the selfish miner exceeds 29.6%.

Eyal and Sirer's define the threshold in terms of γ, the probability that other miners adopt the block of the selfish miner above a competing block. For this to happen two steps have to succeed: (1) the selfish miner has to receive the competing block before the other miners, (2) the block sent by the selfish miner in response has to arrive before the competing block. Given that all delays use the same memoryless distribution both steps succeed with a 50% chance, giving an overall chance of 25%. Eyal and Sirer predict a threshold of 30% for this case, while in Fig. 7 the share of the 30% selfish miner is 29.6%.

Figure 8 shows how this evolves over 24 h for a selfish miner with a 50% network share. Initially, the selfish miner will appear to have a share that is below its 50% network share, as it is secretly mining blocks. As the day progresses its share will quickly exceed 80%.

All results of this section are based on a propagation delay of 4 s. For the expected rewards the propagation delay has little to no influence. The next subsection discusses the effect of different propagation delays in more detail.

Orphaned Blocks. An essential aspect of selfish mining is to create forks such that other miners waste computational resources on blocks that are bound to be orphaned. To compare the models with data from the actual Bitcoin blockchain,

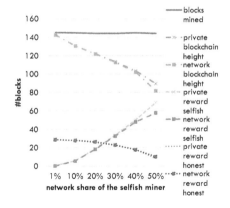

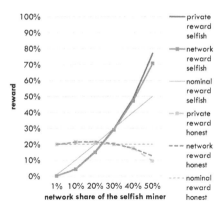

Fig. 6. Height and rewards of selfish and honest miner after 24 h.

Fig. 7. Share of rewards for selfish and honest miner after 24 h.

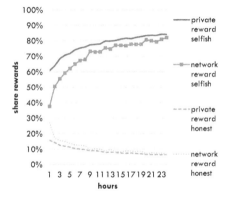

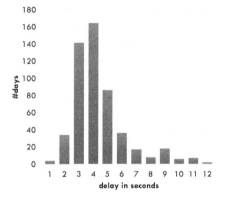

Fig. 8. Share of rewards per hour for the honest and selfish miner over 24 h.

Fig. 9. Histogram of the propagation delays in the selected data set.

we combined the data on orphaned blocks [2] with data on propagation times [1]. This gave 528 usable data points in the period from 18 March 2014 to 22 March 2017, i.e. days with both data on orphaned blocks and propagation times. Figure 9 shows the distribution of days over different propagation times, rounded to the nearest integer second. This leaves us with a reasonable data set for propagation delays in the interval from 2 to 7 s.

Figure 10 shows the number of expected orphans if we have a network without any selfish miner. The figure includes, for reference, the number of orphans from the real data set, labelled *real*. The results show that as the delay increases, the number of orphans increases as well. Except for the data point for 7 s, the real data falls into the range given by the simulation.

This picture changes once we introduce a selfish miner as depicted in Fig. 11. Even a selfish miner with only a 1% network share leads to more orphans than for

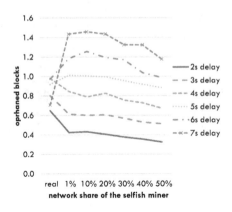
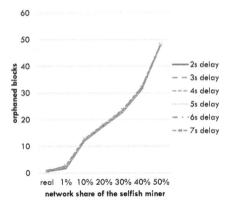

Fig. 10. Number of orphaned blocks in network w/o selfish miner after 24 h.

Fig. 11. Number of orphaned blocks in network with selfish miner after 24 h.

any scenario with only honest miners or the real data. This comparison suggests that there is no evidence in the real data of a prolonged presence of a selfish miner with a significant network share.

6   Conclusion

This paper's contributions are twofold: on modelling a selfish mining attack, and on the outward effects of such an attack.

On Modelling. In [9], Eyal and Sirer provide a pseudocode algorithm for selfish mining. The analysis uses a separate state transition model that captures the presence and length of a fork. Based on this model they manually derived state probabilities and expected rewards for each state. To validate the overall reward they use Monte Carlo Simulation. Their combination of models assumes a single view of the public chain where blocks are propagated instantly to provide estimates of the rewards a selfish miner can expect in the long run.

This paper presented a single unified modelling artefact. It also includes propagation delays, a block model with rewards, and a distributed blockchain. It does not separate the pseudo-code from the transition probabilities, rewards, and the analysis of the evolution of the network over time. This allowed an automated analysis from the perspective of different participants, and compare these to the theoretical results by Eyal and Sirer, as well as to real-world data.

On Selfish Mining. The analysis confirms the known result that selfish mining becomes profitable for networks shares above 30%. The model in this paper additionally shows that while a selfish miner may go undetected for the first few hours, it would be obvious after that and difficult to conceal. The number of forks is unlike anything that could occur naturally by propagation delay. Real-world data provides no evidence of a prolonged presence of a selfish miner with a significant network share.

Future Work. Future work would need to investigate how to identify a short-term attack on a blockchain. For this type of analysis, it is especially important to distinguish between the different views of the blockchain of different participants, as it is done in this paper. Such an analysis could consider real or pathological network topologies, such as a Sybil attack.

Resources. All UPPAAL-SMC models, simulation data and more detailed results are available on https://wwwhome.ewi.utwente.nl/~fehnkera/Q19.

References

1. Bitcoinstats, network propagation times. http://bitcoinstats.com/network/propagation/. Accessed 06 July 2019
2. Bitcoin.info, number of orphaned blocks (2008). https://blockchain.info/charts/n-orphaned-blocks?timespan=all. Accessed 06 July 2019
3. Bitcoin protocol rules (2019). https://en.bitcoin.it/wiki/Protocol_rules. Accessed 06 July 2019
4. Blockchain.info, hashrate distribution (2019). https://blockchain.info/pools. Accessed 06 July 2019
5. Coinmarketcap: Cryptocurrency market capitalizations (2019). https://coinmarketcap.com/. Accessed 06 July 2019
6. Andrychowicz, M., Dziembowski, S., Malinowski, D., Mazurek, Ł.: Modeling bitcoin contracts by timed automata. In: Legay, A., Bozga, M. (eds.) FORMATS 2014. LNCS, vol. 8711, pp. 7–22. Springer, Cham (2014). https://doi.org/10.1007/978-3-319-10512-3_2
7. Bulychev, P., et al.: UPPAAL-SMC: statistical model checking for priced timed automata. EPTCS 85 (2012)
8. Chaudhary, K., Fehnker, A., van de Pol, J., Stoelinga, M.: Modeling and verification of the bitcoin protocol. In: MARS 2015 (2015). EPTCS
9. Eyal, I., Sirer, E.G.: Majority is not enough: bitcoin mining is vulnerable. In: Christin, N., Safavi-Naini, R. (eds.) FC 2014. LNCS, vol. 8437, pp. 436–454. Springer, Heidelberg (2014). https://doi.org/10.1007/978-3-662-45472-5_28
10. Fehnker, A., Chaudhary, K.: Twenty percent and a few days – optimising a bitcoin majority attack. In: Dutle, A., Muñoz, C., Narkawicz, A. (eds.) NFM 2018. LNCS, vol. 10811, pp. 157–163. Springer, Cham (2018). https://doi.org/10.1007/978-3-319-77935-5_11
11. Heilman, E., Kendler, A., Zohar, A., Goldberg, S.: Eclipse attacks on bitcoin's peer-to-peer network. In: SEC 2015 (2015). USENIX Association
12. Nakamoto, S.: Bitcoin: a peer-to-peer electronic cash system (2008). http://bitcoin.org/bitcoin.pdf
13. Neudecker, T., Andelfinger, P., Hartenstein, H.: A simulation model for analysis of attacks on the bitcoin peer-to-peer network. In: INM 2015 (2015)
14. Sapirshtein, A., Sompolinsky, Y., Zohar, A.: Optimal selfish mining strategies in bitcoin. In: Grossklags, J., Preneel, B. (eds.) FC 2016. LNCS, vol. 9603, pp. 515–532. Springer, Heidelberg (2017). https://doi.org/10.1007/978-3-662-54970-4_30

Towards a Verified Model of the Algorand Consensus Protocol in Coq

Musab A. Alturki[1], Jing Chen[2], Victor Luchangco[2], Brandon Moore[1],
Karl Palmskog[3(✉)], Lucas Peña[4], and Grigore Roşu[4]

[1] Runtime Verification, Inc., Urbana, IL, USA
{musab.alturki,brandon.moore}@runtimeverification.com
[2] Algorand, Inc., Boston, MA, USA
{jing,victor}@algorand.com
[3] KTH Royal Institute of Technology, Stockholm, Sweden
palmskog@acm.org
[4] University of Illinois at Urbana-Champaign, Urbana, IL, USA
{lpena7,grosu}@illinois.edu

Abstract. The Algorand blockchain is a secure and decentralized public ledger based on pure proof of stake rather than proof of work. At its core it is a novel consensus protocol with exactly one block certified in each round: that is, the protocol guarantees that the blockchain does not fork. In this paper, we report on our effort to model and formally verify the Algorand consensus protocol in the Coq proof assistant. Similar to previous consensus protocol verification efforts, we model the protocol as a state transition system and reason over reachable global states. However, in contrast to previous work, our model explicitly incorporates timing issues (e.g., timeouts and network delays) and adversarial actions, reflecting a more realistic environment faced by a public blockchain.

Thus far, we have proved *asynchronous safety* of the protocol: two different blocks cannot be certified in the same round, even when the adversary has complete control of message delivery in the network. We believe that our model is sufficiently general and other relevant properties of the protocol such as liveness can be proved for the same model.

Keywords: Algorand · Byzantine consensus · Blockchain · Coq

1 Introduction

The Algorand blockchain is a scalable and permissionless public ledger for secure and decentralized digital currencies and transactions. To determine the next block, it uses a novel consensus protocol [1,3] based on pure proof of stake. In contrast to Bitcoin [6] and other blockchains based on proof of work, where safety is achieved by making it computationally expensive to add blocks, Algorand's consensus protocol is highly efficient and does not require solving cryptographic puzzles. Instead, it uses *cryptographic self-selection*, which allows each user to individually determine whether it is selected into the committees responsible

© Springer Nature Switzerland AG 2020
E. Sekerinski et al. (Eds.): FM 2019 Workshops, LNCS 12232, pp. 362–367, 2020.
https://doi.org/10.1007/978-3-030-54994-7_27

for generating the next block. The self-selection is done independently by every participant, with probability proportional to its stake. Private communication channels are not needed; committees propagate their messages in public. They reach Byzantine consensus on the next block and certify it, so that all users learn the next block without ambiguity. That is, rather than waiting for a long time so as to be sure that a block will not disappear from the longest chain, as in Bitcoin, the Algorand blockchain does not fork: a certified block is immediately final, and transactions contained in it can be relied upon right away. The Algorand blockchain guarantees fast generation of blocks as long as the underlying propagation network is not partitioned (i.e., as long as messages are delivered in a timely fashion). The Algorand consensus protocol, its core technology, and mathematical proofs of its safety and liveness properties are described in [1–3].

The focus of this work is to formally model and verify the Algorand consensus protocol (described in [2,3]) using the Coq proof assistant. Automated formal verification of desired properties adds another level of assurance about its correctness, and developing a precise model to capture the protocol's runtime environment and the assumptions it depends on is interesting from a formal-methods perspective as well. For example, [11] proves state machine safety and linearizability for the Raft consensus protocol in a non-Byzantine setting, and [7] focuses on safety properties of blockchains and, using a largest-chain-based fork-choice rule and a clique network topology, proves eventual consistency for an abstract parameterized protocol. Similar to previous work, we define a transition system relation on global protocol states and reason inductively over *traces* of states reachable via the relation from some initial state. We abstract away details on cryptographic primitives, modeling them as functions with the desired properties. We also omit details related to blockchain transactions and currencies.

However, our goal and various aspects of the Algorand protocol present new challenges. First, our goal is to verify the protocol's asynchronous safety under Byzantine faults. Thus, we explicitly allow arbitrary adversarial actions, such as user corruption and message replay. Also, rather than assuming a particular network topology, the Algorand protocol assumes that messages are delivered within given real-valued deadlines when the network is not partitioned (messages may be arbitrarily delayed and their delivery is fully controlled by the adversary when the network is partitioned). We capture this by explicitly modeling global time progression and message delivery deadlines in the underlying propagation network. Moreover, as mentioned above, the Algorand protocol uses cryptographic self-selection to randomly select committees responsible for generating blocks. As mechanizing probabilistic analysis is still an open field in formal verification, instead of trying to fully capture randomized committee selection, we identify properties of the committees that are used to verify the correctness of the protocol without reference to the protocol itself. We then express these properties as axioms in our formal model. Pen-and-paper proofs that these properties hold (with overwhelming probability) can be found in [1,3].

It is worth pointing out that our approach is based on reasoning about *global* states, in contrast to [8], which formally verifies the PBFT protocol under arbitrary local actions. While it is possible to model coordinated actions as in [8], our model explicitly allows an adversary to arbitrarily coordinate actions (at the network level) among corrupted users using both newly forged and valid past messages. Finally, [10] uses distributed separation logic for consensus protocol verification in Coq with non-Byzantine failures. Using this approach to verify protocols under Byzantine faults is an interesting avenue of future work.

Thus far, we have proved in Coq *asynchronous safety*: two different blocks can never be certified in the same round, even when the adversary has complete control of the network. We believe that our model is sufficiently general to allow other relevant properties of the protocol such as liveness to be proved.

2   The Algorand Consensus Protocol

In this section, we give a brief overview of the Algorand consensus protocol with details salient to our formal model. More details can be found in [1,3,5].

All users participating in the protocol have unique identifiers (public keys). The protocol proceeds in *rounds* and each user learns a *certified* block for each round. Rounds are asynchronous: each user individually starts a new round whenever it learns a certified block for its current round.

A round consists of one or more *periods*, which are attempts to generate a certified block. A period consists of several *steps*: users propose blocks and then vote to certify a proposal. Specifically, each user waits a fixed amount of time (determined by network parameters) to receive proposals, and then votes to support the proposal with the best *credential*, as described below; these votes are called *soft-votes*. If it receives a quorum of soft-votes, it then votes to certify the block; these votes are called *cert-votes*. A user considers a block certified if it receives a quorum of cert-votes. If a user doesn't receive a quorum of cert-votes within a certain amount of time, it votes to begin a new period; these votes are called *next-votes*. A next-vote may be for a proposal, if the user received a quorum of soft-votes for it, or it may be *open*. A user begins a new period when it receives a quorum of next-votes from the same step for the same proposal or a quorum of open next-votes; and repeats the next-vote logic otherwise.

Committees. For scalability, not all users send their messages in every step. Instead, a committee is randomly selected for each step via a technique called *cryptographic self-selection*: each user independently determines whether it is in the committee using a *verifiable random function* (VRF). Only users in the committee send messages for that step, along with a *credential* generated by the VRF to prove they are selected. Credentials are totally ordered, and the ones accompanying proposals are used to determine which proposal to support.

Network. Users communicate by propagating messages over the network. Message delivery is asynchronous and may be out-of-order, but delivery times are bounded: any message sent or received by an honest user is received by all honest users within a fixed amount of time unless the network is *partitioned*. (There is no bound on message delivery time if the network is partitioned.)

Adversary. The adversary can corrupt any user and control and coordinate corrupted users' actions: for example, to resend old messages, send any message for future steps of the adversary's choice, and decide when and to whom the messages are sent by them. The adversary also controls when messages are delivered between honest users within the bounds described above, and fully controls message delivery when the network is partitioned. The adversary must control less than 1/3 of the total stake participating in the consensus protocol.

3   Model

Our Coq model of the protocol, which is an abstracted version of the latest Algorand consensus protocol described in [2,3], is a transition system encoded as an inductive binary relation on global states. The transition relation is parameterized on finite types of user identifiers (`UserId`) and values (`Value`); the latter abstractly represents blocks and block hashes.

User and Global State. We represent both user state and global state as Coq records. For brevity, we omit a few components of the user state in this paper and only show some key ones, such as the Boolean indicating whether a user is corrupt, the local time, round, period, step, and blocks and cert-votes that have been observed. The global state has the global time, user states and messages via finite maps [4], and a Boolean indicating whether the network is partitioned.

```
Record UState := mkUState {        Record GState := mkGState {
 corrupt: bool; timer: R;           network_partition: bool;
 round: N; period: N; step: N;      now: R;
 blocks: N → seq Value;             users: {fmap UserId → UState};
 certvotes: N → N → seq Vote;       msgs: {fmap UserId → {mset R * Msg}};
 (* ... omitted ... *)              msg_history: {mset Msg};
}.                                  }.
```

State Transition System. The transition relation on global states g and g', written $g \leadsto g'$, is defined in the usual way via inductive rules. For example, the rule for adversary message replay is as follows:

```
step_replay_msg : ∀ (pre:GState) uid (ustate_key : uid ∈ pre.(users)) msg,
  ¬ pre.(users).[ustate_key].(corrupt) → msg ∈ pre.(msg_history) →
  pre ⤳ replay_msg_result pre uid msg
```

Here, `replay_msg_result` is a function that builds a global state where `msg` is broadcast. We call a sequence of global states a *trace* if it is nonempty and $g \leadsto g'$ holds whenever g and g' are adjacent in the sequence.

Assumptions. To express assumptions about committees and quorums, we introduce a function `committee` that determines self-selected committees. For example, the following statement says that for any two quorums (i.e., subsets of size at least `tau`) of the committee for a given round-period-step triple, there is an honest user who belongs to both quorums:

```
Definition quorum_honest_overlap_statement (tau:N) :=
 ∀ (trace:seq GState) (r p s:N) (q1 q2:{fset UserId}),
   q1 ⊆ committee r p s → #|q1| ≥ tau →
   q2 ⊆ committee r p s → #|q2| ≥ tau →
   ∃ (honest_voter : UserId), honest_voter ∈ q1 ∧ honest_voter ∈ q2 ∧
   honest_during_step (r,p,s) honest_voter trace.
```

Similarly, we capture that a block was certified in a period as follows (the value 3 indicates the third step, the `certvote` step, in period p and round r):

```
Definition certified_in_period (trace:seq GState) (tau r p:N) (v:Value) :=
 ∃ (certvote_quorum:{fset UserId}),
   certvote_quorum ⊆ committee r p 3 ∧ #|certvote_quorum| ≥ tau ∧
   ∀ (voter:UserId), voter ∈ certvote_quorum →
   certvoted_in_path trace voter r p v.
```

This property is true for a trace if there exists a quorum of users selected for cert-voting who actually sent their votes in that trace for the given period (via `certvoted_in_path`, which we omit). This is without loss of generality since a corrupted user who did not send its cert-vote can be simulated by a corrupted user who sent its vote but the message is received by nobody.

4   Asynchronous Safety

The analysis of the protocol in the computational model shows that the probability of forking is negligible [1,3]. In contrast, we specify and prove formally in the *symbolic* model with idealized cryptographic primitives that at most one block is certified in a round, even in the face of adversary control over message delivery and corruption of users. We call this property *asynchronous safety*:

```
Theorem asynchronous_safety : ∀ (g0:GState) (trace:seq GState) (r:N),
   state_before_round r g0 → is_trace g0 trace →
   ∀ (p1:N) (v1:Value), certified_in_period trace r p1 v1 →
   ∀ (p2:N) (v2:Value), certified_in_period trace r p2 v2 →
   v1 = v2.
```

Here, the first precondition `state_before_round r g0` states that no user has taken any actions in round r in the initial global state g0, and the second precondition `is_trace g0 trace` states that `trace` follows ⤳ and starts in g0.

Note that it is possible to end up with block certifications from multiple periods of a round. Specifically, during a network partition, which allows the adversary to delay messages, this can happen if cert-vote messages are delayed enough for some users to advance past the period where the first certification was produced. However, these multiple certifications will all be for the same block.

Proof Outline. The proof of asynchronous safety proceeds by case-splitting on whether the certifications are from the same period or different periods. For the first and easiest case, p1 = p2, we use quorum hypotheses to establish that there is an honest user that contributed a cert-vote to both certifications.

Then, we conclude by applying the lemma `no_two_certvotes_in_p`, which establishes that an honest user u cert-votes at most once in a period (proved by exhaustive analysis of possible transitions by an honest node):

```
Lemma no_two_certvotes_in_p : ∀ (g0:GState) (trace:seq GState) u (r p:ℕ),
 is_trace g0 trace →
∀ idx1 v1, certvoted_in_path_at idx1 trace u r p v1 →
  user_honest_at idx1 trace u →
∀ idx2 v2, certvoted_in_path_at idx2 trace u r p v2 →
  user_honest_at idx2 trace u → idx1 = idx2 ∧ v1 = v2.
```

The second case (p1 ≠ p2) uses an invariant which first holds in the period that produces the first certification, say, p1 for v1, and then keeps holding for all periods of the round. The invariant is that no step of the period produces a quorum of open next-votes, and any quorum of value next-votes must be for v1. (Please refer to [9] for the full definitions of predicates appearing in the lemma).

5   Conclusion

We presented a model in Coq of the Algorand consensus protocol and outlined the specification and formal proof of its asynchronous safety. The model and the proof open up many possibilities for further formal verification of the protocol, most directly of *liveness* properties. Our Coq development is available on GitHub [9] and contains around 2000 specification lines and 4000 proof lines.

References

1. Algorand blockchain features (2019). https://github.com/algorandfoundation/specs/blob/master/overview/Algorand_v1_spec-2.pdf
2. Chen, J., Gorbunov, S., Micali, S., Vlachos, G.: ALGORAND AGREEMENT: super fast and partition resilient Byzantine agreement. Cryptology ePrint Archive, Report 2018/377 (2018). https://eprint.iacr.org/2018/377
3. Chen, J., Micali, S.: Algorand: a secure and efficient distributed ledger. Theor. Comput. Sci. **777**, 155–183 (2019)
4. Cohen, C.: Finmap (2019). https://github.com/math-comp/finmap
5. Gilad, Y., Hemo, R., Micali, S., Vlachos, G., Zeldovich, N.: Algorand: scaling byzantine agreements for cryptocurrencies. In: SOSP, pp. 51–68 (2017)
6. Nakamoto, S.: Bitcoin: a peer-to-peer electronic cash system (2008)
7. Pîrlea, G., Sergey, I.: Mechanising blockchain consensus. In: CPP, pp. 78–90 (2018)
8. Rahli, Vincent, Vukotic, Ivana, Völp, Marcus, Esteves-Verissimo, Paulo: Velisarios: byzantine fault-tolerant protocols powered by Coq. In: Ahmed, Amal (ed.) ESOP 2018. LNCS, vol. 10801, pp. 619–650. Springer, Cham (2018). https://doi.org/10.1007/978-3-319-89884-1_22
9. Runtime Verification Inc: Algorand verification (2019). https://github.com/runtimeverification/algorand-verification/releases/tag/release-1.1
10. Sergey, I., Wilcox, J.R., Tatlock, Z.: Programming and proving with distributed protocols. PACMPL **2**(POPL), 28:1–28:30 (2018)
11. Woos, D., Wilcox, J.R., Anton, S., Tatlock, Z., Ernst, M.D., Anderson, T.: Planning for change in a formal verification of the Raft consensus protocol. In: CPP, pp. 154–165 (2016)

Mi-Cho-Coq, a Framework for Certifying Tezos Smart Contracts

Bruno Bernardo, Raphaël Cauderlier, Zhenlei Hu, Basile Pesin,
and Julien Tesson(✉)

Nomadic Labs, Paris, France
{bruno.bernardo,raphael.cauderlier,zhenlei.hu,
basile.pesin,julien.tesson}@nomadic-labs.com

Abstract. Tezos is a blockchain launched in June 2018. It is written in OCaml and supports smart contracts. Its smart contract language is called Michelson and it has been designed with formal verification in mind. In this article, we present Mi-Cho-Coq, a Coq framework for verifying the functional correctness of Michelson smart contracts. As a case study, we detail the certification of a Multisig contract with the Mi-Cho-Coq framework.

Keywords: Certified programming · Programming languages · Blockchains · Smart contracts

1 Introduction

Tezos is a public blockchain launched in June 2018. An open-source implementation, in OCaml [16], is available [3]. Tezos is an account based smart-contract platform with a Proof-of-Stake consensus algorithm [2]. Each account has a balance of tokens (called *tez*) and some of them, named *smart contracts*, can also store code and data. A smart contract's code is triggered when a transaction is sent to the associated account. Tezos' smart contracts language is called Michelson.

Our long-term ambition is to propose certified code in the whole Tezos codebase as well as certified smart contracts. The choice of OCaml as an implementation language is an interesting first step: OCaml gives Tezos good static guarantees since it benefits from OCaml's strong type system and memory management features. Furthermore, formally verified OCaml code can be produced by a variety of tools such as F* [21], Coq [22], Isabelle/HOL [17], Why3 [13], and FoCaLiZe [18]. Another specificity of Tezos is the use of formally verified cryptographic primitives. Indeed the codebase uses the HACL* library [23], which is certified C code extracted from an implementation of Low*, a fragment of F*.

This article presents Mi-Cho-Coq, a framework whose ultimate purpose is two-sided: giving strong guarantees – down to the interpreter implementation – related to the semantics of the Michelson language; and providing a tool able to prove properties of smart contracts written in Michelson.

© Springer Nature Switzerland AG 2020
E. Sekerinski et al. (Eds.): FM 2019 Workshops, LNCS 12232, pp. 368–379, 2020.
https://doi.org/10.1007/978-3-030-54994-7_28

Currently, the correspondence between Mi-Cho-Coq's Michelson interpreter implemented in Coq and the Michelson interpreter from a Tezos node implemented in OCaml is unproven. However, in the long run, we would like to lift this limitation by replacing the interpreter in the node with the extraction of Mi-Cho-Coq's interpreter. It would provide a strong confidence that all properties proven in Mi-Cho-Coq would actually hold for on-chain executions. Note that achieving this will not only require engineering efforts, but also the approval of Tezos token holders. Indeed, Tezos has an on-chain governance mechanism: changes to the *economic ruleset*, a subset of the codebase that contains amongst other things the Michelson interpreter, must be approved by a vote of token holders.

In this paper we will present how Mi-Cho-Coq can be used to prove functional properties of smart contracts. It is organised as follows: Section 2 gives an overview of the Michelson smart contract language, the Mi-Cho-Coq framework is then presented in Sect. 3, a case study on a Multisig smart contract is then conducted in Sect. 4, Sect. 5 presents some related work and finally Sect. 6 concludes the article by listing directions for future work.

The Mi-Cho-Coq framework, including the Multisig contract described in Sect. 4, is available at https://gitlab.com/nomadic-labs/mi-cho-coq/tree/FMBC_2019.

2   Overview of Michelson

Smart contracts are Tezos accounts of a particular kind. They have private access to a memory space on the chain called the *storage* of the smart contract, each transaction to a smart contract account contains some data, the *parameter* of the transaction, and a *script* is run at each transaction to decide if the transaction is valid, update the smart contract storage, and possibly emit new operations on the Tezos blockchain.

Michelson is the language in which the smart contract scripts are written. The Michelson language was designed before the launch of the Tezos blockchain. The most important parts of the implementation of Michelson, the typechecker and the interpreter, belong to the economic ruleset of Tezos so the language can evolve through the Tezos amendment voting process.

2.1   Design Rationale

Smart contracts operate in a very constrained context: they need to be expressive, evaluated efficiently, and their resource consumption should be accurately measured in order to stop the execution of programs that would be too greedy, as their execution time impacts the block construction and propagation. Smart contracts are non-updatable programs that can handle valuable assets, there is thus a need for strong guarantees on the correctness of these programs.

The need for efficiency and more importantly for accurate account of resource consumption leans toward a low-level interpreted language, while the need for contract correctness leans toward a high level, easily auditable, easily formalisable language, with strong static guarantees.

To satisfy these constraints, Michelson was made a Turing-complete, low level, stack based interpreted language (*à la* Forth), facilitating the measurement of computation costs, but with some high level features *à la* ML: polymorphic products, options, sums, lists, sets and maps data-structures with collection iterators, cryptographic primitives and anonymous functions. Contracts are pure functions that take a stack as input and return a stack as output. This side-effect free design is an asset for the conception of verification tools.

The language is statically typed to ensure the well-formedness of the stack at any point of the program. This means that if a program is well typed, and if it is being given a well-typed stack that matches its input expectation, then at any point of the program execution, the given instruction can be evaluated on the current stack.

Moreover, to ease the formalisation of Michelson, ambiguous or hidden behaviours have been avoided. In particular, unbounded integers are used to avoid arithmetic overflows and division returns an option (which is None if and only if the divisor is 0) so that the Michelson programmer has to specify the behaviour of the program in case of division by 0; she can however still *explicitly* reject the transaction using the **FAILWITH** Michelson instruction.

2.2   Quick Tour of the Language

The full language syntax, type system, and semantics are documented in [1], we give here a quick and partial overview of the language.

Contracts' Shape. A Michelson smart contract script is written in three parts: the parameter type, the storage type, and the code of the contract. A contract's code consists of one block of code that can only be called with one parameter, but multiple entry points can be encoded by branching on a nesting of sum types and multiple parameters can be paired into one.

When the contract is deployed (or *originated* in Tezos lingo) on the chain, it is bundled with a data storage which can then only be changed by a contract's successful execution. The parameter and the storage associated to the contract are paired and passed to the contract's code at each execution. The execution of the code must return a list of operations and the updated storage.

Seen from the outside, the type of the contract is the type of its parameter, as it is the only way to interact with it.

Michelson Instructions. As usual in stack-based languages, Michelson instructions take their parameters on the stack. All Michelson instructions are typed as a function going from the expected state of the stack, before the instruction evaluation, to the resulting stack. For example, the **AMOUNT** instruction used to obtain the amount in μtez (*i.e.* a millionth of a *tez*, the smallest token unit in Tezos) of the current transaction has type 'S $\rightarrow$ mutez:'S meaning that for any stack type 'S, it produces a stack of type mutez:'S. Some instructions, like comparison or arithmetic operations, exhibit non-ambiguous ad-hoc polymorphism: depending on the input arguments' type, a specific implementation of the instruction is selected, and the return type is fixed. For example **SIZE** has

the following types:

bytes:'S → nat:'S
string:'S → nat:'S

set 'elt:'S → nat:'S
map 'key 'val:'S → nat:'S
list 'elt:'S → nat:'S

While computing the size of a string or an array of bytes is similarly implemented, under the hood, the computation of map size has nothing to do with the computation of string size.

Finally, the contract's code is required to take a stack with a pair *parameter-storage* and returns a stack with a pair *operation list-storage*:

(parameter_ty*storage_ty):[] → (operation list*storage_ty):[].

The operations listed at the end of the execution can change the delegate of the contract, originate new contracts, or transfer tokens to other addresses. They will be executed right after the execution of the contract. The transfers can have parameters and trigger the execution of other smart contracts: this is the only way to perform *inter-contract* calls.

A Small Example - The Vote Contract. We want to allow users of the blockchain to vote for their favorite formal verification tool. In order to do that, we create a smart contract tasked with collecting the votes. We want any user to be able to vote, and to vote as many times as they want, provided they pay a small price (say 5 *tez*). We originate the contract with the names of a selection of popular tools: Agda, Coq, Isabelle and the K framework, which are placed in the long-term storage of the contract, in an associative map between the tool's name and the number of registered votes (of course, each tool starts with 0 votes).

In Fig. 1a, we present a voting contract, annotated with the state of the stack after each line of code. When actually writing a Michelson contract, development tools (including an Emacs Michelson mode) can interactively, for any point of the code, give the type of the stack provided by the Michelson typecheck of a Tezos node.

Let's take a look at our voting program: First, the description of the storage and parameter types is given on lines 1--2. Then the code of the contract is given. On line 5, **AMOUNT** pushes on the stack the amount of (in μtez) sent to the contract address by the user. The threshold amount (5 *tez*) is also pushed on the stack on line 6 and compared to the amount sent: **COMPARE** pops the two top values of the stack, and pushes either $-1, 0$ or 1 depending on the comparison between the value. **GT** then pops this value and pushes true if the value is 1. If the threshold is indeed greater than the required amount, the first branch of the **IF** is executed and **FAIL** is called, interrupting the contract execution and canceling the transaction.

If the value was false, the execution continues on line 9, where we prepare the stack for the next action: **DUP** copies the top of the stack, we then manipulate the tail of the stack while preserving it's head using **DIP**: there, we take the right

```
1   storage (map string int); # candidates
2   parameter string; # chosen
3   code {
4     # (chosen, candidates):[]
5     AMOUNT; # amount:(chosen, candidates):[]
6     PUSH mutez 5000000; COMPARE; GT;
7     # (5 tez > amount):(chosen, candidates):[]
8     IF { FAIL } {}; # (chosen, candidates):[]
9     DUP; DIP { CDR; DUP };
10    # (chosen, candidates):candidates:candidates:[]
11    CAR; DUP; # chosen:chosen:candidates:candidates:[]
12    DIP { # chosen:candidates:candidates:[]
13      GET; ASSERT_SOME;
14      # candidates[chosen]:candidates:[]
15      PUSH int 1; ADD; SOME
16      # (Some (candidates[chosen]+1)):candidates:[]
17      }; # chosen:(Some (candidates[chosen]+1)):candidates:[]
18    UPDATE; # candidates' :[]
19    NIL operation; PAIR # (nil, candidates' ):[]
20  }
```

(a)

{Elt "Agda" 0 ; Elt "Coq" 0 ; Elt "Isabelle" 0 ; Elt "K" 0}

(b)

Fig. 1. A simple voting contract a and an example of initial storage b

element of the (chosen, candidates) pair with **CDR**, and we duplicate it again. By closing the block guarded by **DIP** we recover the former stack's top, and the following line takes its left element with **CAR**, and duplicates it.

On line 12, we use **DIP** to protect the top of the stack again. **GET** then pops chosen and candidates from the stack, and pushes an option containing the number of votes of the candidate, if it was found in the map. If it was not found, **ASSERT_SOME** makes the program fail. On line 15, the number of votes is incremented by **ADD**, and packed into an option type by **SOME**.

We then leave the **DIP** block to regain access to value at the top of the stack (chosen). On line 18, **UPDATE** pops the three values remaining on top of the stack, and pushes the candidates map updated with the incremented value for chosen. Finally, we push an empty list of operations with **NIL operation**, and pair the two elements on top of the stack to get the correct return type.

3   Mi-Cho-Coq: A Verification Framework in Coq for Michelson

Mi-Cho-Coq consists of an implementation of a Michelson interpreter in Coq as well as a weakest precondition calculus à la Dijkstra [12].

Michelson Syntax and Typing in Coq. Michelson's type system, syntax and semantics, as described in the main documentation, are fully formalised in Mi-Cho-Coq.

The abstract syntax tree of a Michelson script is a term of an inductive type which carries the script type:

```
Inductive instruction : list type → list type → Set :=
| NOOP {A} : instruction A A
| FAILWITH {A B a} : instruction (a :: A) B
| SEQ {A B C} : instruction A B → instruction B C → instruction A C
| IF {A B} : instruction A B → instruction A B → instruction (bool :: A) B
| LOOP {A} : instruction A (bool :: A) → instruction (bool :: A) A ...
```

A Michelson code is usually a sequence of instructions (SEQ), which is one of the instruction constructors. It has type instruction stA stB where stA and stB are respectively the type of the input stack and of the output stack.

The stack type is a list of Michelson type constructions, defined in the type inductive:

```
Inductive comparable_type : Set :=
| nat | int | string | bytes | bool | mutez | address | key_hash | timestamp.

Inductive type : Set :=
| Comparable_type (a : comparable_type) | key | unit | signature | operation
| option (a : type) | list (a : type) | set (a : comparable_type)
| contract (a : type) | pair (a b : type) | or (a b : type) | lambda (a b : type)
| map (key : comparable_type) (val : type)
| big_map (key : comparable_type) (val : type).
```

A full contract, for a given storage type storage and parameter type params is an instruction of type

```
instruction ((pair params storage) :: nil) ((pair (list operation) storage) :: nil).
```

Thanks to the indexing of the instruction inductive by the input and output stack types, only well-typed Michelson instructions are representable in Mi-Cho-Coq. This is very similar to the implementation of Michelson in the Tezos node which uses a similar feature in OCaml: generalised algebraic datatypes.

To ease the transcription of Michelson contracts into Mi-Cho-Coq AST we use notations so that contracts in Mi-Cho-Coq look very similar to actual Michelson code. The main discrepancy between Michelson and Mi-Cho-Coq syntax being that due to parsing limitations, the Michelson semi-colon instruction terminator has to be replaced by a double semi-colon instructions separator.

The ad-hoc polymorphism of Michelson instructions is handled by adding an implicit argument to the corresponding instruction constructor in Mi-Cho-Coq. This argument is a structure that carries an element identifying the actual implementation of the instruction to be used. As the argument is *implicit and maximally inserted*, Coq's type unifier tries to fill it with whatever value can fit with the known types surrounding it, *i.e.* the type of the input stack. Possible values are declared through the Coq's canonical structures mechanism, which is very similar to (Coq's or Haskell's) typeclasses.

Michelson Interpreter in Coq. Michelson semantics is formalised in Coq as an evaluator eval of type forall {A B : list type}, instruction A B → nat → stack A → M (stack B) where M is the error monad used to represent the explicit failure of the execution of a contract, and where stack A (resp. stack B) is the type of a stack data whose type matches A (resp. B), the list of types. As the stack is implemented as a tuple, stack constructs a product of types. The argument of type nat is called the *fuel* of the evaluator. It represents a bound on the depth of the execution of the contract and should not be confused with Michelson's cost model which is not yet formalised in Mi-Cho-Coq.

Some domain specific operations which are hard to define in Coq are axiomatised in the evaluator. These include cryptographic primitives, data serialisation, and instructions to query the context of the call to the smart contract (amount and sender of the transaction, current date, balance and address of the smart contract).

A Framework for Verifying Smart Contracts. To ease the writing of correctness proofs in Mi-Cho-Coq, a weakest precondition calculus is defined as a function eval_precond of type forall {fuel A B}, instruction A B → (stack B → Prop) → (stack A → Prop) that is a Coq function taking as argument an instruction and a predicate over the possible output stacks of the instruction (the postcondition) and producing a predicate on the possible input stacks of the instruction (the precondition).

This function is proved correct with respect to the evaluator:

```
Lemma eval_precond_correct {A B} (i : instruction A B) fuel st psi :
  eval_precond fuel i psi st <→
    match eval i fuel st with Failed _ _ => False | Return _ a => psi a end.
```

Note that the right-hand side formula is the result of the monad transformer of [5] which here yields a simple expression thanks to the absence of complex effects (exceptions, state, etc.) in Michelson.

A Small Example - The Vote Contract. We give below a formal specification of the voting contract seen previously, written in pseudo-code to keep it clear and concise. Section 4 presents a case study with a more detailed Coq specification.

We want the contract to take into account every vote sent in a transaction with an amount greater than 5 *tez*. Moreover, we want to only take into account the votes toward an actual available choice (the contract should fail if the wrong name is sent as a parameter). Finally, the contract should not emit any operation.

In the following specification, the *precondition* is the condition that must be verified for the contract to succeed. The *postcondition* fully describes the new state of the storage at the end of the execution, as well as the potentially emitted operations. amount refers to the quantity of μtez sent by the caller for the transaction.

Precondition: amount $\geq$ 5000000 $\wedge$ chosen $\in$ Keys(storage)
Postconditions: returned_operations = [ ] $\wedge$
$\qquad\qquad\qquad\quad$ $\forall$ c, c $\in$ Keys(storage) $\Longleftrightarrow$ c $\in$ Keys(new_storage) $\wedge$
$\qquad\qquad\qquad\quad$ new_storage[chosen] = storage[chosen] + 1 $\wedge$
$\qquad\qquad\qquad\quad$ $\forall$ c $\in$ Keys(storage), c $\neq$ chosen $\Rightarrow$ new_storage[c] = storage[c]

Despite looking simple, proving the correctness of the vote contract still needs a fair number of properties about the map data structure. In particular we need some lemmas about the relations between the mem, get and update functions, which we added to the Mi-Cho-Coq library to prove this contract.

Once these lemmas are available, the contract can easily be proved by studying the three different situations that can arise during the execution: the contract can fail (either because the sender has not sent enough tez or because they have not selected one of the possible candidates), or the execution can go smoothly.

4   A Case Study: The Multisig Contract

The *Multisig* contract is a typical example of access-control smart contract. A Multisig contract is used to share the ownership of an account between several owners. The owners are represented by their cryptographic public keys in the contract storage and a pre-defined *threshold* (a natural number between 1 and the number of owners) of them must agree for any action to be performed by the Multisig contract.

Agreement of an owner is obtained by requiring a cryptographic signature of the action to be performed. To ensure that this signature cannot be replayed by an attacker to authenticate in another call to a Multisig contract (the same contract or another one implementing the same authentication protocol), a nonce is appended to the operation before signing. This nonce consists of the address of the contract on the blockchain and a counter incremented at each call.

Michelson Implementation. To be as generic as possible, the possible actions of our Multisig contract are:

- produce a list of operations to be run atomically
- change the threshold and the list of owner public keys

The contract features two entrypoints named default and main[1]. The default entrypoint takes no parameter (it has type unit) and lets unauthenticated users send funds to the Multisig contract. The main entrypoint takes as parameters an action, a list of optional signatures, and a counter value. It checks the validity and the number of signatures and, in case of successful authentication, it executes the required action and increment the counter.

The Michelson script of the Multisig contract is available at [9]. The code of the default entrypoint is trivial. The code for the main entrypoint can be divided in three parts: the header, the loop, and the tail.

---

[1] i.e. the parameter of the contract is a sum type branching two elements, cf. Sect. 2.2.

The header packs together the required action and the nonce and checks that the counter given as parameter matches the one stored in the contract.

The loop iterates over the stored public keys and the optional signatures given in parameter. It counts and checks the validity of all the signatures.

Finally the contract tail checks that the number of provided signatures is at least as large as the threshold, it increments the stored counter, and it runs the required action (it either evaluates the anonymous function passed in the contract parameter and emits the resulting operations or modifies the contract storage to update the list of owner public keys and the threshold).

Specification and Correctness Proof. Mi-Cho-Coq is a functional verification framework. It is well suited to specify the relation between the input and output stacks of a contract such as Multisig but it is currently not expressive enough to state properties about the lifetime of a smart contract nor the interaction between smart contracts. For this reason, we have not proved that the Multisig contract is resistant to replay attacks. However, we fully characterise the behaviour of each call to the Multisig contract using the following specification of the Multisig contract, where env is the evaluation environment containing among other data the address of the contract (self env) and the amount of the transaction (amount env).

```
Definition multisig_spec (parameter : data parameter_ty) (stored_counter : N)
          (threshold : N) (keys : Datatypes.list (data key))
          (new_stored_counter : N) (new_threshold : N)
          (new_keys : Datatypes.list (data key))
          (returned_operations : Datatypes.list (data operation))
          (fuel : Datatypes.nat) :=
  let storage : data storage_ty := (stored_counter, (threshold, keys)) in
  match parameter with
  | inl tt ⇒
    new_stored_counter = stored_counter ∧ new_threshold = threshold ∧
    new_keys = keys ∧ returned_operations = nil
  | inr ((counter, action), sigs) ⇒
    amount env = (0  Mutez) ∧ counter = stored_counter ∧
    length sigs = length keys ∧
    check_all_signatures sigs keys (fun k sig ⇒
          check_signature env k sig
            (pack env pack_ty (address_ env parameter_ty (self env),
                          (counter, action)))) ∧
    (count_signatures sigs >= threshold)%N ∧
    new_stored_counter = (1 + stored_counter)%N ∧
    match action with
    | inl lam ⇒
      match (eval lam fuel (tt, tt)) with
      | Return _ (operations, tt) ⇒
        new_threshold = threshold ∧ new_keys = keys ∧
        returned_operations = operations
      | _ ⇒ False
```

```
      end
    | inr (nt, nks) ⇒
      new_threshold = nt ∧ new_keys = nks ∧ returned_operations = nil
    end end.
```

Using the Mi-Cho-Coq framework, we have proved the following theorem:

```
Lemma multisig_correct (params : data parameter_ty)
      (stored_counter new_stored_counter threshold new_threshold : N)
      (keys new_keys : list (data key))
      (returned_operations : list (data operation)) (fuel : nat) :
  let storage : data storage_ty := (stored_counter, (threshold, keys)) in
  let new_storage : data storage_ty :=
    (new_stored_counter, (new_threshold, new_keys)) in
  17 * length keys + 14 $\leq$ fuel →
  eval multisig (23 + fuel) ((params, storage), tt)
    = Return _ ((returned_operations, new_storage), tt) <→
  multisig_spec params stored_counter threshold keys
    new_stored_counter new_threshold new_keys returned_operations fuel.
```

The proof relies heavily on the correctness of the precondition calculus. The only non-trivial part of the proof is the signature checking loop. Indeed, for efficiency reasons, the Multisig contract checks the equality of length between the optional signature list and the public key list only after checking the validity of the signature; an optional signature and a public key are consumed at each loop iteration and the list of remaining optional signatures after the loop exit is checked for emptiness afterward. For this reason, the specification of the loop has to allow for remaining unchecked signatures.

5 Related Work

Formal verification of smart contracts is a recent but active field. The K framework has been used to formalise [15] the semantics of both low-level and high-level smart contract languages for the Ethereum and Cardano blockchains. These formalisations have been used to verify common smart contracts such as Casper, Uniswap, and various implementations of the ERC20 and ERC777 standards.

Note also a formalisation of the EVM in the F* dependently-typed language [14], that was validated against the official Ethereum test suite. This formalisation effort led to formal definitions of security properties for smart contracts (call integrity, atomicity, etc).

Ethereum smart contracts, written in the Solidity high-level language, can also be certified using a translation to F* [7].

The Zen Protocol [4] directly uses F* as its smart contract language so that smart contracts of the Zen Protocol can be proved directly in F*. Moreover, runtime tracking of resources can be avoided since computation and storage costs are encoded in the dependent types.

The Scilla [19,20] language of the Zilliqa blockchain has been formalised in Coq as a shallow embedding. This intermediate language is higher-level (it is based on λ-calculus) but also less featureful (it is not Turing-complete as it does not feature unbounded loops nor general recursion) than Michelson. Its formalisation includes inter-contract interaction and contract lifespan properties. This has been used to show safety properties of a crowdfunding smart contract. To the best of our knowledge, no tool currently exists for interactive functional verification of Scilla smart contracts but Scilla's framework for writing static analyses can be used for automated verification of some specific properties.

6   Limits and Future Work

As we have seen, the Mi-Cho-Coq verification framework can be used to certify the functional correctness of non-trivial smart contracts of the Tezos blockchain such as the Multisig contract. We are currently working on several improvements to extend the expressivity of the framework; Michelson's cost model and the semantics of inter-contract interactions are being formalised.

In order to prove security properties, such as the absence of signature replay in the case of the Multisig contract, an adversarial model has to be defined. This task should be feasible in Coq but our current plan is to use specialised tools such as Easycrypt [6] and ProVerif [8].

No code is currently shared between Mi-Cho-Coq and the Michelson evaluator written in OCaml that is executed by the Tezos nodes. We would like to raise the level of confidence in the fact that both evaluators implement the same operational semantics. We could achieve this either by proposing to the Tezos stakeholders to amend the economic protocol to replace the Michelson evaluator by a version extracted from Mi-Cho-Coq or by translating to Coq the OCaml code of the Michelson evaluator using a tool such as CoqOfOCaml [11] or CFML [10] and then prove the resulting Coq function equivalent to the Mi-Cho-Coq evaluator.

Last but not least, to ease the development of certified compilers from high-level languages to Michelson, we are working on the design of an intermediate compilation language called Albert that abstracts away the Michelson stack.

References

1. Michelson: the language of Smart Contracts in Tezos. https://tezos.gitlab.io/whitedoc/michelson.html
2. Proof-of-stake in Tezos. https://tezos.gitlab.io/whitedoc/proof_of_stake.html
3. Tezos code repository. https://gitlab.com/tezos/tezos
4. An introduction to the zen protocol. https://www.zenprotocol.com/files/zen_protocol_white_paper.pdf (2017)
5. Ahman, D., et al.: Dijkstra monads for free. CoRR abs/1608.06499 (2016). http://arxiv.org/abs/1608.06499
6. Barthe, G., Dupressoir, F., Grégoire, B., Kunz, C., Schmidt, B., Strub, P.-Y.: EasyCrypt: a tutorial. In: Aldini, A., Lopez, J., Martinelli, F. (eds.) FOSAD 2012-2013. LNCS, vol. 8604, pp. 146–166. Springer, Cham (2014). https://doi.org/10.1007/978-3-319-10082-1_6

7. Bhargavan, K., et al.: Formal verification of smart contracts: short paper, pp. 91–96. PLAS 2016. ACM, New York (2016). https://doi.org/10.1145/2993600.2993611

8. Blanchet, B.: Modeling and verifying security protocols with the applied pi calculus and proverif. Found. Trends Priv. Secur. 1(1–2), 1–135 (2016). https://doi.org/10.1561/3300000004

9. Breitman, A.: Multisig contract in Michelson. https://github.com/murbard/smart-contracts/blob/master/multisig/michelson/generic_multisig.tz

10. Charguéraud, A.: Characteristic formulae for the verification of imperative programs. In: ICFP 2011, pp. 418–430. ACM, New York (2011)

11. Claret, G.: Program in Coq. Theses, Université Paris Diderot - Paris 7, September 2018. https://hal.inria.fr/tel-01890983

12. Dijkstra, E.W.: Guarded commands, nondeterminacy and formal derivation of programs. Commun. ACM 18(8), 453–457 (1975). https://doi.org/10.1145/360933.360975

13. Filliâtre, Jean-Christophe, Paskevich, Andrei: Why3—where programs meet provers. In: Felleisen, Matthias, Gardner, Philippa (eds.). ESOP 2013. LNCS, vol. 7792, pp. 125–128. Springer, Heidelberg (2013). https://doi.org/10.1007/978-3-642-37036-6_8. https://hal.inria.fr/hal-00789533

14. Grishchenko, Ilya, Maffei, Matteo, Schneidewind, Clara: A semantic framework for the security analysis of ethereum smart contracts. In: Bauer, Lujo, Küsters, Ralf (eds.) POST 2018. LNCS, vol. 10804, pp. 243–269. Springer, Cham (2018). https://doi.org/10.1007/978-3-319-89722-6_10

15. Hildenbrandt, E., et al.: KEVM: a complete semantics of the ethereum virtual machine. In: 2018 IEEE 31st Computer Security Foundations Symposium, pp. 204–217. IEEE (2018)

16. Leroy, X., Doligez, D., Frisch, A., Garrigue, J., Rémy, D., Vouillon, J.: The OCaml system release 4.08: documentation and user's manual. User manual, Inria, June 2019. http://caml.inria.fr/pub/docs/manual-ocaml/

17. Nipkow, Tobias, Wenzel, Markus, Paulson, Lawrence C. (eds.): Isabelle/HOL: A Proof Assistant forHigher-Order Logic. LNCS, vol. 2283. Springer, Heidelberg (2002). https://doi.org/10.1007/3-540-45949-9

18. Pessaux, F.: FoCaLiZe: inside an F-IDE. In: Workshop F-IDE 2014. Proceedings F-IDE 2014, Grenoble, France, May 2014. https://doi.org/10.4204/EPTCS.149.7

19. Sergey, I., Kumar, A., Hobor, A.: Scilla: a smart contract intermediate-level language. CoRR abs/1801.00687 (2018). http://arxiv.org/abs/1801.00687

20. Sergey, I., Nagaraj, V., Johannsen, J., Kumar, A., Trunov, A., Hao, K.C.G.: Safer smart contract programming with scilla. PACMPL 3(OOPSLA), 185:1–185:30 (2019). https://doi.org/10.1145/3360611

21. Swamy, N., et al.: Dependent types and multi-monadic effects in F*. In: POPL, pp. 256–270. ACM, January 2016. https://www.fstar-lang.org/papers/mumon/

22. The Coq development team: The Coq Reference Manual, version 8.9, November 2018. http://coq.inria.fr/doc

23. Zinzindohoué, J.K., Bhargavan, K., Protzenko, J., Beurdouche, B.: HACL*: a verified modern cryptographic library. Cryptology ePrint Archive, Report 2017/536

Smart Contract Interactions in Coq

Jakob Botsch Nielsen⊙ and Bas Spitters$^{(\boxtimes)}$⊙

Concordium Blockchain Research Center, Computer Science,
Aarhus University, Aarhus, Denmark
{botsch,spitters}@cs.au.dk

Abstract. We present a model/executable specification of smart contract execution in Coq. Our formalization allows for inter-contract communication and generalizes existing work by allowing modelling of both depth-first execution blockchains (like Ethereum) and breadth-first execution blockchains (like Tezos). We represent smart contracts programs in Coq's functional language Gallina, enabling easier reasoning about functional correctness of concrete contracts than other approaches. In particular we develop a Congress contract in this style. This contract – a simplified version of the infamous DAO – is interesting because of its very dynamic communication pattern with other contracts. We give a high-level partial specification of the Congress's behavior, related to reentrancy, and prove that the Congress satisfies it for all possible smart contract execution orders.

Keywords: Blockchain · Coq · Formal verification · Smart contracts

1 Introduction

Since Ethereum, blockchains make a clear separation between the consensus layer and the execution of interacting smart contracts. In Ethereum's Solidity language contracts can arbitrarily call into other contracts as regular function calls. Modern blockchains further separate the top layer in an execution layer and a contract layer. The execution layer schedules the calls between the contracts and the contract layer executes individual programs. The choice of execution order differs between blockchains. For example, in Ethereum the execution is done in a synchronous (or depth first) order: a call completes fully before the parent continues, and the parent is able to observe its result. Tezos and Scilla use a breadth first order instead, where observing the result is not possible.

We provide[1] a model/executable specification of the execution and contract layer of a third generation blockchain in the Coq proof assistant. We use Coq's embedded functional language Gallina to model contracts and the execution layer. This language can be extracted to certified programs in for example Haskell or Ocaml. Coq's expressive logic also allows us to write concise proofs.

---

[1] https://gitlab.au.dk/concordium/smart-contract-interactions/tree/v1.0.

© Springer Nature Switzerland AG 2020
E. Sekerinski et al. (Eds.): FM 2019 Workshops, LNCS 12232, pp. 380–391, 2020.
https://doi.org/10.1007/978-3-030-54994-7_29

The consensus protocol provides a consistent global state which we treat abstractly in our formalization.

We work with an account-based model. We could also model the UTxO model by converting a list of UTxO transactions to a list of account transactions [12]. Like that work, we do not model the cryptographic aspects, only the accounting aspects: the transactions and contract calls.

Section 2 describes the implementation of the execution layer in Coq. In Sect. 3 we provide a simple principled specification for the Congress. By using such specifications one avoids having to deal with reentrancy bugs in a post-hoc way. Section 4 discusses related and future work.

2   Implementation

2.1   Basic Assumptions

Our goal is to model execution of smart contracts. To do so we will require some basic operations that are to be used both by smart contracts and when specifying our semantics. We do this with a typeclass in Coq:

```
Class ChainBase :=
  { Address : Type;
    address_countable :> Countable Address;
    address_is_contract : Address → bool; ... }.
```

We require a countable `Address` type with a clear separation between addresses belonging to contracts and to users. While this separation is not provided in Ethereum its omission has led to exploits before[2] and we view it as realistic that future blockchains allow this. Other blockchains commonly provide this by using some specific format for contract addresses, for example, in Bitcoin such pay-to-script-hash addresses always start with 3.

All semantics and smart contracts will be abstracted over an instance of this type, so in the following sections we will assume we are given such an instance.

2.2   Smart Contracts

We will consider a pure functional smart contract language. Instead of modelling the language as an abstract syntax tree in Coq, as in [2], we model individual smart contracts as records with (Coq) functions.

Local State. It is not immediately clear how to represent smart contracts by functions. For one, smart contracts have local state that they should be able to access and update during execution. In Solidity, the language typically used in Ethereum, this state is mutable and can be changed at any point in time. It is possible to accomplish something similar in pure languages, for example by

---

[2] See for instance https://www.reddit.com/r/ethereum/comments/916xni/how_to_pwn_fomo3d_a_beginners_guide/.

using a state monad, but we do not take this approach. Instead we use a more traditional approach where the contract takes as input its state and returns an updated state which is similar to Liquidity.

Different contracts will typically have different types of states. A crowdfunding contract may wish to store a map of backers in its state while an auction contract would store information about ongoing auctions. To facilitate this polymorphism we use an intermediate storage type called `SerializedValue`. We define conversions between `SerializedValue` and primitive types like booleans and integers plus derived types like pairs, sums and lists. Additionally we provide Coq tactics that can automatically generate conversions for custom user types like inductives and records. This allows conversions to be handled implicitly and mostly transparently to the user.

Inter-contract Communication. In addition to local state we also need some way to handle inter-contract communication. In Solidity contracts can arbitrarily call into other contracts as regular function calls. This would once again be possible with a monadic style, for example by the use of a promise monad where the contract would ask to be resumed after a call to another contract had finished. To ease reasoning we choose a simpler approach where contracts return actions that indicate how they would like to interact with the blockchain, allowing transfers, contract calls and contract deployments only at the end of (single steps of) execution. The blockchain will then be responsible for scheduling these actions in what we call its execution layer.

With this design we get a clear separation between contracts and their interaction with the chain. That such separations are important has been realized before, for instance in the design of Michelson and Scilla [9]. Indeed, a "tail-call" approach like this forces the programmer to update the contract's internal state before making calls to other contracts, mitigating by construction reentrancy issues such as the infamous DAO exploit.

Thus, contracts will take their local state and some data allowing them to query the blockchain. As a result they then optionally return the new state and some operations (such as calls to other contract) allowing inter-contract communication. Tezos' Michelson language follows a similar approach.

The Ethereum model may be compared to object-oriented programming. Our model is similar to the actor model as contracts do not read or write the state of another contract directly, but instead communicate via messages instead of shared memory. Liquidity and the IO-automata-based Scilla use similar models.

The Contract. Smart contracts are allowed to query various data about the blockchain. We model this with a data type:

```
Definition Amount := Z.
Record Chain := { chain_height : nat;
                  current_slot : nat;
                  finalized_height : nat;
                  account_balance : Address → Amount; }.
```

We allow contracts to access basic details about the blockchain, like the current chain height, slot number and the finalized height. The slot number is meant to be used to track the progression of time; in each slot, a block can be created, but it does not have to be. The finalized height allows contracts to track the current status of the finalization layer available in for example the Concordium blockchain [5]. This height is different from the chain height in that it guarantees that blocks before it can not be changed. We finally also allow the contract to access balances of accounts as is common in other blockchains. In sum, the following data types model the contracts:

```
Record ContractCallContext :=
  { ctx_from : Address;
    ctx_contract_address : Address;
    ctx_amount : Amount; }.
Inductive ActionBody :=
| act_transfer (to : Address) (amt : Amount)
| act_call (to : Address) (amt : Amount) (msg : SerializedValue)
| act_deploy (amt : Amount) (c : WeakContract) (setup : SerializedValue)
with WeakContract :=
| build_weak_contract
  (init : Chain → ContractCallContext → SerializedValue (* setup *)
          → option SerializedValue)
  (receive : Chain → ContractCallContext → SerializedValue (* state *)
             → option SerializedValue (* message *)
             → option (SerializedValue * list ActionBody)).
```

Here the `ContractCallContext` provides the contract with information about the transaction that resulted in its execution. It contains the source address (`ctx_from`), the contract's own address (`ctx_contract_address`) and the amount of money transferred (`ctx_amount`). The `ActionBody` type represents operations that interact with the chain. It allows for messageless transfers (`act_transfer`), calls with messages (`act_call`), and deployment of new contracts (`act_deploy`). The contract itself is two functions. The `init` function is used when a contract is deployed to set up its initial state, while the `receive` function will be used for transfers and calls with messages afterwards. They both return option types, allowing the contract to signal invalid calls or deployments. The `receive` function additionally returns a list of `ActionBody` that it wants to be scheduled, as we described earlier. This data type does not contain a source address since it is implicitly the contract's own address. Later, we will also use a representation where there *is* a source address; we call this type `Action`:

```
Record Action := { act_from : Address; act_body : ActionBody; }.
```

This type resembles what is normally called a transaction, but we make a distinction between the two. An `Action` is a *request* by a contract or external user to perform some operation. When executed by an implementation, this action will affect the state of the blockchain in some way. It differs from transactions since `act_deploy` does not contain the address of the contract to be deployed. This models that it is the implementation that picks the address of a newly deployed contract, not the contract making the deployment. We will later describe our `ActionEvaluation` type which captures more in depth the choices made by the implementation while executing an action.

The functions of contracts are typed using the `SerializedValue` type. This is also the reason for the name `WeakContract`. This makes specifying semantics simpler, since the semantics can deal with contracts in a generic way (rather than contracts abstracted over types). However, this form of "string-typing" makes things harder when reasoning about contracts. For this reason we provide a dual notion of a *strong* contract, which is a polymorphic version of contracts generalized over the setup, state and message types. Users of the framework only need to be aware of this notion of contract, which does not contain references to `SerializedValue` at all.

One could also imagine an alternative representation using a dependent record of setup, state and message types plus functions over those types. However, in such a representation it is unclear how to allow contracts to send messages to other contracts when the blockchain itself does not have any knowledge about concrete contracts.

2.3   Semantics of the Execution Layer

Environments. The `Chain` type shown above is merely the contract's view of the blockchain and does not store enough information to allow the blockchain to run actions. More specifically we need to be able to look up information about currently deployed contracts like their functions and state. We augment the `Chain` type with this information and call it an `Environment`:

```
Record Environment :=
  { env_chain :> Chain;
    env_contracts : Address →  option WeakContract;
    env_contract_states : Address →  option SerializedValue; }.
```

It is not hard to define functions that allow us to make updates to environments. For instance, inserting a new contract is done by creating a new function that checks if the address matches and otherwise uses the old map. In other words we use simple linear maps in the semantics. In similar ways we can update the rest of the fields of the `Environment` record.

Evaluation of Actions. When contracts return actions the execution layer will need to evaluate the effects of these actions. We define this as a "proof-relevant" relation `ActionEvaluation` in Coq, with type `Environment → Action → Environment → list Action → Type`. This relation captures the requirements and effects of executing the action in the environment. It is "proof-relevant", meaning that the choices made by the execution layer can be inspected. For example, when an action requests to deploy a new contract, the address selected by the implementation can be extracted from this relation.

We define the relation by three cases: one for transfers of money, one for deployment of new contracts, and one for calls to existing contracts. To exemplify this relation we give its formal details for the simple transfer case below:

```
| eval_transfer :
    forall {pre : Environment} {act : Action} {new_env : Environment}
           (from to : Address) (amount : Amount),
      amount ≤ account_balance pre from →
      address_is_contract to = false →
      act_from act = from →
      act_body act = act_transfer to amount →
      EnvironmentEquiv new_env (transfer_balance from to amount pre) →
      ActionEvaluation pre act new_env []
```

In this case the sender must have enough money and the recipient cannot be a contract. When this is the case a transfer action and the old environment evaluate to the new environment where the `account_balance` has been updated appropriately. Finally, such a transfer does not result in more actions to execute since it is not associated with execution of contracts. Note that we close the evaluation relation under extensional equality (`EnvironmentEquiv`).

We denote this relation by the notation $\langle \sigma, a \rangle \Downarrow (\sigma', l)$. The intuitive understanding of this notation is that evaluating the action a in environment σ results in a new environment σ' and new actions to execute l.

Chain Traces. The `Environment` type captures enough information to evaluate actions. We further augment this type to keep track of the queue of actions to execute. In languages like Solidity this data is encoded implicitly in the call stack, but since interactions with the blockchain are explicit in our framework we keep track of it explicitly.

```
Record ChainState := { chain_state_env :> Environment;
                       chain_state_queue : list Action; }.
```

We now define what it means for the chain to take a step. Formally, this is defined as a "proof-relevant" relation `ChainStep` of type `ChainState → ChainState → Type`. We denote this relation with the notation $(\sigma, l) \rightarrow (\sigma', l')$, meaning that we can step from the environment σ and list of actions l to the environment σ' and list of actions l'. We give this relation as simplified inference rules:

STEP-BLOCK	STEP-ACTION	STEP-PERMUTE
b valid for σ $acts$ from users	$\langle \sigma, a \rangle \Downarrow (\sigma', l)$	$\text{Perm}(l, l')$
$(\sigma, []) \rightarrow (\text{add\_block } b\ \sigma, acts)$	$(\sigma, a :: l') \rightarrow (\sigma', l ++ l')$	$(\sigma, l) \rightarrow (\sigma, l')$

The STEP-BLOCK rule allows the addition of a new block (b) containing some actions ($acts$) to execute. We require that the block is valid for the current environment (the "b valid for σ" premise), meaning that it needs to satisfy some well-formedness conditions. For example, if the chain currently has height n, the next block added needs to have height $n + 1$. There are other well-formedness conditions on other fields, such as the block creator, but we omit them here for brevity. Another condition is that all added actions must come from users (the "*acts* from users" premise). This models the real world where transactions added in blocks are "root transactions" from users. This condition is crucial to ensure that transfers from contracts can happen only due to execution of their associated code. When the premises are met we update information about the current block (such as the current height and the balance of the creator, signified by the add_block function) and update that the queue now contains the actions that were added.

The STEP-ACTION rule allows the evaluation of the first action in the queue, replacing it with the resulting new actions to execute. This new list (l in the rule) is concatenated at the beginning, corresponding to using the queue as a stack. This results in a depth-first execution order of actions. The STEP-PERMUTE rule allows an implementation to use a different order of reduction by permuting the queue at any time. For example, it is possible to obtain a breadth-first order of execution by permuting the queue so that newly added events are in the back. In this case the queue will be used like an actual FIFO queue.

Building upon steps we can further define *traces* as the proof-relevant reflexive transitive closure of the step relation. In other words, this is a sequence of steps where each step starts in the state that the previous step ended in. Intuitively the existence of a trace between two states means that there is a semantically correct way to go between those states. If we let ε denote the empty environment and queue this allows us to define a concept of *reachability*. Formally we say a state (σ, l) is *reachable* if there exists a trace starting in ε and ending in (σ, l). Generally, only reachable states are interesting to consider and most proofs are by induction over the trace to a reachable state.

2.4   Building Blockchains

We connect our semantics to an executable definition of a blockchain with a typeclass in Coq:

```
Class ChainBuilderType := {
 builder_type : Type;
 builder_initial : builder_type;
 builder_env : builder_type → Environment;
 builder_add_block (builder : builder_type) (header : BlockHeader)
  (actions : list Action) : option builder_type;
 builder_trace (builder : builder_type) :
  ChainTrace empty_state (build_chain_state (builder_env builder) []); }.
```

A chain builder is a dependent record consisting of an implementation type (builder_type) and several fields using this type. It must provide an initial builder, which typically would be an empty chain, or a chain containing just a genesis block. It must be convertible to an environment allowing to query information about the state. It must define a function that allows addition of new blocks. Finally, the implementation needs to be able to give a trace showing that the current environment is reachable with no more actions left in the queue to execute. This trace captures a definition of soundness, since it means that the state of such a chain builder will always be reachable.

Instantiations. We have implemented two instances of the `ChainBuilderType` typeclass. Both of these are based on finite maps from the std++ library used by Iris [4] and are thus relatively efficient compared to the linear maps used to specify the semantics. The difference in the implementations lies in their execution model: one implementation uses a depth-first execution order, while the other uses a breadth-first execution order. The former execution model is similar to the EVM while the latter is similar to Tezos and Scilla.

These implementations are useful as sanity checks but they also serve other useful purposes in the framework. Since they are executable they can be used to test concrete contracts that have been written in Coq. This involves writing the contracts and executing them using Coq's `Compute` vernacular to inspect the results. In addition, they can also be used to give counter-examples to properties. In the next section we will introduce the *Congress* contract, and we have used the depth-first implementation of our semantics to formally show that this contract with a small change can be exploited with reentrancy.

3 Case: Congress – A Simplified DAO

In this section we will present a case study of implementing and partially specifying a complex contract in our framework.

The Congress Contract. Wang [11] gives a list of eight interesting Ethereum contracts. One of these is the *Congress* in which members of the contract vote on *proposals*. Proposals contain transactions that, if the proposal succeeds, are sent out by the Congress. These transactions are typically monetary amounts sent out to some address, but they can also be arbitrary calls to any other contract.

We pick the Congress contract because of its complex dynamic interaction with the blockchain and because of its similarity to the infamous DAO contract that was deployed on the Ethereum blockchain and which was eventually hacked by a clever attacker exploiting reentrancy in the EVM. The Congress can be seen as the core of the DAO contract, namely the proposal and voting mechanisms.

We implement the logic of the Congress in roughly 150 lines of Coq code. The type of messages accepted by the Congress can be thought of as its interface since this is how the contract can be interacted with:

```
Inductive Msg :=
  | transfer_ownership : Address → Msg
  | change_rules : Rules → Msg
  | add_member : Address → Msg
  | remove_member : Address → Msg
  | create_proposal : list CongressAction → Msg
  | vote_for_proposal : ProposalId → Msg
```

```
| vote_against_proposal : ProposalId → Msg
| retract_vote : ProposalId → Msg
| finish_proposal : ProposalId → Msg.
```

The Congress has an owner who is responsible for managing the rules of the Congress and the member list. By default, we set this to be the creator of the Congress. The owner can transfer his ownership away with the `transfer_ownership` message. It is possible to make the Congress its own owner, in which case all rule changes and modifications to the member list must happen through proposals (essentially making the Congress a democracy).

Anyone can use the `create_proposal` and `finish_proposal` messages. We allow proposals to contain any number of actions to send out, though we restrict the actions to only transfers and contract calls (i.e. no contract deployments). This restriction is necessary because deployments would require the state of the Congress to contain the contracts to deploy. Since contracts are functions in our shallow embedding this would require storing higher order state which we do not allow in the framework. This is a downside to the shallow embedding – with a deep embedding like [2], the code could be stored as an AST or bytes.

The rules of the Congress specify how long proposals need to be debated. During this period, members of the Congress have the ability to vote on the proposal. Once debated, a proposal can be finished and the Congress will remove it from its internal storage and send out its actions if it passed.

A Partial Specification. The DAO vulnerability was in reward payout code in which a specially crafted contract could reenter the DAO causing it to perform actions an unintended number of times. Specifically, the attacker was able to propose a so-called *split* and have the original DAO transfer a disproportionate amount of money to a new DAO contract under his control. Congress does not allow splits, but the same kind of bug would be possible in code responsible for carrying out proposals.

Previous research such as [3] has focused on defining this kind of reentrancy formally. Such (hyper-)properties are interesting, but they also rely heavily on the benefit of hindsight and their statements are complex and hard to understand. Instead we would like to come up with a natural specification for the Congress that a programmer could reasonably have come up with, even without knowledge of reentrancy or the exploit. Our goal with this is to apply the framework in a very concrete setting.

The specification we give is based on the following observation: any transaction sent out by the Congress should correspond to an action that was previously created with a `create_proposal` message. This is a temporal property because it says something about the past whenever an outgoing transaction is observed. Temporal logic is not natively supported by Coq, so this would require some work. Therefore we prefer a similar but simpler property: the number of actions in previous `create_proposal` messages is always greater than or equal to the total number of transactions the Congress has sent out. Our main result about the Congress is a formal proof that this always holds after adding a block:

```
Corollary congress_txs_after_block {ChainBuilder : ChainBuilderType}
         prev creator header acts new :
  builder_add_block prev creator header acts = Some new →
  forall addr,
    env_contracts new addr = Some (Congress.contract : WeakContract) →
    length (outgoing_txs (builder_trace new) addr) ≤
    num_acts_created_in_proposals (incoming_txs (builder_trace new) addr).
```

This result states that, after adding a block, any address at which a Congress contract is deployed satisfies the property previously described. The number of actions created in previous `create_proposal` messages is calculated by function `num_acts_created_in_proposals`. The `incoming_txs` and `outgoing_txs` functions are general functions that finds transactions (evaluation of actions) in a trace. In this sense the property treats the contract as a black box, stating only things about the transactions that have been observed on the blockchain.

This is not a full specification of the behavior of the Congress but proving this property can help increase trust in the Congress. In particular it would not have been provable in the original DAO contract because of the reentrancy exploit where the DAO sent out an unbounded number of transactions. Note also that we do not want to exclude reentrancy entirely: indeed, in the situation where the Congress is its own owner reentrancy is required for changing rules and the member list.

We prove the property by generalizing it over the following data:

- The internal state of the contract; more specifically, the current number of actions in proposals stored in the internal state.
- The number of transactions sent out by the Congress, as before.
- The number of actions *in the queue* where the Congress is the source.
- The number of actions created in proposals, as before.

This results in a stronger statement from which the original result follows. The key observations are that
1. When a proposal is created, the number of actions created in proposals goes up, but so does the number of actions in the internal state of the Congress.
2. When a proposal is finished, the number of actions in the internal state goes down, but the number of actions in the queue goes up accordingly (assuming the proposal was voted for). In other words, actions "move" from the Congress's internal state to the queue.
3. When an outgoing transaction appears on the chain it is because an action moved out of the queue.

Especially observation 3 is interesting. It allows us to connect the evaluation of a contract in the past to its resulting transactions on the chain, even though these steps can be separated by many unrelated steps in the trace.

The proof of the stronger statement is straightforward by inducting over the trace. When deploying the Congress we need to establish the invariant which boils down to proving functional correctness of the `init` function and the use of some results that hold for contracts which have just been deployed (for instance, such contracts have not made any outgoing transactions). On calls to the Congress the invariant needs to be reestablished, which boils down to proving functional correctness of the `receive` function. Crucially, we can reestablish the invariant because the implementation of the Congress clears out proposals from its state *before* the actions in the proposal are evaluated (the DAO was vulnerable because it neglected to do this on splits).

4   Conclusions

We have formalized the execution model of blockchains in Coq and used our formalization to prove formally a result about a concrete contract. Our formalization of blockchain semantics is flexible in that it accounts both for depth-first and breadth-first execution order, generalizing existing blockchains and previous work, while remaining expressive enough to allow us to prove results about complex contracts. We showed for a Congress – a simplified version of the DAO, which still has a complex dynamic interaction pattern – that it will never send out more transactions than have been created in proposals. This is a natural property that aids in increasing trust that this contract is not vulnerable to reentrancy like the DAO.

Related Work. Both Simplicity [7] and Scilla [9] are smart contract languages with an embedding in Coq. Temporal properties of several smart contracts have been verified in Scilla [10], although our Congress contract is more complex than the contracts described in that paper. We are unaware of an implementation of such a contract in Scilla. Scilla, as an intermediate language which includes both a functional part and contract calls, uses a CPS translation to ensure that every call to another contract is done as the last instruction. In our model, the high-level language and the execution layer are strictly separated.

The formalization of the EVM in F* [3] can be extracted and used to run EVM tests to show that it is a faithful model of the EVM. However, they do not prove properties of any concrete contracts. Instead they consider classes of bugs in smart contracts and try to define general properties that prevent these. One of these properties, call integrity, is motivated by the DAO and attempts to capture reentrancy. Intuitively a contract satisfies call integrity if the calls it makes cannot be affected by code of other contracts. VerX [8] uses temporal logic and model checking to check a similar property. Such statements are not hard to state in our framework given Coq's expressive logic, and it seems this would be an appropriate property to verify for the Congress. However, even a correct Congress does not satisfy this property, since it is possible for called contracts to finish proposals which can cause the Congress to perform calls. This property could potentially be proven in a version of the Congress that only allowed proposals to be finished by humans, and not by contracts.

Future Work. More smart contracts are available in Wang's PhD thesis [11] and specifying these to gain experience with using the framework will help uncover how the framework itself should be improved. In this area it is also interesting to consider more automatic methods to make proving more productive. For example, temporal logics like LTL or CTL can be useful to specify properties on traces and model checking these can be automated; see e.g. [8].

Finally, while our current framework is inspired by and generalizes existing blockchains, there is still more work to be done to get closer to practical implementations. Gas is notoriously difficult to deal with in our shallow embedding because tracking costs of operations can not be done automatically. However, perhaps a monadic structure can be used here [6]. We have connected our work with a deep embedding of a functional language [1] and explored pros and cons of shallow and deep embeddings in that work. We plan to use this deep embedding to explore reasoning about gas. In the other direction it is interesting to consider extraction of the execution layers we have shown to satisfy our semantics and extraction of verified contracts into other languages like Liquidity, Oak or Solidity.

Acknowledgements. We would like to thank the Oak team for discussions.

References

1. Annenkov, D., Nielsen, J.B., Spitters, B.: ConCert: a smart contract certification framework in Coq. In: CPP 2020: Proceedings of the 9th ACM SIGPLAN International Conference on Certified Programs and Proofs, pp. 215–228. January 2020 (2020)
2. Annenkov, D., Spitters, B.: Deep and shallow embeddings in Coq. TYPES (2019)
3. Grishchenko, I., Maffei, M., Schneidewind, C.: A semantic framework for the security analysis of ethereum smart contracts. In: Bauer, L., Küsters, R. (eds.) POST 2018. LNCS, vol. 10804, pp. 243–269. Springer, Cham (2018). https://doi.org/10.1007/978-3-319-89722-6_10
4. Jung, R., Krebbers, R., Jourdan, J.H., Bizjak, A., Birkedal, L., Dreyer, D.: Iris from the ground up: a modular foundation for higher-order concurrent separation logic. J. Funct. Program. **28**, e20 (2018)
5. Magri, B., Matt, C., Nielsen, J.B., Tschudi, D.: Afgjort - a semi-synchronous finality layer for blockchains (2019). Cryptology ePrint 2019/504
6. McCarthy, J., Fetscher, B., New, M.S., Feltey, D., Findler, R.B.: A Coq library for internal verification of running-times. Sci. Comput. Program. **164**, 49–65 (2018)
7. O'Connor, R.: Simplicity: a new language for blockchains. In: Proceedings of the 2017 Workshop on Programming Languages and Analysis for Security (2017)
8. Permenev, A., Dimitrov, D., Tsankov, P., Drachsler-Cohen, D., Vechev, M.: Verx: safety verification of smart contracts. In: Security and Privacy 2020 (2019)
9. Sergey, I., Kumar, A., Hobor, A.: Scilla: a smart contract intermediate-level language. arXiv:1801.00687 (2018)
10. Sergey, I., Kumar, A., Hobor, A.: Temporal properties of smart contracts. In: Margaria, T., Steffen, B. (eds.) ISoLA 2018. LNCS, vol. 11247, pp. 323–338. Springer, Cham (2018). https://doi.org/10.1007/978-3-030-03427-6_25
11. Wang, P.: Type system for resource bounds with type-preserving compilation. Ph.D. thesis, MIT (2018)
12. Zahnentferner, J.: Chimeric ledgers: translating and unifying UTXO-based and account-based cryptocurrencies (2018). Cryptology ePrint 2018/262

Formal Specification of a Security Framework for Smart Contracts

Mikhail Mandrykin[1(✉)], Jake O'Shannessy[2], Jacob Payne[2],
and Ilya Shchepetkov[1]

[1] ISP RAS, Moscow, Russia
{mandrykin,shchepetkov}@ispras.ru
[2] Daohub, San Francisco, USA
joshannessy@gmail.com, jacob@daohub.io

Abstract. As smart contracts are growing in size and complexity, it becomes harder and harder to ensure their correctness and security. Due to the lack of isolation mechanisms a single mistake or vulnerability in the code can bring the whole system down, and due to this smart contract upgrades can be especially dangerous. Traditional ways to ensure the security of a smart contract, including DSLs, auditing and static analysis, are used before the code is deployed to the blockchain, and thus offer no protection after the deployment. After each upgrade the whole code need to be verified again, which is a difficult and time-consuming process that is prone to errors. To address these issues a security protocol and framework for smart contracts called Cap9 was developed. It provides developers the ability to perform upgrades in a secure and robust manner, and improves isolation and transparency through the use of a low level capability-based security model. We have used Isabelle/HOL to develop a formal specification of the Cap9 framework and prove its consistency. The paper presents a refinement-based approach that we used to create the specification, as well as discussion of some encountered difficulties during this process.

Keywords: Formal specification · Smart contracts · Isabelle · Security.

1 Introduction

Ethereum [6] is a global blockchain platform for decentralised applications with a built-in Turing-complete programming language. This language is used to create smart contracts—automated general-purpose programs that have access to the state of the blockchain, can store persistent data and exchange transactions with other contracts and users. Such contracts have a number of use-cases in different areas: finance, insurance, intellectual property, internet of things, voting, and others.

However, creating a *reliable* and *secure* smart contract can be extremely challenging. Ethereum guarantees that the code of a smart contract would be executed precisely as it is written through the use of a consensus protocol, which

© Springer Nature Switzerland AG 2020
E. Sekerinski et al. (Eds.): FM 2019 Workshops, LNCS 12232, pp. 392–403, 2020.
https://doi.org/10.1007/978-3-030-54994-7_30

resolves potential conflicts between the nodes in the blockchain network. It prevents malicious nodes from disrupting and changing the execution process, but does not protect from the flaws and mistakes in the code itself. And due to the lack of any other control on the execution of the code any uncaught mistake can potentially compromise not only the contract itself, but also other contracts that are interacting with it and expect a certain behavior from it.

Such flaws can be turned into vulnerabilities and cause a great harm, and there are many examples of such vulnerabilities and attacks that exploit them [2]. Developers can ensure the security of a contract using auditing, various static analysis tools [11,15], domain-specific languages [5,7], or formal verification [3]. These are excellent tools and methods that can significantly improve the quality of the code. But they are not so effective during the upgrades, which is a common process for almost every sufficiently sophisticated smart contract. Upgrades are necessary because it is the only way to fix a bug that was missed during the verification process. However, they can also introduce their own bugs, so after each upgrade the code needs to be verified again, which may cost a lot of time and effort.

These issues are addressed by the Cap9 framework [4]. It provides means to isolate contracts from each other and restrict them from doing dangerous state-changing actions unsupervised, thus greatly reducing risks of upgrades and consequences of uncaught mistakes. Cap9 achieves this by using a low level capability-based security model, which allows to explicitly define what can or can not be done by any particular contract. Once defined, such capabilities, or permissions, are visible to anyone and can be easily understood and independently checked, thus increasing transparency of the system.

In order to be trusted, the Cap9 framework itself needs to be formally verified. The specification of the framework must be formalised and proved, in order to show that it is consistent and satisfies the stated properties. Then the implementation, which is a smart contract itself, must be proved to be compliant with its specification. In this paper we are focusing only on the first part—on developing and proving a formal specification of the Cap9 framework using the Isabelle/HOL theorem prover [17] The paper presents a refinement-based approach that we used to create the specification, and evaluates the chosen formal method by describing encountered difficulties during this process.

The following section outlines the features and capabilities of the Cap9 framework. Section 3 presents the Isabelle/HOL specification, as well as the difficulties we have encountered and the refinement process we used to develop it. Related work is reviewed in Section 4. The last section concludes the paper and considers future work.

2   Cap9 Framework

The Cap9 framework achieves isolation by interposing itself between the smart contracts that are running on top of it and potentially dangerous actions that they can perform, including calling other smart contracts, writing to the storage and creating new contracts. Such actions can be performed only using special

"System Call" interface provided by the framework. Via this interface it has complete control over what contracts can and cannot do. Each time a system call is executed Cap9 conducts various runtime security checks to ensure that a calling contract indeed has necessary rights to perform a requested action. It works similar to how operating system kernels manage accesses of programs to the hardware (like memory and CPU) and protect programs from unauthorised accesses to each other.

In order to ensure that a contract correctly uses the system call interface and does not perform any actions bypassing the framework its source code needs to be verified. Cap9 does it on-chain and it checks that the source code does not contain any forbidden instructions, like ones allowing to make state changes, make an external call, or self destruct. The check is called procedure bytecode validation. The valid code is essentially only allowed to perform local computations (those not involving any calls or modifications of the store) and delegate calls to a special predefined kernel address. This is a very simple property that can be ensured by an efficient dynamic check that is performed only once upon the registration of the newly deployed code. Once the code is validated the corresponding contract can be registered in the framework as a *procedure* and thus access its features.

There are system calls available to securely perform the following actions:

- Register new procedure in the framework;
- Delete a registered procedure;
- Internally call a registered procedure;
- Write data to the storage;
- Append log record with given topics;
- Externally call another Ethereum address and/or send Ether;
- Mark a procedure as an *entry* procedure—one that would handle all the incoming external calls to this contract system or organisation.

As a typical smart contract, Cap9 has access to the storage—a persistent 256×256 bits key-value store. A small part of it is restricted and can be used only by the framework itself. It has a strict format and is used to store the list of registered procedures, as well as procedure data, addresses of entry and current procedures and the Ethereum address of the deployed framework itself. This part is called the *kernel storage*. The rest of the storage is open to use by any registered procedure either directly (in case of read) or through a dedicated system call (in case of write).

Traditional kernels have a lot of abstraction layers between programs and hardware. Unlike them, Cap9 exposes all the underlying Ethereum mechanisms directly to the contracts, with only a thin permission layer between them. This layer implements a capability-based access control, according to which in order to execute a system call a procedure must posses a *capability* with an explicit permission. Such capability has a strict format, which is different for each available type of system calls.

Capabilities can be used to restrict components of a smart contract system and thus to implement the principle of least privilege. They can also be used as base primitives to create a custom high-level security policy model to better fit a particular use case. Such policy would be simple to analyze and understand, but able to limit possible damage from bugs in the code or various malicious actions (including replacing the code of a contract via the upgrade mechanism).

Cap9 is compatible with both EVM and Ewasm applications.

3   Formal Specification

The main goal of formalizing the interface specification of the Cap9 security framework was to ensure internal consistency and completeness of its description as well as to provide a reliable reference for all of its implementations. The reference should eventually serve as an intermediate between the users and the developers of any Cap9 implementation ensuring full compatibility of all further system uses and implementations. The source specification itself is formulated as a detailed textual description of the system interface [19], which is language-agnostic and relies on the binary interfaces of the underlying virtual machine. Thus all the data mentioned in the specification is given an explicit concrete bit-level representation, which is intended to be shared by all system users and implementations.

3.1   Consolidation of Low-Level Representation with High-Level Semantics

One of the immediately arising challenges of formally verifying a system with very explicit specifications on concrete data representation is efficiently establishing a correspondence between this representation and the corresponding intended semantics, which is used for actual reasoning about the system and therefore for the actual proof.

A particular example in our case is the representation and the semantics of capability subsets. Each capability of every procedure in the system logically corresponds to a set of admissible values for some parameter configuration, such as kernel storage address (for writing to the storage), Ethereum address and amount of gas for external procedure call, log message with several special topic fields etc. Each such set is composed of a (not necessarily disjoint) union of a number of subsets, which in their turn directly correspond to some fixed representations. A subset of writable addresses, for example, is represented as a pair of the starting address and the length of a continuous range of admissible addresses. Thus the entire write capability of any kernel procedure is a union of such continuous address ranges.

But it's important to note that while on one hand we clearly need to state the set semantics of the write capability (as a generally arbitrary set of addresses), in particular this is especially convenient semantics to be used for proofs of generic capability properties, such as transitivity; on the other hand, however, we have a clearly indicated format of the corresponding capability representation stated in the system specification, which is not a set, but a range of storage cells holding the bit-wise representations of the starting addresses and lengths of the corresponding ranges.

If we stick with the specified representation, we will be unable to efficiently use many powerful automated reasoning tools provided with Isabelle/HOL, such as the classical reasoner and the simplifier readily pre-configured for the set operations. However, if we just use the set interpretation, the specification on the concrete representation will be notoriously hard to express. Hence we likely need several different formalizations of a notion of capability on several levels of abstraction. We actually used three representations: the concrete bit-wise representation, the more abstract representation with the length of the range expressed as natural number (and with an additional invariant), and finally the set representation. By using separate representations we ended up with small simple proofs for both generic capability properties and their concrete representations.

3.2 Correspondence Relation vs. Representation Function

Eventually we decided to employ the same refinement approach with several formalizations for the entire specification, thus obtaining two representations of the whole system: the structured high-level representation with additional type invariants and the low-level representation as the mapping from 32-byte addresses to 32-byte values, i.e. the state of the kernel storage. However, using separate representations raises a problem of efficiently establishing the correspondence between them. Initially we tried a more general approach based on the correspondence relation. Yet to properly transfer properties of the high-level representation to the low-level one, the relation should enjoy at least two properties: injectivity and non-empty image of every singleton:

lemma $rel\_injective$: $"[\![s \Vdash \sigma_1;\ s \Vdash \sigma_2]\!] \Longrightarrow \sigma_1 = \sigma_2\ "$
lemma $non\_empty\_singleton$: $"\exists\ s.\ s \Vdash \sigma\ "$

Here $\Vdash$ stands for the correspondence relation, σ—for the high-level representation and s—for the concrete one. We noticed that proving the second lemma essentially requires defining a function mapping an abstract representation to the corresponding concrete one. Thus this approach results in significant redundancy in a sense that both the function defined for the sake of proving the second lemma and the correspondence relation itself repeat essentially the same constraints on the low-level representation. For a very simple example consider:

definition $models$ :: $"(word32 \Rightarrow word32) \Rightarrow kernel \Rightarrow bool"\ ("\_ \Vdash \_")$ where
$\quad "s \Vdash \sigma \equiv unat\ (s\ (addr\ Nprocs)) = nprocs\ \sigma"$
definition $"witness\ \sigma\ a \equiv case\ addr^{-1}\ a\ of\ Nprocs \Rightarrow of\_nat\ (nprocs\ \sigma)"$

Here not only we need to repeatedly state the relationship between the value of kernel storage at address $addr\ Nprocs$ and the number of procedures registered in the system ($nprocs\ \sigma$) twice, but we also potentially have to define the address encoding and decoding functions ($addr$ and $addr^{-1}$) separately and to prove the lemma about their correspondence. We discuss our approach to address encoding in the following section and here only emphasize the redundancy arising from the approach based on the correspondence relation.

It also worth noting that merely transferring or lifting the properties stated for one representation to another is insufficient as we would like to also be able to conveniently represent mixed properties such as a property specifying the result of an operation on the high level, but also stating an additional constraint on its concrete representation e.g. that some irrelevant bits in the representation should be zeroed and some others remain unchanged.

At the same time, the major reason for introducing the correspondence relation instead of using a function is an inherent ambiguity of the encoding of the high-level representation into the low-level one. However, after carefully revisiting the initial specification of the system we noticed that the ambiguity of representation in our system actually arises only from the unused storage memory rather than from the presence of any truly distinct ways of representing the same state. But this particular kind of ambiguity can be efficiently expressed using a representation function with an additional parameter—i.e. the state of the unused memory.

Let's illustrate our formalization approach that is based on representation functions on the example of Procedure Call capability. The specification of this capability is as follows:

The capability format for the Call Procedure system call defines a range of procedure keys which the capability allows one to call. This is defined as a base procedure key b and a prefix s. Given this capability, a procedure may call any procedure where the first s bits of the key of that procedure are the same as the first s bits of procedure key b.

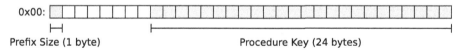

0x00:

⊢⊣
Prefix Size (1 byte)   **Procedure Key (24 bytes)**

Here the unused space is left blank. Beforehand we strive to make the actual formulation of the arising injectivity lemma as simple as possible by eliminating premises of the lemma and turning them into type invariants. So we introduce the following definitions:

typedef $prefix\_size = \text{"}\{n :: nat.\ n \leq LENGTH(key)\}\text{"}$
definition $\text{"}prefix\_size\_rep\ s \equiv of\_nat\ \lfloor s \rfloor :: byte\text{"}$ for $s :: prefix\_size$
type_synonym $prefixed\_capability = \text{"}prefix\_size \times key\text{"}$
definition — set interpretation of single write capability
    $\text{"}set\_of\_pref\_cap\ (sk :: prefixed\_capability) \equiv let\ (s,\ k) = sk\ in$
    $\{k' :: key.\ take\ \lfloor s \rfloor\ (to\_bl\ k') = take\ \lfloor s \rfloor\ (to\_bl\ k)\}\text{"}$
adhoc_overloading $rep\ prefix\_size\_rep$ — $prefix\_size\_rep$ is now denoted as $\lfloor \cdot \rfloor$
definition — low-level (storage) representation of single write capability
    $\text{"}pref\_cap\_rep\ (sk :: prefixed\_capability)\ r \equiv let\ (s,\ k) = sk\ in$
    $\lfloor s \rfloor_1 \Diamond\ k\ OR\ r \upharpoonright \{LENGTH(key)..<LENGTH(word32) - LENGTH(byte)\}\text{"}$

Here the parameter r represents some arbitrary memory state being overwritten by the representation of the capability. The binary representation of r is truncated (by bit-wise conjunction with a mask) to fill the range of unused bits before combining it with the zero-padded representation. The value of unused memory r is propagated across all representation functions in a composable way, so all low-level representations are formalized with plain single-valued functions. This approach not only allows for a simple transfer of all high-level properties to the low-level representation, but also avoids the need in explicit definitions of the corresponding inverse (decoding) functions. A single definition is enough to reuse the encoding functions (along with their injectivity proofs) for the specifications of operations that require decoding of representations:

definition "*maybe_inv f y* ≡ *if y* ∈ *range f then Some (the_inv f y) else None*"

Since we don't verify the actual implementation of the decoding functions, this implicit definition is sufficient and greatly simplifies proofs.

There is, though, one potential weakness in this approach in that it's still possible to accidentally lose some non-determinism when propagating the values of the unused memory by unintentionally identifying different values of the additional parameters. Each occurrence of the representation function should be provided its own separate instance of an additional parameter so that e.g. encoding of the whole kernel storage is supplied with the whole previous state of the store as an additional parameter rather than just a single additional default value. To systematically guarantee absence of such losses of non-determinism we prove additional lemmas of the form:

lemma *cap_rep_unused*: "⌊*c*⌋ *r* ↾ *unused* = *r*",

where *unused* is the set of unused bits and ↾ restricts the range of bits by zeroing out bits with indices not in the specified set. These lemmas, though, are proved very easily for all our representation function definitions.

3.3 Disjointness of Addresses

Another problem arising from detailed low-level specifications of memory layout, such as the layout of the kernel storage, is the problem of reasoning about non-intersecting memory areas. While in the context of program verification there are such well-known approaches to reasoning about disjoint memory footprints as separation logic [18] and dynamic frames [12], in our context of formalizing the specification (rather than the implementation) of the system these approaches turned out to be both too abstract and too heavyweight. Too abstract since in separation logic the particular concrete layout of the memory footprints is left entirely abstract, while we needed to formalize the actual mapping of the data structures to the mostly fixed address ranges they should occupy. Too heavyweight since to represent the encoding of the whole kernel state with either separation logic or dynamic frames we would need to use some additional means to set up the embedding of the corresponding reasoning mechanism into plain HOL, while not having any real need in verifying code involving updates to the system state. In our approach we simply treated kernel addresses as semantic entities with some ascribed low-level representations (concrete values). Then following our general use of representation functions we defined the representation of addresses and its inverse. The inverse then can be directly used to specify the storage layout and prove the injectivity of the overall encoding with minimal effort. Here's an illustrative example:

typedef *offset* = "{ $n :: nat. n < 2 \hat{} LENGTH(byte)$}" morphisms *off_rep off*
datatype *address* = *Nprocs* | *Curr_proc* | *Proc_heap offset*
definition "*addr_rep a* ≡ *case a of*
     Nprocs   ⇒ *0x0000*
   | *Proc_heap offs* ⇒ *0x0200 OR of_nat (off_rep offs)*"
definition "*addr_inv* ≡ *maybe_inv addr_rep*"
definition "*encode σ r a* ≡ *case addr_inv a of*
     Some a'   ⇒ *case a' of*
        Nprocs   ⇒ *of_nat (nprocs σ' OR (r a)* ⌈ ...
     | *Proc_heap offs* ⇒ *encode_heap σ offs r*
   | *None*   ⇒ *r a*"

Also note the filler of the unused memory r being passed over in a top-down manner starting from the outermost representation function.

Now we move from the problems arising from the detailed low-level specification of our target system to some more general issues of formalization and formal proofs within the Isabelle/HOL framework that we encountered during verification.

3.4 General Isabelle/HOL Limitations

Bit-Vector Concatenation. An example of a minor, though noticeable limitations of the simple Hindley-Milner type system employed within the Isabelle/HOL framework is its inability to express type-level sum (and other simple arithmetic operations), while still being able to express type-level numbers. For an illustration of the issue consider the following definition of bit-vector concatenation function from the HOL-Word library that comprises an extensive Isabelle/HOL formalization of fixed-size bit-vectors, corresponding operations and their various properties:

definition *word_cat* :: "*'a::len0 word* ⇒ *'b::len0 word* ⇒ *'c::len0 word*" ...

The annotation of the form *'a::len0* constrains the type parameter *'a* to belong to the *len0* type class, which has the corresponding associated operation *LENGTH('a)* returning a natural number. Thus we essentially gen type-level numbers that can be injected into terms as natural numbers with the use of the *LENGTH* operation. However, as we can see in the definition of *word_cat*, the result of this function has the type *'c::len0* that is generally unrelated to the parameter types *'a* and *'b*. This has two basically unavoidable, but undesirable consequences:

- Since there is no way of further constraining the resulting parameter type *'c::len0*, the function *word_cat* is forced to be partial. Generally, there is nothing particularly special about handling of partial functions within the Isabelle/HOL framework, but their presence has at least one undesirable consequence for formalization of system interface specifications, which we discuss further in this section.
- Since the resulting type parameter *'c::len0* cannot be automatically inferred from the arguments of *word_cat*, if has to be explicitly specified. Normally, this doesn't lead to a significant type annotation burden since the parameter can be propagated by type inference from some term with a known type. But in case of consecutive (nested or chained) *word_cat* applications, the inner type parameters become essentially inaccessible for further type propagation or inference and have to be specified explicitly e.g.

  definition "*entry_proc_addr* ≡ *word_cat*
  (*word_cat* (*word_cat* (*k_prefix* :: *32 word*) (*0x04* :: *byte*) :: *40 word*)
  (*0* :: *192 word*) :: *232 word*) (*0x000000* :: *24 word*) :: *256 word*"

This can be slightly mitigated by introducing some ad-hoc monomorphic notation for hexadecimal numbers (e.g. syntactically reconstructing the type annotation from the length of the input hexadecimal representation), but this approach still quickly becomes unwieldy in practice, especially in the context of the great available variety of Ethereum bit-vector types with various lengths.

First we propose a relatively simple remedy for the second problem. We actually used our own definition of a concatenation function with a fixed result type (the largest needed length of 256 bits) and parameter types of arbitrary length that is ignored. Instead we provided the necessary length of the second argument as an additional explicit parameter. Thus the whole issue of dealing with lengths was shifted from the type to the term level eliminating the need in any type-level representations altogether. This resulted in more approachable definitions e.g.

definition "*entry_proc_addr* ≡
  (*k_prefix* :: *32 word*) $\bowtie_{224}$ *0x04* $\bowtie_{216}$ (*0* :: *192 word*) $\bowtie_{24}$ *0x000000*"

Here $\cdot \bowtie \cdot$ denotes our concatenation function. In our opinion in the lack of dependent types or other expressive capabilities of the type system the use of logical (term-level) constraints may be often preferable to some limited meta-logical (e.g. type-level) extensions such as the use of type classes. Now we move to the second problem.

Partiality. The presence of partial functions in the specification of an interface of the system has a subtle undesirable property—unpredictability stemming from the undefined results returned by the partial functions. Consider the following very typical and general preservation lemma:

lemma *preservation*: "*I s* $\implies$ *I* (*op s a*)"

Here I is an invariant of the system and op is an operation on the system with an argument a. Let's imagine an example instance of this kind of lemma: Let s be a natural number, $I\,s$ be the predicate $s > 0$ and op correspond to the operation $s \leftarrow s + s \operatorname{div} a$. Looking at the general statement of the lemma, a rather natural interpretation of such a preservation property would be that any application of the operation op to the system is "safe" as it preserves its invariant. However in our particular example it's obvious that even though the application of op with $a = 0$ provably preserves the invariant, it actually has entirely unpredictable consequences for the system. So specifications of operations on the system involving partial functions may considerably mislead the reader of the specification while remaining perfectly correct form the purely logical perspective. If the formal specification is to serve as a formal documentation on the system this fact may significantly undermine the value of applying the formal methodology for that purpose. Fortunately, there are various ways to strengthen the specification to exclude such unintuitive definitions. For our specification we additionally proved the following injectivity-like lemmas for every operation:

lemma *injectivity_like*: "*op s a = op s b* $\Longrightarrow$ *a ˜ b* "

Here $\sim$ denotes some notion of equivalence for arguments of the operation in a sense that equivalent arguments produce equivalent results. In case the operation op actually involves some non-determinism, the formulation of the lemma should be adjusted accordingly, thus making this non-determinism explicitly exposed for the reader. The proof of such a lemma is enough to exclude any hidden non-determinism, since for any non-trivial equivalence relation $\sim$ ($\exists a'.\ a' \not\sim a$) if the op has non-deterministic result on a, $op\ a$ may be arbitrarily chosen to be equal to $op\ a'$ and the relation $a \sim a'$ then cannot be established.

Dependent Products. Another limitation arising from the lack of dependent types or other expressive type system features is inability to directly express dependent products i.e. types of the form $\prod_{x::'a} f(x)$, where f is a type-level function on the value x of some type $'a$. A typical example of a situation, where this seems very natural is a list of pairs of the form "*capability_type* × *capability_representation*" (e.g. if the value of the first member is "*Write*", than the type of the second member should be "*write_capability*"). Such types cannot be directly expressed within the Isabelle/HOL framework. A typical workaround is to use injection into some universal type with additional well-formedness predicates stated as preconditions to the operations or as type invariants. Here we were able to directly reuse our representation functions for injecting different types of capabilities into the same universal bit-level representation.

Finally it's important to note an essential benefit of a logical framework with a very limited type system, which is its amenability to automation using existing readily available tools such as saturation-based provers (E-prover, Vampire, Metis) and SMT solvers (Z3, CVC4). In our experience their use within the Isabelle framework lead to great advantages ultimately outweighing all the limitations mentioned above. Overall, the formalized specification with proofs took about 4500 lines of Isabelle based on 25 pages of the original textual description.

4   Related Work

There are many examples of using formal methods for developing specifications of various systems. Isabelle/HOL was used to prove functional correctness of the seL4 operating system microkernel [13], providing a proof chain from the high-level abstract specification of the kernel, down to the executable machine code. The B-method was applied to create formal models of various safety-critical railway systems [14]. A dedicated specification language for defining the high-level abstract models was introduced in [20].

On the other hand, verification of smart contracts is almost exclusively concentrated on the contract implementation, omitting the separate formalisation of their specification. It is a valid approach if the specification is simple enough, which is not the case for the Cap9 framework.

There are several examples of formalisation of the Ethereum virtual machine: using the K framework [9], the Lem language [10], F* [8], and Isabelle [1], which can serve as a basis for formal verification of the contract code. Why3 platform for deductive program verification was recently applied for writing and verifying smart contracts [16].

5   Conclusion and Future Work

We have developed a formal specification[1] of the Cap9 framework using the Isabelle/HOL theorem prover and proved its internal consistency. To create it we have employed a refinement approach based on representation functions, which allowed us to efficiently use powerful automated reasoning tools provided with Isabelle. We have found Isabelle/HOL to be suitable for developing specifications of smart contracts, although some minor issues were identified and outlined.

The next step is formal verification of the Ewasm implementation of the Cap9 framework for its compliance with the Isabelle/HOL specification, which may require developing some additional tools. Other possible direction is to develop and verify a higher level permission system that is based on the Cap9 primitives.

References

1. Amani, S., Bégel, M., Bortin, M., Staples, M.: Towards verifying ethereum smart contract bytecode in Isabelle/HOL. In: Proceedings of the 7th ACM SIGPLAN International Conference on Certified Programs and Proofs, pp. 66–77. CPP 2018. ACM, New York (2018). https://doi.org/10.1145/3167084
2. Atzei, N., Bartoletti, M., Cimoli, T.: A survey of attacks on ethereum smart contracts (SoK). In: Maffei, M., Ryan, M. (eds.) POST 2017. LNCS, vol. 10204, pp. 164–186. Springer, Heidelberg (2017). https://doi.org/10.1007/978-3-662-54455-6_8

---

[1] The specification is publicly available at https://github.com/Daohub-io/cap9-spec.

3. Bhargavan, K., et al.: Formal verification of smart contracts: short paper. In: Proceedings of the 2016 ACM Workshop on Programming Languages and Analysis for Security - PLAS 2016, pp. 91–96. ACM Press, Vienna (2016)
4. Cap9 white paper. https://cap9.io/docs/Whitepaper.pdf. Accessed 2 Jul 2019
5. The Ergo language for smart legal contracts. https://www.accordproject.org/projects/ergo. Accessed 2 Jul 2019
6. Ethereum white paper. https://github.com/ethereum/wiki/wiki/White-Paper. Accessed 2 Jul 2019
7. Frantz, C.K., Nowostawski, M.: From institutions to code: towards automated generation of smart contracts. In: 2016 IEEE 1st International Workshops on Foundations and Applications of Self* Systems (FAS*W), pp. 210–215, September 2016
8. Grishchenko, I., Maffei, M., Schneidewind, C.: A semantic framework for the security analysis of ethereum smart contracts. In: Bauer, L., Küsters, R. (eds.) POST 2018. LNCS, vol. 10804, pp. 243–269. Springer, Cham (2018). https://doi.org/10.1007/978-3-319-89722-6_10
9. Hildenbrandt, E., et al.: KEVM: a complete formal semantics of the ethereum virtual machine. In: 2018 IEEE 31st Computer Security Foundations Symposium (CSF), pp. 204–217. IEEE, Oxford, July 2018
10. Hirai, Y.: Defining the ethereum virtual machine for interactive theorem provers. In: Brenner, M., et al. (eds.) FC 2017. LNCS, vol. 10323, pp. 520–535. Springer, Cham (2017). https://doi.org/10.1007/978-3-319-70278-0_33
11. Kalra, S., Goel, S., Dhawan, M., Sharma, S.: ZEUS: analyzing safety of smart contracts. In: Proceedings 2018 Network and Distributed System Security Symposium. Internet Society, San Diego, CA (2018)
12. Kassios, I.T.: Dynamic frames: support for framing, dependencies and sharing without restrictions. In: Misra, J., Nipkow, T., Sekerinski, E. (eds.) FM 2006. LNCS, vol. 4085, pp. 268–283. Springer, Heidelberg (2006). https://doi.org/10.1007/11813040_19
13. Klein, G., et al.: Comprehensive formal verification of an OS microkernel. ACM Trans. Comput. Syst. **32**(1), 1–70 (2014)
14. Lecomte, T., Servat, T., Pouzancre, G.: Formal methods in safety-critical railway systems. In: 10th Brasilian Symposium on Formal Methods, p. 10 (2007)
15. Luu, L., Chu, D.H., Olickel, H., Saxena, P., Hobor, A.: Making smart contracts smarter. In: Proceedings of the 2016 ACM SIGSAC Conference on Computer and Communications Security, pp. 254–269. CCS 2016. ACM, New York (2016)
16. Nehai, Z., Bobot, F.: Deductive proof of ethereum smart contracts using why3. Research report, CEA DILS, April 2019. https://hal.archives-ouvertes.fr/hal-02108987
17. Nipkow, T., Paulson, L.C., Wenzel, M.: Isabelle/HOL: a proof assistant for higher-order logic. Lecture Notes in Computer Science. Springer, Heidelberg (2002). https://www.springer.com/gp/book/9783540433767
18. Reynolds, J.C.: Separation logic: a logic for shared mutable data structures. In: Proceedings 17th Annual IEEE Symposium on Logic in Computer Science, pp. 55–74, July 2002
19. Specification of the Cap9 framework. https://github.com/Daohub-io/cap9/blob/master/docs/spec/Cap9Spec.pdf. Accessed 2 Jul 2019
20. Xu, F., Fu, M., Feng, X., Zhang, X., Zhang, H., Li, Z.: A Practical verification framework for preemptive OS kernels. In: Chaudhuri, S., Farzan, A. (eds.) CAV 2016. LNCS, vol. 9780, pp. 59–79. Springer, Cham (2016). https://doi.org/10.1007/978-3-319-41540-6_4

FMIS 2019 - 8th Formal Methods for Interactive Systems Workshop

FMIS 2019 Organizers' Message

Reducing the risk of human error in the use of interactive systems is increasingly recognised as a key objective in contexts where safety, security, financial or similar considerations are important. These risks are of particular concern where users are presented with novel interactive experiences through the use of ubiquitous mobile devices in complex smart environments. Formal methods are required to analyse these interactive situations. In such complex systems analysis and justification that risk is reduced may depend on both qualitative and quantitative models of the system.

The aim of FMIS 2019 (The 8th International Workshop on Formal Methods for Interactive Systems) was to bring together researchers from a range of disciplines within computer science (including Human-Computer Interaction – HCI) and other behavioural disciplines, from both academia and industry. People interested in both formal methods and interactive system design presented papers or attended.

The focus of the workshop included general design and verification methodologies, which take account of models or accounts of human behaviour. Papers presented addressed issues of how formal methods can be applied to interactive system design. Also welcomed were papers with a focus on theory, provided a link to interactive systems was made explicit. Application areas considered included: pervasive and ubiquitous systems, cyber-physical systems, augmented reality, scalability and resilience, mobile devices, embedded systems, safety-critical systems, high-reliability systems, shared control systems, digital libraries, eGovernment, human-robot interaction. An invited talk by Michael D. Harrison (Newcastle) reflected on the tools that are used to support the application of formal methods to interactive systems and the problems that hinder their accessibility, commenting on tool developments that could lead to wider use of these techniques.

FMIS 2019, co-located with FM'19 (The 3rd World Congress on Formal Methods), was held in Porto on October 7, 2019. The World Congress on Formal Methods is organised every ten years by Formal Methods Europe as a platform for researchers and practitioners from a diversity of backgrounds and schools to exchange their ideas and share their experience. FM'19 brought together more than 30 events, between conferences, workshops, tutorials, two Festschrifts, a Doctoral Symposium and an Industry Day event.

The workshop was one of a series which aims to grow and sustain a network of researchers interested in the development and application of formal methods and related verification and analysis tools to interactive computing systems, providing a venue at which specifically formal techniques, as applied to problems with the design, modelling or implementation of interactive systems, can be presented and discussed. The previous seven editions were: FMIS 2006 (co-located with ICFEM 2006, Macau), FMIS 2007 (co-located with HCI 2007, Lancaster), FMIS 2009 (co-located with FM 2009, Eindhoven), FMIS 2011 (co-located with FM 2011, Limerick), FMIS 2013 (co-located with EICS 2013, London), FMIS 2017 (co-located with APSEC 2017, Nanjing) and FMIS 2018 (co-located with STAF 2018, Toulouse).

The reviewing for this eighth FMIS was single-blind, and each paper had three reviewers. There were eight papers submitted, seven were given at the workshop day and five have been further reviewed and appear in this post-workshop proceedings.

November 2019   José Creissac Campos
                                                              Steve Reeves

Organization

General Chairs and Program Committee Chairs

José Creissac Campos   University of Minho & HASLab/INESC TEC,
                                 Portugal
Steve Reeves   University of Waikato, New Zealand

Program Committee

Oana Andrei   University of Glasgow, UK
Judy Bowen   University of Waikato, New Zealand
Antonio Cerrone   Nazarbayev University, Kazhakstan
David Chemouil   ONERA & Université fédérale de Toulouse,
                                 France
Horatiu Cirstea   Loria, France
Bruno d'Ausbourg   ONERA, France
Alan Dix   Swansea University, UK
Stefania Gnesi   CNR, Italy
Michael Harrison   Newcastle University, UK
C. Michael Holloway   NASA, USA
Kris Luyten   Hasselt University, Belgium
Paolo Masci   National Institute of Aerospace, USA
Mieke Massink   CNR-ISTI, Italy
Dominique Mery   Université de Lorraine, France
Philippe Palanque   University Toulouse 3, France
Steve Reeves   University of Waikato, New Zealand
Benjamin Weyers   Trier University, Germany

Examples of the Application of Formal Methods to Interactive Systems

Michael D. Harrison[(✉)] ![ORCID]

School of Computing, Newcastle University, Newcastle upon Tyne, UK
michael.harrison@ncl.ac.uk
http://www.ncl.ac.uk/computing/people/profile/michael.harrison

Abstract. Formal methods in interactive systems can be used to analyse how systems support use with a clarity that is not possible with more traditional development approaches. However, the processes involved are complicated and do not fit well with those whose primary concern is user interfaces. The paper reflects on the tools that are used and the problems that hinder their accessibility. It comments on tool developments that could lead to wider use of these techniques. The role that existing methods and tools can play in analysing interactive systems will be explored through concrete examples involving the use of the PVS theorem proving assistant and the IVY toolset. Examples will focus on:

- the formulation and validation of models of interactive systems;
- the expression of use related requirements, particularly in the context of usability engineering and safety analysis;
- the generation of proofs that requirements hold true and making sense when proof fails.

Examples will be taken from existing standalone medical devices including examples from part of a safety analysis of a device leading to product.

Keywords: Formal verification · Automated reasoning tools · Interactive computing systems

1 Introduction

The analysis of interactive systems using formal methods can provide benefits in the development and analysis of interactive systems. However many of these benefits are potential rather than actual because of the many obstacles to their use. This is of particular significance in the context of interactive systems because the developers and analysts of such systems may not be computer scientists. Their focus and expertise may be the domain for which the system is to be designed or the role of the user in understanding how such systems should be designed. The paper explores two specific tools that support formal methods using examples of interactive systems to illustrate some of these issues.

This exploration considers two examples both of which concern medical devices. Medical devices are of particular interest. They are often safety critical and use related errors are a particular concern for the community. Also, the

© Springer Nature Switzerland AG 2020
E. Sekerinski et al. (Eds.): FM 2019 Workshops, LNCS 12232, pp. 409–423, 2020.
https://doi.org/10.1007/978-3-030-54994-7_31

teams involved in their development are often small. It is common that a new medical device is built by a research team who focus on the science associated with the device rather than its usability. The paper explores the following issues through the examples:

- the formulation and validation of the models that are intended to capture the key characteristics of the use of these devices;
- the expression of use related requirements: these requirements could be for example design heuristics or safety requirements derived from a risk log;
- the process of proving and demonstrating that a requirement holds true of the model and, by extension, is true of the existing or intended device.

It is not intended that the paper be exhaustive in its consideration of these issues. The examples are used to illustrate some aspects of the development and analysis of interactive systems. The paper will be concluded by briefly considering extensions to tools that would aid their use.

2   Formal Verification of Interactive Computing Systems

Formal verification, applied to interactive computing systems, has seen considerable development, mostly at the model-based level [1,6,16,27,30]. In [14] it was argued that formal verification has a role to play in systematic usability analysis. Criticisms of formal methods include:

1. use depends on specific knowledge of the complicated formalisms and tools required;
2. application is limited in that they are unable to manage the scale of real systems and consequently they tend to be used in a way that is narrow in scope.

The advantage however is that within the focus of their use, analysis is exhaustive. Use centred requirements may be identified informally by domain or human factors experts and formulated precisely as properties that may be proved of a formal model of the interactive system under investigation. It is envisaged that formal analysis techniques can be used as part of the design process involving a team who have complementary expertise. This paper uses examples of where formal techniques have been used to explore what additional tools would improve the acceptability of formal methods in the development of interactive systems.

Tools such as the IVY workbench have been shown to be applicable to real systems [4] and to contribute to the risk analysis of an actual medical device [15]. IVY focuses on model-based analysis of interactive computing system designs, with particular reference to aspects related to their behaviour. Other tools also aim at supporting the analysis of these systems, each with its particular focus (see [11] for a comparison of CIRCUS and PVSio-web).

The illustrations described in this paper and proposals that will be made can be seen as consistent with the agenda of research in "lightweight formal methods" (LFM). According to Zamansky et al.'s review [31] a key feature of developments in lightweight techniques is a focus on partial models and analyses—the ability to use formal methods to model and analyse components of the software, for example the control component, or in the present context, the user interface component. Analyses can then contribute to parts of the required analysis or program development allowing other techniques, for example testing, to be used for other parts.

3   Tools That Are Used in the Examples

The illustrations in this paper use two toolsets: PVS which uses a theorem proving approach and IVY which provides a front end to a model checking approach (NuSMV [7]). By describing how the tools were used in the example, gaps in user support will indicate the need for further tools.

3.1   PVS

The theorem proving system used in this paper is the *Prototype Verification System (PVS)* [28]. It combines an expressive specification language based on higher-order logic with a theorem proving assistant. PVS has been used extensively in several application domains. A specification in PVS is expressed as a collection of *theories* which consist of declarations of names for types and constants, and expressions in terms of these names. Theories can be parametrised with types and constants, and can use declarations of other theories by importing them.

Properties of a PVS specification are expressed as named formulae declared using the keyword THEOREM. Structural induction will often be used to prove that a given property is an invariant of the system model. This process involves proving a property is true of all relevant *reachable* states when universal quantification is not possible. In the particular context of the analyses discussed in the paper, states are reachable by user actions—a specification is described in terms of states where the focus of their transformation is user action.

The interactive theorem prover of PVS provides a collection of powerful primitive inference procedures that are applied interactively under user guidance within a sequent calculus framework. These include propositional and quantifier rules, induction, rewriting, simplification using decision procedures for equality and linear arithmetic, data and predicate abstraction. Additional information about the PVS theorem proving assistant can be found in [25].

3.2   IVY

IVY provides a front-end to the NuSMV model checker. It supports a notation for describing models, Modal Action Logic (MAL) which is a deontic logic of actions. The IVY tool [9] uses this notation as a front end to the NuSMV model checker [7]. The IVY tool provides plugins that aim to ease the expression of properties (see Fig. 1) and to interpret counter-examples that result when a property fails (see Fig. 6). Properties are expressed in CTL [8].

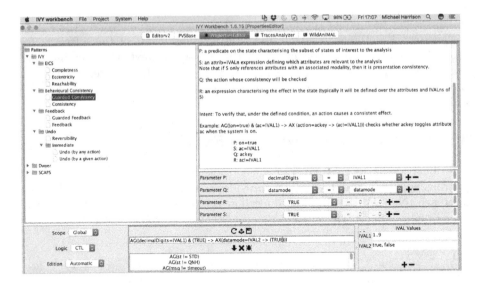

Fig. 1. Constructing guarded consistency properties

4   Models for Systems and Their Validation

In this section we consider briefly the construction of models in two contexts: the first is when a system already exists and analysis is proceeding retrospectively, for example to demonstrate that the system is acceptably safe; the second is when the model is being developed during the design process for the system.

4.1   The Neonatal Dialysis Machine: An Existing System

The analysis of the dialysis machine was carried out as part of the process of making the device ready as a product. This process has included clinical trials but it has also involved a safety analysis of the device hardware and software. The machine had already been used experimentally at the Royal Victoria Infirmary in Newcastle-upon-Tyne for some time. This first example [15] is a simple illustration of a post-hoc analysis of the machine's control component. This component involved the use of a control table to drive the software, providing a flexible and modifiable means of controlling the dialysis cycle and potential failures. The controller software (depicted as a component in Fig. 2) detects and warns about error conditions that need attention, as well as issuing hardware interrupts that prevent the machine from behaving in a dangerous manner according to its risk profile. All critical errors (bubbles, clots) are protected by both hardware and software safety systems. The controller is capable of controlling the system, however the core safety of the device is in the hardware. The control table (Fig. 3) describes the attributes of the state of the device that control the dialysis process, as well as how the state of the device changes in response to events, including warnings displays for example. The developers use a spreadsheet to record the content of the control structure. This spreadsheet was easy to convert to MAL, a translation that was automated after an initial manual conversion (see [12]). The control table includes 93 states and 30 events. More details of the attributes described in the table or their values, can be found in [15].

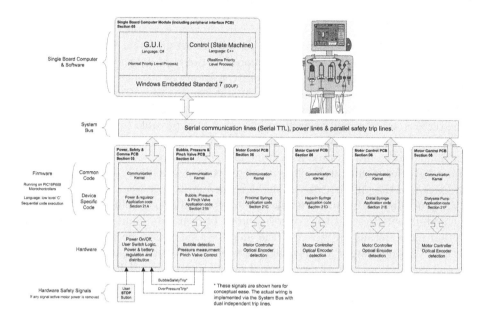

Fig. 2. The software architecture

The use of a control table such as the one described here is common in software development. A challenge therefore is to identify common software structures, particularly user interface structures, that can be used to facilitate the process of model development. This approach is also discussed in Osaiweran et al. [24]. The use of structures would enable the development of tools that aid the instantiation of structure patterns as well as the possible development of predefined properties. A tool that would offer the patterns and enable their access would provide an important step towards the construction of formal models.

* NAME	Power	Motor1	Motor2	Hep	Peri	Valve	Alarm	WashTimer	DialysisTimer	Flash	Mode	HardFault	Overpressure	Bubble	12Voff	M1stall
ST_PowerOn	TRIP12V	M1UNSTALL	M2UNSTALL	HEPUNSTALL	PERIUNSTALL	UNLATCH	INHIBIT	ZERO	ZERO	DISABLE	RESET	HardFault				
ST_ColdStart	TRIP12V	M1SAFE	M2SAFE	HEPSAFE	PERISAFE	UNLATCH	INHIBIT	ZERO	HOLD	ENABLE	RESET	HardFault	ST_ColdStart	ST_ColdStart		
ST_WarmStart	TRIP12V	M1SAFE	M2SAFE	HEPSAFE	PERISAFE	UNLATCH	INHIBIT	ZERO	HOLD	ENABLE	WASH	HardFault				
* RESET stuff																
RST_Start	TRIP12V	M1SAFE	M2SAFE	HEPSAFE	PERISAFE	VALVESAFE	QUIET	ZERO	HOLD	ENABLE	RESET	HardFault	RST_Errors	RST_Errors	RST_Ready	
RST_Ready	ALLOW12V	M1SAFE	M2SAFE	HEPSAFE	PERISAFE	VALVESAFE	QUIET	ZERO	HOLD	ENABLE	RESET	HardFault	RST_Errors	RST_Errors		
RST_InitS1	ALLOW12V	M1FWDMAX	M2SAFE	HEPSAFE	PERISAFE	PREP	ACTIVE	ZERO	HOLD	ENABLE	RESET	HardFault	RST_Errors	RST_Errors	ST_ColdStart	RST_InitS2
RST_InitS2	ALLOW12V	M1STOP	M2FWDMAX	HEPSAFE	PERISAFE	FLUSH	ACTIVE	ZERO	HOLD	ENABLE	RESET	HardFault	RST_Errors	RST_Errors	ST_ColdStart	
RST_InitHep	ALLOW12V	M1STOP	M2STOP	HEPBCKMAX	PERISAFE	FLUSH	ACTIVE	ZERO	HOLD	ENABLE	RESET	HardFault	RST_Errors	RST_Errors	ST_ColdStart	
RST_Relax	ALLOW12V	M1SAFE	M2SAFE	HEPSAFE	PERISAFE	FLUSH	ACTIVE	ZERO	HOLD	ENABLE	RESET	HardFault	RST_Errors	RST_Errors	ST_ColdStart	
RST_All	ALLOW12V	M1RESET	M2RESET	HEPRESET	PERISAFE	VALVESAFE	ACTIVE	ZERO	HOLD	ENABLE	RESET	HardFault	RST_Errors	RST_Errors	ST_ColdStart	
* RESET errors																
RST_Errors	TRIP12V	M1UNSTALL	M2UNSTALL	HEPUNSTALL	PERIUNSTALL	VALVESAFE	WARN	HOLD		HOLD	ENABLE	RESET	HardFault	RST_Overpress	RST_Bubble	
RST_Overpressure	TRIP12V	M1UNSTALL	M2UNSTALL	HEPUNSTALL	PERIUNSTALL	UNLATCH	WARN	HOLD		HOLD	VALVE	RESET	HardFault	RST_Overpressure		
RST_AckOverpressure	TRIP12V	M1UNSTALL	M2UNSTALL	HEPUNSTALL	PERIUNSTALL	VALVESAFE	WARN	HOLD		HOLD	ENABLE	RESET	HardFault	RST_Overpressure		
RST_Bubble	TRIP12V	M1UNSTALL	M2UNSTALL	HEPUNSTALL	PERIUNSTALL	UNLATCH	WARN	HOLD		HOLD	ENABLE	RESET	HardFault		RST_Bubble	
RST_AckBubble	TRIP12V	M1UNSTALL	M2UNSTALL	HEPUNSTALL	PERIUNSTALL	VALVESAFE	WARN	HOLD		HOLD	ENABLE	RESET	HardFault		RST_Bubble	

Fig. 3. A fragment of the control table

4.2   The Pill Dispenser: A Model Under Construction

Much of our work has focussed on the development of models of existing systems. This preoccupation arises through a desire to demonstrate that the use of formal methods can be scaled up to real systems and used to analyse safety related use requirements [18]. For this reason models have been produced to demonstrate that the approach does scale. However, in another example [17], we chose to develop a full model iteratively from an initial sketch design (Fig. 4). The initial sketch prototype and subsequent more functional prototypes were developed using PVSio-web [21]. The logic of the transitions in the design was captured using Emucharts (a simplified version of statecharts [13]). State transition diagrams are a simple way of describing, at a superficial level, the flow of a model. The screens are specified at each node so that it is possible to use the model as a sketch. A web animation was developed using PVSio-web to generate a first exemplar that could be used as a stage in a user centred design process to provide a basis for techniques such as cooperative evaluation [22]. As a result of the evaluation of the pill dispenser design a refined prototype was constructed using PVS, providing both a more detailed prototype and also enabling the analysis of the system with respect to properties based on usability heuristics. In the next section more details are given of the analysis that was done on this emerging design. The motivation for this analysis was to consider the possibility of using formal methods as part of user centred design, discussed briefly in [17].

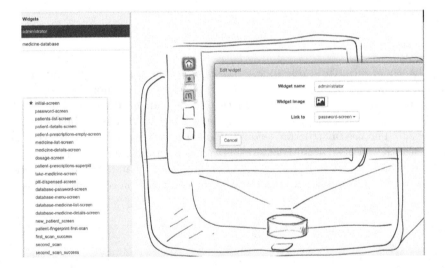

Fig. 4. Phase of the creation of the initial sketch design using PVSio-web.

As is typical in user centred design, iterative evaluations lead to more and more detail in the design. At each step PVSio-web enables the visualisation and therefore successive evaluation. At the same time it is possible to prove properties that enable an understanding of the plausibility of the model as well as demonstrating that the evolving design continues to satisfy the same usability heuristics. In this case the initial simple transition model provides a structure that can be used as a basis for the initial more detailed PVS model.

5   Formulating Requirements as Properties

Part of modelling the device involves demonstrating that requirements are satisfied by the proposed design. Requirements include non-functional requirements relating to use issues and safety requirements. The two examples illustrate how the process of developing formalisations of suitable requirements can be supported so that a wider community might develop appropriate requirements for their formal models.

5.1   Applying Templates: The Pill Dispenser Example

One way of helping the analyst formulate requirements is to provide templates that can help to generate relevant properties. A user centred design process such as the one considered in the case of the pill dispenser often involves the consideration of usability heuristics [23] for example. Templates that aid the process of developing these heuristics have been found useful in the pill dispenser example, but also other examples, see [3] for IVY examples and [18] for PVS examples.

In the case of the IVY tool, templates are offered and can be instantiated directly with the attributes of the model using a similar plug-in to that described in [20]. The *guarded consistency* template is shown in Fig. 1. The left hand side of the display shows the templates that are available in the current version of the IVY tool. The right hand side describes the template (in the form of a pattern [10]) and provides the means to assign parameters that are provided in the general form of the template, thus instantiating it as a CTL property that can be used to check the model. The bottom of the display shows the instantiated property (as well as other properties) that can then be checked. Note that CTL properties may also be entered without using the templates as an intermediary. PVS does not, as yet, provide automated support for templates but this is planned. In the example of the pill dispenser an illustrated example would be the guarded consistency property described in the display of Fig. 1.

The example, used for illustration in the pill dispenser, was *action consistency* and is based on a PVS model. The following is the definition of action consistency referred to in [18].

Action Consistency ────────────────────────

$\forall a \in Act, s \in S, m \in MS :$

  ● $guard(s, m) \wedge$
     $pre\_filter(s, m)\ \varphi\ post\_filter(a(s), m)$ (1)

───

Action consistency is formulated as a property of either a single action, or of a group of actions (they are referred to as *Act*) which may exhibit similar behaviours. A relation $\varphi : C \times C$ connects a filtered state, before an action occurs (captured by $pre\_filter : S \times MS \rightarrow C$), with a filtered state after the action (captured by $post\_filter : S \times MS \rightarrow C$). *MS* refers to possible modes that limit the validity of the filter.

In the case of the pill dispenser a *quit* action is designed to enable the user to quit a sequence without affecting the key data that are being manipulated by the device—for example, two databases that store patient and medication data. The action consistency template can be used to prove that the quit action is consistent in this sense. In fact this property is not true of the device as is discussed in a little more detail in Sect. 6.2. Further details can also be found in [17].

5.2   Taking Requirements from a Risk Log: The Dialyser Example

In the case of the dialyser safety case, a risk log had already been produced describing requirements that would mitigate potential hazards. Requirements often involve several components of the system, for example hardware and software components, and may be mitigated in a variety of ways, for example by means of an operations manual or through some hardware barrier. These requirements were expressed in natural language. In a sense the requirements were already instantiated, it was not appropriate to attempt to fit the requirements to templates. A fragment of the risk log shown in Fig. 5 was used in the safety analysis of the dialyser. The requirements that were mapped to CTL properties that could be proved of the MAL model are labelled with identifiers so that they can be used in the safety argument. The fragment shown represents a stage in the development where a property MAL.GENERROR has been found to be false. As illustration we consider a different property that is a requirement focussed entirely on the software controller. It is labelled MAL.GEN2S1 and is a formulation expressed in the risk log as:

"During DIALYSIS, when the distal syringe is moving forwards then the proximal syringe is necessarily moving backwards."

The property MAL.GEN2S1 was formulated as a result of a series of meetings between the developers and the IVY user. Through discussion a partial translation of the property was produced using a notation with which the developers were comfortable:

If M2 in {M2Fwd} → M1 in {M1Bck}

The informal property contains no temporal dimension, and although *M2Fwd* and *M1Fwd* are meaningful in terms of the developers' understanding of the

Ref	Requirement	
MAL.GENINHIBIT	The alarm is only inhibited during the RESET phase.	It is always the case that wh
MAL.GENBABY	The BABY valve can only be open while the system is in DIALYSIS mode.	It is always the case that wh
MAL.GENS1MOVE	During access to the baby, the BABY valve is open.	It is always the case that wh M1 IN { M1Withdraw, M1Re
MAL.GENS2STOP	During access to the baby, the distal syringe is never running.	It is always the case that wh M1 IN { M1Withdraw, M1Re
MAL.GENERROR	For all error conditions and all system states, the next state will be an ERROR state.	For all error conditions and Note this condition logically all errors have been cleared IF ErrorCondition THEN Nex
MAL.GENS2S1	During DIALYSIS, when the distal syringe is moving forwards then the proximal syringe is necessarily moving backwards.	It is always the case that wh IF M2 IN { M2Fwd } -> M1 II
MAL.GENS1S2	During DIALYSIS, when the distal syringe is moving backwards then the proximal syringe is necessarily moving forwards.	It is always the case that wh IF M2 IN { M2Bck } -> M1 IN

Fig. 5. Snippet of the risk log of the NIDUS device

device, the precise nature of the sets $\{M2Fwd\}$ and $\{M1Bck\}$ was not clear. The two sets $\{M2Fwd\}$ and $\{M1Bck\}$ were then articulated by the formal analyst as MAL definitions:

$$M2FWD := \{ \text{ M2FWDMAX, M2FWDUNUF } \}$$
$$M1BCK := \{ \text{ M1BCKMAX, M1BCKUF, M1WITHDRAW } \}$$

It was confirmed by the developers that these attribute states comprised all those relating to forward and backward motion in the two motors. Having defined the relevant state attributes as specified in the spreadsheet model, the next step was to formulate a precise version of the property as a basis for the analysis. The requirement was formulated in CTL as:

$$AG(Motor2 \ in \ M2FWD \rightarrow Motor1 \ in \ M1BCK) \tag{1}$$

This property turned out to be false and will be explored in more detail in Sect. 6.

Amongst these requirements some properties related to use. The use related requirements had the characteristic, in this particular case, that a state of the controller could only be reached if a state or combinations of states had happened in the past. The controller includes a *Flash* attribute that has values identifying different displays associated with warnings. For example, $Flash = HEPCLOSE$ is true if the display which requests that the heparin clip be closed is displayed. There are a variety of ways in which this property can be expressed using CTL. We chose to adopt a simple approach that had the merits of being easy to explain although it involved some modification to the model. An attribute was introduced *hepclipopen* that was true when $Flash = HEPOPEN$ is the last display. The attribute becomes false when *Flash* has values $HEPCLOSE$ or $HEPSYRINGE$. For example, the following fragment involving the *Hepin* action specifies a transition to the state *HEPClip*. This state includes a change to the *Flash* attribute $Flash' = HEPCLOSE$ and therefore *hepclipopen* is set to false. It is assumed therefore that the clinician will recall the last display relating to the opening or closing of the clip. The requirement that was under consideration was the following:

> "MAL.HEPCLIP: The user is instructed to close clip before changing syringe, and re-open afterwards."

The requirement was therefore expressed simply as

$$AG(Mode = DIALYSING \rightarrow hepclipopen)$$

In other words (in the language of the model) if the controller reaches a mode in which it is dialysing then the *Flash* display "HEPOPEN" has occurred and has not been superseded by any display relating to the heparin clip which would lead to a different conclusion.

The process of property development from the requirements in the risk log is an interactive process. Each step involves agreement—the developers agree to the formulation of the property and, as will be discussed, later scrutinise counter-examples and identify the contexts in which the property may fail. Here support is required to document the path from informal requirement in the risk log to a formal property that can be proved of the model. This documentation might involve checks that: the formal property is consistent with the natural language description; links to counter-examples; rationale for changing the requirement. These are not currently supported by IVY or PVS but could be.

6   Proving Properties

The final step of the paper explores the business of proof. Proof of the properties discussed in the previous section are now considered. The first example indicates the facilities provided by the IVY tool to visualise the results of checking a property.

6.1   Checking Properties: The Dialysis Machine

The property described in Sect. 5.2 checks that for all states, when *Motor2* is in a forward state, then *Motor1* is in a backward state. This expression of the requirement fails. The IVY tool provides a visualisation of a counter-example (shown in Fig. 6). The tool offers alternative styles of visualisation (matrix as in this case and sequence diagrams are examples) all of which indicate one path in which the property fails. The figure shows a sequence starting from an initial state (column 1), ending at a state where the property fails (column 6). Columns indicate values held by attributes. These are named in the left hand column (i.e., column 0). For example, the attribute *Power* has value *ALLOW12V* in column 4. Colour is used to indicate that a state attribute has changed value between successive states. The path indicates (as shown in the row marked *main.action*) that from the initial state the device defaults (that is it takes the action *acDefault*) because there are no events in the queue. This action is followed by *Key2*, followed by *12voff*, *12von* and *M1stall* which leads to the state where the property fails.

main.action	1	2	3	4	5	6
		acDefault	acKey2	ac12Voff	ac12Von	acM1stall
Alarm	INHIBIT	INHIBIT	QUIET	QUIET	ACTIVE	ACTIVE
DialysisTimer	ZERO	HOLD	HOLD	HOLD	HOLD	HOLD
Flash	DISABLE	ENABLE	ENABLE	ENABLE	ENABLE	ENABLE
Hep	HEPUNSTAL	HEPSAFE	HEPUNSTAL	HEPSAFE	HEPSAFE	HEPSAFE
Mode	RESET	RESET	RESET	RESET	RESET	RESET
Motor1	M1UNSTALL	M1SAFE	M1UNSTALL	M1SAFE	M1FWDMAX	M1STOP
Motor2	M2UNSTALL	M2SAFE	M2UNSTALL	M2SAFE	M2SAFE	M2FWDMAX
Peri	PERIUNSTAL	PERISAFE	PERISAFE	PERISAFE	PERISAFE	PERISAFE
Power	TRIP12V	TRIP12V	TRIP12V	ALLOW12V	ALLOW12V	ALLOW12V
Valve	UNLATCH	UNLATCH	VALVESAFE	VALVESAFE	PREP	FLUSH
WashTimer	ZERO	ZERO	ZERO	ZERO	ZERO	ZERO

Fig. 6. Counter-example to property P1

Discussion during the risk meeting explored the implications of the sequence and came to the conclusion that this exception was acceptably safe and could therefore be excluded. The considered property was therefore refined by excluding this case, and the analysis continued. Several other cases were found where the property failed. The risk analysis team considered each of these exceptions and noted that the common property of these counter-examples was that they occurred when the device was not in dialysis mode, hence the following property was constructed:

$$AG((Motor2 \ in \ M2FWD \ \& \ Mode \ in \ \{DIALYSE, DIALYSING\})$$
$$\rightarrow Motor1 \ in \ M1BCK)$$

The property formulated, as a result of this observation, is true for the model. It should be noted that this observation about the exceptions was a problem of formulation, the property could be expressed more simply. It could be argued that visual inspection of the spreadsheet would have been sufficient to indicate the problem in this particular case. However this systematic approach to finding paths to potentially hazardous states provides an exhaustive approach. At the same time it makes it clear to the team the circumstances in which the property fails.

6.2   Proving Properties: The Pill Dispenser

PVS provides relatively little support for the proof of properties. In Sect. 5.1 the property, that was developed initially, assumed that the quit action never changed the patient or meds database. The formulated theorem requires that for all states, the state after the quit action has been applied leaves the meds database and the patients database unchanged. The function select takes an action and the state and produces a new state that contains the effect that the action makes on the state. This theorem expressed below cannot be proved.

```
attemp_quit_consistency_thm: THEOREM FORALL (st: state):
  LET st1 = select(quit, st)
   IN (st`meds_db = st1`meds_db AND st`patients_db = st1`patients_db)
```

Attempts to prove the theorem using the PVS *grind* function generates the following result.

```
 Rule? (grind)
Trying repeated skolemization, instantiation, and if-lifting,
this simplifies to:
attempt_quit_consistency_thm.2.1 :

{-1}   st!1`action(quit)
{-2}   creation_success?(mode(st!1))
  |-------
{1}    st!1`patients_db =
       p_insert(st!1`p_current, temp_patient(st!1), patients_db(st!1))

Rule?
```

The counter-example indicates that when the mode of the state is the mode that signifies successful creation (mode is creation_success) the patients database is updated. The new database includes the patient temp_patient that was generated in the preceding sequence. When a new version of the theorem is generated which excludes this mode, the theorem is true. The question for the analysis team is to recognise whether this exception is acceptable or whether the design of the pill dispenser must be changed.

7 Conclusions and Future Challenges

If formal methods are to be a practical proposition in the analysis of interactive systems then the following are required:

- models at an appropriate level of detail so that requirements can be expressed as suitable properties while at the same providing a basis for an executable prototype;
- tools such as PVSio-web that ease the development of prototypes that capture precisely the model;
- the development of properties from requirements, with the ability to generate documentation to support rationale;
- aids to proof and diagnosis of reasons for failure when properties fail.

The paper has explored some of these issues through the two examples. However further work is required.

Support for Modelling: It seems clear that there are model patterns relating to interactive systems. Patterns already exist at the implementation level (for example MVC [19]) and the graphical user interface level (see, for example [29]). Further patterns could undoubtedly be realised to, support the specification of, for example: moving between display modes; direct manipulation; forms interfaces. Developing patterns can ease the process of constructing formal models, and make the process possible with limited knowledge of formal methods. An initial exploration of these ideas can be found in [2] where "callback", "iterator", and "update" patterns are explored. Their work focuses on interaction techniques rather than patterns for structures of interactive systems.

Ease of Constructing Prototypes from Models: PVSio and PVSio-web [21] provide important steps in this direction. However further work is required to smooth the transition between simulation tools provided by PVSio and the rendering of the simulation.

Developing Properties from Requirements: The pattern approach found in IVY may be extended, producing a larger set of patterns. The process of developing formal properties from informal requirements described in relation to the neonatal dialysis machine can be supported by tools to aid the development of rationale, and to provide confidence that the map from informal requirements to formal properties preserves meaning. It could also provide documentation of rationale for property failure and changes that result.

Supporting the Proof Process: Here work is required to make counter-examples easier to interpret. This can be done through animation facilities, as discussed in the context of AniMAL [5] or using PVSio-web [21]. Further support can be provided for the construction of proof. This can be done through the use of generic tactics [26]. The style of specification lends itself to specific kinds of proof.

Acknowledgments. Josè Creissac Campos and Paolo Masci have made very substantial contributions to the work illustrated in this paper.

References

1. Bolton, M.L., Bass, E.J., Siminiceanu, R.I.: Generating phenotypical erroneous human behavior to evaluate human-automation interaction using model checking. Int. J. Hum. Comput Stud. **70**, 888–906 (2012)
2. Bowen, J., Reeves, S.: Design patterns for models of interactive systems. In: 2015 24th Australasian Software Engineering Conference (ASWEC), pp. 223–232. IEEE (2015)
3. Campos, J.C., Harrison, M.D.: Model checking interactor specifications. Autom. Softw. Eng. **8**, 275–310 (2001)
4. Campos, J.C., Sousa, M., Alves, M.C.B., Harrison, M.D.: Formal verification of a space system's user interface with the IVY workbench. IEEE Trans. Hum. Mach. Syst. **46**(2), 303–316 (2016)
5. Campos, J., Sousa, N.: The MAL interactors animator: supporting model validation through animation. In: Proceedings of the ACM SIGCHI Symposium on Engineering Interactive Computing Systems, pp. 11:1–11:7. ACM (2018)
6. Campos, J.C., Harrison, M.D.: Formally verifying interactive systems: a review. In: Harrison, M., Torres, J. (eds.) Design, Specification and Verification of Interactive Systems 1997, pp. 119–134. Springer, Vienna (1997). https://doi.org/10.1007/978-3-7091-6878-3_8
7. Cimatti, A., et al.: NuSMV 2.3 user manual. Technical report, ITC-IRST, Trento, Italy (2007). http://nusmv.irst.itc.it/NuSMV/tutorial/v23/tutorial.pdf
8. Clarke, E.M., Grumberg, O., Peled, D.A.: Model Checking. MIT Press, Cambridge (1999)

9. Couto, R., Campos, J.: IVY 2 - a model-based analysis tool. In: The 11th ACM SIGCHI Symposium on Engineering Interactive Computing Systems - EICS 2019, pp. 5:1–5:6. ACM (2019)

10. Dwyer, M., Avrunin, G., Corbett, J.: Property specification patterns for finite-state verification. In: Ardis, M. (ed.) 2nd Workshop on Formal Methods in Software Practice, pp. 7–15, March 1998

11. Fayollas, C., et al.: Evaluation of formal IDEs for human-machine interface design and analysis: the case of CIRCUS and PVSio-web. In: Proceedings of the Third Workshop on Formal Integrated Development Environment. Electronic Proceedings in Theoretical Computer Science, vol. 240, pp. 1–19 (2017). https://doi.org/10.4204/EPTCS.240.1

12. Freitas, L., Stabler, A.: Translation strategies for medical device control software. Technical report, Newcastle University, August 2015

13. Harel, D.: Statecharts: a visual formalism for complex systems. Sci. Comput. Program. **8**, 231–274 (1987)

14. Harrison, M.D., Campos, J.C., Loer, K.: Formal analysis of interactive systems: opportunities and weaknesses. In: Cairns, P., Cox, A. (eds.) Research Methods for Human Computer Interaction, Chap. 5, pp. 88–111. Cambridge University Press, Cambridge (2008)

15. Harrison, M.D., Freitas, L., Drinnan, M., Campos, J.C., Masci, P., di Maria, C., Whitaker, M.: Formal techniques in the safety analysis of software components of a new dialysis machine. Sci. Comput. Program. **175**, 17–34 (2019)

16. Harrison, M.D., Thimbleby, H.W. (eds.): Formal Methods in Human Computer Interaction. Cambridge University Press, Cambridge (1990)

17. Harrison, M.D., Masci, P., Campos, J.C.: Formal modelling as a component of user centred design. In: Mazzara, M., Ober, I., Salaün, G. (eds.) STAF 2018. LNCS, vol. 11176, pp. 274–289. Springer, Cham (2018). https://doi.org/10.1007/978-3-030-04771-9_21

18. Harrison, M., Masci, P., Campos, J.: Verification templates for the analysis of user interface software design. IEEE Trans. Software Eng. **45**(8), 802–822 (2019)

19. Krasner, G.E., Pope, S.T.: A cookbook for using the model-view controller user interface paradigm in smalltalk-80. JOOP **1**(3), 26–49 (1988)

20. Loer, K., Harrison, M.: An integrated framework for the analysis of dependable interactive systems (IFADIS): its tool support and evaluation. Autom. Softw. Eng. **13**(4), 469–496 (2006)

21. Masci, P., Oladimeji, P., Zhang, Y., Jones, P., Curzon, P., Thimbleby, H.: PVSio-web 2.0: joining PVS to HCI. In: Kroening, D., Păsăreanu, C.S. (eds.) CAV 2015. LNCS, vol. 9206, pp. 470–478. Springer, Cham (2015). https://doi.org/10.1007/978-3-319-21690-4_30

22. Monk, A., Wright, P., Haber, J., Davenport, L.: Improving Your Human-Computer Interface: A Practical Technique. Prentice-Hall, New York (1993)

23. Nielsen, J., Molich, R.: Heuristic evaluation of user interfaces. In: Chew, J., Whiteside, J. (eds.) ACM CHI Proceedings CHI 1990: Empowering People, pp. 249–256 (1990)

24. Osaiweran, A., Schuts, M., Hooman, J., Groote, J.F., van Rijnsoever, B.: Evaluating the effect of a lightweight formal technique in industry. Int. J. Softw. Tools Technol. Transfer **18**(1), 93–108 (2016). https://doi.org/10.1007/s10009-015-0374-110.1007/s10009-015-0374-1

25. Owre, S., Rushby, J.M., Shankar, N.: PVS: a prototype verification system. In: Kapur, D. (ed.) CADE 1992. LNCS, vol. 607, pp. 748–752. Springer, Heidelberg (1992). https://doi.org/10.1007/3-540-55602-8_217

26. Owre, S., Shankar, N.: Writing PVS proof strategies. In: Design and Application of Strategies/Tactics in Higher Order Logics (STRATA 2003), Number CP-2003-212448 in NASA Conference Publication, pp. 1–15 (2003)
27. Palanque, P., Paternò, F. (eds.): Formal Methods in Human-Computer Interaction. Formal Approaches to Computing and Information Technology Series. Springer, London (1998). https://doi.org/10.1007/978-1-4471-3425-1
28. Shankar, N., Owre, S., Rushby, J.M., Stringer-Calvert, D.: PVS System Guide, PVS Language Reference, PVS Prover Guide, PVS Prelude Library, Abstract Datatypes in PVS, and Theory Interpretations in PVS. Computer Science Laboratory, SRI International, Menlo Park, CA (1999). http://pvs.csl.sri.com/documentation.shtml
29. van Welie, M., van der Veer, G.C., Eliëns, A.: Patterns as tools for user interface design. In: Vanderdonckt, J., Farenc, C. (eds.) Tools for Working with Guidelines, pp. 313–324. Springer, London (2001). https://doi.org/10.1007/978-1-4471-0279-3_30
30. Weyers, B., Bowen, J., Dix, A., Palanque, P. (eds.): The Handbook of Formal Methods in Human-Computer Interaction. HIS. Springer, Cham (2017). https://doi.org/10.1007/978-3-319-51838-1
31. Zamansky, A., Spichkova, M., Rodríguez-Navas, G., Herrmann, P., Blech, J.O.: Towards classification of lightweight formal methods. In: Damiani, E., Spanoudakis, G., Maciaszek, L. (eds.) Proceedings of the 13th International Conference on Evaluation of Novel Approaches to Software Engineering (ENASE 2018), pp. 305–313 (2018)

Modelling Human Reasoning in Practical Behavioural Contexts Using Real-Time Maude

Antonio Cerone[1]([✉]) [iD] and Peter Csaba Ölveczky[2]

[1] Department of Computer Science, Nazarbayev University, Nur-Sultan, Kazakhstan
`antonio.cerone@nu.edu.kz`
[2] Department of Informatics, University of Oslo, Oslo, Norway
`peterol@ifi.uio.no`

Abstract. In this paper we present an approach for modelling human reasoning using rewrite systems and we illustrate our approach in the context of human behaviour using a car driving example. Reasoning inference rules and descriptions of human activities are expressed using the Behaviour and Reasoning Description Language (BRDL). The BRDL model is then translated into Real-Time Maude. The object-oriented and equational logic aspects of Maude are exploited in order to define alternative semantic variations of BRDL that implement alternative theories of memory and cognition.

Keywords: Human reasoning · Human behaviour · Formal methods · Rewrite systems · Real-time maude

1 Introduction

One of the main challenges in human-computer interaction (HCI) is that the way humans use devices is not always consistent with the use for which such devices have been designed and built. In fact, although a systematic exploration of the concept of "plausible" behaviour may provide a good baseline for understanding the interaction [5,11], some forms of "plausible" behaviour emerge only in specific contexts and cannot be predicted *a priori*. Cognitive architectures [12], formal methods [19,20] and several other approaches, including machine learning and control theory [19], have been used to tackle this problem.

However, cognitive architectures tend to be specialised, each with a specific scope, which is normally academic and seldom practical [12], formal methods are "regarded as requiring too much expertise and effort for day-to-day use, being principally applied in safety-critical areas outside academia" [19, Ch. 7, page 187], and machine learning and control theory focus on the interaction process rather than human behaviour. Moreover, although emulating reasoning

Work partly funded by Seed Funding Grant, Project SFG 1447 "Formal Analysis and Verification of Accidents", University of Geneva, Switzerland.

E. Sekerinski et al. (Eds.): FM 2019 Workshops, LNCS 12232, pp. 424–442, 2020.
https://doi.org/10.1007/978-3-030-54994-7_32

is one of the main objectives of some cognitive architectures, past and current efforts in this sense either do not consider human errors or are detached from the practical context of human behaviour [12]. Furthermore, high-level reasoning is not supported by control theory and, although it may emerge using machine learning, the way it emerges cannot be explained.

Our approach builds on the *Behaviour and Reasoning Description Language (BRDL)* [10] and on the use of the Maude rewrite system [16–18] to model the dynamics of human memory and memory processes [8,9]. The semantics of BRDL is based on a basic model of human memory and memory processes and is adaptable to different cognitive theories. This allows us, on the one hand, to keep the syntax of the language to a minimum, thus making it easy to learn and understand without requiring expertise in mathematics or formal methods and, on the other hand, to use alternative semantic variations to compare alternative theories of memory and cognition. BRDL, is equipped with the linguistic constructs to specify reasoning goals, inference rules and unsolved problems. We use rewrite systems [14,17] to implement such constructs. Specifically, BRDL is translated into Real-Time Maude [16,18], thus combining human components with the system components that model the environment in which humans operate [9].

Real-Time Maude was used to model and analyse human multitasking by Broccia *et al.* [3,4], who adopted the initial cognitive framework underlying BRDL [8] and extended it with a number of time-related and other quantitative aspects. In their work, basic activities (also called basic tasks [3,4,8]) incorporate non-cognitive aspects, such as the duration and the difficulty of the task, which are interface-dependent outcomes of the interaction process, as well as external aspect, such as the delay in executing the basic activity, which is possibly due to the switching from one task to another. In fact, this was an *ad hoc* extension for modelling human multitasking. In contrast to Broccia *et al.* we model just one time aspect within basic activities, the duration of the mental process, which is the only time aspect characterising the basic activity. Broccia *et al.*, instead, neglect this time aspect.

The rest of the paper is structured as follows. Sections 2 and 3 present overviews of Real-Time Maude and the way it models BRDL syntax, respectively. Section 4 presents the Real-Time Maude implementation of the model of human memory and memory processes that provide the dynamics of BRDL constructs. Section 5 illustrates the rewrite rules to emulate human reasoning and the environment in which humans operate. Section 6 concludes the paper.

2   Real-Time Maude

Real-Time Maude [16,18] is a formal modeling language and high-performance simulation and model checking tool for distributed real-time systems. It is based on Full Maude, the object-oriented extension of Core Maude, which is the basic version of Maude.

An algebraic equational specification (specifying sorts, subsorts, functions and equations defining the functions) defines the data types in a functional programming style. Labeled rewrite rules crl [*l*]: *t* => *t'* if *cond* define local transitions from state *t* to state *t'*, and tick rewrite rules crl [*l*]: {*t*} => {*t'*} in time Δ if *cond* advance time in the *entire* state *t* by Δ time units.

We briefly summarize the syntax of Real-Time Maude and refer to Ölveczky's work [16,18] for more details. Maude *equational logic* supports declaration of *sorts*, with keyword sort for one sort, or sorts for many. A sort A may be specified as a subsort of a sort B by subsort A < B. Operators are introduced with the op and ops keywords: op *f* : $s_1 \ldots s_n$ -> *s*. They can have user-definable syntax, with underbars '_' marking the argument positions. Some operators can have equational *attributes*, such as assoc, comm, and id, stating that the operator is associative, commutative and has a certain identity element, respectively. Such attributes are used by the Maude engine to match terms *modulo* the declared axioms. An operator can also be declared to be a constructor (ctor) that defines the carrier of a sort. Equations and rewrite rules are introduced with, respectively, keywords eq, or ceq for conditional equations, and rl, or crl for conditional rules. The mathematical variables in such statements are declared with the keywords var and vars, or can be introduced on the fly in a statement without being declared previously, in which case they have the form *var*:*sort*. An equation $f(t_1, \ldots, t_n) = t$ with the owise (for "otherwise") attribute can be applied to a subterm $f(\ldots)$ only if no other equation with left-hand side $f(u_1, \ldots, u_n)$ can be applied.

A declaration class *C* | att_1 : s_1, ..., att_n : s_n declares a class *C* with attributes att_1 to att_n of sorts s_1 to s_n. An *object* of class *C* is represented as a term < *O* : *C* | att_1 : $val_1, ..., att_n$: val_n > of sort Object, where *O*, of sort Oid, is the object's *identifier*, and where val_1 to val_n are the current values of the attributes att_1 to att_n. The state is a term of sort Configuration, and is a *multiset* of objects and messages. Multiset union is denoted by an associative and commutative juxtaposition operator, so that rewriting is *multiset rewriting*.

Real-Time Maude specifications are executable, and the tool provides a variety of formal analysis methods. The *timed rewriting* command (tfrew *t* in time <= *timeLimit* .) simulates *one* of the system behaviours by rewriting the initial state *t* up to duration *timeLimit*.

3   Behaviour and Reasoning Description Language

The Behaviour and Reasoning Description Language (BRDL) [10] originates from and extends the *Human Behaviour Description Language (HBDL)* introduced in previous work [8,9]. HBDL aims at the modelling of automatic and deliberate human behaviour while interacting with an environment consisting of heterogenous physical components. It requires reasoning and problem solving aspects to be modelled explicitly in a procedural way, whereby the reasoning process and the problem solution are explicitly described with the language. BRDL, instead, is equipped with the linguistic constructs to specify reasoning goals, inference rules and unsolved problems. It is then the cognitive engine that implements the language to emulate the reasoning and problem solving processes.

BRDL is based on Atkinson and Shiffrin's *multistore model* of human memory [1]. This model is characterised by three stores between which various forms of information flow: *sensory memory*, where information perceived through the senses persists for a very short time, *short-term memory (STM)*, which has a limited capacity and where the information that is needed for processing activities is temporarily stored with rapid access and rapid decay, and *long-term memory (LTM)*, which has a virtually unlimited capacity and where information is organised in structured ways, with slow access but little or no decay. A usual practice to keep information in memory is *rehearsal*. In particular, *maintenance rehearsal* allows us to extend the time during which information is kept in STM, whereas *elaborative rehearsal* allows us to transfer information from STM to LTM [2]. We consider a further decomposition of LTM: *semantic memory*, which refers to our *knowledge* of the world and consists of the *facts* that can be *consciously* recalled, and *procedural memory*, which refers to our *skills* and consists of *rules* and *procedures* that we *unconsciously* use to carry out tasks, particularly at the motor level.

BRDL has a concise, appealing syntax, which is presented elsewhere [10]. In order to show how BRDL is translated to Maude, in this section we introduce an ASCII, verbose version of the syntax, as it is implemented in Maude. Both HDBL and BRDL describe human behaviour through the manipulation of three kinds of entities:

perceptions are sensed in the environment and enter human input channels;
actions are performed by the human on the environment;
cognitive information consists in the items we store in our STM, including information retrieved from the LTM, goals, recent perceptions or planned actions.

3.1   BRDL Entities and Cognitive Control

BRDL entities are modelled with Maude using the following sort structure.

```
sorts Perception Action Cognition BasicItem Item Goal .
subsorts Cognition Perception Action < BasicItem < Item .
subsort Goal < Item .
```

where `Perception`, `Action` and `Cognition` model perceptions, actions and cognitive information, respectively. Sort `Item` models anything that can be stored in STM and sort `BasicItem` is its subsort that excludes goals (from sort `Goal`). All these entities may also be elements of sets that define further sorts as follows:

```
subsorts Perception < PerceptionSet < BasicItemSet .
subsorts Cognition < CognitionSet < BasicItemSet .
subsorts Action < ActionSet < BasicItemSet .
```

```
subsort BasicItem < BasicItemSet .
subsorts EmptyItemSet < PerceptionSet CognitionSet ActionSet
                       < BasicItemSet < ItemSet .
subsort Item < ItemSet .
op none : -> EmptyItemSet [ctor] .
op _;_ : BasicItemSet BasicItemSet ->
                       BasicItemSet [ctor assoc comm id: none] .
op _;_ : PerceptionSet PerceptionSet ->
                       PerceptionSet [ctor assoc comm id: none] .
op _;_ : ActionSet ActionSet ->
                       ActionSet [ctor assoc comm id: none] .
op _;_ : ItemSet ItemSet -> ItemSet [ctor ditto] .
```

We use semicolon ";" as the general operator to add elements or subsets to a set, starting from an empty set (none in this case).

We extend Perception to DefPerception and Action to DefAction by including as default values noPerception and noAction to model the absence of perception and action, respectively.

```
sorts DefPerception DefAction .
subsort Perception < DefPerception . subsort Action < DefAction .
op noAction : -> DefAction [ctor] .
op noPerception : -> DefPerception [ctor] .
```

Only relevant perceptions are transferred, possibly after some kind of processing, to the STM using *attention*, a selective processing activity that aims to focus on one aspect of the environment while ignoring others. *Explicit attention* is associated with our goal in performing a task. It focusses on goal-relevant stimuli in the environment. *Implicit attention* is grabbed by sudden stimuli that are associated with the current mental state or carry emotional significance. Inspired by Norman and Shallice [15], we consider two levels of cognitive control:

automatic control
fast processing activity that requires only *implicit attention* and is carried out outside awareness with no conscious effort implicitly, using rules and procedures stored in the procedural memory;

deliberate control
processing activity triggered and focussed by *explicit attention* and carried out under the intentional control of the individual, who makes explicit use of facts and experiences stored in the declarative memory and is aware and conscious of the effort required in doing so.

In order to model automatic and deliberate control as well as reasoning, we introduce the following sorts and operations.

```
sorts Automatism KnowledgeDomain .
op automatism : KnowledgeDomain -> Automatism [ctor] .
op goal : KnowledgeDomain BasicItemSet -> Goal [ctor] .
op infer : KnowledgeDomain -> Inference [ctor] .
```

We define automatic behaviour in terms of a specific knowledge domain (sort `KnowledgeDomain` and operation `automatism`). Automatic behaviour is driven by the knowledge domain, which gives a focus to implicit attention.

Deliberate behaviour is driven by a goal, which not only depends on the knowledge domain but also on a representation of the goal achievement. This representation may be given by a combination of perceptions, actions and cognitive information. For example,

- during the interaction with an ATM (automatic teller machine) with the goal of withdrawing cash, we achieve the goal when we perform the action of collecting the cash;
- if our goal is to switch a light on, we achieve the goal when we perceive the light being on;
- if our goal is to solve a mathematical puzzle, we achieve the goal when the solution is represented by the cognitive information in our STM.

Inference is driven by the knowledge domain on which we are reasoning.

3.2 Basic Activities

Human behaviour is modelled in BRDL (and HTDL) as a set of *basic activities*, defined through the following sorts and operations

```
sorts  AutomaticActivity DeliberateActivity Knowledge .
op _:_>|_-->_|>_duration_ : Automatism BasicItemSet DefPerception
           DefAction ItemSet Time -> AutomaticActivity . [ctor]
op _:_>|_-->_|>_duration_ :Goal BasicItemSet DefPerception
           DefAction ItemSet Time -> DeliberateActivity [ctor] .
op _:_>|-->|>_duration_ : Inference BasicItemSet
           ItemSet Time -> Knowledge [ctor] .
```

An automatic basic activity within a given knowledge domain *domain* is modelled in BRDL and HTDL as

automatism(*domain*) : *info1* >| *perception* --> *action* |> *info2* **duration** *d*

where *info1* is the triggering cognitive information in the STM, *perception* is the triggering perception, *action* is the performed action, *info2* is a new cognitive information stored in the STM, and *d* is the duration of the mental processing. Symbol ">|" denotes that *info1* is removed from the STM and "|>" denotes that *info2* is stored in the STM. Using derived operations (i.e. not defined as constructors but through equations) we have the following syntactic sugar

automatism(*domain*) : *info1* | *perception* -->
    action |> *info2* **duration** *d*

where *info1* acts as a trigger but is not is removed from STM, and

automatism(*domain*) : *info* | *info1* >| *perception* -->
    action |> *info2* **duration** *d*

where the union *info;info1* acts as a trigger but only *info1* is removed from STM.

A deliberate basic activity within a given knowledge domain *domain* is modelled in BRDL and HTDL as

goal(*domain, info*) : *info1* >| *perception* --> *action* |> *info2* duration *d*

where *info* is the information denoting the achievement of the goal.

An inference within a given knowledge domain *domain* is modelled in BRDL as

inference(*domain*) : *info1* >|-->|> *info2* duration *d*

where *info1* is the premise and *info2* is the consequence.

Syntactic sugar for deliberate basic activities and inferences is defined similarly to automatic basic activities.

Procedural memory is modeled as the sort ProcMem, which is a set of automatic basic activities

```
sort ProcMem . subsort AutomaticActivity < ProcMem .
op emptyPM : -> ProcMemory [ctor] .
op _;_ : ProcMemory ProcMemory -> ProcMemory
     [ctor assoc comm id: emptyPM] .
```

Semantic memory is modeled by two sort, sort ActivMem, which is a set of deliberate basic activities,

```
sort ActivMem . subsort DeliberateActivity < ActivMem .
op emptyAM : ->  ActivMem [ctor] .
op _;_ :  ActivMem  ActivMem ->  ActivMem [ctor assoc comm id: emptyASM] .
```

and sort InferMem , which is a set of inferences,

```
sort InferMem . subsort Knowledge < InferMem .
op emptyIM : ->  InferMem [ctor] .
op _;_ :  InferMem  InferMem  ->  InferMem [ctor assoc comm id: emptyIM] .
```

3.3   Zebra Crossing Example

As an example to illustrate these forms of human behaviour and reasoning, let us consider car driving. The knowledge domain is given by constant operation

```
op driving : -> KnowledgeDomain [ctor] .
```

Automatic control is essential in properly driving a car and, in such a context, it develops throughout a learning process based on deliberate control. During the learning process the driver has to make a conscious effort that requires explicit attention. For example, the learner has to explicitly pay attention to the other cars, the pedestrian walking on the footpath, who may be ready to walk across the road, the presence of zebra crossings, traffic lights, road signals, etc. These are goals that drive explicit attention. Moreover, the information gathered through this process has to be deliberately used to achieve goals (deliberate control), which continuously emerge while driving as a learner.

For instance, let us define perceptions, actions and cognitive information of a driver dealing with a zebra crossing as follows:

```
ops static moving ped zebra : Oid -> Perception [ctor] .
ops stop go : Action [ctor] .
ops givenWayPed waitForPed leftZebraCrossing : -> Cognition [ctor] .
```

The role of such constructors will be explained later in this section.

A learner's perception of an approaching zebra crossing, normally by seeing a road signal, either a horizontal or vertical one, triggers the storage of the cognitive representation of this perception in STM. We may model this instance of explicit attention as

```
goal(driving,zebra) : none | zebra --> noAction |> zebra duration d1
```

where zebra denotes the perception of the zebra crossing and occurs three times for modelling, from left to right: the achievement of the goal of explicitly perceiving the presence of the zebra crossing, the actual perception and the representation of the perception in STM. There is no resultant action since here we are modelling attention.

When also pedestrians ready to cross are perceived, the cognitive representation of this perception is stored in STM.

```
goal(driving,ped) : none | ped --> noAction |> ped duration d2
```

Once the cognitive representations of perceptions zebra and ped are in STM, if the car is moving and the driver is (cognitively) aware of it (modelled by moving in the STM), this composite mental state triggers the retrieval of the following inference, which models the road code rule concerning zebra crossings:

```
inference(driving) :
     moving ; zebra ; ped |-->|> goal(driving,givenWayPed) duration d3
```

Retrieving the rule results in adding goal goal(driving,givenWayPed) to the STM without removing moving, zebra and ped. Such a goal dictates the prescribed behaviour of giving way to pedestrians (whose achievement is denoted by givenWaypPed). This behaviour is 'implemented' by the human as modelled by the following deliberate basic activity:

```
goal(driving,givenWayPed) :
     none | none --> stop |> waitForFree duration d4
```

where stop is the action of stopping the car and waitForFree denotes the driver's mental state of waiting for the zebra crossing to be free.

Once automaticity in driving is acquired, the driver is no longer aware of low-level details and resorts to implicit attention to perform them (automatic control). In general, also an expert driver always starts driving with a precise goal in mind, which normally is that of reaching a specific destination, possibly as a subgoal of the reason for reaching it. Although such a goal is kept in the driver's STM, most driving activities are carried out under automatic control, with no need to retrieve the learned rules. Therefore, the behaviour of an expert driver is modelled as follows:

```
automatism(driving) : none | zebra --> noAction |> zebra duration d1
automatism(driving) : none | ped --> noAction |> ped duration d2
```

```
automatism(driving) :
    moving ; zebra |> ped --> stop |> ped ; waitForFree duration d3
automatism(driving) :
    moving ; ped |> zebra --> stop |> zebra ; waitForFree duration d3
```

The first two automatic activities model implicit attention, which results in the storage of the perception of zebra crossing and pedestrians, respectively. The last two automatic activities model the automatic reaction to the perception of pedestrian in combination with the awareness of the presence of a zebra crossing or the perception of zebra crossing in combination with the awareness of the presence of pedestrian, depending on which perception occurs first.

We can note that automatic behaviour is more efficient than deliberate behaviour for the following reasons:

- there are no goals in STM to drive explicit attention (low cognitive load);
- there is an immediate reaction to perceptions, when in the appropriate mental state (faster reaction);
- there is no recourse to inference (decreased access to LTM).

4   Dynamics of BRDL Models

We model the structure of the human memory using the following Real-Time Maude class.

```
class Human | cognitiveLoad : Nat,
              shortTermMemory : TimedItemSet,
              inferSemMem : InferMem,
              activSemMem : ActivMem,
              procMem : ProcMem .
```

The STM is modelled by attribute shortTermMemory with cognitiveLoad being its current load, the semantic memory by the two attributes inferSemMem and activSemMem and the procedural memory by the single attribute procMem.

4.1   STM Model with Real-Time Maude

The limited capacity of the STM requires the presence of a mechanism to empty it when the stored information is no longer needed. In fact, information in the STM decays very quickly, normally in less than one minute, unless it is reinforced through maintenance rehearsal. To implement STM decay, we need to associate a time to the elements of sort Item

```
sorts TimedItem TimedItemSet .
subsort TimedItem < TimedItemSet .
op _decay_ : Item Time -> TimedItem [ctor] .
op emptyTIS : -> TimedItemSet [ctor] .
op _;_ : TimedItemSet TimedItemSet -> TimedItemSet
         [ctor assoc comm id: emptyTIS] .
op maxDecayTime : -> Time .
eq maxDecayTime = 20000 .
```

Therefore the STM is modelled as an element of sort `TimedItemSet`, the set of elements of sort `TimedItem`. A piece of information in the STM is associated with a *decay time*, which is initialised to the *maximum decay time* (`maxDecayTime`, for example set to 20000 ms) when the information is stored in the STM. Then decay time decreases along with the passage of time. A piece of information disappears from the STM once its decay time has decreased to 0.

Additionally, every time a goal is achieved, a process called *closure* may determine a subconscious removal of information from the STM: the information used to complete the task is likely to be removed from the STM, since it is no longer needed. Therefore, when closure occurs, a piece of information may disappear from the STM even before its decay time has decreased to 0. Conversely, maintenance rehearsal resets the decay time to the maximum decay time.

In order for a goal with `BIS` as parameter of sort `BasicItemSet` to be achieved

- the entire cognitive information included in `BIS` has to be in STM;
- one of the perceptions (if any) has to be the trigger of the occurring basic activity (which may be automatic or deliberate);
- one of the actions (if any) has to be performed by the occurring basic activity.

This is implemented by operations

```
op removeTime : TimedItemSet -> ItemSet .
op goalAchieved : Goal ItemSet DefPerception DefAction -> Bool .
```

where operation `removeTime` removes the time from the elements of the STM and operation `goalAchieved` returns `true` if the goal is achieved.

It is not fully understood how closure works. We can definitely say that once the goal is achieved, it is removed from the STM. However, it is not clear what happens to the information that was stored in STM in order to achieve the goal. We said at the end of Sect. 3.1 that if an ATM is used with the goal of withdrawing cash, the goal is achieved when the user collects the cash delivered by the ATM [8]. However, old ATM interfaces (some still in activity) deliver the cash before returning the card to the user. There is then the possibility that the user collects the cash and, feeling the goal achieved, abandons the interaction forgetting to collect the card. This cognitive error is known as *post-completion error* [6,7,13]. It could be explained by the loss of the information that was stored in STM, when the user inserted the card in the ATM, as a reminder to collect the card at a later stage. In fact, such a loss of information is the result of the closure due to the achievement of the goal when the user collects the cash.

In practice, however, a user interacting with an old ATM interface does not always forget the card. This may be explained by assuming that the likelihood to forget the card depends on the user's cognitive load. Therefore we define the following thresholds

```
op closureThresholdLow : -> Nat . eq closureThresholdLow = 4 .
op closureThresholdHigh : -> Nat . eq closureThresholdHigh = 6 .
```

and force closure to occurs if the cognitive load is at least `closureThreshold High` and prevent its occurrence if the cognitive load is less than `closure ThresholdLow`. In all other cases closure may occur non-deterministically.

Finally, a piece of information may also non-deterministically disappear from the STM when the STM has reached its maximum capacity and it is needed to make space for the storage of new information. This is implemented by allowing the STM to temporarily exceed its capacity, thus reaching an unstable state in which the only applicable rule is

```
crl [forgetSomethingIfSTMfull] :
      < H : Human | shortTermMemory : (ITEM decay NZT) ; STM,
                    cognitiveLoad : CL >
   =>
      < H : Human |   shortTermMemory : STM,
                      cognitiveLoad : sd(CL, 1) >
    if CL > stmCapacity .
```

where `sd` is the symmetric difference between natural numbers.

4.2   Model of the Environment

A specific environment with which the human interacts is defined as an object of class

```
class Environment | state : TimedEnvState,
                    transitions : EnvTransitions .
```

The `state` attribute characterises the environment and its time aspects by means of the following sort structure

```
sort EnvState .
sorts TimedEnvState ExpiringEnvState TimedEnvStateSet .
subsort EnvState < ExpiringEnvState < TimedEnvState < TimedEnvStateSet .
op _expiring'in_ : EnvState Time -> ExpiringEnvState [ctor] .
op _expired : EnvState -> ExpiringEnvState [ctor] .
op _in'time_ : ExpiringEnvState Time -> TimedEnvState [ctor right id: 0]
var STATE : EnvState .
eq STATE expiring in 0 = STATE expired .
op noEnvState : -> TimedEnvStateSet [ctor] .
op _;_ : TimedEnvStateSet TimedEnvStateSet -> TimedEnvStateSet
                 [ctor assoc comm id: noEnvState] .
```

where

- sort `EnvState` of environmental states is user-defined and application-specific;
- sort `ExpiringEnvState` add a *life time* to the environmental state;
- sort `TimedEnvState` add a *delay time* to the (possibly expiring) environmental state.

Note that 0 is right identity in the construction of timed environmental states out of expiring environmental states. Thus a timed environmental state with delay 0 is actually an expiring environmental state (with no delay). Moreover, expiring environmental states are characterised by a postfix constructor `expired` in order to determine different transitions with respect to the non-expired states.

The sort `EnvTransitions` models environmental transitions as follows:

```
sort EnvTransitions .
sort EnvTransition .
subsort EnvTransition < EnvTransitions .
op noTrans : -> EnvTransitions [ctor] .
op _-->_ : ExpiringEnvState TimedEnvState -> EnvTransition [ctor] .
op _--_-->_ : EnvState Action TimedEnvState -> EnvTransition [ctor] .
op _;_ : EnvTransitions EnvTransitions -> EnvTransitions
                  [ctor assoc comm id: noTrans] .
```

Obviously interactions (`_--_-->_`) are associated with actions, internal actions (`_-->_`) are not.

The sort `EnvTransitions` is populated through the user-defined, application-specific operation

```
op transitions : Cid Oid -> EnvTransitions .
```

where `Cid` is a class identifier and `Oid` is an object identifier.

States of the environment may be observable by humans. Such observability is modelled as

```
op observability : ExpiringEnvState -> PerceptionSet .
eq observability(STATE expired) = none .
eq observability(STATE expiring in NZT) = observability(STATE) .
```

with the rest of operation `observability` user-defined and application-specific.

4.3   Zebra Crossing Environment

In order to define the behaviour of the environment for the example in Sect. 3.3, we need two environments, one to model the car behaviour and one to model the zebra crossing behaviour. Both car and zebra crossing have a location, which is variable for the car and fixed for the zebra crossing. They also need to have additional state components to characterise whether the car is moving or is static and whether the zebra crossing has pedestrians or is free.

Environment and Observability. If we assume to have only one human, one car and one zebra crossing

```
ops driver1 car1 zebra1 : -> Oid [ctor] .
```

then the environmental state is defined as follows:

```
sorts Location AdditionalState .
ops atInit atZebra atFinal : -> Location [ctor] .
ops hasPed isFree isMoving isBraking isStatic : -> AdditionalState [ctor] .
op state : Location AdditionalState -> EnvState [ctor] .
```

The meanings of the operations that define locations and additional state components are obvious. An environmental state consists of a location and an additional state.

The observability operation is defined as follows:

```
eq observability(state(LOC,isStatic)) = static .
eq observability(state(LOC,isMoving)) = moving .
eq observability(state(zebra1,AS)) = zebra .
eq observability(state(zebra1,isFree)) = zebra ;    noPed .
eq observability(state(zebra1,hasPed)) = zebra1 ; ped .
```

Transition System. The environmental transition systems are defined as

```
class Car . subclass Car < Environment .
var C : Oid .
eq transitions(Car, C) =
   (state(atInit,isMoving) --> state(atZebra, isMoving)
                                    expiring in 1 in time 30000) ;
   (state(atZebra,isMoving) -- stop(C) --> state(atZebra, isBraking)) ;
   (state(atZebra,isBraking) --> state(atZebra, isStatic) in time 2000) ;
   (state(atZebra,isStatic) -- go(C) --> state(atZebra, isMoving)) ;
   (state(atZebra,isMoving) --> state(atFinal, isMoving)
                                    expiring in 1 in time 30000) ;
   (state(atFinal,isMoving) -- stop(C) --> state(atFinal, isBraking)) ;
   (state(atFinal,isBraking) --> state(atFinal, isStatic in time 2000) .
```

for the car, and

```
class Zebra . subclass Zebra < Environment .
var Z : Oid .
eq transitions(Zebra, Z) =
   (state(Z,isFree) expired --> state(Z, hasPed) expiring in 5000) ;
   (state(Z,hasPed) expired --> state(Z, isFree) expiring in  20000) .
```

for the zebra crossing.

The timings mean that the car takes time 30000 to move between two consecutive locations and time 2000 to brake, being in an unstable state until these times are elapsed and, once stable, expiring immediately (in time 1) if not taken, and that there are pedestrian crossing every 25000 time units ($25000 = 20000 + 5000$) who take time 5000 to cross.

Initial Configuration. Let us consider a driver who has already acquired a general automatism in driving, in which implicit attention controls the storage of information in STM, but still needs to perform inferences to apply road code rules. The initial configuration of the overall system is

```
op init : -> Configuration .
eq init = < cerone : Human |
   cognitiveLoad : 2,
   shortTermMemory : emptyTIS,
   proceduralMemory :
(automatism(driving) : none | moving --> noAction |> moving duration 1) ;
(automatism(driving) : none | static --> noAction |> static duration 1) ;
(automatism(driving) : none | zebra --> noAction |> zebra duration 1) ;
(automatism(driving) : none | ped --> noAction |> hasPed duration 1) ;
(automatism(driving) : none | freePed --> noAction |> freePed duration 1),
   knowledge :
(infer(driving) : (moving ; zebra ; hasPed) |-->|>
      goal(driving,givenWayPed) duration 10) ;
(infer(driving) : (static ; zebra ; freePed) |-->|>
      goal(driving,leftZebraCrossing) duration 10),
   activity :
(goal(driving,givenWayPed) :
      (moving ; zebra ; hasPed) | noPerception -->
         stop(car1) |> waitForPed) duration 10) ;
      (goal(driving,leftZebraCrossing) :
         (zebra ; waitForPed) > (static ; freePed) | noPerception -->
            go(car1) |> none duration 10)
>
< zebra1 : Zebra | transitions : transitions(Zebra, zebra1),
                   state : state(zebra1,zebraPed) expiring in 5000
>
< car1 : Car | transitions : transitions(Car, car1),
               state : state(initLoc,moving)
> .
```

5   Rewrite Rules

At the end of Sect. 4.1 we have introduced the `forgetSomethingIfSTMfull`
rewrite rule. In this section we illustrate three more rewrite rules: `internal`,
`reasoning` and `timePassing`. Other rewrite rules not presented here involve the
automatic and deliberated activities, including special cases such as implicit and
explicit attention, which are characterised by the presence of perception and
absence of action, and cognition, which are characterised by the absence of both
perception and action. Such rules are duplicated for the closure and non-closure
cases.

5.1   Internal Action Rewrite Rule

Internal actions are modelled by the following rewrite rule.

```
crl [internal] :
     {< E : Environment | >
```

```
    REST}
  =>
    {< E : Environment | state : TESTATE >
    REST}
  if ALL-TESTATES := fireTransitions(< E : Environment | >)
    /\ TESTATE ; OTHER-TESTATES := ALL-TESTATES .
```

The rule makes use of the `fireTransitions` operation, which is defined as follows:

```
op fireTransitions : Configuration -> TimedEnvStateSet .
eq fireTransitions(< E : Environment |
                state : ESTATE,
                transitions : (ESTATE --> TESTATE) ; TRANSES > REST ) =
  TESTATE ; fireTransitions( < E : Environment |
                state : ESTATE,
                transitions : TRANSES > REST ) .
eq fireTransitions( REST ) = noEnvState [owise] .
```

The `fireTransitions` operation returns the set of the environmental states generated by the firing of the enabled internal transitions. In the `internal` rewrite rule, such a set is assigned to variable `ALL-TESTATES`, which is matched to `TESTATE ; OTHER-TESTATES`, thus giving the rewritten state `TESTATE`.

5.2   Reasoning Rewrite Rule

Reasoning is modelled by the following rewrite rule.

```
crl [reasoning] :
    {< H : Human |
        cognitiveLoad : CL,
        shortTermMemory : (TIS1 ; TIS2),
        inferMem : (infer(KD) : BIS >| -->|> IS duration T) ; KNOW >
      REST}
  =>
    {< H : Human |
        cognitiveLoad : card(NEW-STM),
        shortTermMemory : NEW-STM,
        inferMem : (infer(KD) : BIS >| -->|> IS duration T) ; KNOW >
      idle(REST, T)}
  in time T
  if BIS == removeTime(TIS1)
    /\ CL < closureThresholdHigh /\ CL <= stmCapacity
    /\ NEW-STM := addTime(BIS ; IS, maxDecayTime)) ; idle(TIS2,T) .
```

In addition to operation `removeTime` introduced in Sect. 4.1, the rule makes use of

- the `addTime` operation, which transforms the untimed sets `BIS` and `IS` into a timed set to be added to the STM;
- the `idle` operation, which models the passage of a given time by decrementing each element of sort `TimedItemSet` of the STM and, for each environment component, the delay and expiration times of the `state` attribute, which is of sort `TimedEnvState`, if positive.

Note that the decay time of the premises in `BIS` is set to the maximum decay time because the use of `BIS` in the inference is an implicit maintenance rehearsal of its timed version `TIS1`.

Let us consider the zebra crossing example introduced in Sects. 3.3 and 4.3. When moving, `zebra` and `ped` are stored in the STM, the road code rule concerning zebra crossing (from Sect. 4.3)

```
inference(driving) :
    moving ; zebra ; ped |-->|> goal(driving,givenWayPed) duration d3
```

is retrieved, thus enabling the application of Maude `reasoning` conditional rule with

```
BIS = moving ; zebra ; ped     and     IS = goal(driving,givenWayPed)
```

The new goal `goal(driving,givenWayPed)` is then added to the STM and triggers the following deliberate basic activity, stored in LTM, which implement the road code rule (from Sect. 4.3):

```
goal(driving,givenWayPed) :
    none | none --> stop |> waitForFree duration d4
```

Such a rule dictates the action of stopping the car (`stop`) and the storage of `waitForFree` in the STM.

5.3   Time Passing Rewrite Rule

```
crl [timePassing] :
      {CONFIG}
   =>
      {idle(CONFIG,1)}
      in time 1
   if nothingEnabled(CONFIG) .
```

where operation `nothingEnabled` is defined as

```
op nothingEnabled enablingSTM : Configuration -> Bool .
eq nothingEnabled(CONFIG) = (fireTransitions(CONFIG) == noEnvState)
                    and (enablingSTM(CONFIG)) == false .
```

and operation `enablingSTM` checks whether the configuration has an object of class `Human` whose STM either exceeds the maximum cognitive load or is enabling an inference rule, an automatic basic activity or a deliberate basic activity. In this way the `timePassing` rewrite rule may be applied only if no other rewrite rule can be applied.

6 Conclusion and Future Work

We have presented a translation of BRDL into Real-Time Maude. In previous work [8,9], a subset of BRDL, the *Human Behaviour Description Language (HBDL)*, was implemented using Core Maude. However, that untimed implementation was limited to automatic and deliberate behaviour powered by a very simple, fixed short-term memory model, with a minimalist, inflexible approach to closure and without decay. Reasoning and problem solving aspects had to be modelled explicitly in a procedural way in a limited, unstructured environment consisting of just one component.

BRDL, instead, is equipped with the linguistic constructs to specify reasoning goals, inference rules and unsolved problems. These linguistic constructs, extensively described in our previous work [10] can be used to model human behaviour in a natural way from the point of view of a psychologist or cognitive scientist. The Real-Time Maude implementation of BRDL presented in this paper provides an engine capable to emulate the human reasoning specified by such constructs, but its knowledge is not needed to use BRDL. Moreover, the object-oriented and real-time aspects of Maude allow us to overcome the limitation of previous work [8] and carry out the implementation of the time aspects envisaged in recent work [9].

Moreover, our work differentiates itself from the work by Broccia *et al.* [3,4] in several respects:

- we have implemented, using Real-Time Maude, a language for the high-level, general description of human behaviour and reasoning (BRDL), whereas the work by Broccia *et al.* is restricted to the modelling and analysis of human multitasking;
- our modelling approach clearly separate human cognition from its environment, with all interaction aspects emerging through the composition of the human component with the operating environment, whereas the framework developed by Broccia *et al.* explicitly incorporates in the human component interaction aspects, such as task duration and difficulty, and delay due to external constraints, such as the presence of other tasks;
- we model the duration of the mental processing, a time aspect that has not been considered by Broccia *et al.*;
- Broccia *et al.* adopt the same minimalist, inflexible approach to closure introduced in Cerone's previous work [8], in which all cognitive information used to achieve the goal is removed independently of the cognitive load, whereas, in our approach, we may use and compare several forms of closure and use thresholds on cognitive load to control the application of closure;
- our components are eager, namely the time passing rewrite rule may be applied only if no other rewrite rule can be applied.

As future work we plan to implement BRDL problem solving constructs [10] and use the model checking capabilities of Real-Time Maude to extend the untimed analysis approach used in previous work [8] to the formal verification of timed properties.

References

1. Atkinson, R.C., Shiffrin, R.M.: Human memory: a proposed system and its control processes. In: Spense, K.W. (ed.) The Psychology of Learning and Motivation: Advances in Research and Theory II, pp. 89–195. Academic Press (1968)
2. Atkinson, R.C., Shiffrin, R.M.: The control of short-term memory. Sci. Am. **225**(2), 82–90 (1971)
3. Broccia, G., Milazzo, P., Ölveczky, P.C.: An executable formal framework for safety-critical human multitasking. In: Dutle, A., Muñoz, C., Narkawicz, A. (eds.) NFM 2018. LNCS, vol. 10811, pp. 54–69. Springer, Cham (2018). https://doi.org/10.1007/978-3-319-77935-5_4
4. Broccia, G., Milazzo, P., Ölveczky, P.C.: Formal modeling and analysis of safety-critical human multitasking. Innov. Syst. Softw. Eng. 169–190 (2019). https://doi.org/10.1007/s11334-019-00333-7
5. Butterworth, R., Blandford, A.E., Duke, D.: Demonstrating the cognitive plausability of interactive systems. Form. Asp. Comput. **12**, 237–259 (2000)
6. Byrne, M.D., Bovair, S.: A working memory model of a common procedural error. Cogn. Sci. **21**, 31–61 (1997)
7. Byrne, M.D., Davis, E.M.: Task structure and postcompletion error in the execution of a routine procedure. Hum. Factors **48**, 627–638 (2006)
8. Cerone, A.: A cognitive framework based on rewriting logic for the analysis of interactive systems. In: De Nicola, R., Kühn, E. (eds.) SEFM 2016. LNCS, vol. 9763, pp. 287–303. Springer, Cham (2016). https://doi.org/10.1007/978-3-319-41591-8_20
9. Cerone, A.: Towards a cognitive architecture for the formal analysis of human behaviour and learning. In: Mazzara, M., Ober, I., Salaün, G. (eds.) STAF 2018. LNCS, vol. 11176, pp. 216–232. Springer, Cham (2018). https://doi.org/10.1007/978-3-030-04771-9_17
10. Cerone, A.: Behaviour and reasoning description language (BRDL). In: SEFM 2019 Collocated Workshops. LNCS. Springer (2019, in press)
11. Harrison, M.D., Campos, J.C., Rukšėnas, R., Curzon, P.: Modelling information resources and their salience in medical device design. In: EICS 2016, pp. 194–203. ACM (2026)
12. Kotseruba, I., Tsotsos, J.K.: 40 years of cognitive architectures: core cognitive abilities and practical applications. Artif. Intell. Rev. **53**(1), 17–94 (2018). https://doi.org/10.1007/s10462-018-9646-y
13. Li, S.W., Blandford, A., Cairns, P., Young, R.M.: The effect of interruptions on postcompletion and other procedural errors: an account based on the activation-based goal memory model. J. Exp. Psychol. Appl. **14**, 314–328 (2008)
14. Martí-Oliet, N., Meseguer, J.: Rewriting logic: roadmap and bibliography. Theoret. Comput. Sci. **285**(2), 121–154 (2002)
15. Norman, D.A., Shallice, T.: Attention to action: willed and automatic control of behaviour. In: Consciousness and Self-Regulation, Advances in Research and Theory, vol. 4. Plenum Press (1986)
16. Ölveczky, P.C.: Real-time maude and its applications. In: Escobar, S. (ed.) WRLA 2014. LNCS, vol. 8663, pp. 42–79. Springer, Cham (2014). https://doi.org/10.1007/978-3-319-12904-4_3
17. Ölveczky, P.C.: Designing Reliable Distributed Systems. UTCS. Springer, London (2017). https://doi.org/10.1007/978-1-4471-6687-0
18. Ölveczky, P.C., Meseguer, J.: Semantics and pragmatics of Real-Time-Maude. High.-Order Symb. Comput. **20**(1–2), 161–196 (2007)

19. Oulasvirta, A., Kristensson, P., Bi, X., Howes, A. (eds.): Computational Interaction. Oxford University Press, Oxford (2018)
20. Weyers, B., Bowen, J., Dix, A., Palanque, P.: Erratum to: the handbook of formal methods in human-computer interaction. In: Weyers, B., Bowen, J., Dix, A., Palanque, P. (eds.) The Handbook of Formal Methods in Human-Computer Interaction. HIS, pp. E1–E3. Springer, Cham (2017). https://doi.org/10.1007/978-3-319-51838-1_21

A Survey of Papers from Formal Methods for Interactive Systems (FMIS) Workshops

Pascal Béger[✉], Sebastien Leriche, and Daniel Prun

ENAC, Université de Toulouse, Toulouse, France
{pascal.beger,sebastien.leriche,daniel.prun}@enac.fr
http://lii.enac.fr/

Abstract. Our research team is specialized in human-computer systems and their engineering, with focus on interactive software systems for aeronautics (from cockpits to control towers). This context stands out by the need for certification, such as DO-178 or ED-12. Today, formal methods are pushed forward, as one of the best tools to achieve the verification and validation of properties, leading to the certification of these systems.

Interactive systems are reactive computer systems that process information from their environment and produce a representation of their internal state. They offer new rich interfaces with sophisticated interactions. Their certification is a challenge, because the validation is often a human based process since traditional formal tools are not always suitable to the verification of graphical properties in particular.

In this paper, we explore the scientific work that has been done in formal methods for interactive systems over the last decade, in a systematic study of publications in the International Workshop on Formal Methods for Interactive Systems. We describe an analytical framework that we apply to classify the studied work into classes of properties and used formalisms. We then discuss the emerging findings, mainly the lack of papers addressing the formal specification or validation of perceptibility properties. We conclude with an overview of our future work in this area.

Keywords: Interactive software · Formal methods · Verification · Graphical properties

1 Introduction

1.1 Aim and Scope of the Article

Interactive systems are reactive computer systems that process information (mouse clicks, data entries, etc.) from their environment (other systems or human users) and produce a representation (sound notification, visual display, etc.) of their internal state [13,59]. They now have an increasingly important place

© Springer Nature Switzerland AG 2020
E. Sekerinski et al. (Eds.): FM 2019 Workshops, LNCS 12232, pp. 443–464, 2020.
https://doi.org/10.1007/978-3-030-54994-7_33

among modern systems in various sectors such as aeronautics, space, medical or mobile applications. These systems offer new rich human machine interfaces with sophisticated interactions.

The preferred method for the verification and validation (V&V) of properties on interactive systems remains largely based on successive testing sessions of prototypes, performed through various experimentations involving representative end-users. For a long time, formal methods have not been very used to the verification of interactive properties. Indeed, historically, formal methods have been developed for distributed and embedded systems. The first properties studied for software and computer systems concerned safety (e.g. absence of unwanted events, boundedness) as well as program liveness (e.g. return to a given state, deadlock freedom) [63]. The main methods used to verify and validate properties of systems are model verification by model checking [25], mathematical proof [18], static analysis [43] and test processes driven by a formal model of the system under tests.

However, more and more work is being done on the development of formal methods to interactive systems. The objective is to study how these methods can be adapted to the modelling and the verification of properties involving human related characteristics. In particular, in the scope of critical domains such as aeronautics, recent updates of standards used for certification strongly recommend to use formal methods for the verification and validation of requirements of new software for aircraft cockpits [72,73].

In this context, the objective of this survey is to study research activities that have been done in formal methods for the modeling, verification and validation of interactive systems, over the last decade. The aim is to draw a faithful picture of formalisms that are used to model interactive systems, set of properties that are verified and formal methods applied. From this picture, the objective is to identify strengths and weaknesses of formal approaches for interactive systems and to identify ways of improvements. More precisely, the survey highlights several points: What interactive related properties are studied? Which ones are more covered and which ones are least addressed? Are there formalisms that are widely used to model systems and study their properties? Are there any new formalisms that have emerged? Are they used on industrial critical systems or only on small academic case studies?

1.2   Methodology

Through this survey we explore the scientific work that has been done in formal methods for interactive systems over the last decade. For this purpose, we perform a systematic study of publications from a specific workshop, the International Workshop on Formal Methods for Interactive Systems (FMIS). We have selected this workshop because it covers exactly our problematic: the articles from this workshop address issues of how formal methods can be applied to interactive system design and verification and validation of their related properties. The workshop also focuses on general design and verification methodologies, and takes models and human behavior under consideration. Moreover, FMIS has reached a critical mass that makes the analysis more significative and reliable. It has taken place seven times from 2006 to 2018. Our study is based on an exhaustive review of the literature from FMIS representing 43 articles.

As we focus on the formal study of properties related to the graphical scene of interactive systems, this survey is based on a table of our choice that classifies the work that has been done about formalisation and verification of properties for interactive systems.

1.3   Plan of the Article

Before reviewing the work from FMIS, we present our analytical framework (2). It is composed by definitions of properties we have sorted in different classes. We also set up a nomenclature of formalisms that have been used for the studies of the properties. From this basis, we propose an analytical grid that allows us to synthesize the review. Then the 43 articles from all the FMIS workshops are presented and analysed (3), analysis mainly directed by the studied properties and the ways of studying them.

The Sect. 4 provides a synthesis of the review and highlights the issues in the research of formal methods for interactive systems. Finally, the Sect. 5 concludes the discussion and presents ongoing work related to the previously highlighted issues.

2   Analytical Framework

The purpose of this section is to define a framework for the analysis of the properties that have been studied for interactive systems. In order to do that, three basic questions must be considered.

- *"What properties are studied?"* This question concerns the nature of properties that have been studied and is the center of our work to determine if some properties have not been studied.
- *"What formalism is being used?"* This question allows us to show what formalisms can be used to study the properties.
- *"What is the case study?"* This question concerns the system used as the case study to illustrate the use of formal methods and its particularities.

We focus on these questions in order to highlight the range of interactive systems properties covered. It provides the means used to cover these properties. Through this survey, we explore these questions by sorting the articles by the properties studied and the means used to study those. We also provide the case study used to illustrate the studies.

2.1 Properties

As stated in the analytical framework, we firstly drive our analysis according to the studied properties. This paper organises interactive systems properties in four classes of our choice: user behavior [2], cognitive principles [29], human-machine interfaces [13], security [70]. We detail these classes below.

Several articles do not directly address interactive properties and so cannot be classified in one of these 4 classes. For these specific papers, we have defined two additional categories:

- **specification/formal definition**: gather papers dealing with the formal modeling of a system, and possibly addressing properties related to the model itself, and not centered on the interaction.
- **testing**: gather papers related to the modeling of interactive systems with the objective to generate test cases from the study of the model.

User Behavior. This user behavior class considers the properties related to a human user. The properties from this class are about user's actions, user's expectations about the system, user's objectives and restrictions.

- A **user goal** is a list of sub objectives that a user has to perform to achieve a greater objective related to the purposes of the system used. This goal can consist on a single task or an overall use case.
  "Insert the card", "authenticate" and "choose the amount of money" are subgoals of "withdraw money".
- **User privileges** are a way to prevent a user with an unauthorized level of accreditation to perform goals the user should not.
  Example: It is only possible to access our e-mails if we are connected to our e-mail system.
- The **user interpretation** can be seen as the set of assumptions of the user about the system. It can lead users to adapt their behavior in accordance with these assumptions.
  For example, we are used to the shortcut Ctrl+C in order to copy some text. A novice user of a terminal could use it to copy text and close the running application because the functionality is not the same.
- The **user attention** is defined as the ability of the user to focus on a specific activity without being disturbed by irrelevant informations.
  This can be seen when driving a car, the driver is focused on traffic signs, on road traffic, etc.
- The **user experience** concerns the knowledge of the user about the system. This knowledge can come from a previous use of the system or a study of the system before using it. This experience can have an impact on user interpretation.
  The example given in user interpretation also illustrates the user experience: an experienced user of a terminal would not make mistakes with the Ctrl+C functionality.

Cognitive Principles. This cognitive principles class considers the properties related to cognitive sciences. The properties from this class are about the human user cognitive salience and load.

- The cognitive **load** is related to the task performed by the user and more specifically to its complexity. It is possible to define two types of cognitive load: intrinsic (complexity of the task) and extraneous (complexity due to the context and distractors).
  For example, a user may lose attention while interacting with too rich a graphical scene.
- The cognitive **salience** represents a user's adherence to an idea. While performing an action, it depends on the action sensory salience, its procedural cueing and the cognitive load related to the task.
  A user will be more focused on an action more in line with his convictions.

Human-Machine Interfaces. In the human-machine interfaces properties class we consider the new properties that have arrived with these new systems. These properties are mainly specific to the problems induced by the display such as verifying the right display of informations or being aware of the latency that can appear between user actions and the display of informations.

- The **latency** is a well-known issue in rich interfaces. It concerns the delay between interactions with an application and the return of informations from it.
  If a computer processes several actions at the same time, it will take a few seconds to start a web browser.
- the **consistency** represents a system constant behavior whether for a display or a functionality regardless the current mode of the system.
  It can be seen as the use of same terminology for functions ("Exit" or "Quit" in order to define a function "close a window").
- The **predictability** is the user's ability to predict the future behavior of the system from its actual state and the way the user will interact with it.
  When closing a word processor with an unsaved document, a user knows that a pop-up will show to ask what to do between saving the document, canceling the closing or closing without saving.
- ISO 9241-11 [80] defines the **usability** as "the extent to which a product can be used by specified users to achieve specified goals with effectiveness, efficiency and satisfaction in a specified context of use."
  It is possible to improve the usability of an "accept/decline" window by adding symbols related to the two notions such as ✓ for accept and × for decline.
- The visual **perceptibility** is based on different properties such as the superposition of components, the distinction of shapes and colours.
  For example, even if a red text is above a red shape, the text will not be perceptible.

Security. This security class considers the properties related to computer security such as the prevention of threats and the link between the user behavior and the possible threats.

- The **integrity** property states that, for a system that may be exposed to threats, hypothesis of the user about the application are correct and the reverse is also true.
  When we log in interfaces with two text fields, if the fields username and password are not in the expected locations, we could type the password in the clear field.
- The **threats** property focuses in defining the differents threats that may be a risk for the system.
  We can note, for example, data leaking or data manipulation.

2.2 Nomenclature of Formalisms

This section will introduce formalisms and formal methods that have been used by FMIS authors in order to formalize and apply verification techniques on the properties defined in the last section. We will define the basic semantic and the properties inherent to these formalisms.

Process Algebra. Baeten [7] gives the history and the definition of process algebra. The author also gives examples of some formalisms from process algebra such as Calculus of Communicating Systems (CCS) or Communicating Sequential Processes (CSP). We can resume from this paper that process algebra is a set of algebraic means used to study and define the parallel systems behavior.

Authors from the FMIS workshop used formalisms from process algebra such as the CWB-NC [34] syntax for the Hoare's CSP notation [48], Language Of Temporal Ordering Specification (LOTOS) [51], probabilistic π-calculus [61], applied π-calculus [69], Performance Evaluation Process Algebra (PEPA) [47].

Specification Language. A specification language [71] is a formal language that can be used to make formal descriptions of systems. It allows a user to analyze a system or its requirements and thus to improve its design.

Authors from the FMIS workshop used specification languages such as SAL [58], Z [79], μCharts [41], Spec# [11], Promela [49], PVS [74], Higher-Order Processes Specification (HOPS) [36].

Refinement. A program refinement consists in the concretisation of a more abstract description of a system. The aim of this method is to verify properties in an abstract level of the description then to concretise this level while conserving the verified properties. These steps have to be done until the concrete description of the system is obtained.

Authors from the FMIS workshop used refinements processes with models such as B-method [3] or with specification languages such as Z and μCharts.

Transition Systems. Transition systems [8] consist in directed graphs composed of states, represented by nodes, and transitions, represented by edges. A state represents an instant in the system behavior or for a program the current value of all the variables and the current state of the program. Crossing a transition involves a change of state.

Authors from the FMIS workshop used transition systems formalisms such as UPPAAL [15], Petri nets (PN) [35], ICO models [60], finite state automata (FSA), Input/Output labeled transition system (IOLTS).

Temporal Logic. Properties to be verified are often expressed in the form of temporal logic formulas [42]. These formulas are based on Boolean combiners, time combiners and for some logics on path quantifiers. Authors from the FMIS workshop used temporal logics such as computation tree logic (CTL) and linear temporal logic (LTL) [25].

3   Review

Here, we review the state of the art of formal methods applied to interactive systems. We consider research work that have been presented in the International Workshop on Formal Methods for Interactive Systems.

Our aim is to present the properties that have been studied with formal methods. From this and the questions that we asked in the Sect. 2, we base our analysis on the grid presented in the Table 6.

This grid highlights the coverage of properties depending on the formalisms. The categories formal definition/specification and testing are not interactive systems properties. However, we want to present how articles address those with formal methods. This explains the fact that there is a double vertical line in the grid. Our work addresses the visual perceptibility property from the HMI class. We highlight this by setting the perceptibility in italic beside the HMI class, separated by a dashed line.

3.1   User Behavior

The Table 1 summarizes the studies of the user behavior class of properties. It sorts the papers according to the properties studied (goals, privileges, interpretation, attention, emotion and experience) and formalisms used.

User Goals. Cerone and Elbegbayan [32] define user goals in the use of a web-based interface that features a discussion forum and a member list. Those are defined with the CWB-NC syntax for CSP from process algebra. These definitions allow authors to model more precisely the attended and unattended use cases.

Rušėnas et al. [66] address the use of an authentification interface with two textboxes (user name and password). They define user goals with the specification language SAL through the definition of a cognitive architecture of user behavior. It allows authors to define the actions a user can do. Rukšėnas et al. [65] further explore the notion of user goals through their cognitive architecture.

Table 1. Study of the **user behavior** class of properties in the FMIS workshops

	Goals	Privileges	Interpretation	Attention	Emotion	Experience
(PA) CWB-NC	[32]	[32]				
(PA) CSP	[30]			[30]		[30]
(PA) LOTOS				[81]		
(PA) PEPA						[33]
(SL) SAL	[65,66]		[66,67]			
(SL) HOPS	[37]					
(other) HTDL				[31]		[31]
ad-hoc formalism					[19]	

Cerone [30] bases his work on the study of two use cases: a driving user and a user interacting with an ATM. He models the user goals with the Hoare's notation for describing CSP (process algebra). It allows him to study cognitive activities such as closure.

Dittmar and Schachtschneider [37] use HOPS (specification language) models to define user tasks and actions while solving a puzzle.

User Privileges. Cerone and Elbegbayan [32] define user privileges with the CWB-NC syntax for CSP. Thus, authors can model wich actions logged or non-logged users are allowed to do. This allows authors to constrain the user behavior by adding new properties in the web interface model.

User Interpretation. Rukšėnas et al. [66] address the user interpretation of an authentification interface. They define it with SAL through the definition of a cognitive architecture of user behavior. It allows authors to highlight the risk for the user of misunderstanding the interface depending on the display of the two textboxes. Rukšėnas and Curzon [67] study the plausible behavior of users interacting with number entry on infusion pumps. They assume that users have their own beliefs about the incremental values. They separately model the users behavior depending on their interpretation and the constraint on cognitive mismatches with LTL and the SAL model checker.

User Attention and User Experience. Su et al. [81] study the temporal attentional limitation in the presence of stimuli on stimulus rich reactive interfaces. The cognitive model of human operators is defined with LOTOS (process algebra). The model of SRRI is based on studies of an AB task [39]. This work presents simulation results focusing on the performance of the interface in user attention.

Cerone [30] addresses user's expectations, which relies on user attention and user experience. He studies cognitive activities such as closure, contention scheduling and attention activation. He models those with the Hoare's notation for describing CSP (process algebra).

Cerone and Zhao [33] use the process algebra PEPA to model a three-way junction with no traffic lights and a traffic situation. They study the user experience in driving in such junctions. They use the PEPA Eclipse plug-in to analyse the model and determine for example the probability of possible collision.

Cerone [31] proposes a cognitive architecture for the modelling of human behavior. This work presents the Human Task Description Language (HTDL). He uses it to model properties related to user behavior such as the automatic (everyday tasks) and deliberate (driven by a goal) control and the human learning, attention and experience.

User Emotion. Bonnefon et al. [19] use their logical framework, an ad-hoc formalism, to model several emotions and the notion of trust. Among the emotions there is joy/distress, hope/fear, satisfaction/disappointment and fear-confirmed/relief. They also model the relation between trust and emotions.

3.2   Cognitive Principles

The Table 2 summarizes the studies of the cognitive principles class of properties. It sorts the papers according to the properties studied (salience and load) and formalisms used.

Table 2. Study of the **cognitive principles** class of properties in the FMIS workshops

	Salience	Load
(SL) SAL	[50, 65]	[50, 65]
(other) GUM	[50]	[50]

Rukšėnas et al. [65] define two cognitive principles, salience and cognitive load. They add those to their SAL cognitive architecture. The authors also define the link between these two principles. They illustrate these principles through the case study of a Fire Engine Dispatch Task.

Huang et al. [50] try to see if their Generic User Model (GUM) can encapsulate all the cognitive principles presented in the Doughnut Machine Experiment [4].

3.3   Human Machine Interfaces

The Table 3 summarizes the studies of the HMI class of properties. It sorts the papers according to the properties studied (consistency, predictability, latency and usability) and formalisms used.

Consistency. Bowen and Reeves [21] use their presentation models and refinement processes with Z to check the equivalence and the consistency between two UI designs. The presentation models allow them to ensure that controls with the same function have the same name and conversely.

Table 3. Study of the **HMI** class of properties in the FMIS workshops

	Consistency	Predictability	Latency	Usability	Perceptibility
(SL) SAL		[56]		[65,66]	
(SL) PVS	[45,46]				
(SL/Re) μCharts				[22]	
(SL/Re) Z	[21]				
(TS) IOLTS	[14]				
(TL) LTL	[14]			[65]	
(TL) CTL	[27,45]				
(other) Tree based WCET			[54]		

Beckert and Beuster [14] provide an IOLTS model of a text-based application to guarantee consistency constraints. Their first model does not satisfy consistency constraints. They refine this model in order to satisfy the consistency constraints.

Campos and Harrison [27] provide consistency a formal definition of consistency of the Alaris GP Volumetric Pump interface in CTL. The global consistency includes: the role and visibility of modes, the relation between naming and purpose of functions, consistency of behavior of the data entry keys. They also present a part of a MAL specification of the Alarais GP infusion pump.

Harrison et al. [45] explore the consistency in the use of the soft function keys of infusion pumps through the use of MAL models translated into PVS. They define consistency properties with CTL and translate those into PVS theorems.

Harrison et al. [46] create a model of a pill dispenser from a specification in PVS. They use this specification with the PVSio-web tool to study the consistency of possible actions.

Predictability. Masci et al. [56] analyse the predictability of the number entry system of Alaris GP and B-Braun Infusomat Space infusion pumps. They use SAL specifications to specify the predictability of the B-Braun number entry system.

Latency. Leriche et al. [54] explore the possibility of using Worst-Case Execution-Time [64] based on trees to study the latency for interactive systems. They also present some works that have been done with graphs of activation to model interactive systems.

Usability. Rukšėnas et al. [66] use their user behavior model in SAL to check usability properties of an authentification interface. They check that the property "the user eventually achieves the perceived goal" is satisfied. Rukšėnas et al. [65] further explore the use of their user model with SAL and LTL properties. They check that the property "the user eventually achieves the main goal" is satisfied in the Fire Engine Dispatch Task.

Bowen and Reeves [22] present a way of applying the specification language μCharts and refinement processes to UI designs. They use presentation models to compare two UI designs and if these UI maintain usability. They also informally describe the refinement process related to UI design.

3.4   Security

The Table 4 summarizes the studies of security class of properties. It sorts the papers according to the properties studied (integrity, usability errors and threats) and formalisms used.

Table 4. Study of the **security** class of properties in the FMIS workshops

	Integrity	Usability errors	Threats
(SL) SAL		[66]	
(TS) IOLTS	[14]		
(TL) LTL	[14]		
(other) BDMP			[52]
others/ad-hoc	[6]	[6]	

Rukšėnas et al. [66] check the risk of security breach in the authentification interface with SAL properties. This highlights the fact that user interpretation can impact the security by entering the password in the wrong textbox for example.

Beckert and Beuster [14] produce a generic IOLTS (transition system) model of a text-based application. They use LTL to describe the properties of components and interpret them with IOLTS. The model is refined to guarantee integrity and to consider the problem of multi-input (if the user enters again a data if the system has not yet processed the last one) risking security breaches.

Arapinis et al. [6] present security properties related to the use of the MATCH (Mobilising Advanced Technology for Care at Home) food delivery system. They define these properties by using different formalisms such as the access control language RW and temporal logic (LTL, TCTL, PCTL).

Johnson [52] studies security properties in terms of threats that may occur on Global Navigation Satellite Systems (GNSS). He models GNSS with Boolean Driven Markov Processes (BDMP) and integrate security threats to the model.

3.5   Specification/Formal Definition and Testing

The Table 5 summarizes the studies of the specification/formal definition and testing classes. It sorts the papers according to the case (specification/formal definition and testing) and formalisms used. This section allows us to present different systems used as case studies.

The references concern the articles that address the formal definition or specification of systems. These articles do not cover the properties previously presented. We only present in this section these articles.

Table 5. Study of the **specification/formal definition** and **testing** classes in the FMIS workshops

	Formal definition	Testing
(PA) CSP	[30]	
(PA) LOTOS	[10]	
(PA) π-calculus	[6]	
(PA) Prob. π-calc	[5]	
(PA) PEPA	[33]	
(PA) TCBS'	[16]	
(SL) SAL	[12,56]	
(SL) Spec#		[75]
(SL) PVS	[45,46,55,62]	
(SL) Promela	[26]	
(SL) HOPS	[37]	
(SL/Re) μCharts	[22]	
(SL/Re) Z	[21,23]	[23]
(Re) B/event-B	[28,40,68]	
(TS) FSM	[82]	
(TS) UPPAAL	[44]	
(TS) Colored PN	[76]	
(TS) GTS	[84]	
(TS) FSA	[83]	
(TS) Event act. graph	[54]	
(TS) ICO	[76]	
(TL) LTL	[6,26]	
(TL) CTL	[45]	
(other) SAT	[26]	
(other) Mark. proc	[5]	
(other) MAL	[27,45]	
(other) GUM	[50]	
(other) BDMP	[52]	
(tool) Spec explorer		[75]
(tool) FEST		[75]
(tool) SMT solver		[23]
(tool) PVSio web	[46,62]	
others/ad-hoc	[6,9,17,20,30,38,77,82]	

Specification/Formal Definition. We sort the articles only focused in specification/formal definition by formalism used.

Process Algebra. Barbosa et al. [10] represent an air traffic control system with a control tower and three aircrafts as CNUCE interactors. They use ad-hoc formalism, a generic approach to process algebra, to define this representation.

Anderson and Ciobanu [5] builds a Markov Decision Process abstraction of a program specification expressed with a probabilistic process algebra (using π-calculus). The abstraction is then used to check the structure of specification, analyze the long-term stability of the system, and provide guidance to improve the specifications if they are found to be unstable.

Bhandal et al. [16] present the language TCBS', strongly based on the Timed Calculus of Broadcasting Systems (TCBS). They give a formal model of a coordination model, the Comhordú system, in this language.

Specification Language. Calder et al. [26] study the MATCH Activity Monitor (MAM), an event driven rule-based pervasive system. They model separately the system behavior and its configuration (rule set) with Promela. They derive Promela rules in LTL properties to check redundant rule with the model checker SPIN.

Bowen and Hinze [20] present early stages work using presentation models to design a tourist information system. This system displays a map on a mobile support (smartphone).

Bass et al. [12] specify in SAL the three subsystems of the A320 Speed Protection: automation, airplane and pilots. This interactive hybrid system has the potential to provide an automation surprise to a user.

Masci et al. [55] specify the DiCoT's information flow model by using PVS. They use three modelling concepts (system state, activities, task) for this specification. The authors use the example of the London Ambulance Service to illustrate their work.

Refinement. Cansell et al. [28] specify an interface of e-voting corresponding to the Single Transferable Vote model without the counting algorithm. This is done by using the B method and a refinement process.

Rukšėnas et al. [68] study the global requirements related to data entry interfaces of infusion pumps. They use Event-B specifications and refinement processes with the Rodin platform to specify these requirements. These refinement processes allow the authors to check if the Alaris GB infusion pump number entry specification validate the global requirements.

Geniet and Singh [40] study an HMI composed by graphical components in form of widgets. They use the Event-B modelling language and refinement processes to model the system and analyse its behavior.

Transition System. Harrison et al. [44] model the GAUDI system [53] with UPPAAL. Through the UPPAAL model, the authors can explore use cases scenario and check reachability properties for example.

Westergaard [84] uses game transition systems to define visualisations of the behavior of formal models. The example of an interoperability protocol for mobile ad-hoc networks to highlight the use of visualisations.

Thimbleby and Gimblett [82] model the interactions possibilities with key data entry of infusion pumps. They use FSM and specify those with regular expressions to model the interactions.

Silva et al. [76] formally define a system and its WIMP and Post-WIMP interactions with ICO models and colored Petri nets. These models allow them to analyse the properties inherent to the formalisms: place transitions invariants, liveness and fairness, and reachability.

Turner et al. [83] generate presentation models describing tasks and widgets based interactions sequences of an infusion pump. It is composed by five buttons (Up, Down, YesStart, NoStop, OnOff) and a display allowing interactions with the user. They use FSA to model these sequences.

Others. Bhattacharya et al. [17] model soft keyboards (on-screen keyboards) with scanning and use the Fitts-Digraph model [78] to evaluate the performance of their model and the system.

Sinnig et al. [77] describe a new formalism based on sets of partially ordered sets. They use it to formally define use cases and task models.

Dix et al. [38] use an ad-hoc formalism to model physical devices (switches, electric kettle, etc.) logical states and their digital effects in another model.

Oladimeji et al. [62] present PVSio-web, a tool which extends the PVSio component of PVS with a graphical environment. They demonstrate its use by prototyping the data entry system of infusion pumps.

Banach et al. [9] consider using an Event-B model in conjunction with an SMT solver in order to proof some invariants on a hardware based components, dedicated to the acquisition and fusion of inputs from various sensors to a visually impaired and blind person's white cane (INSPEX project).

Testing. Silva et al. [75] highlight a way of testing model-based graphical user interfaces. The testing process presented is as follows: a FSM model called Presentation Task Sets (PTS) is generated from a task model (CTT) with the TERESA tool [57], a Spec# oracle is generated from the FSM model with their Task to Oracle Mapping (TOM) tool, then a testing framework is used to test the system against the oracle.

Bowen and Reeves [23] use the specification language Z for specifying a calendar application. They explore the way to apply testing processes on this application. They use their presentation and interaction models to derive tests such as ensuring that the relevant widgets exist in the appropriate states and ensuring that the widgets have the required behaviors.

4   Findings

Through this survey, we have explored the study of interactive systems with formal methods. Several classes of properties have been studied and cover different aspects of interactions.

The Table 6 summarizes the studies of the articles from the International Workshop on Formal Methods for Interactive Systems that has taken place seven times from 2006 to 2018. It gives a distribution of the articles in our analytical grid. We note: $\checkmark$: 1–5 articles; $\checkmark\,\checkmark$: 6–10 articles; $\checkmark\,\checkmark\,\checkmark$: 10+ articles.

Table 6. Study of interactive systems properties in the FMIS workshops

	User behav.	Cogn. pr.	HMI Percept.	HMI Others	Security	Formal def.	Testing
Process algebra	$\checkmark$					$\checkmark\checkmark$	
Spec. language	$\checkmark$	$\checkmark$		$\checkmark\checkmark$	$\checkmark$	$\checkmark\checkmark\checkmark$	$\checkmark$
Refinement				$\checkmark$		$\checkmark$	$\checkmark$
Transition systems	$\checkmark$			$\checkmark$	$\checkmark$	$\checkmark\checkmark$	
Temporal logic		$\checkmark$		$\checkmark$	$\checkmark$	$\checkmark$	
Other/ad-hoc	$\checkmark$	$\checkmark$		$\checkmark$	$\checkmark$	$\checkmark\checkmark$	$\checkmark$

High Proportion of Works on Formal Definitions and Specifications. We highlight the high proportion of articles that address the formal definition and the specification of interactive systems (classified in "Formal def." column of Table 6). Among the 43 articles from the FMIS workshops, 34 are related to this aspect (representing approximately 80%). More than the half of those specifically address the formal definition of properties inherent to the formalisms used (invariant for B, reachability for transition systems, etc.).

Perceptibility Unstudied. We can note that even if several properties related to HMI have been studied, no paper addresses perceptibility properties (cf. "Perceptibility" column). In the FMIS workshops, we have not spotted studies addressing visual, sound or haptic based interactions.

Common Formalisms. If we look at the formalisms used (Table 5), it appears that some are in the majority.

We can see that PVS and SAL are the most widely used specification languages. Over the 14 articles that use specification languages, we find that SAL is the most used with 5 articles using it. PVS is also widely used with 4 articles using it. Those two cover more than the half of the articles using specification language.

B and event-B models are still the most used for refinement processes. 6 articles present refinement processes and half of those use B and event-B models. We find 2 articles using Z and 1 article using μCharts.

New Formalisms. During this analysis, we have seen some formalisms close to the nomenclature we have set (see Sect. 2.2). But other formalisms could not be easily classified in one of the proposed families. We identified 8 papers that use ad-hoc formalisms or formalisms out of the nomenclature.

In those we find, for example, the formal definition of task models and use cases by using an ad-hoc formalism based on sets of partially ordered sets. We also find the modelling of several physical devices with a new and ad-hoc formalism. Another paper presents the formal definition of different emotions by using an ad-hoc formalism. An article presents security properties and the different means (access control language RW, ProVerif's query language, applied π-calculus) of formalising those.

Maturity of Case Studies. A main case study is frequently presented: the "infusion pump" system. Other systems are presented and considered as "textbook" cases, representing more than half of the papers.

The infusion pump is a safety critical medical device and is used by 7 out of 43 articles. 3 of those study the data part of the whole system by modelling it and validate some properties on a sub-system only. 3 other articles study the full system. They model the final device or its specification in order to check whether the device or its specification validate the global requirements of infusion pump. The last article studies the possible interactions between a user and the system. They model those in the form of interaction sequences corresponding to the human user tasks.

This approach demonstrated the feasibility of the proposed methods but remains limited. We note that even if an infusion pump is a safety critical system, the studies made for this system do not necessarily address safety critical aspects. Indeed, only 3 articles focus on the full system and its certification oriented requirements. Only those demonstrate the scalability of the formalisms used.

16 out of 43 articles focus on "textbook" cases and address the user interface part (web application, smartphone application, e-voting system, etc.). Those allow authors to easily illustrate the use of several formal methods and the properties inherent to those. The systems are modelled, several properties, inherent to the formalisms or to the systems, are studied. However, these articles only illustrate the formal methods and do not allow authors to demonstrate the potential scalability of these formal methods.

5   Conclusion

Aim and Contribution of This Article. The aim of this article is to review different research work on formal methods applied to interactive systems. The overall contribution is to provide a review of the literature, 43 articles, from the International Workshop on Formal Methods for Interactive Systems. This workshop took place seven times from 2006 to 2018. First we propose an analytical framework based on a few questions. Then we present several properties of interactive systems and classify them. We set a classic nomenclature of formalisms. This analytical framework is provided with an analysis grid of our own. Those highlight the following points: formalisms used, properties studied, case study used to illustrate the analysis. Finally, we highlight the findings and the outgoing issues.

Discussion. Interactive systems are increasingly used in several sectors and propose several kinds of interactions with human users. The interactions can be from the system to the user by using sound notifications or display notifications in order to provide information to the user about the actual internal state of the system. They can also be from the user to the system with many interaction solutions such as mouse clicks, data entries with keyboards or buttons on the system or soft keyboards and buttons on the display of the system interface. All these interactions are source of new challenges when when the objective is to perform the formal verification and validation of their related properties.

During the last decade, a substantial work has been done in order to study how formalisms and methods can be applied to interactive system. A lot of them have demonstrated that it is possible to take into account a lot of classes of properties. High level properties such as those related to the tasks the user may accomplish or those related to the abstract interface have been studied. The classical formalisms relying on state and transition paradigm can be easily used to model these elements. However, properties related to the concrete part of the interface (involving characteristics of the graphical scene) remain largely uncovered by studies. As we highlighted in the Sect. 4, we note that the properties related to the perceptibility have not yet been studied. This is not a real surprise: these properties require to model characteristics of the system which are not traditionaly handled by formal models: color of graphical objects, forms, dimension, visibility, collision etc. Modeling them remains a big challenge.

Perspectives. Our research team works in the aeronautics sector. Thus, we focus on interactive and critical systems related to this sector. Interfaces with a very rich graphical scene are becoming increasingly important in aircraft cockpits. In this context, we develop a reactive language, Smala[1], allowing us to develop interfaces and interactions at the same level.

The issue related to visual perceptibility properties is then important in our opinion. In Béger et al. [24] we propose elements for formalising graphical properties. We set three basic properties that compose the node of our formalism: the display order depending on the display layer of graphical elements, the intersection depending on the domain of graphical elements and the colour equality. We also present a scene graph we extract from the Smala source code. It models interactive systems and their graphical interface in a new way. It also gives information about graphical elements and their variables (position, colour, opacity, etc.).

From those, we can formally define graphical requirements for an aeronautic system specified in a standard (ED-143 [1]). The formalism defines requirements such as the colour equality/inequality, the authorized/unauthorized positions and the display order. The scene graph defines requirements we can not write with our formalism such as the shape of graphical elements.

We aim at defining new graphical properties in order to express with our formalism requirements related to the shape and the relative positions of graphical elements. In order to automatically validate the requirements, we want to link our formalism to the Smala source code by using code annotations.

Acknowledgments. This work is partly funded by the ANR project FORMEDICIS, ANR-16-CE25-0007.

---

[1] http://smala.io/.

References

1. Ed 143 - minimum operational performance standards for traffic alert and collision avoidance system ii (tcas ii), April 2013
2. Bargh, J.A.: The four horsemen of automaticity: awareness, efficiency, intention, and control in social cognition, vol. 2, January 1994
3. Abrial, J.R.: The B-book: Assigning Programs to Meanings. Cambridge University Press, New York (1996)
4. Ament, M., Cox, A., Blandford, A., Brumby, D.: Working memory load affects device-specific but not task-specific error rate. In: CogSci 2010: Proceedings of the Annual Conference of the Cognitive Science Society, pp. 91–96 (2010)
5. Anderson, H., Ciobanu, G.: Markov abstractions for probabilistic pi-calculus. Electr. Commun. EASST **22** (2009). https://doi.org/10.14279/tuj.eceasst.22.317
6. Arapinis, M., et al.: Towards the verification of pervasive systems. Electr. Commun. EASST **22** (2009)
7. Baeten, J.: A brief history of process algebra. Theoretical Computer Science **335**(2), 131–146 (2005). Process Algebra
8. Baier, C., Katoen, J.P.: Principles of Model Checking (Representation and Mind Series). The MIT Press, Cambridge (2008)
9. Banach, R., Razavi, J., Debicki, O., Mareau, N., Lesecq, S., Foucault, J.: Application of formal methods in the inspex smart systems integration project. In: FMIS 2018, May 2018
10. Barbosa, M.A., Barbosa, L.S., Campos, J.C.: Towards a coordination model for interactive systems. Electr. Notes Theoret. Comput. Sci. **183**, 89–103 (2007). Proceedings of the First International Workshop on Formal Methods for Interactive Systems
11. Barnett, M., Leino, K.R.M., Schulte, W.: The Spec# programming system: an overview. In: Barthe, G., Burdy, L., Huisman, M., Lanet, J.-L., Muntean, T. (eds.) CASSIS 2004. LNCS, vol. 3362, pp. 49–69. Springer, Heidelberg (2005). https://doi.org/10.1007/978-3-540-30569-9_3
12. Bass, E.J., Feigh, K.M., Gunter, E., Rushby, J.: Formal modeling and analysis for interactive hybrid systems. ECEASST **45** (2011)
13. Beaudouin-Lafon, M.: Designing interaction, not interfaces. In: Proceedings of the Working Conference on Advanced Visual Interfaces, AVI 2004, pp. 15–22. ACM, New York (2004)
14. Beckert, B., Beuster, G.: Guaranteeing consistency in text-based human-computer-interaction. In: proceedings of the First International Workshop on Formal Methods for Interactive Systems (2007)
15. Behrmann, G., David, A., Larsen, K.G.: A tutorial on UPPAAL. In: Bernardo, M., Corradini, F. (eds.) SFM-RT 2004. LNCS, vol. 3185, pp. 200–236. Springer, Heidelberg (2004). https://doi.org/10.1007/978-3-540-30080-9_7
16. Bhandal, C., Bouroche, M., Hughes, A.: A process algebraic description of a temporal wireless network protocol. ECEASST **45** (2011)
17. Bhattacharya, S., Basu, A., Samanta, D., Bhattacherjee, S., Srivatava, A.: Some issues in modeling the performance of soft keyboards with scanning. In: proceedings of the First International Workshop on Formal Methods for Interactive Systems (2007)
18. Boldo, S., Lelay, C., Melquiond, G.: Formalization of real analysis: a survey of proof assistants and libraries. Math. Struct. Comput. Sci. **26**(7), 1196–1233 (2016)

19. Bonnefon, J.F., Longin, D., Nguyen, M.H.: A logical framework for trust-related emotions. Electr. Commun. EASST **22** (2009). https://doi.org/10.14279/tuj. eceasst.22.315.312

20. Bowen, J., Hinze, A.: Supporting mobile application development with model-driven emulation **45** (2011)

21. Bowen, J., Reeves, S.: Formal models for informal GUI designs. Electr. Notes Theoret. Comput. Sci. **183**, 57–72 (2007). Proceedings of the First International Workshop on Formal Methods for Interactive Systems

22. Bowen, J., Reeves, S.: Refinement for user interface designs. Electr. Notes Theoret. Comput. Sci. **208**, 5–22 (2008). Proceedings of the 2nd International Workshop on Formal Methods for Interactive Systems

23. Bowen, J., Reeves, S.: Ui-design driven model-based testing. Electr. Commun. EASST **22** (2009). https://doi.org/10.14279/tuj.eceasst.22.314

24. Béger, P., Becquet, V., Leriche, S., Prun, D.: Contribution á la formalisation des propriétés graphiques des systèmes interactifs pour la validation automatique. In: Afadl 2019. Toulouse, France, June 2019

25. Bérard, B., et al.: Systems and Software Verification: Model-Checking Techniques and Tools, 1st edn. Springer Publishing Company Incorporated, Heidelberg (2010). https://doi.org/10.1007/978-3-662-04558-9

26. Calder, M., Gray, P., Unsworth, C.: Tightly coupled verification of pervasive systems. Electr. Commun. EASST **22** (2009). https://doi.org/10.14279/tuj.eceasst. 22.320

27. Campos, J., Harrison, M.: Modelling and analysing the interactive behaviour of an infusion pump. ECEASST **45** (2011)

28. Cansell, D., Gibson, J.P., Méry, D.: Refinement: a constructive approach to formal software design for a secure e-voting interface. Electr. Notes Theoret. Comput. Sci. **183**, 39–55 (2007). Proceedings of the First International Workshop on Formal Methods for Interactive Systems

29. Cartwright-Finch, U., Lavie, N.: The role of perceptual load in inattentional blindness. Cognition **102**(3), 321–340 (2007)

30. Cerone, A.: Closure and attention activation in human automatic behaviour: a framework for the formal analysis of interactive systems. ECEASST **45** (2011)

31. Cerone, A.: Towards a cognitive architecture for the formal analysis of human behaviour and learning. In: Mazzara, M., Ober, I., Salaün, G. (eds.) STAF 2018. LNCS, vol. 11176, pp. 216–232. Springer, Cham (2018). https://doi.org/10.1007/978-3-030-04771-9_17

32. Cerone, A., Elbegbayan, N.: Model-checking driven design of interactive systems. Electr. Notes Theoret. Comput. Sci. **183**, 3–20 (2007). Proceedings of the First International Workshop on Formal Methods for Interactive Systems

33. Cerone, A., Zhao, Y.: Stochastic modelling and analysis of driver behaviour. ECEASST **69** (2013). https://doi.org/10.14279/tuj.eceasst.69.965.946

34. Cleaveland, R., Li, T., Sims, S.: The Concurrency Workbench of the New Century. User's manual SUNY at Stony Brook, Stony Brooke (2000)

35. David, R., Alla, H.: Discrete, Continuous, and Hybrid Petri Nets, 2nd edn. Springer Publishing Company Incorporated, Heidelberg (2010). https://doi.org/10.1007/978-3-642-10669-9

36. Dittmar, A., Hübner, T., Forbrig, P.: HOPS: a prototypical specification tool for interactive systems. In: Graham, T.C.N., Palanque, P. (eds.) DSV-IS 2008. LNCS, vol. 5136, pp. 58–71. Springer, Heidelberg (2008). https://doi.org/10.1007/978-3-540-70569-7_5

37. Dittmar, A., Schachtschneider, R.: Lightweight interaction modeling in evolutionary prototyping. ECEASST **69** (2013). https://doi.org/10.14279/tuj.eceasst.69.961

38. Dix, A., Ghazali, M., Ramduny-Ellis, D.: Modelling devices for natural interaction. Electronic Notes in Theoretical Computer Science **208**, 23–40 (2008). Proceedings of the 2nd International Workshop on Formal Methods for Interactive Systems

39. Raymond, E.J., Shapiro, K., Arnell, K.: Temporary suppression of visual processing in an RSVP task: An attentional blink? J. Exp. Psychol. **18**, 849–860 (1992). Human perception and performance

40. Geniet, R., Singh, N.K.: Refinement based formal development of human-machine interface. In: Mazzara, M., Ober, I., Salaün, G. (eds.) STAF 2018. LNCS, vol. 11176, pp. 240–256. Springer, Cham (2018). https://doi.org/10.1007/978-3-030-04771-9_19

41. Goldson, D., Reeve, G., Reeves, S.: μ-chart-based specification and refinement. In: George, C., Miao, H. (eds.) ICFEM 2002. LNCS, vol. 2495, pp. 323–334. Springer, Heidelberg (2002). https://doi.org/10.1007/3-540-36103-0_34

42. Goranko, V., Galton, A.: Temporal logic. In: Zalta, E.N. (ed.) The Stanford Encyclopedia of Philosophy, Winter 2015 Edn. (2015)

43. Gosain, A., Sharma, G.: Static analysis: a survey of techniques and tools. In: Mandal, D., Kar, R., Das, S., Panigrahi, B.K. (eds.) Intelligent Computing and Applications. AISC, vol. 343, pp. 581–591. Springer, New Delhi (2015). https://doi.org/10.1007/978-81-322-2268-2_59

44. Harrison, M.D., Kray, C., Campos, J.C.: Exploring an option space to engineer a ubiquitous computing system. Electr. Notes Theoret. Comput. Sci. **208**, 41–55 (2008). Proceedings of the 2nd International Workshop on Formal Methods for Interactive Systems

45. Harrison, M.D., Masci, P., Campos, J.C., Curzon, P.: Automated theorem proving for the systematic analysis of an infusion pump. ECEASST **69** (2013). https://doi.org/10.14279/tuj.eceasst.69.962

46. Harrison, M.D., Masci, P., Campos, J.C.: Formal modelling as a component of user centred design. In: Mazzara, M., Ober, I., Salaün, G. (eds.) STAF 2018. LNCS, vol. 11176, pp. 274–289. Springer, Cham (2018). https://doi.org/10.1007/978-3-030-04771-9_21

47. Hillston, J.: A Compositional Approach to Performance Modelling. Cambridge University Press, New York (1996)

48. Hoare, C.A.R.: Communicating Sequential Processes. Prentice-Hall Inc., Upper Saddle River (1985)

49. Holzmann, G.: The SPIN Model Checker: Primer and Reference Manual, 1st edn. Addison-Wesley Professional, Boston (2011)

50. Huang, H., et al.: Capturing the distinction between task and device errors in a formal model of user behaviour **45** (2011)

51. ISO-8807:1989: Information processing systems - open systems interconnection - LOTOS - a formal description technique based on the temporal ordering of observational behaviour (1989)

52. Johnson, C.W.: Using assurance cases and boolean logic driven markov processes to formalise cyber security concerns for safety-critical interaction with global navigation satellite systems. ECEASST **45** (2011)

53. Kray, C., Kortuem, G., Krüger, A.: Adaptive navigation support with public displays. In: Proceedings of the 10th International Conference on Intelligent User Interfaces, IUI 2005, pp. 326–328. ACM, New York (2005)

54. Leriche, S., Conversy, S., Picard, C., Prun, D., Magnaudet, M.: Towards handling latency in interactive software. In: Mazzara, M., Ober, I., Salaün, G. (eds.) STAF 2018. LNCS, vol. 11176, pp. 233–239. Springer, Cham (2018). https://doi.org/10.1007/978-3-030-04771-9_18

55. Masci, P., Curzon, P., Blandford, A., Furniss, D.: Modelling distributed cognition systems in PVS. ECEASST **45** (2011)

56. Masci, P., et al.: On formalising interactive number entry on infusion pumps. ECE-ASST **45** (2011)

57. Mori, G., Paterno, F., Santoro, C.: Design and development of multidevice user interfaces through multiple logical descriptions. IEEE Trans. Software Eng. **30**(8), 507–520 (2004). https://doi.org/10.1109/TSE.2004.40

58. de Moura, L., Owre, S., Rueß, H., Rushby, J., Shankar, N., Sorea, M., Tiwari, A.: SAL 2. In: Alur, R., Peled, D.A. (eds.) CAV 2004. LNCS, vol. 3114, pp. 496–500. Springer, Heidelberg (2004). https://doi.org/10.1007/978-3-540-27813-9_45

59. Myers, B.A., Rosson, M.B.: Survey on user interface programming. In: Proceedings of the SIGCHI Conference on Human Factors in Computing Systems, CHI 1992, pp. 195–202. ACM, New York (1992)

60. Navarre, D., Palanque, P., Ladry, J.F., Barboni, E.: Icos: a model-based user interface description technique dedicated to interactive systems addressing usability, reliability and scalability. ACM Trans. Comput.-Hum. Interact. **16**(4), 18:1–18:56 (2009)

61. Norman, G., Palamidessi, C., Parker, D., Wu, P.: Model checking the probabilistic π-calculus. In: Proceedings 4th International Conference on Quantitative Evaluation of Systems (QEST 2007), pp. 169–178. IEEE Computer Society (2007)

62. Oladimeji, P., Masci, P., Curzon, P., Thimbleby, H.: PVSIO-web: a tool for rapid prototyping device user interfaces in PVS. ECEASST **69** (2013). https://doi.org/10.14279/tuj.eceasst.69.963

63. Owicki, S., Lamport, L.: Proving liveness properties of concurrent programs. ACM Trans. Program. Lang. Syst. **4**(3), 455–495 (1982)

64. Puschner, P., Burns, A.: A review of worst-case execution-time analyses. Real-time Systems - RTS Jan 1999

65. Rukšėnas, R., Back, J., Curzon, P., Blandford, A.: Formal modelling of salience and cognitive load. Electr. Notes in Theoret. Comput. Sci. **208**, 57–75 (2008). Proceedings of the 2nd International Workshop on Formal Methods for Interactive Systems

66. Rukšėnas, R., Curzon, P., Blandford, A.: Detecting cognitive causes of confidentiality leaks. Electr. Notes Theoret. Comput. Sci. **183**, 21–38 (2007)

67. Rukšėnas, R., Curzon, P.: Abstract models and cognitive mismatch in formal verification. ECEASST **45** (2011)

68. Rukšėnas, R., Masci, P., Harrison, M.D., Curzon, P.: Developing and verifying user interface requirements for infusion pumps: a refinement approach. ECEASST **69** (2013). https://doi.org/10.14279/tuj.eceasst.69.964.945

69. Ryan, M.D., Smyth, B.: Applied pi calculus. In: Formal Models and Techniques for Analyzing Security Protocols. IOS Press (2011)

70. Sabelfeld, A., Myers, A.C.: Language-based information-flow security. IEEE J. Sel. A. Commun. **21**(1), 5–19 (2006)

71. Sannella, D., Wirsing, M.: Specification languages. Algebraic Foundation of Systems Specification. IFIP State-of-the-Art Reports, pp. 243–272, July 1999

72. SC-205, R.F., 71, E.A.W.G.: Rtca/do-178c software considerations in airborne systems and equipment certification, December 2011

73. SC-205, R.F., 71, E.A.W.G.: Rtca/do-333 formal methods supplement to do-178c and do-278a, December 2011

74. Shankar, N.: PVS: combining specification, proof checking, and model checking. In: Srivas, M., Camilleri, A. (eds.) FMCAD 1996. LNCS, vol. 1166, pp. 257–264. Springer, Heidelberg (1996). https://doi.org/10.1007/BFb0031813

75. Silva, J.L., Campos, J.C., Paiva, A.C.: Model-based user interface testing with spec explorer and concurtasktrees. Electr. Notes Theoret. Comput. Sci. **208**, 77–93 (2008)

76. Silva, J.L., Fayollas, C., Hamon, A., Palanque, P., Martiinie, C., Barboni, E.: Analysis of wimp and post wimp interactive systems based on formal specification. ECEASST **69** (2013). https://doi.org/10.14279/tuj.eceasst.69.967

77. Sinnig, D., Chalin, P., Khendek, F.: Towards a common semantic foundation for use cases and task models. Electr. Notes Theoret. Comput. Sci. **183**, 73–88 (2007)

78. Soukoreff, R.W., Mackenzie, I.S.: Theoretical upper and lower bounds on typing speed using a stylus and a soft keyboard. Behav. Inf. Technol. **14**(6), 370–379 (1995)

79. Spivey, J.M.: The Z Notation: A Reference Manual. Prentice-Hall Inc., Upper Saddle River (1989)

80. Standardization, I.: ISO 9241–11: Ergonomic Requirements for Office Work with Visual Display Terminals (VDTs): Part 11: Guidance on Usability (1998)

81. Su, L., Bowman, H., Barnard, P.: Performance of reactive interfaces in stimulus rich environments, applying formal methods and cognitive frameworks. Electr. Notes in Theoret. Comput. Sci. **208**, 95–111 (2008). Proceedings of the 2nd International Workshop on Formal Methods for Interactive Systems

82. Thimbleby, H., Gimblett, A.: Dependable keyed data entry for interactive systems. ECEASST **45** (2011)

83. Turner, J., Bowen, J., Reeves, S.: Using abstraction with interaction sequences for interactive system modelling: STAF 2018 Collocated Workshops, Toulouse, France, 25–29 June 2018, Revised Selected Papers, pp. 257–273, June 2018

84. Westergaard, M.: A game-theoretic approach to behavioural visualisation. Electr. Notes Theoret. Comput. Sci. **208**, 113–129 (2008). Proceedings of the 2nd International Workshop on Formal Methods for Interactive Systems

Formal Modelling of Safety-Critical Interactive Devices Using Coloured Petri Nets

Sapna Jaidka[1]([✉]), Steve Reeves[2], and Judy Bowen[2]

[1] Waikato Institute of Technology, University of Waikato, Hamilton, New Zealand
sapnajaidka87@gmail.com
[2] University of Waikato, Hamilton, New Zealand
{stever,judy.bowen}@waikato.ac.nz

Abstract. Formal modelling is now widely applied for creating models of safety-critical interactive systems. Most approaches built so far either focus on the user interface or on the functional part of a safety-critical interactive system. This paper aims to apply formal methods for modelling and specifying the user interface, interaction and functional aspects of a safety-critical system in a single model using Coloured Petri Nets (CPN). We have used CPNs because of its expressive graphic representation and the ability to simulate the system behaviour. The technique is illustrated through a case study of the Niki T34 Infusion Pump.

Keywords: Formal modelling · Formal method integration · Coloured Petri Nets

1 Introduction

Safety should be a central consideration in the development of safety-critical interactive systems. There are many systems that are considered as safety-critical interactive systems where the interaction occurs via a user or, perhaps, via an automatic manufacturing system (production cell) where sensors are interacting among themselves. It is very important to ensure that all these types of system behave correctly because failure can cause significant damage to property, the environment or even human life. Researchers have been working for many years to solve problems or issues in safety-critical systems due to poor user interfaces or functional errors. The use of formal methods for modelling is often recommended as a way of raising confidence in such systems. The focus of this paper is on user interfaces as well as the underlying system functionality of safety-critical interactive systems.

The work here aims to apply formal methods for modelling and specifying the user interface, interaction and functional aspects of the system in a single model. This technique has its starting point in several formal specification techniques: Z, Presentation Interaction Models (PIMs) and Presentation Models (PMs)

© Springer Nature Switzerland AG 2020
E. Sekerinski et al. (Eds.): FM 2019 Workshops, LNCS 12232, pp. 465–485, 2020.
https://doi.org/10.1007/978-3-030-54994-7_34

(as for instance in [5]). From this (existing) basis we create a Coloured Petri Net (CPN) model of a system which will have the required aspects of Z, PMs and PIMs expressed within it. To specify safety-critical systems adequately, all three aspects, behavioural, functional and user interface/interaction must be taken into account, hence our investigation of the combination of models. In summary, our plan here is to show how an existing, accepted way of formally modelling systems via PM/PIM/Z can be re-cast in the single formalism of CPN, and then in future, having shown the CPN models are as expressive as the PM/PIM/Z models, we can move straight from the system to a CPN model of it.

We have chosen CPNs mainly because of the state space analysis-based methods made possible within the CPN Tool, based on support for the state space graph and the strongly connected components graph to be automatically generated. Once we have these then functions can be written in the SML-subset available in CPN Tools which allow many useful further checking and testing mechanisms. Comparing this with other possibilities, there is a tool called RENEW for Reference Nets but it does not generate the state space graph [18]. Also we find in the literature that the Reference Net models or even Object Petri Nets models get transformed into behaviourally equivalent CPNs for adapting CPN analysis techniques, as mentioned in [19].

This way of investigating and model-checking properties by writing SML functions to define a process for computing a check contrasts with the more usual (for ProB users, for example) method of writing temporal logic statements which are statements of properties. It may be that this more "procedural" way of expressing properties is more attractive to "conventional" programmers, compared with having to learn and then express temporal logic statements in a "declarative" way.

The motive for doing this work is two-fold: the existing method results in three separate models, and the drawback with this is that a lot of work is required to do the coupling of functional behaviour with interactive elements to ensure consistency [8,26]. Moreover, these models need to be combined in order to verify safety properties which might relate to functional constraints, interface constraints or both. The new technique results in a single model capturing all three aspects and all the connections between them. So, the benefit of having all aspects in a single model is that there is no work required to combine them for analysis.

2   Related Work

In the early years, the main focus of formal methods was on modelling and specifying the functional part of a system. User-interfaces and interaction were not considered important because systems used to be very simple. But now as the interfaces have become more complex, so their design and analysis is very obviously important. There were some formal methods which were used to model and verify both user-interface and interaction, for example, Jacob in [13] has used techniques based on state transition diagrams and BNF to specify the user-interface and Dix and Runciman in [11] focused on creating abstract models for user interfaces and interaction. However, formal methods for system development and those for modelling user interfaces and interaction were considered separate. There exists far less work on the combination of both these aspects.

The Food and Drug Administration (FDA) has been working with academic collaborators to develop model-based engineering methods [1]. Figueiredo et al. [2] presented the main advantages of a formal language that is able to be used in the construction of reference models for the medical devices domain and conducted a case study on a specification of a medical device. Masci et al. also presented a case study on a generic PCA infusion pump in [21] and verified the user-interface using the Prototype Verification System (PVS) and also formally modelled the requirements of the interface in [23]. Campos and Harrison presented a case study on modelling and analysis of the Alaris infusion pump using their IVY tool [9].

Petri nets form a powerful modelling language and higher level nets, like Coloured Petri Nets, are used for modelling critical scenarios like railway systems and other safety-critical systems [3,14]. There exist formalisms like HAMSTERS [20] that focus on task models, and also ICOs [22] and the APEX framework [24]. The main difference concerning ICOs is around levels of abstraction, because they take an object-oriented view whereas we are committed to more abstract prior models. All these studies either focus on the functional part of the system or on the user-interface and interaction. We present a technique to combine all aspects in a single model.

3   Coloured Petri Nets and Their Extensions

Coloured Petri Nets (CPN) is a language used for the modelling and validation of hardware and software systems. The existing CPN Tool [16] helps in constructing a model and performing syntax checking. Also simulations can be performed and we can see at every step how the model is behaving. Automatic generation of full and partial state spaces helps in analyzing and verifying the net model.

We will commence with the formal definition of Coloured Petri Nets [16]. The following are assumed to be defined: $EXPR$ denotes the set of expressions provided by the inscription language, i.e., CPN ML [15]. Given an expression $e \in EXPR$, the **type** of e is represented by $Type[e]$. The set of **variables** in an expression e is denoted by $Var[e]$. V denotes the set of (all) variables. By S_{MS}, we denote the set of all *multi-sets* over the set S [15].

Definition 1. *A Coloured Petri Net is a tuple* $(CS, P, T, A, N, C, G, E, I)$ *such that [15]:*

(i) *CS is a finite set of non-empty types, called colour sets.*
(ii) *P is a finite set of places.*
(iii) *T is a finite set of transitions.*
(iv) *A is a finite set of directed arcs such that connect places and transitions.*
(v) *N is a node function. It is defined from A into* $P \times T \cup T \times P$ *and shows, for each arc, which places and transitions are connected by that arc.*

(vi) C is a colour function. It is defined from P into CS.
(vii) G is a guard function. It is defined from $T \rightarrow EXPR$ such that: $\forall t \in T$:
  $Type[G(t)] = Bool \wedge Type[Var[G(t)]] \subseteq CS$.
(viii) E is an arc expression function. It is defined from A into expressions such
  that: $\forall a \in A : Type[E(a)] = C(p(a))_{MS} \wedge Type[Var[E(a)] \subseteq CS]$ where
  $p(a)$ is a place of $N(a)$.
(ix) I is an initialization function. It is defined from P into closed expressions
  such that $\forall p \in P : Type[I(p)] = C(p)_{MS}$.

Definition 2. *A distribution of tokens on the places is called a **marking**. A marking M is a function that maps each place p into a multi-set of values $M(p)$ representing the marking of p. The **initial marking** is denoted by M_0.*

Definition 3. *The **variables of a transition t** is denoted, by overloading function V, as $Var[t] \subseteq V$ and is defined so it consists of the free variables appearing in the guard of t and in the arc expressions of arcs connected to t. A **binding** of a transition t is a function b that maps each variable $v \in Var[t]$ into a value $b(v) \in Type[v]$. It is extended to expressions from EXPR in the obvious way. The application of binding b to expression e is written $e\langle b \rangle$. The set of all bindings for t is denoted by $B(t)$.*
*A **binding element** is a pair (t, b) where $t \in T$ and $b \in B(t)$.*
We often write an arc expression $E(a)$ as $E(p, t)$ or $E(t, p)$ when $N(a) = (p, t)$ or $N(a) = (t, p)$, respectively, as a suggestive shorthand.

Definition 4. *For a binding element (t, b) to be **enabled** in a marking M there are two conditions to satisfy: firstly, the corresponding guard expression must evaluate to True. Secondly, for each place p, an arc expression $E(p, t)$ has to be evaluated using the binding b so that $E(p, t)\langle b \rangle \leq M(P)$. This means that for each place p there should be enough tokens there of the right form so that transition t can remove the required number of tokens.*
This means that in an enabled binding element (t,b), the multi-set of tokens removed from an input place p when t occurs with a binding b is given by $E(p, t)\langle b \rangle$, and similarly $E(t, p)\langle b \rangle$ is the multi-set of tokens added to an output place p.

Definition 5. *A **step** Y is a non-empty, finite multi-set of binding elements. A step Y is **enabled** in a marking M iff the following property is satisfied [15]:*
$$\forall p \in P : \sum_{(t,b) \in Y} E(p, t)\langle b \rangle \leq M(p).$$
When a step Y is enabled in a marking M_1 it may occur, changing the marking M_1 to another marking M_2, defined by: $\forall p \in P : M_2(p) = (M_1(p) - \sum_{(t,b) \in Y} E(p, t)\langle b \rangle) + \sum_{(t,b) \in Y} E(t, p)\langle b \rangle$, which is to say that when a step happens, tokens are removed from the starting place of a transition and placed in the ending place of that transition.

3.1   Hierarchical Coloured Petri Nets

Hierarchical Coloured Petri Nets allow models to be divided into modules. This allows the model to be organized into several pages. There are two ways to interconnect these several pages: *substitution transitions and fusion places* [17]. In this paper we are using *fusion places*. *Fusion places* are places which are functionally identical, so they have the same marking.

4   Presentation Model

A *Presentation Model* (PM) [6] describes the existence, category and behaviour of the widgets (interactive elements) of a user interface. Widgets are categorized using the widget categorization hierarchy given in [4]. A presentation model typically consists of several component presentation models which could be understood as the states of the user interface.

Presentation models consist of two parts: declaration and definition.

$$\langle declaration \rangle \ ::=$$
$$WidgetName\{\langle ident \rangle\}^+ \ Category\{\langle ident \rangle\}^+ \ Behaviour\{\langle ident \rangle\}^*$$

The declarations introduce the three sets of identifiers which can be used within the definitions. *WidgetName* is a list of names of widgets. *Category* refers to the description of widget categories. *Behaviour* shows what behaviour a widget has associated with it (and it can be empty). Behaviours are divided into two categories. The first is called a system behaviour (S-behaviour) which refers to the underlying non-interactive system and the second category is called an interactive behaviour (I-behaviour) that represents user interface functionality, which changes things about the user interface itself, like changing screens.

A definition consists of one or more identifiers for presentation models.

$$\langle definition \rangle \ ::= \{\langle pname \rangle is \langle pexpr \rangle\}^+ \ where \ \langle pname \rangle \ ::=$$
$$\langle ident \rangle \ and \ \langle pexpr \rangle \ ::= \{\langle widgetdescr \rangle\}^+$$

Each state of the system is described in a separate component presentation model by the means of widget descriptions. A widget description consists of a triple, the widget name, the category and the set of behaviours associated with the widget. The syntax of a widget description is as follows:

$$\langle widgetdescr \rangle \ ::= (\langle widgetname \rangle, \langle category \rangle, (\{\langle behaviour \rangle\}^*))$$

Consider a device as shown in Fig. 1 having two buttons *ON* an *OFF* and one *Display*. Pressing the *ON* button will display a start message and the *OFF* button will switch off the device. A PM for the device is given in Table 1. The model has three widgets and each widget falls under one of the two categories (*ActCtrl* or *Responder*). *ActCtrl* is shorthand for action control. The simple device's PM has one S-behaviour and two I-behaviours. In Table 1, *init*, *ON*, *OFF* are three component presentation models. Each component presentation model consists of a set of widget triples. For example, the *ON* component presentation model comprises of three sets of widget triples. The first set of triples means that the widget *Display* is of category *Responder* and has the *S_startmessage* behaviour associated with it. Notice that the behaviour *Quit* is not labelled as an I-behaviour or S-behaviour as it is a special behaviour that terminates both the system and the user interface.

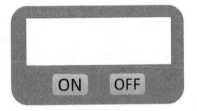

Fig. 1. A simple device

Table 1. Presentation Model of a simple device

WidgetName	Display ONButton OFFButton
Category	ActCtrl Responder
Behaviour	S_startmessage I_ON
	I_OFF Quit
Init is	(Display, Responder, ())
	(ONButton, ActCtrl, (I_ON))
	(OFFButton, ActCtrl, (I_OFF))
ON is	(Display, Responder, (S_startmessage))
	(ONButton, ActCtrl, ())
	(OFFButton, ActCtrl, (I_OFF))
OFF is	(Display, Responder, ())
	(ONButton, ActCtrl, (I_ON))
	(OFFButton, ActCtrl, (Quit))

4.1   Expressing Presentation Models in CPN

We will first look at the declaration part of a PM which introduces the three sets of identifiers: *WidgetName*, *Category* and *Behaviour*. These three sets of identifiers can be modelled in CPN by:

$$colset\ WidgetName\ =\ with\ wid_1\ |\ wid_2\ |\ ...\ |\ wid_n;$$
$$colset\ Category\qquad =\ with\ cid_1\ |\ cid_2\ |\ ...\ |\ cid_n;$$
$$colset\ Behaviour\qquad =\ with\ bid_1\ |\ bid_2\ |\ ...\ |\ bid_n;$$
$$colset\ Behaviours\qquad =\ list\ Behaviour;$$

where wid_s are the names of the widgets, cid_s are the names of the category of the widgets and bid_s are the names of the S-behaviours and I-behaviours associated with the widgets.

Now we look at the definition part of the presentation model [6]. A widget description which we call as *widgetdescr* is described as a tuple consisting of the widget name, the category and the list of behaviours associated with the widget. A widget description can be written in CPN as:

$$colset\ widgetdescr\ =\ product\ WidgetName\ *\ Category\ *\ Behaviours;$$

Consider again the example shown in Fig. 1 and Table 1. The model of this presentation model in CPN is shown in Tables 2 and 3. Each state of the system is described in a separate *component presentation model* by the means of *widgetdescr*. This can be written in CPN as:

$$colset\ pmodel\ =\ list\ widgetdescr;$$

Table 2. Presentation model declarations of the simple device in CPN

colset WidgetName =	with Display |
	ONButton |
	OFFButton;
colset Category =	with ActCtrl |
	Responder;
colset Behaviour =	with S_startmessage |
	I_ON |
	I_OFF |
	Quit;
colset Behaviours =	list Behaviour;

To define the component presentation model we will use the value declaration feature of CPN. A value declaration binds a value to an identifier. The component presentation models for the simple device of Fig. 1 are given in CPN in Table 3. We can now see what the states of the device are and what widgets are available to the user in every state and what the behaviours of those widgets are. But to understand the navigational possibilities, it is always better to have some graphical representation. Another model, i.e., a presentation and interaction model (PIM), is used for this purpose.

Table 3. Presentation model definition of the simple device in CPN

val	Init =	[(Display, Responder, [ ]),
		(ONButton, ActCtrl, [I_ON]),
		(OFFButton, ActCtrl, [I_OFF])];
val	ON =	[(Display, Responder,
		[S_startmessage]),
		(ONButton, ActCtrl, [ ]),
		(OFFButton, ActCtrl, [I_OFF])];
val	OFF =	[(Display, Responder, [ ]),
		(ONButton, ActCtrl, [I_ON]),
		(OFFButton, ActCtrl, [Quit])];

5   Presentation Interaction Models

A presentation and interaction model (PIM) describes the transitions between states [6]. A PIM is the combination of a presentation model and a finite state machine (FSM). A PIM gives a formal meaning to I-behaviours given in the presentation model. The PIM is derived by creating a single state for each of the component presentation models and creating transitions between states based on the relevant I-behaviours, so transitions give the meaning of I-behaviours.

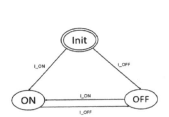

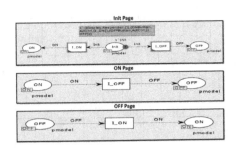

Fig. 2. PIM of simple device   **Fig. 3.** CPN model of PIM of simple device

The PIM for the simple device in Fig. 1 is given in Fig. 2. There are three states: *Init, ON* and *OFF*. Fig. 1 show what states can be reached from a current state via those I-behaviours.

We now look at a way of expressing all this within CPN. The number of pages in a CPN model of a PIM is the same as the number of component presentation models in the PIM. For example, the simple device PIM shown in Fig. 1 has three component presentation models, so there are three pages in the CPN model of this device as shown in Fig. 3. These pages represent the individual component presentation models. The names of the places are exactly the names of the component presentation models. For the simple device, there are three places: *Init*, *ON* and *OFF*. These places have fusion tags (in blue) named the same as the corresponding component presentation models as shown in Fig. 3. The component presentation model *Init* has two I-behaviours, which means that from the place *Init* a user can go to two other states *ON* and *OFF*. The page *Init* will have three places: *Init*, *ON* and *OFF* where *Init* is the current state and *ON* and *OFF* are the states a user can go to from *Init*. Every place in the model will be of one type, i.e. *pmodel*. The transitions give formal meaning to the I-behaviours in the presentation model and have the same name as the respective I-behaviours in the presentation model.

5.1   Formal Definition of CPN for Modelling PM/PIM

In this section we formalize the definition of how we represent the combination of presentation models and presentation interaction models.

Definition 6. *A non-hierarchical Coloured Petri Net for modelling a PM/PIM combination is a tuple* $(PM, K, P, T, I, CS, A, C, G, E)$ *such that:*

(i) *PM is a finite set of colour sets for representing presentation model declarations from the PM, such that:*

$$PM = \{WidgetName, Category, Behaviour, Behaviours, widgetdescr, pmodel\}$$

    where
- *colset WidgetName = with wid_1 | wid_2 | ... | wid_n;*
  - • *where wid_s are the names of the widgets in the various component presentation models in PM.*
- *colset Category = with cid_1 | cid_2 | ... | cid_n;*
  - • *where cid_s are the names of the category of the widgets in the various component presentation models in PM.*
- *colset Behaviour = with bid_1 | bid_2 | ... | bid_n;*
  - • *where bid_s are the names of the S-behaviours and I-behaviours associated with the widgets.*
- *colset Behaviours = list Behaviour;*
- *colset widgetdescr = product WidgetName ∗ Category ∗ Behaviours;*
- *colset pmodel = list widgetdescr;*

(ii) *K is a finite set of constants that represents the component presentation models by their names and is such that Type[K] = pmodel.*

(iii) *P is a finite set of places, the same size as K, representing the component presentation models where the names of the places and names of the constants are same.*

(iv) *T is a finite set of transitions representing the I-behaviours of the PIM.*

(v) *I is an initialization function that assigns an initial marking to each place. The initialization function $I : P \to EXPR$ assigns an initialization expression $I(p)$ to each place p such that: $I(p) = k \in K$, i.e., $I(p)$ can be a constant, k, representing a component presentation model.*

(vi) CS is a finite set of non-empty types, called colour sets with $PM \subseteq CS$.
(vii) A is a finite set of arcs as given in Definition 1.
(viii) C is a colour function. It is defined from P into CS as given in Definition 1.
(ix) G is a guard function as given in Definition 1.
(x) E is an arc expression function such that:
- *For an arc $(p, t) \in A$, connecting a place $p \in P$ and a transition $t \in T$, it is required that the arc expression $E(p, t)$ is the constant $k \in K$ which represents the component presentation model of the place p.*

Having modelled the PM/PIM combination in CPN, we now move to modelling the functionality.

6   Z

Z is a formal specification language which is used to specify and model systems. Z specifications can be recognized by the use of the schema. More detailed information can be found in [10,25]. Z operation schemas are used to give formal meaning to the S-behaviours of a presentation model. A Z specification for the simple device in Fig. 1 is as follows:

This definition introduces a type *MESSAGE* that contains (only) a value *InitializingDevice*.

$$MESSAGE ::= InitializingDevice$$

The schema *SimpleDevice* is the state space of the model. It says that in each state in the state space there is one observation *display* which can have a value of type *MESSAGE*. In its initial state, the value of the *display* is set to *InitializingDevice*. The schema *Startmessage* refers to the *S_startmessage* behaviour of the presentation model.

$$
\begin{array}{l}
\hline
\underline{\;SimpleDevice\;} \\
display : MESSAGE \\
\hline
\end{array}
$$

$$
\begin{array}{l}
\hline
\underline{\;Init\;} \\
SimpleDevice \\
\hline
display = InitializingDevice \\
\hline
\end{array}
$$

$$
\begin{array}{l}
\hline
\underline{\;Startmessage\;} \\
\Xi SimpleDevice \\
display! : MESSAGE \\
\hline
display! = InitializingDevice \\
\hline
\end{array}
$$

Now we have a Z specification that gives meaning to the S-behaviours in the presentation model. As we will now see, instead of having three separate models, we can actually include the S-behaviours (functionality) in the CPN model by expressing a Z in CPN and have a single model.

6.1   Expressing Z in CPN

In this section we will explain how the kinds of Z specification [10] used in the existing PM/PIM/Z models can be expressed in CPN using colour sets, an initial expression and arc inscriptions. Notice that we give rules for the small subset of Z which is adequate for our purposes. We do not need all of Z to be modelled.

Cartesian Product: It is a type consisting of ordered pairs. We can use the product colour set of CPN to represent such Z types and can be written in CPN as:

$$colset \; \langle z\_type\_name \rangle =$$
$$product \; \langle colset\_name_1 \rangle * \langle colset\_name_2 \rangle * ... * \langle colset\_name_n \rangle;$$

where $colset\_name_1...colset\_name_n$ are already defined colour sets which represent types in Z.

Built-in Type: Z provides a single built-in type, namely the type of integers $\mathbb{Z}$. We can write this in CPN using the integer colour set. So the declarations

$$colset \; INT = int; \quad var \; n : INT;$$

will create a colour set INT which defines INT as integers, and a variable n such that the value of n is an integer.

Power Sets: The power set operator $\mathbb{P}$ (giving "the set of all subsets" of a set) is an elementary type constructor often used in Z. If we want to write such a type in CPN, then in this work we have decided that the list colour set is used[1]. The syntax for writing power sets of Z based on this decision in CPN is:

$$colset \; \langle z\_type\_name \rangle = list \; \langle colset\_name \rangle;$$

Axiomatic Definition: If we have an axiomatic definition:

$$\begin{array}{|l}
hours : \mathbb{P}\,\mathbb{N} \\
\hline
hours = 0 \mathrel{.\,.} 24
\end{array}$$

This can be written in CPN as: $colset \; hours = int \; with \; 0..24;$

---

[1] We model only systems with finite components, so modelling the power set with lists is no restriction on our expressiveness.

Z Schemas: Z schemas are used to specify the state space and operations of the system. To write the declaration part of a Z schema in CPN, we use the record colour set:

$$colset\langle Z \rangle = record\ id_1 : type_1 * ... * id_n : type_n;$$

where $id_1..id_n$ are Z observations and $type_1..type_n$ are their corresponding types (which are already declared colour sets using the rules as explained above) as they appear in the declarations of the schema we are modelling. The initialization schema of a Z specification is represented as an initial marking in Coloured Petri Nets. The predicate part of a schema will give us expressions on arcs of certain transitions, as we will see later.

6.2   Formal Definition of CPN for Modelling PM/PIM/Z

Definition 7. *A non-hierarchical Coloured Petri Net for modelling a PM/PIM/Z model is a tuple $(Z, PM, K, P, T, I, CS, A, C, G, E)$ such that:*

(i) *Z is a finite set of colour sets representing the Z state schema of the original model with declarations $id_1 : type_1...id_n : type_n$, such that:*

$$Z = \{type_1, type_2, ..type_n, Z\}$$

where colset $type_1$;.....colset $type_n$; colset Z = record $id_1 : type1...*id_n :$ $type_n$;*

(ii) *PM is a finite set of colour sets representing PM declarations as given in Definition 6.*

(iii) *K is a finite set of constants representing component presentation models as in Definition 6.*

(iv) *P is a finite set of places such that $| P | = | K | + 1$. The constant k in the set K can be mapped to the place p in the set of P with the same name. There is an additional place named Z that represents the state schema.*

(v) *T is a finite set of transitions representing both I-behaviours and S-behaviours.*

(vi) *I is an initialization function that assigns an initial marking to each place.*

(vii) *CS is a finite set of non-empty types, called colour sets, with $PM \subseteq CS$ and $Z \subseteq CS$.*

(viii) *A is a finite set of arcs as given in Definition 6.*

(ix) *C is a colour function as given in Definition 6.*

(x) *G is a guard function as given in Definition 6.*

(xi) *E is an arc expression function such that:*

  – *For an arc $(p, t) \in A$, where t is an I-behaviour transition, it is required that the arc expression $E(p, t)$ is the name $k \in K$ which represents the component presentation model. Similarly for a directed arc from a transition representing an I-behaviour to a place.*

– *For an arc* $(p, t) \in A$ *where p represents a state in the Z state space, and a transition* $t \in T$, *representing an S-behaviour, it is required that the arc expression* $E(p, t)$ *assigns each observation name appearing in S to a new, unique variable (say s).*

7   Case Study: NIKI T34 Infusion Pump

The T34 is a compact and lightweight syringe pump used to deliver drugs. Figure 4 shows an image of the pump. More information about the pump can be found in [12]. There are ten widgets in the T34 infusion pump as shown in Fig. 4 : *LeftFFSK, RightBackSK, OnOffButton, UpPlusSK, DownMinusSK, Display, NoStopSK, InfoSK, YesStartSK* and *Timeout.*

There is a total of nineteen states, one of which the pump can be in at any given point in time which are: *LoadSyringe, Init, BatteryLevel, SetVolume, SetDuration, RateSet, RateConfirm, ConfirmSettings, StartInfusingConfirm, Infusing, Paused, Inittwo, Resume, InfusionStatus, BatteryStatus, EventLog, ChangeSetUp* and *TimeOut.* We can, typically, get to know this by actually experiment-

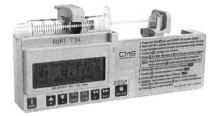

Fig. 4. Niki T34 syringe pump

ing with the device. We might also read the user manuals, but this is not recommended since user manuals are, worryingly, notoriously unreliable [7].

7.1   Modelling T34 Pump in CPN

The declaration part of the presentation model is given in Table 4. *WidgetName* is an enumeration type and represents the names of the widgets of the pump. *Category* is an enumeration type that describes the categories of the widgets. *Behaviour* is an enumeration type that represents a set of all behaviours. Because of space restrictions only a few of the full set of behaviours are given here[2]. *Behaviours* is of type list, so a widget can have more than one behaviour. *Behaviours* is a list of behaviours where the names of the behaviours is taken from the *Behaviour* colour set. *widgetdescr* is of type product. It represents a triple (*WidgetName, Category, [Behaviours]*). *pmodel* is a list colour set and represents the component presentation model. Now we look at the definition part of the presentation model for the Niki T34 infusion pump. As there are nineteen states, the number of component presentation models will be the same. We give component presentation models for *LoadSyringe* and *Info* as representative of those for the whole T34 in Table 5.

---

[2] See https://github.com/sapnajaidka/NikiT34-CPN-Model for complete details.

Table 4. Modelling of the presentation model declarations

colset WidgetName =	with LeftFFSK | RightBackSK | OnOffButton | UpPlusSK | DownMinusSK | Display | NoStopSK | InfoSK | Timeout | YesStartSK;
colset Category =	with ActionControl | MValResponder | System | display;
colset Behaviour =	with S_SyringeWarnings | S_MoveActuatorFwd | S_ArmWarning | I_Init | S_SyringeDisplay | S_ScrollSyringeList | I_SetVolume |...;
colset Behaviours =	list Behaviour;
colset widgetdescr =	product WidgetName * Category * Behaviours;
colset pmodel =	list widgetdescr;

Table 5. CPN version of the PMs

val LoadSyringe = [(Display, MValResponder, [S_SyringeWarnings]), (InfoSK, ActionControl, [I_Info]), (UpPlusSK, ActionControl, []), (DownMinusSK, ActionControl, []), (YesStartSK, ActionControl,[]), (NoStopSK, ActionControl, []), (LeftFFSK, ActionControl, [S_MoveActuatorFwd,S_ArmWarning]), (RightBackSK, ActionControl, [S_MoveActuatorBwd, S_ArmWarning]), (OnOffButton, ActionControl, [Quit]), (Timeout, System, [I_Init])];

val Info = [(Display, MValResponder, [S_InfoList]), (InfoSK, ActionControl, [S_KeypadLock]), (UpPlusSK, ActionControl, [S_ScrollInfoListUp]), (DownMinusSK, ActionControl, [S_ScrollInfoListDown]), (YesStartSK, ActionControl, [I_BatteryLevel,I_Init,I_RateSet,I_EventLog, I_ChangeSetUp]), (NoStopSK, ActionControl, [I_Init]), (LeftFFSK, ActionControl, [ ]), (RightBackSK, ActionControl, [ ]), (OnOffButton, ActionControl, [Quit, I_Init]), (Timeout, System, [ ])];

The complete Z specification for the T34 pump can be found in[3]. The Z types for the T34 pump expressed in CPN are shown in Table 6. *YesNo* is declared as the enumerated colour set that can have exactly two values *yes* or *no*. *SyringeBrand* is declared as enumerated colour set with one value *BDPlastipak*. *PerCent, millilitres, millimeters, hours* and *minutes* are declared as integer colour sets. *Z* is a record colour set with a record of all the observations of the state schema with their corresponding types. It represents the *T34* state

---

[3] https://github.com/sapnajaidka/Niki-T34-Z-specification.

Table 6. Colour sets and variables for T34 pump

---

colset YesNo = with yes | no;

colset SyringeBrand = with BDPlastipak;

colset PerCent = int with 0..100;

colset millilitres= int with 0..100;

colset millimeters = int with 0..10;

colset hours = int with 0..24;

colset minutes = int with 0..59;

colset millilitresperhour = int with 0..100;

colset Z = record BC:PerCent * KP:YesNo * PL:YesNo * TL:YesNo *
BD: SyringeBrand * SS: millilitres * VL: millilitres * PP : millimeters *
SOK: YesNo * BCPOK: YesNo * SR: YesNo * VTBI: millilitres * HH: hours *
MM: minutes * IR: millilitresperhour;

---

schema[4]. As the Z operation schemas would be expressed as arc inscriptions so we need to declare variables which could be bound to different values of their respective colour sets during simulation. There are fifteen variables *BC*, *KP*, *PL*, *TL*, *BD*, *SS*, *VL*, *PP*, *SOK*, *BCPOK*, *SR*, *VTBI*, *HH*, *MM* and *IR*.

There are nineteen component presentation models for the Niki T34 infusion pump, therefore, the CPN model of the pump has nineteen pages which are interconnected by fusion places. Using the CPN Tool, we now create a model that shows all the states with I-behaviours (which show navigational possibilities representing interactivity) and S-behaviours (which represent underlying system functionality). The resulting CPN model has all the important aspects (functional, user-interface and interaction) of the original PM/PIM/Z expressed within it.

The structure of the *LoadSyringe* page is shown in Fig. 5. The three places: *LoadSyringe*, *Init* and *Info* represent the states of the system. The marking on the place *LoadSyringe* shows the definition of the *LoadSyringe* component presentation model which gives information about the available widgets. The marking on the *LoadSyringe* page also shows that there are four S-behaviours: *S_SyringeWarnings* and *S_ArmWarning* display warning messages on the screen and *S_MoveActuatorBwd* and *S_MoveActuatorFwd* are the functions that move the syringe plunger forward and backward. The Z specification[5] for these S-behaviours are not modelled here to keep the size of the state space small, so just the fusion place *Z* is added to the page and represents only the Z *Init* schema.

---

[4] To make the description short and easy to read we have used abbreviated names for the Z observations. In this declaration *BC* stands for *BatteryCharge*, *KP* is for *KeyPadLocked*, *PL* is for *ProgramLocked*, *TL* is for *TechMenuLocked*, *BD* is for *Brand*, *SS* is for *SyringeSize*, *VL* is for *VolumeLeft*, *PP* is for *PlungerPosition*, *SOK* is for *SyringeOK*, *BCPOK* is for *BarrelOK*, *CollarOK*, *PlungerOK*, *SR* is for *SystemReady*, *HH* is for *Hours*, *MM* is for *Minutes* and *IR* is for *InfusionRate*.

[5] See https://github.com/sapnajaidka/Niki-T34-Z-specification.

The component presentation model for the *LoadSyringe* has two I-behaviours: *I_Init* and *I_Info* as shown in Table 3 and as shown by the initial marking on that place, so there are two transitions, namely *I_Init* and *I_Info*. Figure 5 clearly shows that from the *LoadSyringe* state, the user can go to either the *Init* state or *Info* state by firing the transitions *I_Init* or *I_Info*.

In Fig. 5, on the arc going into place/state *Init*, we have the expression *Init* which tells us the relevant presentation model for this state and on the arc going into place *Info*, we have the expression *Info* which tells us the relevant presentation model for the state *Info*. If the user asks for information, i.e., if *I_Info* transition is fired, then the user goes to the *Info* state. Figure 6 shows the structure of the *Info* page. The *Info* state shows a list of options that a user can select to see status and change settings. There are seven places in the *Info* page: *Info, BatteryLevel, Init, ChangeSetUp, Eventlog, RateSet* and *Z*. The marking on the place *Info* is a token showing the definition of a component presentation model *Info* which provides information about the available widgets and tells us which button press results in what state. The marking shows that there are five I-behaviours and four S-behaviours. As we are not modelling the S-behaviours which just display messages on the screen, the page *Info* has just one S-behaviour transition *S_KeyPadLocked*. There are six transitions: *I_BatteryLevel, I_ChangeSetUp, I_Init, I_EventLog, I_RateSet* and *S_KeyPadLocked*. These transitions give meaning to the I-behaviours and S-behaviours given for the definition of the component presentation model *Info*.

If the user gives a long press to the *Info* button on the device, the keypad gets locked or unlocked. This behaviour changes the value of the observation *KP* from *no* to *yes* and vice-versa. In the CPN model, the transition *S_KeyPadLocked*

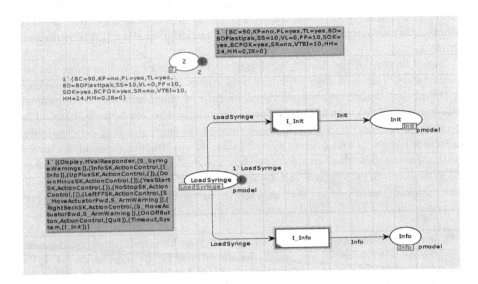

Fig. 5. LoadSyringe page with Z

represents this behaviour. There are two arcs needed to model this (going to and from the place Z). The arc from Z to $S\_KeyPadLocked$ simply contains assignments which set each variable to its current value (where the variables are the ones that model the observations from the Z operation schema $KeyPadLocked$ where they will appear on the left of each equation in primed form). This set of assignments "picks up" the current values of the variables ready to be used by the second arc. This second arc, the one from $S\_KeyPadLocked$ to Z, assigns each variable to its *new* value, as given by the right-hand side of each equation in the $KeyPadLocked$ operation schema. Taken together these two arcs express the intent of the equations in the operation schema $KeyPadLocked$. Users can go to any of the five states by firing the I-behaviour transitions which will update the markings on the corresponding places. If the value of KP is *yes*, i.e., if the keypad is locked, then a user cannot go to any further possible states. For that reason, we have a guard $[KP = no]$ on transitions $I\_BatteryLevel$, $I\_EventLog$, I_Init, $I\_RateSet$ and $I\_ChangeSetUp$. These transitions would not be enabled if the keypad is locked. In a similar manner we model the rest of the pages[6] which are interconnected via fusion places and a user can go from one state to another by firing the I-behaviour transitions and the operations can be observed by firing the S-behaviour transitions.

8   Benefits of Formal Method Integration

There are several benefits accruing from using CPN and its tool and combining what was previously done via three different formalisms (PM/PIM/Z). First, CPNs have a simple graphical representation which is useful for illustrating the concepts, and the CPN Tool allows us to visualize the models and structure them in useful ways. The CPN model provides a better understanding of how the system will behave by means of interactive simulation which provides a way to walk through a CPN model, investigating different scenarios in detail and checking whether the model works as expected. It is possible to observe the effects of the individual steps directly in the graphical representation of the CPN model. The models in CPN can be used to specify different aspects (functional or control flow) of a system and can specify different types (concurrent, sequential or distributed) of a system, all in one model.

When we build a Coloured Petri Nets model, any non-determinism present can be exposed and can be corrected. The appealing graphical representation of Coloured Petri Nets allows us to consider all the navigational possibilities in a model. It gives a good indication of the complexity of the user-interface and its navigation by way of the number of places and transitions. Having aspects of Z modelled in CPN has benefits in the development process as a developer can have a better idea of the user interface and interactivity as well as the functionality of a modelled system.

---

[6] See https://github.com/sapnajaidka/NikiT34-CPN-Model.

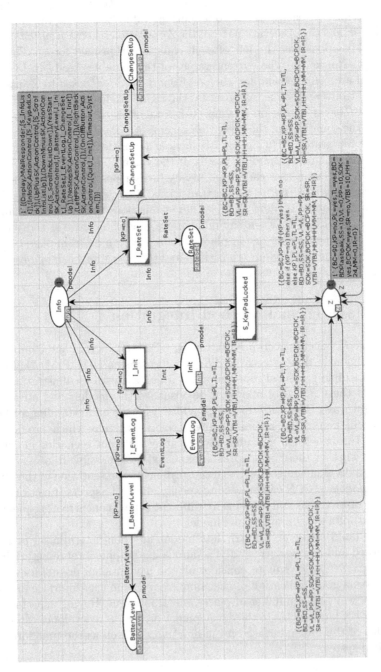

Fig. 6. Info page with Z

9 Conclusion and Future Work

We have used CPNs to model the user-interface and interaction of a medical infusion pump. This shows the navigational properties of the system, but also allows us to include the underlying system functionality in the model as well. By means of simulation we can actually see what widgets are available and what happens when the user interacts with them. Also we can actually *see* how the behaviours change the underlying system functionality. By these means we can check to see if the model is working as expected. If it seems that it is not then we can look deeper and see what the flaws are in the model and what changes should be made to make the model work correct in all situations: this is the most important thing for safety-critical devices.

Now that we can build CPN models there are certain properties that can be *verified* with the CPN's state space analysis method. This method provides information about the dynamic properties of a system, for example, dead transitions, and dead markings. It also gives information about the fairness and liveness properties of a modelled system. Therefore it is possible to investigate the behaviour of the system in sophisticated and useful ways: this includes the safety requirements of the system. With the state space method, in conjunction with suitable queries, it is possible to verify that queries hold, so safety requirements (like detecting livelocks, total reachability, desired terminal states etc.) for safety-critical systems can be proved. In the future it would be interesting to see if the safety properties proposed by the FDA[7] can be proved using this combined model.

References

1. Arney, D., Jetley, R., Jones, P., Lee, I., Sokolsky, O.: Formal methods based development of a PCA infusion pump reference model: generic infusion pump (GIP) project. In: Joint Workshop on High Confidence Medical Devices, Software, and Systems and Medical Device Plug-and-Play Interoperability, 2007. HCMDSS-MDPnP, pp. 23–33. IEEE (2007)
2. Barbosa, P.E., et al.: Towards medical device behavioural validation using petri nets. In: 2013 IEEE 26th International Symposium on Computer-Based Medical Systems (CBMS), pp. 4–10. IEEE (2013)
3. Boudi, Z., Collart-Dutilleul, S., Khaddour, M., et al.: High level Petri Net modeling for railway safety critical scenarios. In: 10th FORMS-FORMAT symposium, Formal Methods for Automation and Safety in Railway and Automotive Systems, pp. p65–75 (2014)
4. Bowen, J.A.: Formal specification of user interface design guidelines. Ph.D. thesis, Citeseer (2005)
5. Bowen, J., Reeves, S.: Using formal models to design user interfaces: a case study. In: Proceedings of the 21st British HCI Group Annual Conference on People and Computers: HCI...but not as we know it-Volume 1, pp. 159–166. British Computer Society (2007)

---

[7] See https://repository.upenn.edu/cgi/viewcontent.cgi?referer=&httpsredir=1&article=1938\&context=cis_reports.

6. Bowen, J., Reeves, S.: Formal models for user interface design artefacts. Innovations Syst. Softw. Eng. **4**(2), 125–141 (2008). https://doi.org/10.1007/s11334-008-0049-0

7. Bowen, J., Reeves, S.: Modelling user manuals of modal medical devices and learning from the experience. In: Proceedings of the 4th ACM SIGCHI Symposium on Engineering Interactive Computing Systems, pp. 121–130. ACM (2012)

8. Bowen, J., Reeves, S.: Generating obligations, assertions and tests from UI models. Proc. ACM on Hum. Comput. Interact. **1**(EICS), 5 (2017)

9. Campos, J.C., Harrison, M.: Modelling and analysing the interactive behaviour of an infusion pump. Electron. Commun. EASST **45**, 16 (2011)

10. Derrick, J., Boiten, E.A.: Refinement in Z and Object-Z: Foundations and Advanced Applications. Springer, Heidelberg (2014). https://doi.org/10.1007/978-1-4471-5355-9

11. Dix, A.J., Runciman, C.: Abstract models of interactive systems. In: People and Computers: Designing the interface, pp. 13–22 (1985)

12. Electronics, C.M.: Niki T34 syringe pump instruction manual. ref. 100–090SS Edition (2008)

13. Jacob, R.J.: Using formal specifications in the design of a human-computer interface. Commun. ACM **26**(4), 259–264 (1983)

14. Jaidka, S., Reeves, S., Bowen, J.: Modelling safety-critical devices: coloured petri nets and Z. In: Proceedings of the ACM SIGCHI Symposium on Engineering Interactive Computing Systems, pp. 51–56. ACM (2017)

15. Jensen, K.: Coloured Petri Nets: Basic Concepts, Analysis Methods and Practical Use, vol. 1, p. 234. Springer, Heidelberg (2013). https://doi.org/10.1007/978-3-662-03241-1

16. Jensen, K., Kristensen, L.M., Wells, L.: Coloured Petri Nets and CPN tools for modelling and validation of concurrent systems. Int. J. Softw. Tools Technol. Transfer **9**(3–4), 213–254 (2007). https://doi.org/10.1007/s10009-007-0038-x

17. Kristensen, L.M., Christensen, S., Jensen, K.: The practitioner's guide to coloured Petri Nets. Int. J. Softw. Tools Technol. Transf. (STTT) **2**(2), 98–132 (1998)

18. Kummer, O., Wienberg, F., Duvigneau, M., Köhler, M., Moldt, D., Rölke, H.: Renew-the reference net workshop. In: Tool Demonstrations, 21st International Conference on Application and Theory of Petri Nets, Computer Science Department, Aarhus University, Aarhus, Denmark, pp. 87–89 (2000)

19. Lakos, C.: From coloured Petri Nets to object Petri Nets. In: De Michelis, G., Diaz, M. (eds.) ICATPN 1995. LNCS, vol. 935, pp. 278–297. Springer, Heidelberg (1995). https://doi.org/10.1007/3-540-60029-9_45

20. Martinie, C., Navarre, D., Palanque, P., Fayollas, C.: A generic tool-supported framework for coupling task models and interactive applications. In: Proceedings of the 7th ACM SIGCHI Symposium on Engineering Interactive Computing Systems, pp. 244–253. ACM (2015)

21. Masci, P., Ayoub, A., Curzon, P., Lee, I., Sokolsky, O., Thimbleby, H.: Model-based development of the generic PCA infusion pump user interface prototype in PVS. In: Bitsch, F., Guiochet, J., Kaâniche, M. (eds.) SAFECOMP 2013. LNCS, vol. 8153, pp. 228–240. Springer, Heidelberg (2013). https://doi.org/10.1007/978-3-642-40793-2_21

22. Navarre, D., Palanque, P., Ladry, J.F., Barboni, E.: ICOs: a model-based user interface description technique dedicated to interactive systems addressing usability, reliability and scalability. ACM Trans. Comput. Hum. Interact. (TOCHI) **16**(4), 18 (2009)

23. Rukšėnas, R., Masci, P., Harrison, M.D., Curzon, P.: Developing and verifying user interface requirements for infusion pumps: a refinement approach. Electron. Commun. EASST **69**, 12 (2014)
24. Silva, J.L., Ribeiro, Ó.R., Fernandes, J.M., Campos, J.C., Harrison, M.D.: The APEX framework: prototyping of ubiquitous environments based on Petri Nets. In: Bernhaupt, R., Forbrig, P., Gulliksen, J., Lárusdóttir, M. (eds.) HCSE 2010. LNCS, vol. 6409, pp. 6–21. Springer, Heidelberg (2010). https://doi.org/10.1007/978-3-642-16488-0_2
25. Smith, G.: The Object-Z Specification Language, vol. 1, 1st edn, p. 146. Springer, Heidelberg (2012). https://doi.org/10.1007/978-1-4615-5265-9
26. Turner, J.D.: Supporting interactive system testing with interaction sequences. Ph.D. thesis, The University of Waikato (2019)

Model-Based Testing of Post-WIMP Interactions Using Object Oriented Petri-Nets

Alexandre Canny[1]([✉]), David Navarre[1], José Creissac Campos[2],
and Philippe Palanque[1]

[1] ICS-IRIT, Université Paul Sabatier – Toulouse III, Toulouse, France
{alexandre.canny,navarre,palanque}@irit.fr
[2] HASLab/INESC TEC, Department of Informatics, University of Minho, Braga, Portugal
jose.campos@di.uminho.pt

Abstract. Model-Based Testing (MBT) relies on models of a System Under Test (SUT) to derive test cases for said system. While Finite State Machine (FSM), workflow, etc. are widely used to derive test cases for WIMP applications (i.e. applications depending on 2D widgets such as menus and icons), these notations lack the expressive power to describe the interaction techniques and behaviors found in post-WIMP applications. In this paper, we aim at demonstrating that thanks to ICO, a formal notation for describing interactive systems, it is possible to generate test cases that go beyond the state of the art by addressing the MBT of advanced interaction techniques in post-WIMP applications.

Keywords: Post-WIMP interactive systems · Software testing · Model-Based Testing

1 Introduction

Model-Based Testing (MBT) of software relies on explicit behavior models of a system to derive test cases [28]. The complexity of deriving comprehensive test cases increases with the inner complexity of the System Under Test (SUT) that requires description techniques with an important expressive power. The modelling of post-WIMP (Windows, Icons, Menus and Pointers) interactive applications (i.e. applications with an interface not dependent on classical 2D widgets such as menus and icons [29]) proves to be a challenging activity as pointed out by [12]. For instance, when using a touch screen, each finger down/up is a virtual input device being added or removed from the systems at runtime and behaves in parallel with the other fingers or input devices. A modelling technique able to describe such interactive systems must support the description of dynamicity.

Beyond the problem of describing the SUT behavior, testing Graphical-User Interface, whether it is WIMP or post-WIMP, is known to be a complex activity [9], especially because of the unpredictability of the human behavior as well as the virtually infinite number of possible interaction sequences. To face such difficulty, model-based testing

© Springer Nature Switzerland AG 2020
E. Sekerinski et al. (Eds.): FM 2019 Workshops, LNCS 12232, pp. 486–502, 2020.
https://doi.org/10.1007/978-3-030-54994-7_35

techniques have been developed to try to generate relevant test sequences without relying on manual scripting or capture and replay of tester's interactions.

The massive adoption of touch screens means advanced touch interactions (e.g. swipe, pinch-to-zoom, etc.) gained in popularity, while most of the existing MBT techniques for interactive applications are designed to deal with events performed on the standard GUI widgets (e.g. button, combo box, etc.) [1, 9, 14, 26]. Lelli et al. [14] identified the need for new MBT techniques for post-WIMP applications by highlighting the need for supporting ad-hoc widgets (i.e. non-standard widgets developed specifically for the application) and advanced interaction techniques.

In this paper, we propose to build upon the work of Hamon et al. [12], which used the ICO [19] formal modelling technique to describe post-WIMP interactive systems, as a support to the generation of test cases for interaction techniques of post-WIMP applications, and to demonstrate that testing can be conducted following the standard process for Model-Based Testing proposed in [28]. As interaction techniques have to cope with the high dynamicity of Input/Output, as well as temporal aspects, they prove to be one of the most difficult components of interactive systems to be described. Thus, they are the prime focus of this paper, even though we will highlight that our proposed approach applies to other components of the interactive systems' architecture as well.

This paper is structured as follows: Sect. 2 presents related work on the MBT of interactive applications; Sect. 3 introduces the interaction technique on which we propose to apply the approach and its modelling in ICO; Sect. 4 discusses the generation of the test cases from the ICO specification and Sect. 5 provides some comments on test execution; Sect. 6 discusses the generalizability of the proposed approach to other components of the SUT; Sect. 7 concludes the paper by discussing future work.

2   Related Work

The classical approaches to interactive applications testing consider that the user's interaction takes place at the GUI widget level (e.g. buttons, icons, label, etc.). While it is the case in the WIMP paradigm, this assertion cannot be used in the post-WIMP paradigm where "at least one interaction technique is not dependent on classical 2D widgets such as menus and icons" [29]. Consider a gesture-based (post-WIMP) drawing tool. One may want to define (and test) whether moving two fingers on the drawing area means zooming (pinch-to-zoom), rotating or drawing. As this may be determined by how the user effectively moves his/her fingers (speed, angle, pressure level, delay between finger down events, etc.), it goes beyond available standard testing techniques for widget level interactions.

In this section, we first introduce the process of MBT and discuss the existing Model-Based Testing techniques for WIMP applications. We then discuss the testing of post-WIMP applications in order to highlight challenges to overcome.

2.1   The Process of Model-Based Testing

In their Taxonomy of Model-Based-Testing Approaches, Utting et al. [28] present the model-based testing process illustrated by Fig. 1. In this process, a model of the SUT is built from informal requirements or existing specification documents (Fig. 1(1)) and test selection criteria (Fig. 1(2)) are chosen to guide the automatic test generation to produce a test suite that fulfils the test policy defined for the SUT. These criteria are then transformed (Fig. 1(3)) into a test cases specification (i.e. a high-level description of a desired test case). Utting et al. [28] use the example of test case specification using state coverage of a finite state machine (FSM). In such case, a set of test case specification {reach s0, reach s1, reach s2...} where s0, s1, s2 are all the states of the FSM is the test case specification.

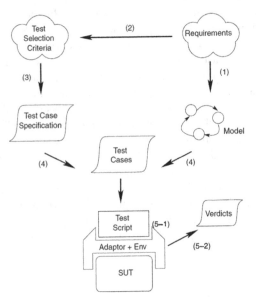

Fig. 1. The process of Model-Based-Testing (from [28])

Once the model and the test case specifications are defined, a set of test cases is generated with the aim of satisfying all the test case specifications (Fig. 1(4)). With the test suite generated, the test cases are executed (either manually -i.e. by a physical person- or automatically thanks to a test execution environment). This requires concretizing the test inputs (Fig. 1(5–1)) and comparing the results against expected ones to produces a verdict (Fig. 1(5–2)).

2.2 Model-Based Testing of WIMP Application

In software engineering, the nearly three-decades-old field [1] that addresses concerns regarding the testing of user interfaces is called "GUI testing". In [1] GUI testing is defined as performing sequences of events (e.g., "click on button", "enter text", "open menu") on GUI widgets (e.g., "button", "text-field", "pull-down menu"). For each sequence, the test oracle checks the correctness of the state of the GUI either after each event or at the end of the sequence. Since the domain is three-decade-old, it naturally focused on WIMP UIs as they were the only available at the time. This focusing is still quite present today.

Some of the research works presented in the following paragraphs do not follow the process of MBT presented by Utting [28], but they propose relevant and inspiring approach for WIMP application testing.

Memon et al. [16] propose a detailed taxonomy of the Model-Based techniques employed to generate test cases in GUI testing. These techniques rely on various kinds of models (state machine, workflow, etc.) that target mono-event-based systems (i.e. systems on which UI events are produced directly as a result of a single action on a widget: key typed, mouse clicked, etc.). They describe the possible test cases by checking reachability of a node. It is important to mention that most of the techniques listed in [16] rely on models built by reverse engineering of the SUT [23].

Another approach based on reverse engineering is the one of Morgado et al. [18] in the iMPAcT tool. This tool uses patterns of common behavior on Android applications to automatically test them. The tool explores the SUT checking for UI patterns using a reverse engineering process. Each UI pattern has a corresponding testing strategy (a Test Pattern) that the tool applies.

Bowen et al. [7] adopt the test-first development approach in which abstract tests are built from formal specification of the system functionality (given using Z [27]) and from a presentation model describing the interactive components (widgets) of the user interface. These abstract test cases are used to produce JUnit and UISpec4J[1] test cases.

Finally, Campos et al. [8] propose an example of approach that matches the outlines of the MBT-process by using task models to perform scenario-based testing of user-interfaces coded in Java using the Synergistic IDE Toucan [15]. The conformance between the application code and the task models is checked at runtime thanks to annotations in the Java code that allow the association of methods calls to the Interactive Input and Output Tasks. The scenarios produced from the task model are then played automatically on the Java application.

2.3 Model-Based Testing of Post-WIMP Application

Testing post-WIMP applications requires going beyond GUI testing as mentioned by Lelli et al. [14]. This requires considering ad-hoc widgets and complex interaction techniques that cannot be performed simply as sequences of events on GUI widgets. For instance, interactions such as gesture-based or voice command activations are not tied to a specific GUI widget.

One of the main references in post-WIMP application testing is Malai [14] that has been proposed as a framework to describe advanced GUI Testing. It allows the description of interaction using Finite State Machine (FSM) with two types of end state: terminal state and aborting state. These states are dedicated to identifying whether the user completed the interaction or aborted it. The output actions associated with completing the interaction (i.e. reaching its terminal state) are described in a specific reification of tools called instruments.

---

[1] https://github.com/UISpec4J/UISpec4J.

However, the use of FSM limits the description of interaction techniques and should be enhanced to support:

- **The description of dynamic instantiation of physical and virtual input/output devices**: on systems with a touchscreen, the display is a physical output device and the touch layer the physical input device. When dealing with multi-touch interaction, a finger is a virtual device that is added/removed whenever it touches the screen or is removed from it;
- **The description of timing aspects** to represent quantitative temporal evolution of the interaction technique (available in timed-automata);
- **The description of concurrent aspect** to represent concurrent usage of input devices by the user; events from these devices might be fused to produce higher-level multimodal event [13];
- **The description of dynamic user interface behavior driven by temporal events** such as animations during transition between states of the system [17];
- **The description of system configurations** as, for instance, using resolution scaling on displays with high pixels densities affects the size, location and translation of the GUI elements on screen. Beyond, this also applies to mobile and web-based UI in which having a responsive-design behaving properly is a concern.

While advances have been made in the description of such aspect, especially in work such as [12], there are not, to the best of our knowledge, techniques taking advantages of them to generate tests cases for interactive applications. In the following of the paper, we introduce and use the ICO formalism to demonstrate the need for advanced modelling techniques for effective testing of interactive applications.

3   Modelling of a Post-WIMP Case Study Using ICO

In this section, we present an architecture for post-WIMP applications and highlight where the interaction techniques take place. We then present the informal requirements for the "finger clustering" interaction technique used as a case study in the remaining of this paper. Thereafter, we introduce the formal description technique we use, ICO [19], and present the models associated to the "finger clustering" interaction technique.

3.1   Architecture of a Post-WIMP Application

Effectively testing an interactive application requires a good understanding of its architecture and of the role of its components to select appropriate test criteria [9]. While a detailed architecture such as MIODMIT [10] is able to describe in detail the hardware and software components of interactive systems, we use in this paper a simpler software architecture (inspired by ARCH [3]) for touch applications, presented in Fig. 2, to detail the role of the component we focus on. The work presented in the remaining of this paper is still applicable to a more complex architecture.

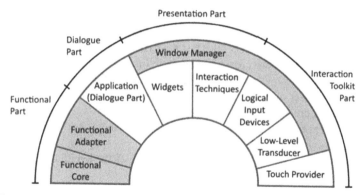

Fig. 2. Example of architecture of a post-WIMP application adapted from [12].

As this paper discusses specific aspects of post-WIMP application, we do not detail the "back-end", or Functional Part, of the application (leftmost part of Fig. 2). The Dialogue Part of the application shares a common role in WIMP and post-WIMP applications, i.e. translating high-level events resulting of the user interaction into invocations on the Functional Part. The main difference between WIMP and post-WIMP applications then resides in the Window Manager that contains, from right to left, the widgets (that share similar roles to widgets of WIMP interfaces), the Interaction Techniques, the Logical Input Device and the Low-Level Transducer.

The Low-Level Transducer is connected to the Touch Provider (rightmost part of Fig. 2), i.e. the driver of the touch screen. The Touch Provider produces the lowest-level events in the input chain as they are directly derived from the touch screen behavior. The role of the Low-Level Transducer is to handle these low-level events and to translate them to make sense for the Window Manager logic. On touch applications, the Low-Level Transducer creates Logical Input Devices (i.e. Fingers) with unique IDs and additional information (coordinates, pressure level, etc.). The Logical Input Devices are added to the Window Manager Interaction Technique(s) that will notify widgets and other subscribers (such as a drawing panel) using high-level events when either simple (e.g. tap) or complex (e.g. pinch) interactions are performed.

While this paper focus on the testing of the Interaction Technique, i.e. on verifying that for a set of Logical Input Device actions, the correct high-level events are produced, we highlight the applicability of our methods to the other components of the architecture and on integration testing of these components.

3.2 Presentation of the "Finger Clustering" Interaction Technique

The case study we use in this paper is a multi-touch interaction technique that produces events when fingers are clustered (i.e. within a given range of each other) and de-clustered according to the requirements presented below. These requirements are the inputs for the MBT Process (top-right of Fig. 1):

- Clusters may either contain two or three fingers;
- Clusters of three fingers are always created in priority over clusters of two fingers (i.e. if 4 fingers are on the screen in a range suitable for creating a cluster of 3 fingers,

a three finger cluster will be created with a finger left alone; in no occasion such circumstance may lead to the creation of two clusters of two fingers);
- The distance between two fingers must be under 100 pixels to create a 2 finger clusters;
- Clusters of three fingers are created when three fingers on the screen form a triangle with each of its edges measuring less than 100 pixels. If it happens that two fingers of an existing cluster of 2 fingers can be part of a three fingers cluster, then the three fingers cluster is created, removing the 2 fingers cluster.
- Clusters of 2 fingers are de-clustered whenever the distance between the 2 fingers it contains goes over 150 pixels;
- Clusters of 3 fingers are never de-clustered because of the length of the edges of the triangle;
- Clusters of 3 fingers are automatically de-clustered after 5 s;
- All the clusters cease to exist, producing the corresponding de-clustering event, whenever a finger contained in this cluster is removed from the screen.

The events produced by this interaction technique are the following ones: *twoFingersClustered, twoFingersDeclustered, threeFingersClustered, threeFingersDeclustered*.

3.3 ICO: A Formal Description Technique Dedicated to the Specification of Interactive Systems

The ICO formalism is a formal description technique dedicated to the specification of interactive systems [19]. It uses concepts borrowed from the object-oriented approach (dynamic instantiation, classification, encapsulation, inheritance and client/server relationship) to describe the structural or static aspects of systems and uses high-level Petri nets to describe their dynamic or behavioral aspects.

ICOs are dedicated to the modeling and the implementation of event-driven interfaces, using several communicating objects to model the system, where both the behavior of objects and the communication protocol between objects are described by the Petri net dialect called Cooperative Objects (CO). In the ICO formalism, an object is an entity featuring four components: a cooperative object which describes the behavior of the object, a presentation part (i.e. the graphical interface), and two functions (the activation function and the rendering function) which make the link between the cooperative object and the presentation part.

An ICO specification fully describes the potential interactions that users may have with the application. The specification encompasses both the "input" aspects of the interaction (i.e. how user actions affects the inner state of the application, and which actions are enabled at any given time) and its "output" aspects (i.e. when and how the application displays information relevant to the user).

This formal specification technique has already been applied in the field of Air Traffic Control interactive applications [19], space command and control ground systems [20], interactive military [5] or civil cockpits [2].

The ICO notation is fully supported by a CASE tool called PetShop [4, 21]. All the models presented in the following of this paper have been edited using it. Beyond, the presented test generation techniques are part of an effort to support MBT in PetShop.

3.4   Modeling of the Interaction Technique Using ICO

Based on the requirements provided in Sect. 3.1, we can build a model of the interaction technique (step 1 of the MBT process) using ICO. Figure 4 presents this model, which is made of places (oval shapes), transitions (rectangular shapes) and arcs. Two communication means are proposed by ICO: a unicast and synchronous communication, represented by method calls, and a multicast asynchronous communication, represented by event handling:

- When an ICO proposes method calls, they are each mapped into a set of three places representing three communication ports (the service input, output and exception ports). For instance, on the top part of Fig. 4, the places called *SIP_addFinger*, *SOP_addFinger* and *SEP_addFinger* are the input, output and exception ports of the method addFinger. When this method is called (for instance, in the *addFingerToInteraction* transition of Fig. 3), a token is created, holding the parameters of the invocation and is put in place *SIP_addFinger*. The transitions that invoke such methods have got a 'I' on the right part of their header.
- When an ICO is able to handle events, it uses special transitions called event handlers such as transition *updateFingerX* in the middle-right of Fig. 4. Such transitions are described using a set of information holding the event source, the event name, extra event parameters and a condition that concerns the event parameters. In the example of transition *updateFingerX*, the event source is fx, a value held by place *FINGERS_MERGED_BY_TWO*, the event name is touchevent_up, the event parameters contain an object called info and there is no condition on the parameter. These event handlers may handle events from outer sources or from other models. When the event source is another model, this model contains transitions that raise events. Events are raised using the keyword raiseEvent in the code part of the transition and an "E->" is put in the right part of the header of the transition (see transition *merge2Fingers* of Fig. 4).

The model illustrated by Fig. 4 represents the behavior of the "Finger Clustering" Interaction Technique described in Sect. 3.2. This behavior may be divided into two different parts according to their role:

- **Managing fingers life cycle:** Each finger is added or removed from the interaction technique model. In between, their coordinates may be updated (i.e. the finger has moved):

  - Adding finger to the interaction technique is done using the method addFinger, implemented using the *SIP_addFinger* place, *addFinger* transition and *SOP_addFinger* place (see Fig. 4). This method is called by a transition of the Low-Level transducer model (see Fig. 3). This invocation is made each time a Finger is created to add it to the interaction technique. When the finger enters the interaction technique, it is placed in the *SINGLE_FINGERS* place. This mechanism allows for dynamic appearance of fingers in the interaction technique. To ease the rest of the discussion, we limited the number of fingers instantiated in the interaction technique to 4 using the place *FINGER_LIMIT*. Removing this place would remove this restriction.

- Removing or updating fingers coordinates is performed by handling events that comes from the Low-Level transducer model (see Fig. 3). When a `touchEvent_up` is received, the corresponding finger is removed from the interaction technique model (this is the case for instance with transition remove1 on the left part of Fig. 4). When a `touchEvent_update` is received, the corresponding point (associated with a finger) is updated (this is the case for instance with transition *updating1Finger* on the top right part of Fig. 4).

- **Detecting clusters of fingers:** Each time a finger is added or removed from the interaction technique model, or each time the coordinates of one finger is updated, the clustering or de-clustering of fingers is computed:

  - For two or three fingers, the principle is the same, supported thanks to the preconditions of the *mergeXFingersX* and *unMergeXFingers* transitions, that compute the proximity of the fingers.
  - The 5 s timeout for de-clustering three fingers is handled thanks to a "timed transition" (note the [5000] - expressed in ms - line at the bottom of the *un-Merge3Fingers* transition) that removes the fingers held by place *FINGERS_MERGED_BY_THREE*.

While we are able to describe the interaction technique, the approach can be applied to other components of the architecture. For instance, Fig. 3 presents the ICO model of the Low-Level Transducer component of the architecture presented earlier. Note that the *addFingerToInteraction* transition contains an invocation on the interaction technique. This invocation is the one associated with the SIP/SOP places in the Interaction Technique Model. To prevent inconsistent input such as two fingers at the same location (which is physically impossible), a test arc allows to check whether a touch down is associated with a touch point of a finger already on the screen.

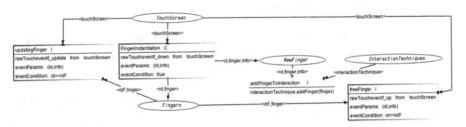

Fig. 3. ICO model for the Low-Level Transducer

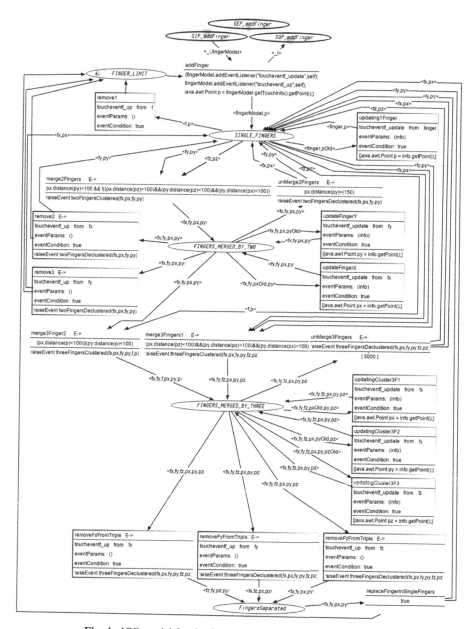

Fig. 4. ICO model for the finger clustering interaction technique.

4 Generating Test Cases from ICO Specifications

In this section, we focus on steps 2, 3 and 4 of the MBT process (see Fig. 1) applied to our case study. We first present our test selection criteria and specification and then present our test generation approach.

4.1   Test Selection Criteria and Test Case Specification

Testing an interaction technique consists in verifying that, for a set of low-level input events, the corresponding high-level event is produced so that components subscribed to it (e.g. application dialogs or widgets) are notified with a well-formed event. This differs from testing the application as done in the work presented in Sect. 2.2. Indeed, in these, the events considered in the test cases are already high-level ones and the verification that is made is that the effect on the UI is the correct one. To perform testing on the interaction techniques requires to i) describe the sequences of actions triggering the events raised by the interaction techniques and to ii) describe the associated events to observe on the interaction technique.

Regarding the finger clustering interaction techniques, this means that we want to be able to identify all the possible sequences of low-level events leading to the raising of the "twoFingersClustered", "threeFingersClustered", "twoFingersDeclustered and "threeFingersDeclustered" events in the interaction technique transitions. For illustration purpose, we focus on the raising of the "threeFingersClustered" event.

4.2   Generating Test Cases for the Interaction Technique

To identify the relevant test cases for the raising of the "threeFingersClustered" event, we use the reachability graph of the Petri-net. A reachability graph of a Petri-net is a directed graph G = (V, E), where v ∈ V represents a class of reachable markings; e ∈ E represents a directed arc from a class of markings to another class of markings [30]. Figure 5 presents the reachability graph of the interaction technique introduced previously. In this graph, each state contains four digits symbolizing the number of tokens contained in the places "FINGER LIMIT", "SINGLE FINGER", "FINGERS MERGED BY TWO" and "FINGERS MERGED BY THREE". For instance, the state "4,0,0,0" at the top means that the "FINGER LIMIT" place contains 4 tokens and that the other places are empty. We take advantage of the APT (Analysis of Petri nets and labelled transition systems) project[2] [6] to generate this graph.

As observable in Fig. 5, the reachability graph is actually a Finite State Machine with no accepting state. Considering that the event we focus on is raised in the "merge3FingersX" transition, we know that the event must be raised whenever a state of the FSM having a "merge3Fingers" incoming edge is reached. Marking these states (i.e. "1,0,0,1" and "0,1,0,1") as accepting ones allows us to describe the actual grammar of the test cases for the "threeFingersClustered" event. This grammar[3] only misses concrete values for fingers coordinates. The following is an example of test case matching this grammar expressed into Backus-Naur Form (BNF):

```
<testCase> ::= <addFinger> <touchEventf_update>
<addFinger> <addFinger> <touchEventf_update>
<merge3Fingers>
```

---

[2] https://github.com/CvO-Theory/apt.

[3] For which the regular expression can be obtained from the FSM using tools such as FSM2Regex (http://ivanzuzak.info/noam/webapps/fsm2regex/).

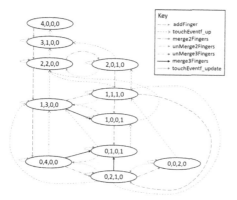

Fig. 5. Reachability graph derived from the ICO model of the interaction technique

The reachability graph we present in this case study contains values for each place as we intentionally limited to 4 the number of fingers in the interaction technique. However, some touch screens support more than 4 fingers and therefore one may want to use multiple clusters of three fingers. It would be possible to remove this restriction while still being able to apply our process by performing our analysis on a symbolic reachability graph. Symbolic reachability graphs use variables instead of concrete values in the states for the analysis of Petri-nets with such infinite marking, making it possible to express infinite number of states.

To prepare the instantiation of the test scripts, we must focus on how the required values are produced, partly supported by the model of the application. This model describes the conditions under which the transitions are fired. In our case, it describes the constraints on the distance between the points, defining the values domain. When instantiating the test scripts, the integration of these constraints relies on a semi-automated support, where the values are checked at editing time. For instance, in the instantiation of the grammar example proposed above, whatever the coordinates of the three added fingers are, the distance between them must fit the precondition of the transitions "merge3Fingers1" and "merge3Fingers2".

5 Test Cases Execution

In this section, we discuss the execution of the test of the interaction technique, i.e. steps 5.1 and 5.2 of the MBT process. While the advances we propose are mostly related to test cases generation, we find it important to emphasis the relevance of selecting the test adapter appropriately and to discuss the possible ways to use our test cases.

5.1 Test Adapter Selection

Testing the interaction technique consists in verifying that for a set of input events the corresponding high-level event is produced. Key in executing such test properly is being able to produce an input event that is actually the event expected by the interaction technique as an input, i.e. an event from the low-level transducer. Assuming that we are testing our interaction technique as part of a JavaFX application, this means producing JavaFX Touch Events[4]. However, testing the interaction technique alone may prove to be insufficient to ensure that the interaction technique will behave properly for the end-user. Indeed, while evaluating our approach, we encountered a known issue that no touch events are forwarded to JavaFX by most popular distributions of Linux using a GTK-based desktop environment[5]. In other words, the Touch Provider of these distributions is not producing relevant events for the Low-Level Transducer that cannot, in turn, produce events for the interaction technique. This means that the JavaFX finger clustering cannot be used on a Linux platform even though tests based on JavaFX Touch Event would have indicated that the interaction technique behaves properly. Therefore, when testing touch applications, one may want to produce Operating System-level events and to perform integration testing of the Low-Level Transducer/Interaction Technique couple. Such tests can be executed on the Windows platform by using the Touch Injection technology of the Windows API[6] to produce OS-level touch events as inputs. Regarding Linux, it is worth mentioning that ARM versions of GTK are not prone to the issue presented earlier.

5.2   Test Execution for the Interaction Technique

The execution of the tests on the SUT is an activity that is highly dependent of the way the SUT is implemented. Overall, testing the interaction technique alone requires i) being able to forward the event sequence of the test script to the interaction technique and ii) being able to subscribe to the events the interaction technique produces. The easiest way to test the interaction technique of the SUT is to do it using white-box or grey-box testing. Indeed, in such cases, it is easy to either instrument the class of the SUT responsible for the interaction technique or to encapsulate it in a test adapter with which the test execution environment can interact. Then, the test execution environment can perform the event sequence described by the test script. The role of the oracle is then to determine whether the test passed based on whether or not it received the expected event from the interaction technique in a timely manner.

6   Generalizability of the Approach

While this paper focused on the interaction technique component of the architecture presented in Sect. 3.1, the ICO notation, alongside with its CASE tool Petshop, support the modelling and the test generation for other components of the architecture, as well as GUI Testing as defined by Banerjee et al. [1]. This section highlights the generalizability of the modelling philosophy and of the test case generation approach. Due to space constraint and to the highly SUT-dependent nature of the tests execution, we will however not develop further on test execution.

---

[4] https://openjfx.io/javadoc/11/javafx.graphics/javafx/scene/input/class-use/TouchEvent.html.

[5] https://bugs.openjdk.java.net/browse/JDK-8090954.

[6] https://docs.microsoft.com/en-us/windows/desktop/api/_input_touchinjection/.

6.1 Generalizability of the Modelling Philosophy

In addition to interaction techniques, we pointed out in Sect. 3.4 that ICO can be used to model the low-level transducer of a post-WIMP application (Fig. 3). Modelling of Logical Input Devices (e.g. fingers) and their dynamic instantiation is covered in [12]. Moreover, [19] demonstrates that ICO allows the description of the Application (dialog part) components, including those with dynamic instantiation of widgets, on examples such as an Air Traffic Control (ATC) plane manager. To validate that our work is compatible with GUI Testing of WIMP application, we modelled the application specified in Memon et al.'s [16] review of advances in MBT for applications with a GUI front-end. We had no trouble describing the behavior of this WIMP application using ICO in Petshop. Combining this with the modelling of post-WIMP interaction techniques demonstrated herein, shows that we are able to model post-WIMP applications.

6.2 Generalizability of the Test Case Generation Approach

Thanks to Memon et al.'s review of advances in MBT [16], we were able to verify that our test generation approach worked for WIMP applications. Indeed, [16] presented various models for the application it specifies, including one being a Finite State Machine. This allowed us to verify that the reachability graph of the Petri-net was the same (name of states aside) as the FSM in [16]. Beyond that, on applications that involve dynamicity such as the ATC plane manager dialog, the approach fits well as each aircraft is added to the dialog model using invocation in the same way as fingers are added to the interaction technique presented in this paper. Yet, as the number of aircraft on the radar visualization is virtually infinite, the use of a symbolic reachability graph is made mandatory, while standard reachability graph can be kept for interaction techniques (as the maximum number of touch points supported by the screen is known).

7 Conclusion and Future Work

Testing interactive applications is known to be a challenging activity, whether we consider WIMP or post-WIMP applications. In this paper, we have shown that while the testing of WIMP applications retained most of the attention of researchers and practitioners in the field of MBT, post-WIMP applications raise new challenges for the community. Indeed, properly testing post-WIMP following the standard Model-Based Testing process requires modelling techniques that are expressive enough to describe the dynamic instantiation of virtual and physical devices, timing aspects, system configuration, etc. Only such models allow the generation of exhaustive enough test cases.

Building on previous work on the Petri-net-based notation ICO (and its associated CASE tool, PetShop), we showed that we are able to propose a toolchain that addresses the need for expressive modelling techniques in order to support the generation of test cases for post-WIMP application following the MBT process. We showed that thanks to the mechanism supported by ICO we are able to support the high dynamicity of post-WIMP applications for all the software components of the architecture. This expressiveness allows for the generation of abstract test case using a grammar derived from the reachability graph of Petri-nets.

As we focused on a specific component of the architecture, i.e. the interaction technique, we found that post-WIMP applications are more sensitive than WIMP applications to the execution platform, as touch event are not always well forwarded to libraries by operating-systems, highlighting the need for integration testing. A future extension to our work would be to implement the generation of integration test cases into PetShop by relying on the different artifacts allowing the communication between models.

Finally, we are currently investigating using such approach for the testing of interactive applications to be deployed in large civil aircraft interactive cockpits. Indeed, following guidance from supplement DO-333 [25] on formal methods to the DO-178C certification process [24], one may use formal specifications during the development of such application. If a formal model of the interactive application is built for supporting reliability arguments (e.g. "low-level requirements are accurate and consistent [24]") we propose to exploit that model to generate test cases from that formal specification (as proposed by Gaudel [11]). Such process could result in more cost-effective test case generation leveraging on available formal models. Beyond, thanks to the expressive power of ICO, such approach could support the adoption of application offering richer interaction techniques (e.g. animations [17] or multitouch [12]) even in safety-critical context (e.g. brace touch [22]).

References

1. Alur, R., Dill, D.: A theory of timed automata. Theoret. Comput. Sci. **126**, 183–235 (1994)
2. Barboni, E., Conversy, S., Navarre, D., Palanque, P.: Model-based engineering of widgets, user applications and servers compliant with ARINC 661 specification. In: Doherty, G., Blandford, A. (eds.) DSV-IS 2006. LNCS, vol. 4323, pp. 25–38. Springer, Heidelberg (2007). https://doi.org/10.1007/978-3-540-69554-7_3
3. Bass, L., et al.: The arch model: Seeheim revisited. In: User Interface Developers' Workshop (1991)
4. Bastide, R., Navarre, D., Palanque, P.: A model-based tool for interactive prototyping of highly interactive applications. In: CHI 2002 Extended Abstracts on Human Factors in Computing Systems, pp. 516–517. ACM, New York (2002)
5. Bastide, R., Navarre, D., Palanque, P., Schyn, A., Dragicevic, P.: A model-based approach for real-time embedded multimodal systems in military aircrafts. In: Sixth International Conference on Multimodal Interfaces (ICMI 2004), USA, 14–15 October 2004. ACM Press (2004)
6. Best, E., Schlachter, U.: Analysis of petri nets and transition systems. Electron. Proc. Theor. Comput. Sci. **189**, 53–67 (2015)
7. Bowen, J., Reeves, S.: Generating obligations, assertions and tests from UI models. Proc. ACM Hum.-Comput. Interact. **1**, 5:1–5:18 (2017)
8. Campos, J.C., Fayollas, C., Martinie, C., Navarre, D., Palanque, P., Pinto, M.: Systematic automation of scenario-based testing of user interfaces. In: Proceedings of the 8th ACM SIGCHI Symposium on Engineering Interactive Computing Systems, pp. 138–148. ACM, New York (2016)
9. Canny, A., Bouzekri, E., Martinie, C., Palanque, P.: Rationalizing the need of architecture-driven testing of interactive systems. In: Bogdan, C., Kuusinen, K., Lárusdóttir, M.K., Palanque, P., Winckler, M. (eds.) HCSE 2018. LNCS, vol. 11262, pp. 164–186. Springer, Cham (2019). https://doi.org/10.1007/978-3-030-05909-5_10

10. Cronel, M., Dumas, B., Palanque, P., Canny, A.: MIODMIT: a generic architecture for dynamic multimodal interactive systems. In: Bogdan, C., Kuusinen, K., Lárusdóttir, M.K., Palanque, P., Winckler, M. (eds.) HCSE 2018. LNCS, vol. 11262, pp. 109–129. Springer, Cham (2019). https://doi.org/10.1007/978-3-030-05909-5_7
11. Gaudel, M.-C.: Testing can be formal, too. In: Mosses, Peter D., Nielsen, M., Schwartzbach, Michael I. (eds.) CAAP 1995. LNCS, vol. 915, pp. 82–96. Springer, Heidelberg (1995). https://doi.org/10.1007/3-540-59293-8_188
12. Hamon, A., Palanque, P., Silva, J.L., Deleris, Y., Barboni, E.: Formal description of multi-touch interactions. In: Proceedings of the 5th ACM SIGCHI Symposium on Engineering Interactive Computing Systems, pp. 207–216. ACM, New York (2013)
13. Ladry, J.-F., Navarre, D., Palanque, P.: Formal description techniques to support the design, construction and evaluation of fusion engines for sure (safe, usable, reliable and evolvable) multimodal interfaces. In: Proceedings of the 2009 International Conference on Multimodal Interfaces, pp. 185–192. ACM, New York (2009). https://doi.org/10.1145/1647314.1647347
14. Lelli, V., Blouin, A., Baudry, B., Coulon, F.: On model-based testing advanced GUIs. In: 2015 IEEE Eighth International Conference on Software Testing, Verification and Validation Workshops (ICSTW), pp. 1–10 (2015)
15. Martinie, C., Navarre, D., Palanque, P., Barboni, E., Canny, A.: TOUCAN: an IDE supporting the development of effective interactive java applications. In: Proceedings of the ACM SIGCHI Symposium on Engineering Interactive Computing Systems, pp. 4:1–4:7. ACM, New York (2018)
16. Memon, A.M., Nguyen, B.N.: Advances in automated model-based system testing of software applications with a GUI front-end. In: Zelkowitz, M.V. (ed.) Advances in Computers, pp. 121–162. Elsevier (2010)
17. Mirlacher, T., Palanque, P., Bernhaupt, R.: Engineering animations in user interfaces. In: Proceedings of the 4th ACM SIGCHI Symposium on Engineering Interactive Computing Systems, pp. 111–120. ACM, New York (2012)
18. Morgado, I.C., Paiva, A.C.R.: The iMPAcT tool for android testing. Proc. ACM Hum.-Comput. Interact. 3, 4:1–4:23 (2019)
19. Navarre, D., Palanque, P., Ladry, J.-F., Barboni, E.: ICOs: a model-based user interface description technique dedicated to interactive systems addressing usability, reliability and scalability. Proc. ACM Hum.-Comput. Interact. 16, 18:1–18:56 (2009)
20. Palanque, P., Bernhaupt, R., Navarre, D., Ould, M., Winckler, M.: Supporting usability evaluation of multimodal man-machine interfaces for space ground segment applications using petri net based formal specification. In: Ninth International Conference on Space Operations, Italy, 18–22 June 2006 (2006)
21. Palanque, P., Ladry, J.-F., Navarre, D., Barboni, E.: High-fidelity prototyping of interactive systems can be formal too. In: Jacko, Julie A. (ed.) HCI 2009. LNCS, vol. 5610, pp. 667–676. Springer, Heidelberg (2009). https://doi.org/10.1007/978-3-642-02574-7_75
22. Palanque, P., Cockburn, A., Désert-Legendre, L., Gutwin, C., Deleris, Y.: Brace touch: a dependable, turbulence-tolerant, multi-touch interaction technique for interactive cockpits. In: Romanovsky, A., Troubitsyna, E., Bitsch, F. (eds.) SAFECOMP 2019. LNCS, vol. 11698, pp. 53–68. Springer, Cham (2019). https://doi.org/10.1007/978-3-030-26601-1_4
23. Pezzè, M., Rondena, P., Zuddas, D.: Automatic GUI testing of desktop applications: an empirical assessment of the state of the art. In: Companion Proceedings for the ISSTA/ECOOP 2018 Workshops, pp. 54–62. ACM, New York (2018)
24. RTCA: DO-178C Software Considerations in Airborne Systems and Equipment Certification (2011)
25. RTCA: DO-333 Formal Methods Supplement to DO-178C and DO-278A (2011)
26. Shneiderman, B.: Direct manipulation: a step beyond programming languages. Computer 16, 57–69 (1983). https://doi.org/10.1109/MC.1983.1654471

27. Spivey, J.M., Abrial, J.: The Z notation. Prentice Hall, Hemel Hempstead (1992)
28. Utting, M., Pretschner, A., Legeard, B.: A taxonomy of model-based testing approaches. Softw. Test. Verif. Reliab. **22**, 297–312 (2012)
29. Van Dam, A.: Post-WIMP user interfaces. Commun. ACM **40**(2), 63–67 (1997)
30. Ye, X., Zhou, J., Song, X.: On reachability graphs of Petri nets. Comput. Electr. Eng. **29**, 263–272 (2003). https://doi.org/10.1016/S0045-7906(01)00034-9

Fortune Nets for Fortunettes: Formal, Petri Nets-Based, Engineering of Feedforward for GUI Widgets

David Navarre[1] , Philippe Palanque[1,2](✉) , Sven Coppers[3] , Kris Luyten[3] , and Davy Vanacken[3]

[1] ICS-IRIT, University of Toulouse, 118 Route de Narbonne, 31062 Toulouse, France
`{navarre,palanque}@irit.fr`
[2] Department of Industrial Design, Technical University Eindhoven, Eindhoven, The Netherlands
[3] Hasselt University - tUL - Flanders Make, Expertise Centre for Digital Media, Diepenbeek, Belgium
`{sven.coppers,kris.luyten,davy.vanacken}@uhasselt.be`

Abstract. Feedback and feedforward are two fundamental mechanisms that supports users' activities while interacting with computing devices. While feedback can be easily solved by providing information to the users following the triggering of an action, feedforward is much more complex as it must provide information before an action is performed. Fortunettes is a generic mechanism providing a systematic way of designing feedforward addressing both action and presentation problems. Including a feedforward mechanism significantly increases the complexity of the interactive application hardening developers' tasks to detect and correct defects. This paper proposes the use of an existing formal notation for describing the behavior of interactive applications and how to exploit that formal model to extend the behavior to offer feedforward. We use a small login example to demonstrate the process and the results.

Keywords: Feedforward · Formal methods · Petri nets · Interactive systems engineering

1 Introduction

Feedback and feedforward are two fundamental mechanisms supporting users' activities while interacting with computing devices. While feedback can be easily solved by providing information to the users following the triggering of an action, feedforward is much more complex as it must provide information before an action is performed. Automatic feedforward presents in a systematic way to the users what can be done without requiring any dedicated action (e.g. greying out an interactive object that is not available). Automatic feedforward is often available in well-designed interfaces. User-triggered feedforward provides localized, contextual information to the users related to the actions that they envision triggering (e.g. painting temporarily a selected object

E. Sekerinski et al. (Eds.): FM 2019 Workshops, LNCS 12232, pp. 503–519, 2020.
https://doi.org/10.1007/978-3-030-54994-7_36

in yellow while hovering over the yellow button for painting objects). User-triggered feedforward is usually not available in user interface, as it requires computing the future state of the application (if a given action is performed) and presenting this future state on the UI.

In [22], the authors exploit Norman's activity theory [16] to explain the importance and the impact of providing users with feedforward in user interfaces, especially in the action selection phase. In poorly designed systems, that kind of user activity can be very cumbersome especially in the upper part of the model of the activity theory (also called semantic distance).

Figure 1 presents a typical system offering limited feedforward. In that system (Microsoft Word) some of the commands for changing text graphical attributes do not propose feedforward (see Fig. 1b) while others do (see Fig. 1c). Figure 1a) presents a snapshot of MS Word software with the word Fortunettes selected and highlighted. In that version of MS Word, when some text is selected, a contextual pop-up menu appears next to the selected text. In Fig. 1a) the cursor has been moved far away from the selected text and thus no pop-up menu is visible. In Fig. 1b) the pop-up menu is displayed and the mouse cursor hovers over the Bold command to change the presentation of the text to Bold. However, in that case, no feedforward is presented so it is not possible to see how the text will be if the Bold command is performed. Surprisingly, Fig. 1c) highlights the fact that for altering the color of the selecting text, hovering over one of the colors displayed in the pop-up menu applies directly the hovered over color to the selected text, thus providing users with feedforward on the color attribute of the text.

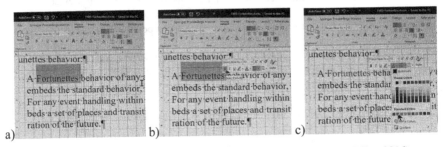

Fig. 1. Inconsistent availability of feedforward in Microsoft Word (Office 2016)

One of the questions that arises immediately is: why such a sophisticated tool as MS Word is not offering feedforward mechanisms for all the functions or at least to all the similar functions (e.g. changing attributes of selected text).

While, as highlighted in [9] and [22], the design of feedforward is an issue. We would argue that its specification and its implementation are the key problem to solve when it is considered as a potential function to add to the system. In that case, we would argue that feedforward is a **usability function** using the pending concept of **security function** [23] or **safety function** [12]. While a safety function can be defined as a function added to a system to prevent undesired safety problems, we would define a usability function as a function added to an interactive system to prevent undesired usability problems. Within this context, feedforward can be considered as a function similar to "undo" and thus requires complex implementation due to its crosscutting nature [12]. This paper argues for the use of a formal approach for the specification and the implementation of feedforward in a systematic way. We present how the expressive power of high-level Petri nets such as ICOs [15] can describe feedforward and how the resulting models are amenable to verification (to identify and check properties on the system offering feedforward). In a nutshell we propose to produce a Petri net model (called *Fortune Net*) in addition to the model describing the behavior of the application. We also argue that a formal model of the initial application can be extended in a systematic way to include feedforward functionality, thus reducing development cost of such a usability function.

This paper is an extension of the work done in [6] to offer feedforward mechanisms in a more general context. Section 2 presents the foundations, interaction and one design for the Fortunettes concept for feedforward usability function. Section 3 presents the illustrative example of a simple widget-based interactive application that is used throughout the paper. Section 4 presents the Petri nets based modeling approach for modeling interactive applications and its application to the modelling of Fortunettes usability function. Section 5 focusses on the formal analysis of the application model and of the Fortune Nets ones. Section 6 concludes the paper and highlight paths for future work.

2 Fortunettes: Design, Foundations and Use

The origin of Fortunettes [6] is the need of providing feedforward about the future state of an application. When including a feedforward usability function in the GUI, the feedforward information does not need to be presented permanently (to avoid visual overload and cluttering of the UI) but instead we propose this specific information display to be triggered by the user on demand (when needed). In our approach, exploring the future may be seen as a four steps process:

- **Look at the present,** when the user explores visually the user interface elements;
- **Peek into the future,** when the user is considering performing an action;
- **Go to the future,** when the user confirms and actually executes the considered action;
- **Return to the present,** when the user is no longer considering the execution of that action.

The choice has been made of providing such feedforward at widget-level as it makes it easier to reuse for any widget-based application. Figure 2 shows an example of this kind of widget-level feedforward: when the user hovers over the Login button (that is currently enabled), the button Logout and the text box (that are currently disabled), show their future state in terms of availability (the button Logout and the textbox will become enabled if the user clicks the button Login, while the button Login will become disabled). With this information, the user knows that to enable the Logout button, the Login button me be pressed first.

The main idea of Fortunettes is to provide the user with an answer to "What will happen if I do that?", by presenting what the result of the user action will be, before the action is actually performed. It thus requires the widgets to be able to present their future state in addition to their current state (enabled or disabled).

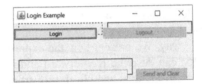

Fig. 2. Illustration of the Fortunettes concept using the case study.

As presented in [6], the user interface of the application presented in Fig. 2 is the following:

- The application is composed of four widgets (the three buttons and a textbox),
- The current state of the widgets is displayed on the forefront, the login button is enabled, "Logout" and "Send and Clear" ones are disabled, and the textbox is disabled too.
- In order to present the feedforward information, users have to hover over the widget of interest. In Fig. 2, the "login" button is hovered and the background display of each widget presents the feedforward information showing the state of the application if the user clicks on the login button. Current feedforward display tells the user that "login" button will be disabled, the textbox will become enabled, "logout" will become enabled and "Send and Clear" will remain disabled. Indeed, as the status of "Send and Clear" will remain the same, no additional feedforward display is presented. We follow here the parsimony principle of user interface designs.

The design choice presented here is one example of the many possible designs of Fortunettes: every widget is decorated with borders to express its future availability (full lines for enabled, dashed lines for disabled) and/or its future values.

This design will not be further discussed as the focus of this paper is on formal description and engineering support. These two aspects are particularly important as the introduction of Fortunettes increases the complexity of the development of an application, and, by consequence its reliability.

3   Illustrative Example

We illustrate the use of the Fortunettes approach with a simple application (as illustrated by Fig. 3) that behaves as follows: when the user is logged in, a message can be written in the textbox or the user can log out. To ensure that the message only contains letters, the edited text is filtered, removing any other characters (numbers, special characters…). If the textbox is not empty, the message can be sent. Sending the message or logging out clear the textbox.

Fig. 3. Screen shots of the illustrative application. On the left, the user is logged out, on the right, the user is logged in and a message is being edited and ready to be sent.

4 Modelling of Fortunettes Behavior

To support the engineering of interactive applications offering a feedforward usability function based on Fortunettes, we propose an approach based on a formal description technique called Interactive Cooperative Objects (ICO). We firstly present in this Section the formal description technique, then we present how it is possible to derive the feedforward behavior of the application from the existing model of the application behavior.

4.1 ICO Formal Description Technique

The ICO formalism is a formal description technique dedicated to the modeling and the implementation of event-driven interfaces [15], using a decomposition of communicating objects to model the system, where both behavior of objects and communication protocol between objects are described by the Petri net dialect called Cooperative Objects (CO) [4]. In the ICO formalism, an object is an entity featuring four components: a cooperative object which describes the behavior of the object, a presentation part (i.e. the graphical interface), and two functions (the activation function and the rendering function) which connects the cooperative object and the presentation part.

An ICO specification fully describes the potential interactions that users may have with the application. The specification encompasses both the "input" aspects of the interaction (i.e. how user actions impact the inner state of the application, and which actions are enabled at any given time) and its "output" aspects (i.e. when and how the application displays state information that is relevant to the user).

This formal description technique has already been applied in the field of Air Traffic Control interactive applications [15], space command and control ground systems [18], or interactive military [3] or civil cockpits [2].

The ICO notation is fully supported by a CASE tool called PetShop [5, 19]. All the models presented in the two next Sects. (4 and 5) have been edited, simulated and analyzed using PetShop tool.

4.2 Principle of Fortunettes Feedforward Modelling Using ICO

As stated in Sect. 2, engineering an application with feedforward capabilities requires to handle extra interaction events (at least three, depending on the widget type). These events allow the user to **peek into the future**, to **go to the future** or to **return to the present**, without affecting the standard behavior of the application, as the objective is to enhance the application (with feedforward) and not to change it. This design choice impacts the modelling of feedforward behavior:

- The feedforward behavior of any application is modelled as an independent object that embeds the standard behavior (as a copy), making it fully compatible with the original application behavior. This Petri net model is called the **Fortune Net** as it allows users to look into the future of the application.
- For any event handling within the standard behavior, the feedforward behavior embeds a pattern described in Petri nets (a set of places and connected transitions) that models the exploration of the future states. The important aspect in this modelling principle is that we exploit the behavior of the application to forecast the future states of the application if the user decides to use feedforward function.

To illustrate these two points, we use an excerpt of the complete behavior presented in the next Sect. (4.3) that only concerns the login action on the user interface (as shown by Fig. 4).

Fig. 4. Excerpt from the Petri net model of the standard behavior of the application: event handling of the login action. In the transition, the text on the left describes the name of the transition while the text on the right describes the name of the event associated the transition.

In Fig. 4, the login transition is the event handler for an event called loginPerformed that represents the use of the button Login. When fired, this transition moves the token from place LoggedOut (1.) to place LoggedIn, setting the state of the application to the new state following the execution of the login (code not represented here).

When introducing the Fortunettes view on this action, the three base actions defined in Sect. 2 (peek into the future, go to the future and return to the present) are represented as three extra event handlers, as shown on Fig. 5, where event handlers {FloginPerformed, UFloginPerformed, InFloginPerformed} are generated from the event handler loginPerformed. In this paper, the name of the generated event handlers for handling Fortunettes mode are built with the name of the corresponding event handler, prefixed by F (that represents entering in Fortunettes mode, e.g. peek into the future), by UF (that represents exiting the Fortunettes mode, e.g. return to the present) and InF (that represents exiting the Fortunettes mode and go to the future).

On Fig. 5, transition f1login (event handler for FloginPerformed) represents the action of peeking into the future of the action login. Basically, it behaves in the same way as the original action (put a token in place LoggedIn) while the standard behavior is still in state LoggedOut. It additionally puts a token in place flogin that represents the entering in feedforward mode (a dedicated rendering may occur).

There are then two possibilities:

- The user decides to really perform the login action (using the login button), producing two events: loginPerformed handled by the standard behavior (making it going to the state LoggedIn) and InFloginPerformed handled by the

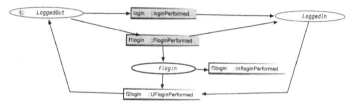

Fig. 5. Extracted from the feedforward behavior of the application: event handling of the login action and peek into its future.

feedforward behavior (discarding the token in place `flogin`, while the token in place `LoggedIn` does not move, placing it in the same state as the standard behavior).
- The user decides to not perform the login action producing an event `UFloginPer-formed`. The standard behavior remains in the same state while in the feedforward behavior, the tokens from places `LoggedIn` and `flogin` are removed and a token goes back to the place `LoggedOut`, making it return to its previous state (leaving the feedforward mode).

This pattern is particularly efficient when describing a feedforward behavior for events that do not handle values or when the widgets are simple such as button. For more complex events, or when the underlying widgets are more complicated, this pattern has to be modified/extended:

- When values are handled by the action of the widget, it is not always possible to peek into the future of these values. One possible improvement is to proceed in two steps. When entering the feedforward mode, an envisioned value must be produced (decided at design time for instance) and when the user really performs the action, a substitution must be done between the envisioned value and the real value. In the feedforward behavior, this can be done by moving tokens (if it was the case in the login example, the first token put in place `LoggedIn` by transition `f1login` would have a design time envisioned value, and when `f3login` would be fired, this token would have been removed and replaced by one holding the correct value).
- When the widget is more complex (in our case, the complexity is related to the event production), extra event handlers may be introduced. For instance, when using a classical textbox, one may be interested by the end of the text edition (validation) and not by the whole process of typing in the text. In this case, in the standard behavior of the application, the only handled event would be the last one (for instance, the event `actionPerformed` of the `JTextField` in Java Swing). On the feedforward behavior side, any text change may be relevant to allow the rendering of text filtering.

Fortunettes requires enhancing widgets with extra means to allow rendering feedforward states and to trigger dedicated events. In our implementation using Java Swing widgets, we embed them within a specialized decorator, but there are many other implementation options at widget level or at application level.

4.3 Application of the Modeling Principle to the Illustrative Example

This Section presents the ICO models for both the standard application and its Fortunettes enhancement. For each model, we present the behavioral part and the two user interface description functions: the activation part and the rendering part.

Standard Behavior

Figure 6 presents the entire behavior of the illustrative example. It may be divided into two parts: the upper part is dedicated to login actions and the lower part is dedicated to the message handling.

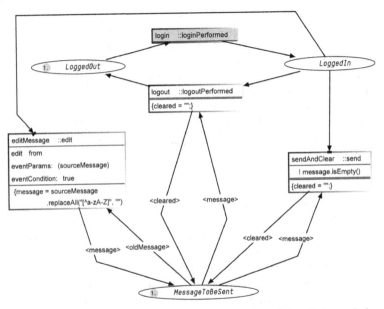

Fig. 6. Behavior of the Login example using the ICO formal description technique.

The upper part of Fig. 6 models what has been explained in the beginning of the Section (see Fig. 4) to introduce Fortunettes and the modelling approach, including the complete behavior of the application i.e. its functional code (inside the transitions). Another difference is the way back from place LoggedIn to place LoggedOut when logging out that clears the edited message (modification of the value of the token held by place MessageToBeSent).

The lower part of Fig. 6 is dedicated to the message editing and to send it. Sending it (transition sendAndClear) can only occur if the message is not empty (precondition !message.isEmpty()). When it occurs, the token held by place MessageToBeSent is destroyed and a new token (with an empty string) is set to that place. The message editing is represented by the transition editMessage that receives an event called edit, and this event holds a string value called sourceMessage. This sourceMessage is then filtered resulting in a string message that only contains characters that belongs to [a-z] and [A-Z] (For instance "a1b2c3" will be transformed into "abc") by the execution of the function replaceAll.

Table 1 represents the activation function of the application. It relates the event production from the application and event handlers described using ICO. When the event occurs, the corresponding transition is fired. If the transition is not available, the corresponding event source must be disabled. This part of the functioning is assumed by the activation rendering method (last column of Table 1) that is provided by the application: for instance, setLoginEnabled changes the enabling of the button Login.

Table 1. Activation function for the ICO model of the Login example.

User event	Event handler	Activation rendering
Edit	editMessage	setEditEnabled
Login	login	setLoginEnabled
Logout	logout	setLogoutEnabled
Send	sendAndClear	setSendEnabled

Table 2 represents the rendering function of the application. It relates any state change within the application behavior to rendering methods call. For instance, when a token enters place MessageToBeSent, the string of this message is set in the text box widget by calling the method showMessage.

Table 2. Rendering function for the ICO model of the Login example.

ObCS node name	ObCS event	Rendering method
MessageToBeSent	marking_reset	showMessage
MessageToBeSent	token_enter	showInitialMessage

Feedforward Behavior

Figure 7 illustrates how feedforward information can be displayed using Fortunettes. Figure 8, Table 3 and Table 4 fully describe the feedforward part of the application. The behavior presented by Fig. 8 is structured similarly to the standard behavior, the upper part being dedicated to the login actions and the lower part, to the message editing.

This Fortune Net behaves according to the pattern explained in the previous Section with the particularity of the filtering of the text while it is being typed in and not only at the end of the interaction with the text box (transition f4editMessage in the lower part of Fig. 8). This allows to present to the user what will happen to the edited value if it is validated (e.g. press ENTER), as illustrated by Fig. 7.

Table 3 presents the activation of the feedforward behavior of the application. The interesting part of this function is that the activation rendering is not related to the

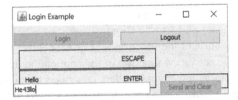

Fig. 7. Illustration of the text filtering while typing in feedforward mode

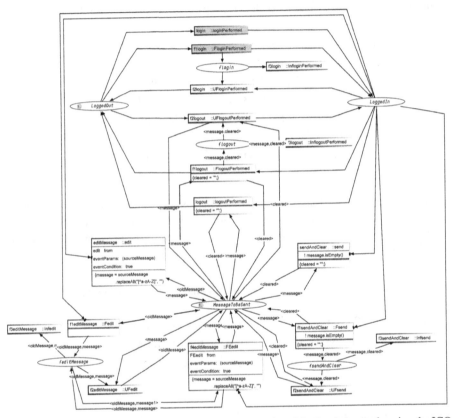

Fig. 8. The Fortune Net describing the feedforward behavior of the Login example using the ICO formal description technique.

immediate availability of the events, but to their availability in the future. Therefore, it does not directly impact the application widgets but only calls functions that have been added to render their Fortunettes appearance. For instance, on Fig. 7, if the edited text is validated (e.g. pressing ENTER), the button "Send and Clear" will become available (represented by the rectangle around it, in the background).

Table 4 presents the rendering function of the feedforward behavior of the application. This function first aims at making the application entering in feedforward mode (a token enters any of the places prefixed f) or at exiting the feedforward mode (a token exits any

Table 3. Activation function for the ICO model of the feedforward behavior of the example.

User event	Event handler	Activation rendering
Edit	editMessage	setFortunettesEditEnabled
Login	login	setFortunettesLoginEnabled
Logout	logout	setFortunettesLogoutEnabled
Send	sendAndClear	setFortunettesSendEnabled

of the paces prefixed by f). This function ensures too that when a new message is under editing, it is rendered on the feedforward part of the interface (each time a token enters the place MessageToBeSent, showFortunettesMessage is called modifying what is rendered in the ENTER rectangle of the text box as illustrated on Fig. 7).

Table 4. Rendering function for the ICO model of the feedforward behavior of the example.

ObCS node name	ObCS event	Rendering method
MessageToBeSent	marking_reset	showFortunettesMessage
MessageToBeSent	token_enter	showFortunettesInitialMessage
fEditMessage	token_enter	startRenderFortunettes
fEditMessage	token_exit	stopRenderFortunettes
fLogin	token_enter	startRenderFortunettes
fLogin	token_exit	stopRenderFortunettes
fLogout	token_enter	startRenderFortunettes
fLogout	token_exit	stopRenderFortunettes
fSendAndClear	token_enter	startRenderFortunettes
fSendAndClear	token_exit	stopRenderFortunettes

This interesting joint behavior between the standard behavior of the application and its Fortunettes ones is highlighted on Fig. 7. Indeed, when the user types some text in, it is rendered directly in the text box while the Fortunettes rendering displays the text, as it will appear if the validation key is pressed. In the case of the login application, we see that all the non-textual characters will be removed and the current text "He43llo" will appear as "Hello" in the future.

5   Formal Analysis on the Illustrative Example

This Section is dedicated to the formal analysis of the models presented above. The fact that we produce two different models for the same application (the standard application model and the Fortune Net) has multiple implications. First, the standard application models must exhibit some properties and it is important to check that they are true. Second, the Fortune Net also needs to exhibit some properties (e.g. each time the user triggers the "peek into the future" there must be two actions available: one to go into that peeked future and one to come back to the current present. Third, the Fortune Nets must implement a "similar" behavior as the standard application and thus we must demonstrate their compatibility. For instance, it is important to demonstrate that all the actions available in the models of the standard application are available in the Fortune Net. This is only an example of the generic properties that have to be checked when a feedforward usability function is added to an application.

With ICOs, as detailed in [21] and [17], there are two different techniques:

- The analysis of the underlying Petri net using results from Petri nets theory. This analysis can be performed using methods and algorithms from the Petri nets community such as the ones presented in [14].
- The analysis of the high-level Petri net (ICO) but this requires manual demonstrations as some of the properties are undecidable [8].

Due to space constraints, we only present here properties that are based on the underlying Petri net model. Some interesting results demonstrate that the high-level nature of the Petri nets with objects only reduce the availability of transitions (for instance when they feature pre-conditions) and thus in order for the high-level Petri net to be live, the underlying Petri net must be live [4].

5.1 Formal Analysis of the Model of the Standard Behavior (Fig. 6)

Table 5 presents the list of traps and siphons of the model in Fig. 6[1]. In a Petri net a siphon is a set of places that never gain tokens whatever transition is fired while a trap is a set of places that never lose tokens [7]. The fact that all the places in the model are both traps and siphons demonstrate that the number of tokens in the model will remain the same as the one in the initial state i.e. two tokens (see Fig. 6).

Table 5. Siphons and Traps from the standard behavior of the application.

Siphons	Traps
MessageToBeSent	MessageToBeSent
LoggedIn, LoggedOut	LoggedIn, LoggedOut

Table 6 analysis is based on the calculation of transition invariants and place invariants. As can be seen all the places in the model belong to a place invariant which means that the total number of tokens in the places of the models will remain the same. One interesting piece of information is that place MessageToBeSent is a single place in a

---

[1] The computing of the results in those tables was done using Petshop tool and are not presented due to space constraints. How to make such computing is presented in [7].

P-invariant. This means that whatever transition is fired the number of tokens in that place will always be the same as the one of the initial marking. In the current example, this means that the place MessageToBeSent will always be marked by a single token.

Table 6. Transitions and Place Invariants from the standard behavior of the application.

T-Invariants	P-Invariants
1 sendAndClear	1 LoggedIn, 1 LoggedOut
1 editMessage	1 MessageToBeSent
1 login, 1 logout	

In terms of behavior, transitions login and transition logout belong to the same t-invariant which means that, if they can be made available from the initial state, there always exists a sequence of transitions in the Petri net to make them available. Their connection with the P-invariant {1 LoggedIn, 1 LoggedOut} (with a bounded value of one token) demonstrates that always one of the two transition will be available and they will never be available at the same time.

5.2 Formal Analysis of the Fortune Net (Fig. 8)

We will not detail the analysis of the Fortune Net, but it is important to check that the properties true in the application model are still holding in the Fortune Net.

If we take as example the property of the mutual exclusion of login and logout transitions, we can easily see in Table 7 and Table 8 that the places and the transitions belong are also listed in siphons, traps, P-invariants and T-invariants.

Table 7. Siphons and Traps from the feedforward behavior of the application.

Siphons	Traps
MessageToBeSent	MessageToBeSent
LoggedIn, LoggedOut	LoggedIn, LoggedOut

Of course, the Fortune Net is more complex and should also exhibit specific properties related to its own semantics. A very simple but important one is that whenever the user triggers a transition to peek into the future (name starting with f1) immediately after a transition to come back to present (name starting with f2) and a transition to go into the future (name starting with f3) will be available. The analysis results in Table 8 demonstrate that a Fortune Net always verifies this fundamental property (any of such transitions is always in a T-Invariant with each other).

Table 8. Transitions and Place Invariants from the feedforward behavior of the application.

T-Invariants	P-Invariants
1 f4editMessage	1 LoggedIn, 1 LoggedOut
1 f1logout, 1 f3logout, 1 login	1 MessageToBeSent
1 f1login, 1 f2login	
1 editMessage	
1 f1editMessage, 1 f2editMessage	
1 f1sendAndClear, 1 f3sendAndClear	
1 f1sendAndClear, 1 f2sendAndClear	
1 f1logout, 1 f2logout	
1 login, 1 logout	
1 f1login, 1 f3login, 1 logout	
1 f1login, 1 f1logout, 1 f3login, 1 f3logout	
1 sendAndClear	
1 f1editMessage, 1 f3editMessage	
1 f1login, 1 f1logout, 1 f2login, 1 f3logout, 1 login	
1 f1login, 1 f2login, 1 login, 1 logout	

6 Related Work

As highlighted in [20] many formal approaches to support the design, specification and verification of interactive systems have been proposed. That book chapter highlights four criteria to compare those approaches: 1) Modeling coverage (how much of the interactive systems can the notation describe); 2) Properties (and their type) supported; 3) Application of the methods in which domain; 4) Scalability (is the notation able to deal with large scale interactive systems).

With respect to the modelling need of Fortunettes, the expressive power of the notation to be used heavily depends on the interactive application itself and does not require specific modelling power. With that respect, if the interactive application does not feature concurrent behavior, dynamic instantiation of objects and does not exhibit quantitative time behavior, automata would be adequate for describing Fortunettes behavior as demonstrated in [6]. If more complex behaviors need to be represented, more expression power will be required. The Table 1 from the book chapter [20] would be then of great help to select the modeling notation.

As Fortunettes feedforward concept is meant to be applied in a systematic way to all the interactions in an interactive system, Fortune Nets need to cover all the aspects of the interactive (from the low-level interaction technique to the functional core according to the MIODMIT architecture [13]. We have only presented here Fortunettes at the application level, but all the layers of the architectures should be taken into account.

7 Conclusion and Perspectives

While research in the field of HCI focuses on adding more functionalities to the user interface, the interaction techniques and the interactive applications to improve usability and user experience, very little work is spent on transferring these improved interactions to the developers of interactive systems. For instance, papers proposing bubble cursor for improving target acquisition [10] or marking menus [11] to improve command selection do not present means for engineering these interaction techniques in a reliable and systematic way.

This paper has proposed an engineering method based on formal methods to support the systematic integration of Fortunettes concepts to provide interactive application with feedforward mechanisms. While the graphical and interaction design of Fortunettes might be improved and could be subject of future research, we have demonstrated that the use of a Petri nets-based approach limits the complexity of adding Fortunettes behavior to an existing application. We have also demonstrated that a formal approach can provide benefits in ensuring that the application with the additional feedforward behavior remains behaviorally compatible with the initial application.

The work presented in the present paper leads to extensions that should be addressed in future work. First, the current design of Fortunettes only deals with WIMP interaction techniques based on a set of identified widgets. While this can be seen as a strong limitation for current user interfaces targeting at better user experience, it is important to note that many applications are still widget-based. In some critical domains it is even not possible to embed other types of interfaces as required by the ARINC 661 specification standard [1] for user interfaces of cockpits of large civil aircrafts. We have previously worked on the formal description of User Application, user interface widgets and servers using Petri net based description [2] and that early work can directly benefit from the work presented in the paper. This means that adding the feedforward usability function to those user applications will result in very limited work (as the Fortune Net is built upon the original behavior and is described with the same language) and would come with assurance means to guarantee their correct behavior.

Second, the current behavior of Fortunettes is to offer the possibility to the user to look only one step into the future. The model-based behavior presented in the paper could be exploited further to look into several step or even to look at the eventual end of the execution, as introduced in [17]. For instance it would be possible to identify a widget (via formal analysis) that would become unavailable forever in five steps from the current state of the application. While graphical design and interaction will be clearly a difficult challenge, the engineering of such applications could be reachable via the analysis of the formal models.

References

1. ARINC 661. Cockpit Display System Interfaces to User Systems. ARINC Specification 661-5. AEEC (2013)

2. Barboni, E., Conversy, S., Navarre, D., Palanque, P.: Model-based engineering of widgets, user applications and servers compliant with ARINC 661 Specification. In: Doherty, G., Blandford, A. (eds.) DSV-IS 2006. LNCS, vol. 4323, pp. 25–38. Springer, Heidelberg (2007). https://doi.org/10.1007/978-3-540-69554-7_3

3. Bastide, R., Navarre, D., Palanque, P., Schyn, A., Dragicevic, P.: A Model-based approach for real-time embedded multimodal systems in military aircrafts. In: Sixth International Conference on Multimodal Interfaces (ICMI 2004) 14–15 October 2004. ACM Press, New York (2004)

4. Bastide R., Sibertin-Blanc C., Palanque P. Cooperative objects: A concurrent, petri-net based, object-oriented language. IEEE Systems Man and Cybernetics Conference-SMC 1993, 286–291

5. Bastide, R., Navarre, D., Palanque, P.: A model-based tool for interactive prototyping of highly interactive applications. In: CHI 2002 Extended Abstracts on Human Factors in Computing Systems, pp. 516–517. ACM, New York (2002)

6. Coppers, S., Luyten, K., Vanacken, D., Navarre, D., Palanque, P., Gris, C.: Fortunettes: feedforward about the future state of GUI widgets. In: Proceedings of the ACM on Human-Computer Interaction, vol 3. ACM SIGCHI (2019)

7. David, R., Alla, H.: Petri Nets and Grafcet - Tools for Modelling Discrete Event Systems, pp. I–XII, 1–339. Prentice Hall, Upper Saddle River (1992). ISBN 978-0-13-327537-7

8. Dietze, R., Kudlek, M., Kummer, O.: Decidability problems of a basic class of object nets. Fundam. Inform. **79**(3–4), 295–302 (2007)

9. Djajadiningrat, T., Overbeeke, K., Wensveen, S.: But how, Donald, tell us how? On the creation of meaning in interaction design through feedforward and inherent feedback. In: Conference on Designing interactive systems: processes, practices, methods, and techniques (DIS 2002), pp. 285–291. ACM, New York (2002)

10. Grossman, T., Balakrishnan, R.: The bubble cursor: enhancing target acquisition by dynamic resizing of the cursor's activation area. In: Proceedings of the SIGCHI Conference on Human Factors in Computing Systems (CHI 2005), pp. 281–290. ACM, New York (2005)

11. Kurtenbach, G., Buxton, W.: User learning and performance with marking menus. In: Conference on Human Factors in Computing Systems (CHI 1994), pp. 258–264. ACM, New York (21994)

12. Lee, S., Yamada, Y.: Strategy on safety function implementation: case study involving risk assessment and functional safety analysis for a power assist system. Adv. Robot. **24**(13), 1791–1811 (2010)

13. Cronel, M., Dumas, B., Palanque, P., Canny, A.: MIODMIT: a generic architecture for dynamic multimodal interactive systems. In: Bogdan, C., Kuusinen, K., Lárusdóttir, M.K., Palanque, P., Winckler, M. (eds.) HCSE 2018. LNCS, vol. 11262, pp. 109–129. Springer, Cham (2019). https://doi.org/10.1007/978-3-030-05909-5_7

14. Murata, T.: Petri nets: properties, analysis and applications. In: Proceedings of the IEEE, vol. 77, no. 4, April 1989 (1989)

15. Navarre, D., Palanque, P., Ladry, J.-F., Barboni, E.: ICOs: a model-based user interface description technique dedicated to interactive systems addressing usability, reliability and scalability. ACM Trans. Comput. Hum. Interact. **16**(4), 18:1–18:56 (2009)

16. Norman, D.A.: The Psychology Of Everyday Things. Basic Books, New York (1988)

17. Palanque, P., Bastide, R., Sengès, V.: Validating interactive system design through the verification of formal task and system models. EHCI 1995. IAICT, pp. 189–212. Springer, Boston, MA (1996). https://doi.org/10.1007/978-0-387-34907-7_11

18. Palanque, P., Bernhaupt, R., Navarre, D., Ould, M., Winckler, M.: Supporting usability evaluation of multimodal man-machine interfaces for space ground segment applications using petri net based formal specification. In: Ninth International Conference on Space Operations, Italy, 18–22 June 2006 (2006)

19. Palanque, P., Ladry, J.-F., Navarre, D., Barboni, E.: High-fidelity prototyping of interactive systems can be formal too. In: Jacko, Julie A. (ed.) HCI 2009. LNCS, vol. 5610, pp. 667–676. Springer, Heidelberg (2009). https://doi.org/10.1007/978-3-642-02574-7_75
20. Oliveira, R., Palanque, P., Weyers, B., Bowen, J., Dix, A.: State of the art on formal methods for interactive systems. In: Weyers, B., Bowen, J., Dix, A., Palanque, P. (eds.) The Handbook of Formal Methods in Human-Computer Interaction. HIS, pp. 3–55. Springer, Cham (2017). https://doi.org/10.1007/978-3-319-51838-1_1
21. Silva, J.-L., Fayollas, C., Hamon, A., Palanque, P., Martinie, C., Barboni, E.: Analysis of WIMP and post WIMP interactive systems based on formal specification. ECEASST **69**, 19–35 (2013)
22. Vermeulen, J., Luyten, K., van den Hoven, E., Coninx, K.: Crossing the bridge over Norman's Gulf of execution: revealing feedforward's true identity. In: SIGCHI Conference on Human Factors in Computing Systems (CHI 2013), pp. 1931–1940. ACM, New York (2013)
23. Yoon, C., Park, T., Lee, S., Kang, H., Shin, S., Zhang, Z.: Enabling security functions with SDN. Comput. Netw. **85**, 19–35 (2015)

Author Index